Human
Resources
Management

# Human Resources Management

Sixth edition

PROF P S NEL (coordinating author)

Authors
DR P S VAN DYK
DR G D HAASBROEK
MS H B SCHULTZ
PROF T J SONO
MS A WERNER

# OXFORD
UNIVERSITY PRESS

Great Clarendon Street, Oxford OX2 6DP

Oxford University Press is a department of the University of Oxford.
It furthers the University's objective of excellence in research, scholarship,
and education by publishing worldwide in

Oxford  New York

Auckland  Bangkok  Buenos Aires  Cape Town  Chennai
Dar es Salaam  Delhi  Hong Kong  Istanbul  Karachi  Kolkata
Kuala Lumpur  Madrid  Melbourne  Mexico City  Mumbai
Nairobi  São Paulo  Shanghai  Taipei  Tokyo  Toronto

Oxford is a registered trade mark of Oxford University Press
in the UK and certain other countries

Published in South Africa
by Oxford University Press Southern Africa, Cape Town

**Human Resources Management**
ISBN 0 19 578680 7

© Oxford University Press Southern Africa 2004

The moral rights of the authors have been asserted
Database right Oxford University Press (maker)

Previously published by Southern Book Publishers (Pty) Ltd
and by International Thomson Publishing Southern Africa (Pty) Ltd
First edition published 1987
Fifth edition published 2001
Sixth edition published 2004
Eighth impression 2005

The authors and publishers gratefully acknowledge permission to reproduce
material in this book. Every effort has been made to trace copyright holders,
but where this has proved impossible, the publishers would be grateful for
information which would enable them to amend any omissions in future editions.

Commissioning editor: Marian Griffin
Editor: Stuart Douglas
Senior editor: Annette de Villiers
Cover design: Christopher Davis/Brigitte Rouillard
Indexer: Mary Lennox

Published by Oxford University Press Southern Africa
PO Box 12119, N1 City, 7463, Cape Town, South Africa

Set in 10 pt Plantin on 12 pt by RHT desktop publishing, Durbanville
Imagesetting by Castle Graphics
Cover reproduction by The Image Bureau
Printed and bound by ABC Press, Kinghall Avenue, Epping Industria II, Cape Town

## Dedication

The sixth edition is dedicated to the memory of our co-author Helen Schultz, who inspired great admiration for her generosity of spirit and unfailing commitment to her family, teaching, writing, and research in the tertiary education sector in South Africa. She made a major contribution to the fifth and sixth editions of the book and the instructor's manual. Helen passed away in September 2003.

# Preface

The new edition of a book usually provides an opportunity to reflect upon the task that was executed and the body of knowledge which was captured to reflect the state of a discipline at a particular point in time. This book documents human resources management theory and practice developments, reflects far-reaching changes in society and practice in the economic and business environment in South Africa. It has now also, after 16 years, achieved the distinction of being one of the longest continuously updated human resources books at tertiary level in South Africa, and has a wide usage at various levels.

The new edition elucidates new challenges in business and human resources management, which mirror the dynamics of South African society at macro and micro level, and reflect turbulent and volatile business, economic and political developments. The authors completely revitalised the book, which led to an enhanced configuration. The new edition includes some consolidated chapters and a completely new satellite chapter on reputation management. This can be viewed at the publisher's website: http://www.oup. com/za/resources/booksites.

The first and last parts of the book were subject to major revision. This repositioning will clearly lead to a more concise overview of the context of human resources management as a discipline. It also incorporates an increased focus on international aspects of human resource management to reflect South Africa's re-entry into the global market.

The authors experienced major upheavals during their work on the new edition. Dr Van Dyk's continued ill health led to a further reduction of his contribution to the sixth edition and the loss of Helen Schultz leaves an irreplaceable void.

The instructors' manual which accompanies *Human Resources Management* sixth edition is intended to guide students to a rapid understanding and application of the relevant theory and practice, which includes a multitude of practical applications as well.

It is very fitting to thank Marian Griffin of Oxford University Press SA in particular for her encouragement and guidance in seeing this edition through. Marian had to contend with authors currently scattered across the globe as well as the death of one of the authors. It is also appropriate to also extend the gratitude of the authors to the following researchers who contributed immensely to the completion of the book on time: Dr Andries du Plessis, Paul Woodfield and Trevor Robinson, all from the School of Management and Entrepreneurship at UNITEC institute of Technology in Auckland, New Zealand.

The authors also wish to thank Elize Nel for typing a major portion of the manuscript including the updated instructors' manual.

Based on the comments and suggestions from a wide range of end-users over the years it is clear that this book fulfils the tertiary level quest for knowledge in this particular field of study – both in its academic and practical context. Furthermore it enhances confidence in the human resources function in all spheres of business endeavours, because organisations have to use their most important resource optimally in the face of increasing global competition, in order to survive and prosper.

Prof. Pieter S Nel
Coordinating author
Auckland, New Zealand
November 2003

# Abridged table of contents

# Contents

# part one

General introduction and basic knowledge prerequisite to human resources management

# 1

# Introduction to Human Resources Management

PS van Dyk

## Learning outcomes

At the end of this Chapter the learner should be able to:

- Schematically present Human Resources Management (HRM) as a body of knowledge in its own right by drawing it in any form.
- Explain in his/her own words:
    - human resources management from a traditional point of view
    - from a quality assurance point of view.
- Practically argue the impact of the environment, i.e. the economic, political, social and technological impact on human resources management in short descriptions.
- Differentiate between the different approaches to structuring human resources making use of line diagrams.
- Prove that an organisation known to him/her is a system by describing it in words.
- Defend the statement that work is also a sub-system of or in the organisation by the use of concentric circles.

- Distinguish individual employee efficiency and effectiveness by describing it in practical terms.
- Write an essay on the skills/brain drain of South African-born human resources.

## Key words and concepts

- body of knowledge
- customer
- discipline
- efficiency/effectiveness
- efficiency approach
- empowerment
- functional approach
- globalisation
- job content/job context
- knowledge
- line/staff
- process
- quality assurance
- service delivery
- systems approach

## Illustrative case

Thandi was a second-year student in business management. During her first year, a compulsory study module was 'General Management', which she found very interesting; and from then on, she applied the general management principles to her personal life. Of particular interest to her was the concept of the organisation as an open system.

Like all undergraduate students, she was quite keen to share the knowledge which she gained through her studies with friends and family.

One Sunday afternoon after lunch, her family, grandparents, and other extended family members were having coffee in the lounge. As most of her family stemmed from an agricultural background, her grandfather, a successful maize farmer, asked her how the theory she was learning could be used to improve his farming ability and skills. She was immediately motivated and told him, as well as the rest of the family, about the efficiency/systems approach to organisations.

Her grandfather listened attentively and, after his second cup of coffee, asked her to explain a few things she had said to him, namely: how his farm was a system; how each individual labourer of his was also a system; how his farm, as a system, differed from their church, as a system; and what the difference was between efficient and effective farming.

If you were in Thandi's shoes, how would you answer her grandfather's questions?

## 1.1    Introduction

More than a decade ago the authors were confronted with new developments in this field of study when this book was first written, and in this spirit endeavoured to be leaders at that stage in new, relevant developments in human resources management and employment relations practices. This edition once again reflects many influences and developments in this field of study.

The study field of HRM has expanded tremendously over the last decades. In the past, then, relevant fields of study and sister disciplines were studied and prescribed as separate subjects or credits. Academics were also very careful not to overstep the border of their strictly demarcated part of the science, and great emphasis was put on the purity of each separate field of study (discipline). However, and rightfully so, science doesn't have rigid barriers. The government's emphasis on a more practical approach to curriculum design at tertiary level basically removed these barriers among sister disciplines to bring about practical curricula which would empower students to apply the theory much faster in their jobs than in the past. This is also what we want to achieve, and you will experience it. How are we going to achieve this?

## 1.2    The point of departure: Demarcating the field of study

To study anything in a meaningful way, we must start with the gestalt. This means the whole. The big picture. Only when we grasp the big picture will we be able to understand the small 'pictures' contained therein. In academic terms, a subject or discipline, like HRM is referred to as 'a body of knowledge'. But you must also remember that a 'body of knowledge', like a human body, consists of many different parts. It is always amongst other relevant bodies of knowledge but, as was explained above, the body of knowledge called Human Resources Management is an applied body of knowledge, i.e. it consists of various relevant parts of other bodies of knowledge (see Figure 1.1).

The authors of this book support the view of many leading authors like Mullins (1997: 398) in the definition of management as:

- Taking place within a structured organisational setting (usually the workplace).
- Consisting of prescribed work roles (selection and job descriptions).

**Figure 1.1**  The study of the field of human resources management as demarcated in this book

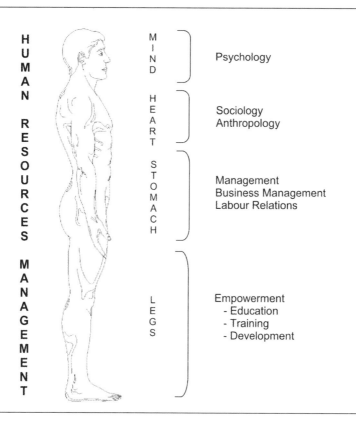

Directed towards the attainment of aims and objectives (organisational efficiency, effectiveness and success), achieved through the efforts of other people (leadership, motivation, groups) and using systems and procedures (culture, policies, communication, performance appraisal).

From this brief description it is evident that management is in itself not an independent discipline. No single discipline can describe the field of management by itself. Management is, however, a science and an art, and must be viewed from our perspective as superimposed on all known disciplines. It is wrapped around any and all 'parcels' of knowledge in the applied sciences.

The second important sister discipline is *psychology*. Psychology is the study of the essence of human nature and human behaviour. It studies the traits of the individual as a whole person, and includes aspects such as perception, attitudes and motives. In the context of this book, its application is confined mainly to the selection process and, to a large degree, to motivational theories.

Thirdly, the field of *sociology* is of great significance, especially in dealing with groups and the cultural aspects of organisational functioning. As the name suggests, sociology is the study of social behaviour and relationships within and among groups (inter- and intra-group behaviour in this book). Leadership as a field of study evolved mainly from this sphere. Together with sociology goes anthropology (traditionally 'the study of humankind'), a discipline of special importance within the South African context. Contemporary legislation and practice requires interventions like affirmative action and equity. The diversity of the South African work force is reflected within organisations. It's an established fact that cultural diversity provides a person with security and stability within the workplace. If the organisational culture does not accommodate diversity within a diversified universe, cultural minorities will suffer adverse reactions to unfamiliar work environments.

*Business economics* or *business management,* as it is referred to these days, is essentially the study of management, firstly from a macro- or corporate point of view, and then functionally. Any business (and most other institutions) carries out its tasks through different specialist fields, which Frederich Taylor termed 'functions'. These functions represent the core activities as well as the supporting activities of a business, and normally manifest in logistics (the procurement of raw material in any form), the production of goods or services from these raw materials, the marketing of these products, and the physical selling and distribution thereof.

Business management includes further activities that must be carried out in support of those already mentioned, such as human resources, finance, public relations and social responsibility, quality control, quality assurance and customer satisfaction. The last-mentioned supporting activity manifests itself in different ways and forms within an enterprise. In this book, much emphasis is placed on quality assurance.

Then there is the field of *employment relations*. In the South African world of work, labour relations is by far the most tangible of all the above sub-disciplines. You perhaps now belong to a registered employment organisation according to the Labour Relations Act (No. 66 of 1995), or you certainly will be when you embark on a career. In South Africa, the labour movement started late in comparison

to the first world countries due to the apartheid legislation that severely restricted management. The labour movement was reactive in nature, and indeed still is if compared to the status quo in leading industrial countries. Given the rise of globalisation and world competitiveness, South Africa's ability to compete successfully in the global market is in the balance if a better dispensation between the leading trade union movements and the Government can't be found in the near future. The neglect of this subtle issue can harm any company tremendously.

Last, but not least, is the field of *empowerment*. Empowerment is an umbrella term referring to education, training and developmental activities to which people, whether young or old, are exposed with a certain purpose in mind, i.e. to uplift and enable them to execute a job more effectively.

## 1.3   Redefining human resources management

In this book, the approach to HRM is future orientated. However, the basics remain the same as they have always been. An approach, which for a long time has complemented the author's view, is that of Hall and Goodale (1986:6). They note that 'human resources management is the process through which an optimal fit is achieved among employee, job, organization, and environment so that employees reach their desired level of satisfaction and performance and the organization meets its goals.' The rise of and focus on HRM in managing the fit between jobs and knowledge capital (to be discussed later) substantiates Hall and Goodale's (1986) view.

It is clear from Figure 1.2 that there are four important components in the definition given by Hall and Goodale, namely: the external environment, the organisation, the work itself, and the individual or employee.

Nowadays, and because the world has become a global market place, the focus of human resources management lies in the integration of the HRM strategy into the global strategy of the organisation. This approach has been needed for a long time, since human resources is the only dynamic production factor an organisation has, and it is also the only factor that reacts when acted upon.

### 1.3.1  The external environment

Every organisation exists inside an external environment that consists of four primary sub-environments, namely:

- The social environment.
- The economic environment.
- The political environment.
- The technological environment.

The economic environment must surely be important from a free market (capitalistic) point of view. In the general literature, the economic environment is taken to mean the external influences that have an effect on an organisation, such as:

- The availability of capital.
- The current interest rates.
- The rate of inflation.
- The level of employment (whether it is above or below national average).

The influence of the social environment of an organisation has been under-estimated to a large extent in the past. Nowadays, it features much more prominently as far as the top management of organisations is concerned.

The social environment is shaped by the society in which the organisation features. Potential customers and employees of the organisation, with their attitudes and values concerning work, products and business, their educational and skill levels, and their expectations, are integral parts of the social environment. To prosper, the organisation must achieve a fine balance between the needs of the employees and customers, and meeting its own organisational goals.

The political environment is particularly important in the present South African context. Every organisation is run according to laws and regulations, whether they originate at central, provincial, or local levels. These laws and regulations influence any organisation from its external environment, regardless of the nature of the business.

Now, more than ever before, the technological environment has an influence on management philosophy, not only in South Africa,

**Figure 1.2** Components of human resources management

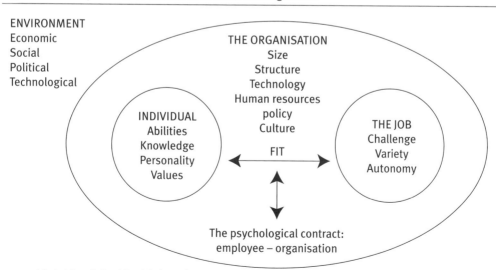

SOURCE: Adapted from Hall and Goodale (1986:4).

but in the general African context, since there is a positive correlation between the technology in use and the productivity of a community.

Technology essentially means the way in which an organisation changes the inputs (raw materials in whatever form is available) into outputs (products or services) by means of an ongoing process.

### 1.3.2  The organisation

Before going on to discuss the role that the organisation plays in this regard, cognisance must be taken of what constitutes an organisation. Schein (1980:15) says that:

> An organization is the planned coordination of the activities of a number of people for the achievement of some common explicit purpose or goal, through division of labor and function, and through a hierarchy of authority and responsibility.

According to Hall and Goodale (1986:5), an organisation has a number of characteristics. One obvious characteristic is size; some people have strong preference about the size of the organisation they want to join. Organisations also differ in their structure. Some are hierarchical while others are structured according to certain functional preferences. Another key characteristic of organisations is the technology that governs how work is done; this determines the profiles that employees must match. The organisation's human

**comment**

In South Africa, labour legislation, affirmative action, as well as laws and regulations with regard to training and development are currently of particular importance to the management of local organisations.

resources policies show its orientation towards people and play a major part in attracting and satisfying employees. Finally, the culture of the organisation is of particular importance. This indicates the way in which things are done in organisations, and is also known as the personality of the organisation. For the success of an organisation it is particularly important that the individual employee's personality and the 'personality' of the organisation are in tune with one another. A mismatch can hamper the attainment of both personal and organisational goals.

### 1.3.3  The work (job) itself

An individual employee joins an organisation by virtue of his/her potential for reaching personal goals in that organisation by supplying work and work potential. The basic motivation of a person (employee) in this context is that s/he sees the opportunity of satisfying his/her intrinsic and extrinsic needs (see Chapter 13).

Hall and Goodale (1986:6) comment in this regard that, among the key characteristics that directly affect employee performance and satisfaction are the degrees of challenge, variety and autonomy they offer to employees. Challenge is the level of difficulty of a job's tasks and activities. Variety refers to the number of different tasks and activities in the job, and autonomy is the extent to which an employee works independently on a job.

### 1.3.4  The individual employee

The last, but undeniably the most important component in Hall and Goodale's conceptualisation (see Figure 1.2) is the individual in an organisation.

The approach of Hall and Goodale (1986) now falls into line with that of the authors. As you get further into the book, the similarity will become more obvious.

However, if one takes the latest thought and emerging philosophy towards human resources management, one can also define it as follows:

Human resources management is the efficient delivery of customised quality assured human resources management services to the internal customers of the organisation through highly efficient knowledge assets (internal or out sourced) to enhance the organisation's global competitiveness (Van Dyk 2002:4).

The key elements contained in this definition, i.e. service delivery, customer satisfaction, quality assurance, internal customers, knowledge assets and globalisation, are discussed in later chapters.

## 1.4 Management approaches to human resources management

### 1.4.1 General

You, as reader or learner, find yourself as part of a family set up. In that sense you experience HRM approaches every day. For example, the traditional role of the father – head of the household, breadwinner and handy man; the mother – wife, housekeeper and cook; the daughter(s) – scholar or student and assistant housekeeper, cook; the son(s) – scholar or student and gardener or refuse man, runner. In other families things are viewed differently, i.e. every family member contributes to the maintenance and upkeep of the family household. The father provides the money, the family use that for everyday needs including food, heat, transport and social matters, and by so

---

**comment**

Note that the term 'employee' is used not only to mean the employee at a low level – even though people in the management of an organisation and who are responsible for its functioning normally dissociate themselves from this designation.

---

**comment**

Each individual brings a unique combination of attributes to an employer. Some personal characteristics that cause people to succeed or fail on a job are their abilities, knowledge, personality, values and expectations. Abilities and knowledge determine an employee's potential to perform specific jobs successfully. Personality, values and expectations are related to an individual's preference for different kinds of jobs and organisations and, therefore, determine the choice of a specific job or employer.

---

doing contribute to society and the economy while the father continues working. Still another form of 'housekeeping' exists where family members view and treat each other as a unique member(s) of the family who possesses the potential and ability to contribute something worthwhile to the household to make it work.

This same phenomena is present in all organisations, and therefore in human resources management. In this regard we refer to this perspective as the functional, systems and efficiency approaches to human resources management. All of these approaches are present in an organisation, although one is perhaps more prominent than the other two. This depends on the governance, nature, size, form of enterprise, composition of the labour force, product or service and target market or customers.

### 1.4.2 The functional approach to human resources management

From a functional perspective, human resources management is a staff function, with the aim of helping other functional managers to apply and utilise the most important production factor, human resources, as effectively as possible within the organisation. The people in an organisation essentially determine how successfully the other means of production will be applied.

Human resources management is a purposeful action of the human resources department, aimed at assisting functional managers in the optimal application and utilisation of the human resources under their control, in accordance with official organisational policy as well as general HRM theory and practice, in order to achieve the goals of the organisation.

Within the organisational framework of the company, the human resources function manifests itself as a human resources department. The human resources function of an organisation refers to a number of ancillary functions carried out in order to achieve the goals of an organisation. A human resources department, responsible for the organisation's human resources management activities, carries out the human resources function. However, the department also gives advice and assistance to the rest of the organisation.

The human resources function is, therefore, a staff function aimed at providing the organisation with labour, and giving it specialised human resources services to help it to achieve its goals. The human resources function should be flexible by implication, and the physical embodiment of this function depends on the nature of the organisation in terms of its size, products, services, and geographical location. The human resources function traditionally includes the following: human resources provisioning, comprising human resources planning, recruitment, selection, placement, induction, and career management; human resources maintenance, comprising the determination of conditions of service, remuneration structures, record keeping, personnel turnover, settlement of disputes, advisory services, employer–employee relations, social responsibility, affirmative action, and performance assessment; and human resources empowerment, with training, education and development as its most important activities.

Theoretically, three functions of the human resources manager may be distinguished:

- A service function.
- A control function.
- An advisory function.

The service function incorporates the everyday tasks of a human resources department, such as:

- recruitment;
- selection;
- remuneration;
- training; and
- health and safety activities.

The control function is more strategic in nature and incorporates activities such as:

- An analysis of key human resources management outputs such as labour turnover, productivity, absenteeism, and resignations.
- The recommendation of appropriate corrective action by line managers, such as training and development, dismissals, and transfers.

The advisory function is associated with the expert advice given by the human resources department in line with human resources policy and procedures with regard to matters such as:

- Which employees are ready for promotion?
- How should a grievance procedure be carried out?
- How should service contracts, and health and safety regulations be carried out?

From the above it is evident that the human resources manager must be a diplomat in the sense that s/he must act as a mediator between management and the employee, between management and management, and between various groups of employees. This role is of particular importance in contemporary South African organisations.

A typical HRM department with its different human resources management functions may be represented as shown in Figure 1.3.

A further distinction must be made between line, functional, and staff authority:

- *Line authority* is the authority vested in managers to give their subordinates orders that they are expected to carry out. In other words, line authority is the direct authority of any manager or supervisor over immediate subordinates. For example, the general manager has line authority over heads of departments who have line authority over employees in their sections, and so forth. Line authority gives the human resources department the right to issue enforceable orders to its functionaries on any matter dealt with by the human resources department.
- *Functional authority* gives the human resources manager the right to issue enforceable instructions on human resources matters throughout the organisation, in order to fulfil duties and responsibilities outside his or her own department. The authority to ensure that human resources policy, regulations and procedures are correctly applied is an example of this functional authority.

- *Staff authority* is only advisory and cannot be enforced. A functionary of the department may, for example, advise a supervisor how to reprimand an employee who is regularly late for work.

### 1.4.3 The systems approach to human resources management

The question arises: What is a system? A system is simply a number of interdependent components that form a whole and work together with a view to attaining a common goal. Thus, for example, you as a person are also a system in your own right (a biological system), and you come into daily contact with various types of systems:

- When you travel to work in the morning by car, bus, or train, you are part of a mechanical system.
- When you are at work, you are in a social system.
- When you come home in the evenings, you are in a micro-social economic system, i.e. your family.

**Figure 1.3** The place of the human resources management function in an organisation

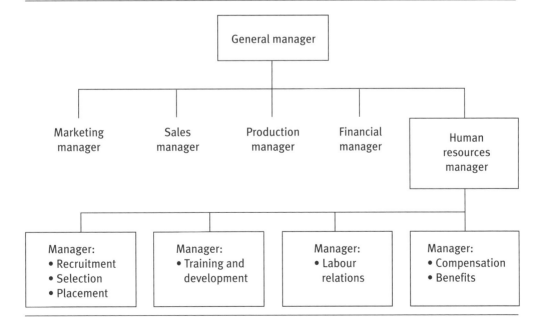

In the literature 'system' is derived from cybernetics, and here a distinction is made between a closed and an open system. A system is closed when it is self-sustaining and independent of external stimuli or input. An example is the development of a test-tube baby from conception (fertilisation) until it is implanted in the womb of a woman. An open system, on the other hand, requires certain input or stimuli from elsewhere, known in technical terms as the environment. A system is open if:

● It is dependent on the environment in which it operates.
● The environment depends on it.
● There is interaction between the system and the environment.

Diagrammatically, an open system can be represented as in Figure 1.4.

Though the human resources management function can be viewed as a sub-system of the organisation as a system, the focus in this discussion is on the human being as a sub-system within the human system of the organisation. In this way, the responsibility of human resources management can be highlighted.

In Chapter 2, the human being as an employee is discussed. However, to put this approach to HRM into perspective we must view human resources management of the individual (micro-) and its management of the function (macro-) as distinct. This will help to distinguish HRM practices aimed at the individual and those aimed at the total labour force of the organisation.

## A micro-systems view of human resources management

The argument presented here stems from the views of French and Bell (1984) and Gardner (1999). We have adapted these authors' stances for the purpose of the book.

The first sub-system is the goal sub-system (or goals, objectives, aims) of the organisation. If we take this as our point of departure, we must assume that work, as the main activity of an organisation's labour force, starts with the mission. The primary goals of the organisation (supporting the mission) are reflected throughout the existence and contents of the different departments. These priority goals, according to Gardner (1999:187), provide the glue that bonds the organisation together. To ensure organisational success, the alignment between organisational goals, departmental goals and mission must be examined continuously. As departments (functions) and processes become more efficient at achieving their own goals they may become further and further removed from obtaining organisational goals.

To accomplish goal integration and to realise the mission of an organisation from a work point of view, we must investigate what we do, how we do it, who does it and through what mechanisms. This proves that all sub-

**Figure 1.4** The basic elements of a system

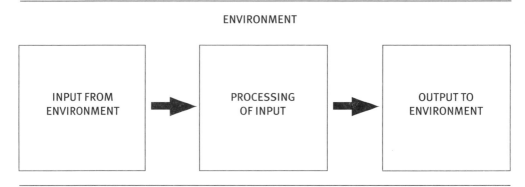

systems are mutually dependent on each other. The interdependence of the following two sub-systems is particularly important (see Figure 1.5):

- The *work task sub-system* of the organisation, consisting of the tasks and duties that employees perform. In a typical manufacturing concern it would include drawing up plans, delivering stock or raw materials, manufacturing a product(s) and selling it. Work task originates from job descriptions or other professional prescriptions and standard operating procedures about which information was gathered through a process called job analysis. Job descriptions form the basis of recruitment, selection and placement, while job analysis data also serve as important information upon which pay (compensation) is determined.

- The *work method sub-system*, i.e. how we do our work. The work method sub-system identifies how we work and how the individualised organisational process

facilitates outcomes for employees. Gardner (1999:189) states that work processes are not important in and of themselves; they are important only if they facilitate outcomes for people.

The difference between work tasks and work processes is illustrated by the distinction between form and function. For example, the selection of employees as a human resources function can take many forms. In a small business where only routine administrative skills are required (the function), the selection method would perhaps be word of mouth (form). The same job in a large organisation may require an intensive headhunt and reference checks.

The people sub-system (the who) consists of the individuals who make up the organisation. According to Gardner (1999:193), this people sub-system is simple to understand because it is about people, but it is difficult to analyse because people are unpredictable and not always as they appear. There are four aspects of this sub-system:

- *Skills and ability of the people.* Developing competent people for quality performance requires some effective combinations of effective recruitment, ongoing staff development, good supervision and opportunity for individual growth and development.

- *Leadership philosophy and style.* A leader's philosophy and style are related to the manner in which decisions are made, information is communicated and coordinated and the degree of concern for human values in the organisation.

- *Formal person systems.* Personnel functions, such as staffing, promotion, rewards, appraisal, performance, bargaining processes and systems for due process and appeal represent the formal person system. The formal system is encoded in the organisation's policies and procedures. The legislative environment of a company presents many aspects of the formal system.

- *Informal system.* The informal part of the people sub-system contains the values,

---

**Figure 1.5** A systems model of work

## WORK AS A SUB-SYSTEM

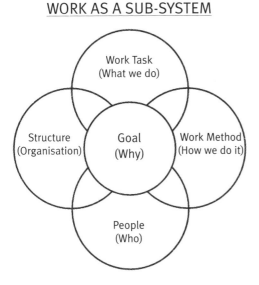

Source: Adapted from Gardner (1999)

norms and assumptions that govern group behaviour. They define the unwritten laws of how the organisation operates and explain the value and status of employees. The informal part of the people sub-system cultivates organisational renewal. Changing values, norms, and assumptions are preconditions for organisational renewal. These factors however cannot be changed by traditional management intervention. Sending managers on management development courses or seminars has no value if it isn't done within a contextual framework that will lead to a new paradigm (a total shift in mind). Organisational renewal requires a mind change within the dominant coalition of an organisation and realignment with organisational mission. It requires an open, painful focus on key issues by the very people who will be affected most by the proposed change.

- *The structural sub-system* is the most visible part of the organisation. This sub-system consists of the grouping of the organisation into units, departments or divisions. It also includes the work protocol, authority mechanisms, reward system and the communication sub-system. The structural sub-system also identifies the formal system policy towards centralisation, standardising and formalisation from which coordinating and decision-making relationships follow.

In conclusion, this micro-view holds certain key principles for quality human resources and organisational renewal:

- Depending on organisational characteristics, the external environment and individual skills, management can initiate change and quality improvement in any of the sub-systems.
- Successful quality improvement and change efforts will cross into other systems and eventually will reach throughout all systems.
- Efforts to define quality improvements and change within the context of a single

sub-system or to contain the change to a single sub-system will fail.

- Mission, principles and values are important; but they are just the starting point of change. Systems thinking reveals that an organisation can start with values, norms, etc., but change in quality improvement will require job content skills, interpersonal skills, understanding of the work and work processes, commitment and endurance.

These four points are what is meant by a futuristic view in human resources management, and constitute the new focus of this edition (which is regarded as an advanced point of departure).

## A macro-systems view of human resources management

A systems model is presented in Figure 1.6. This model has two main purposes. First, it focuses on the employee as a sub-system within the organisation as a system, with specific reference to the inputs which an employee brings into an organisation, the throughput process, and the outputs produced by employees. And, second, it focuses on those HRM sub-processes aimed at the management, maintenance, and development of an employee as a sub-system within an organisation. The purpose of these human resources management processes is to obtain optimal utilisation of the employee, as well as optimal outputs.

The individual employee is the smallest system within the organisation as a system. As can be deduced from the systems approach to organisations, there is a critical relationship between inputs, outputs, and throughputs in the organisation. As is the case with any organisation, individuals as a system also have certain inputs with which they join an organisation and which they release as long as they are part of the organisation.

These inputs are released mainly during the throughput phase where they are utilised and transformed by general and human resources

**Figure 1.6** A management systems model of the employee as a sub-system and human resources management processes affecting the individual employee

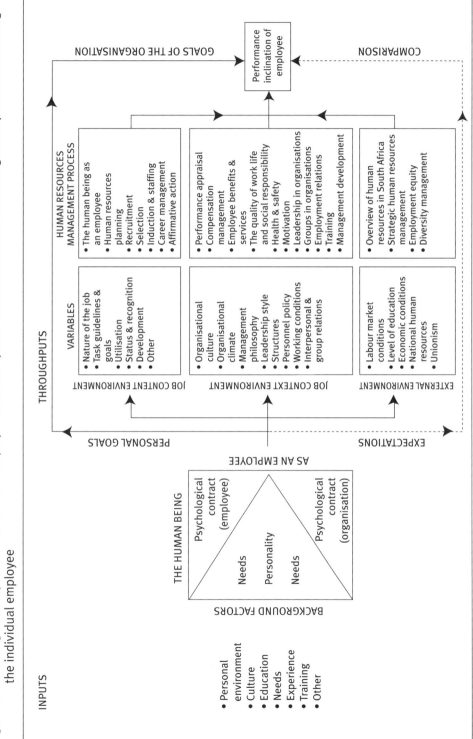

management processes. The quality of application of these processes determines the individual employee's outputs. These phenomena will become clearer during the course of this discussion.

The input process of individual employee functioning within the organisation is discussed at length in Chapter 2, but a few clarifying remarks are deemed necessary here:

- Each employee has a unique personality, and employees' personalities differ from one another. These differences mean that employees are not the same and do not necessarily experience the same needs at the same times. An employee's personality is the result of numerous variables, which have affected him/her since birth. These variables include aspects such as the personal environment in which the individual grew up, the culture to which s/he was exposed, and their needs, which, in turn, are the result of numerous other factors.
- Individuals' personality and needs constitute the basis of their expectations of their job (and of life in general). Because individuals have different personalities they also have different expectations in life. This may be observed in the way in which individuals pursue their personal goals in an organisation.
- Individuals set certain personal goals they wish to achieve in life on the basis of their unique personalities, needs, and expectations. To satisfy these needs and expectations, and to achieve these goals, individuals have to work and earn money. Individuals join organisations with the sole purpose of achieving their personal goals, as this results in need satisfaction. Individuals' personal goals, in turn, motivate them to behave in certain ways in the organisation. This behaviour is personal and is aimed at satisfying individuals' own needs and goals, irrespective of the group with which they identify. Therefore, individuals continuously interact with the organisation where they are employed in order to achieve their personal goals.

- Before an individual joins an organisation, a psychological negotiation process takes place, which takes the form of a psychological contract between the individual and the organisation. During this negotiation process, the individual states his/her expectations and personal goals, and the organisation similarly states its expectations and goals. If this negotiation process results in an agreement, the individual is employed and joins the organisation as an employee.

An employee's personal goals, together with her/his aptitude, qualifications, ability, experience, and potential, constitute the input process of individual functioning within the context of the organisation. This input phase is indicated on the left-hand side of the model in Figure 1.6.

In terms of the throughput process of individual employee functioning within the organisation, we may say that individuals with unique personalities join organisations with certain expectations, and formulate personal goals on the basis of a negotiation process resulting in a psychological contract. They try to achieve their personal goals while also pursuing the goals of the organisation.

There are three environments that exert an influence on employee functioning within the organisation. These environments are the job content environment, the job context environment, and the external environment:

- *The job content environment* may also be referred to as the psychological work environment, and may thus be regarded as the most significant environment in terms of its relation to individual performance as the basic cornerstone of success in the organisation. The job content environment is related to the psychological satisfaction experienced by the employee while doing the job for which s/he applied and was appointed. This is related to the cognitive, affective, and conative functions of people. The cognitive function refers to the stimulus value of the job, i.e. the extent to which it creates interest. The affective function refers to the emotional aspect, the employee's feeling or attitude and inclination towards the job as such. The conative function refers to the volitional aspect of people. It follows, then, that the job content environment refers to personal job satisfaction.

Different authors use different terms for these concepts; however, what is important is that they concur to a large extent on the elements present in the job content environment which exert an influence on the employee's inclination to perform.

One definition that may be closely related to what we term the job content environment concerns Herzberg's so-called motivators.

Herzberg (1966) found that factors relating to the job itself could have a positive effect on job satisfaction and result in increased output. He called these motivators or satisfiers, and identified them as the work itself, recognition, advancement, and the possibility of growth, responsibility, and achievement.

Ford (1969) emphasises job characteristics rather than individual differences: jobs with opportunities for achievement, recognition, responsibility, promotion and growth in competence are jobs that will promote motivation and job satisfaction. Turner et al. (in Wanous 1974: 616) identify six attributes that jobs need to have (job content environment) namely: variety, autonomy, compulsory interaction, optional interaction, required knowledge and skills, and responsibility.

In view of the aforementioned, an employee's job content environment consists of five important elements, i.e. the nature of the job, job guidelines and goals, utilisation, status and recognition, and development. These elements are now briefly discussed.

- *Nature of the job:* The nature of the job means what the job entails. Does it afford the employee the opportunity to utilise his/her abilities to their full potential? Does the employee find the opportunity for self-actualisation in the job? Does s/he have the opportunity to be creative and use initiative? Is the job interesting and in line with what s/he wants to do? Is there the opportunity for independent decision-making? Does the job offer variety?

- *Job guidelines and goals:* This element entails directing an employee's work behaviour in accordance with the goals of the organisation. An important element often neglected is linking job goals to the goals of the organisation. HRM processes relate to the job content environment and need to answer the following questions: Do employees know what they have to do? Do they know how to do it? Do they know why they are doing it? Is there a logical relation between what employees do and the goals of the organisation? Do employees know what is expected of them? Do they know what they are accountable for and what standards they are to maintain? Job guidelines and goals not only enable the employee to assess his/her activities within the functioning of the organisation, but they also spell out how s/he should attempt to achieve personal goals.

- *Utilisation:* Vroom (1966:143) states that the self-actualisation need is represented by the opportunity people are given to utilise their capabilities. We distinguish between qualitative and quantitative utilisation, however. Quantitative utilisation refers to the amount of time an employee actually spends on the job daily, whereas qualitative utilisation refers to the utilisation of an employee's potential such as intelligence, skills, and qualifications. Over- and under-utilisation may occur in both instances. Questions to be addressed in this respect in order to ensure optimal employee functioning are: Are employees busy every day all day? Is the extent of an employee's job such that s/he can cope with what has to be done? Are employees utilised according to their abilities, qualifications, experience and training?

■ *Status and recognition:* There is a causal relation between the types of job an employee has and the status enjoyed. Vroom (1966:141) describes it as follows:

The job is a description or a tag, which marks the person, both at his place of employment and in the world outside.

Status in this respect refers to the job content status, which means the relative status value linked to the job within a specific organisation by the organisation itself and by other employees of the organisation. Recognition in this respect comes from two sources. Firstly, it refers to the respect an employee enjoys among colleagues in the organisation, which is the result of the status value of the job. Secondly, it is the recognition the organisation affords an employee for good performance. The most critical question to be addressed by human resources management processes in this respect is whether employees are proud of their jobs, as this is the best indication of the status and recognition they themselves give to the job.

■ *Development:* Modern work life is characterised by technological and other changes placing increasing demands and pressure on employees. When employees are unable to meet changed job expectations or requirements, they become superfluous and redundant. In this respect, development refers to development possibilities within a job or position for a specific employee, with reference to the employee's personal growth and personal goals. In our opinion, development has a number of dimensions applicable to any work situation with-

in any organisation. Human resources management processes must assess the opportunities for training and development, whether the training offered is applicable to the execution of tasks and whether the work an employee is doing at present is preparing him/her for a higher position, i.e. whether there is career preparation.

Individual employee performance is the cornerstone of success in an organisation and takes place mainly in carrying out tasks given by the organisation. The extent to which employees experience psychological or personal job satisfaction within the job content environment determines to a large extent the quality and quantity of these employees' outputs.

● *The job context environment* has an extremely important influence on the throughput process in the employee's job context environment. This environment contains two important factors:

■ The leadership element in the job context environment consists of the employee's superiors, and the management cadre within the organisation. The leadership element determines numerous aspects of the job content, for example, the nature of the job. Therefore, the leadership element has a significant effect on the employee's job content environment.

■ Those elements that Herzberg terms the hygiene factors (discussed in detail in Chapter 13) are primarily satisfiers of lower-order needs that include physiological, safety, and social needs. According to Herzberg, examples of hygiene factors are salaries, promotion policy, and fringe benefits. These hygiene factors are an essential prerequisite for motivation to pursue the goals of the organisation. This is mainly because they are related to job content factors that become prominent once job context aspects are such that lower-order needs are reasonably satisfied, so that the employee will look for the opportunity to satisfy his/her higher-order needs within the job.

We must regard all the influences exerted on an employee (with the exception of the job content and external influences) because of his/her presence in the organisation, as job context influences affecting the employee in the job context environment. Porter et al. (1975:211) emphasise the significance of these influences on individual employee behaviour as follows:

Among the many influences on the work behaviour of individuals in organizational settings, none is more important or more pervasive than the design of the organization itself. By 'organization design' we mean primarily the particular arrangements of the structural factors that constitute the basic form and nature of the organisation.

In our opinion, the job context environment refers to the interpersonal as well as the intra-group job satisfaction individual employees experience because of their membership of an organisation. An employee derives interpersonal job satisfaction through interaction with peers, superiors, subordinates, and clients in the execution of the job. Schein (1980:88) calls this the employee's interaction context. In other words, interpersonal job satisfaction refers to satisfaction experienced by an employee within the context of the formal organisation, i.e. within the formal execution of his/her tasks. Intra-group satisfaction refers to the satisfaction an employee experiences through membership of informal groups.

Because humans are social beings, they will always try to establish informal interaction. Within the context of Maslow's (1954) theory, people are social beings and need to belong to groups and to be accepted by those groups. When a social need becomes dominant, a person will strive to establish favourable relationships with other persons. The need for social interaction may be satisfied in the work situation to a large extent, but it is very difficult to develop strategies that would translate this need into an incentive for improved performance.

We regard the following elements, that can have either a positive or a negative effect on the individual employee's functioning and her/his inclination to perform, as important within the job context environment: organisational culture, organisational climate, management philosophy, leadership style, structure and personnel policy, working conditions, and interpersonal and group relations.

- *Organisational culture:* We define the concept of organisational culture simply as 'the manner in which things are done in the organisation'. It is also known as the personality of the organisation. Irrespective of what it is called, the culture of an organisation develops over time, and employees are often not even aware of its existence. Organisational culture is, however, of particular importance to management because it helps them understand how employees feel about their work. Culture involves general assumptions about the manner in which work should be done, appropriate goals for the organisation as a whole and for departments within the organisation, and personal goals for employees. It is particularly the latter that makes the nature of the psychological contract (discussed in Chapter 2) of special importance in the pursuit of organisational success. It is represented by formal goals, structures, policy and communication.
- *Organisational climate:* In our opinion, organisational climate is an all-encompassing concept that could be regarded as the result of all the elements contained in the job context environment. For example, the climate within a specific organisation is the result of the

management philosophy of that organisation as shown in the style of management practised in the organisation. In this respect, human resources management processes should be directed at monitoring the outputs of the organisation, such as labour turnover, absenteeism, grievances, complaints, and productivity, as there is a correlation between these variables and organisational climate. This is the invisible side of organisational culture and represents the working of the informal organisation.

- *Management philosophy:* The origin of management philosophy lies in the assumptions people make in respect of others, and the way in which they perceive and interact with others. Irrespective of whether they are aware of it or not, people's social behaviour is based on the way in which they believe other people behave. Managers, as human beings, do not differ from other human beings. All managers direct their behaviour and actions according to the way they believe others (employees) behave. Human resources management processes must use management and organisational development to determine the prevailing management philosophy and its effect on the work behaviour of the worker corps, and to change this philosophy if necessary.

- *Leadership style:* In our opinion, leadership style is the way in which management philosophy manifests itself in practice. The important relationship between leadership style and employee outputs should be emphasised. There is no doubt that managerial leadership and supervision have an important impact on the motivation, commitment, adaptability, and satisfaction of employees. The human resources manager must ensure that the leadership of the management cadre in the work situation is sound,

as leadership behaviour has a significant effect on the functioning of individual employees.

- *Structures and personnel policy:* It is generally accepted that the structures of an organisation are related to the management style of its management cadre. The structures of an organisation may be defined as the sum total of the way in which its labour is divided into specified tasks, and the degree of coordination achieved between these tasks. The purpose of management is to bring about an effective organisation. There are various examples of the way in which management may use structures in order to achieve desirable results. For example, management may design compensation systems, especially bonus systems, to promote performance and goal achievement; or they may implement job specialisation to promote closer supervision to counteract deviations from instructions. It is clear that all these aspects are related to HRM processes. Personnel policy is a result of human resources management as a sub-system within an organisation. Therefore, personnel policy has a direct influence on employee functioning. Examples of this influence are: the effects of the compensation policy of the organisation, its promotion policy, and its labour relations policy on the individual employee. Numerous human resources management processes use these means to retain employees.

- *Working conditions:* Working conditions are created by the interaction of employees with their physical work environment. It is that environment that impacts on employees' senses and which is related to their lower order needs, which in turn affect their physiological functioning. Various sub-elements of working conditions should be distinguished.

The first sub-element is the *physical working conditions.* This aspect refers to the amount of work and the availability of facilities, such as production machinery and protective clothing, and to aspects of the physical environment in which the employee works, such as ventilation, lighting and space. There are, thus, two important considerations in the physical work environment, i.e. aids and the physical work environment per se. Aids refer to the equipment and appliances at the employee's disposal for the execution of a task, irrespective of its nature. What is important is the extent to which these aids enable employees to function effectively. The physical work environment per se refers to the attractiveness of the work environment – the aesthetic element and other aspects involved in the physical execution of tasks.

The second sub-element is the *psychological working conditions.* According to our view, this refers to the psychological effect of work pressure on individuals and groups. Psychological working conditions also include the psychological expectations of employees as to the psychological contract in respect of their working conditions, compared to what they actually experience.

The last sub-element is the *physical layout of the job,* which refers to the neatness, organisation, convenience, attractiveness, and stimulus value of an employee's personal micro-work environment. This affects the employee's physical interaction with these work aids, and this interaction affects physical and sensory functions.

It seems clear, therefore, that human resources management processes are faced with a number of problems which may affect employee functioning within the job context environment.

- *Interpersonal and group relations:* In our opinion interpersonal and group relations are a sub-section of working conditions and, more specifically, social working conditions. Interpersonal relations can be defined as the whole range of human conduct between individuals who interact, as

they are involved in relationships of communicating, cooperating, changing, problem-solving, and motivation. In these relationships, each employee tries to influence and adapt the behaviour of other employees in order to satisfy his/her own needs. Therefore, we should take a brief look at the role of the individual employee within the group context.

An organisation depends on groups for the achievement of its goals, therefore it is organised accordingly. Continuous interaction is a characteristic of groups within an organisation. The ideal state for each group is one of harmonious cooperation in order to achieve the goals of the organisation. In practice, however, groups are continuously in a state of conflict, mainly because they are often competing with one another. If this competition does not coincide with or follow the direction of the goals of the organisation, it will adversely affect the organisation. Competition should be in line with the goals of the organisation, and this means that group objectives need to be associated with these goals, bearing in mind that groups, as sub-systems of the organisation, have their own goals. In addition to the formal groups and the reasons they compete on a formal basis, there are informal groups within an organisation, and these probably have the strongest influence on formal groups. Informal group formation determines group functioning and sets informal group goals, which may either help or hinder the achievement of the goals of the organisation. Interpersonal and group relations present a great challenge for human resources management because of their effect on the functioning of an organisation.

To summarise, individual motivation and, therefore, individual performance, is either positively or negatively affected by the individual's job context environment. The philosophy of the management cadre or the leadership element determines to a large extent the nature and content of the influencing process within the job context. The leadership style of the management cadre in an organisation is a primary factor influencing employee functioning and performance. Structure and policies within an organisation must be such that they will not only promote the achievement goals of the organisation, but also enhance the achievement of individual goals within the framework of the psychological contract. Physical, psychological, and social working conditions are important in any organisation. In this book we regard these conditions as even more important than is generally maintained among theorists. The quality of interpersonal and group relationships is equally important in view of the significant effect this has on the achievement of employee goals and the goals of the organisation.

However beneficial individual employees' job content environment may be to individual performances, influences from the job context environment, together with the external environment, are jointly responsible for their motivation and performance. The last environment in the throughput process of HRM is the individual employee's external environment.

- *The external environment* that exerts an influence on individual employee functioning will now be discussed in broad terms only. The term external environment refers to areas outside the organisation that affect employees via the organisation, as well as areas within the organisation that affect individual employees. We refer specifically to the effect of labour demand and supply on an

employee's period of service with a particular organisation. For example, an employee may be unhappy with her/his job content and job context environments in an organisation, but is forced to stay with that organisation because of labour market conditions. Such an employee will probably do just enough work not to be dismissed. In this respect, the economic conditions of South African organisations and the entire country are highly relevant, as well as the effects of these conditions on individual employees. For example, the state of the economy has a direct effect on employees' compensation packages. Furthermore, technological change plays an important part. Owing to the lack of skilled employees in the country, organisations are sometimes forced to mechanise, and this often leads to unemployment. These factors have an indirect effect on employees' performance inclinations.

## Summary

Figure 1.6 indicates the three environments, i.e. an employee's job content environment, job context environment and external environment, as illustrated on the left-hand side of the model. The dotted line indicates the psychological contract, with specific reference to the extent to which an employee progresses towards the achievement of personal goals. The solid line at the top of the model is also related to the process of comparison mentioned above, with specific reference to the opportunity an employee perceives in an organisation to achieve personal goals while at the same time pursuing the goals of the organisation. If the opportunity is provided, the employee will integrate personal goals with the goals of the organisation, which will serve as a foundation for motivated employee behaviour. The extent to which personal goals coincide with the goals of the organisation determines the employee's inclination to perform. This inclination has a direct bearing on the employee's real outputs in terms of efficiency and effectiveness, which ultimately determine the success of the employee.

### 1.4.4 The efficiency approach to human resources management

**General**

The success of an organisation means the extent to which it succeeds in achieving its organisational goals, as measured against set standards of achievement. According to the systems approach to organisations, organisations have multiple goals. To be successful, they must therefore work towards the optimal achievement of multiple goals.

**Multiple goals in an organisation**

The goals of an organisation are usually divided into three broad categories: long-, medium-, and short-term goals:

- Long-term goals focus on the organisation's ability to adapt to changes in the economy. They include: situation, technological development, social responsibilities, statutory and political responsibilities, human resources requirements, etc.
- Short-term goals are set, measurable goals with regard to production (for example, returns, sales, and market share); efficiency (for example, labour costs, unit costs, refuse, and waste); and employee satisfaction (for example, morale, attitudes, labour turnover, absenteeism, fatigue, and grievances).
- Medium-term goals are formulated to fill the gap between set long- and short-term goals; for example, to increase market share by 30 per cent over a period of three years, at a rate of 10 per cent per annum.

A question that might arise is how this relates to the study of human resources management. The relation between HRM and the success of an organisation is now discussed in detail.

**The cornerstones of organisational success**

The success of an organisation is based on two cornerstones: efficiency and effectiveness. This is illustrated in Figure 1.7.

In simple terms, the efficiency of an organisation means doing things the right way and is closely related to ratios. Examples of ratios are the input-output ratios of individual employees, sections, and departments, in other words, the cost-effectiveness ratios in the production process and other processes within the organisation. The efficiency of an organisation also refers to the nature and quality of the interpersonal, inter- and intra-group relationships within the organisation. Beer (1980:29) defines organisational efficiency as follows:

> [Organisational efficiency] may be defined as the extent of fit between the

**Figure 1.7** The relation between efficiency and effectiveness and the success of an organisation

internal components of the social system. The more congruity exists between these components the more the organisation will function smoothly, with relatively little dissatisfaction on the part of organisation members.

Beer's definition (as adapted by the authors of this book) has many implications; among other things, it demands thorough internal management of the organisation.

Effectiveness means doing the right things, which is primarily determined by setting goals for the organisation. These goals are not set in isolation, but are directly linked to the demand for an organisation's product or service. A study of this demand must also be based on the systems approach, with particular attention to the background of the organisation's supra-system. Only thorough identification and analysis of the needs of groups interested in the organisation will enable top management to interpret the demand correctly, and formulate goals for the organisation accordingly.

The following comments can be made with regard to organisational effectiveness: Effectiveness may be defined as the extent of fit between the organisation's environment and all the internal components of the social system. The more congruity exists between the internal social system components and the environment, the more the organisation is likely to exchange favourably with its environment.

In view of the above we can place organisational success in perspective, as follows: Organisational health (success) may be defined as the capacity of an organisation to engage in ongoing self-examination aimed at identifying incongruities between social system components and developing plans for needed change in strategy (environment), structure, process, people, culture and the dominant coalition. Such a healthy organisation is likely to maintain organisational efficiency and effectiveness in the long term.

If organisational managers carry out the tasks assigned to them in an effective manner, and set aside organisational politics, they should be able to transform their organisations in the interests of their employees and shareholders, and ultimately to the benefit of South Africa.

However, these goals (and therefore the success of the organisation) cannot be achieved of their own accord. Goals cannot be achieved without the necessary resources. Resources such as capital, raw materials, and machinery are static and can only take on a dynamic character through the intervention of labour resources (i.e. human resources). For this reason there is a causal relationship between the success of an organisation and the utilisation of its resources, in particular human resources, which activate the other resources. Therefore it seems essential that HRM be studied from a management point of view, especially in the light of the purpose of human resources management (namely to provide the organisation with a more efficient and effective worker corps). Every organisation's worker corps consists of individual workers, groups, and management. In this respect, the task of human resources management may be defined as follows:

Human resources management implies the proactive creation, maintenance and development of individual and group efficiency and effectiveness in order to improve individual and group performance (output).

Figure 1.8 clearly shows that organisational success is the result of interaction between a number of variables. As mentioned, an organisation cannot be successful unless it accurately identifies the demand for the product or service within its external environment (effectiveness of the organisation). An organisation may accurately identify and define the demand for its product or service, and yet not be successful if it does not 'do things in the right way' (efficiently). This is illustrated in the following example.

Suppose the management of an organisation determined, on the basis of their strategic

**Figure 1.8** The relation between the success of the organisation and individual and group
performance

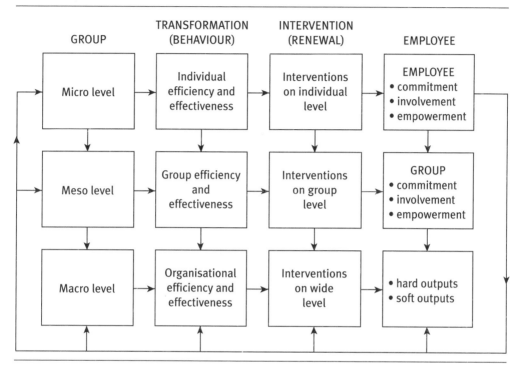

planning and market research, that there was
a great demand for a less expensive version of
a popular bicycle for children, and decided to
produce it. They supplied according to
demand, and sales forecasts were topped
within a short period. Within the course of a
few months, the organisation's management
learnt from the media and through complaints from their outlets that their version of
the bicycle had been responsible for many
injuries among children using it. A thorough
internal investigation found that the strength
of the metal used for the bicycle was in accordance with the predetermined standards, but
that the quality maintained during the assembly process was poor. As a result of these incidents the demand for this particular bicycle
dropped sharply, and the organisation also
became less successful with regard to the
other products it marketed. On further investigation it was found that, for various reasons,

the motivation of production personnel was
very low, which resulted in a negative attitude
towards their work and the organisation and
its goals. In other words, although the management of the organisation was doing 'the
right thing', they were not doing it 'in the right
way'.

This example may also be approached from
the point of view of the effectiveness of the
organisation. Suppose the demand for that
particular bicycle had indeed been identified,
but the price was set so high that the greatest
portion of the market (parents) could not
afford it despite the fact that it was an example of exceptionally fine workmanship. In this
case, the organisation would not have been
successful either, as it was not 'doing the right
thing' even though it was 'doing it in the right
way'.

Figure 1.8 also shows that the efficiency of
the organisation depends on group perform-

ance. Organisations consist of groups of employees, and employees are grouped on the basis of joint activities at work. For these reason organisations have different departments, such as production, marketing and personnel, based on a functional approach. This implies that groups (whether departments, divisions, sections or plants) produce the organisation's product or render its service according to the demand, as identified, with a view to the effectiveness of the organisation. Group performance, however, is the result of group efficiency and effectiveness. Group effectiveness refers to the extent to which groups 'do the right things'. Here, the extent to which the formal activities of groups coincide with the goals pursued by the organisation is relevant (from the point of view of the effectiveness of the organisation). In other words, are they doing the right things in terms of the goals set for them by the management of the organisation?

Group efficiency refers to the extent to which groups carry out their tasks in the right way (i.e. in the most cost-effective way). This includes the quality and quantity of work produced.

The next point to be dealt with is the relationship between individual performance and the success of the organisation. Figure 1.9 illustrates that individual performance (which is the result of individual efficiency and individual effectiveness) is the cornerstone of the success of an organisation. Therefore, the main responsibility of human resources management lies in this area. One might ask how human resources management is involved here.

Human resources management is mainly concerned with establishing, maintaining and improving individual performance, as individual performance is the key to the success of an organisation.

Figure 1.9 also illustrates a number of different aspects of the efficiency of an organisation and its success. In addition, it indicates that individual performance is the result of

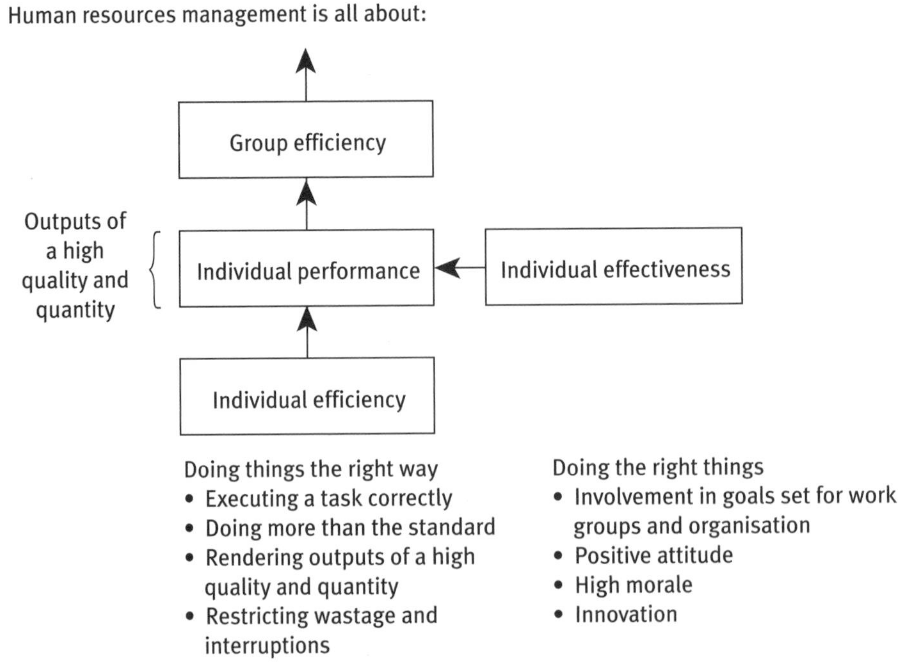

**Figure 1.9** The relationship between individual performance and group efficiency

the interaction between an unlimited number of the elements of both individual effectiveness and individual efficiency. From this point of view, quality individual performance is regarded as the cornerstone of the efficiency of an organisation and its success.

## 1.5    Challenges to human resources management entering a global era in organisations

### 1.5.1    General

The South African business and institutional world is facing two major challenges from an international point of view, i.e. globalisation and knowledge management. From an African and regional point of view, issues such as the SADEC (Southern African Development and Economic Community) agreement and NEPAD (New Economic Plan for African Development) – which are intertwined – together with the new African Union bring new continent-wide challenges closer to home. And then, of course, there is HIV/AIDS and the so-called brain drain. However, and against a multitude of counter-arguments, to meet these challenges Africa needs globalisation and, especially to succeed in the global market place, the creation of knowledgeable organisations with quality human resources covering all fields of economic activity together with technological transformation where most needed.

### 1.5.2    Globalisation

Globalisation can be defined as the ever-increasing integration of national economics into the global economy through trade and investment rules and privatisation, aided by technological advancement. In the Northern Hemisphere, and also in East Asia, globalisation can be regarded as highly successful. However, we live in Africa where the benefits of globalisation are questioned even by Kofi

Annan: 'How can we say that half the human race which has yet to make a telephone call, let alone use a computer, is taking part in globalization? We cannot without insulting their poverty' (in Mahiaini 2002:1).

Annan's statement must be seen against the following background (Guilford 2002):

- The share of the poorest fifth of the world population in global income has dropped from 2.3 per cent to 1.4 per cent over the past 10 years.
- The proportion taken by the richest fifth has risen from 70 per cent to 85 per cent.
- In sub-Saharan Africa, 30 countries have lower incomes per head in real terms than they did 20 years ago.
- 340 million Africans live on less than 60p (R7.50) a day.

It is a well-known fact that the major beneficiary of globalisation in Africa is South Africa with a share of 40 per cent of sub-Saharan GDP. In dollar terms, our own GNP per capita is US$3010 in sharp contrast to Zambia's US$350, Malawi's US$145, and Mozambique's US$80.

From the point of view of globalisation, South African business within the African (and especially within the SADEC) context is doing very well. From an international perspective, South Africa is lagging behind, and labour issues which have recently turned into political issues are harming the South African business world and are responsible for a decelerated pace towards a bigger bite in globalised profit-sharing.

The dilemma, as we see it, is the way this phenomenon is affecting and will be effecting HRM in South African companies and situations. Globalisation has especially placed business everywhere in new and different competitive situations. South Africa's present competitive ability in terms of management, and especially human resources management, is still alarmingly low. To become an effective and competitive global player (and not only an African Union player) is a significant stumbling block in the national quest for a better quality of life for all.

### 1.5.3  Knowledge management

A definite key to becoming and remaining a global contributor for any business is to unlock and unfold the human capacity in its service or employment. Viewing a company's human resources as knowledge capital brings a new focus to the management thereof. Wiig (1999:155) states that a competitive edge can be obtained in different competitive situations with knowledgeable, effective behaviour of its employees.

The concept of knowledge has been subdivided by Nonaka (1991) between knowledge as we have always known it (education, training for knowledge, insight and application) and knowledge as tacit. According to Nonaka (1991:8), tacit knowledge consists of:

> highly personal and hard to formalize subjective insights, intuitions, and hunches ... Tacit information is deeply rooted in an individual's action and experiences as well as the ideals, values or emotions he or she embraces.

Explicit and systematic knowledge management (KM) methods are internationally or globally recognised as important approaches to improve organisational performance, either through knowledgeable people delivering quality work more effectively, or through other ways of leveraging intellectual capital.

South African companies cannot avoid the increased requirements for better knowledge in the workplace to deliver competitive knowledge-intensive work. Demands have increased for customised and more sophisticated products and services. Globalisation pressure has changed business – and correspondingly work – worldwide. In this regard, Wiig (1999:156) remarks that nations which earlier supplied manual labour have started to compete with Europe, Japan, and North America (the so-called developed countries) by offering competent intellectual work.

From the HRM perspective, knowledge management subscribes to the basic compo-nents of organisational success, namely organisational effectiveness and efficiency. Suffice is to say that knowledge management requires the organisation and systematisation (the systems approach to human resources management) of work and individuals to apply to all required resources effectively. Hence, and according to Wiig, among proactive enterprises, there are increased efforts to make individuals and therefore the enterprise itself act as effectively as possible.

### 1.5.4  SADEC, NEPAD and the new African Union

The view that globalisation can never work for the poor and that integration into global markets will inevitably cause more poverty and inequality (referred to as 'globa phobia') is unjustified. Equally untrue is the opposite: 'globa philia', that holds that increased integration through trade and openness is an almost automatic passport to more rapid growth and poverty reduction. In our understanding, the approach that SADEC and NEPAD have to follow with reference to all aspects of the national economy is to reinforce and empower, with the aid of foreign capital, those national human resources enterprises which are close to, on the verge of, and already fit to compete on the international open markets and especially in those niche markets which are unique to Africa. In South Africa, the motor-industry is a very good example of optimising national resources to the benefit of the total SADEC region, even though South Africa has no motor vehicle of its own. We can only hope that those rich countries that invest in SADEC and NEPAD will appreciate the lesson demonstrated by such success: teach local and African producers and organisations how to fish rather than encourage them to buy fish. This is especially applicable to human resources and information technologies. A small contingent of highly efficient and effective knowledgeable companies delivering quality products from SADEC and NEPAD countries on the open global market can have numerous spin-offs, of which the upliftment of national human resources is the most important.

## 1.5.5  HIV/AIDS

There are so many predictions of the number of people who will die of HIV/AIDS that in terms of strategic human resources planning, companies and governmental institutions can only use 'guestimate' figures. One such figure states that in Africa there were 28 million people living with HIV/AIDS in 2002, while in 2000, according to the same source, there are 1500 deaths per day in South Africa (Guilford 2002:2). However, what is true is that HIV/AIDS in Africa primarily kills those people between 25 and 35 years of age who are economically active. We must assume that any person who is economically active would have received some degree of education and training. Globalisation, however, places a premium on intellectual property, which must be identified and developed within African companies if other SADEC countries and NEPAD want to obtain a larger share of the growth as a consequence of globalisation.

## 1.5.6  The flight of skills or 'brain drain'

The South African labour force, especially that sector that possesses high intellectual capacity, is leaving the country and the national economy at an alarming rate. These people go to first world countries where they assist in keeping up and expanding the globalised effort of such countries. As a result, back home the situation either remains the same or further stagnates. This phenomenon is a reflection of the current national state of depression in South Africa, where the focus on affirmative action and also super-taxation is frightening away intellectual capital.

According to *South Africa Survey's* 'millennium edition' (Potter 1999) 170 000 people emigrated to first world countries, especially Great Britain, Canada, Australia and New Zealand. Thousands of these people are among the best-educated professionals in the world. In fact, South Africans have such a high status as quality employees that the demand and financial offers grow at an alarming rate. How South African companies are going to maintain their professionals and this capital human resources investment in the future is unsure if they do not compete effectively on the international intellectual capital market.

Also in many sub-Saharan countries, skilled people emigrate to first world countries only to perform menial work with much better spin-offs than the educated and skilled work activities that they were involved in, in their home countries. This state of affairs has an adverse effect on the globalisation ability of Africa.

## 1.5.7  Summary

There are many other smaller issues that impact on human resources management's quest for efficiency and effectiveness. The South African challenges mentioned above are, however, so critical that it is hard to envisage sustainable growth in SADEC. Even the future of NEPAD and the new African Union is questionable – not from the first world, but from inside Africa. The heart of the problem is the competency of the continent's human resources.

## 1.6    The structure of the book

This book is presented, as far as possible, consistent with the layout of the body of knowledge depicted in Figure 1.1. It consists of six parts and twenty-four chapters including this chapter.

- *Part 1: General introduction and basic knowledge prerequisite to human resources management.* This part consists of three chapters. Every science or discipline contains basic theoretical truths that must be understood in full before the dissecting of the subject can move to different topics. With reference to Figure 1.1, Chapter 2 address both 'mind and heart' issues of the individual employee. It concludes with a chapter on quality assurance as the perspective from which HRM is approached in this book.

- *Part 2: Human resources management and the legislative environment.* This part consists of three chapters. Chapter 4 deals with the various statutes and theory of employment relations, while Chapter 5 addresses the important interdependency between employment relations and human resources management (and it includes handling mechanisms). The contemporary emotional issues of affirmative action and diversity management are prominent in South Africa. All people come from different cultural backgrounds. Even people with the same culture differ in accordance with the diverse family contexts in which they grew-up. This is referred to as cultural diversity, and these aspects all together deserve a chapter on its own, namely Chapter 6. With reference to Figure 1.1, this part represents the stomach as this has a direct bearing on individual employees' quality of life.

- *Part 3: Staffing the organisation and maintaining people.* Six chapters are contained in this part. They cover the spectrum from job vacancies to company regulations regarding safety on the job (accident prevention) and healthy physical work environments. Pay and benefits play a critical part in every employee's mental make-up, and determining and differentiating between compensation levels will surely remain a headache for management till the end of time. With reference to Figure 1.1, this too is represented by the stomach of the body because, as is frequently said, it deals with bread and butter issues.

- *Part 4: Behavioural aspects of human resources management.* This part consists of three chapters. With reference to Figure 1.1, this part discusses sociological and anthropological aspects. However, Chapter 13 addresses motivation-related mind-issues, which are a direct conse-

quence of the human being as employee, discussed in Chapter 2. Different motivational theories (particularly those of Maslow and Herzberg) underlie the contents of Chapter 2. People or employees are social beings that flock together, and this phenomenon is referred to as grouping or groups within organisational context. In this respect, the science of HRM differentiates between formal and informal groups of people. People in any organised context are held together by the phenomenon of leadership.

All of these points refer to different types of human behaviour that are found in any structural context. Later in the book, Chapter 15 deals with the important aspects of group and teamwork.

- *Part 5: Employee, group and organisational empowerment through human resources management interventions.* This part consists of five chapters. During the course of this book you will be made aware of the absolute necessity of continuously empowering employees in new work technologies due to the accelerated pace of development. This human resources investment culminates in training and development, performance management, and organisation renewal and change management. Employees have become known as 'knowledge assets', and these assets must be protected and developed to enable organisations to become and remain 'knowledge entities' that are 'globally competent'. In this globalised age there is no place for incompetence, and it is the responsibility of HRM to intervene in a proactive way in the skills and knowledge levels of companies. The legs in Fig 1.1 represent labour mobility. These days, qualified and knowledgeable employees have the bargaining chip in their hands. A lack of empowerment leads to the negative organisational outcome known as labour turnover.

- *Part 6: Strategic and international human resources management.* Five chapters in this part conclude the body of knowledge presented in Fig 1.1. Strategic human resources management has grown in importance with the paradigm shift to employees as 'knowledge assets'. The loss of one 'knowledge asset' can ruin the global competitive advantage of a company overnight. There are no gentlemanly agreements in the business world of today, and the proverb 'one man's loss is another one's gain' is truer than ever. Therefore, strategic planning in this regard is paramount. It is also important to focus on information systems in human resources management (Chapter 22), as well as the important issue of reputation management in organisations. This part is concluded with reference to human resources in the wider context, in other words, the international aspect, and concludes with a future perspective on the human resources function in organisations.

## 1.7    Conclusion

This first chapter's purpose was to introduce the learner or reader to the study field of human resources management as an applied science. The various sub-disciplines of this body of knowledge will be evident in the contents of the chapters which make up this book. By the end of the book you should be able to confidently orient yourself within the field of HRM. Of importance to this chapter is the foundation of human resources management in definition and manifestation. The challenges to HRM are not distant or remote, and in most cases they are already part of the quest for better and improved practices within human structures so as to uplift quality of life outcomes in organisations, but perhaps more importantly, to contribute more directly to an increased GDP for all SADEC countries.

## Chapter questions

1   Explain in your own words what you understand by the concept 'body of knowledge'.

2   Define human resources management from both a traditional and quality assurance point of view.
3   Draw a functional chart of a human resources department known to you.
4   Explain by means of a practical example how the work that you do can be regarded as a sub-system.
5   Relate the different chapters in the book to the components of the body of knowledge depicted in Figure 1.1.
6   What is meant by globalisation?
7   Contrast the line function to the staff function. Why is human resources classified as a staff function?

## Bibliography

BEER, M. 1980. *Organization change and development: A systems view.* Goodyear, Santa Monica, California.

DRUCKER, P.F. 1979. *Management.* Heinemann, New York.

FORD, R.N. 1969. *Motivation through the work itself.* American Management Association, New York.

FRENCH, W. & BELL, C. 1984. *Organization development: Behavioural science interventions for organization empowerment.* (Prentice-Hall), Pearson Education Inc.

GARDNER, J.F. 1999. 'Organizations as systems'. In Gardner, J.F. & Nudler, S. (eds.) *Quality performance in human services: Leadership, values and vision.* Paul H. Brookes, Baltimore.

GUILFORD, P. 2002. *Journal of African Christianity.* (Photocopy – other details not available).

HALL, D.T. & GOODALE, J.G. 1986. *Human resources management: Strategy, design and implementation.* (Scott-Foresman), Pearson Education Inc.

HERZBERG, F. 1966. *Work and the nature of man.* World Publishing Company, Cleveland.

MAHIAINI, W. 2002. 'How globalization has affected Africa'. *Global connections conference.* Conference paper.

MASLOW, A.H. 1954. *Motivation and personality.* Harper and Row, New York.

MULLINS, L.J. 1997. *Management and organizational behavior.* (Pitman), Pearson Education (UK).

NONAKA, I. 1991. 'The knowledge creating company'. *Harvard Business Review,* November–December, 96:10.

PORTER, W.W., LAWLER, E.E. & HACKMAN, J.R. 1975. *Behavior in organizations.* McGraw-Hill Companies, New York.

POTTER, E. 1999. *South Africa Survey 1999–2000.* South African Institute of Race Relations, Johannesburg.

SCHEIN, E.H. 1980. *Organizational psychology.* (Prentice-Hall) Pearson Education Inc.

SWANEPOEL, B.J., ERASMUS, B.J., VAN WYK, M. & SCHENK, H. 2003. *South African human resource management: Theory and practice, 3rd edition.* Juta, Cape Town.

VAN DYK, P.S. 2002. *Strategic inputs for quality assurance in hospitality services.* Unpublished confidential report, Botswana.

VROOM, V.H. 1966. *Work and motivation.* Wiley, New York.

WANOUS, J.P. 1974. 'Individual differences and reactions to job characteristics'. *Journal of Applied Psychology,* 59(5):616–22.

WHITESIDE, A. & SUNTER, C. 2000. *AIDS. The challenge for South Africa.* Human & Rousseau (NB Publishers, Cape Town).

WIIG, K.M. 1999. 'What future knowledge management users may expect'. *Journal of Knowledge Management,* 3(2):155–165.

# 2

# The human being as an employee

PS van Dyk and PS Nel

## Learning outcomes

At the end of this chapter the learner should be able to:

- Explain the concept of personality in theory.
- Describe and evaluate the difference between the traditional and contemporary psychological contract between the employee and the organisation.
- Explain the authors' view of 'motivation' from a personal framework of reference.
- Describe the attachment to and involvement in the goals of an organisation from personal experience.
- Critically discuss the role of employees to add value as well as shareholder value to an organisation as a contribution to organisation goals.
- Critically evaluate the HRM approach to quality management described in this chapter.

## Key words and concepts

- adding value
- attachment
- bottom line
- expectations
- individual interaction
- involvement
- motivation
- organisational expectations
- organisational goals
- personality
- personal goals
- psychological contract
- shareholder value

## Illustrative case

'ONCE A GAUTENGER, ALWAYS A GAUTENGER'

**Background**
It is a common problem when moving from one province to another that the rest of the family often does not settle well, or alternatively settles too well. It is hard not to complete a posting once entered into, and therefore consideration must be given to the effect on an employee's continued psychological

attachment to the organisation. This would also include the effect on the family, and how it in turn affects the psychological contract.

The following is a case study of a family that was posted from Pretoria to Cape Town by a brewery.

After the negotiation of a re-location package, which included consideration for the children's schooling, Andre arrived at his destination in Cape Town, with the great expectation that the assignment given would be relatively straightforward without too much cultural integration required. For him and his family, as born and bred 'Gauties', and mad about their local rugby and soccer teams, it was tough. Andre's role was to assist the Cape Town subsidiary in the new financial systems and monitor the outcomes of quality control and business relationships for a three-year period as Dark Gauteng Lager Beer (Pty) Ltd. wanted to make in-roads into the Cape liquor market – which is, of course, predominantly a wine lover's paradise. The position in the beer business called for good exposure to clients as well as staff at the growing subsidiary.

The first two years went by slowly as he established training programmes and learning modules for staff to continually upgrade their knowledge of the new system in tune with the upgrades and additions of software inevitable in a growing organisation. At this time Andre stepped back and reviewed his first year. His work was fulfilling, but he found Cape Townians to be reproachful and having unanticipated differences in culture (such as rugby and food tastes). They also gave him the nickname of 'beer Gautie'.

These were relatively minor annoyances, but it was difficult to see the children not fitting in as well as expected and not being able to play the style of rugby they had grown up to love. Andre's wife, Jenna, was finding that Cape Townians were friendly, but did not enjoy the type of work she was doing, and was also concerned that the children were not doing as well at school as they had been

doing in Pretoria. At one stage Andre thought of resigning and moving back to Gauteng on their own, as his wife already started talking about moving back on her own. The family was not concerned when Andre was called back to the head office in Pretoria in his third year with the praise that his objectives were achieved admirably, and therefore a return to Pretoria was speedier than the original stipulated contract period. The experience of relocating to Cape Town was worthwhile, but any longer would have found the family finding it very hard to integrate back into Pretoria, as they had already lost a lot of friends due to their long absence and the changes in school syllabi. One of the children barely scraped through at the end of the first year and had to take lower-grade courses the following year.

What observations can you make from this in terms of Andre's psychological contract?

## 2.1    Introduction

This chapter focuses on the individual as an employee. In other words, the essence of this chapter is the inputs with which an individual joins an organisation as an employee. Discussions in this chapter will be presented in accordance with Figure 2.1. Each employee has a unique personality, and this aspect is dealt with briefly without giving too much psychological detail. Nevertheless, the emphasis in this chapter falls on the psychological contract, and the personal expectations and goals with which an individual joins an organisation and functions as an employee. As motivated employee behaviour is only possible when employee goals are integrated with the goals of an organisation, attention is also given to this most vital recipe for success. In recent literature, this integration is referred to as the human resources approach. The success of an employee depends primarily on him-or herself. You should therefore study this chapter very well before continuing with the others.

## 2.2 The individual employee as a human being

Personality is certainly one of the most exhaustively researched concepts in the field of behavioural science. The relationship between employee behaviour and personality requires knowledge and insight on the part of superiors to enable them to guide their subordinates effectively in their pursuit of the goals of the organisation.

According to Swanepoel et al. (2003:80–1), personality includes aspects such as emotions, interests, attitudes, values, behaviour and mental characteristics.

Personality refers to the way in which the biological, physical, social, psychological and moral traits of an individual are organised into a whole, and also to the relatively stable set of behavioural patterns which flow from the dynamic interaction between the individual and his/her environment in a particular situation.

Various personality traits can therefore be identified, each referring to a relatively stable characteristic responsible for some form of consistency in behaviour. For example, temperament, as a trait, refers to the individual's characteristic speed and way of reacting to stimuli and situations, to his/her emotional nature and total disposition, and is usually linked to physiological factors such as the individual's nervous system, endocrine and gland system, and also genetic factors.

It is generally believed that an individual's

**Figure 2.1** Major factors affecting personality

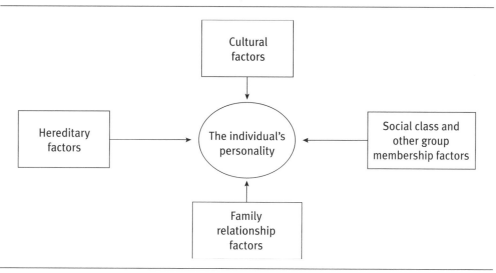

**Figure 2.2** The relation between personality and behaviour in organisations

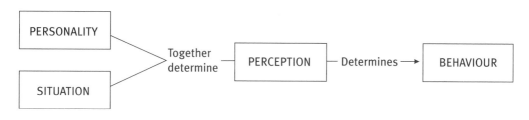

personality can have a marked influence on his/her work performance and on the extent to which such a person adjusts to her/his job. In this regard two aspects apply:

- First, it is reasonable to assume that in some circumstances personality factors do have an influence on job-related behaviour via a motivational route. One could thus expect individuals with certain personality traits to be more inclined to seek certain types of employment and to be better suited to such jobs than people with other personality traits.

- Secondly, it is reasonable to assume that, in some kinds of jobs, personality factors will have a direct bearing on the proficiency with which the individual will be able to perform his/her functions. This is particularly true of jobs that require a great deal of personal contact with other people, such as in public relations work, some management activities, interviewing, and so on.

It has been shown that hereditary factors do play a role in the shaping of personality, but that this role differs from one characteristic to the next. Heredity usually plays a more significant role in temperament than in values and ideals. Culture, however, has a major effect on the shaping of personality.

Culture impacts on peoples' personalities. It shapes personality gradually, and usually there is no alternative but to accept the culture. The stable functioning of a society requires that there be shared patterns of behaviour among its members and that there is some basis for knowing how to behave in certain situations. To ensure this, the society institutionalises various patterns of behaviour. The institutionalisation of some patterns of behaviour means that most members of a culture will have certain common personality characteristics. (Readers are referred to Chapter 23 where culture is discussed in more detail.)

This description poses many challenges for the management of people and human resources. A diversified worker corps requires a more scientific human resources management practice than a homogeneous worker corps. The South African labour market is not only characterised by wide national diversity, but also by international diversity. This state of affairs results in human resources policies and practices having to be based on well-considered scientific principles. (Readers are referred to Chapter 6 of this book where these aspects are discussed in more detail.)

Many authors conceptualise the influence of variables on personality as in Figure 2.1.

Social class is also important in the shaping of personalities. The environment in which a person grows up largely determines what s/he will learn about life. Social class affects a person's self-perception, perception of others and perception of work, authority and money. Such things as the nature of people's expectations of others, the way in which they try to achieve satisfaction, the way in which they express their feelings and solve emotional conflict, are acquired within interpersonal contexts. A key factor in this respect is the parent-child relationship, which serves as a model of behaviour patterns for the child and a frame of reference for her/his future.

The relation between an individual's personality and individual behaviour is shown in Figure 2.2.

This simple conceptualisation shows that the situations in which people are involved from time to time affect their perception of these situations, which in turn determines their behaviour (employee behaviour) in the execution of a task or job.

When one considers the factors contributing to the shaping of personality (as set out in Figure 2.1), it seems that superiors within organisations have very little control over these factors. The significance of this will become clear in the following discussion of our view.

## 2.3   The authors' view of personality

Our view of the employee as a person with his/her own personality is set out in Figure 2.3. Each individual has personal needs, expectations and goals. Each individual also has a unique personality that differs from that of others. These differences mean that people are distinct and do not necessarily experience the same needs at specific times. Consequently, people also have different expectations in life, and this is shown in the way in which they pursue personal goals in organisations. In practice we find that some individuals are happy if they can merely satisfy their basic needs and the minimum needs of the organisation, while others wish to satisfy social and status needs, and yet others are constantly trying to improve themselves and achieve self-actualisation. These behaviour patterns are the result of differences between individuals, as each individual constitutes a unique personality.

Personality is known to be the result of many factors, of which the most dominant are those shown in Figure 2.3.

An individual's personality is primarily the result of his/her personal environment from

**Figure 2.3** Human resources inputs in organisations

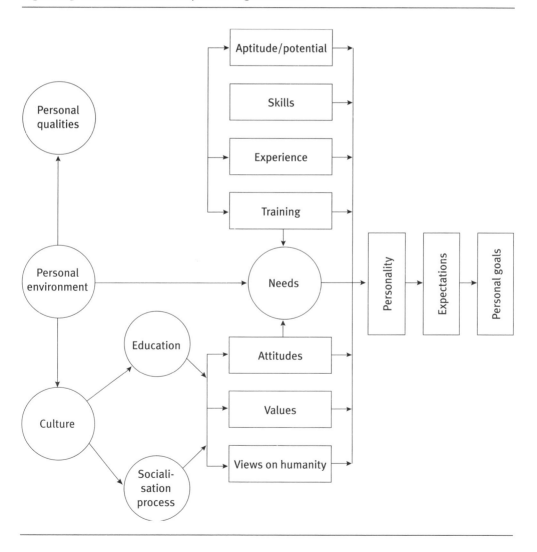

the day of birth until the day of joining the particular organisation with which s/he has entered into a psychological contract. Through personal environment an individual is exposed to a certain culture in terms of which s/he is educated. This culture influences the person through a process of socialisation during which certain behaviour patterns, values, attitudes, and views of humanity are acquired.

Individuals acquire certain personal qualities such as skills, training, experience and ability within their personal environment, whereas the personal quality 'aptitude' is a congenital characteristic, the full realisation of which is the result of their personal environment. Certain needs are congenital (physiological needs) while others are acquired. In addition, it is characteristic of human beings that needs develop in the course of time and change in accordance with levels of development. All these factors together shape the personality of a person who has certain expectations of life and work, which are transformed into the personal goals with which the person joins an organisation.

## 2.4    The psychological contract between the human being as an employee and the organisation (management) as employer

Individual performance is the result of motivated employee behaviour. It is known that motivated employee behaviour is best achieved by integrating personal goals with the goals of the organisation. Personal goals can only be integrated with those of the organisation if employees' expectations of their employer, as well as the employer's expectations of individual employees, are clearly spelt out during the negotiation phase of the psychological contract. The psychological contract does, however, imply that individual expectations and those of the organisation change in the course of time. In other words, it is not a static agreement.

### 2.4.1    Types of psychological contract

It is generally accepted that three types of psychological contracts can be identified, namely:

- *The coercive contract* is where individuals are held as organisation members against their will (for instance, in prison).
- *The calculative contract* is where the two parties discuss specific terms and all aspects of the contract are agreed to and probably written down (like the normal employment contract).
- *The cooperative contract* is open-ended and less clear-cut, the parties to it operating on the basis of mutual trust and interdependence and sharing the same broad goals and intentions (for example, a person working as a family member in a small family business).

In order to gain perspective on the important role of the psychological contract in producing motivated employee behaviour, we will now deal with:

- The nature of the psychological contract.
- The nature of the expectations of individual employees.
- The result of the needs of individual employees.
- The nature of the expectations organisations have of their employees.

## Encounter 2.1

THE EFFECT OF PERSONAL CONSTRUCTS ON THE WORK SITUATION

Whenever we are interacting with other people at work, we are fitting whatever they say into our own personal constructs of how the company should work, what the workforce is like, and so on. This means that we select bits from what the other person says – the bits that we think make sense, or are relevant – and ignore the rest. Moreover, if we have accepted some overall goal, such as a production target, or some kind of innovation, we immediately bring our personal constructs about the organisation into play and use these to judge whether it is practical or not.

SOURCE: Hayes (2002:43)

All these aspects have a positive or negative effect on the employee's quality of life. It is important to bear in mind that the traditional psychological contract has evolved in a contemporary context, which has a variety of implications for organisations and employees alike.

### 2.4.2  The nature of the psychological contract

When individuals join an organisation they have certain expectations about promotion opportunities, salary, status, office and decor, the amount of challenging work as opposed to the amount of boring work – things they expect to receive. They also have expectations about their technical skills, time and energy, involvement, communication skills, supervisory skills and so on – things they expect to give.

The management of organisations has certain expectations about what it will receive from the employee (in the same way as the employee expects to receive things from the organisation), as well as expectations about what it can offer the employee, examples of which are similar to what the employee expects to receive.

These two sets of expectations may therefore either correspond with or differ from each other. The psychological contract also differs from legal and labour agreements. In reality it could contain an indefinite number of items even though the employee may only be aware of a few expectations about his/her most pressing needs.

The first group of expectations represents what an individual expects to receive from an organisation and what the organisation expects to give the individual. In other words, for each item on the list an individual has expectations of what the organisation will offer and what s/he will receive. Similarly, the organisation has expectations of what it will offer or give the individual in that area:

- A meaningful job.
- Opportunities for personal development.
- Interesting work that will generate curiosity and excitement on the part of the individual.
- Challenging work.
- Authority and responsibility at work.
- Recognition and approval for work of a high standard.
- Status and prestige at work.
- Friendly people and equality in the work group.
- Compensation.
- The extent to which the environment is structured, for example, general practices, discipline or regimentation.
- Security at work.
- Promotion possibilities.
- The amount and frequency of feedback and assessment.

In the contemporary context, Ison and Barton (2003:35) highlight what organisations will provide to employees as a modern psychological contract, which differs from the traditional approach:

- A flexible, innovative work environment.
- Clear leadership and accountabilities.
- A customer-focused environment.
- Open communication channels.
- Effective recruitment processes.
- Retention focused on key skills.

- Effective performance management.
- Competitive guaranteed rewards.
- Flexible packages with an appropriate mix of total rewards.
- Pay linked to business performance.
- Ownership opportunities.

The second group of expectations includes what an individual expects to offer an organisation and what the organisation expects to receive from employees. In other words, for each item on the list the individual has an expectation of what s/he is willing or able to offer or give the organisation. Similarly, the organisation has certain expectations of what it will receive from the individual in that area:

- The ability to execute tasks that are not socially related and that require a certain degree of technical knowledge and skills.
- The ability to learn to execute various aspects of a job in the work situation.
- The ability to invent new methods of task performance and the ability to solve problems.
- The ability to state an opinion effectively and convincingly.
- The ability to work productively with groups of people.
- The ability to present well organised and clear reports orally or in writing.
- The ability to supervise and guide others in their work.

- The ability to make good, responsible decisions without assistance.
- The ability to plan and organise his/her own work as well as the work of other employees.
- The ability to use time and energy to the benefit of the organisation.
- The ability to accept instructions and requirements from the organisation that are incompatible with personal prerogatives.
- Social interaction with other employees outside the working environment.
- Conforming to the norms of the organisation applicable to the job in areas not directly related to the job.
- Self-study outside normal working hours.
- Maintaining a good public image of the organisation.
- Accepting the organisation's values and goals as own values and goals.
- The ability to realise what has to be done and to take the appropriate steps.

The psychological contract may contain an infinite number of items. More important than these items, however, is an understanding of the nature of the psychological contract, and the communication of these mutual expectations.

Decades ago Porter et al. (1975:109) referred to the psychological contract as the

**Figure 2.4** The dynamics of organisation/individual interaction

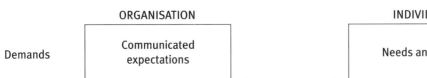

| | ORGANISATION | INDIVIDUAL |
|---|---|---|
| Demands | Communicated expectations | Needs and goals |
| Resources | Organisational resources (people, activities, things) | Skills and energy |

SOURCE: Porter et al. (1975:109)

'dynamics of organisation/individual interactions', and conceptualised it as in Figure 2.4.

As indicated by the arrows in Figure 2.4, the different requirements of the individual and the organisation represent a tapping of common resources. In other words, the communicated expectations of the organisation make demands on the skills and energy of individuals, while the satisfaction of individuals' needs depends on certain resources of the organisation. It seems obvious that if a working relationship is to be developed and maintained between the individual and the organisation, both parties will have to respond to mutual expectations and needs.

From the preceding discussion it is clear that whether a person is working effectively, whether s/he generates commitment, loyalty, and enthusiasm for the organisation and its goals, and whether s/he obtains satisfaction from her/his work, depends to a large measure on two conditions: First, the degree to which a person's own expectations of what the organisation will provide him/her and what s/he owes the organisation match what the organisation's are of what it will give and get; and, second, assuming there is agreement on expectations, what actually is to be exchanged – money in exchange for time at work; social-need satisfaction and security in exchange for work and loyalty; opportunities for self-actualisation and challenging work in exchange for high productivity, quality work and creative effort in the service of organisational goals; or various combinations of these and other things. Ultimately the relationship between the individual and organisation is interactive, unfolding through mutual bargaining to establish a workable psychological contract. The psychological dynamics cannot be understood if we look only to the individual's motivations or only to organisational conditions and practices.

The psychological contract is therefore dynamic and changes in the course of time. This change takes place in accordance with changed needs of both the individual employee and the organisation.

What an employee expects of an organisation or the employer at age twenty-five differs

dramatically from what that same employee expects at age fifty. A newly married employee of twenty-five is primarily interested in career prospects and a good salary so that s/he may provide his/her family with housing and a good standard of living, while at 50 the same person would pay more attention to what the organisation can offer on retirement.

In the same way, the organisation's expectations of its employees differ from time to time. For example, the organisation may expect its members to do their very best and remain loyal and diligent in times of economic recession, or to promote the organisation's image in times of economic prosperity.

---

## Encounter 2.2
### THE ROLE OF THE EMPLOYEE IN ORGANISATIONS

New rules will have to be invented in the event of change if an organisation wishes to transcend its existing parameters of competition. To achieve this, all employees and the organisation must think like entrepreneurs. Both organisation and employees must leave behind the image of the 'unpleasant manipulators' of the past and become the 'nice guys' of the future.

This can be summed up by saying to employees: 'Be excellent in what you do, learn and develop new skills, be special in your organisation (in other words create your own personal trade mark in the organisation), keep growing in your job, be creative and innovative, keep on marketing your skills and yourself, and choose jobs that will help you to build your career to the benefit of the organisation as well.'

For the organisation: 'Do research, appoint highly talented people, enhance creativity and innovation, talk to your clients, manage diversity, reward active success, monitor ongoing change and projects, evaluate what your organisation is achieving, and enhance enthusiasm.'

SOURCE: Nel (2003)

---

In most cases, the needs of employees starting a career revolve around 'self-testing'. Employees would like to determine whether they have all the skills needed to do the job for which they are appointed. Therefore they expect organisations to provide them with challenges to test their skills and knowledge in terms of goal achievement. This is where the problem of conflicting goals comes to the fore. Employees are usually disappointed if they are kept in meaningless training programmes for too long, or if they are occupied with tasks that bear no relation to the primary goals of the organisation. In such cases neither the organisation nor the individual employee is in a position to determine the employee's actual abilities in terms of the goal achievement of the organisation, and this results in a feeling of uncertainty.

During a later phase of employees' work lives, their needs and expectations move into an area where they may feel that they are contributing to the organisation, and where they are enabled to develop in their area of speciality. At this stage employees expect the organisation to acknowledge their contributions. Most employees reach this position in the middle of their career, usually when they are at their most productive and consequently expecting the most recognition and remuneration. At a later stage, when the employee is doing less crucial work, his/her need for security increases and expectations in the psychological contract change to not wanting to be sidelined or sent on early retirement. Retired employees often complain that the psychological contract has been broken because they could still make a positive contribution to the organisation.

## 2.5 The integration of personal goals with those of the organisation

The expectations of the employee and the manager are, among other things, the result of what they have learnt from others of prevailing traditions and norms and of previous experience. As needs and other external factors change, expectations also change, and this gives the psychological contract a dynamic character that requires constant re-negotiation. Although the psychological contract is unwritten, it remains the critical determinant of the work behaviour of employees.

The question then arises how the psychological contract can contribute to the process of motivation. This important aspect is explained in the following section.

Individuals, as employees, have certain personal goals that are the result of the expectations contained in the psychological contract. In keeping with the nature and content of the psychological contract, it is also clear that organisations expect certain things from their employees. The individual and the organisation are thus in constant interaction with one another, with the aim of attaining their mutual goals.

An individual employee enters an organisation with a certain set of needs. If the organisation has an organisational climate that promotes need satisfaction, an employee should show positive employee behaviour. If such a climate is not present, employees will tend to subordinate organisational goals to their personal goals for need satisfaction.

It should thus be clear that there is a critical link between the successful integration of personal goals and the goals of the organisation, as well as organisational success.

## 2.6 Contemporary views on the psychological contract

The dynamics of organisations and the relationship between employees and the organisation has dramatically changed over the last two decades. Many organisations nowadays have different characteristics from yesteryear. Similarly the psychological contract has also changed from the traditional to a contemporary format. This is due to the new generation of employees that has steadily been entering the world of work. This evolvement is discussed below.

### 2.6.1 The new world of work and new millennium employees

Most organisations worldwide are nowadays

characterised by a heterogeneous workforce with diverse approaches to the way in which they live and view the concept of work. This is a consequence of the rapid changes and advances in technology, new mindsets and increased global labour mobility opportunities during the last three decades of the 20th century in most market-driven economies. What is the employee and organisation of the future, however, going to look like?

According to Allen (2003:27), the immediate future generation starting to enter the labour market is going to have a greater influence on global business than ever before. The South African workforce (and probably all over the world) is predicted to become more diverse in terms of age, ethnicity, and racial background, due to the world becoming a global village. It is also unlikely that one set of values will characterise all employees. For example, 'traditionalists', born between 1927 and 1945, tend to be uncomfortable challenging the status quo and authority; 'baby boomers', born between 1946 and 1960 view work as a means to self-fulfilment and 'baby busters' (the so-called 'generation X'), born between 1961 and 1979, value unexpected rewards for work accomplishments, opportunities to learn new things, praise and recognition. Lastly, 'generation Y', also known as 'Millennials', 'Echo Boomers' and 'Nexters', were born between 1980 and 1995. The characteristics of 'generation Y' employees are, amongst others: free agent, lifestyle driven, no loyalty to employers, and a job for life is not in their make-up.

Due to uncertainty in the world, values have also changed. Previously, values were (in order of priority): career, wealth, health, family and home. Probart (2002:32) states that after the terror attacks like September 11 and the Bali bombing these values changed to: Family, health, country and home. This analysis reveals that softer issues such as religion and family are also substituting tangible values such as money and careers. Dahmen (2002:29) confirms this by saying that organisations are also refocusing by attempting to outsource and reduce labour costs, and to change the culture so as to enhance the organ-

isation's performance and provide a far more intensive focus on the bottom line than before. During the past five years, a growing body of research has suggested that interaction between co-workers is one of the primary sources of job stress. Organisations are also increasingly adopting flat hierarchies to enhance productivity. However, as they do so, the potential for conflict increases.

The background to the contemporary workforce, outlined above, needs to be taken cognisance of, and it is over and against this that HRM and organisation leaders should view the psychological contract since it is clear that what employees and employers want and expect from each other will change dramatically in the new work environment.

## 2.6.2 The contemporary psychological contract

The contemporary psychological contract is dynamic, voluntary, subjective, informal, and it accomplishes two tasks: first it defines the employment relationship; and second, it manages the mutual expectations.

According to Brewster et al. (2000:7):

Perhaps the most significant change in the new work environment is the lack of job security offered to employees. In the old paradigm, an employee's current and future position was very clear and predictable, which resulted in employee loyalty being fostered. For this loyalty, employers would provide good pay, regular promotion and benefits, and would also invest in the training and development of their staff. The relationship between the employer and the employee was a good one. However, this happy marriage has become strained in the new work environment, in which cutting costs and improving productivity are management goals. The flexible, de-layered, slimmer organisation is constantly changing to suit volatile and shifting markets, and can logically no longer sustain secure career progression.

The contemporary approach to the psychological contract is also confirmed by research undertaken by Buyens et al. (1997:13), where they reached the conclusion that the traditional psychological contract of industrial security for employees has been replaced by a contract where employees have to look after their own security. The security provided by organisations has decreased, and the focus is now more on the talents and commitments of the individual. The contemporary psychological contract could therefore be compared with a 'forced blind date' due to the uncertainties involved therein, yet the necessity for the parties to be in contact with and dependent on each other remains. The 'blind date' aspect comes from the fact that regardless of all the selection instruments, the future behaviour of both parties cannot be predicted.

Hiltrop (1995:7) has provided the most comprehensive definition of the contemporary psychological contract, namely:

> There is no job security, the employee will be employed as long as he/she adds value to the organisation, and is personally responsible for finding new ways to add value. In return the employee has the right to demand interesting and important work, has the freedom and resources to perform it well, receives pay that reflects his or her contribution and gets the experience and training needed to be employable here or elsewhere.

Lastly, it is also clear that in terms of research reported by Vinassa (2003:20–1), based on a recent review of 30 international studies, organisations worldwide that provide Employee Assistance Programmes to their staff earn a return of between three and seven times the amount they invest in terms of increased motivation and productivity and reduced absenteeism, accidents and staff turnover. These aspects also have an influence on the contemporary psychological contract.

## 2.7  Attachment to the organisation and involvement with the goals of the organisation

An employee's behaviour within an organisation may be regarded as the function of his/her perception of the content of the psychological contract entered into with the organisation. Organisations expect their employees to accept the goals allocated to them, and to be motivated to achieve these goals. On the other hand, individual employees expect the organisation to fulfil its part of the contract too.

The results of this interaction can be seen as leading to two equally important outcomes:
- An individual's desire to maintain her/his membership in a particular organisation (termed here attachment).
- An individual's desire to perform on the job and contribute to organisational goal attainment.

An organisation can only expect its employees to be attached to the organisation and to be involved with their personal goals if it fulfils the following commitments:
- It must be able to attract (recruit) the workers required and retain them. This involves not only the recruitment, selection, employment and induction of workers, but ensuring that individual employees receive sufficient compensation, commensurate with their individual contribution and need satisfaction, in order to retain them.
- The organisation must also be able to ensure that each employee executes the tasks allocated to him/her. This implies that employees should not merely do their work, but should do it with responsibility.
- A third requirement, which is often neglected and that is not formally included in individual employees' goals, but which does promote the goal achievement of the organisation, is innovation and sponta-

neous cooperation on the part of employees.

Organisations must ensure that employees become involved and give their spontaneous and continuous cooperation.

The recruitment and maintenance of the required human resources are related to attachment to organisations. In other words, it has to do with why an individual joins a particular organisation, and what motivates him/her to stay with that organisation.

The second and third commitments on the part of the organisation – to ensure that employees are responsible and that their behaviour is spontaneous and innovative – are related to the quality of employee functioning or their performance level. Research has shown that in the study of human behaviour as it relates to organisational effectiveness, employee attachment and performance emerge as the key variables to be examined. Although structure, technology and environment contribute to and often constrain effectiveness, such variables are largely overshadowed by the role of employee behaviour. If employees are not motivated to remain with and contribute to an organisation, questions of effectiveness become academic.

This underlies the approach followed in this book. Therefore it seems necessary to take a closer look at the concepts of attachment and involvement, as applied to organisations.

## 2.7.1  Employees' attachment to the organisation

Attachment to organisations may be divided into two components. The first is formal attachment. This refers to methods to reduce labour turnover, absenteeism and other forms of withdrawal from the work environment, and to increase time spent at work. A simple statement that employees are attached to organisations does not necessarily imply that they are strongly drawn to the organisation, nor that they have positive feelings about the organisation, but involves only the question of why they retain their membership of organi-

sations. The second component, namely involvement, is discussed in section 2.7.2.

At this point one might well ask why individuals retain their membership of organisations. In general, it may be said that organisations can expect employees to be attached to them and less prone to withdrawal if the employees experience job satisfaction. This is related to the variables contained in the job content and job context environments.

According to Kelemen (2003:43), there are five possible states of attachment of employers to the organisation, depending on whether the employee embraces organisational goals and/or institutionalised means for achieving them. These are: identification, innovation, ritualism, resilience and rebellion:

- *Identification* occurs when employees accept both the goal of quality and the organisational means for achieving it. The employees believe they are one with the company, embracing their organisational role with conviction.
- *Innovation* occurs when employees may agree with organisational goals but reject the 'one best way' of doing things as enforced by top management. Thus, employees may embrace the goal of quality, but the ways of achieving it are challenged on various counts.
- *Ritualism* is that situation where employees conform to prescribed organisational routines, but do not believe in organisational goals. Thus employees may not make quality a personal goal, but conform to it for calculative reasons, out of comfort, or out of fear.
- *Resilience* occurs when employees are opposed to organisational goals and institutionalised means for achieving them. Resilient employees invoke rational or emotional reasons for rejecting the goal of quality and the organisational means for achieving it.
- *Rebellion* takes place when employees want to replace organisational goals with something else and want to achieve that quite differently. Rebellion is an ideal state which cannot be sustained in prac-

tice as it leads either to the dismantling of the organisation or to people quitting their work. In most cases, rebellion and resilience become re-defined in terms of ritualism.

Another question arising at this stage is how the success of an organisation is affected if individuals terminate their membership of the organisation permanently or temporarily. Withdrawal (in particular permanent withdrawal) often has specific consequences for organisations and eventually for their efficiency. Many studies claim that increased labour turnover often leads to the employment of more administrative personnel in proportion to production personnel. It can also have a negative effect on innovation and creativity. Labour turnover gives rise to undesirable outputs and is directly related to the success or failure of organisations. On the other hand, organisations do benefit from getting rid of unproductive workers. Some labour turnover is desirable as it ensures that new workers with new ideas join the organisation, thus preventing stagnation.

The withdrawal of performance-inclined employees, in particular, poses a difficult problem for management.

## 2.7.2 Involvement with the organisation

Involvement, the second component of attachment, represents a state where individuals feel strongly drawn to the objectives, values and goals of their employer. In other words, it goes much deeper than mere membership of an organisation, in the sense that it makes goal achievement possible by ensuring a positive attitude towards the organisation, as well as the willingness to make a bigger effort on behalf of the organisation.

Involvement in organisations and organisational goal achievement indicate the nature of the individual employee's relationship with the organisation. A performance-orientated employee generally shows the following work behaviour:

> **comment**
>
> Successful organisations are characterised by performance-inclined, innovative and creative employees. The 'price' that an organisation has to pay for the withdrawal of such an employee is irrecoverable. It is therefore a challenge to human resources management to retain such successful employees as well as less successful employees and to develop them further to the advantage of the organisation and its stakeholders.

- A strong desire to remain a member of the organisation.
- A willingness to do more than is expected for the sake of the organisation.
- A definite acceptance of the organisational culture and goals.

Involvement refers to an active relationship between employee and employer, where the employee is willing to make sacrifices in pursuit of the employer's goals. An individual might now ask how increased involvement with organisations would affect the success of the organisation, or in different terms, what is the result of real involvement in organisations? We are of the opinion that involvement is closely related to at least four effectiveness variables, which are briefly discussed below.

- *Increased attendance:* Employees who are deeply involved with the goals and values of an organisation are more inclined to increase their participation in the activities of the organisation. In general, their attendance will only be prevented by events such as illness. With employees such as these, voluntary absenteeism will be lower than with employees who are less involved.
- *Employee retention:* A second variable related to increased attendance is reduced labour turnover (employee retention). This implies that employees who feel committed to an organisation have a strong desire to stay with that organisation, so that they

may continue their contribution to goal achievement with which they identify.

- *Work involvement:* Increased identification with and belief in the goals of the organisation will increase employees' involvement in their work, as work is the key mechanism by which individuals contribute to the achievement of the goals of the organisation.
- *Increased effort:* This variable implies that individuals who are deeply involved will be willing to make a bigger effort on behalf of the organisation. In some cases such increased efforts will result in outstanding achievement.

## 2.8   Employees' contribution to the organisation's bottom line

In the contemporary world of work and with the turbulent business environment with uncertain horizons and a widely oscillating ebb and flow of business, the pressure on the employee as the most valued asset in the organisation is greater than before. The emergence of the learning organisation and complex adaptive systems (CASs) management theory developments, has also guided thinking on how the employee is viewed in an organisation. The employee, as human being, is therefore under great pressure to perform and to contribute to an organisation's survival. Two important contemporary developments in which the employee plays a primary role that are promoted by human resources departments, is adding value and contributing to shareholder value.

### 2.8.1   Adding value

Despite the rather radical changes in the environment, there has been a strong recognition of the links between how people are managed, the bottom line, and the satisfaction of the employee. The 'softer side' of competitiveness reflects the involvement of the employee and also a shift towards a knowledge-based econ-omy. In the industrial world today, roughly 15 per cent of the active population physically touch a product in the production process. The other 85 per cent add value by the creation, management and transfer of information. A modem economy, thus, depends heavily on the employee factor as a key to success.

Dahmen (2002:29) came up with some answers to the question of how employees can add value to the business bottom line and what is best practice to capitalise on the inputs of employees. It includes aspects such as the ability to identify with the organisation's objectives to being retained in service by the organisation.

The concept of added value is also focused on by another global 'guru', namely Lawler (1996:33), who states that the new logic turns the traditional equation of who adds value to the organisation's products and services upside down. It constantly pushes for individuals throughout the organisation to add more value by:

- Doing more complicated tasks.
- Managing and controlling themselves.
- Coordinating their work with the work of other employees.
- Suggesting ideas about better ways to do the work.
- Developing new products and ways to serve customers.

### 2.8.2   Contributions to shareholder value

A major recent development is to determine the contribution of the employee to value in the organisation so as to indirectly contribute to shareholder value. According to Grigg (2003:30–1), this is not only in terms of internal efficiency, but should also be reflected in HRM's contribution to shareholder value. In other words, what is the return on investment in human capital?

Grigg's (2003:30) research shows that the following dimensions contribute to an organisation's share value, and therefore market value:

- Total reward and accountability and value creation.

- Collegiality and flexibility.
- Recruitment and retention excellence.
- Communication integrity.
- Focused human resources service technology.

It is clear that in the modern world of today the context has changed dramatically and that the employee as human being has a vastly different role from that which was regarded as traditional a mere decade or two ago.

### 2.8.3  Quality assurance

The theme of this book is the support of the individual employee at the end of the day so as to provide quality inputs. The quality assurance function is, however, executed by the human resources department. The actual execution of quality work, however, remains on the shoulders of the employee. This approach has been recurring in various writings of a number of authors, such as Burton (2003), Charlton (2000), Dawson (2003), Kelemen (2003), Lawler (1996), and Parmenter (2002). This approach is also the theme of Chapter 3, where how the human being as an employee forms the focus of an organisation's survival efforts, by providing quality inputs which become quality outputs, and the thrust of an organisation's competitive edge is outlined.

### 2.9    Conclusion

In this chapter we have attempted to explain why individuals join a particular organisation and what motivates them to stay with that organisation. Organisations must, therefore, not only recruit, employ, and induct new individuals, but also ensure that they are attached to the organisation, and in particular that they become involved in the pursuit of the goals of the organisation. Employees will feel attached to or involved with organisations if factors such as their immediate work environment, job content and so on are satisfactory. This will result in fewer resignations and reduced absenteeism, with the resultant positive effect on the success of the organisation. Involvement also means that employees will identify with the overall goals of the organisation, and they will consequently make a bigger effort in their pursuit of the goals of the organisation.

The chapter also deals with the individual employee as a human being with a unique personality, and his/her individual needs, expectations and personal goals. A person joins and enters into a psychological contract with an organisation on the basis of his/her personal needs and goals. Both the individual employee and the organisation have certain expectations that must be met in order to uphold this contract. The integration of personal goals with the goals of the organisation seems to be the best way to uphold this contract. This provides the basis for motivated employee behaviour, which is essential to the success of the organisation. Attachment to organisations and involvement with the goals of the organisation greatly contribute to the success of the organisation. In other words, the inputs with which an employee joins an organisation must be utilised by that organisation in order to achieve optimal employee functioning.

## Summary

- From a human resources perspective, the heart of any employment contract is the psychological contract. This is usually an informal and often unstated, shared (organisational and personal) commitment to a goal or variety of objectives.
- Employee motivation depends on the respect that s/he receives from the organisation. The prosperity of the organisation depends on the respect and commitment it receives from the individual employee. Overall success hinges around mutual expectations and commonly understood definitions and measures of performance and success.
- All relationships, be they interpersonal and/or those between the company and the individual, are dynamic. Human resources policies and practices must take

full cognisance of the fact that employees and employers change over time. The psychological contract between employer and employee is therefore an ongoing process of definition and redefinition.

- Dialogue is essential if the psychological contract is to have integrity and be amicable and dignified. Personal and organisational objectives must be clearly communicated, and individual and corporate goals must be openly integrated.

- The present generation of employers demands financial success and a strong, inoffensive, and popular brand. The present generation of employees wants financial reward but also informality, freedom, room for innovation and creativity, and the opportunity to look after itself. There are no longer mutual expectations of long-term careers and deep-seated, unquestioning loyalty.

## Case study
## Employee affiliations at Fast Comp (Pty) Ltd.

Fast Comp Ltd. in Midrand, is a South African computer assembly and consulting company. It was formed in 1986 and employs 194 people. Dudu Pachuhoe has been working for the company as an assembler, and since last year as a quality controller. Dudu originally qualified with an Advanced National Diploma in Computer Science from Sebokeng Technical College and was also the Student of the Year who received a Compaq prize as the best final year student in the Faculty of Computing and Information Technology. Directly after completing her studies she worked for three years as a programmer, occasionally acting as a relief assembly quality controller at a small Germiston-based computer assembly plant called Gyrostics cc. After four years with the present company she is in line for promotion to superintendent in the assembly and quality control section, since the retirement of the present incumbent becomes effective at the end of the year. Bongani Mabote, who has been with the company for four years and who has occasionally acted as relief superintendent for short periods, is also being considered for the position of superintendent.

The assembly team consists of twenty males and five females who represent most race groups in South Africa. Men have traditionally occupied the position of superintendent since the company's formation.

In view of diversity sensitivity and quality consciousness, Steven Nyamane, the human resources manager, is convinced that Dudu is the appropriate person for the job. This is particularly so because the company may in future tender for Government contracts regarding computer advisory services to Government departments, and it is well known in Government circles that only companies that are diversity sensitive and have ISO 9000 quality clearance are allowed to tender for these contracts. Steven therefore keenly interviewed her for the job and hoped that she would accept it.

Dudu responded rather favourably to the idea, but admitted that she was worried that the men in the section may not accept her authority as superintendent. Furthermore she specifically voiced her concern that her priority is to care for her four children and her husband (who is partly paralysed and who only works temporarily at the local telephone exchange) as opposed to taking on more career responsibility – although the extra income would come in handy. Steven Nyamane became very determined and insisted that she accept the position, pointing out that an attitude survey recently conducted by consultants indicated that 90 per cent of the males at Fast Comp Ltd. would accept a woman superintendent if she was suitably qualified.

The negative responses recorded in the survey revolved around opinions that women may become more emotional when conflict erupts. Some respondents also indicated that women work merely to supplement the family's income and may resign once the financial need no longer exists. Some also indicated that women put a priority on their family and children instead of their jobs, leading to lower productivity and ultimately negative attitudes in a company.

The factory manager, Ian Klaver, thought that Dudu was capable of doing the job, but was worried about her priority concerning her family responsibilities, which may detract her from being successful in the job. It was also rumoured that Dudu was not determined enough to put up with the hassles of the job, particularly regarding regular difficult demands from the Amalgamated Assembly and Computer Workers' Union, which is unaffiliated but is nationally organised, and has 23 500 members country-wide.

Ian remarked to Steven that they should try their level best to get Government contracts because Fast Comp Ltd. desperately needed contracts of this nature to survive the four-year long recession which has eroded all the company's financial reserves. Ian also indicated that it would be better to put the company's interests first and to focus on quality and effective management in order to survive.

## Questions

1　Discuss the potential implications of the psychological contract on Dudu in terms of her family responsibilities and her apparent reluctance to put work before family.
2　How would the contemporary psychological contract trends influence the company's thinking if Dudu refused an offer made to her?

## Chapter questions

1　What do you understand by its concept 'personality'?
2　Critically discuss the authors' view of personality.

3　In not more than 500 words, explain what you understand by the psychological contract.
4　One of the key factors in individual motivation is achieving personal goals. Critically discuss this statement.
5　What do you understand by attachment to organisations?
6　Discuss the relationship between the traditional and the contemporary approach to the psychological contract. Will the contemporary psychological contract contribute to or detract from the commitment of employees to pursue the organisation's goals fully?
7　Is it fair for employees to be pressurised to add value and contribute to shareholder value? Is this not the task of line management and the human resources department? Discuss critically.

## Bibliography

ALLEN, C. 2003. 'You should care'. *Employment Review, Australia*, 1(1):27.

BREWSTER, C., Dowling, P., Grober, P., Holland, P. & Warnich, S. 2000. *Contemporary issues in human resources management. Gaining a competitive advantage.* Oxford University Press, Cape Town.

BURTON, L. 2003. 'The next big thing'. *People Dynamics*, 21(2):22–23.

BUYENS, D., VAN SCHELSTRAETE, S., DE VOS, A. & VANDENBOSSCHE, T. 1997. *HRM in transitie.* Jan van den Nieuwenhuijzen, Antwerpe.

CHARLTON, G. 2000. *Human habits of highly effective organisations.* Van Schaik, Pretoria.

DAHMEN, C. 2002. 'The recipe for HR success'. *New Zealand Management*, 49(10):29.

DAWSON, P. 2003. *Understanding organizational change. The contemporary experience of people at work.* Sage Publications, London.

GRIGG, V. 2003. 'Linking HR to shareholder value'. *Employment Review, Australia*, 1(1):30–31.

HAYES, N. 2002. *Managing teams. A strategy for success.* Thomson Learning, Australia.

HILTROP, J.M. 1995. 'The changing psychological contract: The human resource challenge of the

1990s'. *European Management Journal*, 13(3):286–294.

ISON, J. & BARTON, P. 2003. 'Future Fillips'. *Employment Review, Australia*, 1(1):35.

KELEMEN, M.L. 2003. *Managing Quality*. Sage Publications, London.

LAWLER, E.E. 1996. *From the ground up. Six principles for building the new logic corporation*. Jossey-Bass Publishers, San Francisco.

NEL, P.S. 2003. *Old wine in new bottles: The human resources management role in new millennium organisation management revisited*. Professorial Inaugural address, UNITEC Institute of Technology, 29 April, Auckland, New Zealand.

PARMENTER, D. 2002. 'How HR adds value'. *New Zealand Management*, 49(10):36–37.

PORTER, L.W., LAWLER, E.E. & HACKMAN, J.R. 1975. *Behavior in organizations*. McGraw-Hill Companies, New York.

PROBART, R. 2002. 'In search of international trends in HR management'. *Management Today*, 18(9):32–33.

SCHULTZ, H.B. 2003. *Organisation behaviour*. Van Schaik, Pretoria.

STONE, R.J. 2001. *Human resource management, 4th edition*. John Wiley & Sons, Australia.

SWANEPOEL, B.J., ERASMUS, B., VAN WYK, M. & SCHENK, H. 2003. *South African human resources management: Theory and practice, 3rd edition*. Juta, Cape Town.

VINASSA, A. 2003. 'Stress management'. *People Dynamics*, 21(3):20–21. Reprinted with permission of Copyright Clearance Center.

## Websites

Society for HR Management: www.shrm.org

World Federation of Personnel Management: www.wfpma.com

International Personnel Management: www.ipma.hr.org

Andersen Consulting: www.ac.com

Ernst and Young: www.ey.com

Towers Perrin: www.towers.com

Work and Family Connection: www.workfamily.com/resource.htm

# 3

# The quality assurance approach to human resource management

PS van Dyk

## Learning outcomes

At the end of this chapter the learner should be able to:

- Differentiate by definition in words between a holistic approach to Quality Assurance (QA) and a process approach to quality assurance.
- Identify five reasons why the quality assurance approach to human resources management has become more prominent.
- Explain, using a diagram, what you understand by human resources management as a process.
- Explain the difference between the Human Resources (HR) department's role as an internal supplier of quality service and as an internal customer of other functional areas by describing it in concrete terms.
- Develop a questionnaire for the assessment of the effectiveness of HRM practices from a quality assurance perspective.
- Describe human resources quality assurance delivery in essay form.

- Indicate how the vision of an organisation serves as a facilitator for quality assurance by listing key aspects thereof.
- Differentiate between the various organisational and managerial choices for quality-assured human resources management service delivery by describing each one's main features.

## Key words and concepts

- continuous improvement
- customisation
- goal achievement
- human resources as a process
- internal supplier or customer
- Key Performance Areas (KPAs)
- Key Performance Indicators (KPIs)
- knowledge assets
- organisational self-assessment
- organisational vision
- process management
- quality assurance

## Illustrative case

A number of retired people formed a business with the capital they received from their pensions. They started a small manufacturing plant that produced PVC water tanks for the water supply of households in the rural areas of Limpopo.

Jack, because of his financial background, managed the business, while Toby, a retired engineer, took charge of the manufacturing process. Dick, who was previously employed by the Department of Trade and Industry, was responsible for marketing and sales.

The business grew slowly and they employed only labourers, for the manufacturing process. Due to Dick's contacts at the Department of Trade and Industry, they landed a government contract to produce several thousand water tanks for distribution to additional areas. This created chaos, and since none of them had any experience in human resources management, they offered Toby's son, John (who had just completed his BCom degree in human resources management) the opportunity of managing the expansion of the company. John, aware of the multitude of legislation in this regard, realised that the company had to be restructured in order to make provision for an effective human resources department.

How would you go about restructuring the business to assure quality?

## 3.1  Introduction

Various concepts central to the quality assurance approach are analysed in this chapter, and definitions are also proposed for the various aspects of quality assurance. Furthermore, the importance of culture and leadership within the quality assurance process is focused upon. With the advent of the Industrial Revolution and consequent mass production, economies of scale, etc., the quest for a workable definition of the word quality shifted from religion and philosophy to engineering, operations research, and statistics. In the modern and contemporary context, the issues of culture and leadership are also recognised as important aspects when dealing with quality assurance.

The interaction of the various quality assurance issues as they relate to human resources management is analysed as the major focus of this chapter.

### 3.1.1  Defining concepts

Nowhere other than in operations management and logistics has the concept of quality assurance been thoroughly analysed. Also, and until recently, no explicit definition was offered in HRM. However, this has changed, and Longford's definition (1995:85) is to the point:

> Quality assurance is a systems engineering discipline which embodies the process of quality control; the art of inspection, and the management philosophy, policies, and oversight procedures that will instil understanding, integration of individual objectives and supportiveness of quality at all levels of the organisation.

From the above it must be evident that quality assurance is a management task, and perhaps in this new dispensation of globalisation, it is the most critical management factor. What makes the whole phenomena contentious is the human resources side of quality. Everything that an organisation produces, whether goods or services, and in whatever form of enterprise, and irrespective of its reason for existence and the dominant coalitions, is conceived, developed, produced and released into the hungry globalised environment through human resources. Quality assurance covers all entrepreneurial activities that aim to satisfy any human or environmental needs.

Although other definitions will be offered or implied in the text to follow, the core issues of Longford's definition are entirely applicable to HRM.

The most recent definitions of quality assurance cover its applicability to more fields than just engineering and logistics, and also contain the crucial element of what is emphasised in this book, i.e. customer satisfaction (Reeves and Bednar 1994). Kelemen (2003), as one of the current generation of theorists regarding this development, devotes a whole book to the approach of managing quality and traces the approach via theoretical perspectives, the origin and evolution thereof, as well as the manner in which quality is applied in contemporary organisations. It is furthermore pointed out how quality can be applied in a variety of conditions, and also how business process engineering as well as total quality management interact. Further aspects, such as leadership, teamwork and organisational culture are also discussed in relation to quality. Furthermore, Kelemen (2003:43) outlines the critical impact of human resources management in an organisation via the application of quality management in that company. These concepts are also supported by Dawson (2003:148), where he outlines quality management as the competitive edge in organisations' quest for excellence.

Albrecht (1992), an expert in organisational behaviour, states that quality in the 21st century will begin with the consumer and not with the products, services, or work processes that create them. This is in line with our view of what quality assurance is, i.e. in this book quality assurance is viewed both from a holistic and process perspective. Accordingly, Van Dyk (1998:3) defines quality assurance as:

> ... a behaviour inclination of the organisation as a whole (organisational cultural dimension) and individual employee behaviour (motivation) as part of any process or sub-process used to pursue quality in the products or services of the organisation.

This definition requires a commitment to quality. Quality, like any productive organisational activity, requires a commitment from top management (leadership) to fully mani-

fest as part of an organisation's culture or 'the way we do things here'. Quality mindedness must become part of every employee's thinking, namely by asking: 'How do I do things here?'

Quality assurance is an abstract phenomenon, and therefore there is difficulty in defining it. However, people claim to know quality when they see it. Therefore, quality (or quality-assured services) has now become one of the dominant criteria for measuring or predicting organisational success. Quality is thus equated with the concept 'customisation'. This stems from the approach that quality is a matter of customer satisfaction and the way customer feedback into service delivery is handled. This is, however, also a leadership function (see Chapter 14 for more detail in this regard).

The following example can be used to explain quality as customer satisfaction: 'Sell a Mercedes Benz with a junk attitude' or 'sell a piece of junk with a Mercedes Benz attitude', and experience the difference. The key is how the service meets customer needs.

From the definition given above, quality is actually much more. What is more important is that part of the definition that refers to the role of the individual: the intangible contribution, which represents a workers pride to the quality of his/her own work. A worker who takes pride in his/her work, who gets intrinsic satisfaction (see Chapter 14) from doing a good job, is more likely to produce high quality results. However, the question is: What makes some workers take pride in their work, when others do not? Elsewhere it is quoted that only dead workers are not motivated. Thus, it is an inborn characteristic of all people to act in a motivated manner. It is only when people enter into an official place of work that motivational problems start, and an inborn desire to quality becomes a dependent variable. Quality work in most organisational settings is of a sub-standard nature (unmotivated) because the organisational culture wherein pride in workmanship is supposed to thrive is secondary to company politics and other bureaucratic red tape. The majority of employees are intrinsically motivated to per-form to the best of their ability because their work represents them, and thus their self-esteem. The self-esteem an employee brings to her/his work represents her/him in task (job) execution. That is why feedback on perform-ance, if not executed in the correct manner (irrespective of whether the employee per-formed above or below the standard), can have serious psychological effects on an employee's emotions. Thus, as Hughes et al. (1993:462) put it: '... a commitment to quality involves cultural change ... the responsibility for changing an organisation's culture belongs to its leadership.'

## 3.1.2 The role of culture

Schein (1985), like Beer (1980) and others, agrees that organisational culture refers to a system of shared beliefs, norms, values and backgrounds of members of a group in an organisation. In Chapter 1, a distinction between culture and environment or climate was made. Organisational climate, amongst other factors, refers to organisational mem-bers' (employees') subjective reactions to the organisation, and can have an adverse effect on efforts to change an organisation's culture and assumptions. In everyday jargon, culture is referred to as 'the way we do things here' (the policies, rules, regulations and operating procedures within formal structures). Sim-ilarly climate refers to the reaction of some people towards 'how things are done here'. Thus, organisational climate is partly a func-tion of or reaction to organisational culture, especially in change efforts. To superimpose quality assurance over all the activities of organisations will naturally lead to both acceptance and rejection thereof. In process management, this phenomenon is of utmost importance due to the nitty gritty elements of culture climate and how employees get along with each other in the pursuance of quality as a primary or critical process out-come.

Hughes et al. (1993) describe culture as phenomenological in nature, i.e. the day-to-day characteristics that are displayed within the organisation as an environment in itself. Culture is also referred to as the 'personality' of the organisation, and can be equated with the self-concept of an individual. It is deter-mined by all the components of the organisa-tion as a system (its structures, people, poli-cies, processes, etc.); but as systems theory asserts, culture is larger than its component parts.

As individual employees, we are in daily interaction with co-workers, clients, etc. Our actions (behaviours) are controlled and guid-ed by structural variables like communication channels, policies, procedures, and the bosses keep strict supervision over our job execu-tion. This is especially true where service delivery takes place. In this fashion, employ-ees naturally develop a perception of basic managerial practice and classify it according to their common perceptions and experience. Over time, names or tags and labels develop amongst employees for certain employees, and work is then executed according to the personal preferences of those people (em-ployees) in charge of organisational activities. Quality, as a measure of managerial or super-visory efficiency, is overshadowed by tangible criteria of performance. And so 'the way we do things around here', whether good, mediocre or bad, becomes the norm. Dis-ciplined employees are expected to follow the norm and formal individual behaviour is directed in this fashion. New employees are subjected to existing cultural anomalies, and before long the effects of this manifest in their work behaviour.

To create an inclination that is positive to quality-assured individual outputs requires change. However, the above state of employee behaviour develops within the informal sys-tem of the organisation. To cultivate quality mindedness requires aggressive transforma-tional leadership. South Africa is not well known for quality, either in products or in the service industry. It is a sad state of affairs when company products or services suffer quality loss due to the strength of a negative informal organisational culture towards quality. Globalised companies need people who sustain and improve quality in order to gain and maintain a competitive edge in global markets.

### 3.1.3  The importance of leadership

To transform organisations from only an output (production) orientation to a quality output inclination requires a paradigm shift and the use of power. Although culture manifests negatively in the informal system where change is more difficult to achieve (because of extreme personal power, for example), dynamic leadership can contribute to a very large extent to reshaping the culture. Where management authority is a structural phenomenon (Pfeffer 1981), leadership is spontaneous and inherent in the person who occupies a position of structural authority. Therefore, the distinction between management and leadership exists. A leader in a position of power can change employee performance. From the full range of leadership theories (see Chapter 14), proponents of quality prefer a Theory-Y approach.

To create the inner pride within an employee, Theory-Y leadership is more inclined to recognise an employee's strengths as well as his/her weaknesses. It tends to oversee and assist employees in their daily work routine and not to police. Rather, it continuously empowers employees in their quest for quality work. This approach is especially applicable where organisational activities are executed in a process management fashion. Further analysis of this type of leadership behaviour reveals actions that relate to intrinsic motivation (see job content factors in Chapter 1). The leader or manager is just like any other organisational member – a member of a specific team. Whether it is called a section, department, function or process is irrelevant. The point is that quality-assured job performance is more dependent on intrinsic motivational leader behaviour than extrinsic actions and policies. Therefore, an organisational culture that is inclined to quality-assured outputs is the result of the sum of intrinsically motivated employee behaviour. Organisational actions and leadership behaviour must be directed towards the empowerment of the positive informal system of the organisation by using customer satisfaction as a formal output criterion. In organisational settings where customer satisfaction is of paramount importance, most employees display a proactive work attitude towards customisation, which we know is a critical success factor in contemporary organisations. Customisation makes customers successful. Successful customers are satisfied customers, and satisfied customers make suppliers of quality service successful. Spontaneous teaming and partnerships develop, and collaboration changes to cooperation. Such organisations have a longterm inclination towards quality and a vivid quality vision.

## 3.2  Quality assurance: From products to service

It is estimated that up to 70 per cent of the employees in developed countries these days are engaged in jobs and careers that have no bearing on the production of tangible goods. The service industry, in the global context, demands more and more jobs in fields only indirectly related to physical production (itself already taken over by machines and robotics). These days, the world market consists primarily of service economies. Moreover, the most important product has become 'knowledge'.

The worldwide growth of service economies and the information revolution have elevated the importance of customer service. Gardner and Nudler (1999:6), as well as other writers (Dawson 2003:112–125 and Kelemen 2003:55), contemplate that customers have individual preferences and needs, and because these change over time, service must be flexible to accommodate the consumer. These criteria are different from those in the manufacturing setting, where quality is defined as conformity with specified standards. Standardisation of quality (have you heard about ISOs, International Standards Office numbers?) is of critical importance in the manufacturing environment. Quality in services, however, varies (as will be discussed below).

Zeithaml et al. (1990:16) identified three differences that distinguish service quality from quality in manufacturing:

- Customers find it more difficult to evaluate service quality than product quality. Quality assurance in these terms is mathematically measured by a number of statistical applications.
- The delivery of the service cannot be separated from the outcome of the service.
- 'Only customers judge quality: all other judgements are essentially irrelevant.'

## 3.3 Quality products or service as a human output

To get closer to the field of study (the body of knowledge) we – and therefore management – must accept the fact that quality assurance is superimposed over all the organisation's activities. Not all over, but over all:

- It is everything.
- It is product development.
- It is production or manufacturing.
- It is finance.
- It is marketing.
- It is sales.
- It is, over and above all else, *management*, and especially human resources management as an empowering service to the organisation's operations.

The author recently had the opportunity to apply the quality assurance approach in two different organisational settings: a purified and fountain water concern in Botswana, and a South African chain of upmarket restaurants (Van Dyk 2002a; 2002b). In both instances the focus was taken away from the product(s) and replaced by a 'need-satisfying service'. It is our opinion that this will become the norm rather than the exception. The competition in terms of product quality is so high that instead of the quality of the product being the focus (if a product doesn't possess certain qualities in this globalised market it will never land in the market place – and if so, only for a very short period), the emphasis must shift to the service that accompanies it. If any of these two variables are out of kilter the product will fail. In the production of services the competition is even stronger. The only way to success is the common denominator, i.e. the human or 'soft' side of the enterprise.

Rosander (1999) supports our view for a new approach to management and quality because of the role that people (employees) and the customer (his/her knowledge and expectations) play in the service industry. Rosander (1999:6) further argues that:

- Service cannot be measured like the physical properties of a manufactured good.
- Service cannot be stored or stockpiled.
- Service cannot be inspected (it can be observed and conclusions drawn).
- Service quality cannot be determined ahead of time. Quality is determined at the moment that the service is rendered. The customer cannot evaluate the service until it is delivered and experienced – the so-called moment of truth.
- Service involves human reliability to a much greater extent than the reliability of products used in performing the service until it is delivered and experienced.
- Services are provided by the lowest paid worker in the company (this really creates a dilemma).

(The reader must please note that the focus of this chapter is not on the service industry but on quality assurance, which is regarded as a service that human resources management delivers to the total organisation, whether it manufactures products or non-tangible goods.)

## 3.4  The scope of quality assurance and human resources management

### 3.4.1  General

Human resources management was elsewhere defined (see Chapter 1). We also now know that as an employee, the individual human being is central to any discussion of HRM. If we talk about the status of employees under management and human resources management practice, the net result is referred to as the current quality of work life in an organisation. Thus, apart from management's task of achieving the goals of the organisation, and human resources management's of empowering management to do so by the release of human skills, it is also the primary task of both line and staff managers to ensure the quality of the workforce. Like all management activities, it starts at the top, and we must therefore investigate how quality assurance, in terms of both product and service delivery, can be achieved through sound HRM practices.

### 3.4.2  How the mix works

Human resources management is a staff function. As a staff function it delivers service to the rest of the organisation. For practical reasons these services have been given names and arranged in an order according to the logical sequence of events. From a functional management perspective it is referred to as HRM functions, which are planning, organising, leading and controlling. From a systems perspective, HRM can also be viewed from a functional point of view, i.e. as a sub-system, like marketing, finance, etc. However, whatever approach (even outsourcing or contracting of external agencies) is used in a particular organisation is irrelevant. From a HRM point of view, quality assurance makes use of both approaches, be they functional or systems.

A further important ingredient from a QA perspective is how the different tasks are viewed. This is the keystone to understanding quality assurance in HRM. It was stated above that HRM is a service. As such, the human resources department is a supplier of services to the operations and goal achievement efforts throughout the organisation. These services are unlike the delivery of physical raw material, a service is rendered mostly by external sources or agencies. If a company doesn't have a human resources department or has sourced it out to different specialised HR agencies, external suppliers render these services. The merit of having or not having a HR department is irrelevant. The focus of this book is, however, on the HR department as an internal supplier of HRM services to all its internal customer (all the other departments within an organisation). The reason is simple. All departments consist of people (irrespective of the nature or size of the organisation) performing certain tasks as an input to the core business of the organisation. Quality assurance in human resources management endeavours to ensure quality performance from each individual employee irrespective of position and title. According to Popp et al. (1999:269), quality performance is a synergetic combination of knowledge, skills, information, systems, facilities and equipment, behaviour, and most important, the outcomes the customer receives.

### 3.4.3  Quality performance starts with organisational vision

Van Dyk (2002:3) states that vision answers the question: What is the big picture? This is a fact of life and applies to all human effort. Visions guide and motivate the behaviour of all people. Humans spend the major part of their lives working in pursuit of a better quality of life for them and their dependants. That is our vision, whether it is spiritual- or material-based, or both. Any place where human activity is present there is also a vision. The simplistic definition of the term 'vision' is an anticipation of a true state of affairs. A vision is not a dream. If it was a dream, people would spend their working time in a dream. Lipton

(1996:85) provides the following insight, which also has bearing on our own personal visions:

> A vision must focus on the future and serve as a concrete foundation for the organisation. Unlike goals and objectives, a vision does not fluctuate from year to year but serves an enduring promise. A successful vision paints a vivid picture of the organisation and, though future-based, is in the present tense, as if it were being realised now. It illustrates what the organisation will do in the face of ambiguity and surprises. A vision must give people the feeling that their lives and work are intertwined and moving toward recognisable, legitimate goals.

It is difficult for organisations to continually improve if the focus is only on the present and on improving the present functions and activities by some stated amount or measurable degree. According to Dykstra (1999a:12), quality performance, reviewed through the perspective of a guiding vision, may require a dramatic departure from present activities. If the vision takes hold, then the organisational emphasis may change dramatically: it changes from programmes to people, from services to supports, from process to outcomes, from details to dynamics, and from buildings to behaviours.

How can such a quantum leap be achieved? Dykstra (1999b:117) has studied this phenomenon of why vision is sustained in one organisation and not in another. Quality assurance through quality performance can only be achieved if the vision is sustained firstly by gaining the commitment of top leadership. Organisational reality suggests that most organisations function with a dominant coalition around the Chief Executive. These key people must believe in the vision if it is to be pursued and become an integral part of corporate life. A second factor present in organisations that sustain their vision is to align organisational practices with the vision. In practical

terms this requires a strategic plan that can be followed and against which progress can be judged. The organisation must set goals and stakeholders must agree on responsibilities. Process management especially lends itself to this management style. Achieving the vision becomes an ongoing process. In this regard human resources reviews offer helpful feedback, and changing hiring practices can contribute to a workforce that can consider and implement the vision creation process. A third factor is that of establishing personal responsibility. Dykstra further explains that a vision perceived in a culture of personal responsibility is much more likely to prevail than a vision introduced into an environment in which dependency and hierarchy are dominant. As far as possible, all employees must be engaged in carrying out their parts (however small) in fulfilling the vision. This is especially true with employees who have an inner self-direction and permission to take significant actions. From all the HRM structures, only process management allows such freedom. However, the organisation must reward creativity, initiative and risk taking. Expanding organisations serves quality performance in human resources. New challenges mean new opportunities. Motivated, future-orientated employees stretch themselves. Nothing is as rewarding as achieving.

### 3.4.4 Quality assurance and the establishment of partnerships

Quality results from human resources employees and other managers and supervisors learning the company's practices and culture. These human resources management activities can be delegated. However, the primary responsibility for relationships can never be delegated. According to Dykstra (1999b:127), relationships are not a matter of information sharing but rather involve emotion, dispute resolution, concerns of fairness, honesty and respect. To put it another way, HRM demonstrates how the people in an organisation care for one another so that they might care about the people whom the organisation serves (customers) and the products it produces.

Human resources practices must support the mission (reason for existence) of the organisation in theory as well as in practice. Employees are constantly watching, observing, and comparing notes whenever the occasion presents itself. Therefore, it is important that organisational goals and values should be continuously addressed through an ongoing dialogue that acknowledges the changing dynamics within the organisation.

Dykstra (1999b:127) further explains that human resources that are founded on a commitment to relationships and partnerships will flourish as part of the quality consciousness of the organisation. These human resources efforts contribute energy to the organisation. On the other hand, efforts that are directed at compliance subvert organisational energy rather than create it. These relationships and partnerships occur through the various levels of organisational influence, among the top executives, middle managers, and front line employees. Time is set aside to review current practices, seek and except feedback, and to make ongoing changes to benefit the workforce. Williams (1996:1) contemplates that partnering puts a new emphasis on the working relationship. It begins with a commitment to cooperation by top management. It is a commitment to fairness and openness. It requires acceptance of one's own mistakes and refraining from exploitation of others' mistakes. It is, in fact, our view that networking is a result of the non-existence of the above.

To put it very simply, partnerships recognise the benefits of cooperation over competition (see Chapter 15), of attachment to goals over withdrawal (see Chapter 2), of thankfulness over manipulation, and equality over hierarchy. Following Dykstra (1999b:128), other qualities of partnerships include:

- Partners do not do bad things to each other, do not exploit each other, and do not say one thing and do another.
- Partners worry about the challenges faced by others. Partners work to strengthen

the organisation. Partners seek to share, not hide their resources.

- Partners come together, enrol in a higher purpose, but it is not to fight against a motivationally manufactured enemy. Partners share responsibility for problem-solving.
- Partners share the losses as well as the gains. They are each other's agents.

An organisation that is serious about pursuing partnerships should have a written partnership agreement that is signed by all the relevant parties.

## 3.5    Quality assurance and human resources management practices

### 3.5.1    General

Quality performance is in many ways predicated on the quality of the human resources practices of the organisation, and therefore determines in many ways the quality of the products or services. According to Kelemen (2003:43–46), the responsibility for any organisational activity in this global era is borne by both employees and the leadership that is vested within senior management of a company.

Some human resources management practices will hence be briefly discussed from a quality assurance and performance perspective. Only the contextual aspects of these topics are relevant to this chapter.

### 3.5.2    From recruitment to promotion

Of all the HRM activities discussed in this book, none is so critical to quality than the appointment or the decision to hire a certain individual. Dykstra remarks in this regard: 'As a matter of organisational management, this principle is self-evident; converting self-evident principles into actual practices is another matter.' The problem in the South African world of work is more complicated than the above statement suggests. The legislative environment in which organisations operate in South Africa requires that experienced senior managers make the hiring decisions. However, in many companies, supervisors and managers who have little experience in hiring and even less training in employee selection hire new employees. The more senior and experienced staff members are usually engaged in 'more important' business matters. The irony is that often these people keep themselves busy with HR practices like discipline, grievance hearings, etc. due to this 'unavailable' attitude.

To ensure quality performance from responsible people in this regard, companies can, according to Dykstra (1999b:130), conduct internal self-assessments on the organisation hiring process by asking questions such as:

- Who does the hiring and why?
- When is it done?
- What is the employment applications process?
- Is the application useful?
- How long is the lag time between application and interview?
- Where do we advertise job openings? To whom?
- What do we want in terms of qualifications?
- How many people apply?
- How many candidates are interviewed?
- How many employees are hired?
- How many applicants turn down job offers?

An organisation concerned with quality not only addresses these questions but many more, including the cost of the problem. Promotional practices are another key human resources consideration. Dykstra lists the following self-assessment questions in this regard:

- Who is promoted?
- Do promotions tend to occur internally or are promotions generally filled from the outside?
- Are employees aware of promotional opportunities? If so, by what mechanism?

The legal environment in South African organisations also limits freedom of appointment and promotion.

### 3.5.3 Human resources management maintenance practices

The first human resources management practice can also be viewed as the primary one, i.e. compensation. Although compensation and benefits will be discussed in consequent chapters, the importance to quality performance, and thus to quality assurance, cannot be overemphasised. Today's world revolves around money – more so than in the past. The accelerated pace of newly acquired needs, the opening of the globe as both a place to shop and to visit, and also the escalatory cost of living have made this topic more important than ever. The average South African worker lives at least two years ahead on debt, and societal demands will only increase. Apart from this, in terms of psychological and motivational theories (Chapter 13), there must be a direct relationship between quality performance and compensation. Dykstra (1999b: 132) suggests the following questions for organisational self-assessment in this regard:

- Will the organisation have differential pay for different shifts? For holidays and weekends? For different assignments? If so, how will the amount be decided?
- How often will the organisation pay its employees? Weekly? Every two weeks? Monthly?
- Who gives employees their cheques? And how do they do it?
- How are payroll errors corrected? Does management take the error seriously? How quickly is it fixed?

The problem is that the personal relationship in the input-outcome (pay) dynamic has become obsolete. To align corporate vision with employee behaviour (quality performance), the trend has been to narrow the spread between highest and lowest paid employees and compensation systems, rather than analyse the difference between the compensation levels within an organisation compared to other similar or geographically close organisations and according to supply and demand factors. (See Chapter 1 – particularly the 'brain drain'.)

### 3.5.4 The performance contract and appraisal

To ensure quality in both personal service and in the products and services that the company produces, a sound and dynamic performance contract must be established and adjusted for each individual employee. This contract contains the majority of the psychological elements discussed in Chapter 2. An individual's alignment with a dynamic corporate mission is founded on this relationship. All organisational and personal variables are included in this agreement. Apart from the compensation considerations discussed in the previous paragraph, the whole issue of employee feedback and further empowerment or termination of service comes to the fore. Future individual quality performance stops, starts or carries on from this human resources management intervention. The international trend to view the human resources of a company as intellectual property and knowledge sources will reach South African run-of-the-mill companies soon. All of this is, and will continue to form, a larger and more important part of performance assessment and future training, development, promotion or termination of human resources activities.

Dykstra (1999b:133) offers the following self-assessment question for managers:
- Is a written document to be used in performance appraisal?
- Is one form used for all employees?
- Does it use a 'check the correct box' approach?
- How often is the form or document completed?
- Where does it go?
- Where is it filed?
- Does the employee have the opportunity to discuss (i.e. agree or disagree with) the evaluation?

To support our view on the importance of this HRM intervention, Jacques and Clement (1991:188) provide the following insight:

> Every managerial leader must be able to recognise the fundamental difference between performance accounting and personal effectiveness appraisals. An individual's performance is the difference between targeted output and achieved output. Personal effective appraisals are judgements made by an individual manager about how objective measures can be used for performance accounting. Personal effectiveness measures call for managerial judgement.

This emphasises the distinction made in Chapter 2 with regard to employee efficiency and employee effectiveness, and lays the foundation for the future movement of the individual.

### 3.5.5 Job design

Job design forms part of both the individual employee's content and contextual work environments. In terms of content, it relates to intrinsic motivating factors like challenge, personal growth and feedback. Within a job position (for which job design is responsible – see Chapter 16) is found a family and hierarchy of jobs. All the jobs together represent a company's total business endeavour. All the jobs are kept together by the organisational structure, policies, company procedures and standard operating procedures. All these are kept alive and dynamic by communication.

In the contemporary world of work many jobs are customised due to the accelerated pace of knowledge creation – a job in itself can these days be regarded as a knowledge creation entity. In such cases the job is 'built' around the individual or 'knowledge base'. Most jobs, however, must be designed by management, or in the case of professional employees like chartered accounts and engineers, by the official accreditation body. However, these kinds of jobs have to fit into an existing job culture, which is the organisation as represented by the employer. The ways formal and non-formal jobs are executed in an organisation is also known as organisational culture. In the past, when blue-collar employees were represented by guilds or specialised unions, such technical professionals brought their own work culture to the work organisation.

What do employees do? Who decides on the tasks? How do the tasks change? According to Dykstra (1999b:130), these are the critical issues of job design. To be effective, employees must be engaged in meaningful activities that are valued by the organisation. Job design is the mechanism whereby critical issues such as the amount of supervision, level of authority and the significance and range of tasks being performed can be evaluated. If properly aligned, these elements are a major force of external motivation and job satisfaction.

## 3.5.6 Leadership and managerial philosophy

The quest in today's globalised companies is for visionary and transformational leaders and for managers with an above average risk profile. Competitiveness and management survival are synonymous. The challenge for managerial leadership is to recognise which things need to be done timeously and which need to be done sequentially. The balance is demanding and ever-changing. The dynamics, however, cannot be neglected.

Factors that can be regarded as leadership and management issues with reference to quality performance are presented below:

- *Age, size and structure of the organisation.* In this regard it can be stated that newly incorporated organisations will approach human resources in a different manner than old, well-established institutions. Such organisations can use informal practices and approaches, which is less possible where different levels of management have been established and specialisation of functions has settled. In the growth stages of a company, human resources can be handled in an informal manner, but as the size increases it must be formalised within the organisational structure. Bureaucratic forces begin to emerge as an organisation grows. Managers should attempt to use the positive elements of bureaucracy and guard against the frivolous aspects.

- *Structure also has an important impact on human resources.* The view that is taken in this book is for an organisational structure that enhances human resources management service delivery and managerial and supervisory empowerment along all 'sharp edges' of all business operations. A bureaucratic structure that is inflexible will not allow such service delivery. However, flatter organisations are more common today. Human resources management practice in a globalised market place will have the possibility to be customised for quality assurance and overall quality performance. As will be seen, process management allows for the delivery of customised human resources management services.

- *Resource availability is an important management issue.* Human resources are often down-sized when resources, especially financial resources, become scarce. Are salary packets, fringe benefits, rewards and promotion directly linked to the availability of financial resources? Other key practices exist and must be addressed, irrespective of financial circumstances. An organisation forced to lay off a portion of its workforce is very different to a rapidly growing and expanding organisation.

- *Staffing levels and succession planning.* Securing qualified staff must be foremost on the agenda of management. Without qualified people no quality service or performance is possible. Middle managers always have the highest turnover in companies. Just after large investments have been made in them, they leave for better offers elsewhere. This also mostly applies to affirmative action appointments. It is likely that this will always be the case, especially with the new global emphasis on employees as knowledge creators. An effective succession and replacement plan must be available at all times.

- *Unionisation status of the workforce.* Dykstra (1999b:139) is of the opinion that unions and the subsequent labour contracts can have a powerful influence on human resources practices. The classic triad of union interests – wages, hours and working conditions – clearly impinges on human resources strategies. Union issues of seniority and past practices usually arrest the opportunity for creativity and variation. The speed of organisational change may be much lower in unionised organisations.

- *Employee empowerment.* Once again globalisation has a severe effect on human resources management practice and quality assurance. As mentioned earlier, if South African businesses want to be successful in the global economy, quality-assured performance by their employees is a prerequisite. However, the opposite is equally true but more important: for any business firm's survival in the South African market place it must be able to compete successfully otherwise its products or services will locally be replaced by other globally competent business firms doing the same things better. Therefore, continuous empowerment of employees must be the first order of business. To be successful, organisations must embark on continuous self-improvement. This can be achieved by life-long empowerment (training and development) of their workforce through quality performance of their HR department.

## 3.5.7 Recognition of employee performance

Where other academics and authors hold the opinion that the hiring decision is perhaps the most important of all human resources actions, we, however, emphasise recognition

as the key to lasting quality employee performance. Recognition is that management and leadership philosophy which can be made tangible in all aspects of organisational activity. In this regard Morrison (1994:62) outlines some practical ways in which managers can recognise their employees (other than the common pay and promotion):

> Participation – inclusion in decision-making; Autonomy – freedom to act on one's own without supervision; Resources – staff, budget and time to do the job; Respect and Credibility – one's priorities and opinions are considered and valued; and Faith – the expectation that one's productivity will continue in increasingly responsible positions.

Dykstra (1999b:136) is of the opinion that quality would not be an issue in an organisation in which all the employees believed that they were needed by their co-workers and bosses. The fulfilment of human need is a powerful motivator and a source of reinforcement. Recognising employees for their contributions is a vital source of individual and corporate self-esteem and commitment. Attachment to and involvement in the organisation, as discussed in Chapter 2, is the net result thereof.

Nothing sustains employee attachment and involvement more than a management culture of appreciation and encouragement. The words 'thank you' work magic. Managers and supervisors must assess and re-assess their attitude towards recognition. Inflexibility in recognition programmes stems from a poor attitude in this regard. According to Dykstra, for recognition to be effective there must be an intellectual as well as an emotional commitment.

Annual recognition of outstanding organisational performance is also crucial. The annual awards should reinforce the organisation's values and vision. Celebrations are vital to organisational renewal. Dykstra (1999b: 137) elaborates and mentions that employee recognition rituals – including decisions with respect to financial awards, frequency, extent of publicity, and ceremonies – should be linked to values and vision. To conclude this important leadership intervention, we support the view of Gellerman (1992:78), who states that: 'every employee is motivated; the only unmotivated employees are dead ones.'

### 3.5.8 Summary of leadership and managerial issues

It seems as if an organisation's vision is the beginning and the end of quality assurance and quality performance from a HRM point of view. To compete and survive in this global era, management must continuously work on the alignment of the human resources work attitudes with the vision of the organisation. Employees who share common values and are knowledgeable, skilled and committed are the key to future organisational success.

## 3.6 Auditing for quality-assured human resources performance

The ability of management, and especially human resources management, to create and sustain organisational renewal and continuous self-improvement and quality performance in their human resources will depend mainly on the results of the following organisational introspection. From these results a viable human resources strategic plan (see Chapter 21) can be devised. Auditing takes place in five human resources management areas, i.e. mission, job content, job infrastructure, organisational structure and people in the workplace.

- *Mission.* Mission flows from vision, and it represents the organisational goals of any institution. From Chapter 2 we have learnt that congruence with organisational goals enhances individual employee efficiency and effectiveness, which ultimately leads to organisational success. In this regard management, under the guidance of HRM, must obtain verifiable data in response to the following:

  ■ Is the mission clear, concise and understood by all employees?
  ■ Are the underlying values clear, concise and shared by all employees?
  ■ Does the mission statement energise staff?
  ■ Are all organisation activities directly related to the mission?

- *Job content.* Management can get direct feedback on their hiring decisions if job content factors are analysed. The motivational side of job content factors has also been mentioned in Chapter 2. However, to get an indication of the status quo of work tasks, the following questions would provide adequate information for decision-making:

  ■ Do work tasks flow from the mission statement?
  ■ Are employees clear about the purpose of the organisation?
  ■ Do employees and consumers have the freedom to make an input with regard to objectives and standards?
  ■ Do employees have a clear understanding of their jobs as linchpins in the achievement of overall organisational goals and purpose?
  ■ Is all employee work behaviour linked to the day-to-day activities of the overall work of the organisation?
  ■ Are work tasks defined and open to employee (job incumbent) suggestions?

- *Job infrastructure.* This refers to all the policies, rules, regulations, and resources that enable a job incumbent to execute tasks without hassles. Supervisory support and guidance in task execution can be determined by obtaining answers to the following questions:

  ■ Do employees have clarity about how they have to perform their tasks with special reference to efficiency, standards and time?
  ■ Is there insight among workers of the relationship of their job execution to other jobs in the organisation?
  ■ Is job execution made challenging by

supervisors?

- Do employees have the correct information, technology, materials and authority to perform tasks?
- Do employees experience a supervisory-friendly job context?
- Is communication accurate, open and friendly in job execution?
- Is there a system of continuous feedback for members with regard to job execution?
- Is completed work inspected or tested and validated, and by whom and in what managerial atmosphere?
- Are prescribed work methods adequate?

- *Structure.* Structure does not only refer to organisational charts, positional titles and job titles. It also includes formal communication, group relationships and authority networks. Prominent questions to be answered in this regard, are the following:
  - Is the organisation structured in a way that promotes the accomplishment of the mission, jobs and technology?
  - Do employees understand the organisational structure?
  - Do they know where and why they fit into a specific slot?
  - Is the organisational structure free from unnecessary bureaucratic layers?
  - Are employees clear on how the various organisational layers relate to each other?
  - Are the right people performing the right duties at the right time and place?
  - Is the organisational structure supportive of the work methods in producing the desired company outcomes?

- *People.* Of course people are the most dominant organisational variable. Organisations are people. From all the resources at the disposal of a company – people or human resources is the only resource that reacts when acted upon. It is management's task to obtain positive reactions from their human resources,

and the HR specialists can ensure such a state of affairs by continuously assisting all managerial and supervisory personnel. Critical questions that must be posed in this regard are the following:

- Is the right person performing the right job?
- Are employees competent to perform the contents of their jobs?
- Is empowerment by means of training and development freely available?
- What is the nature and time-frame for employee feedback and recognition?
- Is a management support system operating and to what effect?
- Are employees aware of the boundaries of their job execution?

To develop and implement a system like this is not difficult. However, of importance are the views of the authorities that are accountable for employee job performance. This refers to perceptions more than attitudes, and must thus be viewed and assessed on an individual or departmental, rather than on an organisation-wide, basis. Caution is the name of the game!

## 3.7 Organisational and managerial choices in quality-assured human resources management service delivery

### 3.7.1 General

As the workforces of companies differ so do the manifestations of human resources as a management function. To agree about the importance of human resources in the contemporary globalised business world is fruitless. Suffice it to say that whereas most modern business products and resources become more and more intangible, human resources becomes more vital because human resources in itself is the organisation, company and, ultimately, the business.

In this section we briefly touch on different

options that are available to contemporary organisations in performing their human resources management function in an effort to deliver quality performance in a customised way. However, the importance of the concept 'knowledge management', and especially the emphasis on tacit knowledge creation, has once again put human resources as well as HRM under the spotlight. This new wave of human resources management activities can also be accommodated in the options discussed below.

### 3.7.2  Personnel agencies

In their present form these agencies will not be able to meet the demands of modern business. The trend in successful global enterprises and other organisations is towards customised human resources management services, which requires much more than what is presently offered by these agencies. However, there will always be a demand for non-technical and daily-required stand-ins.

### 3.7.3  Professional agencies

Though registered human resources practitioners have the qualifications to act as headhunters, psychologically screening and subjecting candidates for companies to more intensive managerial and other advanced behavioural testing, they basically fulfil the same function as personnel agencies. These agencies will be found in every city and as close as possible to central businesses and manufacturing locations. Over the past few decades these professionals have expanded their professional services and a company can satisfy its total human resources management needs by making use of various agencies. These agencies specialises in the total field of human resources.

### 3.7.4  HRM through the Internet

As in all organisational activities, the Internet by itself can satisfy some companies' HRM

needs (see www.ahrd.org, the Academy of Human Resources Development; www.cipd. co.uk, the Chartered Institute of Personnel and Development; www.sabpp.co.za, the South African Board of Personnel Practice; and www.opd.net, Organisational Performance Dimensions). Suppliers on the Internet provide for every major human resources activity. Some of these are: recruiting, CV's and CV comparisons, testing and selection, performance management, compensation management, and career management and training and development. Even labour management issues can be satisfied. Various websites exist in South Africa (like www.p-net. co.za; www.jobnavigator. co.za; www.career-junction.co.za; www.movestar.co.za; www. salarislyn.co.za; www.arbeidsregforum. co.za).

### 3.7.5  Outsourcing

A distinction must be drawn between internal and external outsourcing. In the case of external outsourcing, an organisation makes full use of a professional human resources management company that delivers all required services as would any external supplier of goods and services. Internal outsourcing is whereby management establishes its own HRM service as a separate Strategic Business Unit (SBU) and cost centre. As is the case with the external side of things, all services are contracted out to this separate business entity.

### 3.7.6  In-house human resources management departments

#### 3.7.6.1  General

Quality-assured human resources management services could be more effectively achieved by in-house high performance HR departments. It is the best way to meet the challenges of organisational success in this global era. However, to achieve this, management must start viewing human resources management as perhaps the most critical department for future quality performance and sustainable growth. No longer can organisations afford to cut human resources management budgets when economic or business conditions decline. The loss of employees who have been selected, hand-picked and empowered and managed as knowledge creators will be disastrous. Also, for quality to be sustained, employees must have within them a culture of quality. This culture is the most important prerequisite for quality performance. It requires time, effort and money to cultivate such a culture, but the return on investment cannot be over-estimated. Furthermore, contemporary literature emphasises the customisation of human resources and quality. For quality to be customised it requires a diagnostic approach to each type of human resources management interaction or human resources service delivery. Anderson et al. (1995) call this customised quality. Danahar and Rust (1996:85) note that in service delivery, the measure of quality is the measure of customisation, while some use the term 'mass customisation' to describe the use of new technology to customise on a large scale. Thus, it is possible to enhance human resources management quality service delivery by individualised internal quality demands through making use of enhanced communication. This leads to relationship building, resource attainment, and the realisation of these resources focused on individual customer desired outcomes. This can be obtained by quality assurance through process management discussed below.

It was mentioned earlier that the process approach to human resources management could be viewed as an evolution of the practice of human resources management over the past few decades. It was also emphasised that process management can only be practised within a structural and functional organisational set-up. The need for a process approach to human resources management stems from the need to empower line and other functional managers at the lowest level of organisational functioning in HRM practices. This is due to the fact that management (worldwide) has realised the value and bene-fits of an efficient and effective human resources management department in view of the realisation that organisational success depends mainly on the human potential of an organisation.

In the following section we will discuss the theory underlying process management and quality assurance within the realm of human resources management.

### 3.7.6.2 Defining the concepts

To understand process management readers have to acquaint themselves with certain concepts.

- *Process.* Inter-related activities that add value to the product(s) and/or service(s) an organisation produces. Process activities have a start and an end, but constitute a never-ending cycle of events unless the organisation or the specific product and/or service which is produced by the process cease to exist due to economic factors (supply and demand).
- *Internal supply chain.* A network of major organisational events directed to produce products and/or services, which represents an organisation's reason for existence or purpose.

---

**comment**

A manufacturing concern, for example, must have a research and development department, logistics department, a marketing department, manufacturing facilities, warehousing, quality control and distribution and sales to enable it to deliver a product to the market place.

---

- *Internal customer.* A person, process, section or department that is affected by processes which contribute to the making of a product or the delivery of a service in the process chain.

> **comment**
>
> The quality of the raw materials that the logistics department delivers to manufacturing has a direct impact on the quality of the products that is produced by manufacturing.

- *Internal supplier.* The opposite of internal customer. The internal supplier delivers material, products, technology or information to some internal customer in the internal supply chain to enable such an internal customer to further add value to the end product or service that the organisation produces.

> **comment**
>
> The marketing research department is expected to provide accurate information with regard to consumer quality expectations of the organisation's products/services. The accuracy of this information determines the sales volume a certain product/service obtains or generates.

- *Process flow chart.* A pictorial representation of steps in a process making use of standard process symbols.
- *External customer.* Those, irrespective of size, composition, market segment, etc. who purchase the products and/or services produced by an organisation.

> **comment**
>
> In a manufacturing concern producing products en masse – especially in the food and beverage industry – important external customers are chain stores like Pick 'n Pay, Checkers, Rite-Value.

- *External supplier.* Entities, institutions or organisations that, on demand, deliver materials, technology or information to an organisation so as to enable the organisation's internal supply chain to produce products or services.

> **comment**
>
> Typical external customers of a manufacturing concern are the producers of the raw materials such a concern needs to produce (the primary products), which reflects its organisational purpose.

- *Continuous self-improvement.* Central to process management is the concept of continuous improvement. It refers to ongoing efforts to meet and exceed the expectations of stakeholders by changing the way work is performed. It means that products and/or services are delivered sooner and at less cost than previously by the concept of a self-renewing entity by means of organisational learning through introspection.

> **comment**
>
> Within the realm of process management, this poses the biggest challenge to human resources management, i.e. to empower managerial, supervisory and ordinary employees involved in the organisation's different processes to continuously improve bottom line results by applying human resources interventions at the point where they are required or needed by preventing future similarities.

- *Internal support chain.* This refers to other functional departments that are not directly involved with the internal supply chain, such as marketing, sales and merchandising.

- *Professional staff chain.* Those functional departments (like human resources, corporate communications, social responsibility, labour relations and legal services) rendering services to the total organisation's core business as key performance areas.

### 3.7.6.3 Process management and human resources operations

Just like the functional and efficiency approach to human resources management, the quality assurance approach must operate within a structure, which in this case is represented by organisational processes. The process structure of the internal supply chain can be depicted as in Figure 3.1.

In traditional management terms, the internal supply chain represents the line function of an organisation. The inter-linking circles represent the interrelatedness and interdependency of the different main processes in the chain, emphasising the systems or efficiency approach to human resources management. These overlapping shackles imply the internal supplier and internal customer relationship (partnership and performance contracts that is built around vision). Both these parties have certain expectations of each other with regard to the inputs and outputs each linkage requires. In managerial terms, these are called Key Performance Areas (KPAs) and Key Performance Indicators (KPIs) as critical organisational success factors of a process. The outputs (KPIs) of a shackle are the input for the next interrelated shackle. For example, the input of the sales department to manufacturing will determine whether inventory levels will be in accordance with sales forecasts.

**Figure 3.1** Organisational structure from a process management perspective

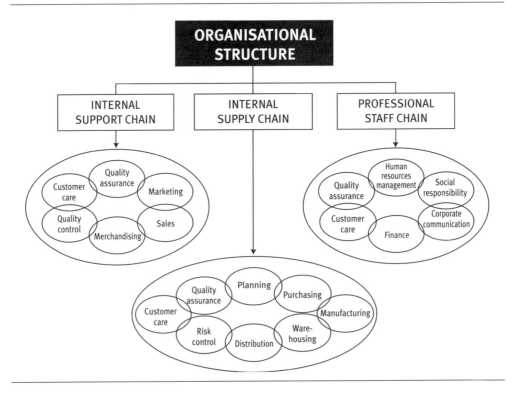

Any discrepancy in this example, whether from sales or manufacturing (under-production or over-production), high labour turnover, or low labour turnover, triggers a red light, and in terms of HRM this refers to under- or sub-performance by the individuals involved in the process. This calls for the human resources department (which is part of the professional staff chain) to implement a continual improvement programme. The nature of the intervention(s) will depend on the diagnosis of the human resources professional and the process managers and may range over the total spectrum of the human resources management function. In Figure 3.2 the human resources function is centrally depicted within the internal supply chain. This implies that any range of services can be offered to the relevant process operators to improve both the quality of their inputs (KPAs) and their outputs (KPIs) in order to assure quality service internally and externally to their internal or external customers.

Ensuring quality service in the organisa-tional processes will require any of the following range of products and services that the human resources department (as an internal supplier) can offer:

- Improved job design, process design and organisational design.
- Improved job descriptions, job specifications and performance contracts.
- Improved human resources planning and management succession planning.
- Ensuring more effective recruitment, selection and placement.
- Improved quality of employee work life by continuously researching compensation trends, motivating experiences and social life expectations.
- Ensuring a labour-friendly work environment by applying and keeping to the rules of the game in terms of relevant governmental legislation.
- Empowering personnel by providing job-related education, training and development.
- Recognising and rewarding employees

**Figure 3.2** Human resources management (internal supplier) and the internal supply chain (internal customers)

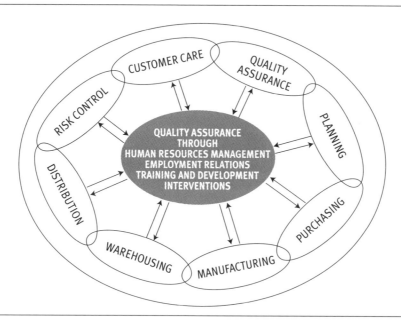

**comment**

- If a process manager is unable to or does not provide accurate job requirements for a certain position, the human resources department's efforts to recruit and employ the most suitable available person, are in vain.
- If a vacancy opens in the accounting department and the financial manager cannot make a decision with regard to whom to appoint, this cannot be laid at the door of the human resources department.

(process members) for attaining or improving on performance standards, but at the same time disciplining under-achievers and providing remedial training intervention.
- Assisting managerial, supervisory and other process employees with accurate human resources information.

This seems like one-way traffic where everything is expected from the human resources department, which is not a true reflection. The effectiveness of the human resources department as an internal supplier of quality service depends on the cooperation and accurate information it receives from its internal customers (partnerships).

However, the shift towards a quality assurance approach from a traditional and efficiency systems approach can be directly attributed to the inability of other functional and process managers to exercise human resources management as part of their normal managerial duties. This has led to human resources management (as an organisational unit) being questioned and challenged by top management. No organisation can do without human resources management, and it is therefore of utmost importance to take human resources management (and not personnel management or personnel administration) to the lowest level of organisational processes. It is

the only way it will survive, but it is also the only way that Southern African organisations will become efficient, effective and successful in a highly competitive global market.

The only way organisations (business or other) can survive is to practise (or endeavour to practise) what successful companies worldwide are practising. That is to ensure the quality of their services and products. If management of Southern African companies can for once and for all come to the realisation that the human resources they employ holds the key to quality and success, the sooner it will deliver improved outcomes for the organisation and its stakeholders. Of utmost importance is the creation by human resources managers of a symbiotic relationship between organisation and work culture where quality assurance is the name of the game in all positions at all levels of employment.

## 3.8   Conclusion

The efficiency and effectiveness approach to HRM has been highlighted by the introduction of quality and knowledge management as core issues in globalised entrepreneurial leadership. Efficiency and effectiveness is viewed by some authors (Gardner and Nudler 1999; Popp et al. 1999) as quality, i.e. quality is the net result of efficient and effective organisational actions. Wiig (1999:156) refers to this as 'effective behaviour', and elaborates as follows: sustained success (organisational) and viability requires effective execution of internal functions (efficiency) and interactions with the environment (effectiveness).

When individual employees act efficiently within an effective framework, the enterprise can act effectively. In practice, effective behaviour means for both people's and the organisation's responses to adjust to context (environment). A major operational objective is to make the customer successful by customising products and services to satisfy individual needs while at the same time attaining organisational goals.

Efficiency is defined according to Wiig (1999:156), but there are, however, others

(Cameron-Bowers and Salas 1998; Klein 1998) who are also of the opinion that organisational success depends on the interplay of many factors – especially those associated with how the enterprise arranges its internal affairs (efficiency). Special factors that have a direct bearing on the individual employee, leadership, groups and especially motivation are as follows (Wiig 1999:164):

- The ability to deliver desired *service paradigms* by individuals, departments and business units, and by the overall organisation. (Service paradigms describe what the organisation and individual units and employees within it, ideally should be able to do for *external* and *internal* customers and how units and people should appear to customers through their behaviour.)
- The ability to act in a timely fashion.
- The capability of employees to deliver the work products for which they are responsible.
- The effectiveness of interpersonal work (teaming and partnership) through coordination, cooperation and collaboration.
- How well work at all levels supports implementation of organisational strategy and direction.
- The ability to create, produce and deliver superior products and services that match present and future market demands.
- The effectiveness of outcome feedback on how well work products perform – in the market place as well as within the enterprise.
- The degree to which innovations occur, are captured, communicated and applied.
- The ability of individuals, teams, units and the enterprise itself to deal with unexpected events, opportunities and threats.
- The effectiveness of organisational systems, procedures and practices.
- The degree to which undesirable and dysfunctional personal or systems behaviours are controlled and corrected.

Wiig (1999:157) is of the opinion that all these factors depend to significant degrees on effective availability and application of good knowledge. We are now learning what motivates individuals and how to integrate individual goals with those of the enterprise, i.e. people and their behaviour contribute much more to enterprise success than conventional assets.

## Summary

- While quality is hard to define, it can be described as an attribute and virtue that manifests in inherent pride and intrinsic satisfaction – on the part of the employer, the employee, and the external customer.
- From a human resources point of view, it can be said that quality is the principal value that underlies human resources management. Quality is the ethic that informs human resources as a crucial service to the organisation. While the organisation might be motivated by other factors, such as the bottom line, human resources is first and foremost motivated by quality assurance.
- Human resources management is part of the company's internal supply chain, and it is that part that ensures the permeation of quality from organisational vision, to mission, to job design and content, research and development, production, logistics and distribution, to marketing, and so on. Quality must be pervasive.
- Quality assurance is best implemented and maintained through process management, a form of control and oversight that is production and product-specific. While the meaning of quality remains constant, the application of quality assurance differs from task to task, job to job. However, process management cannot be separated from continuous self-improvement of the organisation and the individual. In this respect, Key Performance Areas (KPAs) must be continuously identified, and Key Performance Indicators (KPIs) constantly analysed.
- In the contemporary knowledge economy, knowledge management is integral to

corporate success (knowledge is power). It is vital that quality assurance focus on the structuring and managing of information and knowledge.

## Case study
## Supreme Corner Shops (Pty) Ltd.

### Background
The South African economy's isolation from the international evolution of business and innovations was broken after the democratic elections in 1994. Various industries, in particular the business sector, have undergone major changes and adaptations since then. Furthermore, organisations like McDonald's, Seven Eleven, and various others, have made their impact felt on the economy and consumers due to their professionalism and quality service.

### Case detail
Vusi Pitjani completed a business degree in 1983 at Virginia Commonwealth University in Richmond, Virginia in the United States. This was after he left South Africa in 1978 because he was expelled from one of the local universities for his political convictions. He then started and managed a wholesale business successfully in Atlanta, Georgia, which he sold very profitably when he decided to return to South Africa in 1997.

He decided to apply his experience and start a new business venture in South Africa, but with a difference to what he did in the USA, in that he intended to integrate small businesses into one powerful organisation, while retaining a retail character. In fact, he was thinking of emulating Molopo foods, but with his own approach and niche market.

His idea was to integrate a number of independent, but currently small businesses into a chain of grocery outlets, under the combined ownership of one newly formed company.

Owners of these businesses would become shareholders in the new company. The outlets would be located primarily in the suburbs and the micro-shopping centres, which are being established throughout Gauteng in particular. He hoped to list this group on the Johannesburg Securities Exchange within eight years, to sell his shares at a handsome profit, and then become involved in community upliftment projects.

After many consultations with various retailers, Vusi convinced the following organisations' management to combine into one powerful corner convenience grocery store chain: Big Bun Pastries cc, Deli Meats and Butchery (Pty) Ltd., Northern Tinned Meats (Pty) Ltd., Pela Canned Fruits and Vegetables, Jabulani Supermarket cc, Sipho's Best Flamed Grilled Chickens cc, and Bob's Best Bread Bakery (Inc.).

He also entered into agreements with a number of manufacturers of well-known retail product brands to supply the various grocery outlets with the necessary products.

Vusi realised from his American experience that quality and service, as well as effective procurement, were key elements to making his business successful. He was also fully aware of the fact that qualified, experienced, and motivated employees form the core component of any business that wishes to be successful.

The number of personnel employed by the businesses listed above varied from seven to seventy-four. Needless to say, conditions of service, pension agreements, medical schemes, quality of service, working hours, benefits, length of service, etc., all varied extensively. To integrate them into an effective chain of grocers, and to provide a uniformly high level of service was to be a major issue for the group's success. Vusi realised that a quality assurance approach to HRM would be essential. It would be the only way to beat similar outlets, based on the 7 am–11 pm (Seven-Eleven) retail shop principle, which have recently established themselves in

South Africa, and which he knew all too well from his experience in the USA.

You have been recruited and appointed as a knowledgeable and competent human resources manager for the group.

## Question

Advise Vusi as to how to go about establishing a quality assurance approach to human resources management by compiling a report to be presented to him. In the report, explain the principles and advantages of managing human resources from this point of view. Also ensure that your report includes the operationalisation of the process approach, which is contained in the Figures towards the end of this chapter.

## Chapter questions

1   Write an essay on the difference between the functional, efficiency, and quality assurance approaches to human resources management. Explain why these three approaches cannot function in isolation.
2   Re-design an organisation with which you are familiar into an integrated functional and process design.
3   Identify and arrange the different human resources activities in your organisation to form a fluent human resources quality service process.
4   Define quality assurance in your own words.
5   Write an essay on how vision can be made practical to keep employees focused on quality assurance.
6   How important is the creation of quality performance?
7   Develop a quality assurance self-assessment system for a company known to you.

## Bibliography

ALBRECHT, K. 1992. *The only thing that matters: Bringing the power of the customer into the center of your business.* Harper Business, New York.

ANDERSON, E.W., FORNELL, C & RUST, R.T. 1995. *Customer satisfaction, productivity, and profitability: Differences between goods and services.* Working Paper. University of Michigan, Ann Arbor.

BEER, M. 1980. *Organization change and development: A systems view.* Goodyear, Santa Monica.

CAMERON-BOWERS, J.A. & SALAS, E. 1998. 'Team performance and training in complex environments: Recent findings from applied research'. *Current Directions in Psychological Research,* March:20–26.

DANAHAR, P.J. & RUST R.T. 1996. 'Rejoinder'. *Quality Management Journal,* 3(2):85–88.

DAWSON, P. 2003. *Understanding organisational change. The contemporary experience of people at work.* Sage Publications, London.

DYKSTRA, A. 1999a. 'Quality performance and organizational vision: The role of vision in leadership and management'. In Gardner, J.F. & Nudler, S. (eds.). 1999. *Quality performance in human services: Leadership, values and vision.* Paul H Brookes, Baltimore.

DYKSTRA, A. 1999b. 'Quality performance and human resources'. In Gardner, J.F. & Nudler, S. (eds.). *Quality performance in human services: Leadership, values and vision.* Paul H Brookes, Baltimore.

GARDNER, J.F. & NUDLER, S. 1999. *Quality performance in human services: Leadership, vision and values.* Paul H Brookes, Baltimore.

HUGHES, R.L., GINNET, R.C. & CURPHY, G.J. 1993. *Leadership: Enhancing the lessons of the past.* Irwin, Boston.

JAQUES, E. 1989. *Requisite organisation: The CEO's guide to create structure and leadership.* Cason Hall, Arlington, Vermont.

JAQUES, E., & CLEMENT, S.D. 1999. *Executive leadership.* Cason Hall, Arlington, Vermont.

KELEMEN, M.L. 2003. *Managing quality.* Sage Publications, London.

KLEIN, D.A. 1998. *The strategic management of*

*intellectual capital.* Butterworth-Heinemann, Boston.

LIPTON, M. 1996. 'Demystifying the development of an organisational vision'. *Vision Management Review.*

LONGFORD, J.W. 1995. *Logistics: Principles and applications.* McGraw-Hill Companies, New York.

MORRISON, A.M. 1994. 'Diversity and leadership development'. In Renesch J. (ed.). *Leadership in a new era*, pp. 53–18. New Leaders Press, Sterling and Store, San Fransico.

PFEFFER, J. 1981. *Power in organizations.* Pitman, Marshfield.

POPP. D.E., AMAN, M.D. & BRAUN, V. 1999. 'Quality performance and information communication'. In Gardner, J.F. & Nudler, S. (eds.). *Quality performance in human services: Leadership, values and vision.* Paul H Brookes, Baltimore.

REEVES, C.A. & BEDNAR, D.A. 1994. 'Defining quality: Alternatives and implications.' *Academy of Management Review*, 19:419–45.

ROSANDER, A.C. 1999. 'The quest for quality in services'. In Gardner, J.F. & Nudler, S. (eds.) *Quality performance in human services: Leadership, values and vision.* Paul H. Brookes, Baltimore.

SCHEIN, E.H. 1985. *Organization and leadership. A dynamic view.* Jossey-Bass, San Francisco.

VAN DYK, P.S. 1998. *The development of a process management system to increase quality service in a large manufacturing concern.* Unpublished confidential research report. UNISA, Pretoria.

VAN DYK, P.S. 2002a. *Strategic inputs for quality assurance in hospitality services.* Unpublished confidential report, Botswana.

VAN DYK, P.S. 2002b. *Quality assurance for an up-market chain of restaurants through South Africa.* Unpublished top management report, Pretoria.

WIIG, K.M. 1999. 'What future knowledge management users may expect'. *Journal of Knowledge Management*, 3(2):155–65.

WILLIAMS, T.D.A. 1996. *Partnering: An overview of the application of the partnering process to the current business environment.* Resolutions International, Washington.

ZEITHAML, V.A., PARASURAMAN, A. & BERRY, L.L. 1990. *Delivering quality services: Balancing customer perceptions and expectations.* The Free Press, New York.

## Websites

Bright on line: www.bright-future.com

Giga Information Group: www.gigaweb.com

Knowledge Exchange: www.knowledge-exchange.com

LearnerFirst, Inc.: www.learnerfirst.com

# part two

# Human resources and the legislative environment

# 4

# Employment law impacting on employment relationships

PS Nel

## Learning outcomes

At the end of this chapter the learner should be able to:

- Explain the components of the employment relations system.
- Motivate and present arguments for the need for the Employment Equity Act.
- Explain the purpose, role and function of the Labour Relations Act (LRA).
- Compile examples on how working hours are applied in terms of the Basic Conditions of Employment Act (BCEA).
- Provide guidelines for effective skills development of employees.
- Consider the influence of the Skills Development Levies Act on employers' need for skilled personnel.
- Explain the role of compensation for occupational injuries to employees.
- Discuss the benefits of the new unemployment insurance dispensation for South Africa's workforce.
- Present positive arguments in favour of personnel law on sound human resources management for organisations.

## Key words and concepts

- bargaining councils and collective agreements
- basic conditions of employment
- CCMA
- closed shop agreements
- compensation for injuries and diseases
- constitution
- dispute resolution
- diverse workforce
- employment equity
- freedom of association
- hours of work
- occupational health and safety
- organisational rights
- political democracy
- skills development
- strikes and lockouts
- unemployment insurance
- unfair dismissals
- workplace forums

## Illustrative case

## Turbulent times at Clearwash Ltd. Manufacturers

Clearwash Ltd. is a Durban based company also owning an independent plant in Tswane, Gauteng, manufacturing washing machines, dishwashers and tumble driers. It employs a total of 1 236 staff of which just over 1 080 are 'unskilled' local workers. The small plant in Tswane employs 175 workers, and only manufactures dishwashers under a patent agreement from a very well known German company. The supervisors, line managers, managers and administrative staff total 156, and most of them belong to three different unions.

The unskilled workers in Durban work on a production line where each worker is responsible for only a tiny part of the manufacturing process to complete an appliance. Many of the workers have little interest or understanding of how their jobs fit into the overall process. They work in a noisy and humid environment, and although it is air-conditioned it is still not ventilated to the satisfaction of the workers and they have complained to no avail. They have even written a letter to the representative of the local branch of the Occupational Health and Safety Directorate.

They work according to a set speed and cannot leave their workstation for any reason without stopping the whole production line. The work is monotonous and boring for most workers. Human resources has not thought of any job-enrichment programmes yet as it is under-staffed and runs on a shoestring.

With the weakening of the Rand currency, Clearwash Ltd. struggled to cope with the competition from cheap Asian imports (it is very expensive to compete favourably with overseas productions in terms of price and quality). Labour costs also went up by 29 per cent over the past three years due to persistent union demands. Conditions of employment, such as unused annual leave and sick leave, higher overtime rates, business and long service bonuses, travelling allowances and housing subsidies were issues that increased costs significantly after negotiations between Clearwash Ltd. and the union over the last three years as a result of recurring threats of industrial action. Due to this, the company is suffering financial losses and it is now locked into a survival battle for the Durban plant. In fact, at a recent shareholders' meeting it was suggested that the company should be sold and only the Tswane operation continue, as it was running profitably. The Manufacturing and Allied Workers Union of Natal (MAWUN) is also insistent on further improving overall working conditions for its members.

In the past, Clearwash Ltd. had a very good working relationship with employees. Even after the union gained representation four years ago, the initial working relationship was reasonably good. However, as time passed the union demanded more and more, and management received a letter last week in which the union requested a meeting to negotiate substantial wage increases and to improve working conditions as part of the annual collective bargaining agreement.

Due to the deterioration in the worker-management relationship, management decided at the beginning of this year to join an employer's organisation and to employ a part time labour relations consultant from Port Elizabeth. The consultant's main tasks would be the negotiations of the annual wage increases and related employment conditions.

The company is also facing additional problems since it has to upgrade its technology to stay competitive, which means that it may have to reduce staff and a number of jobs may also have to be declared redundant. The employees are suspicious, and the shop stewards have already said that the company is only going to upgrade to have less union members and thereby undermine their bargaining power. The union, resentful about what may happen to its redundant workmates, is anxious about the future of the company and the number of members it may loose due to the possible redundancies.

Management, on the other hand, is frustrated with the wastage of materials resulting in higher production costs, the high level of absenteeism and the 'deliberate' misuse of machinery. Management has already communicated to the union that a serious drop in efficiency and productivity has occurred during the last four months.

As the labour relations consultant, what advice would you give the management of Clearwash Ltd. to resolve the conflict and looming labour demands in the context of the relevant employment law?

## 4.1 Introduction

Its own history and influences from other countries shape a country's labour or management system and its employment law. South Africa is no exception, and the system in its broader context and employment relationships in particular have always been a reflection of the socio-political system and the development of the trade union movement, all of which is closely linked to the prevailing political dispensation.

It must also be noted that no country operates in isolation, and therefore international bodies and issues greatly impact on a country (for example, international trade accords, sovereignty agreements like those specific to the IMF and G8, defence treaties like the NATO, and the multiplicity of laws and conventions orchestrated via the United Nations). Furthermore, the Universal Declaration of Human Rights, which provides many of the guidelines regarding relations, and which is a centrepiece in the point of departure for the United Nations, is also subscribed to by South Africa. Of particular interest, however, are the laws governing employment relations, which fall under the auspices of the International Labour Organisation (the ILO, a division of the United Nations). Of concern in this chapter of the book would therefore be the background pro-

vided by the United Nations' and in particular the ILO's Conventions and Recommendations concerning labour law in particular, which would, for example, provide guidelines for collective bargaining, health and safety in the workplace, unemployment, etc. All of these principles are subscribed to by South Africa, being a member of the United Nations and a signatory to the ILO's policies.

The non-sexist, non racial and equality-based democratic society which is the basis of the current environment within which South Africa operates has evolved considerably since the 1994 general elections. Numerous legislative reforms in the labour field have also taken place to reinforce the new dispensation. The current state of employment law is thus reflected in this chapter.

Employment relationships are also influenced by various sources of law, namely common law, the contract of employment, collective agreements negotiated by trade unions and management, guidelines of the ILO in the form of conventions, and the South African Constitution (RSA 1996a).

Readers or learners must note that it is essential to understand the interdependence between HRM and employment relations. This is presented in this and the next chapter, which should be studied as a unit.

### 4.1.1 Government policy and the Constitution

It is important to take note of South Africa's Constitution (RSA 1996a) in that it is the supreme Act of the country. The provisions of all South African statutes must conform to the basic principles contained in the Constitution. Parliament, as well as the private and public sectors, are all subordinate to the Constitution. Since the Constitution is the supreme law, it means that any action that is in contravention thereof can be challenged. So much so, that any Act of parliament can be challenged and declared null and void if found to be unconstitutional (Swanepoel et al. 2003:99). Therefore, the principle is that sovereignty no longer belongs to Parliament and that it resides in the

Constitution, which gives the Constitutional Court the authority to overrule Parliament.

It is, for example, clearly stated in Chapter 2 of the Constitution that various rights are important to the peoples of South Africa, such as human dignity, equality and freedom, and so on. The Constitution also provides very clear guidelines with regard to employment relations. So, for example, Section 23 of the Constitution stipulates the following provisions:

- Everyone has the right to fair labour practices.
- Every worker has the right to form and join a trade union, to participate in the activities of a trade union, and to strike.
- Every employer has the right to form and join an employers' organisation and to participate in the activities of an employers' organisation.
- Every trade union and employers' organisation has the right to determine its own activities, to organise, to bargain collectively and to form and join a federation.
- Every trade union, employers' organisation and employer has the right to engage in collective bargaining. National legislation may be enacted to regulate collective bargaining. To the extent that the legislation may limit a right in this chapter, the limitation must comply with Section 36(1) on page 16 of the Constitution (RSA 1996a).

It is clear that the Constitution and Government policy set the scene for the practice of employment relations in South Africa, in that they emphasise that employment law should also facilitate worker participation and decision-making in the workplace.

Roodt (1999:10) made comments concerning how Mbeki's government ought to go about transforming South African society within the 'African renaissance', as well as the focus on African-ness in the next millennium, namely:

- Enhance fundamental social delivery and transformation.
- Spread a new understanding of what it

means to live in a democracy in order to counter the 'myopic view that democracy engenders rights to citizens while responsibilities and duties reside with the government alone.'
- Emphasise effectiveness, efficiency and delivery in respect of government initiatives and actions. (This includes cuts to the civil service, which Roodt links to the need for economic growth as the engine for job creation: 'The fundamental base on which we can create meaningful, sustainable jobs is by ensuring the economy grows in a way that creates jobs. One of the things that will have to be done is to reduce the number of people in the public service.')
- Take a tougher approach to dealing with law and order, including partnerships between state, communities and business in preventing and combating crime and corruption.
- Accelerate initiatives to stimulate job creation, in alliance with business and labour.
- Provide a world outlook for South Africa on its position in the region, in Africa and in the rest of the world – also in particular in relation to bringing about an African renaissance.

In terms of the above, and according to Marais (2002:28–30), Government policy and sentiments should be traceable via its statutes. The labour legislation needs to reflect fairness, both to management and labour. These sentiments reflect the changes in employment law in South Africa, which amended the LRA, BCEA and Unemployment Insurance Act (UIA) in particular the last few years. All of these are discussed in the following sections.

## 4.1.2 Relationship between the Constitution and labour laws

In the previous section, the highest level of law in South Africa was referred to. The connection with employment relations was also alluded to in terms of Section 23 of the Constitution, and the international context was also briefly mentioned. In the South African context, however, readers must be aware that regardless of the hundreds of other laws governing the country's activities and resources (such as marine, mining, agriculture, local authorities, etc.), there are also various layers of laws governing the tripartite relationship between state, employers (represented via employers' organisations) and employees (represented via employee organisations) within the business context. The labour laws in South Africa in particular regulate this relationship.

In Figure 4.1 the various levels of law including labour law as well as common law are outlined.

From the figure it is clear that the highest level of law is the Constitution, followed by the centrepiece of labour law, which is the Labour Relations Act. All other labour laws,

such as the Basic Conditions of Employment and the Skills Development Acts, are subordinate to the Labour Relations Act. Readers must, however, also note that an important element of employment relations is the relationship between employer and employee, and therefore the contract of employment is an important regulatory element in the relationship between the parties, but is of course also subject to and regulated by the labour legislation. (Readers or learners are referred to Chapter 5 where the Contract of Employment is discussed in detail.)

It must furthermore be noted that the lowest level of law is the common law. According to Swanepoel et al. (2003:98–9), the common law of South Africa originates from Roman/Dutch law, which was of course the system brought into the country with the arrival of Jan van Riebeeck. In a broad sense, common law is therefore the law, which is applicable throughout the country, unless it is superseded by any particular statute. Common law, for example, is the point of departure for a contract of employment which refers to a contract of letting and hiring and that stipulates that a wage is to be paid – all of which is of course fine-tuned by the Basic Conditions of Employment Act (the latter is superseded by a collective agreement according to the Labour Relations Act, and so it goes on).

The actual applicable employment laws, which influence employment relations within the business context, are presented in Figure 4.2.

Readers or learners must take careful note that the employment law discussed in the next sections is presented in summarised format. It merely sensitises readers or learners to the major provisions, and focuses on the broad context applicable to the world of work in South Africa. Should readers require a legal interpretation of a particular situation and law, they must refer to the original text of the applicable law signed by the President (and which was subsequently published).

Readers or learners must also note that the sequence in which the acts are discussed is not in terms of their importance, but from

**Figure 4.1** Levels of labour law application in South Africa

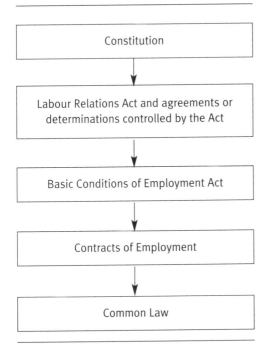

Constitution

Labour Relations Act and agreements or determinations controlled by the Act

Basic Conditions of Employment Act

Contracts of Employment

Common Law

the perspective of a human resource recruitment process following the path a prospective employee would follow of entering an organisation up to a point where the employee exits the organisation. This can be illustrated by the employment decisions an organisation needs to take in terms of policy before employing somebody, for example: What is the composition of its workforce in terms of equity? Therefore, the Employment Equity Act (RSA 1998a) will come into play first, and then of course, the specific conditions under which an employee will accept employment. Thereafter other elements kick in via the Labour Relations Act, then the question of health and safety in the workplace comes into play. Training needs to take place, and of course an accident could only take place once an employee is employed, etc. With all of this in mind it is easy to understand why unemployment insurance is discussed last.

## 4.2    The Employment Equity Act, No. 55 of 1998

There was a long run-up to the signing of this Act on 12 October 1998. The Green Paper on Employment and Occupational Equity, which was published on 1 July 1996 and paved the way to becoming the core of labour legislation, does away with all forms of discrimination in employment in South Africa. The preamble to the promulgated Act illustrates its focus and importance in promoting equity and non-discrimination in the employment sector in South Africa (RSA 1998a).

The preamble states that:

- As a result of apartheid and other discriminatory laws and practices, there are disparities in employment, occupation and income within the national labour market.
- Those disparities create such pronounced disadvantages for certain categories of

**Figure 4.2**  Statutes impacting on the employment relationship

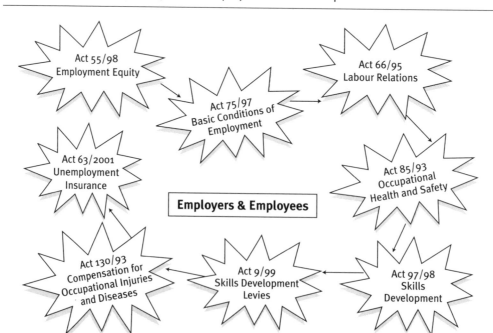

people that simply repealing discriminatory laws cannot redress them.

Therefore, the Act has a particular purpose in order to:

- Promote the constitutional right of equality and the exercise of true democracy.
- Eliminate unfair discrimination in employment.
- Ensure the implementation of employment equity to redress the effects of discrimination.
- Achieve a diverse workforce broadly representative of our people.
- Promote economic development and efficiency in the workforce.
- Give effect to the obligations of the Republic as a member of the International Labour Organisation.

## 4.2.1 The purpose and scope of the Act

Section 2 contains the major purpose of the Act, namely to achieve equity in the workplace by:

- Promoting equal opportunity and fair treatment in employment through the elimination of unfair discrimination.
- Implementing affirmative action measures to redress the disadvantages in employment experienced by designated groups, in order to ensure their equitable representation in all occupational categories and levels in the workforce.

The Act excludes members of the South African National Defence Force (SANDF), the National Intelligence Agency (NIA) and the South African Secret Services (SASS). The anti-discriminatory provisions of the Act apply to all other employers and employees, but the affirmative action provisions only apply to 'designated employers' and members of 'designated groups'. This has a direct bearing on the anti-discrimination prohibitions outlined in Chapter 2 and affirmative action in Chapter 3 of the Act. The drawing up of employment equity plans and the achieve-

ment of numerical goals are also crucial aspects of the Act.

## 4.2.2 Commencement dates of provisions

The commencement dates of the various provisions of the Act (RSA 1998a) are outlined as follows:

- Establishment of the Commission for Employment Equity: 15 May 1999.
- Chapter 2 of the Act (anti-discrimination provisions): 9 August 1999.
- Chapter 3 of the Act (affirmative action provisions): 1 December 1999.
- Submission of employment equity plans for more than 150 employees being employed: The first report by June 2000.
- Submission of employment equity plans for less than 150 employees being employed: The first report by December 2000.
- Awarding of state contracts to employers who employ 150 or more employees: 1 September 2000.
- Awarding of state contracts to employers who employ fewer than 150 employees: 1 April 2001.

## 4.2.3 Human resources impact of the Act

The Act impacts greatly on employment policies and practices in all sectors of the South African economy. The impacts also include, but are not limited to: recruitment procedures, advertising and selection criteria; appointments and the appointment process; job classification and grading; remuneration, employment benefits and terms and conditions of employment; job assignments; the working environment and facilities; training and development; performance evaluation systems; promotion; transfer; demotion; disciplinary measures other than dismissal; and dismissal.

The Act is instrumental in breaking the employment discrimination the country experienced previously in order to propel it into the international community's acceptance of what an equal society represents in the world of work. This also includes how diversity and transformation in the workplace ought to be managed.

Further detail concerning employment equity and applications thereof, is provided in the discussion of cultural diversity and change management in Chapter 18, and the exploration of employment equity and affirmative action in Chapter 7.

## 4.3    Basic Conditions of Employment Act, No. 75 of 1997

Due to the importance of this Act (RSA 1997) – as well as the Labour Relations Act (RSA 1995a) – more attention is paid to these than other acts in this chapter.

The Act replaced the Wage Act of 1957 when it became operational on 1 December 1998 in respect of the private sector and on 1 May 2000 in the public sector. An important amendment to the Act became effective on 1 August 2002 in the form of the Basic Conditions of Employment Amendment Act, No. 11 of 2002 (RSA 2002a). The amendments are included in the discussion of the Act below.

### 4.3.1   Purpose and scope of the Act

The purpose of this Act is to advance economic development and social justice by establishing and enforcing basic conditions of employment. The primary objectives of the Act are to:

- Give effect to and regulate the right to fair labour practices as contained in Section 23(1) of the Constitution by establishing and enforcing basic conditions of employment.
- Give effect to obligations incurred by the Republic as member state of the International Labour Organisation.

The Act applies to all employees and employers except members of the National Defence Force, National Intelligence Agency, South African Secret Service and unpaid charitable workers.

A further focus of the Act is to promote 'regulated flexibility', which is an attempt to balance the protection of minimum standards and the requirements of labour market flexibility.

According to various writers (Landman 2002a:41–7 and Nel 2002:87), it must also be noted that the basic conditions of employment established by the Act form part of every contract of any employment of an employee in South Africa, and represent the minimum standards unless they have been replaced, varied or excluded in accordance with the Act, or unless the employee has personally or via a bargaining council agreement contracted for more favourable terms of employment.

However, these minimum standards enforced by the Act place a further burden on especially smaller employers and may hamper the creation of jobs and flexibility in employment and the doing of business. The restrictions are, for example, the wage levels, structured by law in terms of minimum wages, which may have a negative effect on employment levels in the country. Various determinations in this regard have been legislated concerning minimum wages, the possible negative effect of which will only become apparent in time to come as far as employment levels and overall business efficiency in South Africa are concerned. Examples in this regard are:

- Sectoral Determination No. 7: Domestic Workers (came into effect on 1 November 2002).
- Sectoral Determination No. 8: Farm Workers (came into effect on 1 March 2003).
- Sectoral Determination No. 9: Wholesale and Retail Sector (came into effect on 1 February 2003).

The working time of employees must be arranged so as not to endanger their health and safety, and with due regard to their family responsibilities.

These are exclusions to the Act: the require-ments with regard to remuneration, deduc-tions and termination do not apply to employees who work less than four hours a week.

## 4.3.2 Work time and rules

- *Ordinary hours of work.* The maximum ordinary weekly hours for all employees are 45. The maximum daily hours that an employee may work are nine for employ-ees who work on five days or less a week, and eight for employees who work six days a week.

  According to Schedule 1 of the Act there must be a progressive reduction of the maximum hours of work. It proposes a procedure to reduce working hours of employees to 40 hours and an eight-hour working day. This is to be achieved through collective bargaining and the publication of sectoral determinations having regard for the impact on existing employment and opportunities of employment creation, economic efficien-cy and the health safety and welfare of all employees in South Africa. It must fur-thermore be noted that if a party to nego-tiations puts the reduction of working hours on the agenda, it must be an issue that must be negotiated.

- *Overtime.* Overtime may only be worked by agreement. Overtime work must be compensated by paying the employee at one-and-a-half times the employee's nor-mal wage or, if agreed, by granting the employee a period of paid time off equiv-alent to the value of the overtime pay. An agreement may provide for a maximum of 12 hours to be worked on any day (instead of the previous maximum of three hours overtime per day). Furthermore, a collective agreement (that is with a trade union) can increase the maximum permitted overtime from 10 hours to 15 hours per week. It can only be implemented for a maximum of two months in any period of 12 months.

- *Extended ordinary daily hours of work.* An agreement may permit an employee to work for up to 12 hours in a day without receiving overtime pay, provided that the weekly limits continue to apply and the employee does not work on more than five days in a week. This allows for the 'compressed work week' to be worked as well, i.e. 11.25 hours for four days to work a 45 hour week. A collective agree-ment may permit the hours of work of an employee to be averaged over a period of up to four months. The average time worked over the agreed period must not exceed 45 ordinary hours and five hours overtime per week.

  The Minister of Labour, on grounds of health and safety, may make regula-tions setting shorter maximum hours of work for any category of employees.

- *Meal intervals.* An employee must have a meal interval of at least 60 minutes after five hours. This may be reduced to 30 minutes by agreement. An employee required to be available for work or to remain on the employer's premises dur-ing the meal interval must be paid.

- *Daily and weekly rest period.* An employee must have a daily rest period of at least 12 hours between ending work and starting work the following day. Every employee must have a rest period of at least 36 con-secutive hours each week. The rest period must include a Sunday, unless otherwise agreed. An employee may agree to have a longer rest period (60 hours) every two weeks.

  An employee who works on a Sunday must receive double pay. However, an employee who normally works on a Sun-day must be paid at one-and-a-half times the employee's normal wage. By agree-ment, an employer may compensate an employee for Sunday work by granting paid time off.

- *Night work.* The Act contains protection for employees for two types of night work. Firstly, night work is defined as work performed between 18h00 and

06h00. Employees must be compensated by the payment of an allowance or by a reduction of working hours. Transportation must be available for employees. Secondly, employers must inform employees who regularly work after 23h00 of the health and safety hazards of night work, and on request provide employees with a free medical assessment. 'Regular' is taken to be at least five occasions per month or 50 times per year.

- *Sunday work and public holidays.* An employee who works on a Sunday must receive double pay. However, an employee who normally works on a Sunday must be paid at one-and-a-half times the employee's normal wage. By agreement, an employer may compensate an employee for Sunday work by granting proportional paid time off. An employee may not be required to work on a public holiday unless by agreement. Work on a public holiday must be remunerated at double rates or the normal daily rate plus the amount, for actual time worked, whichever is the greater. The limits on hours of work do not apply to senior managers and travelling sales personnel. The Minister of Labour may exclude or vary the application of the provisions in Chapter 3 of the Act to employees earning above a certain amount.
- *Emergency work.* The limits on ordinary and overtime working hours and the requirements for meal intervals and rest periods do not prevent the performance of emergency work.
- *Annual leave.* Employees are entitled to three weeks (21 consecutive days) fully paid leave after every 12 months of continuous employment. This may also be calculated as one day's (or one hour's) leave for every 17 days (or 17 hours) of employment. Leave is extended by one day for every public holiday that falls in the leave period. An employer must not pay an employee instead of granting annual leave. However, an employee whose employment is terminated must be paid out any leave pay due that the employee has not taken.
- *Sick leave.* An employee is entitled to six weeks' paid sick leave for every 36 months of continuous employment. However, during the first six months of employment an employee is entitled to only one day's paid sick leave for every 26 days worked. An employer may require a medical certificate from an employee who is regularly away from work for more than two days, or after two occasions of absence within an eight-week period before paying the employee for sick leave. Sick leave cannot run concurrently with annual leave.

  An employee's daily pay for sick leave may be reduced by agreement, provided the number of days' sick leave is increased. The pay may not be reduced below 75 per cent of ordinary pay.
- *Maternity leave.* A pregnant employee is entitled to consecutive months' maternity leave. This leave may begin up to four weeks before the expected date of birth, unless otherwise agreed or if the employee is required to do so for health reasons. An employer may not require an employee to return to work for six weeks after the birth of a child. During this period, an employee may elect to return to work if a medical doctor or midwife certifies that she is fit to do so.

  An employee who has a stillborn child or a miscarriage in the third trimester of pregnancy may remain on maternity leave for six weeks or for longer if a doctor certifies it necessary for her health. During pregnancy and for six months after birth, an employer must offer suitable alternative employment to an employee who works at night or whose work may endanger her health or safety or that of her child.

  The Act does not prescribe payment for maternity leave, in other words maternity leave is unpaid leave. However, an employee is entitled to claim maternity benefits in terms of the Unemployment Insurance Act (RSA 2001).

- *Family responsibility leave.* An employee who has worked at least four months is entitled to three days' paid family responsibility leave. This only applies to employees who work on four or more days in a week. The employee may take this leave in the event of the birth of the employee's child, if the employee's child is sick or if a member of the employee's immediate family dies. An employer may require reasonable proof of the purpose for which this leave is taken before paying the employee. Unused days do not accrue nor are they transferable to another member of a family working in the same organisation.

The provisions of Chapter 3 of the Act do not apply to leave granted by an employer in excess of the requirements of the Act. The provisions of Chapter 3 of the Act do not apply to employees who work less than 24 hours a week.

### 4.3.3 Payment of remuneration and deductions

An employer must pay an employee according to arrangements made between them. Payment may take place daily, weekly, fortnightly or monthly, and must take place at the workplace unless otherwise agreed and during, or within 15 minutes of the employee's working time. An employer may only deduct money from an employee's pay if permitted or required to do so by law, collective agreement, and court order or arbitration award.

A deduction for loss or damage caused by the employee in the course of employment may only be made by agreement and after the employer has established, by a fair procedure, that the employee was at fault. An employee may agree in writing to an employer deducting a debt specified in the agreement.

### 4.3.4 Termination of employment

During the first six months of employment, an employment contract may be terminated on one week's notice. The notice period during the remainder of the first year of employment is two weeks. It is four weeks for employees with more than a year's service.

The notice period for a farm worker or domestic worker who has worked for more than six months is four weeks. The notice period may be varied by a collective agreement to a minimum of two weeks after one year of service.

Notice must be given in writing. If the recipient cannot understand the notice, it must be explained to the employee in a language s/he can understand. An employer may pay the employee the remuneration for the notice period instead of giving notice. An employee who occupies accommodation situated on the employer's premises or supplied by the employer may elect to remain in the accommodation for the duration of the notice period.

The termination of employment by an employer on notice in terms of the Act does not prevent the employee challenging the fairness or lawfulness of the dismissal in terms of the Labour Relations Act.

Note that Section 41 of the Act is amended to state that when an employee is dismissed the employer must pay an employee who is dismissed for reasons based on the employer's operational requirements or whose contract of employment terminates or is terminated in terms of Section 38 of the Insolvency Act (Act No. 24 of 1936), severance pay equal to at least one week's remuneration for each completed year of continuous service with that employer.

In the event of the termination of an employee who is on probation (in terms of amendments to the LRA) for failure to meet the required standard of performance, despite having given a reasonable opportunity to do so, the employer's reasons for dismissal will not be judged as strictly as might otherwise have been the case.

However, note that an employer would be required to prove procedural fairness, i.e. opportunity by the employee to state her/his case, the opportunity to be assisted by fellow employees, and at least one weeks' notice. Less strict, however, are the reasons that would be required for the substantive fairness of the dismissal during probation than after the probationary period.

On termination of employment, an employee must be paid:

- For any paid time off that s/he is entitled to and which s/he has not taken, for example, time off for overtime or Sunday work.
- Remuneration for any period of annual leave due and not taken.
- In respect of annual leave entitlement during an incomplete annual leave cycle, for example, one day's remuneration in respect of every 17 days on which an employee has worked.

### 4.3.5 Administrative obligations

The employer must:

- Give the employee written particulars of employment when the employee starts employment. The Minister of Labour must prescribe the required particulars.
- Keep these particulars of employment for four years after the end of the contract of employment.
- Must give employee information concerning remuneration, deductions and time worked with their pay.
- Keep a record of the time worked by each employee and their remuneration.
- Display at the workplace a statement of employees' rights under the Act.

On termination of employment, an employee is entitled to a certificate of service, and simplified provisions apply to employers who have less than five employees and to employers of domestic workers.

### 4.3.6 Prohibition of employment of children and forced labour

Children under 18 may not be employed to do work inappropriate for their age or that places them at risk. No person may employ a child under 15 years of age and the Minister of Labour may make regulations prohibiting or placing conditions on the employment of children over 15 years of age.

The Minister of Labour may further make regulations concerning medical examinations for children in employment. The use of forced labour is prohibited, unless any other law permits it.

### 4.3.7 Variation of basic conditions of employment

A collective agreement concluded by a bargaining council or between an employer's organisation and a trade union might replace or exclude any basic condition of employment.

The Minister of Labour may make a determination that varies or excludes any basic condition of employment. A determination that applies to a category of employers or employees must be made on the advice of the Employment Conditions Commission. The Minister of Public Service and Administration must make a determination that applies to the public sector.

Bargaining council agreements take preference over other collective agreements, and the latter in turn take preference over individual agreements.

A bargaining council agreement may vary any provision of the Act, except the core rights of an employee, which are:

- The employer's duty to arrange working time with due regard to the health and safety and family responsibilities of employees.
- Protection of the health and safety of night workers.
- The 45-hour week or its averaged equivalent.
- The employee's entitlement to maternity and sick leave.
- The prohibitions on child and forced labour.
- Annual leave may not be reduced to less than two weeks.

Other collective agreements may vary only those conditions of employment that the Act specifically allows, including:

- Averaging of hours of work.
- Family responsibility leave.
- Deductions from an employee's wages.
- Shorter notice period for the termination of employment.
- Removal of labour inspector's ability to issue a compliance order if the collective agreement provides for arbitration.
- Certain conditions of employment within the limits set by the Act, for example, overtime, weekly rest periods, Sunday work, and sick pay.

### 4.3.8 Monitoring, enforcement and legal proceedings

The Minister of Labour may appoint labour inspectors. Labour inspectors perform their functions subject to the direction and control of the Minister. The function of labour inspectors is to promote, monitor or enforce compliance with employment laws. Labour inspectors must advise employees and employers on their rights and obligations in terms of employment laws. They may also conduct inspections, investigate complaints and secure compliance with employment law.

A dispute concerning the exercise of these rights may be referred to a bargaining council or the Commission for Conciliation, Mediation and Arbitration (CCMA) for conciliation. If this does not resolve the dispute, it may be referred to the Labour Court.

## 4.4 Labour Relations Act, No. 66 of 1995

### 4.4.1 The purpose, scope and application of the Act

The purpose of the Act is to advance economic development, social justice, labour peace and a democratisation of the workplace by fulfilling the primary objectives of the Act, which are to realise and regulate the fundamental rights of workers and employers in the Constitution (RSA 1996a, Section 23) – which was discussed elsewhere in this chapter (RSA 1995a). Readers

must also note that the contents of the Labour Relations Amendment Act (RSA 2002e), which came into operation on 1 August 2002 is also included in the discussion of the Act. The major focus of the amendments was firstly, to correct practices that undermine the application of the Act (unintended consequences); secondly, to ensure effective alignment of laws with the changing labour market environment; and thirdly, to sensitise the legal framework to the need for job creation in South Africa.

Regarding the scope of the Act, it applies to all employment relationships between employers and employees and it makes no distinction whether these relationships are in the private sector or the public sector. All previous exclusions of employees from the ambit of the Labour Relations Act have been removed, but the National Defence Force, the National Intelligence Agency and the South African Secret Service are now specifically excluded (Section 2). This brings an entirely new dimension to the Labour Relations Act, as the public service, the South African police, the nursing and teaching professions as well as agricultural and domestic employees now have virtually the same rights as other employees. However, in certain instances, specific procedures are established for these sectors.

Regarding the application of the Act, it should be noted that the amendment in 2002 refined it considerably in outlining a new Section 200A, defining what an employee is. It is stated that a person who works for, or renders services to, any other person is presumed, regardless of the form of the contract, to be an employee, if any one or more of the following factors are present:

- The manner in which the person works is subject to the control or direction of another person.
- The person's hours of work are subject to the control or direction of another person.
- In the case of a person who works for an organisation, the person forms part of that organisation.
- The person has worked for that other

person for an average of at least 40 hours per month over the last three months.

- The person is economically dependent on the other person for whom s/he works or renders services.
- The person is provided with tools of trade or work equipment by the other person.
- Or, the person only works for or renders services to one person.

The above description does not apply to any person who earns in excess of the amount determined by the Minister in terms of Section 6(3) of the Basic Conditions of Employment Act (RSA 1997). In 2002, this amount was assessed to be R89 455.00.

If a proposed or existing work arrangement involves persons who earn amounts equal to or below the amounts determined by the Minister in terms of Section 6(3) of the Basic Conditions of Employment Act (RSA 2002a), any of the contracting parties may approach the Commission for an advisory award on whether the persons involved in the arrangement are employees.

It must furthermore be noted that the question of an 'independent contractor' also comes into play. An independent contractor is a worker who works for another person to complete a specific task for a specified remuneration or fixed rate, for instance, a building contractor, a tax consultant, or a freelance filmmaker. An independent contractor is not regarded as an 'employee' for purposes of the LRA, and subsequently does not enjoy the protection of the LRA. Clarity in this regard rests on the following issues:

- Whether the person rendering the service is under the authority of an employer.
- The result of the work being executed is the objective and not the rendering of services personally to the employer.
- Three tests are used for the distinction, namely:
  - *The control test.* Is the employer entitled to exercise control?
  - *The organisational test.* In what way is the worker incorporated in the organisation?

- *The dominant impression test.* Favoured test because it evaluates the relationship as a whole, taking into account the true intention of parties, right of supervision, manner of payment, right to discipline, etc.

The status of the Act is such that in the case of any conflict between the provisions of the Labour Relations Act and any other act (except the Constitution), priority will be given to the provisions of the Labour Relations Act. The Labour Relations Act automatically supersedes the Basic Conditions of Employment Act. This exclusion enables bargaining councils to enter into agreements which contain conditions of employment less favourable than those provided for in the Basic Conditions of Employment Act (excluding the core rights of employees).

The following schedules are contained in the Act, which greatly simplifies the execution and understanding thereof:

- Schedule 1. It entails the establishment of a bargaining council for the public service.
- Schedule 2. It entails the establishment and constitution of workplace forums.
- Schedule 3. It contains aspects regarding the CCMA.
- Schedule 4. It entails 14 flow diagrams to enable users to determine how different disputes should be dealt with.
- Schedule 5. It entails technical amendments to the Basic Conditions of Employment Act and the Occupational Health and Safety Act.
- Schedule 6. It contains provisions of the Acts which have been repealed.
- Schedule 7. It contains transitional arrangements, for example, those relating to residual unfair labour practices.
- Schedule 8. It entails the Code of Good Practice: Dismissal, which is of cardinal importance to employment relations practitioners.

In order to gain a holistic perspective of the South African system of labour relations, a schematic presentation (but strictly not technically accurate) adapted from Nel (2002), is presented in Figure 4.3 to assist readers or learners to understand how the components of the Act fit together.

Readers or learners must also note that the presentation sequence of the LRA in this section is presented according to the chapters contained in the Act itself, namely Chapter 1, the general provisions and scope; Chapter 2, aspects on freedom of association; Chapter 3, collective bargaining; Chapter 4, strikes and lock-outs; Chapter 5, workplace forums; Chapter 6, trade unions and employers' organisations; Chapter 7, dispute resolution; Chapter 8, unfair dismissal and unfair labour practices; and Chapter 9, general provisions. The focus, however, is on the major issues only.

## 4.4.2 Freedom of association and general protections

Freedom of association and general protections is discussed in Chapter 2 of the Labour Relations Act. One of the stated objectives of the Act is to give effect to the Constitution. One of the provisions contained in Section 23 of the Constitution is that workers have the right to form and to join trade unions, and employers have the right to form employers' organisations. This freedom of association is also enshrined in the International Labour Standards of the ILO.

Union members further have the right to elect office bearers, officials or trade union representatives (shop stewards), to be elected and appointed as office bearers or officials and, if elected or appointed, to hold office. The functions of a trade union representative must be carried out subject to the union's constitution.

### Protection of employees and persons seeking employment

Section 5 of Chapter 2 of the Act states clearly that no person may discriminate against an employee for exercising any right conferred by the Act. In addition, nobody may force an employee or a person seeking employment not to be or become a member of a trade union or workplace forum, or to give up membership of a trade union or workplace forum or for his/her omission or failure to do anything which the employer by law may not compel or allow him/her to do, for the publicising of information which an employee may lawfully give to another person, for the employee's assertion of any rights in terms of the Act or for his/her participation in any activities of the Act. Furthermore, no one may offer or promise an employee favourable treatment if s/he waives any rights granted to her/him or desists from any activities in terms of the Act.

According to Section 6 of the Act, every employer has the right to assist in forming an employers' organisation or a federation of employers' organisations and to join an employers' organisation. Its members have the right to participate in its lawful activities and the election of office bearers or officials.

### Protection of employers' rights

In terms of Section 7 of the Act, no person may discriminate against an employer with regard to the following: force an employer not to be or become a member of an employers' organisation or to give up membership of an employers' organisation or to take part in such an organisation's activities.

In any disputes regarding victimisation or interference with freedom of association, the complainant merely has to prove that s/he has been compelled, threatened, prohibited or detrimentally affected in any manner, and it is then up to the defendant to prove that her/his action was not contrary to any of the provisions of the Act (Section 10).

### Rights of trade unions and employers' organisations

Employers are granted essentially the same rights as employees in respect of freedom of association and freedom from victimisation. Trade unions and employers' associations likewise have the right to establish independently constituted bodies, to organise their own ad-

**Figure 4.3** Aspects of the employment relations system presented visually

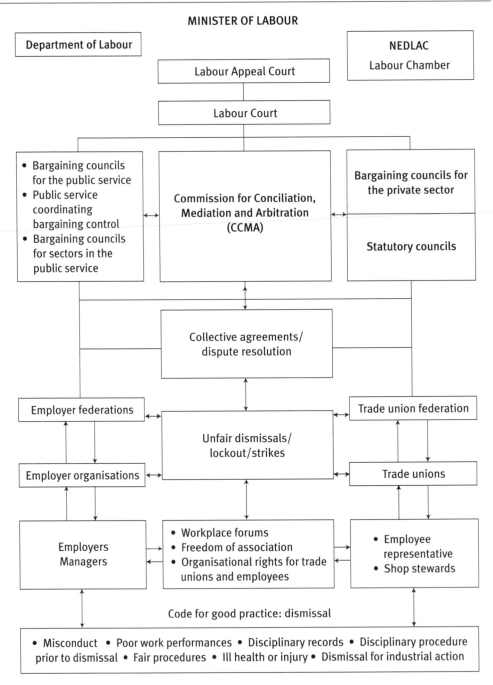

ministration and activities, to take part in the establishment of federations and to affiliate to other bodies, both locally and internationally.

Every trade union and employers' organisation has the right to determine its own constitution and rules and to elect office bearers, officials and representatives subject to the provisions of the Act, and this links up with Chapter 6 of the Act.

### 4.4.3 Collective bargaining

In Chapter 3, the Act promotes collective bargaining and in particular, sectoral level collective bargaining, as the desired method of settling wages and conditions of employment. The Act, however, strongly promotes centralised collective bargaining at industrial or sectoral level.

Although the Act does not contain a statutory right to bargain in the strict sense of the word, a duty to bargain is strongly promoted, given the statutory organisational rights now afforded trade unions.

#### Organisational rights

Unions are accorded 'sufficiently representative' rights, such as the right to access, to hold meetings with employees outside working hours (Section 12), to conduct an election at the workplace, and to be granted stop order facilities (Section 13). A majority union, or more than one union which together represent a majority of employees at the workplace, may also appoint shop stewards, may be given information necessary for the purpose of representation or collective bargaining and, in consultation with the employer, establish thresholds for representation.

Due to their importance, more attention is focused on access to the workplace, leave for trade union activities and disclosure of information, since they have far-reaching implications for human resources managers.

#### Trade union access to workplace

A 'representative trade union' means any reg-istered trade union or two or more registered trade unions acting jointly that are sufficiently representative of employees. According to Le Roux (1995:21), there is no definition of 'sufficiently representative', and if there is a dispute in this regard it should be resolved through arbitration undertaken by the 'Commission' (CCMA).

Any office bearer or official of a representative trade union is entitled to enter the employer's premises to recruit, communicate with its members or just to serve their interests. Trade unions shall be entitled to hold meetings with employees outside their working hours at the employer's premises, and with members of a representative trade union are entitled to vote at the employer's premises, in any election or ballot in terms of that trade union's constitution.

The right of access to an employer's premises does not, however, include the right to enter the home of a domestic worker's employer, for which his/her consent is necessary.

#### Leave for trade union activities

In terms of Section 15 of the Labour Relations Act, an employee who is an office bearer of a representative trade union, or a federation of trade unions to which the representative trade union is affiliated, is entitled to take reasonable leave during working hours to perform the functions of that office and to be trained in any subject relevant to the performance of those functions.

The employer may agree to the number of days' leave and the number of days' paid leave, and the conditions of leave may be agreed between the employer and trade union representative.

#### Disclosure of information

In terms of Section 16, an employer must disclose to a trade union representative all relevant information needed for the effective performance of the functions. Whenever an employer consults or bargains with a representative trade union, the employer must disclose all information necessary for the representative trade union to engage effectively in such consultation or collective bargaining.

The employer must notify the trade union representative or the representative trade union in writing if any information disclosed is confidential. An employer is not required to disclose information that:

- Is legally privileged.
- Cannot be disclosed without contravening a prohibition imposed on the employer by any law or order of any court.
- Is confidential and, if disclosed, may cause substantial harm to an employee or the employer.
- Is private, personal information relating to an employee unless that employee consents to the disclosure of that information.

In a dispute about what information is required to be disclosed in terms of this section, any of the parties may refer the dispute in writing to the CCMA. The party that does so must satisfy the Commission that a copy of the referral has been served on all other parties to the dispute.

It is interesting to note that the right to disclosure of information (Section 16 of the Labour Relations Act) does not apply in the domestic sector.

A 2002 amendment to the Act concerning the disclosure of information states that an employer who does not wish to disclose information when a retrenchment is in question would have to prove that the information is not relevant. It must also be noted that employees, on the other hand, are supported by the Protected Disclosures Act (RSA 2000), in that it would be automatically unfair for a worker to be dismissed for making a disclosure which is thus in alignment with the Labour Relations Act.

## The exercise of organisational rights

According to Section 21 of the Act, any registered trade union may notify an employer in writing at any time that it wishes to exercise organisational rights in a workplace. A certi-fied copy of the trade union's certificate of registration must accompany the notice, which must specify:

- The workplace where the trade union seeks to exercise the rights.
- The representatives of the trade union in that workplace, and the facts that show that it is a representative trade union.
- The rights that the trade union seeks to exercise and how they will be exercised.

The employer must meet the registered trade union within 30 days of receiving the notice and must attempt to conclude a collective agreement on how the trade union will exercise the rights in that workplace.

If a collective agreement is not concluded, either the trade union or the employer may refer the dispute in writing to the CCMA. The Commission must appoint a commissioner to attempt to resolve the dispute through conciliation.

An employer who alleges that a trade union is no longer a representative trade union may apply to the Commission to withdraw any of the organisational rights via the conciliation and arbitration process, should there be a dispute about it.

## Collective agreements

The Act defines a collective agreement very widely as a written agreement between, on the one hand, one or more registered trade unions and, on the other, between one or more employers, or one or more registered employers' organisations, or one or more employers together with one or more registered employers' organisations, concerning terms and conditions of employment or any other matter of mutual interest.

A collective agreement binds employees who are not members of the registered trade union or trade unions to the agreement if the employees are identified in the agreement. The agreement expressly binds them if the majority of employees in the workplace are members of the trade union(s).

In terms of the amendment in 2002 to the

**Figure 4.4** Collective agreements

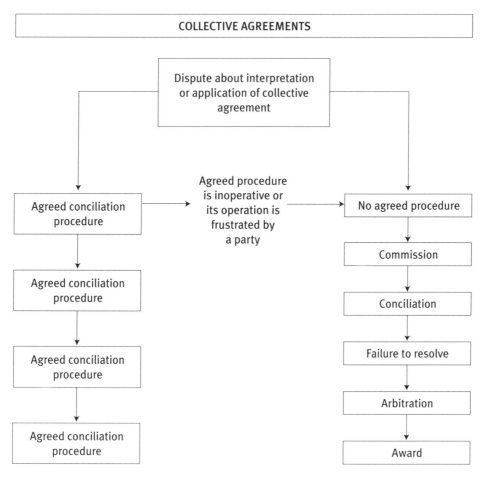

SOURCE: Government Gazette, 13 December 1995.

Act, the Minister can request that a bargaining council appoint a designated agent to promote, monitor and enforce compliance with any agreement concluded in a bargaining council. The designated agent may secure compliance with collective agreements by:

- Publicising the contents of the agreements.
- Conducting inspections.
- Investigating complaints.
- Any other means the council may adopt.
- Perform any other functions that are conferred or imposed on the agent by the council, and also has all the powers as set out in Schedule 10 of the Act.

A further amendment, which was introduced in 2002, was when ownership of a business is transferred, collective agreements and arbitration awards that bound the old employer will bind the new employer.

The diagram in Figure 4.4, contained in the Labour Relations Act (RSA 1995a:238), indicates how a dispute about the interpretation or application of a collective agreement should be executed.

## Agency shop agreements

According to Section 25 of the Act, a representative trade union and an employer or employers' organisation may conclude an agency shop agreement, whereby the employer will deduct an agreed agency fee from the wages of employees who are identified in the agreement and who are not members of the trade union.

An agency shop agreement is binding only if it makes provision for representative employees not to be compelled to become members of the trade union and the agreed agency fees are paid. The amount deducted must be paid into a separate account administered by the representative trade union and no part of it may be paid to a political party as an affiliation fee, contributed in cash or kind to a political party or a person standing for election to any political office, or used for any expenditure that does not advance or protect the socio-economic interests of employees.

An employer does not need employees' authorisation to deduct the agreed agency fee from their wages. A conscientious objector may request the employer to pay the amount deducted into a fund administered by the Department of Labour (see RSA 1995a, Section 25(4)(b)).

## Closed shop agreements

Arguments still rage that the freedom of disassociation of an employee is violated in the sense that s/he is compelled to belong to a certain union on joining a certain employer in a certain industry.

A representative trade union and an employer or employers' organisation may conclude a closed shop agreement, requiring all employees covered by the agreement to be members of the trade union and its agreements.

A registered trade union and a registered employers' organisation may conclude a closed shop agreement in respect of a sector and area.

## Bargaining councils

Bargaining councils (Sections 27 to 34) were introduced to replace industrial councils under the old Labour Relations Act. Registered trade unions and registered employers' organisations may establish a bargaining council for a sector and area. The registrar of Labour Relations may establish a statutory council provided that there is not a bargaining council for the industry and if the trade union involved is registered and enjoys a 30 per cent representivity amongst the employees.

The state may be a party to a bargaining council if it is an employer in the sector and area in respect of which the bargaining council is established. The process of designating, establishing and amalgamating and varying the scope of bargaining councils in the public sector was also clarified and greater autonomy was given to the public service coordinating bargaining council as a result of the 2002 amendments to the Act.

Various other bargaining councils may also be formed, for example, public sector and statutory councils, but are not discussed in this chapter.

Other amendments are that bargaining councils must also address the interests and concerns of small businesses and must provide a report on an annual basis to the Registrar of Labour regarding their activities. The Registrar may also investigate irregularities and non-compliance with the Act. Furthermore, the services and functions of bargaining councils are to be extended to workers in the informal sector as well as home workers. The authority to register as a trade union or employer organisation in order to participate in bargaining council activities has been tightened by giving the Registrar of Labour Relations greater authority. It will prevent unscrupulous bodies or persons from abusing the framework of bargaining councils. (In particular, consultants who registered as one of the aforementioned are now more tightly regulated to prevent abuse of the formal structures of the bargaining council.) The Registrar must therefore be satisfied that applicants are genuine organisations for bargaining council purposes.

According to Section 28 of the Act, a registered bargaining council may, amongst others, do the following:

- Conclude and enforce collective agreements.
- Prevent and resolve labour disputes.
- Perform the dispute resolution functions.
- Establish and administer a fund to be used for resolving disputes.
- Promote and establish training and education schemes.
- Establish and administer pension, provident, medical aid, sick pay, holiday, unemployment and training schemes for the benefit of the parties to the bargaining council or their members.

A collective agreement concluded in a bargaining council binds only those who are parties to the collective agreement to the bargaining council. According to Section 32 of the Labour Relations Act, a bargaining council may ask the Minister in writing to extend such a collective agreement to non-parties to the collective agreement within its registered scope, and identify in the request, if at a meeting of the bargaining council:

- The members of one or more of the major registered trade unions in the bargaining council vote in favour of the extension.
- The members of one or more of the major registered employers' organisations in the bargaining council vote in favour of the extension.

The Minister must extend the collective agreement within 60 days, as requested, by publishing a notice in the Government Gazette declaring that the agreement will bind the non-parties stipulated in the notice from a specified date and for a specified period.

## 4.4.4 Strikes and lockouts

Industrial action, especially in the form of strikes, is discussed in Chapter 4 of the Act, and is a common occurrence in South Africa. Most strikes occur as a result of wage disputes, followed by dismissal disputes.

In terms of the Act, every employee has a fundamental right to strike. This right is subject to certain limitations (which are mentioned below). This is also strictly in line with the letter and spirit of the Constitution of the Republic of South Africa. In the Act, the definition of a strike is essentially similar to that in the old Act, with one major exception: voluntary or compulsory overtime bans are included in the definition.

### Defining strikes and lockouts

The Act (RSA 1995a:214) defines a strike as:

> The partial or complete considered refusal to work or the retardation or obstruction of work by persons who are or have been employed by the same employer or by different employers, for the purpose of remedying a grievance or resolving a dispute in respect of any matter of mutual interest between employer and employee, and every reference to 'work' in this definition includes overtime work, whether it is voluntary or compulsory.

Regarding a work stoppage itself, when a group of employees lay down their tools during working hours and decline to resume work, there is no question that their action amounts to a 'concerted refusal to work'. With one exception, a stoppage entails a refusal to do work, which the employees are contractually obliged to perform. The exception is overtime, the refusal of which amounts to a strike if the overtime is compulsory (i.e. in terms of a contract or collective agreement). There is no requirement as to the duration of the stoppage. Partial strikes such as work-to-rules, go-slows and 'grasshopper' (intermittent) stoppages also clearly amount to strikes. Joint action by employees, aimed against the employer and for a recognised purpose, or protest action, may also constitute a strike.

The Act (RSA 1995a:212–13) defines protest action as follows because it is different from strike action:

A partial or complete concerted refusal to work, or the retardation or obstruction of work, for the purpose of promoting or defending the socio-economic interests of workers, but not for a purpose referred to in the definition of strike.

Although the Act does not openly indicate that the purpose of a strike is to force an unwilling employer to do something, the definition does imply force: the joint action of employees must aim at remedying a grievance or resolving a dispute.

In terms of the Act (RSA 1995a:212) the definition of a lockout is:

Lock-out means the exclusion by an employer of employees from the employer's workplace, for the purpose of compelling the employees to accept a demand in respect of any matter of mutual interest between employer and employee, whether or not the employer breaches those employee's contracts of employment in the course of or for the purpose of that exclusion.

## Forbidden strikes and lockouts

The Act forbids strikes, lockouts and conduct aiming at or promoting them in terms of Section 65, if:
- A collective agreement that binds that person prohibits a strike or lockout for the issue in dispute.
- A collective agreement or an arbitration award that binds that person regulates the issue in dispute, unless the collective agreement permits it.
- There is a collective agreement that became a determination by the Minister, unless the collective agreement permits it.
- An agreement binds that person to use compulsory arbitration on the issue in dispute.
- During the first year of a wage determination made in terms of the Basic Conditions of Employment Act that regulates the issue in dispute.

- A party has the right in terms of the Act to refer the issue in dispute to arbitration or to the Labour Court.
- A person is engaged in an essential service, for example, an interruption that will endanger lives, personal safety, etc. or a maintenance service, such as physical destruction of a working area, machinery, etc.

## Procedures to be followed to engage in protected strike action

According to Section 64, various procedures must be followed for an employee to embark on a protected strike action or for an employer to lock out his/her employees:
- The dispute must be referred to either a bargaining or statutory council (if there is one) or to the CCMA, and a certificate must be issued stating that the dispute remains unresolved. These institutions have 30 days, or any further period as agreed by the parties, to attempt to resolve the dispute.
- If the dispute concerns a refusal to bargain (which includes a refusal to recognise a trade union as a collective bargaining agent, or the withdrawal of such recognition or a dispute about appropriate bargaining units, levels or subjects) then an advisory award by the commission is required in addition to the requirements.
- At least 48 hours written notice of either strike or lockout must be given to the other party or parties.
- Strikes or lockouts instituted after compliance with these procedures are referred to as 'protected strikes or lock-outs'.

## Legitimate and compliant strikes and lockouts

According to Section 67, any person who takes part in a strike or lockout, which complies with the required procedures, or conducts his- or herself in contemplation or in furtherance of such strike or lockout does not thereby commit a delict or a breach of contract.

An employer is not compelled to pay employees not working as a result of a strike or lockout, whether protected or not (i.e. the 'no work, no pay' rule still applies). Where pay includes payment in kind, for instance, accommodation, food, etc., this shall not be discontinued at the request of the employee. The employer may afterwards recover the monetary value by way of civil proceedings in, the Labour Court.

An employer may not dismiss an employee by virtue of the fact that the employee has participated in a protected strike. The following very important exceptions do however apply, in which case employees may be dismissed:

- For a fair reason connected with the employee's conduct during the strike e.g. theft, wilful damage to property, assault, endangering the safety of the employer, other employees, the public, etc.
- For a reason based on the employer's operational requirements. In this case, the normal consultation procedures for retrenchment must be followed. The 2002 Amendment Act (RSA 2002) extends the right to a protected strike by unions in Section 189A to organisations where dismissals for operational requirements by employer with more than 50 employees take place. However, it must be noted that should such a strike commence, the employer can retaliate with a lockout.

The Act contains an indemnity that no civil legal proceedings may be brought against any person who participates in or for conduct in furtherance of, a procedural or protected strike or lockout. The indemnity shall, however, not apply to any act which is an offence. A contravention of the Basic Conditions of Employment Act does not constitute an offence for the purpose of this provision (such as the non-payment of wages during a strike).

## Secondary strikes (sympathy strikes)

A secondary strike is one that supports other workers who are on strike against their employer. In other words, the employees in this instance go on strike to pledge their solidarity with fellow unionists who are on strike and their action has nothing to do with their own employer and is not even directed at their employer. However, a strike is not regarded as a secondary strike if it pursues a demand referred to a council as a dispute in which the striking employees have a material interest, and if they are employees within the registered scope of that council.

## Picketing

According to Nel (2002:191), rules for picketing are set out in Section 69 of the Act to accommodate picketing in the South African business environment. Provision is made for a registered trade union to authorise a peaceful picket by its members and supporters in support of a protected strike or in opposing any lockout. Pickets under the authority of the Act may be held regardless of any laws regulating the right of assembly.

Employees participating in a picket are protected from any delictual action or breach of contract, from dismissal and from any civil legal proceedings. The right to picket is now guaranteed in the Constitution of the Republic of South Africa. The Act extends this right further by making provision for picketing on the employer's premises. The picket may be at any place outside the premises of an employer where the public has access, unless the employer has consented for it to take place inside the premises. The employer may not withhold this permission unreasonably.

## Essential and maintenance services

The Act outlaws strikes in essential services or maintenance services in terms of Sections 71 to 75. Employers and employees engaged in essential services and maintenance services are prohibited from embarking on industrial action or socio-economic protest action. Both are briefly discussed below:

- *Essential services.* Essential services are defined as those services whose interruption would endanger the life, personal safety or the health of the whole or part of the population. The Act does not provide a specific list of essential services to provide an element of certainty as to which services are essential. The only two exceptions are the South African Police Services and the parliamentary service.

- *Maintenance services.* The concept of maintenance services is also introduced by the Act. In this case strike and socio-economic protest action is also outlawed. In terms of the Act, a service is a maintenance service if its interruption has the effect of the material physical destruction of any working area, plant or machinery. The need to contain industrial action, which goes beyond the infliction of economic harm alone, to the complete destruction of the wealth-generating capacity of the working area, plant or machinery, is the justification for this prohibition.

### Protest action

Section 77 of the Act grants the right to every employee, except those in essential or maintenance services, to take part in protest action to promote or defend the socio-economic interests of workers. This type of action is more commonly referred to in South Africa as 'mass action'.

The Labour Court has jurisdiction to grant an interdict or restraining order in respect of protest action not in conformity with the Act. The Labour Court has the power to lift the protection referred to earlier, depending on circumstances such as the nature and duration of the protest action and the conduct of the parties. Readers or learners must also read the relevant sections of Chapter 6 of the Act, where the management of strikes is also discussed.

## 4.4.5  Workplace forums

Workplace forums are outlined in Chapter 5 of the Act, and are structures made up of representatives of workers and non-senior man-

agement employees. In terms of the Act, the role of a workplace forum is to promote the interests of all employees in the workplace, irrespective of whether they are trade union members – but excluding senior managerial employees (whose contracts of employment or status authorise them to hire and fire, to formulate policy, to represent the employer's interests in interactions with workplace forums, and who may thus make decisions that may be in conflict with the representation of employees in the workplace). The term 'employee' in Chapter 5 of the Act specifically precludes senior managerial employees who are viewed as being 'employers'. Workplace forums must strive to enhance efficiency in the workplace. They have to be consulted by the employer with a view to reaching consensus about certain issues, and they must be respected as joint decision-making structures in respect of specific matters.

In terms of Section 79, the functions of a workplace forum are to:

- Promote the interests of all employees in the workplace, whether or not they are trade union members.
- Enhance efficiency in the workplace.
- Be consulted by the employer, with a view to reaching consensus, about the specific matters referred to in Section 84 (for example, restructuring the workplace, partial or total plant closure, and job grading).
- Participate in joint decision-making about the matters referred to in Section 86 (for example, disciplinary codes and procedures, conferring on a workplace forum the right to joint decision-making and refer a dispute to arbitration).

In terms of Section 80, only a majority registered union, or two or more registered unions acting jointly, can initiate a workplace forum. The employer cannot initiate or impose such a forum.

## 4.4.6  Trade unions and employers' organisations

In Chapter 6 of the Act, the registration and

regulation of trade unions and employers' organisations are discussed.

For the purpose of this book, the reader's or learner's attention is only drawn to the stipulations regulating the registration of trade unions and employers' organisations. For more detail, the sections outlined above are to be consulted.

A trade union is independent if it is not controlled (directly or indirectly) by an employer or employers' organisation and is free of any interference or influence from an employer or employers' organisation. If not, it will be perceived as being a 'sweetheart' union that has little credibility amongst employees.

The constitution of any trade union or employers' organisation, which intends to register, may not discriminate directly or indirectly against any person on the grounds of race or sex.

Every trade union and employers' organisation has the right to determine its own constitution and rules and to elect office bearers, officials and representatives subject to the provisions of the Act (Chapter 6).

Readers should refer to Chapter 5 of this book for details regarding the actual functioning of employers' organisations and trade unions (including those of shop stewards).

## 4.4.7  Dispute resolution

In Chapter 7 of the Act various forums are discussed to resolve disputes in an efficient and cost saving manner at the lowest possible level. The way in which disputes should be resolved depends on the reason for the dispute. These forums are now discussed with reference to the terms in which they are presented in the Act. Readers or learners should note that the detail and procedures of dispute resolution are, however, discussed in Chapter 6 of this textbook.

In Chapter 7 of the Act, the establishment of the Commission for Conciliation, Mediation and Arbitration (CCMA) referred to as 'the Commission', is discussed. The 2002 amendments to the Principal Act refined previous processes and mainly focused on improvements to processes and procedures and addressing application problems.

Because of the human resources focus of this book, only the most important elements of the Act with regard to dispute resolution are discussed, as they provide guidance to human resources and employment relations officials.

## The Commission for Conciliation, Mediation and Arbitration (CCMA)

The CCMA is an independent body with jurisdiction in all the provinces of South Africa.

In terms of Section 115, the CCMA's main functions are to:

- Attempt to resolve, through conciliation, any dispute referred to it in terms of the Labour Relations Act.
- Arbitrate the dispute if the Act requires arbitration or if it remains unresolved after conciliation, or any party has requested that the dispute be resolved through arbitration.
- Assist in the establishment of workplace forums.
- Compile and publish information and statistics about its activities.
- Enable a commissioner to make any order as to costs in any arbitration.
- Regulate the right of any person or category of any persons to represent any party in any conciliation or arbitration proceedings.
- Regulate the circumstances in which the commission may charge a fee in relation to any conciliation or arbitration proceedings or for any services the commission provides.

The CCMA may give advice or provide training on matters relating to the primary objectives of the Act, among others:

- Establishing collective bargaining structures.
- Designing, establishing and electing workplace forums and creating deadlock-breaking mechanisms.
- The functioning of workplace forums.

- Preventing and resolving disputes and employees' grievances.
- Disciplinary procedures.
- Procedures in relation to dismissals.
- The process of restructuring the workplace.
- Affirmative action and equal opportunity programmes.
- Sexual harassment in the workplace.

The CCMA must attempt to resolve disputes either through conciliation or arbitration. These approaches are briefly outlined below.

## Resolution of disputes through conciliation

When a dispute has been referred to the CCMA, it must appoint a commissioner to attempt to resolve it through conciliation (Section 135). The commissioner must attempt to resolve the dispute within 30 days of the CCMA receiving the referral. However, the parties may agree to extend the 30-day period.

The commissioner must determine a process to attempt to resolve the dispute, which may include mediating the dispute, conducting a fact-finding exercise, and making a recommendation to the parties (for example, an advisory arbitration award).

At the end of the 30-day period or the period agreed between the parties:

- The commissioner must issue a certificate stating whether or not the dispute has been resolved.
- The CCMA must serve a copy of that certificate on each party to the dispute or his/her representative.
- The commissioner must file the original of the certificate with the CCMA.

## Arbitration of disputes

If the Act requires a dispute to be resolved through arbitration, the CCMA must appoint a commissioner to arbitrate that dispute. The commissioner may decide on the most appropriate way to conduct the arbitration in order to resolve the dispute fairly and quickly, but must deal with the substantial merits of the dispute with the least legal formalities.

A party to the dispute may give evidence, call witnesses, and question witnesses of any other party and address concluding arguments to the commissioner.

If all the parties consent, the commissioner may suspend the arbitration proceedings and attempt to resolve the dispute through conciliation. A party to the dispute may appear in person or be represented only by a legal practitioner, a co-employee or a member, office bearer or official of that party's trade union or employers' organisation and, in the case of a juristic person, by a director or an employee.

Within 14 days of the conclusion of the arbitration proceedings, the commissioner must issue and sign an arbitration award with brief reasons.

If a dispute about a matter of mutual interest proceeds to arbitration and any party is engaged in an essential service (Section 139), the commissioner must, within 30 days of the date of the certificate or within a period agreed between the parties to the dispute, complete the arbitration and issue and sign an arbitration award with brief reasons.

If the dispute being arbitrated is about fairness of a dismissal (Section 140 of the Labour Relations Act) and a party has alleged that the reason for the dismissal relates to the employee's conduct or capacity, the parties are not entitled to be represented by a legal practitioner in the arbitration proceedings unless all the other parties and the commissioner consent thereto.

The commissioner concludes that it is unreasonable to expect a party to deal with the dispute without legal representation, after considering the:

- Nature of the questions of law raised by the dispute.
- Complexity of the dispute.
- Public interest.
- Comparative ability of the opposing parties or their representatives to deal with the arbitration of the dispute.

If a dispute remains unresolved after conciliation, the CCMA must arbitrate the dispute, if any of the parties would otherwise be entitled to refer the dispute to the Labour Court for adjudication, but instead all the parties agree to arbitration under the auspices of the CCMA.

An arbitration award is final and binding and may be made an order of the Labour Court, unless it is an advisory award. Any party to a dispute who alleges a defect in any arbitration proceedings under the auspices of the CCMA may apply to the Labour Court within six weeks to set aside the decision. The Arbitration Act, No. 42 of 1965, does not apply to any arbitration under the auspices of the CCMA.

The 2002 Amendments to the Principal Act also aim at improving conciliation and arbitration in general, but particularly for small business employers and/or vulnerable workers. They include the following:

- Introducing an efficient one-stop process of conciliation and arbitration for individual unfair dismissals and unfair labour practices. This 'con-arb' process will allow conciliation and arbitration to take place as a continuous process, on the same day, if necessary. This was made possible by means of an amendment to Section 191 (5A) of the Act.
- Employers and employees will have an option to request (by mutual consent) that the CCMA or a bargaining council appoint an arbitrator to conduct a final and binding disciplinary enquiry. This will eliminate the duplication of proceedings involved in having both an internal inquiry and arbitration at the CCMA or Labour Court hearing. The employer will be charged a fee.
- Arbitration awards made by the CCMA, bargaining councils and accredited agencies in terms of the Act will be final and binding and immediately enforceable, and they will be capable of being enforced in the same way as a court order. This will therefore alleviate the need for an employee whose award is not complied with to approach the Labour Court, but would be able to directly

approach the Sheriff of the Court for a warrant of execution in the case of a compensation award. Other awards, such as an award of reinstatement, would be enforceable by the Labour Court on the basis of contempt proceedings.

- Aligning the powers of bargaining council arbitrators with those of the CCMA.
- Giving the Minister the power to make regulations, after consulting the National Economic and Development Labour Council (NEDLAC) and the CCMA, to determine matters such as representation of parties and the charging of fees by the CCMA.
- Giving commissioners at the CCMA the power to deal with contemptuous conduct by one of the parties by referring their findings to the Labour Court, which can confirm the findings and, if appropriate, impose a sanction for contempt.
- Giving commissioners broader powers to issue cost awards when frivolous and hopeless cases are brought to the CCMA by means of an amendment of Section 138 (10) of the Act after considering any relevant Code of Good Practice issued by NEDLAC in terms of Section 203.
- Consent or contract by employers and workers to have a final and binding disciplinary hearing conducted by a CCMA commissioner.
- The CCMA Director is enjoined to make arbitration awards of the CCMA, bargaining councils or accredited agency arbitrators orders of the Labour Court.
- A commissioner may pay a witness in terms of a subpoena the prescribed witness fee on good cause instead of the person who subpoenaed the witness.

Readers or learners are also referred to Chapter 5 of this book for more detail regarding the conciliation and arbitration of disputes via means additional to the CCMA.

## The Labour Court

In relation to matters under its jurisdiction,

the Labour Court is a court of law and a superior court with authority, inherent powers and standing equal to a court of a provincial division of the Supreme Court. The proceedings in the Labour Court are open to the public, but it may exclude people in any case where a court of a provincial division of the Supreme Court could have done so.

Any party may appeal to the Labour Appeal Court against any final judgement or final order of the Labour Court. If the application is refused, the applicant may petition the Labour Appeal Court for leave to appeal. Leave to appeal may be granted subject to any conditions that the court concerned may determine.

Readers or learners are also referred to Chapter 5 of this volume for further detail regarding dispute resolution by the Labour Court.

Labour Court judges will be concurrently appointed as judges of the High Court and would thus have life-long tenure. This will enable the Labour Court to attract and retain suitable judges.

### The Labour Appeal Court

In terms of Section 167, the Labour Appeal Court is a court of law and equity, and also the final court of appeal in respect of all judgements and orders made by the Labour Court on matters within its exclusive jurisdiction. The Labour Appeal Court is a superior court and has authority, inherent powers and standing, in relation to matters under its jurisdiction, equal to that of the Appellate Division of the Supreme Court.

The Labour Appeal Court has the power to receive further evidence, either orally or by deposition before a person appointed by it, or to remit the case to the Labour Court for further hearing, with any instructions on taking of further evidence or otherwise it may consider necessary. The Labour Appeal Court may further confirm, amend or set aside the judgement or order that is the subject of the appeal and give a judgement or make an order according to the circumstances.

## 4.4.8  Unfair dismissals and unfair labour practice

In Chapter 8 of the Act, dismissal and unfair labour practice is dealt with as well as Schedule 8, Code of Good Practice: Dismissal. The aforementioned was substantially updated by means of the Labour Relations Amendment Act, No. 12 of 2002 (RSA 2002e). The intention of the Act, however, is to deal with all aspects of individual and collective labour law. Readers or learners must, however, note that anti-discriminatory measures are dealt with in detail via the Employment Equity Act, No. 55 of 1998 (RSA 1998a).

In this section the meaning is first discussed and thereafter the definitions of dismissal and unfair labour practice. Other elements such as retrenchment, pre-dismissal, arbitration and the transfer of a business are also addressed in Chapter 8 of the Act.

According to Section 185 of the Act, as amended, every employee has the right not to be:

- Unfairly dismissed.
- Subjected to unfair labour practice.

These concepts are outlined in more detail below in terms of the Act.

Dismissal, according to Section 186, means that:

- An employer has terminated a contract of employment with or without notice.
- An employee reasonably expected the employer to renew a fixed term contract of employment on the same or similar terms, but the employer offered to renew it on less favourable terms, or did not renew it.
- An employer refused to allow an employee to resume work after she:
  - took maternity leave in terms of any law, collective agreement or her contract of employment
  - was absent from work for up to four weeks before the expected date, and up to eight weeks after the actual date, of the birth of her child.
- An employer who dismissed a number of

employees for the same or similar reasons has offered to re-employ one or more of them, but has refused to re-employ another.

- An employee terminated a contract of employment with or without notice because the employer made continued employment intolerable for the employee.
- An employee's contract of employment is terminated with or without notice, because a new employer, after the transfer of a business, provided the employee with conditions or circumstances at work that are substantially less favourable than those which were provided by the old employer.

Unfair labour practice, in terms of the amended Section 186 – by adding a Sub-section (2), introduced by the 2002 amendment to the Principal Act – means an unfair act or omission that arises between the employer and an employee involving the following:

- Unfair conduct relating to the promotion, demotion, probation or training of an employee, or relating to the provision of benefits to an employee. (Note that this excludes disputes about dismissals for a reason pertaining to the probation of an employee.)
- Unfair suspension or other unfair disciplinary action short of a dismissal of an employee.
- A failure or refusal by an employer to reinstate or re-employ a former employee in terms of any agreement.
- An occupational detriment, other than a dismissal in contravention of the Protected Disclosures Act (RSA 2000) on account of the employee having made a protected disclosure in that Act.

Concerning unfair labour practice, Le Roux (2002a:91) comments as follows:

In 1998, the Employment Equity Act removed unfair discrimination from the definition of an unfair labour practice as it appeared in item 2 of Schedule 7. The new amendments to the Labour Relations Act return the concept of the unfair labour practice to the fold of rights and duties – no longer contained in a transitional schedule and no longer 'residual', the unfair labour practice now finds its place in [Section] 186(2) of the Labour Relations Act as amended.

In a further discussion concerning the new unfair labour practice, Le Roux (2002a:95) makes the concluding comment that because of its constitutional origin, the new unfair labour practice could lead to significant developments in our law: the possibility of other forms of employer conduct (such as the redeployment or transfer of employees) amounting to unfair labour practices, or even the possibility of employee actions against the employer as constituting unfair labour practices. It may even be wide enough to develop a law relating to the relationship between a trade union member and the union. 'Unwittingly, it seems South African labour law has returned to a point from which it sought to escape – an open-textured, wide in scope and interpretation-dependent unfair labour practice.'

## Unfair dismissal applications

In terms of Section 187 of the Act, a dismissal is regarded as automatically unfair if the employer, when dismissing the employee, states the reason for the dismissal as:

- The employee participated in or supported or indicated an intention to participate in or support a strike or protest action that complies with the provisions of Chapter 4 of the Act. That the employee refused or indicated an intention to refuse to do any work normally done by an employee who at the time was taking part in a strike that complies with the provisions of Chapter 4 or was locked out, unless that work is necessary to prevent an actual danger to life, personal safety or health.
- The employee was compelled to accept a

demand in respect of any matter of mutual interest between the employer and employee.

- The employee took action, or indicated an intention to take action, against the employer allowed by the Act.
- The employee's pregnancy, intended pregnancy, or any reason related to her pregnancy.
- The employer unfairly discriminated against an employee, directly or indirectly on any arbitrary ground, including, but not limited to race, gender, sex, ethnic or social origin, colour, sexual orientation, age, disability, religion, conscience, belief, political opinion, culture, language, marital status or family responsibility.
- A transfer, or a reason related to a transfer, contemplated in Section 197 or 197A.
- Or, a contravention of the Protected Disclosures Act (RSA 2000) by the employer, on account of an employee having made a protected disclosure defined in that Act.

In this regard, see the flow diagram in Figure 4.5, contained in the Act (RSA 1995a:245), to indicate the procedure to be followed.

*A fair dismissal* occurs when the reason for the dismissal is based on an inherent requirement for the job. This is when, for example, the dismissal is based on age, which is fair if the employee has reached the normal agreed retirement age for persons employed in that capacity.

In terms of Section 188, a dismissal that is not automatically unfair is unfair if the employer fails to prove that:

- The reason for the dismissal is a fair reason and is related to:
  - the employee's conduct or capacity; or
  - the employer's operational requirements.
- The dismissal was effected in accordance with a fair procedure.

Any employer, or for that matter the relevant official, considering whether or not the reason

for dismissal is a fair reason, or whether or not the dismissal took place in accordance with a fair procedure, must bear in mind the contents of the Code of Good Practice: Dismissal which is contained in Schedule 8 of the Act. Readers should note that the Schedule was substantially amended as a result of the 2002 amendments to the Principal Act where detailed guidelines regarding probation of employees were included under the section dealing with incapacity based on poor work performance. Guidelines contained in Schedule 8 include the following topics:

- Fair reasons for dismissal.
- Misconduct and the disciplinary procedures that should be followed prior to dismissal.
- What a fair procedure would entail.
- A review of disciplinary records.
- Dismissals for industrial action.
- Guidelines for dismissal for misconduct.
- Incapacity based on poor work performance and probation.
- Dismissal based on incapacity due to ill health or injury.
- Guidelines for dismissal for both poor work performance and ill health or injury.

The handling of discipline in terms of procedures, penalties and so on is discussed in Chapter 5 of this textbook where the interdependency between human resources and employment relations management is addressed.

A new Section 188A was also introduced via the 2002 Amendments to the Principal Act. This introduced the concept of *pre-dismissal arbitration* and enhances the concept that an employer may, with the consent of an employee, request a council, an accredited agency or the commission to conduct and arbitration into allegations about the conduct or capacity of an employee provided that the request must be on the prescribed form and that the aforementioned parties appoint an arbitrator on receipt of the following:

- Payment of the prescribed fee by the employer.

- The employee's written consent to the enquiry.

It must be noted that employees earning more than the amount determined by the Minister in terms of the Basic Conditions of Employment Act (during 2002 it was R89 455 pa) may also consent to the holding of a pre-dismissal arbitration.

According to Landman (2002b:71), the rationale but also advantage of this approach is:

It is a little like having a TV umpire decide whether a batsman is out before the ball has been delivered. On the other hand it is not unlike a LBW decision which requires an umpire to gauge whether the

---

**Figure 4.5** Unfair dismissal (automatically unfair reasons)

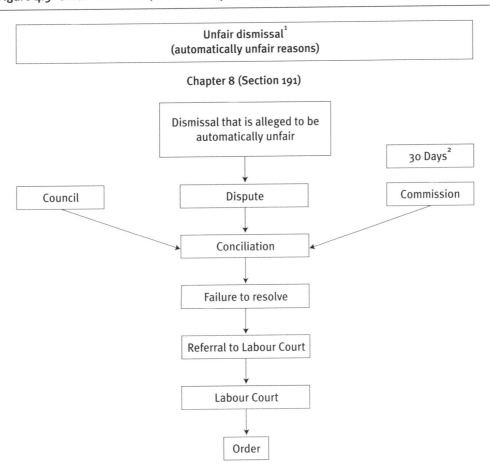

1 Examples of dismissals that are automatically unfair include dismissal for participation in a protected strike, dismissal on account of pregnancy and dismissal that amounts to discrimination.
2 The time limit is designed to ensure that disputes are dealt with as soon as possible. Condonation can be granted if there is a good cause to do so.

ball, which has not stuck the wickets, would have done so save for the interposition of the batsman's pad.

*Probation*, which was inserted in Item 8 entitled 'probation' of Schedule 8 via the 2002 amendment: an employee must be in a position to prove procedural fairness, i.e. be given the opportunity to state his/her case, the opportunity to be assisted by a fellow employee, and one weeks' notice. Less strict, however, would be the requirement for the substantive fairness of the dismissal during probation rather than after the probationary period.

Section 191 was also amended, whereby a continuous process of conciliation followed by arbitration in all probation disputes and all dismissal disputes relating to misconduct and incapacity takes place. This is the so-called 'con-arb' where conciliation failure could be followed immediately by arbitration (on the same day) in order to expedite matters in the CCMA.

## Dismissals based on operational requirements

Section 189 of the Act was substantially amended. The major amendments were that the Act now distinguishes whether retrenchments deal with individuals, small enterprises or large enterprises, and are as follows in that the parties are obliged in accordance with two things:

- The employer and the other consulting parties must, in the consultation process, engage in a meaningful joint consensus seeking process concerning dismissals for operational reasons.
- The employer must issue a written notice inviting the other consulting party to consult with it and disclose in writing all relevant information. The employer has the duty to show why certain information is not relevant.

The new Section 189A introduced dismissals based on the requirements by employers with more than 50 employees.

Two aspects are of importance to determine substantive and procedural fairness in this regard, namely the size of the undertaking and the size of the dismissal. A small employer employs 50 or less employees. A large employer employs more than 50 employees. The size of dismissal is determined as follows (as being large scale):

- 10 employees dismissed, if 50 up to 200 employees are employed.
- 20 employees dismissed, if more than 200–300 (max) employees are employed.
- 30 employees dismissed, if more than 300–400 (max) employees are employed.
- 40 employees dismissed, if more than 40–500 (max) employees are employed.
- 50 employees dismissed, if more than 500 employees are employed.

Employees dismissed for operational requirements in the 12 months prior to their employer dismissing again, must also be taken into consideration.

Le Roux (2002b:102) maintains that the amendments dealing with dismissals for operational requirements are the most controversial of all the amendments to the Labour Relations Act, since small and large scale employer retrenchments are included. Furthermore, employees will in certain circumstances acquire the right to strike in opposition to the proposed retrenchments. Le Roux (2002b:108) further states:

> When viewed as a whole, there appears to be little doubt that, in many situations the new law of retrenchments will make it more difficult, if not more expensive, for employers to restructure their operations. This is reinforced by the new [Section] 197 dealing with the transfers of businesses as a going concern in terms of which, outsourcing may become more difficult and expensive to accomplish.

In addition, Marais (2002:30–1) states that '…identifying the practical consequences of Section 189A 7 & 8 in regards to exactly when an employer may give notice to terminate, one is unfortunately faced with conflicting interpretations.' The consequences are that numerous litigations may result from this in future. Readers or learners are referred to Chapter 5 where more detail on dismissals for operational requests (retrenchment) is discussed.

## Limits on compensation for dismissal

It is important for human resources and employment relations practitioners to take note of the penalties for an unfair dismissal, since they could have far-reaching financial implications for an organisation over and above severance pay.

In terms of Section 194 of the 2002 Amendment to the Principal Act, the limits on compensation for dismissal have been simplified and the Labour Court or CCMA would have a broader discretion regarding compensation. The maximum total compensation for both procedural and substantive unfairness would be 12 months in cases other than automatically unfair dismissals. Prior to this amendment there was an unrealistically high amount of compensation that was awarded, especially in cases affecting workers with short service.

The compensation awarded to an employee whose dismissal is automatically unfair must be just and equitable in all the circumstances, but not more than the equivalent of 24 month's remuneration calculated at the employee's rate of remuneration on the date of dismissal.

An award of compensation made as above is in addition to and a substitute for any amounts to which an employee is entitled in terms of any law, collective agreement or contract of employment (for example, overtime pay which is due, performance bonuses, etc.).

## Transfer of a business

Government's initial objective in respect of this issue was to provide greater certainty and flexibility to local and foreign investors who want to acquire local businesses. In the course of negotiations, provisions have been added to prevent transfers being used as a device to deprive employees, who have been transferred to a new employer, of accrued benefits.

A major adjustment via the 2002 amendment to the Principal Act concerns the transfer of a contract of employment by the substitution of Section 197 of the Act, which spells out in detail the way in which employers and employees should go about addressing matters when this happens. It is furthermore augmented by a Section 197A, which deals with the transfer of a contract of employment in terms of insolvency, and Section 197B, which deals with the disclosure of information concerning insolvency.

The transfer of a business 'as a going concern', according to the amendment of Section 197 of the Principal Act, is explained as follows in *Rapport* (1 September 2002) (translated text):

- A business is interpreted as part of or a whole business depending on the sale being made.
- Automatic substitution of new employer for old employer.
- The rights and obligations of the employee and the new employer remain the same as they were between the employee and the old employer.
- Terms and conditions of employment may be changed, provided that they are on the whole not less favourable (except where there is a collective agreement, in which case terms and conditions may not be changed).
- Transfer to pension, provident, retirement or similar funds would be in order.
- Resignation due to terms and conditions of employment being changed could amount to constructive dismissal.
- The new employer would be bound to collective agreements and arbitration awards that bound the old employer.
- The old employer would have to take reasonable steps to ensure that the new employer can meet the obligations in respect of leave pay, severance pay and other monies payable to employees.
- In the case of insolvency or scheme of arrangement, the new employer (liquid-

ator) would be automatically substituted for the old employer, but rights and obligations would not be transferred.

- Create a new obligation on the employer who is transferring employees to *take reasonable steps to ensure that the new employer is capable* of taking over the benefit obligations that have already accrued to the employees.

### Amendments to the Insolvency Act

Notification: Employees or unions would have to be notified of an application to sequestrate in terms of Section 197B of the Principal Act.

### Employment contracts

Contracts of employment would be suspended (not automatically terminated) pending consultations with the appointed trustee regarding ways to save or rescue the organisation. The contract would terminate 21 days after appointment of trustee.

### Severance pay

Employees would be able to claim severance pay from the insolvent estate.

## 4.5   Occupational Health and Safety Act, No. 85 of 1993

The Occupational Health and Safety Act (RSA 1993a) ensures that no party can agree that work will be conducted in unsafe conditions. The Act applies to all agricultural workers, domestic servants, public servants and students. The general public that may be affected in terms of its health or safety is also included in the Act. The ambit of the Act is much wider than that of the other acts, since it covers everybody in South Africa, except the mining industry and merchant shipping (which includes load-line ships, fishing, sailing and whaling boats) which are separately legislated. (For more detail see also chapter 12 of the book.)

### 4.5.1   The purpose and scope of the Act

The Act covers all areas of employment and the use of machinery, which means that employers like designers, suppliers and installers of machinery and equipment are also included. Other persons are also protected from hazards to their health and safety caused by activities of persons at work. It also includes the establishment of an advisory council.

Persons in any form of work activity, except a one-person business are included in the definitions of employer and employee. Included are unpaid helpers, employees paid by some other agency and independent contractors or sub-contractors. An employee is defined in the Act as 'any person who is employed by or works for an employer and who receives or is entitled to receive any remuneration or who works under the direction or supervision of an employer or any other person.'

The Act may be extended in terms Subsection (2) of Section 1, which states:

> The Minister may by notice in the Gazette declare that a person belonging to a category of persons specified in the notice shall for the purposes of this Act or any provision thereof be deemed to be an employee, and thereupon any person vested and charged with the control and supervision of the said persons shall for the said purposes be deemed to be the employer of such person.

The definition of 'employer' and 'employee' in this Act are thus the same as those contained in the Labour Relations Act and in the Basic Conditions of Employment Act.

Victimisation is forbidden in this Act in terms of Section 26, in that no employer shall be allowed to dismiss an employee, or reduce the rate of his/her remuneration, or alter the terms of conditions of his/her employment to terms or conditions because an the employee has supplied information to the Minister, inspector or any other party, regarding accidents, threats to occupational health and safety, and so on.

The Act makes provision for an advisory council on occupational safety, the duties of employers, employees and safety representatives. It furthermore focuses the attention on safety committees, the reporting of incidents, enquiries, and prohibition on victimisation and stipulations regarding offences and penalties. Only the major aspects are focused on here.

## 4.5.2 The duties of employers concerning health and safety

The duties of employers are as follows:
- To ensure that systems of work, plant and machinery are reasonably safe and without health risks.
- To initiate steps to eliminate possible health and safety hazards or risks before resorting to the use of protective equipment.
- To ensure, as far as is reasonably practicable, that the production, use, handling, storage or transport of articles and substances does not endanger health and safety.
- To establish which hazards or risks are involved in any type of work and in the handling of any substance, and what precautionary measures should be taken.
- To provide the necessary information, instruction, training and supervision.
- To ensure that precautionary measures and the requirements of the Act are implemented.
- To ensure that work is performed and plant or machinery is used under the supervision of a trained person with sufficient authority to ensure that safety measures are implemented.
- In the area of 'listed' work (so declared by the Minister), to ensure not only that all safety measures are taken, but also that occupational hygiene and biological monitoring programmes are undertaken.
- To inform safety representatives of the steps taken to identify the hazards and evaluate the risks entailed in 'listed' work, and of the monitoring and occupational hygiene programmes and their results.
- To inform all employees of the danger involved in their work.
- To provide facilities, assistance and training to health and safety representatives.
- To inform health and safety representatives beforehand of inspections, investigations, formal inquiries and applications for exemption.
- To inform representatives of any incident which occurs at the workplace ('incident' is defined as an occurrence as a result of which a person dies, becomes unconscious, loses a limb or part of a limb, becomes so ill that s/he is likely to die or be disabled, or will not be able to work for a period of more than 14 days).
- To see that the safety committee performs its functions.

## 4.5.3 The duties of employees concerning health and safety at work

Employees themselves have a duty to care for their own health and safety, to obey the safety regulations, to cooperate with the employer in this regard, to report any unsafe situation to the safety representative of the employer and to report to the employer, his/her mandatory or a safety representative, any incident which has caused an injury to his- or herself. Thus the maintenance of safety is the joint responsibility of the employer, the safety representative, the employees and (if one exists) the safety committee. The greater responsibility, however, still falls on the employer.

The general duties of employees at work are set out in Section 14. These are that every employee shall at work:
- Take reasonable care for the health and safety of his- or herself and of other persons who may be affected by his/her acts or omissions.
- As regards any duty or requirement imposed on his/her employer or any

other person by this Act, cooperate with such employer or person to enable that duty or requirement to be performed or complied with.

- Carry out any lawful order given to her/him, and obey the health and safety rules.

### 4.5.4 The Advisory Council for occupational health and safety

The functions of the Council are as follows:

- Advise the Minister of Labour concerning matters of policy in relation to the application of the Act and any matter relating to occupational safety and health.
- Perform other functions referred to it by the Minister of Labour.
- Conduct research and investigations which it considers to be necessary.
- Make rules concerning the conduct of meetings of the Council and technical committees established by the Council.
- Advise the Department of Labour concerning the formulation and publication of standards, specifications and other forms of guidance, the promotion of education and training in, and the collection of dissemination of information about, occupational health and safety.

### 4.5.5 Penalties for offences

No one may tamper with, discourage, deceive or unduly influence somebody who is to give evidence, and no one may prejudice or precipitate proceedings, tamper with or misuse safety equipment or wilfully or recklessly do anything, which endangers health or safety. These offences are subject to fines of up to R50 000 or one year's imprisonment, or both. Finally, anyone who commits or omits to do an act and thereby injures another person in such a way that, if s/he were to die, the perpetrator would have been guilty of culpable homicide can (irrespective of whether or not the person dies) be subject to a fine of up to R100 000 or two years' imprisonment, or both.

Further details of the Occupational Health and Safety Statute and applications thereof, are discussed in Chapter 12 of this textbook.

## 4.6 Skills Development Act, No. 97 of 1998

Training is of critical importance in South Africa, and a major overhaul took place in recent years. The forerunner to this Act was the South African Qualifications Authority Act (RSA 1995b), which put in place the South African Qualifications Authority (SAQA) and its functions. SAQA pursues the objectives of the National Qualifications Framework (NQF). The objectives of the NQF, according to Section 2 of the Act (RSA 1995b), are to:

- Create an integrated national framework for learning achievements.
- Facilitate access to and mobility and progression within education, training and career paths.
- Enhance the quality of education and training.
- Accelerate the redress of past unfair discrimination in education, training and employment opportunities, and thereby contribute to the full personal development of each learner and the social and economic development of the nation at large.

The NQF provided the backdrop for the Skills Development Act, No. 97 of 1998 (RSA 1998b), which came into effect on 1 February 1999 and replaced the Manpower Training Act as well as the Guidance and Placement Act.

### 4.6.1 The purpose of the Act

According to Section 2, the purpose of the Act is to:

- Develop the skills of the South African workforce.
- Increase the levels of investment in education and training in the labour market and to improve the return on investment.

- Use the workplace as an active learning environment, to provide employees with the opportunities to acquire new skills, to provide opportunities for new entrants to the labour market to gain work experience.
- Employ persons who find it difficult to be employed.
- Encourage workers to participate in leadership and other training programmes.
- Improve the employment prospects of persons previously disadvantaged by unfair discrimination and to redress those disadvantages through training and education.
- Ensure the quality of education and training in and for the workplace.
- Assist work-seekers to find work, retrenched workers to re-enter the labour market and employers to find qualified employees.
- Provide and regulate employment services.

According to Section 2(2), the purpose of the Act is to be achieved by establishing the following mechanisms:

- An institutional and financial framework comprising: the National Skills Authority; the National Skills Fund; a skills development levy-grant scheme as stipulated in the Skills Development Levies Act (RSA 1999a, see Section 15.6); Sector Educational and Training Authorities (SETAs); labour centres; and a Skills Development Planning Unit.
- Partnerships between the public and private sectors of the economy to provide education and training in and for the workplace.
- Cooperative relationships with the South African Qualifications Authority.

With regard to the further enhancement of skills development in South Africa, the Skills Development Levies Act was passed in 1999. Its function, amongst others, is to regulate the imposition and collection of levies for training purposes, the role of SETAs and the commissioner as well as the distribution of levies,

recovery of levies by SETAs, etc. In terms of the Act, every employer must pay a skills development levy from 1 April 2000 at a rate of half a per cent of the leviable amount (meaning the total amount of remuneration payable to an employee during any month as determined in the Fourth Schedule of the Income Tax Act, but excluding pensions, superannuations or retirement allowances) and one per cent from 1 April 2001 for the training and education of employees. The South African Revenue Services (SARS) is to be the national collection agency.

### 4.6.2  Application of the Act

Various managerial challenges and implications of the Training Legislation should be taken note of. These are:

- Ensure that all stakeholders in the organisation are aware of the different acts and the employer's responsibilities.
- Participate in the bodies as set out by the South African Qualifications authority, for example, standards generating bodies and Education Training Quality Assurers.
- Participate in the process of establishing a SETA, and in the planning thereof.
- Align the organisation's human resource strategy, and in particular Education and Training strategy, with the overall business strategy.
- Make finances and personnel available to involve themselves in the NQF alignment process as well as for paying levies.

Further details regarding Training and Development Legislation and applications thereof, are discussed in Chapters 17 and 18 of this textbook.

## 4.7  The Compensation for Occupational Injuries and Diseases Act, No. 130 of 1993

The Act (RSA 1993b) allows for compensation to be paid to an employee who, as a result of her/his activities in the work situation, is partially or totally disabled or contracts an occupational disease. In the event that the employee dies as a result of the accident, injury or disease, the compensation will be paid to her/his dependants. The Act is focused on all employees, including casual and seasonal workers, and directors who have a contract of employment. It must be noted that the Act also includes members of the Permanent Force of the SANDF except persons performing military service who are not members of the Permanent National Defence Force and members of the SA Police Services while employed on service in defence of the Republic. It also applies to independent contractors and domestic workers.

The Act utilises a system of no-fault compensation for employees who are injured in accidents that arise out of and in the course of their employment or who contract occupational diseases. This means that employees are compensated whether their injuries or illness were caused by their own fault or due to their employer's negligence or that of any other person. At the same time, the employee may not institute a claim of damages against the employer or any other person for the damage suffered.

The duties of employers are as follows:
- They must register with the Compensation Commissioner and provide detail regarding his/her business and employees.
- They must keep records of wages, time worked as well as payment for overtime and piecework and retain these records for four years.
- By 31 March of every year, the total salary bill for the previous financial year must be submitted to the commissioner in the prescribed form.
- They must report accidents within seven days and any occupational disease within fourteen days of its coming to his/her attention.
- They must pay an assessed amount into the Compensation Fund since no contributions may be deducted from an employee's pay.

Benefits are paid to three categories of claimants:
- Employees who suffer temporary disability.
- Employees who are permanently disabled.
- The dependants of employees who have died as a result of their injuries or an occupational disease.

An important aspect is the provision for the payment of medical aid required by the temporary or permanent disablement of an employee. A further obligation is that employers must pay employees who are temporarily disabled their compensation for the first three months of absence from work. Employers must report all accidents within seven days and all occupational diseases within 14 days. However, a claim for compensation must be lodged within 12 months after the accident or illness has occurred or the employee has died.

A Compensation Commissioner administers the Act. A Compensation Fund consists of payments and contributions made by employers, and is used for compensation and administration costs. The Compensation Board comprises 16 members who represent the state, employers, employees, and two mutual associations operating in the mining and building industry and the medical profession. The board advises the Minister and decides on the minimum and maximum amounts to be paid in compensation for temporary or permanently disabled employees.

Further details of occupational injuries and diseases legislation and applications thereof, are discussed in various chapters of this book.

## 4.8 The Unemployment Insurance Act, No. 63 of 2001

This Act came into operation on 1 April 2002 after it was published in Government Gazette No. 23064 of 28 January 2002 (see RSA

2002f). It repealed the Unemployment Insurance Act, No. 30 of 1966.

This Act provides for the payment of benefits for a limited period to people who are ready and willing to work, but are unable to get work for whatever reason. In terms of the Act, some employees (those who qualify as contributors in terms of Section 2 of the Act) contribute one per cent of their monthly wage to the Unemployment Insurance Fund, which is administered by the Department of Labour. Employers also pay one per cent of their labour bill of all the employees who are contributors in terms of the Act. The contributors are workers who earn up to a maximum of R97 108 per year.

It should be noted that the Act must be read in conjunction with the regulations in terms of Section 54 of the Act (Government Gazette No. 23283 of 28 March 2002 [RSA 2002g]) and the Unemployment Insurance Contributions Act, No. 4 of 2002 (RSA 2002f).

It must also be noted that domestic and seasonal workers and their employers came under the Act on 1 April 2003. To place this in context, readers or learners should consult the media release by the Department of Labour of 12 November 2002 at www.labour.gov.za.

### 4.8.1  The scope of the Act

The Act is a compulsory insurance scheme through which the Unemployment Insurance Fund is established. The fund assists unemployed contributors by paying out benefits to contributors. Only contributors to the fund are entitled to benefits. A contributor is a natural person who has previously contributed to the fund.

The Act only applies to certain categories of people. In this regard, the following persons are not covered by the Act:
- Employees employed for less than 24 hours per month with a particular employer, and their employers.
- Employees who receive remuneration under a learnership agreement registered in terms of the Skills Development Act 97 of 1998, and their employers.

- Employers and employees in the national and provincial spheres of government.
- Persons who enter the Republic for the purpose of carrying out a contract of service, apprenticeship or learnership within the Republic and if upon the termination thereof the employer is required to repatriate that person by leaving the Republic, and their employers.

In terms of the provisions, the following persons are, however, not entitled to benefits that might apply to contributors:
- Contributors who receive a monthly pension/disability grant from the state or benefits in terms of the Compensation for Occupational Injuries and Diseases Act.
- A contributor who has refused to accept appropriate available work must undergo vocational training and will be subject to a penalty of 13 weeks during which benefits are not paid out.
- A person who has voluntarily resigned from employment. (In this regard an exemption exists where an employee resigns because the employer made work impossible and the employee therefore had no other choice and the dispute has been referred to the CCMA for a case of constructive dismissal.)

### 4.8.2  Duties of employers

An employer has the following duties when s/he commences to be an employer:
- Provide the street address of the business (and of its branches) of the employer. The names, identification numbers and monthly remuneration of each of its employees, stating the address at which the employee is employed.
- The Commissioner must be informed before the seventh day of each month of any change during the previous month with regard to information that has been furnished previously.
- Employers must pay to the Fund the required amount from the employer and every contributor in his/her employ. Note

that the employer must pay both the employer and the employee contribution at monthly intervals to the Unemployment Insurance Fund by the seventh of the month.

Readers or learners must note that the traditional 'Blue Card' (in terms of UF 74), which employers had to apply for in respect of each contributor, has now become obsolete. It will no longer be used to apply for benefits. The 'Blue Card' has been replaced by the information in the employee database, which forms the basis of the information required to claim benefits. The forms needed for claims in terms of Section 54 of the Act are published in the regulations contained in the Government Gazette, No. 23283 (RSA 2002g). Employers must keep their employee database up to date in terms of Section 37 of the Act.

### 4.8.3  Benefits and allowances

In terms of Chapter 3 of the Act, contributors who lose their jobs (or their dependents) fall into the following categories for claiming benefits.

- *Illness benefits.* Unable to work, prescribed requirements in respect of the illness have been complied with. The period of illness should be more than 14 days. All applications for illness benefits must be applied for within six months of the start of the illness. Benefits must be calculated in terms of the difference between sick leave in terms of any collective agreement or service contract and the maximum benefit in terms of this Act.

  Backer (in *Rapport*, 1 September 2002) stresses that employers must be careful that an illness benefit is not more than what an employee would have received in income if the employee was not ill. The benefit is therefore only applicable when an employee does not receive full salary during an illness.

- *Maternity benefits.* In terms of Section 24, expectant mothers are entitled to benefits during period of pregnancy and delivery

as prescribed by the UIF. An application for maternity leave must be made at least eight weeks before delivery.

- *Adoption benefits.* In terms of Section 27, persons are entitled to benefits if a child has been adopted in terms of the Child Care Act of 1983, and the two-year period that the contributor has not worked was spent on caring for the child. The age of the adopted child must be less than two years. Application in accordance with prescribed requirements.

- *Dependant's benefits.* In terms of Section 30, the surviving spouse or life partner of a deceased contributor is entitled to the contributor's benefits within six months of the death. If there is no spouse, a dependent child is entitled to the benefits of the deceased.

- *Unemployment benefits.* These are described in Sections 15 to 18 of the Act. They apply to any period of unemployment lasting more than 14 days. They also apply if the reason for the unemployment is the termination of a contract, dismissal or insolvency, and if the contributor is registered as a work-seeker with a labour centre established under the Skills Development Act and is capable of and available for work.

The benefit to which a contributor is entitled is calculated in one of two ways, depending on a contributor's income before the person becomes unemployed.

One, contributors who earned less than the particular amount (known as the 'benefit transition income level') are entitled to a percentage of their previous pay.

Two, contributors who earned more than the benefit transition income level are entitled to a flat benefit, equal to the entitlement of a contributor who was previously paid at the benefit transition income level.

The benefit transition income level is currently R8 099 per month. The Minister may, however, change the benefit transition income level from time to time to reflect changing patterns of income.

Note that the income replacement rate (IRR) is at its maximum when income equals zero, and its reaches its minimum where income is equal to the benefit transition income level. The maximum IRR is fixed at 60 per cent. The minimum IRR is currently set at 38 per cent.

A contributor is eligible to receive one day's benefit for every six completed days of employment, up to a maximum of 238 days (34 weeks). A contributor will therefore be eligible to claim benefits for the maximum duration after being continuously employed for four years. If a contributor has already drawn benefits (other than maternity benefits) in terms of this Act in the preceding four years, the number of days for which the contributor is eligible to claim benefits will be reduced accordingly.

### 4.8.4 Unemployment Insurance Board

In Chapter 6 of the Act, the provision governing the Board is outlined. The Board is instituted by the Minister, and consists of 12 members from various representative bodies such as labour, business, the state (which includes the chair), etc. They are appointed for three years.

Functions of the board are advising the Minister on unemployment insurance policy, policies arising out of the application of the UIA, policies for minimising unemployment and the creation of schemes to alleviate the effects of unemployment.

Recommendations can be made to the Minister on changes to legislation in so far as they impact on policy on unemployment or policy on unemployment insurance.

### 4.8.5 The Unemployment Insurance Contributions Act, No. 4 of 2002

Readers or learners must note that this act (RSA 2002f) is in support of the Un-

employment Insurance Act itself, and the application thereof is the same. It also indicates that it is mandatory for any employer and employee to contribute to the Unemployment Insurance Fund.

Others aspects dealt with, for example, are that it is mandatory for every employer and employee to contribute to the Unemployment Insurance Fund (see RSA 2002f). It is, however, clearly stated that the onus for the payment of contributions rests on the shoulders of the employer.

Furthermore, the contributions are stipulated in this act, namely one per cent of an employee's monthly remuneration, whilst the employers' contributions must also be an amount equal to one per cent of the remuneration paid to any one employee.

It is clear that government is adamant to regulate contributions to and the processes regarding unemployment (and the benefits associated with it in terms of payouts) more tightly than before by regulating it more stringently than before.

## 4.9   Conclusion

Since the 1994 total overhaul of all legislation and subsequent adjustments, the overall labour legislation picture is now vastly different in South Africa from that of a decade ago. It now reflects a model and system that is comparable to democracies the world over as far as the application of employment relations is concerned.

Current employment law in South Africa is structured in the spirit and prescriptions of the Constitution. It includes directives from the international community, and particularly the ILO, to structure a modern and acceptable set of laws in line with worldwide modern-day practices.

The background to the promulgation of the current employment law is discussed in this chapter, and the most recent amendments are also included. Labour legislation in South Africa is discussed, namely the Employment Equity, Basic Conditions of Employment, the Compensation for Occupational Injuries and

Diseases, Skills Development for employees, and Unemployment Insurance Acts.

It is evident from the discussion in this chapter that the Labour Relations Act in particular makes legal requirements and provisions accessible and understandable to as many members of the population as possible. This is achieved by using straightforward and non-legalistic language. It is augmented with various schedules, flow diagrams, codes of good practice, and so on to describe the procedures and mechanisms in a clear and concise manner.

The Labour Relations Act, as the principal act, focuses on issues such as freedom of association, the registration and constitution requirements of trade unions and employers' organisations, and organisational rights. Further attention was also given to bargaining councils, statutory councils, bargaining councils in the public service, collective agreements, and the Commission for Conciliation, Mediation and Arbitration. The Labour Court and Labour Appeal Court were also discussed. Various structures such as workplace forums and the CCMA were instituted to ensure participation by both management and labour in seeking solutions to workplace conflict. Dispute handling and dismissal were also dealt with.

Should readers or learners wish to further understand the context of employment law, which forms the basis for effective human resources management, it is appropriate to continue with Chapter 5, where human resources practices as they impact on employment relations (and vice versa) are examined. Only then can a study be made of the staffing and other functions of HRM, which then follow in subsequent parts of the book.

## Summary

- While the previous chapter looked at a decisive but informal and implicit aspect of organisations, namely quality assurance (the very nub of HRM), this chapter examined the formal and explicit conditions under which South African organisations operate.

- There are a number of pivotal Acts in accordance with which all South African companies must function: the Basic Conditions of Employment Act, the Employment Equity Act, the Labour Relations Act, the Occupational Health and Safety Act, the Skills Development Act, and the Unemployment Insurance Act. It is vital that the reader or learner study and understand these pieces of legislature.

- Law that specifies procedures pertaining to labour relations, terms of employment, working conditions, dispute resolution, collective bargaining, and so forth, is not discriminatory: it is to the benefit of all – the organisation and the individual, the employer and the employee. Rather than seeing the law as a burden and hindrance to effective and efficient business, it presents an opportunity for a free and fair workplace.

- Human resources management must be committed to ensuring a work environment that is anti-discriminatory, democratic, respectful of rights, mindful of dignity, and legally sound or legitimate.

## Case study
### Staff problems at Mega Earthworks Ltd.

The company was founded in 1970 and operates in Gauteng. Contracts were easily obtained for major work, such as earthworks at construction sites, provincial road construction and shopping mall excavation. The company employs 835 staff, headed by a CEO and a general manager in charge in each division.

There are 622 union members of the National Union of Heavy Construction Workers (NUHCW) working at different sites. They all have a collective employment contract with disciplinary codes and procedures as part of the agreement.

It is common practice that an employee can, with the written consent of the appropriate general manager, use the company's equipment, such as a concrete mixer, wheelbarrows, chain saws, etc., during weekends. It is a manager's privilege to have certain work done at their homes by employees during the normal working hours of Mega Earthworks Ltd., using the company's equipment and materials for the work. The company pays for the equipment cost. This has been a common practice for years to enhance employee loyalty and extend quality of life in terms of the CEO's personal motivation philosophy.

On Thursday morning Alex, a maintenance supervisor and his crew of six were working at the CEO's home. During their work session, Alex's wife called him on his cellular phone screaming that a water pipe in the bathroom had burst and was flooding their house. He immediately took two of his crew members and the company's truck and raced off to his house to fix the problem. He used the company's equipment and materials to replace the leaking pipe.

The site manager, Reuel, who is a cousin of the CEO, phoned Alex to find out how long he was still going to be at the manager's house only to learn that Alex was working at his own home, fixing the burst water pipe. After three hours the pipe was fixed, the mess cleaned up and Alex and his two workers returned to the manager's house to carry on with their work.

Back at the site office at knock-off time Alex filled out the daily work sheet for his crew, without entering any work done at his own house. The following morning Reuel confronted Alex with his work sheet asking him if he was going to alter it by entering the three hours he spent at his own house. Alex refused because it was an emergency situation at his house, as he told Reuel when he phoned him.

Reuel pointed out to Alex that to leave his workstation without permission was a dismissible offence. Furthermore to be dishonest in filling out the worksheet (as if they were working at the manager's house for the full shift) is also a dismissible offence according to the disciplinary code. Alternatively, it can be seen

as falsifying of documents, which is also a dismissible offence.

Reuel then gave Alex a last chance to rectify the records for the previous day, but Alex refused and started walking out of the office. Reuel then loudly told Alex that he and his two crew members are summarily dismissed for dishonesty, leaving their workstation without permission, doing private work in the company's time and falsifying worksheets.

Alex did not respond to this, but he and his crew went to the onsite full-time shop steward and reported that they had been summarily dismissed.

The union official, Sam, investigated and found that work had been done for the CEO to re-gunnite the swimming pool because it had a leak, but the worksheet was filled in for 'general maintenance' on the advice of Reuel.

Sam also found that two weeks before Christmas, two supervisors used a company vehicle to travel to the Spur steakhouse where they had lunch with a representative of one of the suppliers. They had an extended lunch until 15h00 and only got a verbal warning from Reuel.

After further investigations of the various disciplinary records lodged during the last three months, Sam found two recent cases of non-union members being dismissed for falsifying documents. One was a medical certificate and the other was an incorrect worksheet. Falsifying is not specifically defined in the disciplinary code of Mega Earthworks Ltd., but is regarded as dishonesty.

Sam could not believe it that Reuel did not consult the human resources department on this issue, and neither did Reuel issue any notices for the attending of a disciplinary hearing.

# Questions

1   What is the Mega Earthworks Ltd.'s legal position with regard to the dismissal?

2   What should the best practice be that the

human resources manager should have followed?

3   Are the procedures and disciplinary code up to standard at Mega Earthworks Ltd.?

4   You are a consultant. Advise the human resources manager regarding his position, taking into consideration the relevant employment legislation, sound human resources and business management practices to resolve this situation with Alex and his fellow workers.

## Chapter questions

1   Explain the importance of the labour legislation's role you have read about in this chapter to promote the comprehensive protection of employees in the workplace.

2   Explain your view regarding the effectiveness of the Skills Development Act to promote training and development of employees.

3   Discuss the application and value of the new UIA (No. 63 of 2001) to both employees and employers in South Africa.

4   Explain the concept 'organisational rights', and indicate how workplace relationships between shop stewards and management will be influenced.

5   Discuss the protection that employees and persons seeking employment have. How will this influence the recruitment practice in your organisation?

6   Are protected strikes beneficial or detrimental to the relationship between labour and management? Evaluate critically.

7   Illustrate and discuss, with the aid of a diagram, the main elements of the Labour Relations Act, No. 66 of 1995.

8   Does the Labour Relations Act serve its purpose to deal effectively with labour disputes? Explain how you would resolve industrial disputes.

9   Do you think that an institution like the CCMA will lead to the faster resolution of the previously high levels of conflict which existed between employers and employees?

10  Can you distinguish between agency shops and closed shop agreements? Thereafter, motivate your view regarding the impact these agreements have on freedom of association.

11  Do you know the functions of the CCMA? List the problems you foresee in the execution of the CCMA's functions.

12  Evaluate the approach to dealing with dismissals followed in the Code of Good Practice: Dismissal contained in Schedule 8 of the Act as well as the 2002 Amendment. Also comment on the prescriptive nature of dismissal as to whether it enhances or restricts the decision-making powers of human resources and industrial relations officials in enterprises.

## Bibliography

BASSON, A., CHRISTIANSON, M., GARBERS, L., LE ROUX, P.A.K., MISCHKE, C. & STRYDOM, E.M.L. 2000. *Essential labour law, 2nd edition*. Labour Publications, Cape Town.

BENDIX, S. 2000. *The basics of labour relations*. Juta, Cape Town.

DU PLESSIS, J.V., FOUCHÉ, M.A. & VAN WYK, M.W. 1998. *A practical guide to Labour Law, 3rd edition*. Butterworths, Durban.

FINNEMORE, M. & VAN RENSBURG, R. 2000. *Contemporary labour relations, revised 1st edition*. Butterworths, Durban.

GROGAN, J. 1999. *Workplace law, 3rd edition*. Juta, Cape Town.

GROSSETT, M. 1999. *Discipline and dismissal, 2nd edition*. International Thomson Publishing, Halfway House.

LANDMAN, L. 1995a. 'The closed shop born again. A surprise from the new Labour Relations Act'. *Contemporary Labour Law*, 5(2):11–17.

LANDMAN, L. 1995b. 'Unfair dismissal: The new rules for capital punishment in the workplace (Part One)'. *Contemporary Labour Law*, 5(5):41–50.

LANDMAN, L. 1996. 'Unfair dismissal: The new rules for capital punishment in the workplace (Part Two)'. *Contemporary Labour Law*, 5(6):51–58.

LANDMAN, A.A. 2002a. 'Setting the threshold for domestic wages. The wage implications of Sectoral Determination No.7'. *Contemporary Labour Law*, 12(5):41–47.

LANDMAN, A.A. 2002b. 'Pre-dismissal arbitration: The new procedures of s188A of the Labour Relations Act'. *Contemporary Labour Law*, 11(8):71–74.

LE ROUX, P.A.K. 1995. 'Organisational rights: The Labour Relations Act, 1995'. *Contemporary Labour Law*, 5(4):21–29.

LE ROUX, P.A.K. 1996. 'Statutory councils: Their powers and functions'. *Contemporary Labour Law*, 5(7):61–72.

LE ROUX, P.A.K. 1999. 'Affirmative action and the individual employee'. *Contemporary Labour Law*, 9(4).

LE ROUX, P.A.K. 2000. 'Mass action strikes and lock-outs. A review of some important cases'. *Contemporary Labour Law*, 9(7):61–67.

LE ROUX, P.A.K. 2002a. 'The new unfair labour practice: The High Court revives the possibility of a wide concept of unfair labour practice'. *Contemporary Labour Law*, 11(10):91–95.

LE ROUX, P.A.K. 2002b. 'The new law of retrenchment: Implications for employers arising out of pending changes to dismissal procedures under the Labour Relations Act'. *Contemporary Labour Law*, 11(11):101–108.

LE ROUX, P.A.K. 2003. 'Severance payments a dismissal for operational requirements'. *Contemporary Labour Law*, 12(12):61–66.

MARAIS, P. 2002. 'Understanding the LRA'. *People Dynamics*, 20(5):28–31.

MISCHKE, C. 2002. 'The interpretation of collective agreements: Making sense of collective intentions'. *Contemporary Labour Law*, 11(10):96–100.

NEL, P.S. (ed.) 2002. *South African employment relations relations: Theory and practice, 4th edition*. Van Schaik, Pretoria.

NEL, P.S., ERASMUS, B.J. & SWANEPOEL, B.J. 1998. *Successful labour relations-guidelines for practice, 2nd edition*. Van Schaik, Pretoria.

ROODT, A. 1999. 'The leadership challenges of Thabo Mbeki'. *Management Today*, 15(5):6–11.

RSA (REPUBLIC OF SOUTH AFRICA). 1993a. *Occupational Health and Safety Act*, No. 85 of 1993. Government Gazette, No. 14918. Government Printer, Pretoria.

RSA (REPUBLIC OF SOUTH AFRICA). 1993b. *Compensation for Occupational Injuries and Diseases Act*, No. 130 of 1993. Government Gazette, No. 15158. Government Printer, Pretoria.

RSA (REPUBLIC OF SOUTH AFRICA). 1995a. *Labour Relations Act*, No. 66 of 1995. Government Gazette, No. 16861. Government Printer, Pretoria.

RSA (REPUBLIC OF SOUTH AFRICA). 1995b. *South African Qualifications Authority Act*, No. 58 of 1995. Government Gazette, No. 16725. Government Printer, Pretoria.

RSA (REPUBLIC OF SOUTH AFRICA). 1995c. *Regulations for the Labour Relations Act*, No. 66 of 1995. Government Gazette, No. 17516. Government Printer, Pretoria.

RSA (REPUBLIC OF SOUTH AFRICA).1996a. *The Constitution*, Act No. 108 of 1996. Government Gazette, Vol. 367. Government Printer, Pretoria.

RSA (REPUBLIC OF SOUTH AFRICA). 1996b. *Labour Relations Amendment Act*, No. 42 of 1996. Government Gazette, No. 17427. Government Printer, Pretoria.

RSA (REPUBLIC OF SOUTH AFRICA). 1997. *Basic Conditions of Employment Act*, No. 75 of 1997. Government Gazette, No. 18491. Government Printer, Pretoria.

RSA (REPUBLIC OF SOUTH AFRICA).1998a. *Employment Equity Act*, No. 55 of 1998. Government Gazette, No. 20626. Government Printer, Pretoria.

RSA (REPUBLIC OF SOUTH AFRICA). 1998b. *Skills Development Act*, No. 97 of 1998. Government Gazette, No. 19420. Government Printer, Pretoria.

RSA (REPUBLIC OF SOUTH AFRICA). 1999. *Skills Development Levies Act*, No. 9 of 1999. Government Gazette, No.19984. Government Printer, Pretoria.

RSA (REPUBLIC OF SOUTH AFRICA). 2000. *Protected Disclosures Act*, No. 26 of 2000. Government Gazette, No. 21453. Government Printer, Pretoria.

RSA (REPUBLIC OF SOUTH AFRICA). 2001. *Unemployment Insurance Act*, No. 63 of 2001. Government Gazette, No. 23064. Pretoria:

Government Pretoria.

RSA (REPUBLIC OF SOUTH AFRICA). 2002a. *Basic Conditions of Employment Amendment Act*, No.11 of 2002. Government Gazette, No.23539. Government Printer, Pretoria.

RSA (REPUBLIC OF SOUTH AFRICA). 2002b. *Sectoral Determination No.7: Domestic Worker Sector*. Government Gazette, No. 23732. Government Printer, Pretoria.

RSA (REPUBLIC OF SOUTH AFRICA). 2002c. *Sectoral Determination No.8: Farm Workers Sector*. Government Gazette, No.24114. Government Printer, Pretoria.

RSA (REPUBLIC OF SOUTH AFRICA). 2002d. *Sectoral Determination No.9: Wholesale and Retail Sector*. Government Gazette, No.24207. Government Printer, Pretoria.

RSA (REPUBLIC OF SOUTH AFRICA). 2002e. *Labour Relations Amendment Act,* No.12 of 2002. Government Gazette, No.23540. Government Printer, Pretoria.

RSA (REPUBLIC OF SOUTH AFRICA). 2002f. *Unemployment Insurance Contributions Act* No. 4 of 2002. Government Gazette, No. 23064. Government Printer, Pretoria.

RSA (REPUBLIC OF SOUTH AFRICA). 2002g. *Regulations for the Unemployment Insurance Act.* Government Gazette, No. 23283. Government Printer, Pretoria.

SLABBERT, J.A., PRINSLOO, J.J., SWANEPOEL, B.J. & BACKER, W. 1998. *Managing Employment Relations in South Africa.* Butterworths, Durban.

SWANEPOEL, B.J., SLABBERT, J.A., ERASMUS, B.J. & BRINK, M. 1999. *The management of employment relations. Conceptual and contextual perspectives.* Butterworths, Durban

SWANEPOEL, B.J., ERASMUS, B.J., VAN WYK, M. & SCHENK, H. 2003. *South African human resources management. Theory and practice, 3rd edition.* Juta, Cape Town.

VAN NIEKERK, A. & LE ROUX, P.A.K. 1995. 'Worker participation-sharing the right to decide'. *Contemporary Labour Law,* 4(6).

VAN NIEKERK, A. 1995. 'Workplace forums'. *Contemporary Labour Law,* 5(4):31–39.

## Websites

Case Law: www.caselaw.co.za
Labour legislation: www.gov.za and
    www.gov.labour.za

# 5

# Interdependency between employment relations and human resources management

## PS Nel

## Learning outcomes

At the end of this chapter the learner should be able to:

- Explain the importance and the complex role of employment relations in human resources management.
- Explain the role of a policy on employment relations in an organisation.
- Explain why employment relations and human resources matters are interdependent and promote general human resources stability and progress in an organisation.
- Explain which policy components are essential to limit labour unrest and strikes.
- Consider the influence of the primary aspects of employment relations on the role of the human resources manager and vice versa.
- Provide guidelines to demonstrate the effect of general employment practices on employment relations in the context of applicable personnel law.

## Key words and concepts

- compensation
- contract of employment
- dispute handling procedures
- employer-employee communication
- employer's association
- employment relations policy
- fringe benefits
- functioning of workplace forums
- grievance and discipline
- human resources policy
- individual, legal, informal and collective dimensions
- influence of AIDS on workplace
- recruitment and selection
- rights and duties
- strike handling
- termination procedures
- training and development

## Illustrative case

### Hanky Panky at Mix 'n Match Nickers and Bra's Inc.

Mix 'n Match Nickers and Bra's Inc. is a small wholesale import company employing 35 people who are mainly women. The business imports women's underwear to a warehouse, which is located in the industrial area of Despatch in the Eastern Cape. It supplies on demand a colour range of women's under-wear to a number of retailers throughout the Eastern and Western Cape.

On Wednesday morning Mr Phakwe, a supervisor in the warehouse packing section, invited Patricia who is in her late 20s, and works as a receptionist in the administration building, to have dinner with him. It was to be at a new restaurant some distance from their workplace, which was unknown to her. She agreed, as it was in the general direction of her home and after work they left by car. She did not know where they were going until they arrived at his home on some pretext that he wanted to pick something up. In his house he made comments of a sexual nature, removed some of his clothing and suggested that she should do the same. She resisted at first, but became scared and decided to play along to prevent further trouble. He then kissed and fondled her and they never got to the restau-rant. An hour later he took her to a bus stop on her route to her home where she got out of the car. Later that night she and her boyfriend, John, wrote to Mr Phakwe telling him to leave her alone and that she doesn't approve of this kind of attention from him. The next day she left the note on his desk and asked one of her colleagues to go with her to their supervisor to complain about the incident.

On Thursday morning the written com-plaint was made to Sipho, a senior manager, and after reading the letter he decided that a formal investigation was to be initiated. Sipho sensed that the complainant was uncomfortable talking to him about the inci-dent, because he and Mr Phakwe play golf together every second Wednesday. He tried to settle the matter by asking Patricia if this was really so serious and whether she would not rather drop the complaint due to the small size of the company and the working relationships that would be strained as a result of it. She was, however, adamant to proceed with the case. Sipho then took advice from a retired friend who is also a Wednesday golfer. He was afraid that his friendship with Mr Phakwe, on the one hand, and the lack of expertise in such cases, on the other hand, was unethical. He would therefore rather have an independent investi-gation conducted to interview her. He did not find anything on a matter of this nature in the Rules and the Regulations of the company and, therefore, was out of his depth as to what decision he should take.

The following Monday an interview was also conducted with Mr Phakwe. Sipho sat in on this interview conducted by a friend from another firm who dealt with the case regard-ing Mr Phakwe and Patricia. After considering the case of the complainant based on the advice of his friend, Sipho decided that it was serious misconduct and he should take dras-tic action to save face.

Mr Phakwe was then advised that he was dismissed immediately or had to resign vol-untarily. He decided to take the latter option. A week later Mr Phakwe brought a claim against the employer arguing that the inquiry conducted was illegal as the incident occurred outside working hours and away from the workplace and was also unrelated to his employment. He was going to sue the company for damages and also demand rein-statement.

Consider whether there was a relationship between the incident and the conducting of employment and human resources manage-ment in the business. If so, what is it and what are the consequences for the employ-ees and the company?

## 5.1   Introduction

It is common knowledge that without taking cognisance of people, no organisation can be effective. In this regard Swanepoel et al. (1999a:1) state that 'the human dimension' is critical. Readers or learners are also reminded that in Chapter 2 of this book this dimension is discussed in detail. To improve the organisation's effectiveness, implies that the work people do must be enhanced, as well as the relationship that exists between people and the organisation improved. Employment relations are thus focused on how organisations manage the relations between itself and its human resources regarding the effectiveness with which the production of goods and services takes place. Three parties are involved in this relationship: directly, the employee and the employer and, indirectly, the state:

- *Workers* sell their labour to the producers of goods and services. Workers may be organised into trade unions, which regulate all matters on their behalf, or they may operate by means of the workplace forum system or on an individual basis in their organisations.
- *Employers* are compelled to ensure an acceptable return on investment for shareholders. This means that they must ensure the most effective application of the scarce resources at their disposal.
- *The state* is both master and servant of the other two participants. On the one hand, the state holds legislative power. On the other, it is expected to give assistance to both the other participants in satisfying their respective needs.

From this point of view, this relationship has existed for thousands of years, but has only during the last few hundred years evolved to the discipline called 'industrial relations' (also called 'labour relations'). In other words, it means that somebody is performing work for someone else (an employer) in return for compensation, which could be monetary, or in the form of housing, clothing, food, etc. In modern use this relationship has evolved to become known as the 'employment relationship' since it primarily focuses on the notion of work and labour.

Furthermore, studying this relationship from a managerial perspective has become the focal point in the modern day business environment. It therefore implies that a cornerstone of employment relations is the employment relationship. This is so because as soon as one person works for another, various dimensions of the employment relationship become operative. There are four dimensions: individual, collective, legal or formal, and informal:

- The *individual dimension* is that each individual worker is in daily contact with the employing body and with different managers at various levels and with workers as individuals. There are therefore individualised interpersonal or human relationships.
- The *collective dimension* is that workers can organise into groups that can interact with management as a group or with groups of employers. This is what is generally referred to as the labour-management or union-employer relationship. Labour mostly organises in groups such as trade unions, who act as representatives of the individual member-workers. Intergroup relations between management and trade unions are involved here.
- The *legal dimension* refers to certain rights and duties that the parties have due to official agreements between themselves, irrespective of whether these are individual or collective. It also means that the contract of employment entered into between the employee and the employer creates a legal relationship between them, which is governed by law.

  Whether the contract of service is written or verbal (individual-formal), it involves a formal agreement being entered into between the parties. This formalises the employment relationship. Swanepoel et al. (1999a:14) state that the employer therefore has a duty 'to pay remuneration for work done, to provide the employee with leave, to provide safe working conditions and many other duties – such as to respect and honour the employee's right to freedom of association and not to victimise or unfairly discriminate (directly or indirectly) against the employee on the basis of (for instance) race, gender, colour, religion, marital status or sexual orientation.' The employee, on the other hand, has duties such as to obey lawful and reasonable instructions with regard to his/her work, and not be dishonest.

- There is also an *informal dimension,* which revolves around dynamic human behavioural aspects. This can be human behaviour within a group context (informal-collective dimension) or within the context of the individual dimension. It includes those aspects and consequences of relationships arising from what various parties feel and think about each other, what their needs and views of life are, their attitudes and perceptions towards each other, and so on. It thus revolves around the day-to-day interaction between employees.

In practice, the collective and individual dimensions occur in combination together with a formal dimension or an informal dimension. The role of trade unions is discussed elsewhere in more detail.

It is clear that the employment relationship within these dimensions is anything but simple. It is thus clear that the individual contract of employment also plays a major role in this relationship apart from the collective relationship.

## 5.2    The individual contract of employment

The contract of employment is usually entered into between one person (the employer) and another person (the employee). In this regard Grogan (1999:23–4) states that:

A contract of employment is an agreement between two legal personae (parties) in terms of which one of the parties (the employee) undertakes to place his or her personal services at the disposal of the other party (the employer) for an indefinite or determined period in return for a fixed or ascertainable wage, and which entitles the employer to define the employee's duties and (usually) to control the manner in which the employee discharges them.

The contract must comply with the requirements set for all valid contracts as outlined by Nel (2002:56), i.e. it must be a voluntary agreement between two legal personae (parties); the parties must have contractual capacity; performance of the contract must be possible (in other words, a person professing to be a welder should be able to do welding according to a certain standard); the contract may not be *contra bonos mores* (against public moral values); the contract must comply with any formalities which may be prescribed (for example, all apprenticeship contracts must be in writing); and the parties must intend to be bound by the contract.

The contents of the contract usually include the following terms to clarify the duties and obligations of both employer and employee:

- Job description.
- Remuneration/basic pay, overtime, bonuses.
- Hours of work.
- Annual leave, sick leave, maternity, compassionate and study leave.
- Benefits/pension, provident fund, medical aid, housing.
- Protection of the company's interests/ confidentiality, restraint of trade.
- The period of the contract/length, retirement age, period of notice required.
- Closed shop or agency shop requirements.
- Safety rules.
- Disciplinary rules.
- Application of any procedural or substan-

tive agreement between employer and union, which may be applicable.

The parties may not agree to terms that are less favourable than those provided for in the Basic Conditions of Employment Act (RSA 1997) as amended by Act No. 11 of 2002 (RSA 2002b, implemented on 1 August 2002), bargaining council agreements or conditions required by the Occupational Health and Safety Act, No. 85 of 1993 (RSA 1993). The contract of employment is therefore subordinate to the various labour laws in South Africa.

Under the collective dimension of employment relations, employment contracts could thus also be entered into via collective bargaining agreements concluded in terms of statutory collective bargaining mechanisms (for example, bargaining council agreements) between employer organisations and trade unions.

Contracts can be entered into by employees at any level in an organisation, from a wage labourer to a top manager. The contract of employment can be terminated in a number of ways, such as the expiry of a fixed period, insolvency of the employer, dismissal and termination by notice. However, under the Labour Relations Amendment Act (RSA 2002a, which was implemented on 1 August 2002) specific guidelines are laid down in, for example, Chapter 8 and Schedule 8, where the Code of Good Practice: Dismissal deals with how to terminate a contract by means of dismissal as well as dealing with personnel who are on probation. It is important to note that Section 186 of the Act defines dismissal in such a way as to embrace common law forms of termination and other forms of termination not recognised by common law. Organisations must therefore take careful note of these guidelines prior to terminating an employee's contract of employment, and human resources managers in particular are advised to pay attention to the detail of the Act in this regard. It is, for example, unacceptable in South Africa for an employer to terminate the contract of employment by notice without giving a reason.

From the above approach it is clear that the employment relationship influences the management of this relationship from two angles, namely the collective as well as the individual dimensions. It therefore means that interdependency between the management of these elements exists. Consequently, human resources managers as well as those managers dealing with the collective and legal dimension (industrial relations) of this relationship must understand the interdependency in order to manage the relationship successfully.

In the rest of this chapter we focus on those general aspects of employment relations with which a human resources manager should be familiar. Today employment relations are so specialised that most organisations employ a labour relations officer or manager to deal with this dimension of employment relations.

## 5.3    The focus of the interdependency

The material presented in this chapter therefore presupposes that the human resources manager has access to an employment relations officer or manager in the organisation. S/he should nevertheless be familiar with some employment relations issues, specifically in the private sector in South Africa. This chapter is therefore not addressed to the labour relations elements the specialist would focus on (and such information is not provided).

Employment relations are of special importance for human resources managers in South Africa, particularly because of the rapid changes that are taking place at present. Human resources managers, particularly in large organisations in South Africa, have, however, handed over this new facet of human resources management to employment relations managers. Employment relations developments are so rapid that the task of the employment relations manager has become just as important as that of the human resources manager.

Not all organisations are lucky enough to have the services of an employment relations manager or officer (particularly smaller organisations), and many do not have a separate employment relations section or department. Here employment relations are the human resources manager's responsibility. It will be detrimental to the progress of the organisation if s/he neglects this responsibility. S/he needs to know the functions of employment relations, and should be willing to do the work of an employment relations officer, should one not be employed by the organisation. Employment relations are crucial in South Africa, and as more specialists in this area become available, human resources managers will become less involved. However, they should remain *au fait* with the general functioning of employment relations in an organisation.

What, then, should human resources managers know about employment relations, and how should they go about integrating this function with the broader context of human resources management in an organisation?

In the modern business world it is essential that organisations have a company policy, a human resources policy and an employment relations policy. An organisation that neglects to synchronise all three policies or draws up, for example, a human resources policy that is not in line with the company policy, commits a grave error. Human resources managers should be aware of the effect that conflict between employees and managers could have on the organisation. They should know the various trade union groupings or federations in South Africa and how the organisation should cope with a strike, should it occur. They should know that collective bargaining is an integral part of the interaction with trade unions, that employment relations training should be continually carried out in the organisation, and that supervisors, in particular, should be trained in human relations to interact with employees on the shop floor. Finally, they should know that an organisation should have specific procedures to deal with grievances and disciplinary matters. These issues form the nucleus of the discussion in the rest of this chapter. Human resources

management issues (such as recruitment and selection) that have a bearing on employment relations will also be discussed, because the application of the new Labour Relations Act necessitates an integration of the functions that deal with broader human resources issues such as the prohibition of discrimination (Section 187 of the Labour Relations Act is an example in this regard).

## 5.4    The rights and duties of employers and workers

There is a division between the ownership (shareholders) and control (management) of capital, and management's (or employer's) need for a certain amount of freedom in their management of organisations if they are to assure an acceptable return on the owners' investment. This means that managers or employers have certain rights (and responsibilities) in managing the organisation successfully.

Employers and workers are completely interdependent and need to cooperate if the running of the organisation is to be successful. Managers and workers, however, have different roles in the organisation, and this means that they have different rights and responsibilities.

### 5.4.1    The rights of management

Managers have a right to manage an organisation and to execute their task successfully. There are, however, two kinds of management rights: exclusive and shared rights. With the advent of worker participation in the affairs of organisations, a re-arrangement of rights has taken place, and is outlined below.

Management has the exclusive right to determine the objectives of the organisation, determine product policies, plan and implement policies, provide financial and material resources, establish and expand facilities, determine the quality of products, determine work standards, determine the content of the workforce, direct and organise the workforce, belong to an employers' association, and manage the organisation. At best, employees could be consulted concerning the implications of these rights for them. Many attempts have been made by workers to take over these rights, but it has never been adequately shown in the Western democratic system that these rights should not be exclusive to management. In South Africa, it could be argued that certain rights belong indisputably to management and must be considered within the context of management prerogatives.

The following rights are shared with workers through the introduction of worker participation and in the spirit of industrial democracy. These rights are to recruit and appoint workers, assign them to jobs, promote or demote them, transfer them, increase or decrease their salaries or wages, discipline workers, discharge or lay them off, establish hours of work (i.e., starting and finishing times), grant or refuse leave of absence, and determine overtime required.

What is important is not so much management's prerogative regarding these rights, but the way in which these rights are exercised. Managers are compelled to share information on issues that affect workers. This is detailed in the issues relating to the functions of workplace forums. In particular, Section 84 prescribes matters for consultation between management and workers, for example, restructuring of the workplace, job grading, criteria for merit increases, education and training. In Section 86 matters for joint consultation are outlined, such as disciplinary codes and procedures, matters regarding the conduct of employees not related to work performance, measures designed to protect and advance persons disadvantaged by unfair discrimination, etc.

It is therefore clear that participation in the affairs of the organisation and the extent of shared rights have taken on a totally new dimension in South Africa – which is in line with international views on the re-arrangement of the rights of management in the workplace.

Rights are never without obligations. Man-agement represents the employers (and therefore the shareholders) of the organisation, and management's obligations to the organisation are to take calculated risks and to render an acceptable return on investment to the shareholders.

## The general modern-day duties of management towards workers

Management has the responsibility of facilitating contact with workers and their respective representative bodies. This means management should:

- Arrange regular meetings with the aim of establishing sound relationships with workers.
- Discuss matters of importance with all parties.
- Positively share important information, such as human resources statistics, human resources turnover, absenteeism, safety arrangements and production targets and achievements.
- Promote the quality of work life, help with housing, assist with education and training, etc.

Aspects such as vacation leave, pension, sick leave, etc. are usually left to the human resources manager or the employment relations manager, who keep relations between management and workers smooth by negotiating with unions or workplace forums, or in the absence of any formal worker representative body, with the workers themselves.

## 5.4.2 The rights of workers

Workers have six internationally recognised categories of rights, namely the right to work, the right to freedom of association, the right to collective bargaining, the right to strike, the right to protection and the right to training.

- *The right to work:* In South Africa the right to work is not a legal right, but rather the democratic right of a worker to find employment and to perform the job willingly. Employment possibilities are determined by the free market economy, which dictates the job market and the rate of remuneration.

In its constitution and labour laws, South Africa does not recognise either the right of a citizen to be placed in employment or the duty of the state to provide work. The Unemployment Insurance Act (RSA 2001, which came into operation on 1 April 2002) makes provision for unemployment pay for a specified period, which is at most an indication of the state's interest in the continued existence of employment relations between employers and workers.

- *Freedom of association:* This right is entrenched in the Labour Relations Act (RSA 1995a). It gives anybody in South Africa the opportunity to join an association, which will protect him/her and negotiate on his/her behalf with the employer for fair and acceptable remuneration and conditions of employment.
- *Collective bargaining:* This right is also protected by the Labour Relations Act. It enables trade unions to represent workers and to bargain on their behalf with representatives of employers about all aspects of the employment contract.
- *Strikes:* This right is also protected by the Labour Relations Act. A strike is usually effective only if it is undertaken collectively regardless of whether or not workers are unionised. Unionised workers usually stage the most effective strikes.
- *Protection:* The right to protection consists of a number of components – the right to fair remuneration and conditions of service, the right to health, safety and security, and the right to protection from unfair labour practices. There are various laws to protect workers in the work environment, for example, the Compensation for Occupational Injuries and Diseases Act, No. 130 of 1993, the Unemployment Insurance Act (RSA 2001), and the Occupational Health and Safety Act, No. 85 of 1993(RSA 1993).
- *Training:* This right is of paramount im-

portance in South Africa today, and the Skills Development Act (RSA of 1998a) gives training prominence. The scope of the Act is to provide an institutional framework to devise and implement national, sector and workplace strategies to develop and improve the skills of the South African Framework contemplated in the South African Qualifications Authority Act (RSA 1995b); and to provide for learnerships that lead to recognised occupational qualifications; to provide for the financing of skills development by means of a levy-grant scheme and a National Skills Fund. Also, see the Skills Development Levies Act (RSA 1999a). (For more information on training, see Chapters 17 and 18 where training and development is discussed in detail.)

A further development of employment equity and dignified treatment of all persons in the workplace is contained in the Employment Equity Act (RSA 1998b). As far as employment equity is concerned, legislation has been passed and has far reaching effects as far as the rights of workers in the workplace are concerned. This aspect is also discussed elsewhere in this chapter as well as in Chapters 4 and 6 in this volume.

## The general duties of workers towards management

Management is responsible for planning, directing and controlling the organisation's human resources. On the other hand, workers are responsible for the implementation of management plans. Without this shared responsibility, an organisation cannot be effective. If workers are to fulfil these responsibilities towards management, they need a worker's representative body which will undertake to:

- Ascertain the views and feelings of workers towards the organisation and brief management on workers' customs and cultures.
- Investigate grievances and resolve them if

this is within their power, and make recommendations to management regarding these grievances (if a grievance is not resolved, a formal grievance must then be lodged with the human resources manager, the employment relations manager or the supervisor of the worker, depending on how the grievance procedure operates).

- Maintain regular communication with workers, transmitting decisions and information from management to workers and explaining the reasons, and to communicate business results to other workers.
- Explain workplace forums and trade union activities and representative procedures and methods.
- Make the responsibilities and limits of authority of these bodies clear and to teach workers about the business they are in.
- Contact new workers and participate in their induction into the organisation.
- Help workers understand the importance of economic considerations and to convey to management how this has been understood, in order to ensure that workers make requests that are economically possible.

**The specific modern-day duties of workers towards management**

The worker's duty to work implies no unnecessary absence from work, not to be late for work, not to leave the work station without permission, not to work under the influence of intoxicating substances, not to indulge in bad behaviour in the workplace, and not to strike without good reason. Workers also have the duty to be subordinate, that is, not to ignore legitimate orders or stir up other workers. Workers must behave well, which means that they must not insult co-workers or become involved in a fight on the organisation's premises. They should never be dishonest or commit fraud. Workers must be loyal to their employer and not reveal the secrets or work methods of the organisation to the opposition.

It is clear from the above that employment relations is a complex field of study and that the relationships between managers and workers are of cardinal importance to the goals of an organisation. Many attempts have been made to establish structures and procedures to formalise the relationship between managers and workers. This can be achieved by drawing up company, human resources and employment relations policies. The contents of these policies and the relation between them are discussed in the next section.

## 5.5 The relation between company, human resources and employment relations policies

### 5.5.1 Company policy and human resources policy

Management and workers have different interests, objectives and needs. It is essential, therefore, that there should be written documentation in the form of a policy to regulate communication and interaction between them. Company policy forms the basis upon which other policies and procedures in the organisation can be drawn up. The various levels of management in an organisation have different policies, and depending on its size, these could vary from simple to very complex. Should an organisation be fairly small, it may combine such documents for its own needs and purposes.

Organisations need to formulate short-term and long-term goals and strategies (corporate planning) to achieve objectives. After this corporate planning is done, the organisation can draw up formal policies.

The employment relations manager or human resources manager never does the formulation of an employment relations policy or a human resources policy only. It is the end product of corporate planning and strategy formulation, and therefore it is a corporate responsibility, like corporate planning.

Policy formulation is top management's responsibility because the area of responsibility of the top executive team is the optimum application and integration of resources. Policy is dependent upon this integration and application of resources, and has at the same time a major effect on it. It must, therefore, be a top executive responsibility, although the human resources or employment relations manager will assist in working out the details.

Once a policy is formulated and accepted it is important to put it in writing and make it public, perhaps by publishing it in the in-house magazine. This step is in itself proof of commitment to the policy. It is easy to deny or reverse a 'policy' that is merely part of the organisation's culture. Such informal policies are also open to manipulation or misinterpretation, either accidentally or intentionally.

The failure of many organisations to develop formal company human resources and employment relations policies could be one of the reasons why there is increasing labour unrest in South Africa. It is of vital importance for the human resources manager to ensure that his/her organisation has such policies and follows them.

A policy provides proof of commitment and of preparedness to declare views and attitudes, and it sets limits of behaviour. It shows the intention of the parties involved to honour these declarations. It implies that there has been conscious and rational consideration of the relationship between management and workers. It recognises the security needs of workers and the interdependence of workers and management in the organisation. It acknowledges that workers are indispensable and that they are more than mere production factors. At the same time, it recognises the rights of workers and the obligations of managers.

The company policy therefore forms the basis for the development of all other processes and procedures that determine the conduct of workers and management in an organisation. An effective disciplinary procedure, for example, can only be drawn up once an employment relations policy has been formulated.

An organisation therefore needs a policy statement that indicates its approach and business philosophy. The company policy statement could look something like the following:

## comment

The Adcorp Group's primary objectives are to maintain growth as one of the top companies in South Africa and to increase its return to shareholders. At the same time it acknowledges its corporate responsibility to contribute to the prosperity and progress of the people of South Africa. It also operates in the education and provision of services fields.

Other terms in the company policy statement could, for example, provide incentives to ensure maximum productivity and encourage worker participation in decision-making that affects workers; make provision for housing and for educational projects for employees and a statement of the organisation's right to manage these.

An organisation should also have a human resources policy. Its terms could include: the aim to assist each employee in developing his/her skills and enable him/her to use these skills to the full, thus ensuring the employee's job satisfaction and ability to contribute to the organisation; the intention to promote and preserve at all times the dignity and self-esteem of each employee and to develop and maintain open lines of communication and personal contact between the organisation and each employee.

An organisation should also have an employment relations policy, but it is important to draw a distinction between a human resources policy and an employment relations policy. A human resources policy addresses the needs of the individual within the organisation; an employment relations policy, on the other hand, is intended to regulate the relationships between management and the workers, between management and organised labour, and between management and the several external agencies that play a part in employment relations.

In practice the distinction between these policies is not always clear, as many organisations combine them.

### 5.5.2 Employment relations policy

The employment relations policy of an organisation is the expression of top management's philosophy towards the human resources of the organisation.

It is a declaration of the fundamental values, beliefs, standards and philosophies (principles) that underlie the behaviour of the organisation, but it is detailed enough to provide specific guidelines for the relationship between the organisation's people.

According to Institute of People Management (IPM) Fact Sheet No. 103, the employment relations policy statement of an organisation should contain the following:

- A statement of the organisation's responsibility to protect worker rights and to provide workers with the opportunity of participating in decisions that directly affect them.
- A commitment to the principle of freedom of association.
- Acceptance of the rights of workers to collective bargaining in industrial disputes.
- Acceptance of the principle of lawful withholding of labour as a result of industrial disputes.
- A statement of the organisation's attitude to the available machinery for collective bargaining (for example, support of bargaining councils and the CCMA).

It is important to bear in mind that a policy reflects values. Therefore the policy objectives should cover the following: development of mutual trust and cooperation; prevention of problems and disputes through agreed procedures; reduction of labour costs; strengthening of managerial control; development of human resources skills and management of

productivity. The policy standards should be universally acceptable to all departments or subsidiaries; they should be in writing, in broad terms and in clear language; they should be justifiable in terms of their impact on profit; they should be approved and authorised by the highest authority so that the policy carries the weight of a directive; and the terms must be inviolate.

Other important considerations in drawing up an employment relations policy are:
- The policy must be unambiguous.
- The policy must be positively phrased and not contain negative statements, for instance, it is preferable to say 'the organisation intends granting equal pay for equal work', rather than 'the organisation will not engage in any discriminatory practices'.
- The policy statement must not require interpretation.
- The rationale behind the policy must be explained.
- The boundaries within which individual discretion may be exercised must be clear.
- A distinction must be drawn between policies (for example, equal pay for equal work) and procedures (such as grievance procedures).
- The use of such words and phrases as 'may', 'generally recommended', 'in most cases', should be avoided as they have a permissive tone.
- No statement of policy that is contradicted by any other confidential policy should be included. It is better to ignore a subject than to say one thing publicly and another privately.
- The policy should meet the relevant legal and government requirements.
- Management should avoid the expedient settlement of disputes that could prejudice long-term interests.
- Collective agreements must be for fixed periods and should set out prescriptions regarding disputes of interest (such as the percentage wage increase employees are bargaining for when they regard the employer's offer as too low) for the full

duration of the agreement. During the period of an agreement there should be no dispute of rights (such as a common law requirement, legal issues, or the interpretation of a clause in the agreement).

- The policy should contain a clause stating that management will not negotiate or make concessions under illegal or non-procedural economic coercion or the explicit threat of it.
- Management must state clearly that the company's employment relations practices will be made known and comprehensible to employees and their representatives, and will always be consistent with the organisation's general human resources policy and company policy.

The employment relations policy statement should contain procedures and guidelines that will provide operational structures in the organisation. Management can then consolidate and strengthen the organisation's position by utilising the procedures set down in the policy for settling grievances, disputes and disciplinary actions. This means that managers can distance themselves from the negative side of the relationship between employer and workers in the sense that they no longer need to be seen as the source of discipline in their personal capacity, but merely as officials carrying out policy prescriptions. It also eliminates many negative emotions associated with employer-worker relationships because the participants in the employment relations policy have agreed to procedures. Conflict is reduced in the work environment when the implementation of policy is seen as an integral part of the relationship between employer and workers, since the relationship is then formalised in writing and known by everybody.

The procedures and structures in the employment relations policy prescribe relations with trade unions, strike handling, grievance procedures and general employment relations issues, such as recruitment, industrial safety and training. These issues are discussed in the next two sections.

## 5.6 The major components of employment relations which are of concern to the human resources manager

An employment relations policy is a document that is instrumental in formalising the relationship between employers and unionised employees, in particular, in any organisation. The structures and procedures in the employment relations policy form a basis for the practical details that govern the day-to-day interaction between management and workers. Issues that need to be precisely spelled out in the employment relations policy include trade union and workplace forum relations, participation in employer associations, dispute-handling procedures, methods of collective bargaining, strike handling, grievance and disciplinary procedures and the channels and role of communication between management and workers.

These issues are discussed separately in the following sections, after the discussion on communication.

### 5.6.1 The essentials of employer-employee communication

Communication and the channels used for it are essential for the survival of any organisation. The communication methods and channels used in organisations usually determine the effectiveness of communication between the various groups, such as supervisors and subordinates, employee groups and the employer. Effective communication at all levels in an organisation is therefore essential. In the employment relations context the means of communication, such as telephones, memos or even personally delivered messages, is not the most important factor. What is important is not what is said, but how it is said. If communication between trade union members and the employer is hostile, unfriendly and based on incorrect assumptions, this will lead to conflict, and the relationship between these parties will be strained. The human resources manager should therefore pay attention to those issues of communication that are important to employers and employees and which, if not contained, could lead to disputes and even strikes.

Communication is indispensable in organisations. It is generally accepted that people spend 70 per cent of their day communicating, and of this 45 per cent is spent listening. It is also known that people normally have only 25 per cent efficiency when listening. It is therefore not surprising that something like 50 per cent of all communication attempts fail. Yet communication in any organisation is essential to reduce conflict to a minimum and to increase the effectiveness of employees in carrying out their daily tasks. Effective communication should therefore be a top priority of the human resources manager so that the full benefit can be derived from it.

Effective communication results in higher productivity and greater cooperation in an organisation. People can give of their best only if they understand what they have to do, why they have to do it and to what extent they are achieving their targets. If communication is not systematic, employees who are affected by change, for example, will not understand the reasons for these changes and will resist them.

So far in this chapter we have dealt with those issues that are important in effective communication between employers and workers. The employment relations policy provides the means to specify the relationship between employer and worker, and provides a structure for communication between them. It also sets procedures for collective bargaining and for dealing with grievances and disciplinary issues – it thus makes known aspects of employment relations within the organisation. The grievance procedure is a form of upward communication from the workers to the employer concerning problems and work-related issues. On the other hand, the disciplinary procedure is a form of downward communication from the employer to the workers about issues that are regarded as unacceptable

behaviour on the part of the workers. The organisation can gain several advantages from employer-to-worker downward communication:

- *Commitment to the job is improved:* The provision of information helps to build trust and motivates workers. Trust and motivation improve the commitment of workers to the work group and cause them to strive to achieve the goals of this group and of their section, and ultimately those of the organisation.
- *'Grapevine' distortion is reduced:* 'Grapevine' distortion is inevitable in informal communication. Regular formal communication serves to reduce such distortion since workers come to expect an official version instead of giving credence to rumours.
- *Feedback is elicited:* Formal communication usually elicits a response from the receiver. This response provides valuable information and feedback to the sender, which enables him/her to assess the opinions and reactions of the interested parties.
- *The status of supervisors is improved:* To possess and to impart information confers status. If management wants its supervisors to enjoy status in the eyes of the workers, one way to achieve this is to make supervisors the bearers of management information to workers.
- *Workers are involved in change:* It is human nature to resist change. Advance communication of a proposed or pending change allows workers time to evaluate it and prepare for it. They are then more likely to cooperate in the proposed changes.
- *The disciplinary system is more effective:* Workers accept the authority of management and see the disciplinary procedure as a means used by management to eliminate unacceptable behaviour in the organisation.

The management of an organisation, in conjunction with the human resources manager, should evolve a definite policy as to what should or should not be communicated to workers. Not all the activities of the organisation should automatically be communicated to everybody. The rights and responsibilities of managers and workers should be taken into consideration when communication structures are established. The following serve as guidelines on what should be communicated to workers:

- *Progress of the organisation, branch or section:* Workers are directly concerned with the results, whether positive or negative, of their efforts in their immediate job environment (section) and they are concerned with the progress of the organisation as a whole. Such results should therefore be communicated to workers as it gives them feedback on their work performance, serves as an indication that management recognises their contribution to the results, and confirms their job security, which is very important in the present economic climate.
- *Movements of people:* Not every appointment, transfer, promotion and resignation is relevant to every worker. But movements of people belonging to their work group, people to whom they report or people with whom they are in frequent contact should be made known to workers.
- *Policy or procedure decisions affecting workers:* All new or revised procedures affecting workers should be communicated to them. Employment relations decisions arrived at between management and union officials or shop stewards, such as bargaining council or workplace forum decisions, are of direct concern to workers. Worker representatives (shop stewards or workplace forum members) as a party to the decisions should, however, report back to the workers through their own channels.

It is clear that aspects of employment relations are major contributors to effective communication. We now describe the most important aspects of employment relations with which the human resources manager should be familiar.

## 5.6.2  The relationship between employer and trade union

In South Africa, the Labour Relations Act guarantees freedom of association. Whether employers or human resources managers like or dislike trade unions is immaterial, since it is a violation of the Labour Relations Act to oppose the efforts of a trade union to recruit members from among the employees of an organisation. However, the human resources manager can, via the employment relations policy of the organisation, place certain reasonable restrictions on trade union officials regarding access to the premises, and so on. Unreasonable restrictions will lead to claims of unfair labour practices or victimisation of employees, and this may result in a Labour Court case against the employer.

Relationships between organisations and unions vary between two extremes. Organisations may be apathetic, yet remain within the limits of the law, or they may be patronising towards any trade union that represents their employees. Neither attitude makes for good relationships. It is important for the organisation and the union to develop a working arrangement whereby their respective goals can best be achieved.

The relationship between the employer and trade union entails an acknowledgement of their conflicting interests and an appreciation of the need to compromise. Earlier we described the relationship between the primary participants in the employment relations system in South Africa. Further aspects of the relationship are now highlighted.

According to Nel (2002:112–14), the objectives of trade unions are to protect and promote the particular goals or interests of individual workers or groups of workers. That is why workers' reactions to trade union membership will indicate the degree to which they believe such membership will decrease their frustration and anxiety, improve their opportunities, and lead to the achievement of a better standard of living.

It is in the employer's interest, on the other hand, to maximise return on investment for shareholders, which means making the maximum profit that seems fair and reasonable to all parties concerned (including workers).

The human resources manager should bear in mind that it is immaterial whether there is a formal relationship with a trade union operating in terms of the Labour Relations Act, or an informal relationship based on a recognition agreement. It is not so much the contractual nature of the relationship with the union that matters, but rather the development of an atmosphere of trust and cooperation between the parties and the establishment of a working arrangement to accommodate each other's needs. There is an apparent contradiction in that the acknowledgement of inherent differences between employers and trade unions actually increases their chances of achieving their respective objectives. In the day-to-day running of the organisation, the human resources manager should therefore ensure that all management and supervisory staff reconcile themselves to the reality of trade unions. Provision should be made for the accommodation of shop stewards. Their role in the organisation is of cardinal importance in the promotion of harmony between the organisation and the trade union. Nel (2002:122) points out:

> The primary role of the shop steward is to ensure and maintain the equilibrium in relations between management and labour within the framework of existing rules, regulations and customs, since it is precisely this that creates efficient liaison across the age-old gulf between the interests of management and workers.

It is the shop steward who represents workers and acts as the link between the workers and the trade union when grievances are lodged or disciplinary action is taken. It is possible that trade union officials who are not employees of the organisation might from time to time wish to enter the premises to communicate with workers. The human resources manager needs to be aware of this and know the organisation's policy on such visits. This should be spelt out in the employment relations policy, which should also clarify further practical issues with regard to access to the organisation's premises. It may be stipulated that trade union officials may enter the organisation's premises only if they meet certain requirements (unless they obtain prior consent from the employer to do otherwise).

Management could consider granting unions other facilities under certain conditions, such as an office at the disposal of trade union officials at certain times, the use of notice boards, or time off for the training of shop stewards (but subject to specific limits, normally five working days per year). Arrangements should be made for interaction with the union if a serious dispute should arise.

Concerning collective bargaining, it is generally not in the interests of management to conduct multiple discussions and negotiations where more than one union represents the same group of workers. The unions should get together to define the issues that they wish to discuss, and should present a single submission to management where possible. The idea is of course to do so via the establishment of a bargaining council as well as a workplace forum. The human resources manager should take note of all these issues and should formulate a policy on them, which can be incorporated into the employment relations policy.

### 5.6.3 Relationships with employers' associations

By law workers can belong to trade unions, while employers can join employers' associations and chambers, such as the Chamber of Mines, the Building Industries Federation of South Africa (BIFSA), the Foundation for African Business and Consumer Services (FABCOS), and can join federated chambers such as the National African Federated

Chambers of Commerce (NAFCOC). These associations also operate under the sanction of the Labour Relations Act. In this chapter, only the philosophy underlying employers' associations is dealt with. Employers' associations can consist of any number of employers in any particular undertaking, industry, trade or occupation, which associate for the purpose of regulating relations in that industry between themselves and their employees or some of their employees.

An important consequence of membership of an employers' association is that as soon as an employer becomes a member of such an association, the provisions of any agreements or awards that are binding upon that association automatically bind it. Employers' associations usually participate in the bargaining council system (discussed in Chapter 4) and participate at this level in collective bargaining with representatives of trade unions in order to enter into agreements. Employers (and trade unions) remain bound to such agreements during their currency, and even if an employer ceases to be a member of the association, it still remains bound to the agreement.

The human resources manager should assess his/her particular organisation's position in the industry and then decide whether or not to join an employer's association. The criterion may be the degree to which the relevant bargaining council is representative of that industry. The organisation's relationship with the employers' association will have an influence on the organisation's employment relations profile, both in the industry and in the eyes of the various trade unions that operate in that industry.

Participation in the employers' association, and finally in the bargaining council system, means that collective bargaining can take place on behalf of the organisation by means of employers' representatives, and that specialists in negotiation and collective bargaining can perform this task on behalf of the organisation. Collective bargaining at bargaining council level is discussed in Chapter 4.

### 5.6.4  Dispute-handling procedures

An important aim of the LRA, and refined by the 2002 amendments (RSA 2002a, which became operational on 1 August 2002), is to facilitate the dispute resolution process and to enable resolution at the lowest possible level. In other words, mechanisms have been instituted to attempt to resolve disputes as close as possible to the level at which the conflict actually took place. It will therefore in future not easily occur that a general dispute is resolved in the Labour Court, because the 'con-arb' process was introduced with the 2002 amendment to the Principal Act (see Chapter 4). Some disputes can, however, only be resolved via the Labour Court. Mechanisms like the CCMA and bargaining councils are geared to attempt to resolve disputes speedily, close to the level where the conflict actually took place. The type of dispute will also determine its route for resolution, as outlined in the Labour Relations Act.

It must be noted that a dispute procedure is distinct from a grievance procedure. A grievance procedure provides employees with a channel for expressing dissatisfaction or feelings of injustice in connection with the employment situation, and acts as an in-house means for an organisation in an attempt to resolve a dispute. (Grievance procedures are discussed in a subsequent section.) If a grievance procedure runs its course without any agreement being reached between the affected parties, a dispute arises. Note that disputes can also arise during the process of collective bargaining or during the normal course of interaction between management and employees or between management and management or between employees and other employees.

A dispute procedure prescribes the action to be taken by both parties during the interval between the start of a dispute and a possible work stoppage or, even worse, a strike. The dispute procedures that are briefly discussed below all operate under the sanction of the Labour Relations Act. (They are discussed in more detail in Chapter 4 of this book.)

The various dispute resolution institutions are: accredited bargaining councils, the Commission for Conciliation, Mediation and Arbitration (CCMA), the Labour Court and Labour Appeal Court and accredited private agencies.

It must, however, be noted that should a bargaining council exist, and if it is accredited by the CCMA, then certain disputes may not be referred to the CCMA, but an attempt must be made to conciliate such a dispute in a bargaining council first. Human resources managers must therefore know which avenue to follow should a dispute arise in their organisation. The Act itself makes provision for a two-step approach to resolve disputes: First, conciliation, which includes mediation, fact-finding or the making of a recommendation to the parties by the conciliator (who decides the more appropriate process), and second, either arbitration or adjudication or industrial action, depending on the type of dispute. Also depending on the type of dispute, various time periods apply.

The technical functions of these mechanisms to resolve disputes were discussed in Chapter 4 of this book.

## The methods of resolving disputes

There are numerous legitimate way to resolve labour disputes:

- *Dispute resolution via bargaining councils (including statutory councils):* The duty of a bargaining council is to maintain industrial peace between all employers and employees under its jurisdiction. Once a council is accredited by the CCMA it can proceed to resolve disputes. It must, however, be noted that the constitution of a council will determine the approach to be followed in an attempt to resolve a dispute.

  Any person who falls under the jurisdiction of a council can refer a dispute to it to be conciliated. Even a non-party who falls within a council's registration must utilise the council to conciliate in a dispute. Should the dispute not be resolved,

a council is entitled to arbitrate the dispute or immediately follow the 'con-arb' process.

Disputes that must be referred to a council for conciliation are, for example, disputes about what an essential service is, a dispute in essential services, disagreement as to what is a maintenance service, unfair suspension or disciplinary action, unfair conduct of an employer relating to promotion, demotion, training or provision of benefits to an employee and matters that may give rise to a strike or lock-out.

- *Dispute resolution via the CCMA:* The CCMA will only conciliate a dispute if there is no council covering the parties in the dispute, or the council is precluded from resolving the dispute, for example, a dispute concerning the interpretation and application of collective bargaining, exercise of picketing rights, disclosure of information to workplace forums, etc. In this regard, the jurisdiction of CCMA commissioners at conciliation proceedings has been clarified by Meyer (2002:31–3), specifically with respect to unfair dismissal claims, and regarding Section 191 of the LRA for the resolution of unfair dismissal disputes. Practitioners in businesses must therefore be aware that proceedings can only be initiated if there was a dispute about the fairness of a dismissal and that there has been an employment relationship between the parties (meaning that one of the parties was defined as an 'employee').

  A commissioner of the CCMA may also arbitrate a dispute should conciliation not be reached between the parties. Such an arbitration decision will be binding on the parties, and no appeal against the decision of an arbitrator is possible, only a review of the decision. An arbitrator must, within 14 days of the conclusion of arbitration proceedings, issue an arbitration award accompanied by brief reasons, which must be served on both parties. Note, however, that in the case of a review as a result of a defect in the arbitration proceedings, the affected party may apply to the Labour Court within six weeks to have the award set aside.

In terms of the LRA Amendment Act of 2002, a predismissal arbitration can now also take place provided that an employer pays the prescribed fee and the employee's written consent is received upon which the CCMA must appoint an arbitrator. The fee may vary according the seniority of the arbitrator or commissioner. A guideline in this regard is that the daily fee, as of 1 April 2002 of a B-level commissioner, was R900 according to Landman (2002:71–4).

- *Dispute resolution by the Labour Court:* Under certain circumstances, as outlined above, the Labour Court (or if a decision of the Labour Court is appealed, the Labour Appeal Court) can adjudicate a dispute. Under certain circumstances only the Labour Court is entitled to resolve a dispute, for instance, breach of fiduciary duty arising from changes in the rules of social benefit schemes, appeals against CCMA arbitration decisions, etc.
- *Dispute resolution by private agencies or private arrangement:* The parties involved in a dispute may decide to have the dispute resolved via an accredited private agency. However, a private agency may only conduct an arbitration in terms of the new Section 188A of the Act if it is accredited for this purpose by the CCMA. It must be noted that the Arbitration Act, No. 42 of 1965, does not apply to any of the dispute processes. However, all other rules as set out by the Act remain the same regarding arbitration. A private agency is, for example, the Arbitration and Mediation Service of South Africa (AMSSA). It appears that there seems to be no reason why potential dismissals, such as retrenchment, can also not follow the same private process in future.

Should parties to a dispute decide to resolve a dispute by private arrangement, they are free to follow their own approach, provided the dispute is resolved. If not, they must follow the normal approach as set out by the Act, either via a council or the CCMA.

- *Dispute resolution via industrial action:* The parties may embark on industrial action, including strikes or lockouts, only if the Act does not provide that the dispute must go to arbitration or adjudication, and specific restrictions (in terms of the Act) do not apply. In this case, readers should refer to and use the information in Chapters 4 and 7 of the Principal Act for specific detail in this regard.

## 5.6.5  Strike handling

Strikes are a fact of life in South Africa and the world over. The human resources or employment relations manager must therefore be prepared for strikes, know what they are and how to handle them when they occur (in other words, there should be a contingency plan), as well as know what to do after a strike. (The more technical and legal aspects of strikes are discussed in Chapter 4.)

In its general preparation for strikes, management needs to obtain information about unions and strikes by asking the following questions:
- Who are the unions?
- How and where do they operate?
- Who are the leaders?
- How strong are they?
- What are their aims or strategies?
- How many members do they have altogether?

Management should then answer the following questions regarding the organisation:
- What are the organisation's labour costs?
- How lean is the staffing and how easily can workers be replaced?
- What are the critical areas in terms of management and effectiveness and the key performance areas in the organisation's overall operations?

Management and the human resources manager can use the answers to these critical questions to prepare for possible strikes by taking proactive measures.

Strikes contain four elements that the human resources manager needs to be aware of. First, a strike is a temporary work stoppage, because strikers plan to resume their work with the same employer. Employers, however, do not always view strikers in the same light. Many employers incorrectly regard strikers as people who have cancelled their employment contracts in an uncalled-for and unseemly manner. Second, a strike is a specific type of work stoppage. Contrary to popular opinion, striking is not easily used as a weapon, since it entails deprivation for the strikers and their families. This means that striking is the final weapon in a trade union's armoury. Third, a strike is carried out by a group of workers; it is a joint action taken by the workers, as opposed to resignation, which is the individual withdrawal of labour. Fourth, a strike is a collective action by workers to express a grievance which may have been disregarded by management for a long time.

In the event of the refusal by a significant number of workers to start or continue working, management should react in the manner most likely to resolve the issues that caused the work stoppage:

- As speedily as possible.
- As near to the point of origin as possible.
- Without injury to personnel and damage to property.

To achieve such an objective requires planning, organising and decision-making in advance to ensure appropriate and uniform behaviour on the part of management. This means that a contingency plan must be drawn up that will cover most of the issues discussed below.

Human resources managers are advised in the IPM Fact Sheet No. 106 to adopt the following procedures in the event of a strike:

- Maintain a chronological diary of events.
- There should be no police involvement if this is at all possible. However, the police are responsible for public law and order and it may become necessary to call

them, should public order be threatened. The police will never become involved in the industrial action dispute as long it remains an internal affair between the organisation and its workers and public order is not threatened in any way whatsoever.

- A reliable two-way channel of communication should be opened with the striking workers. Mass meetings to negotiate the issues should be avoided and an attempt should be made to identify representatives with whom management can communicate. The options available to management are:
  - The existing channels of communication.
  - An acceptable and neutral party.
  - Elected representatives who can speak on behalf of the workers.
  - A body (such as a trade union) that claims to represent the interests of the workers.
- Report-back facilities and a time schedule should be agreed on. Where necessary, workers should be allowed to hold meetings with their representatives to facilitate the process of resolving the grievances. Management must listen to and address any expressed grievances or demands.
- The Department of Labour could be informed. Its role would only be to provide advice and information on legal procedures and not to intervene.
- A single spokesperson should be appointed to liase with the press. The media should be kept informed as much as possible regarding the developments and the information they receive should be factually correct. Incorrect reporting should be avoided.
- Normal facilities such as food, accommodation and transport should be provided where possible, and any form of confrontation should be avoided.
- A strike develops a personality of its own, and management should acknowledge this and not immediately attempt to suppress the strike. A request for striking

workers to cease striking before negotiations can take place constitutes a contradiction, as it implies that the workers must forfeit their bargaining power in order to bargain, and as such, the request is highly unlikely to be successful.

Once the workers return to work, management should see to the following:
- The promises that were made must be carried out.
- Managers and supervisors must be carefully briefed and requested to be tactful, without relinquishing essential controls (such as promptness).
- Workers are to clock in, in recognition of legal and civilised norms. They must be treated tactfully yet firmly, otherwise all previous efforts may have been in vain and the strike may flare up again.
- Management should inform all non-strikers of what happened, commend them on their responsible decision not to strike, and express appreciation for their loyalty to the organisation. Management should, at the earliest opportunity, give consideration to the following:
  - The time and cause of the strike.
  - The role communication played in causing and resolving the strike.
  - The role of shop stewards and members of the workplace forum, should it exist.
  - Current channels for handling grievances and for disciplinary action, as well as those used by line managers for communication.
  - Mistakes that were made and the lessons to be learnt from them.
  - The adjustment of plans to handle strikes better in the future. (This may include a change to the contingency plan.)
- The employment relations policy may have to be reviewed. It is therefore important that all workers should understand the following:
  - Current procedures for the handling of grievances and discipline.
  - The role of shop stewards and workplace forums.
  - The organisation's employment relations policy as set out in the employment contract.

It is clear that the human resources manager can do a great deal to prevent strikes, and can do even more once a strike is in progress. This is contrary to the general belief that there is little that can be done while a strike is in progress. The biggest task, however, starts when the strike is over, when management has to re-establish relations with the workers and the trade union and investigate and eliminate the issues that caused the strike.

## 5.6.6 Grievance and discipline handling

Grievance and discipline are dispute resolution methods at the individual level, and are essential tools of good human resources management practices in any organisation. Organisations not in possession of such procedures are bound to suffer continuous conflict with their employees. Fortunately, the Labour Relations Act makes it easy for organisations to practice sound grievance and discipline handling by means of the guidelines provided in the Act (particularly Schedule 8 noting the changes brought about by Amendment Act, No. 12 of 2002). Human resources and employment relations officials should take careful note of its functioning.

Written grievance and disciplinary procedures obviate the need for management to become involved in skirmishes about relationship procedures with labour, thereby allowing management to get on with running the organisation. The grievance procedure is discussed first, followed by the disciplinary procedure.

### Handling of grievances

There is no doubt that grievance procedures are the most important institutional system that can be used to support an organisation's employment relations. This can be deduced from the definition of a grievance: an occurrence, situation or condition that justifies the lodging of a complaint by an individual. In the usual context of an organisation's employment relations activities, a grievance would constitute a real, perceived or alleged breach of the terms of the employment contract. While this refers in most cases to the formal collective contract between employer and employees, it could also include both the individual's conditions of employment and the psychological contract between him/her and the employer.

If a sound grievance procedure does not exist, managers will not be aware of grievances or sources of dissatisfaction. This does not mean, however, that there are no grievances. It only means that they simmer under the surface. When they eventually erupt, the effect on the organisation is usually out of proportion to the extent of the underlying causes. Managers who profess to 'know the workers' and maintain that they follow an 'open-door policy' that is adequate for meeting workers' needs, are living in a fool's paradise and will eventually reap the bitter fruits of this short-sighted policy.

Furthermore, managers who limit the scope of the grievance procedure to those grievances relating to the formal human resources policy, or to the items contained in the collective agreement, are ignoring the complexity and uniqueness of individual human beings. It should be recognised that because of the complexity of human nature and the behaviour resulting from it, many issues that could constitute grievances fall beyond the scope of a written company policy and employment relations policy. Such issues need to be assessed on merit, and management must be flexible in this regard.

The grievance procedure starts when the worker raises a grievance with his/her immediate supervisor and should end at the highest authority in the organisation, the managing director or someone of similar rank. The roles of the employee representative and of the human resources department must be speci-

fied, as should the time limits within which grievances must be lodged and appeals heard. Employees need to be taught during their induction how to utilise the procedure, and employee representatives and supervisors need to be trained in the performance of their respective roles. Furthermore, records of proceedings must be kept and the human resources department, which should provide advice and assistance (when requested) on its operation, must monitor the execution of the procedure.

Human resources managers need to realise that the key to successful grievance resolution is prompt action. A delayed or neglected grievance is often the origin of a new grievance. If specific time limits are laid down in the procedure, workers will be prepared to allow the process to be completed, and will even wait longer if facts are difficult to establish. They must, however, be kept continually informed.

An effective grievance procedure is an integral part of the organisation's total communications system. It keeps both workers and managers aware of each other's needs, desires, attitudes, opinions, values and perceptions. However, more important than handling grievances, is preventing them. Being sensitive to potential causes of dissatisfaction and taking steps to eliminate them will obviate the need to apply the grievance procedure. This means getting rid of poor human resources practices, adjusting managerial behaviour, and improving worker morale.

Finally, it must be noted that if no solution to a grievance can be found, external intervention follows, for example, by the CCMA or the new conciliation arbitration process (the so-called 'con-arb' process), which was introduced with the 2002 amendments to the Act (RSA 2002a). Various external sources up to the level of the Labour Court may be solicited to solve disputes of this nature, but the process should be according to the prescribed dispute procedure as set out in the Labour Relations Act.

Grievance procedures can consist of various stages, which will depend on the size and complexity of the organisation. However, their operation should be just and fair, from the employee's interaction with his/her supervisor (the first stage) to the point where the grievance is lodged with the managing director, which would be the final stage in the attempt to solve the grievance within the organisation. Thereafter it is forwarded to external sources, as mentioned above.

## Handling of discipline

Any organisation, irrespective of its nature, structure or objectives, needs to have rules and a standard of conduct, and its members have to observe these if the organisation is to function successfully. It is important to realise that these rules determine permissible behaviour for all the employees in the organisation. The rules should apply to all personnel, from the highest to the lowest level, if they are to have maximum effect, although there would be some exemptions, such as exemption from clocking in and out and working shifts for some personnel in an organisation. Discipline in the employment context is to ensure that individual employees contribute effectively and efficiently to the goals of the business. Production and the provision of services will certainly be impeded if employees are free to stay away from work when they please, to work at their own pace, to fight with their fellow employees, or to disobey their employers' instructions. It is therefore the employer's right and duty to ensure that its employees adhere to reasonable standards of efficiency and conduct. This is stated as follows in Basson et al. (2000:69):

> There can be no doubt that the employer's unfettered legal right to dismiss forms the basis of his disciplinary power. His answer to the employee who contests his disciplinary power, his answer to the employee who contests his disciplinary rules, can always be: 'If you don't like it here, go and find another employer'.

Disciplinary action is usually initiated by management in response to unsatisfactory work performance or unacceptable behaviour on the part of workers. This is downward communication. (When a worker has problems and initiates a grievance procedure, this is upward communication.) It is thus evident in the context of current employment law that discipline is regarded as a corrective rather than punitive measure. A disciplinary code therefore endorses the concept of corrective or progressive discipline, which regards the purpose of discipline as a means for employees to know and understand what standards are required of them. It empowers employers to seek to correct employees' behaviour by a system of graduated discipline measures like counselling and warnings.

The duty of the employer to maintain discipline is also highlighted in the case Atlantis Diesel Engines (Pty) Ltd. vs. Roux & Another ([1988] 9ILJ 45[C]). A proper procedure must, however, be followed when exercising discipline. This duty is furthermore recognised in the Labour Relations Act in Schedule 8, entitled The Code of Good Practice: Dismissal and Unfair Labour Practice. In Schedule 8, broad guidelines for dismissal and unfair labour practice with regard to misconduct, etc. are set out, but are also relevant to the general maintenance of discipline which should be observed by human resources and employment relations officials in organisations. Note that the unfair labour practice also clearly spells out what the case may be and various alleged disciplinary transgressions by employees have been overturned because the unfair labour practice was actually misunderstood by the employer in the past.

It is obvious from the above statements that the power to prescribe standards of conduct for the workplace and to initiate disciplinary steps against transgressors is one of the most jealously guarded assets of managers everywhere, forming, as it does, an integral part of the broader right to manage which was discussed elsewhere in this chapter. It must, however, be borne in mind that in the context of the participative spirit of the new Labour Relations Act, the exercise by employers of their power to prescribe standards and to impose discipline will invariably be challenged by individuals and the trade unions representing them.

Discipline can consequently be defined as action or behaviour on the part of the authority in an organisation (usually management) aimed at restraining all employees (including managers) from behaviour that threatens to disrupt the functioning of the organisation.

---

## comment

**Example of a policy statement on disciplinary procedures**

To ensure consistent and fair discipline in the organisation and promote disciplined behaviour among all employees, it is the organisation's policy to vest disciplinary action and accountability in line management, to ensure that disciplinary action is immediate in response to the transgression of defined limits, to commence, and, where possible, to settle disciplinary action at the lowest possible level, and to ensure that it is consistently applied.

---

The Labour Relations Act (RSA 1995a), Sections 187 to 196 and Schedule 8, are regarded as the basis for policy statements to be followed for discipline and subsequent possible dismissal. (Dismissal is dealt with in detail elsewhere in this chapter under the heading Termination procedures.) However, it is essential that human resources and employment relations officials take cognisance of the detail proposed in the relevant sections of the Labour Relations Act. In the Code of Good Practice of the Labour Relations Act (Section 3.1 to 3.6) it is stated that various procedures prior to dismissal should be followed. These are:

- All employers should adopt disciplinary rules that establish the standard of conduct required of their employees. The form and content of disciplinary rules will obviously vary according to the size and nature of the employer's business. In general, a larger business will require a more formal approach to discipline. An employer's rules must create certainty and consistency in the application of discipline. This requires that the standards of conduct are clear and made available to employees in a manner that is easily understood. Some rules or standards may be so well established and known that it is not necessary to communicate them.

- The courts have endorsed the concept of corrective or progressive discipline. This approach regards the purpose of discipline as a means for employees to know and understand what standards are required of them. Efforts should be made to correct employees' behaviour through a system of graduated disciplinary measures such as counselling and warnings.

- Formal procedures do not have to be invoked every time a rule is broken or a standard is not met. Informal advice and correction is the best and most effective way for an employer to deal with minor violations of work discipline. Repeated misconduct will warrant warnings, which themselves may be graded according to degrees of severity. More serious infringements or repeated misconduct may call for a final warning, or other action short of dismissal. Dismissal should be reserved for cases of serious misconduct or repeated offences.

- Generally, it is not appropriate to dismiss an employee for a first offence, except if the misconduct is serious and of such gravity that it makes a continued employment relationship intolerable. Examples of serious misconduct, subject to the rule that each case should be judged on its merits, are: gross dishonesty or wilful damage to the property of the employer, wilful endangering of the safety of others, physical assault on the employer, a fellow employee, client or customer, and gross insubordination. Whatever the merits of the case for dismissal might be, a dismissal will not be fair if it does not meet the requirements of Section 188 and especially bearing in mind Section 188A.

- When deciding whether or not to impose the penalty of dismissal, the employer should, in addition to the gravity of the misconduct, consider factors such as the employee's circumstances. These include: the length of service, previous disciplinary record and personal circumstances, the nature of the job and the circumstances of the infringement itself.
- The employer should apply the penalty of dismissal consistently with the way in which it has been applied to the same and other employees in the past, and consistently as between two or more employees who participate in the misconduct under consideration.

Furthermore, it is important to note that a fair procedure must be applied when disciplinary action is to take place. In terms of Schedule 8, the employer should conduct an investigation to determine whether there is grounds for dismissal should an offence of such a grave nature occur. However, this need not be a formal enquiry. Section 4.1 of Schedule 8 provides the following guidelines:

The employer should notify the employee of all the allegations using a form and language that the employee can reasonably understand. The employee should be allowed the opportunity to state a case in response to the allegations. The employee should be entitled to a reasonable time to prepare the response and to the assistance of a trade union representative or fellow employee. After the enquiry, the employer should communicate the decision taken, and preferably furnish the employee with written notification of that decision.

The following needs to be observed when the employer considers the appropriateness of a penalty, namely:

- The gravity of the misconduct.
- The nature of the misconduct.

- The employee's state of mind, both at the time of the misconduct and during the investigation.
- The employee's previous disciplinary record.
- The guidelines of the applicable disciplinary code.
- The employee's personal circumstances.
- The consistency of the penalty in comparison with similar past cases.

Employers should keep records for each employee specifying the nature of any disciplinary transgressions, the actions taken by the employer, and the reasons for the actions.

At the end of a disciplinary enquiry, the employer must tell the employee of its decision and should preferably confirm it in writing. If the employee is dismissed, the employee should be given the reason for dismissal and be reminded of any rights to refer the matter to a council with jurisdiction or to the Commission or to any dispute resolution procedures established in terms of a collective agreement. In exceptional circumstances, if the employer cannot reasonably be expected to comply with these guidelines, the employer may dispense with pre-dismissal procedures.

It must be borne in mind that disciplinary action entails various progressive levels, i.e. verbal warnings followed by written warnings and final written warnings prior to dismissal. Other measures, which could be applied short of dismissal, are the denial of privileges for a short time, for example, loss of a portion of discretionary bonuses, etc. Another approach is demotion or suspension instead of dismissal. It goes without saying that where this method is used, the employee must have committed a dismissible offence.

Dismissal is considered the most serious disciplinary penalty that can be lawfully imposed by an employer on an employee. (This aspect is discussed elsewhere in this chapter of the book.)

The advantages to an employer of a consistent disciplinary procedure are threefold: first, it contributes to the stability of the workforce;

second, labour turnover is minimised; and third, it promotes productivity. The advantages to an employee of a consistent disciplinary procedure are also threefold: first, the people who are able to dismiss employees are competent to do so; second, those who are able to dismiss employees have a strong sense of responsibility; and third, employees need not automatically distrust every manager and every dismissal and disciplinary measure.

Three components are necessary for the effective maintenance of a disciplinary procedure in an organisation: consultation or negotiation, communication with everybody concerned regarding the exact way in which the system operates, and training of the individuals involved in a disciplinary process.

Grievance and disciplinary procedures are primarily aimed at interaction between employees and their supervisors where they have contact most often, i.e. on the shop floor. It is at that level that the foundations of a sound employment relations policy should be laid. The fulfilment of the needs of both workers and management is made possible through the grievance and disciplinary procedures, because these structures minimise conflict between the workers and management.

Readers must note that unfair labour practice is re-introduced by means of Section 186(2) of Amendment Act, No. 12 of 2002, to the Principal Act (RSA 2002a). It has an influence on the disciplinary procedure and possible subsequent dismissal. Readers are referred to Chapter 4 of this book, where this aspect is discussed.

## 5.7    Workplace forums

This mechanism contained in Chapter 5 of the Labour Relations Act, is supposed to make a great impact on employment relationships since it aims to promote the interests of all workers and efficiency in the workplace. It was specifically introduced to replace the inefficient works council system, but to date has not been very successful.

Managers must realise that if South African businesses are to compete in the global economy, major restructuring of the workplace is required. Management and labour have to find new ways of relating to each other. Consequently there needs to be a shift towards joint problem-solving and better communication on certain issues.

Therefore, human resources and employment relations officials need to take careful note of how workplace forums operate and how they can benefit their organisations.

### 5.7.1   Setting up a workplace forum

A workplace forum may be established in any workplace with more than 100 workers. Registered unions that have a majority membership in the workplace may apply to the CCMA for the establishment of a workplace forum.

### 5.7.2   How will workplace forums work?

Members of a workplace forum must meet regularly with all the workers in that workplace. The workplace forum must also meet regularly with the employer. At these meetings, the employer must present a report on its financial and employment situation, its performance since the last report, and its expected performance in the short term and in the long term. The employer must then consult with the workplace forum on any matters arising from the report that may affect workers at the workplace.

The employer must provide the workplace forum with facilities so that it can perform its functions. Forum members are entitled to reasonable time off during working hours with pay, either to perform their functions or to undergo training so as to perform these functions. Union officials are entitled to attend meetings of the forum. The forum can also call on experts for assistance.

There are two ways in which a workplace forum provides for this shift in promoting participative management and improving relations between management and employees: consultation and joint decision-making. Human resources and employment relations officials must ensure that they understand the magnitude and consequences of consultation and joint decision-making, both of which are briefly discussed below.

### 5.7.3  Consultation

The employer is obliged to consult and try to reach agreement with the workplace forum on particular issues.

Some examples of the matters on which an employer is required to consult are:

- Restructuring the workplace.
- Partial or total plant closures.
- Mergers and transfers of ownership, where these affect workers.
- Retrenchments.
- Exemptions from any collective agreement or law.
- Education and training.

### 5.7.4  Joint decision-making

On other matters the employer cannot take a decision alone. The decision must be made jointly with the workplace forum. If no agreement can be reached between the workplace forum and the employer on joint decision-making issues, the issue must be referred for conciliation. If no conciliation is reached the issue must be referred for arbitration. Matters specified for joint decision-making include disciplinary codes and procedures, affirmative action, and changes to the rules of benefit funds.

### 5.7.5  Effectiveness of workplace forums in practice

Research by Kirsten and Nel (2000) investigated the empirical effectiveness of workplace forums three years after its introduction in terms of its potential usefulness and value to organisations. The project involved organisations employing more than 100 employees in the Gauteng Province during 1999 and was based on the results of 1 039 organisations.

Until then, only 17 workplace forums had been established and were operating in South Africa. The objective was to uncover the limited use of this mechanism and to improve participation and cooperation between management and employees. The research project concluded that the value of workplace forums to promote industrial democracy and participation was either under-estimated or not pursued. In order to utilise workplace forums more effectively in industry, the following recommendations were made:

- Workplace forums should not have to be initiated by majority representative trade unions. They should be worker-driven rather than trade union-driven.
- Workplace forums should be prohibited by statute from using strikes as the final solution, since this cannot be conducive to the process of participation.
- It would be possible to set up statutory workplace forums in organisations with fewer than 100 employees. The minimum number of employees should therefore be reduced so that smaller organisations can also enjoy the benefits of protected worker participation.
- Employers, employees and trade unions should receive training regarding the role of workplace forums. Workplace forum representatives should also receive specific training to enable them to carry out their task effectively.
- A supervisory council should be established to exercise control over important strategic decisions. All role-players should be represented on this council. These decisions should be incorporated into the constitution of the workplace forum. This will prevent decisions from being taken by workers who do not have the necessary knowledge, skills and experience.
- Workplace forums should function completely independently of trade unions.
- The role of workplace forums and that of collective bargaining should be very clearly spelled out if workplace forums are to be successful.
- There should be trade union representa-

tion at board level. This would counteract the 'us/them' approach that is prevalent between management and trade unions in some businesses.

## 5.8    General employment practices that affect employment relations

In this section, human resources management issues that are commonly considered to be general employment practices are covered. The manner in which they are handled in an organisation can hamper harmonious relations between management and workers. Therefore, their handling must feature in the employment relations policy to assist human resources and employment relations officials to effectively deal with workplace relations.

Readers or learners must note that the Labour Relations Act includes various sections regarding workplace relations between the various parties, for instance, no unfair recruitment and employment practices are permitted. Various refinements in terms of the 2002 amendments to the Principal Act were introduced, for example, unfair labour practice dealing with probations and adjustment to retrenchments has refined the relationship between employers and employees considerably. These and other important areas for human resources and employment relations managers are discussed below.

Transgression of these will constitute discrimination and therefore unfair labour practice. A further refinement of this is included in the Employment Equity Act (RSA 1998b), where unfair discrimination is prohibited in Chapter 2, Section 6(1), namely:

> No person may unfairly discriminate directly or indirectly, against an employee in any employment policy or practice on one or more grounds, including, race, gender, sex, pregnancy, marital status, family responsibility, ethnic or social origin, colour, sexual orientation, age, dis-

ability, religion, HIV status, conscience, belief, political opinion, culture, language and birth.

It is, however, in terms of Sections 6(2), 7(1), and 7(2) of the Employment Equity Act not unfair discrimination to: take affirmative action measures consistent with the purpose of this Act, or distinguish, exclude or prefer any person on the basis of an inherent requirement of a job. Harassment of an employee is a form of unfair discrimination and is prohibited on any one, or a combination of, grounds of unfair discrimination listed above. Furthermore, medical testing and psychological testing and other similar assessments are also prohibited unless certain requirements are met.

Readers or learners must note that some of the above provisions were originally contained in Schedule 7 of the Labour Relations Act, but were repealed and re-appeared as provisions in the Employment Equity Act (RSA 1998b).

### 5.8.1    Recruitment

Recruitment has two stages: the defining of requirements and the attracting of candidates. Both are affected by the employment relations standpoint of an organisation. For example, if an organisation professes to offer equal employment opportunities to employees, it is unlikely that it will tolerate any prohibitions in the recruitment of certain employees.

Prejudices and preferences in an organisation show in the manner in which recruitment is conducted. An organisation also has an opportunity, through the recruitment process, to advertise its employment practices and state for individual employees its public relations policy.

There is a direct overlap of the employment relations policy of an organisation and its recruitment practices in the case of a closed shop agreement. In such an instance, an organisation is bound to employ only those individuals in certain occupations who are members of the appropriate trade union representing that occupation. This means that the organisation's recruitment criteria for that occupation include membership of the union. This in turn gives a degree of cooperation between the two organisations. There is even more overlap between an organisation's employment relations policy and its recruitment policy if the organisation uses a trade union as a recruitment agent.

Organisations should be extremely careful when drafting a recruitment policy to prevent unfair discriminatory practices being entered into, as it would transgress the Employment Equity Act and also lead to a retardation of its relationship with its employees in terms of the Labour Relations Act. In this regard Nel (2002: 278–9) provides the following guidelines:

- All jobs should be open to all applicants irrespective of race, sex or other grounds of discrimination prohibited by law.
- Recruitment of candidates for affirmative action positions should be done according to the provisions of the Constitution and relevant labour legislation.
- An objective and fair recruiting procedure should be followed at all stages of recruitment.
- In the case of a closed shop agreement, a representative trade union is to be informed timeously of all vacancies.
- Internal recruitment should take precedence over external recruitment.
- Information regarding vacancies must clearly state the relevant selection criteria to be applied.
- The selection criteria should be valid and appropriate for the needs of the job, the employer and the society as a whole.
    - All vacancies should be advertised internally, by the following methods:
    - Information regarding vacancies to be posted on special vacancy notice boards in all applicable languages, in all plants and distribution outlets in the same region.
    - All workers to be advised of details of vacancies by a notice in their wage packets.
- Procedures and time limits for application should be clearly stated.

- Where an employer is unable to recruit internally, and where retrenchment has occurred, the organisation should make all attempts to recruit workers from the ranks of workers retrenched by the organisation.
- Press advertisements should be placed in newspapers that are accessible to all population groups, and the necessary criteria for the job, and procedures and time limits should be clearly stated.
- Priority should be given to local South Africans. Foreign skilled labour may only be recruited after negotiation with the trade union(s) and after it has been established that there are no local South Africans capable of occupying the position.
- Referrals ('word of mouth') are never to be the sole method of recruitment, since this may cause unfair promotion or disadvantaging of a particular group or individual.

By following these principles, the chances of negatively influencing employment relations are minimised. For more detail regarding recruitment, readers or learners are referred to Chapter 8 in this book.

### 5.8.2 Selection and induction

The selection procedures practised by an organisation also reflect its employment relations policy.

---

**comment**

**Typical policy statement on selection**
The organisation undertakes to fill vacancies with the most suitable individuals, and such individuals will be selected in accordance with established criteria for each job. Each individual's suitability will be measured against the job requirements by means of tests, past performance, education and biographical data.

---

Selection practices may be specified in an employment relations agreement with worker representatives. Organisations may make provision for shop stewards to witness any testing procedures to ensure that the process is objective and no labour group's interests are being promoted or prejudiced.

The following guidelines could be followed to prevent unfair advancement or discrimination during interviews:

- Questions should be related to job requirements.
- The interview should be structured: fixed pre-planned questions should be asked. Questions ought to be consistent across interviews.
- An interviewer should not ask for information that can be easily and more accurately assessed by application forms, tests or reference checks.
- The interview atmosphere should be free from patronising approaches and intimidation.
- Records of interviews, questions and applicants' answers should be retained for justifying decisions.
- The purpose of the interview should be explained – whether it is an initial screening device or the final step in selection.

Selection and promotion are closely intertwined, especially if the organisation follows a policy of filling vacancies from within where possible. Worker representatives have an interest in such promotion of employees: unions might prefer seniority as a criterion for promotion rather than performance, since this furthers the interests of their long-term members. Other unions may attempt to restrict occupation of certain positions to a limited group of individuals defined in their constitutions, and as such will oppose promotion from within of anyone who does not meet these requirements. During the selection process psychometric testing is often resorted to, but must be conducted according to statutory laws which have specific guidelines on the design, registration and use of tests in South Africa. It should be noted that only reg-

istered psychologists are allowed to interpret psychometric tests, and that interpretation of a test by someone other than a psychologist may be a breach of the applicable professional code and the applicable laws regulating the use of psychometric tests. A non-standardised psychometric test may lead to unfair discrimination, and care should be taken to use tests that have been validated for specific applications, and will surely attract the attention of a trade union representative if not properly validated.

The following guidelines should be followed to avoid unfair selection practices which, according to Nel (2002:280), could lead to strained employment relations and even conflict with a union's representatives in an organisation:

- Selection criteria should be objective, related to the inherent requirements of the job and consistently applied to applicants irrespective of their race or sex.
- Non-job-related qualifications and higher than necessary qualifications such as educational degrees, linguistic abilities or length of service should not be used to justify selection of a person from an advantaged group over a person from a disadvantaged group.
- Any qualification or condition that has the effect of restricting a position to persons from an advantaged group must be clearly justified as job-related and necessary, before it is applied.
- Qualifications required for a position should be based on current job descriptions or skill requirements that accurately identify the nature, purposes and functions, the job without traditional notions of who should be performing the job.
- Qualifications for a position should not be adapted to meet the qualifications of any particular individual whose application is anticipated.
- An objective and clearly specified procedure should be used so that a quantified score on an individual's suitability is available. A correction factor must be applied to scores of disadvantaged indi-

viduals to boost their scores to be determined through negotiation by the parties in consultation with a committee of experts.

- The mere existence of a prior detention, arrest or criminal record should not constitute sufficient grounds for refusal to select any applicant for employment.
- Recognition of Prior Learning should be considered if requested by an applicant.

During induction, new employees should be informed of the employment relations policy of the organisation. They should be trained in the use of employment relations structures, such as grievance and disciplinary procedures. Furthermore, it is during the induction process that new employees are informed of all the specific conditions of employment. A union has probably negotiated many of these, such as working hours and holidays, and new employees will therefore be able to gauge the employment relations climate in the organisation.

The induction process provides the employer, and specifically the human resources manager, with an opportunity to sow the seeds for a harmonious working environment, and therefore contribute towards the maintenance of industrial peace in the organisation.

## 5.8.3  Training and development

Training serves a dual role in that it helps management meet its human resources requirements, while at the same time increasing the market value or marketability of those being trained, and hence their bargaining power. Guidelines for employer and employee are provided in the Skills Development Act (RSA 1998a), and guidelines for the payment of levies are contained in the Skills Development Levies Act (RSA 1999a), all of which are discussed in Chapter 4 of this book. Training, therefore, is a matter of mutual interest to both workers and management. Policy statements on training may include the following:

- Employees are encouraged to develop to their full potential in the best interests of

both the organisation and themselves.
- In the event of technological changes, retraining will be provided for affected employees.
- Training and retraining affecting union members will be implemented with the cooperation and support of the union concerned.

Employment relations training is necessary if the procedures and programmes outlined in the employment relations policy are to be successfully implemented. Employees who are to use such procedures and programmes must be trained in the actions required.

According to Van Dyk et al. (2001), personnel at the appropriate management and supervisory levels need to receive training in the application of policies and procedures. This would specifically include training in employment relations matters to promote management and labour harmony. Employee and employer representatives should be trained in the functioning of workplace forums, conducting meetings, and so on. Employees who are not involved in a workplace forum should also be informed about its functioning and made aware that it is a medium for communication. If employment relations training involves members of a trade union, management should consult with the union involved about training material, and where necessary should conduct joint training. For more detail on training and development, readers are referred to Chapters 17 and 18 of this book.

## 5.8.4  Job evaluation

Job evaluation is a formal system for determining the relative worth of jobs in an organisation. Steps must be taken to ensure that all employees are familiar with the job evaluation system and that members of the job evaluation committee (including the worker representative) have received the necessary training.

In the sphere of employment relations, job evaluation provides information that could have a profound influence on an organisation's management style. This is because employees, in terms of the job evaluation structures available to them, can assess management decisions on things like remuneration. This highlights the employment relations issues subject to management prerogative.

In the negotiation process over salaries and wages, trade unions should acknowledge both phases in the job evaluation process. Phase 1 is the process of grading jobs according to a particular job evaluation technique, such as the Paterson or Peromnes systems (see Chapter 11 of this volume). Phase 2 is the process of attributing a pay structure to the graded hierarchy of jobs established in phase 1. It is only in phase 2 that there can be flexibility and negotiation.

Today it is critically important to realise that job evaluation has become a focal point in the unionised environment. This is so because union pressure on job evaluation skills is nothing other than an attempt to get more money, rather than a concrete objection to the scheme itself.

## 5.8.5 Compensation

Various aspects should be considered before policy and procedures for determining remuneration are decided upon. According to Nel (2002:286), it is a widely recognised fact that in South Africa, inconsistencies in this regard very easily lead to industrial disputes and strikes. In fact, industrial action concerned with wages in one way or another is one of the biggest causes of industrial action in South Africa. Particular note should be taken of the following:

- No discrimination should exist in the area of payment and remuneration that is based on discriminatory factors or principles. The principle of equal pay for work of equal value should pertain.
- Methods of evaluating jobs should be in accordance with methodologies that accord with accepted standards. These systems should be published and be available for inspection by all employees and their organisations. Schedules for the grading of all jobs in the organisation should be available.
- Salary scales, payment systems and wage rates should be non-discriminatory, and all relevant information regarding the salary range, wage rates, etc. for all posts in the organisation should be made available to any employee, or any employee organisation on request.
- Where differentiation does exist, this should be permissible only as far as it pertains to the level, status and content of the job, and/or the level of performance of the incumbent, evaluated by generally acceptable means.

Employers should consider including a code on equal remuneration in service conditions. This code will guarantee fair remuneration practice, and should include the following requirements:

- Rates and types of remuneration should not be based on an employee's race or sex. The basis should be equal remuneration for work of equal value.
- Job classification, grading systems and pay structures should be based on objective skill criteria, irrespective of the race or sex of the employee doing the job.
- Any reference to race or sex should be eliminated in all remuneration criteria in payment systems, salary schedules, bonus systems, medical schemes, and other fringe benefits.
- Any remuneration system or structure that has the effect of grouping blacks and women in a specific job classification and salary levels should be reviewed and adjusted to ensure that other employees are not doing work of equal value in a different job classification and salary level.
- The employers and their associations must undertake to correct any incidents of unequal remuneration and to negotiate with the trade unions concerned on measures, including compensation, for eliminating inequality.
- Wage and salary structures should be sufficiently flexible to allow for all eventuali-

ties and for the necessary mobility, otherwise dissatisfaction and conflict are certain to result. The date of payment and the method of payment should be negotiated to avoid unnecessary mistakes on delays.

It must also be noted that issues such as the cost of living, productivity, the skills gap, seniority and minimum wages also relate to the salary scales applied by employers, and are likely to be raised during negotiations with unions.

For more detail on compensation, readers or learners are referred to Chapter 11 of this book.

### 5.8.6  Fringe benefits

Fringe benefits are compensation other than wages and salaries. Law, such as unemployment insurance and workmen's compensation, mandates some fringe benefits. In other cases, benefits result from negotiations between management and labour, and are then specified in bargaining council agreements, wage regulating measures, private

### Case-in-point

ABC company is a consulting concern, which provides employees with 30 calendar days leave per year. They also allow 10 days research leave per year. The regulation states that employees can carry over 12 days to the following year, but it must be taken within six months or need to have it paid out. If they do not exercise their option they will lose their leave carried over. In terms of the Basic Conditions of Employment Act, the question is whether it is permissible. The answer lies in the fact that it is over and above the minimums prescribed by law and if negotiated, the above arrangement is legal.

employment contracts, and so on. Leave arrangements, for example, are a benefit specified in this way.

Some employers voluntarily introduce other fringe benefits with the object of maintaining a stable and contented labour force, such as a canteen, additional leave, parking, medical benefits or club membership fees.

### 5.8.7  Employee promotion

Promotion – assigning an employee to a job of higher rank – is an area of management where trade unions can actively promote the interests of their members since they now have the backing of the new Labour Relations Act to ensure that fair promotion procedures are followed for employees. Examples of the manner in which trade unions can assert themselves are:

- Unions can press for seniority as the criterion for promotion.
- Unions can insist that employees be promoted from within the organisation before outsiders are hired.
- Unions can press for the promotion of a specific individual, subject to the grievance procedure.
- Pressure on employers to start applying broad banding to job evaluation for remuneration purposes, to give employees upward movement in their jobs, which is tantamount to a promotion.

### 5.8.8  Labour turnover and absenteeism

The monitoring of absenteeism and labour turnover is a human resources function which is often neglected, and which also has employment relations implications if not properly managed. High turnover and absenteeism rates often show poor management and/or conflict within the relationship with labour. Accurate labour turnover figures lead to better labour planning and the avoidance of intermittent redundancies.

The human resources department should not only monitor turnover and absenteeism rates, but also establish the reasons for turnover and absenteeism. Managers should, however, bear in mind that the employee may be exposed in the work situation to quite a variety of factors that may lead to illness, and of course, poor employee health will lead to high absenteeism and low productivity. It is the responsibility of management to see to it that the workplace is equipped so that occupational health is promoted.

Other sources of absenteeism may be personal problems, such as family problems, divorce, alcoholism, and stress. Management should try to reduce or eliminate the factors that cause personal problems, i.e. overtime, fatigue, job-related stress, and extensive employee travel. Some form of Employee Assistance Programme (EAP) can be implemented. The exit interview or a follow-up questionnaire may be used to fathom the reasons for absence from work. Neglect of these aspects is fertile for and conducive to labour unrest, and sometimes strike action.

## 5.8.9   Industrial health and safety

The health and safety of workers in the working environment is of cardinal importance. Trade unions, in particular, focus strongly on this point. If a union were to take an organisation to court on a matter of health and safety, the union would be on safe ground since there would be no question of the union's moral right to ensure that proper safety and health standards are maintained.

Consequently, health and safety can play an important part in union-management relations. On the other hand, showing concern for workers' health and safety is to management's benefit in employment relations because it enhances the image of the employer. The application and effect of the Occupational Health and Safety Act, No. 85 of 1993, should also be borne in mind in this regard.

Issues that might be the subject of union bargaining include: the provision of protective clothing, protection from industrial diseases, first aid provisions, and the appointment of a safety official who represents the union's (hence workers') interests. For more detail on

industrial health and safety, readers or learners are referred to Chapter 12 of this book.

## 5.8.10   Retrenchment

Retrenchment becomes unavoidable when there are redundant workers. It is the removal of an employee from the payroll because of factors beyond his/her control, and relates to negative external issues facing an enterprise in its totality. Such factors might include loss of sales, shortages of materials, seasonal changes, economic fluctuation, production delays and technological change. Readers must note that the technical aspects were discussed in Chapter 4 of this book, where unfair dismissals and unfair labour practice, but specifically dismissal based on operational requirements (retrenchment), were focused upon.

Updated amendments in 2002 to the principal Act have far reaching implications for human resource practitioners, should they wish to retrench employees (RSA 2002a).

The Department of Labour engaged in prolonged negotiations in NEDLAC (National Economic and Development Labour Council) to reach agreement between organised business and labour at the Millennium Labour Council (MLC). The final outcome relates to the regulation of retrenchments, and is out-

### Case-in-point

Provided that a decision is made in good faith with regard to substantive unfairness, the courts are unwilling to intervene and consider the merits of this type of decision.

In the recent decision of BMD Kitting Mills (Pty) Ltd. vs. SACTWU (2001) [7 BLLR 705 (LAC)], a slightly stricter test is formulated for determining substantive fairness, namely that the decision must have a reasonable basis. Nevertheless, even this approach leaves managers with a large degree of discretion to take decisions which may lead to retrenchments.

SOURCE: Le Roux (2002:101)

lined below (other amendment issues such as the transfer of businesses and liquidations or insolvencies are not discussed in this section).

Employers gained from the changes because they do not have to worry about drawn-out litigation over the substantive fairness of a retrenchment in the Labour Court, albeit that there are new inconsistencies created by the amendments.

Previous practices, the amendments to Section 189, as well as a new Section 189A of the Act together with the Code of Good Practice, set the scene for practitioners with regard to retrenchments. The following need to be taken note of when practitioners are faced with retrenchments:

- Parties to a retrenchment dispute are obliged to engage in a 'meaningful joint consensus seeking process' and it should be an attempt to achieve the following:
  - Appropriate measures to avoid the dismissals, minimise the number of dismissals, change the timing of dismissals and mitigate the adverse effects of the dismissals.
  - Consensus on an appropriate method to select the employees to be dismissed.
  - Reach agreement on the severance pay for dismissed employees.
- Where an employer employs more than 50 employees and contemplates retrenching more than a defined number of employees (it depends on the numbers employed or likely to be effected in terms of Section 189A(1(a)), then the parties can agree to the appointment of a facilitator (RSA 1995a). Marais (2002:30) points out that 'if the facilitator has started and/or not completed his/her facilitation, or has been appointed but for whatever reason has not started the facilitation process, it seems that the employer is able to dismiss after the said 60 days and there is no clear specification in this regard.' The confusion that exists here is also highlighted in an article by Le Roux (2002:101–3), mentioned in Chapter 4 of this volume.
- If the process of meaningful interaction

fails after a period of no less than 60 days, workers in companies which employ over 50 employees can elect whether they want to go on strike or take their dispute to the Labour Court in respect of dismissals.
- At least 30 days after issue, the notice (inviting consultation) must elapse to allow for consultation. In the case where a facilitator has been appointed this period is 60 days.
- If workers elect to refer a dispute about the substantive fairness of a dismissal for operational requirements to the Labour Court, the Labour Court may consider whether the dismissal was in fact a retrenchment, whether it was operationally justifiable on rational grounds, whether there was a proper consideration of alternatives, and whether the selection criteria were fair and objective.
- If workers elect to strike, the existing strike procedures apply, except that 14 days' notice must be given of a secondary strike.
- The onus is on the employer to prove that information that it refuses to disclose to trade unions during consultation is not relevant. This will improve the ability of unions to gain access to information, which will allow them to participate meaningfully in retrenchment consultations.
- Workers can also apply to the Labour Court on an expedited basis to compel an employer to comply with the retrenchment procedures.
- Individually retrenched employees have the right to choose whether they want to go to the Labour Court or the CCMA for arbitration.
- Employers must issue in writing a notice to the other party to consult, and also disclose in writing all relevant information which is, amongst others, the reason for the dismissal, alternatives which were considered, severance pay, the number of employees employed, etc. in terms of Section 189 of the LRA.

Note that the technical aspects with regard to the retrenchments of employees by employers who employ more than 50 employees, were discussed in the previous chapter.

In light of the above, trade unions can therefore negotiate with management to minimise reductions in the workforce, yet maintain the efficient operation of the organisation. Measures might include: the restriction of overtime, training and retraining, transfers between departments, division of work, reduced working hours, rotation of appointments and dismissals, and spreading the retrenchments over a certain period.

How to deal with and assist those workers who are retrenched, may also be negotiated. Issues in this regard include: redundancy payments, reappointment with or without the retention of seniority, putting retrenched workers in touch with other employers, offering potential employers facilities to interview on the organisation's premises, waiving the notice period of retrenched workers who have found alternative employment, assisting workers in obtaining unemployment insurance benefits, helping workers compile a curriculum vitae in order to find employment, and giving redundancy counselling.

All in all, human resources practitioners must do their best to maintain good relations with the relevant unions and workers. They are therefore well advised to comply with these changes by proactively considering what aspects of a collectively negotiated retrenchment agreement or policy ought to be adapted in consultation with the union, and also to consider the unwritten practices that are normally used when retrenchment is contemplated.

## 5.8.11  Termination procedures

The employment relations policy usually contains a disciplinary procedure and a disciplinary code, and these structures make provision for dismissal as a possible disciplinary step. There are nevertheless certain constraints on termination, which may be high-lighted in an employment relations context. Proper legal procedures must be followed when a person is dismissed, and matters such as notice of the termination of contract, payment on termination, payment in lieu of notice and commencement of the notice period must be handled with great care and preferably in consultation with the organisation's lawyers.

Termination of service is discussed in Chapter 8 of the Labour Relations Act – entitled Unfair Dismissal and Unfair Labour Practice (RSA 1995a). The chapter covers issues such as: what is regarded as dismissal, the right not to be unfairly dismissed, what is regarded as an unfair dismissal and so on. The Act deals with the Code of Good Practice: Dismissal and Unfair Labour Practice as per Schedule 8. Detailed guidelines are provided as to how fair dismissal should be dealt with, and include what would constitute fair reasons for dismissal. Dismissals based on operational requirements were dealt with earlier in this chapter. Specific information regarding the following types of dismissal in Schedule 8 of the Act, is included:

- Dismissal for industrial action.
- Guidelines in cases of dismissal for misconduct.
- Incapacity: poor work performance, including probation.
- Incapacity: Ill health or injury.

Human resources and employment relations officials should take careful note of Section 194 of the Act. It stipulates that if an employee was dismissed unfairly and the employer cannot prove that the dismissal was for a fair reason related to the employee's conduct, capacity, or based on the employer's operational requirements, the employee will have to be paid not more than the equivalent of 12 months' remuneration calculated at the employee's rate of remuneration on the date of dismissal. This has been confirmed with the amendments in 2002 to the Principal Act. However, if an employee's dismissal falls under the category of Automatic Unfair Dismissals, the remuneration to the employee of not more than 24 months is calculated at the employee's rate of remuneration on the date of dismissal.

Section 195 of the LRA also states that an order or award of compensation made in terms of Chapter 8 is in addition to and not a substitute for any other amount to which the employee is entitled in terms of any law, collective agreement or contract of employment.

## 5.8.12  Codes of employment

Various codes of employment have been designed to encourage organisations to promote the social and economic development of South Africa's people. They are a contribution to employment relations outside of the law. (Employment practices are discussed in Chapter 4 of this book.)

It must be noted that a code of employment is not an employment relations policy in its own right. Subscribers or signatories to a code may well model their employment relations policy on the objectives laid down in their code, but the code itself is a policy statement with a much broader base, which merely expresses the organisation's intentions with regard to its labour force. A code of employment is sometimes used instead of a human resources policy.

## 5.8.13  Quality of work life and social investment (also called social responsibility)

The quality of work life and social investment are also important. In the application of employment relations to these issues, quality of work life is discussed first and then social investment. Quality of work life reflects an organisation's concern for its employees. Whether or not formalised, it is usually marked by one, some, or all of the following:
- Recreation facilities are provided.
- Precautions are taken to protect the health of employees.

- Training facilities are provided.
- Opportunities are provided for career advancement and security of employment is regarded as a priority.
- Satisfactory working conditions are provided.
- Ethical employment practices are maintained.

Whether they are motivated by altruistic intent or provided as a means towards increased profitability, such benefits contribute both directly and indirectly towards the fulfilment of employees' social needs.

If an organisation meets its obligations to its employees (as outlined above), this will foster cooperation and trust, which are necessary for collective bargaining, as well as generally better relations between management and employees in the organisation. It may also reduce mistrust and the threat of strikes, and increase both parties' chances of achieving their respective objectives.

### Corporate social investment

Both social conscience and expedience motivate the organisation in its concern for the external environment. It is expedient in that by maintaining environmental conditions at a satisfactory level, an organisation safeguards its own future. An organisation may discharge its social investment towards the external environment in the following ways: through concern for the effects of ecological imbalances and pollution, through sponsorship of public recreation and entertainment, through research, by providing housing and electricity, and by promoting community development and welfare in the communities in which its employees live.

Trade unions are showing increasing concern for community affairs and are likely to monitor organisations' commitment in this regard. Such issues could be included in collective bargaining. Taking this process one step further, management and worker representatives in an organisation could jointly determine the allocation of corporate resources for social projects through joint committees. This would lead to better relationships between the organisation and the trade union, with resultant better employment relations.

### 5.8.14  The monitoring of employment relations

There are two dimensions to the monitoring of employment relations programmes and procedures: first, the assessment of whether employees are implementing the required procedures; second, an assessment of whether the procedures that are implemented are effective.

To determine whether an employment relations policy and all the procedures that accompany it are being effectively implemented, the human resources or employment relations manager can circulate questionnaires to staff, interview staff, or observe interpersonal relationships in the organisation. However, the responsibility for the practical implementation of employment relations policy lies with line management. This should be included in their job description, and their effectiveness in its execution should be reflected in their performance appraisals. If this approach is not used, employment relations procedures will not be effectively implemented. It should be remembered that the human resources or employment relations manager performs a staff function in the organisation and therefore can only advise management on how things should be done with regard to employment relations, but cannot mandate action.

It is equally important that grievances (their nature and number), written disciplinary warnings, etc. should be examined to determine whether the procedures and programmes that have been implemented are effective. Other indices of the effectiveness of the employment relations policy in its totality are rates of labour turnover, rates of absenteeism, the number of hours lost through work stoppages, the production rate for a certain period, exit interviews, and the attitudes of employees towards management and towards their employment conditions.

The monitoring of employment relations in an organisation is of cardinal importance if the human resources or employment relations manager wishes to determine the effectiveness of this function. In fact, it is crucial to the survival of the organisation in the turbulent times South Africa is experiencing. The human resources or employment relations manager can make or break his/her career by the way s/he manages employment relations in the organisation, because of the direct effect it has on the profitability of the organisation.

## 5.9   Employment equity

A very important development, which has a major impact on employment relations and which human resources managers should take careful note of, is employment equity in terms of the Employment Equity Act (RSA 1998b). South Africa has a legacy of discrimination in relation to race, gender and disability that has denied access to opportunities for education, employment, promotion and wealth creation for most South Africans.

The Act has two main objectives, namely to ensure that the workplace is free from discrimination and that employers take active steps to promote employment equity. The purpose of the Act in terms of Chapter 1 is to achieve equity in the workplace by:

- Promoting equal opportunity and fair treatment in employment through the eliminating of unfair discrimination.
- Implementing affirmative action measures to redress the disadvantages in employment experienced by designated groups in order to ensure their equitable representation in all occupational categories and levels in the workforce.

Human resources managers should furthermore note that the question of the prohibition of unfair discrimination is contained in this Act. (This was already outlined earlier in this chapter. The detail of the Act concerning diversity is also discussed in detail in another chapter elsewhere in this book.)

A major aspect of applying employment equity in the workplace is the preparation of the employment equity plan. Detail in this regard has been published as a Users Guide by the Department of Labour.

Only the essentials concerning the compilation of an organisation's plan to coincide with the provisions of the Act, and which must be addressed by employers, are, according to Tinarelli (2000: 58–85):

- Objectives that should be achieved each year.
- Affirmative action measures that should be implemented.
- Numerical goals, timetables and strategies that should be achieved.
- A timetable for the achievement of the goals and objectives other than the numerical goals for each year should be established.
- The duration of the plan should be stipulated.
- Procedures to monitor and evaluate the implementation should be in place.
- Internal procedures for dispute resolution should be established.
- Persons responsible for the plan, including senior management, should be identified.
- Any other prescribed matter should be included.

To comply with the provisions listed above, specific strategies should thereafter be selected, such as procurement (recruitment and selection) and maintenance interventions like specific job competency training and development – skills training career management, mentorship programmes and formal training.

This should be followed by specific organisational development techniques for the facilitation and support of the process, like sensitivity training, survey feedback information, process consultation, team building, intergroup development, management development, diversity management, and conflict resolution techniques.

In addition, top management must commit itself to an equitable system of employment and employment equity should form part of the organisation's strategic management plan. Line management should drive the project and human resources should support it.

Concerning the affirmative action elements of employment equity, employers must, in terms of the Employment Equity Plans of the Department of Labour (2000:4), and according to Chapter 3 of the Labour Relations Act:

- Consult with unions and employees in order to make sure that the plan is accepted by everybody.
- Analyse all employment policies, practices and procedures, and prepare a profile of their workforce in order to identify any problems relating to employment equity.
- Prepare and implement an employment equity plan setting out the affirmative action measures they intend taking to achieve employment equity goals.
- Report to the Department of Labour on the implementation of their plan in order for the Department to monitor their compliance.
- Display a summary of the provisions of the Act in all languages relevant to their workforce.

There is, however, another angle concerning Chapter 3 of the Act which human resource managers must take cognisance of, and that is the emphasis on employment equity within group context. Le Roux (1999:31) states:

Some individuals within a designated group may not have suffered disadvantages, or that some groups may have been exposed to lesser degrees of disadvantage, is irrelevant. The emphasis is on the representivity of the designated groups within the workforce.

The dilemma is now that many employees, especially employees who do not fall within the designated groups, will certainly expect and demand that their needs and interests as individuals must be acknowledged. Le Roux (1999:31) makes the point that these 'individual interests are protected in Chapter 2 of the EEA [Employment Equity Act], which prohibits discrimination against an employee in any employment policy and practice on the basis of a wide range of grounds, including race, sex, gender and disability.' The result is that human resources managers must take note of group and individual rights, which creates many pitfalls in the workplace and which could lead to unfair labour practices if not carefully observed.

## 5.10  Conclusion

An updated view is presented in this chapter with regard to those employment relations issues that pertain specifically to human resources managers and with which they need to be familiar to perform their job effectively. We have stressed that human resources managers are subject to numerous pressures regarding employment relations because it is a complex and rapidly changing field in South Africa's business environment. This area of human resources management is a daunting one, and human resources managers have to be *au fait* with all the rapid developments in trade unionism and legislation in South Africa. Changes to legislation defining the parameters within which employers and employees operate also mean that human resources practitioners have to be even more alert to manage and enhance sound relations between employers and employees.

Human resources managers need to know how components of employment relations affect them, such as relations with trade unions and dispute-handling procedures. They should be able to manage these critical issues confidently, particularly if they have to make do without the services of an employment relations manager. However, human resources managers can manage these components of employment relations effectively only if they understand the value of company, human resources, and employment relations policies. They also need to understand that the relationship between employers and workers is based on their various rights and responsibilities.

As far as general employment practices are concerned, if issues such as recruitment, job evaluation, and remuneration and industrial safety are ineptly handled, this will have an extremely negative effect on the organisation. This will be compounded if the employment relations elements contained in all general employment practices are disregarded or under-estimated by the human resources manager. The employment relationship should be given special consideration if general employment practices that affect human resources management in the employment relations context are to be effectively managed.

Moreover, in this chapter, the human resources manager's role was discussed at the micro-level as it applies in terms of the Labour Relations Act. The employment relations system should also be discussed at the macro-level to complete the picture of employment relations in South Africa. However, aspects of the macro-level were discussed in Chapter 4 of this book.

## Summary

- Human resources deals with the individual, at whatever level in the organisation, as a human and social, yet also professional, being. Employment relations addresses the employer-employee or the management-workers relationship. It is imperative that human resources and employment relations are integrated if an organisation is to function at its optimum.
- The immediate work environment consists of the following parties: the owners of the organisation (who are shareholders), those who control the everyday operations or management, workers who manufacture goods or offer services at the primary level of production, and the state (in the form of a multitude of laws and

provisions). While employment relations concentrates on the management-worker interface, human resources includes managers and workers in recognising that both parties are employees (directed by the owners or shareholders) and citizens (with legal socio-economic rights and obligations).

- Neither the hand-maiden of the state nor the lackey of shareholders, human resources professionals must provide a human face to the official, formal, and structural relationships that characterise the workplace. A free and fair work environment, content employees, and satisfied employers and owners, requires a dynamic interdependency between human resources management operations and employment relations policy and procedure.

## Case study
## Strained worker relationship at Finezza Restaurant

Alice graduated last year with distinctions in her major subjects after a three-year course from the Hospitality and Tourism Department at the local Technikon. She also won the national trophy for the top final year student in hospitality at the Technikon, which was sponsored by the Tropical Twin Palms Resorts Group. She immediately got a job at Finezza Restaurant as trainee manager. The manager/owner is Mandla Seloane who is an ex-foreign trade organisation representative of the South African Government, and who was stationed in Milan, Italy, for four years. Mandla opened the restaurant two years ago, which now employs 30 full time staff members. It is located just off the M1 highway at a very busy shopping centre midway between Sandton and Alexandra. Finezza is an upper-market restaurant catering for celebrities, weddings and formal parties. The restaurant is subject to the Restaurant, Catering and Hotel Bargaining Council for the Central Gauteng region.

Mandla already received a warning from the employment relations inspector regarding the lack of policy and procedures to manage the staff in terms of the bargaining council's agreement stipulations.

Mandla employed Alice on a three month probation period. Soon after Alice jointed the restaurant, she fell in love with the chief chef who is a Swedish national, but loves the ruggedness of Africa's natural beauty and game parks. He is a master at the fine art of providing the best international delicacies, but is also an expert at preparation and presenting exotic venison gourmet dishes. Andrio graduated from a very reputable Swedish Chef's academy and moved to South Africa 10 years ago, but got divorced recently. He is also the shop steward representative of the union which represents most employees at the restaurant.

After 10 weeks at the restaurant, Alice was unhappy working long hours and complained to Mandla. He was of the opinion that it is part of a trainee manager's job, and if she wants to become a manager she should either stop complaining about perceived long working hours or she should find other employment. Mandla, however, said that he would review her salary after completing six months' service instead of one year. He furthermore told her that a number of customers have complimented her on her cuisine knowledge and excellent customer relations.

As time went by, Alice at times became tired and frazzled as she tried to cope with her job and her intensified love life, which reached the point where she and Andrio thought of getting engaged. She recently had two arguments with Mandla in front of the staff. The one argument was about the shortage of staff and the other was about her perception of impossible workloads that seem to compromise service standards. Two days after her last outburst, Mandla called her to his office and said that he decided to extend her probationary period for another three months to six months. Alice questioned the reason for the extension of her probation after she had a chat to Andrio. Mandla, however, said that she became too argumentative and that she is challenging his authority in front of the other employees and that this damages relations in terms of the Bargaining Council's Code of Customer and Employee Conduct. She wanted to argue more, but Mandla said she could consider herself lucky that he did not fire her two days ago when she argued with him in front of the employees. Alice was really upset when she heard this from Mandla, but managed to keep her cool.

The next morning she tried again to reason with Mandla about her work situation. He refused to budge, and told her that she was summarily dismissed and challenged her to take her case to the bargaining council if she so desired. He said she was fired for insubordination and regarded this as so serious that she had to leave the premises immediately. She left without saying anything.

Later that day Mandla phoned her and apologised for his outburst and asked her to come back immediately. They should then forget what happened and she could carry on with her duties as if nothing had happened and even her probationary period would not be extended. She asked what made him change his mind and he replied that there was nothing in particular, but that a group of celebrities accompanied by an international trade delegation from Italy, which totalled 100 persons, had just booked the restaurant for the night. Alice received no training, evaluation or counselling with regard to her work performance while she was employed at Finezza. Alice declined the offer to have her job back and said she will get a job somewhere else and would never contact Mandla again.

## Questions

1   Did Mandla give good reason for extending her probation period by three months?
2   What human resources and employment

relations implications are you able to identify from this case?
3   What suggestions can you make to Mandla to improve relations at the restaurant, and what possible legal consequences is he facing as a result of his actions?
4   Draw up a performance management procedure to evaluate Alice's competency in the job at the restaurant in order to satisfy the requirements of Schedule 8 of the Labour Relations Act.

## Chapter questions

1   Describe the relationship between the state, employers and employees in South Africa. Pay special attention to the primary participants in the employment relations system.
2   Critically discuss the issues of interdependency you can identify between human resources and employment relations management that have been addressed by means of the amended legislation of 2002. Does this interdependency improve or strain relations between labour and management?
3   Does your organisation have company, human resources and employment relations policies? If not, draw up such policies to reflect your organisation's culture, while still being acceptable to both top management and the relevant trade unions.
4   Which general employment practices in your organisation have resulted in disputes? Why? What solutions can be suggested for human resources managers?
5   Draw up a profile of the trade unions with which you deal. How would you describe your relations with these unions? How can you go about developing mutual trust and cooperation on common issues?
6   Compile an approach your organisation could follow to ensure that employment equity is effectively practised in terms of the Department of Labour's Employment Equity Plan.

7   Review the areas in remuneration that
    may cause unfair discrimination and
    employment relations conflict. Propose
    measures for the prevention of these
    practices in your organisation.

# Bibliography

BACKER, W.A. 1999. *Die dienskontrak.
Perspektiewe vanuit die Wet op Basiese
Diensvoorwaardes.* Bactas Personeel
Konsultante, Pretoria.

BASSON, A., CHRISTIANSON, M., GARBERS, C.,
LE ROUX, PAK., MISCHKE, C. & STRYDOM
EML. 2000. *Essential labour law. Volume 1:
Individual labour law, 2nd edition.* Labour Law
Publications, Groenkloof.

BOTHA, E. 1999. 'The next revolution in organisations'. *Management Today,* 15(6):30–31.

Department of Labour. 2000. *Preparing an
Employment Equity Plan. User's Guide.*
Department of Labour, Pretoria.

EDITORIAL COMMENT. 2000. 'So staan sake nou
in SA'. *Finansies en Tegniek,* 7 January.

GROGAN, J. 1999. *Workplace law, 3rd edition.* Juta,
Cape Town.

INSTITUTE FOR PERSONNEL MANAGEMENT.
n.d. 'Fact Sheet Supplements', Nos. 103–107
and 232, *IPM Journal.*

KIRSTEN, M. & NEL, P.S. 2000. ,Workplace
forums in South Africa: Are they effective?'
*South African Journal of Labour Relations,*
24(1):35–55.

LANDMAN, A. 2002. 'Pre-dismissal arbitration:
The new procedures of s188A of the Labour
Relations Act'. *Contemporary Labour Law,*
11(8):71–74.

LE ROUX, P.A.K. 1999. 'Affirmative action and
the individual employee'. *Contemporary Labour
Law,* 9(4):31–38.

LE ROUX, P.A.K. 2002. 'The new law of retrenchment: Implications for employers arising out
of pending changes to dismissal procedures
under the Labour Relations Act'. *Contemporary
Labour Law,* 11(11):101–108

MARAIS, P. 2002. 'Understanding the LRA'. *People
Dynamics,* 20(5):28–31.

MEYER, N. 2002. 'The jurisdiction of CCMA

Commissioners at conciliation proceedings'.
*Contemporary Labour Law,* 12(4):32–36.

NEL, P.S., ERASMUS, B.J. & SWANEPOEL, B.J.
1998. *Successful labour relations: Guidelines for
practice, 2nd edition.* Van Schaik, Pretoria.

NEL, P.S. (ed.) 2002. *South African employment
relations: Theory and practice, 4th edition.* Van
Schaik, Pretoria.

RSA (REPUBLIC OF SOUTH AFRICA). 1993.
*Occupational Health and Safety Act,* No. 85 of
1993. Government Gazette, No. 14918.
Government Printer, Pretoria.

RSA (REPUBLIC OF SOUTH AFRICA). 1995a.
*Labour Relations Act,* No. 66 of 1995.
Government Gazette, No. 16861. Government
Printer, Pretoria.

RSA (REPUBLIC OF SOUTH AFRICA). 1995b.
*South African Qualifications Authority Act,* No.
58 of 1995. Government Gazette, No. 16725.
Government Printer, Pretoria.

RSA (REPUBLIC OF SOUTH AFRICA). 1995c.
*Labour Relations Act, Regulations.* Government
Gazette, No. 17516. Government Printer,
Pretoria.

RSA (REPUBLIC OF SOUTH AFRICA). 1996.
*Labour Relations Amendment Act,* No. 42 of
1996. Government Gazette, No. 17427.
Government Printer, Pretoria.

RSA (REPUBLIC OF SOUTH AFRICA).1997. *Basic
Conditions of Employment Act,* No. 75 of 1997.
Government Gazette, No. 18491. Government
Printer, Pretoria.

RSA (REPUBLIC OF SOUTH AFRICA). 1998a.
*Skills Development Act,* No. 97 of 1998.
Government Gazette, No. 19420. Government
Printer, Pretoria.

RSA (REPUBLIC OF SOUTH AFRICA). 1998b.
*Employment Equity Act,* No. 55 of 1998.
Government Gazette, No. 20626. Government
Printer, Pretoria.

RSA (REPUBLIC OF SOUTH AFRICA). 1998c.
*Labour Relations Amendment Act,* No. 127 of
1998. Government Gazette, No. 19542.
Government Printer, Pretoria.

RSA (REPUBLIC OF SOUTH AFRICA). 1999a.
*Skills Development Levies Act,* No. 9 of 1999.
Government Gazette, No. 19984. Government
Printer, Pretoria.

RSA (REPUBLIC OF SOUTH AFRICA). 1999b.

*Employment Equity Act, Commencement Notice, Regulations and Code.* Government Gazette, No. 20626. Government Printer, Pretoria.

RSA (REPUBLIC OF SOUTH AFRICA). 2001. *Unemployment Insurance Act,* No. 63 of 2001. Government Gazette, No. 23064. Government Printer, Pretoria.

RSA (REPUBLIC OF SOUTH AFRICA). 2002a. *Labour Relations Amendment Act,* No. 12 of 2002. Government Gazette, No. 23540. Government Printer, Pretoria.

RSA (REPUBLIC OF SOUTH AFRICA). 2002b. *Basic Conditions of Employment Amendment Act,* No. 11 of 2002. Government Gazette, No. 23539. Government Printer, Pretoria.

SWANEPOEL, B.J. 1995. *'n Strategiese benadering tot die bestuur van die diensverhouding.* Unpublished D.Com. thesis. UNISA, Pretoria.

SWANEPOEL, B.J., SLABBERT, J.A., ERASMUS, B.J. & BRINK, M. 1999(a). *The management of employment relations. Conceptual and con-*textual perspectives. Butterworths, Durban.

SWANEPOEL, B.J., SLABBERT, J.A., ERASMUS, B.J. & NEL, P.S. 1999(b). *The management of employment relations. Organisational-level per-*spectives. Butterworths, Durban.

TINARELLI, S. 2000. *Employers' guide to the Employment Equity Act.* Van Schaik, Pretoria.

VAN DYK, P.S., NEL, P.S., LOEDOLFF, P. VAN Z. & HAASBROEK, G.D. 2001. *Training management: A multidisciplinary approach to human resources development in Southern Africa,* 3rd edition. Oxford University Press, Cape Town.

WHITESIDE, A. & SUNTER, C. 2000. *AIDS. The challenge for South Africa.* (Human & Rousseau), NB Publishers, Cape Town.

## Websites

Caselaw: www.caselaw.co.za
South African Government: www.gov.za
Department of Labour: www.gov.labour.za
Business Day: www.bday.co.za

# 6

# Employment equity and diversity management

T Sono and A Werner

## Learning outcomes

At the end of this chapter the learner should be able to:

- Explain employment equity and relate it to affirmative action.
- Discuss the pros and cons of employment equity programmes.
- Discuss the requirements of the Employment Equity Act.
- Define the issues in the McWhirter Thesis on affirmative action.
- Explain the Zelnick Thesis on affirmative action.
- Outline the Sono Thesis on the weaknesses of affirmative action.
- Compare and contrast the international experiences of affirmative action.
- Present a business case for the management of diversity in organisations.
- Use Hofstede's dimensions of cultural differences to explain differences between managers in South Africa, and particularly between male and female managers in South Africa.
- Discuss a systematic best practice model for building a diversity-valuing culture.

## Key words and concepts

- compliance costs or orders
- diversity management
- employment equity
- Employment Equity Act
- employment equity plan
- empowerment (economic or political)
- equal employment opportunity
- equality before the law
- fair or unfair discrimination
- group rights
- McWhirter Thesis
- non-racial or non-racialism
- preferential policies or treatment
- previously disadvantaged groups
- protected categories of people
- race population register
- racial preferences
- racial privileges
- societal discrimination
- Sono Thesis
- Sowell Thesis
- workforce diversity
- workforce harassment
- Zelnick Thesis

## Illustrative case

### Juggling equity and injustice

Recently the Labour Court ruled that the failure of the South African Police Service to promote white male explosive experts to the rank of captain amounted to unfair discrimination.

Eligible captains in the explosives unit were, as promised, promoted to the rank of superintendent. Inspectors, who were promised promotion to the rank of captain, were not promoted. Instead, due to a change in the employment process, the posts were advertised. The SAPS recommended that posts be divided into designated (70 per cent) and non-designated (30 per cent) groups. After advertising and re-advertising, 20 posts (about 70 per cent of the posts) were still not filled. The commander of the explosives unit requested that at least 17 of these posts be filled by members of the non-designated group. The reasoning was that due to a shortage of qualified and experienced personnel in the explosives unit, the SAP could not afford to lose critical experts, and training was very expensive. The national commissioner turned down the request.

The case was taken to the Labour Court, which ruled that the SAPS failed to justify the discrimination due to the following reasons:

- There was no specific affirmative action plan for the explosives unit. The general employment equity plan did not make provision for an interim plan for specialised units.
- The national commissioner did not give consideration to the constitutional requirement that the police service 'discharge its responsibilities (to maintain law and order) effectively'.

The SAPS was ordered to institute the promotion of the affected employees.

Although this case is unique due to the constitutional requirements that govern the police services, the moral is that employers should have appropriate plans and training programmes in place to achieve employment equity.

SOURCE: 'The job of juggling equity and injustice', *Sunday Times*, 16 March 2003

## 6.1     Introduction

In racially and culturally diverse societies, organisations and companies will ideally be similarly diverse because of their demographics. South African organisations have generally been skewed in terms of their workforce, especially at the middle to upper levels of management.

Since the 1994 general elections, South Africa has been well on its way towards establishing political and social democracy. Affirmative action, employment equity and diversity management are strategies employed by the government and business to remove all forms of apartheid and to give everybody the opportunity to actualise his/her potential.

Affirmative action and employment equity are legally enforced in South African organisations. Organisations might willingly or unwillingly submit to the law. Diversity management, on the other hand, is seen by more and more organisations as a competitive advantage and a strategic necessity to survive in a globally diverse environment. It involves a fundamental change in attitude and behaviour that cannot be prescribed by law.

In this chapter we define employment equity, consider the need for employment equity, and discuss the Employment Equity Act and its application. We also present arguments for and against affirmative action and employment equity, as well as various international applications of employment equity. In the last part of this chapter we look at diversity management with special emphasis on cultural diversity and how it could be leveraged to give an organisation a competitive advantage.

## 6.2     Employment equity

Affirmative action and employment equity are not clearly defined in the South African context. Definitions of affirmative action generally reflect labour market policy aimed at addressing past imbalances that are a direct result of discrimination, while definitions of employment equity reflect labour market policy aimed at preventing future discrimination (Van Dyk et al. 2001:357–8).

Affirmative action and employment equity are two related concepts now fully formulated as law in the Employment Equity Act, No. 55 of 1998. Affirmative action precedes employment equity both in time and legislative enactment. The Employment Equity Act (EEA) is largely a rehash of Chapter 23 of the Canadian Constitution. Nearly everything, from 'designated groups' to 'employment equity plans' to the concept 'employment equity' itself comes from Chapter 23 (Second Supplement) of the Constitution of Canada.

The EEA has become an ambitious social engineering workplace programme to determine the composition of company workforces. Its aim, as the South African government's Department of Labour puts it (Department of Labour 1997:7), is to undo the huge disparities in the labour market brought about by apartheid. Although the EEA does not define equity, it may be defined as 'present fair discrimination to prevent future unfair discrimination'. Affirmative action, on the other hand, is present 'fair' discrimination to correct past 'unfair' discrimination.

Both the EEA and affirmative action emphasise groups. Chapter 3 of the EEA emphasises employment equity in a group context. Unfair discrimination could be construed on several grounds.

## 6.2.1  Unfair discrimination

The Act prohibits direct and indirect discrimination on a number of grounds, including:
- Race, ethnic or social origin, colour, and culture.
- Gender, sex, pregnancy, and sexual orientation.
- Disability and HIV status.
- Religion, conscience, belief, and language.

According to Section 10 of the EEA, discrimination on one or more of the above grounds is unfair unless it is established that the discrimination is fair. In other words the burden of proof of innocence on a charge of unfair discrimination rests with the employer.

The following are regarded as forms of discrimination:
- Harassment.
- Medical testing if not permitted by law or justifiable in light of certain conditions.
- Psychological testing if not valid, reliable and applied fairly to all employees.

The EEA regards harassment of an employee as a form of discrimination, and it is prohibited. This includes harassment based on sex, sexual orientation, race and religion. If a worker is found guilty of harassment in the workplace, his/her employer may also be held liable. A perpetrator may face disciplinary action, while employers may be faced with claims for compensation by the victims for failing to ensure that the work environment is safe and non-hostile. It would be prudent for employers to develop clear policies and procedures regarding workplace harassment and to publicise these broadly to all employees.

Discrimination is not unfair if it is:
- part of affirmative action measures which are in line with the Act; or
- an inherent requirement of the job.

Disputes in this regard are referred to the CCMA.

In light of the above, the following observation could be made: It will be unfair to discriminate against blacks, for instance, in favour of non-blacks, but fair to discriminate against non-blacks in favour of blacks for the purpose of racial preferences.

## 6.3    Why the need for employment equity?

Employment equity, according to the authors of the law, i.e. Department of Labour (1997), is based on the following:
- Disparities in the labour market in:
  - employment
  - occupation
  - income
- Pronounced disadvantages for certain categories of people.

- Repealing discriminatory laws is not enough to redress disadvantages.

The purpose of the EEA is thus to achieve equity in the workplace by: first, promoting equal opportunity and fair treatment in employment through the elimination of unfair discrimination; and second, implementing affirmative actions to redress the disadvantages in employment experienced by designated groups in order to ensure their equitable representation in all occupational categories and levels in the workforce in terms of the Act. Protected 'categories of people' are blacks (i.e. Africans, Indians/Asians and Coloureds), women, and people with disabilities.

## Case-in-point

Challenges to affirmative action measures are beginning to be mounted, especially in the public service. For instance, in Public Servants of South Africa vs. the Minister of Justice & others (1997) 18 ILJ 241(w), the applicant challenged the decision of the Department of Justice to reserve certain posts for affirmative action candidates.

Le Roux (1999:32–3), from whom this entire case is cited, states that the case revolved around the interpretation of various statutory provisions. The first was Section 212 of the Interim Constitution (1993), which stated that the Public Service should promote an efficient public administration broadly representative of the South African community. The second was Section 8 of the Interim Constitution, which entrenched equality rights and prohibited discrimination. Section 8 (3)(a), which was of particular importance, stated that the Interim Constitution did not: '... preclude measures designed to achieve the adequate protection and advancement of persons or groups or categories of persons disadvantaged by unfair discrimination, in order to enable their full and equal enjoyment of all rights and freedoms.'

Le Roux (1999) points out that the court adopted the formal approach to equality and accepted that affirmative action measures constituted discrimination, but that they could, in the correct circumstances, be fair. Taking into account the above provisions, the Court formulated the following principles with regard to affirmative action measures:

- The affirmative action measures must be specifically designed to achieve the goal of the adequate protection and advancement of persons subject to past unfair discrimination. The action taken must not be haphazard or random.
- There must be a causal connection between the affirmative action measures that have been designed and their objectives.
- Although the affirmative action measures must be designed to provide adequate protection and advancement, the rights of others and the interest of the community should also be taken into account.
- The requirement that the Public Service must ensure an efficient public administration should not be compromised.

The Court found that these principles had not been adhered to and that the affirmative action measures adopted by the Department of Justice were therefore invalid. What are the comparisons between this case and the one cited at the beginning of this chapter?

## 6.4  Requirements set out by the Employment Equity Act

### 6.4.1  Prohibition of discrimination

Chapter 2 of the EEA requires every employer to 'take steps to promote equal opportunity in the workplace by eliminating unfair discrimination in any employment policy or practice.'

'Eliminating unfair discrimination' leads, of course, to the inference that the under-representation of blacks, women and the disabled is evidence of discrimination in the past. This places the onus on the employer to justify the composition of his/her workforce.

## 6.4.2 Affirmative action for designated groups

Chapter 3 of the EEA deals with affirmative action. 'Designated groups', as we have seen, are black people, women and people with disabilities, and 'designated employers' are the focus of this category of employers.

To achieve employment equity, every designated employer must implement affirmative action measures for people from designated groups in terms of this Act (Section 13). These measures are contained in Section15, and are those measures designed to ensure that 'suitably qualified' people from designated groups have equal employment opportunities and are equitably represented in all occupational categories and levels in the workforce of a designated employer.

The measures implemented by a designated employer must include:

- Measures to identify and eliminate employment barriers, including unfair discrimination, which adversely affect people from designated groups.
- Measures designed to further diversity in the workplace based on the equal dignity and respect of all people.
- Making reasonable accommodation for blacks, women and people with disabilities so that they enjoy equal opportunities and are equitably represented in the workforce of a designated employer.

## 6.4.3 Five steps to employment equity

The following steps should be taken to ensure employment equity:

- Consult with employees (Section 16 of the EEA).
- Conduct an analysis (Section 19).

- Prepare an employment equity plan (Section 20).
- Implement the plan (Section 20).
- Report to the Director-General of the Department of Labour on progress made (Section 7).

## 6.4.4 Employment equity plan

A major requirement of the 'designated employer' by the EEA, is an employment equity plan. Section 20(1) states that a designated employer must prepare and implement an employment equity plan which will achieve reasonable progress towards employment equity in that employer's workforce. Such employment equity plan must, inter alia, state:

- Annual objectives to be attained.
- Affirmative action measures to be implemented.
- Where under-representation of people from designated groups has been identified by the analysis, the numerical goals to achieve the equitable representation of 'suitably qualified' people from designated groups within each occupational category and level in the workforce, the time-table within which this is to be achieved, and the strategies intended to achieve those goals.
- The time-table for each year of the plan for the achievement of goals and objectives other than numerical goals, as well as the duration of the plan covering a period within five years but not less than a year.
- The procedures that will be used to monitor and evaluate the implementation of the plan and whether reasonable progress is being made towards implementing employment equity.
- The internal procedures to resolve any dispute about the interpretation or implementation of the plan.
- The persons in the workforce, including senior managers, responsible for monitoring and implementing the plan.

### 6.4.5 Reporting to the Director-General

Reports to the Director-General are due on the first working day of October every year, for organisations employing more than 150 employees, and the first working day of October every second year for those with less than 150 employees.

The report must contain the prescribed information and be signed by the CEO of the designated employer. A summary of the report must be published in the designated employer's annual financial report, as it is regarded as a public document.

### 6.4.6 The Department of Labour

The Department is required to:
- Assess whether or not employers comply with the provisions of the EEA.
- Issue compliance orders to employers who do not comply.
- Issue guidelines on developing and implementing affirmative action plans and say what the reporting requirements are.

### 6.4.7 Designated Employers

According to Section 24 of the EEA, each designated employer must:
- Assign one or more senior managers to take responsibility for monitoring and implementing.
- Provide the managers with the authority and means to perform their functions.
- Take reasonable steps to ensure that the managers perform their functions.

### 6.4.8 Compliance costs and maximum fines for contravening the EEA

Compliance costs of the EEA are not inconsiderable. A major aspect of these high compliance costs emanates from policies that drive current South African legislation. That is, labour legislation too often proceeds from the apparent assumption that employees need protection from unscrupulous employers who, if the law did not prevent them, would exact maximum labour for minimum benefits.

Consequently, the compliance costs would be exorbitant for most companies. For instance, the implementation of an employment equity plan would require not only additional staff, but also staff highly qualified to undertake the complex requirements of the Act. Chapter 5 of the EEA, 'Monitoring, Enforcement and Legal Proceedings', makes explicit the responsibilities of the designated company in terms of compliance. Merely complying with the equity plan would require additional budgetary allocations for many companies. Bigger companies would easily meet the costs, simply adding them as part of the cost of labour. Such costs would invariably be passed over to the consumer. Smaller companies, however, could even be compelled to close down. But more onerous are the fines for contravening the EEA, as Schedule 1 of the Act shows (see Appendix 6.1).

## 6.5 Arguments for affirmative action: The McWhirter thesis

- The first and, in the minds of many, the most legitimate justification for engaging in affirmative action, is the need to compensate for specific instances of race and gender discrimination in the past by particular organisations. This is termed 'specific discrimination'.
- The need to remedy 'societal discrimination'. By this McWhirter means that though some organisations may not have 'engaged in intentional discrimination in the past ... [other] entities in society have'.
- The justification for affirmative action is the need to create more diversity in a particular organisation.
- Affirmative action programmes have

increased the labour force participation rate for women and blacks. (See McWhirter 1996:6–8.)

## 6.6   Arguments against affirmative action: The Zelnick thesis

- Zelnick (1996) regards affirmative action as a racially discriminatory practice against whites and other non-favoured ethnic groups. It favours the less qualified over the more qualified, and it is therefore a systematic attack upon objective merit selection criteria. Zelnick concurs with the view that while it increases black enrollment at selective universities and also expands somewhat the pool of black entrepreneurs, it has brought little employment, educational or income benefits to those most in need of help. He holds that it has 'distracted attention from the real causes of misery among [really poor] blacks'. He sees affirmative action more as an ideology than as a programme. As such 'it has proven impervious to overwhelming evidence'. Zelnick thus sees it as counter-productive. 'It legitimizes negative stigmas and panders to the darker instincts of racial animosity'.
- Affirmative action, argues Zelnick, 'has been broadened for political purposes to include beneficiaries who lack the historical claim of blacks for relief'. Zelnick concludes that affirmative action has not been successful in other societies. It is being challenged, and successfully so, in the courts as well as in the political arena. (See Zelnick 1996:18.)

## 6.7   Weaknesses of affirmative action: The Sono thesis

- Every employee is now a representative of a group. Affirmative action is a contrived programme of preferential policies based on membership of a specific group.
- Specific individuals are conferred the rights of groups. There thus seem to be no more specific individual rights, but only generic group rights.
- Affirmative action is based on political empowerment and not on economic empowerment.
- Contrary to the view of the ANC Department of Economic Policy (1990), affirmative action has no expiry date. It is without a cut-off date nor is it, so far, a 'transient method', as was once claimed by the ANC Department of Economic Policy.
- It discriminates against one group and prefers another group. It is an employment discrimination law.
- It adopts the doctrine that the end justifies the means. It argues that if the intentions are noble, then the means to attain those ends must also be noble.
- The re-emphasis on race is also its strong point. A racial preference is termed a non-racial condition. That is, it is non-racial to prefer some people over others on the basis of race. Moreover it would depend on a racial population register.
- It fails to accommodate the least privileged of blacks and women. It tends to increase the economic status among blacks and women of those already relatively advanced in comparison to the poorest of the poor.
- All forms of affirmative action violate the principles of equal opportunity before the law and thus contravene the rule of law.

## 6.8   International affirmative action and employment equity experiences

The report of the commission to investigate the development of a comprehensive labour market policy indicates that international experience, as far as equal opportunity and affirmative action is concerned, differs substantially from that of South Africa. Nearly all previous experiences in this area had to do with addressing discrimination against a minority. The situation in South Africa is the reverse. International experience, while valuable, will be of limited direct application to the South African situation. One possible exception is the experience of Malaysia, where bold steps were taken to reorganise public employment in favour of the majority Malays.

Where international experience has proved more valuable is with regard to affirmative action as it relates to gender and disability, and therefore the experiences of Malaysia, the USA and Namibia are discussed in this chapter.

## 6.8.1 The Malaysian experience

Castle (1995:19–20) indicates that in Malaysia, affirmative action is defined in ethnic rather than racial or gender terms. Statutory affirmative action policies favour the Malays, who constitute 55 per cent of the population of 17 million, over the 35 per cent Chinese and 10 per cent Indian. Emsley (1996:7) is of the opinion that Malaysian affirmative action has been both the world's most extensive programme and one of its most successful.

Charlton and Van Niekerk (1994:41–2) are of the opinion that the Malaysian model is of particular interest to South Africa. Many parallels exist in terms of a majority benefiting from affirmative action programmes and religious differences coinciding with ethnic ones. Malaysia had made significant strides in implementing affirmative action when the minority Chinese and the Malay majority, anticipating a coalition government, set up a comprehensive plan to implement affirmative action while still maintaining economic standards. Although much credit must go to the political and economic bargain struck in Malaysia, it needs to be borne in mind that its affirmative action success was in large part due to a high economic growth rate, enabling resources to be distributed.

Emsley's (1996:102–3) view is that the lessons for South Africa of the Malaysian experience imply the overarching importance of economic growth. The Malaysian affirmative action programme had four aspects, and economic growth was critical to each. The same will be true for similar programmes in South Africa:

- *Poverty reduction.* The Reconstruction and Development Programme (RDP) was to address workers by equipping excluded workers with much of what is needed to participate in the formal sector. The speed with which poverty is reduced will depend critically on the ability of the economy to create employment opportunities. But the RDP poverty reduction programmes have so far had minimal effect.

- *Increased racial representation across the economy.* This is not as big a problem in South Africa as it was in Malaysia, as much of the black population is urbanised and ready to work in the formal economy.

- *Equity ownership.* Any attempt to replicate the Malaysian scheme without exceptionally buoyant government revenues would surely constitute a grave misallocation of resources.

- *Black middle-class.* Malaysia has followed a course of organic growth of Malays in the private corporate sector, where affirmative action had been largely eschewed.

## 6.8.2 The USA experience

There are essential differences between circumstances in South Africa and in the USA, but South Africa can learn a great deal from the American experience. The USA was the first country to make affirmative action as an anti-discriminatory measure compulsory by law.

In 1961, President Kennedy declared that specific affirmative action should be taken to counteract discrimination. President Johnson defined in more detail what was meant by affirmative action. To a large extent this coincides with the current approach to affirmative action in the Western world.

The Civil Rights Act of 1957 was amended in 1964 to make discrimination based on race, sex, colour, religious belief or national origin by both private and public employers illegal. This law may be regarded as the forerunner of modern affirmative action legislation.

Schmitt and Noe (1986:71) outline the most important stipulation of the Civil Rights Act, Title 7, which spells out equal opportunities as follows:

> It shall be an unlawful employment practice for an employer ... to fail or refuse to hire or discharge any individual, or otherwise to discriminate against any individual with respect to his compensation, terms, conditions, or privileges of employment, because of such individual's race, colour, religion, sex or national origin ...

However, Sowell (1983:200) also says, 'while affirmative action results were impressive in gross terms, a finer breakdown shows disturbing counter-productive trends.' In his opinion, these counter-productive results include the following (which we call the Sowell Thesis):

- The least privileged black people are even worse off with affirmative action than before, while the more privileged black people rapidly increase their economic status.
- Reverse discrimination takes place because the demand for qualified black people is higher than the demand for qualified white people. In 1980, graduated black couples earned more than graduated white couples.

It is therefore clear that South Africa can learn a number of lessons from the USA experience.

### 6.8.3  The Namibian experience

Namibia's legislation on affirmative action is of particular importance to South Africa, regardless that contrary to expectations, legislation on South African affirmative action has unexpectedly preceded its Namibian counterpart. The International Labour Organisation (1991:113) states the following:

> By virtue of their history, the issue of equality of opportunity and treatment is one to which the Namibians are particularly sensitive. Consequently, Article 23 of the Constitution, entitled 'Apartheid and Affirmative Action', provides for parliament to enact legislation to facilitate the advancement of those 'socially, economically or educationally disadvantaged' as a result of past laws or practices.

The Namibian government took a decision at the 31st meeting of Cabinet (held on 14 September 1993) to prepare and implement an affirmative action policy as soon as was procedurally possible. The Namibian bill on affirmative action has now been promulgated into law.

The Office of the Labour Commission of Namibia published the following policy statement on affirmative action during 1995:

> The Government of the Republic of Namibia (Ministry of Labour) has decided that the Legislation of Affirmative Action in Employment will be based on the following principles:
>
> a) The goal of affirmative action is to create equal employment opportunities.
> b) The target groups of affirmative action are the disadvantaged groups of Namibian society: blacks, women and the disabled.
> c) Employment quotas and any other measures which require the hiring of unqualified persons are rejected.
> d) Preferential treatment under carefully planned affirmative action programmes should only be given to suitably qualified persons. Special concern of affirmative action is to benefit the least well off persons from the relevant target groups.
> e) Affirmative action measures should

not be used as an absolute bar on the employment or career prospects of those who are not members of target groups.

f) Legislation of affirmative action should cover both the public and private sectors.

g) Affirmative action should be administered by an independent agency which can further the dialogue between social partners and other stakeholders.

The Namibian Cabinet had instructed the Minister of Labour to:

- Prepare a draft bill on affirmative action in employment which is consistent with the seven key principles listed above and which takes into account the submissions to the Consultation Document.
- Carry out, where necessary, further consultations on the draft bill with the social partners and other stakeholders.

The office of the Labour Commission of Namibia published a document on affirmative action in *Employment Consulting* in September 1995, and it is this document which was sent to 'social partners' and stakeholders for their comments. These comments have subsequently been incorporated into law. Chapter 1 explains the concept of affirmative action, Chapter 2 sets out the constitutional and legal framework, Chapter 3 summarises the government's approach to affirmative action, and Chapter 4 focuses on specific issues regarding the implementation of affirmative action.

More recently, the government of Namibia published the Affirmative Action (Employment) Act (No. 29 of 1998), which outlines the measures that relevant employers should adhere to in order to ensure that persons in designated groups enjoy equal opportunities and are fairly represented in the various positions of employment (van Rooyen 2001). An overview of the Act and guidelines for the practical implementation thereof can be found on the Internet (www.nid.org.na/pdf/aff-action.pdf).

## Case-in-point
### Companies are losing skilled blacks at a rapid rate

According to a 2001 *Global Business Solutions* study, companies were losing skilled blacks at a rapid rate. The study revealed that 74 per cent of all new appointments comprised black recruits. Although it created the impression that South African firms actively addressed employment equity, 67 per cent of service terminations also involved black employees, which resulted in a retention rate of only seven per cent.

The following reasons were given to explain the situation:

- A lack of commitment from top management to employment equity.
- A lack of cultural sensitivity as new recruits are expected to assimilate into the current organisational culture.
- A lack of cultural awareness (only 24 per cent of companies have implemented diversity management programmes to support employment equity).
- A white male dominant organisational culture that excludes black recruits.
- The appointment of black recruits as tokens without real responsibility and decision-making powers.
- An absence of a systematic training and development programme for black staff.

SOURCE: Booysen et al. (2002:22–4)

## 6.9 Diversity management

In the past, debate in South Africa around employment equity typically centred on the moral, social and legal obligations of employers. However, there is a new paradigm emerging that perceives diversity as a valuable attribute that provides an organisation with a competitive edge, provided that a business environment conducive to the appreciation and utilisation of diversity is created.

Not only does the diverse population of South Africa contribute to workplace diversity, but organisations are also becoming global in orientation and outlook. A homogeneity of workforce backgrounds is giving way to heterogeneity; a homogenisation of the human race, in terms of technological culture, is taking place. Unicultural groups, in which virtually all members come from the same background, are no longer the norm in workplaces. This is a paradox, though, because a 'world culture' is simultaneously also evolving.

Biculturality and multiculturality, not only of the workforce in general, but of workforce management in particular, are now the trend, unlike the previously predominant unicultural workforce management. Technology is rendering human culture similarly paradoxical, even as workforces are becoming bicultural or multicultural. In a bicultural workforce, more members represent one or other of two distinct cultures, whereas in a multicultural workforce, members represent three or more ethnic backgrounds (Adler 1991).

## 6.9.1  Diversity: A definition

Diversity encompasses all forms of difference among individuals, including culture, gender, age, ability, religious affiliation, personality, economic class, social status, military attachments, and sexual orientation (Nelson and Quick 1997:39). In South Africa, we may add political affiliation, which is a subtle but powerful force in the diversity stakes. It now plays a critical role in affecting the composition, and thus the diversity, of the workforce in both the public and private sectors.

Diversity is the opposite concept to universality, a generalisation which may be made about all cultures. Certain activities occur across cultures; that is, they are common to all cultures, but their manifestation may be unique to a particular society. Workforce diversity is a powerful force for change in organisations, and change itself is a force to be reckoned with in companies.

## 6.9.2  The influence of cultural diversity on organisational behaviour

The importance of cultural diversity should not be minimised, since an organisation's culture, as a system of shared values and beliefs, leads people, decision-making processes and procedures, and control systems to interact so as to produce behavioural norms. A strong culture guides behaviour and gives meaning to activities and, thus, contributes significantly to the long-term success of organisations. Strong cultures attract, reward, and hold the allegiance of people performing essential roles and meeting relevant goals (Kast and Rosenzweig 1985:680).

There is no doubt that culture impacts on every aspect of life, from the way people relate to the natural environment to how they behave towards one another. Beliefs and values, assumptions and perceptions, all are cultural influences on behaviour. Culture, in other words, is communicable knowledge for coping with a particular environment that is passed on for the benefit of present inhabitants of that environment, as well as future generations.

Culture can be an asset or a liability. It is an asset when shared beliefs ease and economise communications and facilitate decision-making. Motivation, cooperation and commitment may also be facilitated by shared values. Organisational efficiency is achieved as a result. However, a strong culture can also be a liability when it is not appropriate to an organisation's environment and overall strategy. Congruence between culture, strategy, and managerial style is important because it facilitates organisational efficiency.

## 6.9.3  Hofstede's model for understanding cultural diversity

Various studies prove that cultural differences translate into different work-related attitudes. It is therefore very important to facilitate inter-cultural understanding in diverse workforces.

A Dutch researcher, Geert Hofstede (and his colleagues), provided a very useful model for understanding differences in cultures. They studied workers from the same company doing similar jobs, but working in different countries. Hofstede found that national culture explained more differences in work-related attitudes than did other diversity issues (such as age, gender, profession, or position within the organisation).

Hofstede also found five dimensions of cultural difference that formed the basis for work-related attitudes (see Figure 6.1).

- *Individualism versus collectivism.* In some cultures individualism predominates, in others it is collectivism that predominates. Individualist cultures foster loose social frameworks among people, whose primary concern is for themselves and their families. The emphasis in these cultures is on individuals looking after their own interests. Personal responsibility is highly valued and individual decision-making is cherished. Collectivist cultures, on the other hand, have different social frameworks which are tightly knit, unlike in individualist cultures. Group cohesion and group decisions are valued and practised. Loyalty and unity, and a group approach to life and work, colour and influence personal conduct in collectivist cultures. The USA is an example of an individualist society, whereas Japan is an example of a collectivist culture.

Individualist cultures encourage initiative, flexibility, and experimentation. Individual achievement is valued. Collectivist cultures, on the other hand, cherish a harmonious fit within the group. Members of the group are characterised by conformity. Team unity is the norm.

- *Power distance.* This cultural dimension deals with the degree of unequal distribution of power. In cultures with a high power distance, managers and superiors have more powers precisely because they are supervisors and managers. This is a significant hierarchy; formality is the norm and titles are valued and used. In low power distance cultures there is a strong belief that social inequality should be reduced to a minimum. There is more trust among people at various power levels. There is a relaxed regard for seniority/juniority dimensions. Superiority is based on merit. Managers without expertise are a contradiction in terms. Employees easily bypass bosses in order to get the work done.

- *Uncertainty avoidance.* Some cultures easily accept uncertainty and ambiguity; others are intolerant of such conditions. Cultures with high uncertainty avoidance are concerned with security and tend to avoid conflict. There is a need for consensus. The inherent uncertainty in life is a threat against which people in such cul-

**Figure 6.1** Hofstede's dimensions of cultural difference

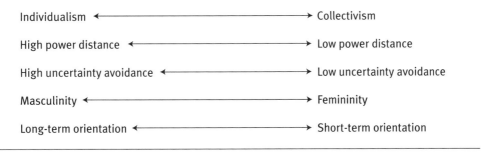

SOURCE: Hofstede (in Schultz et al. 2003:25)

tures struggle constantly. Cultures with low uncertainty avoidance are more tolerant of ambiguity. Here people are risk-takers and are not perturbed by individual differences. Conflict is not a threat, but is seen as constructive. There is no fear of dissenting views. Such cultures place a premium on job mobility, unlike those of Japan and Italy, which place a premium on high uncertainty avoidance and thus emphasise career stability.

- *Masculinity versus femininity.* Cultures that encourage masculinity expect their members to be strong, powerful, assertive, competitive and directive. These behaviours are traditionally associated with males. Cultures that encourage femininity expect their members to be relationship-orientated, nurturing, supportive and empathetic. These behaviours are traditionally associated with females.
- *Long-term versus short-term orientation.* Some cultures encourage tactical decision-making and spontaneous action, while others foster strategic and well-planned, long-thought about, conduct. Spur of the moment business practice has distinct advantages (opportunities are immediately capitalised upon and exploited) and disadvantages (no thorough planning for management of opportunities, whether successful or unsuccessful). So too does long-term and often slower business practice have pros (good consideration of all parties involved and all scenarios) and cons (too constrained, stifling, and inflexible).

How do these cultural dimensions manifest themselves in the South African workforce? Research done revealed that the cultural values of white South Africans emphasised competition, high work orientation, free enterprise, individual self-sufficiency, self-fulfillment, exclusivity and the use of planning and methodology (Booysen et al. 2002:22–4). The cultural values of black managers emphasised collective solidarity, inclusivity, collaboration, consensus, group significance, concern for people, patri-

archy, respect and dignity. Differences in gender, irrespective of race, were also found. South African male managers valued performance, competition and winning, domination, control and directive leadership. Leadership was perceived as a rational, unemotional and objective transaction. South African female managers emphasised collaboration, participation, intuition, empathy, empowerment, self-disclosure, and subtle forms of control. Female managers perceived follower-leader relationships as interactional and transformational.

According to Booysen et al. (2002:22–4), the challenge is to create a work environment that blends the diverse cultural expectations of people in such a way that all employees share in the vision for organisational success.

### 6.9.4 A best practice model for creating an organisational culture that appreciates and values diversity

Booysen et al. (2003:33–6) provide a systematic model for the management of diversity, which is based on theory, best practices and their collective consulting experiences. A systematic approach is mostly use when an organisation is perceiving diversity as a strategic and transformational issue.

- *Step 1: Top management commitment.* The commitment from top management is imperative in an organisation that takes diversity seriously. Top management should demonstrate the link between valuing diversity and business excellence. They should wholeheartedly participate in the planning and implementation of the diversity initiative, commit resources to the process and demonstrate personal commitment.
- *Step 2: Establish a diversity leadership team to guide the diversity initiative.* The diversity leadership team should comprise a vertical and horizontal cross-section of the company, reflect the demographic diversity and include representatives from top management

and other stakeholders. This team should develop a team charter, familiarise itself with diversity and act as a role model for the rest of the organisation.

- *Step 3: Conduct an assessment of the organisational climate, needs and issues.* The diversity leadership team oversees the assessment of the organisational climate, needs and issues. The purpose of the assessment is to gain an understanding of the perception organisational members have of diversity issues, and to determine to what extent diversity is perceived as an equity issue and to what extent it is valued. The results from the assessment should be fed back to the entire organisation to raise awareness for the need to change and therefore reduce resistance.
- *Step 4: Craft a vision that values diversity.* A vision describes a future desired state. Typically, a diversity vision has two dimensions: it touches the heart and mind of each employee, and it states why it is important to the organisation (makes a business case for valuing diversity). Buy-in is achieved through organisation-wide face-to-face discussion of the meaning of the vision, its acceptance, and how it translates into everyday work life.
- *Step 5: Develop and implement a strategic plan for valuing diversity.* Using the issues raised in the assessment as a baseline, objectives, strategies and plans are developed. Training features in most organisational diversity plans, but should be linked with the assessment needs, and carefully designed and presented. Training typically includes awareness training, knowledge training and the transference of specific diversity skills, such as communication skills. Other strategic plans include changing existing human resources practices, such as recruitment, orientation, performance management and promotion policies.
- *Step 6: Evaluate and measure results.* The impact of the diversity initiative on the business, attitudes and organisational culture is measured by comparing progress against the baseline data from the first assessment.
- *Step 7: Ensure integration and accountability.* A successful diversity initiative results in an organisational culture that really values diversity. The values and skills of the initiative should become an integral part of the fabric of the organisation, its values, operations, systems, policies and everyday practices. Management should be held accountable for leading diversity throughout the organisation. Pioneering companies incorporate diversity goals into the performance review and reward systems of managers. The developers of this diversity model emphasise the importance of creating open channels of communication throughout the process.

### 6.9.5 The advantages of managing cultural diversity effectively

Diversity can only have a positive effect if knowledge is combined with action. The existence of diversity must be acknowledged and capitilised upon (Chang 1996:7). Cultural diversity needs to be managed if its positive influences are to be harnessed. The effective management of cultural diversity holds the following advantages:

- It stimulates, rather than stifles, individual participation and creativity.
- It increases the flow of ideas.
- It attracts and retains the best skills.
- It improves employer-employee relations.
- It increases the morale of the workforce, rather than create suspicions and hostilities amongst employees.
- It reduces tension, confusion and counter-productivity in the workforce.
- It leads employers to view differences as valuable assets rather than unwanted liabilities.
- It increases the motivational levels of organisational members.

## 6.10  Conclusion

Affirmative action and employment equity aim to redress discrimination of the past and prevent future discrimination. It should, however, not become a number and quota game, but be regarded and utilised as a strategy to create a just society in which every individual gets a fair opportunity to contribute constructively to the economy and his/her individual prosperity.

Managing diversity in the workforce and workplace requires effective management. Cultural diversity is an important aspect of diversity. The challenges posed by diversity and transformation demand that human resources managers intervene proactively by recognising the nature of diversity and channel them in a positive direction.

## Summary

- South Africa is well on its way to establishing true political and social democracy after the 1994 elections. Affirmative action, employment equity and diversity management are strategies employed by the government and business to remove all forms of apartheid and past discrimination, and to give everybody the opportunity to actualise his/her potential. Employment equity seeks to prevent future discrimination while affirmative action addresses past discrimination.
- The EEA requires organisations to draw up an employment equity plan and submit a report to the Director-General of the Department of Labour. Failure to submit a report results in heavy fines. Employment equity and affirmative action can be viewed from various perspectives (both for and against), but whatever the case, they are a reality and their success depends in large measure on effective management, and hence, HRM.
- South Africa is in a unique position due to the past political dispensation. However, we can learn from international experiences in employment equity, espe-

cially in relation to gender and disability.
- Diversity management is seen by more and more organisations as a strategic necessity to survive in a globally diverse environment. It involves a fundamental change in attitude and behaviour that cannot be prescribed by law.
- Hofstede (in Schultz et al. 2003) provides a model for understanding socio-cultural diversity by considering cultural dimensions such as power distance, collectivity-individualism, masculinity-femininity, and risk avoidance.
- A best practice model for building a culture that values diversity provides guidelines for companies that perceive diversity as a strategic issue.

## Case study
### Terry's Appliances Inc.

You are a consultant who has been approached by the management of Terry's Appliances Incorporated to assist them with the performance problems experienced in their company. The company has achieved its employment equity goals for the last two years and has a workforce that is almost representative of the population, and it hopes to have it fully representative within the next three years. However, due to increased diversity, the company is also experiencing more conflict, dissatisfaction and apathy from certain groups. You have been requested to help due to your extensive knowledge and experience in the field of diversity management.

Initial talks with managers and employees revealed the following:
- Policies that are discriminatory in certain instances.
- Employees from various groups are not equally involved in decision-making.
- Communication and relationship problems.
- Physically challenged employees are excluded from certain activities.
- Some managers feel that diversity issues

should be separated from operational issues, and that only the human resources department should deal with diversity.

You are convinced that there are many other issues that also need attention. You also realise that the management of Terry's Appliances has failed to establish a culture that is appreciative of diversity. You inform senior management that you would like to schedule a meeting with them to discuss a best practice model for the establishment of a culture that values diversity. To your surprise, one of the male managers suggests that you finish the meeting with a round of golf at the nearest country club.

## Question

Comment on the above situation and suggest a plan of action to establish a culture that will value diversity.

## Experimental exercise

Purpose: To illustrate a shared value system amongst participants from diverse groups.

Introduction: In America, in the South Dakota's Black Hills, a sculptor, Gutzon Borglum, created the world's largest mountain carving. Borglum's creation depicts the faces of four exalted American presidents: George Washington, Thomas Jefferson, Theodore Roosevelt, and Abraham Lincoln. A picture of his artwork can be found on the following website: www.travelsd.com/parks/rushmore/

Task 1 (15 minutes): Each individual gets an opportunity to decide that, if s/he could have the faces of four well-deserved people carved into a mountain, who s/he would have chosen for this honour. It could be anybody who the person has a high regard for, such as a family member, sports hero, teacher, or any other person who has set a good example or influenced the participant in a positive manner. The person then makes a list of the attrib-

utes in these people that they admire.

Task 2 (15 minutes): Form diverse groups of five members each. Compare the lists drawn up and identify common attributes from everybody's list. These attributes represent shared values in the group.

Task 3 (15 minutes): Compile one global list from the common attributes identified in each group.

## Chapter questions

1   Discuss the requirements of the Employment Equity Act.
2   Audit your organisation's employee component. What adjustments will you make to reflect the spirit of the Employment Equity Act?
3   Compile and describe an employment equity plan for your organisation that will meet all prescriptions of the Act.
4   Discuss Hofstede's cultural dimensions and indicate how they apply to South African managers.
5   How will you establish a work environment that values diversity and makes business sense?

## Bibliography

ADAMS, C. (ed.) 1993. *Affirmative Action in a Democratic South Africa*. Juta, Cape Town.

ANC (AFRICAN NATIONAL CONGRESS). 1990. *Discussion Document on Economic Policy by the ANC Department of Economic Policy*. Department of Economic Policy Workshop, Harare, 20–23 September.

ADLER, N.J. 1991. *International Dimension of Organizational Behavior, 2nd edition*. PWS Kent, Boston.

BELZ, H. 1991. *Equality transformed: A quarter-century of affirmative action*. Transaction Books, New Brunswick.

BLACK MANAGEMENT FORUM (BMF). 1993. *Affirmative action blue print*. BMF, Johannesburg.

BOOYSEN, L., NKOMO, S. & BEATY, D. 2002. 'Breaking through the numbers game: High impact diversity (part1)'. *Management Today*,

18(9):22–24.

BOOYSEN, L., NKOMO, S. & BEATY, D. 2003. 'A best practice model for building a valuing diversity culture'. *Management Today,* 19(1):33–36.

CASTLE, J. 1995. 'Affirmative action in three developing countries, lessons from Zimbabwe, Namibia, and Malaysia'. *South African Journal of Labour Relations,* 19(1):6–33.

CHANG, R.Y. 1996. *Capitalizing on workplace diversity: A practical guide to organizational success through diversity.* Richard Chang Associates, Irvine, California.

CHARLTON, G.D. & VAN NIEKERK, N. 1994. *Affirmative action beyond 1994.* Juta, Cape Town.

CHRISTIANSON, M. 'The job of juggling equity and injustice'. *Sunday Times,* www.sunday-times.co.za (accessed 16 March 2003).

DAVIE, E. 2000. *Directors' report.* Free Market Foundation Documents, Sandton.

DEPARTMENT OF LABOUR. 1997. *Employment Equity Bill.* Department of Labour, Pretoria (www.gov.labour.za).

EMSLEY, I. 1996. *The Malaysian experience of affirmative action: Lessons for South Africa.* (Human & Rousseau), NB Publishers, Cape Town.

GERBER, P.D., NEL, P.S., & VAN DYK, P.S. 1999. *Human resources management, 4th edition.* Oxford University Press, Cape Town.

GOVERNMENT OF SOUTH AFRICA. 1998. *Employment Equity Bill* B–60–98, Government Printer, Pretoria.

HUMAN, L. (ed.) 1991. *Educating and developing managers for a changing South Africa: Selected essays.* Juta, Cape Town.

HUMAN, L. 1993. 'Women in the workplace: A Programme to counteract gender discrimination at work'. In Adams, C. (ed.) *Affirmative action in a democratic South Africa.* Juta, Cape Town.

INTERNATIONAL LABOUR ORGANISATION. 1991. *Social and Labour Bulletin of Namibia.* Government of Namibia, Windhoek.

JEFFREY, A.J. 1996. *Business and affirmative action.* South African Institute of Race Relations, Johannesburg.

JORDAN, B. n.d. *The Star* advertisement supple-ment.

KAST, R. & ROSENWEIG, J.E. 1985. *Organization and management: A system and contingency approach, 4th edition.* McGraw-Hill Companies, New York.

LE ROUX, P.A.K. 1999. 'Affirmative action and the individual employee'. *Contemporary Labour Law,* 9(4):31–40.

MAPHAI, V.T. 1993. 'One phrase, two distinct concepts'. *Die Suid-Afrikaan,* Special focus: Affirmative action in action, May/June (44):6–8.

MCWHIRTER, D.A. 1996. *The end of affirmative action: Where do we go from here?* Carol Publishing Group, New York.

NELSON, D.L. & QUICK, J.C. 1997. *Organisational behaviour: Foundations, realities and challenges.* West Publishing Company, Minneapolis.

NJUGUNA, M. 1992. *A Kenyan case study: Focusing on a country where affirmative action has been introduced.* Juta, Cape Town.

PERON, J. 1992. *Affirmative action, apartheid and capitalism.* Free Market Foundation, Sandton.

RSA (REPUBLIC OF SOUTH AFRICA). 1998. *Employment Equity Act,* No. 55 of 1998. Government Gazette, No. 20626. Government Printer, Pretoria.

SACHS, A. 1990. *Protecting human rights in a New South Africa.* Oxford University Press, Cape Town.

SCHMITT, N. & NOE, R.A. 1986. 'Personnel selection and equal employment opportunity'. In Cooper, C.L. & Robertson, I.T. (eds.) *International review of industrial and organizational psychology.* John Wiley & Sons, Chichester.

SCHULTZ, H., BAGRAIM, J., POTGEITER, T., VIEGDE, C. & WERNER, A. 2003. *Organisational behaviour.* Van Schaik, Pretoria.

SONN, F. 1993. 'Afrikaner nationalism and black advancement as two sides of the same coin'. In Adams, C. (ed.) *Affirmative action in a democratic South Africa,* pp. 1–10. Juta, Cape Town.

SOWELL, T. 1983. *The economics of politics and race.* Quill, New York.

THOMAS, A. 1996. *Beyond affirmative action.* Knowledge Resources, Randburg.

VAN DYK, P.S., NEL, P.S., VAN Z LOEDOLFF, P. & HAASBROEK, G.D. 2001. *Training manage-*

*ment, 3rd edition.* Oxford University Press, Cape Town.

VAN ROOYEN, J.W.F. 2001. *Implementing affirmative action in Namibia, 3rd edition.* Namibia Institute for Democracy, Namibia (www.nid.org.na/pdf/aff-action.pdf).

ZELNICK, B. 1996. *Backfire.* Regnery Publishing, Washington D.C.

## Websites

Diversity at PepsiCo:
www.pepsico.com/diversity/
The Employment Equity Act: www.labour.gov.za

# Appendix 6.1

The following schedule which reflects the fines prescribed by the Act also emphasises the tone thereof and the extent to which it should be taken seriously.

SCHEDULE 1
Maximum permissible fines that may be imposed for contravening this act

This Schedule sets out the maximum fine that may be imposed in terms of this Act for the contravention of certain provisions of this Act.

| Previous contravention | Contravention of any provision of Sections 16,19, 20, 21, 22 and 23 |
|---|---|
| No previous contravention | R500 000 |
| A previous contravention in respect of the same provision | R600 000 |
| A previous contravention within the previous 12 months or two previous contraventions in respect of the same provision within three years | R700 000 |
| 1   Three previous contraventions in respect of same provision within three years | R800 000 |
| 1   Four previous contraventions in respect of the same provision within three years | R900 000 |

# part three

## Staffing the organisation and maintaining people

# 7

# Job analysis

## HB Schultz

## Learning outcomes

At the end of this chapter the learner should be able to:

- Discuss job analysis as the basis of all human resources activities.
- Identify the components of a job.
- Perform the process of strategic job analysis.
- Decide whether to use job-orientated or worker-orientated methods of job analysis in an organisation.
- Evaluate various problems in job analysis.
- Develop a job description and job specification based on the principles of ergonomics.
- Explain the ergonomic relationship in the work environment.
- Briefly describe the influence of quality assurance in job analysis.

## Key words and concepts

- Critical Incident Technique (CIT)
- ergonomics
- Functional Job Analysis (FJA)
- job analysis
- job description
- job specification
- job-orientated approach
- knowledge, skills, and abilities (KSAs)
- Management Position Description Questionnaire (MPDQ)
- Position Analysis Questionnaire (PAQ)
- strategic job analysis
- systematic activity log
- worker-orientated approach

**Illustrative case**
## Cookies for Julian

Julian Louw joined the staff of Cookes Biscuit Manufacturers in 1980 at the age of 30. For 10 years he was employed as a packer on the Gypsey Creams production line, before being transferred to the warehouse as an order-filler. This job required him to lift sealed cardboard boxes weighing up to 35 kilograms and place them on pallets in a designated area, ready for collection by the fork-lift drivers. Julian enjoyed this job until a back injury laid him off work for a month. Covered by workers' compensation, he received physiotherapy treatment for several weeks and then returned to his job. After a short time, however, he re-injured his back and was laid off work again to receive physiotherapy and treatment. Julian returned to work a second time, only to have the same back injury flare up again.

He was frustrated by the back injury that kept him away from his job. He was a loyal worker and a valued employee, and his employer was paying thousands of Rands in injury-related costs. Unfortunately the company had lost the benefit of having him at work. It was obviously time for a new strategy.

The human resources manager felt that they should search for an underlying reason for Julian's recurring injury. Each time he returned to work after physiotherapy, his doctor and therapist pronounced him fit for duty, only to see him fall prey to the back injury within the first few days. The HR manager was perplexed and decided to call in the services of a health management consultant who conducted a complete job analysis of Julian's job. The analysis broke down the tasks and components of the job, as well as the aptitudes, skills, physical environment, and work schedule. This revealed that the amount of weight that Julian had to lift was only part of the problem. The compounding factor was that his job required mandatory overtime which, coupled with the 45-hour week he was working, proved to be too much, too soon. Without a thorough job analysis, Julian could have continued the cycle of injuries, perhaps culminating in termination of his job. It was the job analysis that uncovered the problem and provided the solution.

Job analysis is more than just a checklist of required abilities and physical demands, it breaks down and catalogues the movements, motions and aptitudes of the tasks that comprise a job. With complete information and understanding of what a job entails, employers have a powerful tool for assisting and placing workers.

At the warehouse where Julian worked, employees were videotaped while they performed their duties, which yielded a wealth of details about the demands of their jobs. Once the problem of the mandatory overtime had been identified, and with input from his doctor, transitional duties were assigned to Julian, who performed his regular job as order filler for the first few hours of the day and then worked as an inventory clerk. The job analysis showed that the skills-set of the inventory clerk matched many of the functions that Julian performed as an order-filler. However, the inventory clerk's job was far less physically demanding. During the next few weeks, Julian's strength and stamina returned, enabling him to eventually work his regular job for a full day and then later the mandatory overtime as well. The job analysis also reaped large savings for his employer, especially as Julian was able to contribute to company productivity.

## 7.1    Introduction

The concept of continuous improvement is accepted as a basic business philosophy in every developed country around the world. This philosophy has encouraged these countries to re-think the fundamental principles that underlie the design of jobs and the way they are carried out. Whether it is called job analysis, job review, or job classification, the systematic process of compiling a description of the skills, duties, knowledge and experience required for various jobs and a forecast of the future direction of the business, is essential in making intelligent decisions in the workplace. Management typically begins by conducting a job analysis, which defines the jobs within the organisation and the behaviours that are necessary to perform those jobs. It is an essential and pervasive human resources technique that reveals important details about selected jobs.

This chapter commences with a discussion of how job analysis forms the basis of all human resources activities. We investigate the process of job analysis, before describing some of the popular methods of data collection. The nature of job descriptions and job specifications is examined, and we take a look at the ergonomic relationship in the work environment, before discussing the impact of quality assurance on the job analysis process.

## 7.2 Job analysis: The basis of human resources activities

Most of the people-related activities that take place in every company would not be effective unless some form of job analysis is undertaken at the start of the exercise. Various authors, such as Gómez-Mejía et al. (1998:62–3), Ivancevich (2001:152) and Mondy and Noe (1996:92–5) provide examples of the questions that job analysis answers (see Figure 7.1) and discuss some of the major uses of job analysis, which are explained below and summarised in Figure 7.2.

- *Workforce planning,* which depends on job analysis to provide the foundation for forecasting current and future human resources needs through incorporation into a Human Resources Information System (HRIS).
- *Job evaluation and compensation,* which requires job analysis to rank or compare jobs in terms of their total value to an organisation.
- *Recruitment and selection,* which relies on job analysis to supply a clear picture of the duties, tasks, and responsibilities, job expectations, skills, knowledge and abilities of the job.
- *Training, development and career planning,* which is based on up-to-date job descriptions and specifications produced through job analysis, in order to ensure that training programmes reflect actual job requirements and that managers and their subordinates plan career paths.
- *Performance management,* which makes use of job analysis to set an employee's

level of performance according to the work standards identified through job analysis. It also allows a manager to effectively develop, assess and maintain a subordinate's performance.
- *Ergonomics,* which calls for the use of job analysis as an aid in efforts to design a job or workspace for more efficient performance.
- *Health and safety procedures,* which depend on job analysis to uncover safety hazards and dangerous operating procedures associated with the job.
- *Organisational restructuring,* which calls for adaptations in the jobs people do and the way they carry out these jobs. Job analysis can be instrumental in re-arranging and re-organising the jobs in a company.
- *Labour relations,* which finds in job analysis a useful tool for employers faced with the implications of labour legislation and employment equity.
- *HR research,* which needs job analysis to provide the researcher with a starting point when investigating organisational variables such as absenteeism, labour turnover and job satisfaction.

## 7.3 The components of a job

Organisations have evolved because the overall mission and objectives of most institutions are far too large for any single person to accomplish. Consequently, groups of people perform particular functions or tasks, providing the mechanism for coordinating and linking the various activities that are necessary for success. These activities unite to form the jobs that the organisation is built upon (Ivancevich 2001:152).

Jobs can be broken down into components and arranged in a hierarchy of work activities. This hierarchy is depicted in Figure 7.3.

## 7.4 The process of job analysis

Job analysis must always be conducted according to a systematic process. An example of this process is offered in Figure 7.4.

**Figure 7.1** Questions that job analysis answers

- What Knowledge, Skills and Abilities (KSAs) does the job-holder need?
- What kinds of behaviours are needed to perform the job?
- What traits and experience does the job-holder require?
- What machines and special equipment must be used?
- How much supervision is necessary?
- Under what working conditions should this job be performed?
- With whom does the job-holder interact?
- How much time is taken to complete important tasks?
- What are the performance expectations for this job?
- How can the information acquired by the job analysis be used in the employee's development?

**Figure 7.2** The major uses of job analysis

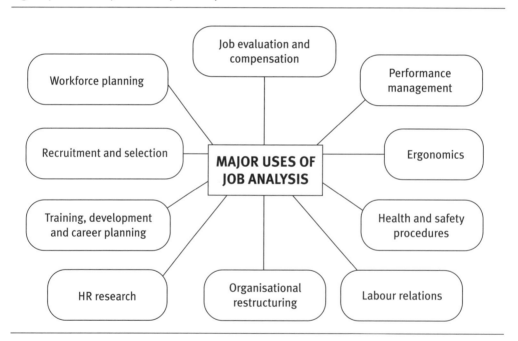

## 7.4.1 The systematic process of job analysis

The following steps form the basis of the job analysis process:

- *Step 1: Involve and empower employees in the process.* Job analysis must never be undertaken without consultation with employees. Certain methods of data collection (for example, direct observation) could raise suspicions if undertaken without communication to the worker of the underlying reasons for the exercise. This could have a great impact on the level of labour relations in the organisation. In addition, consultation affords employees

**Figure 7.3** A hierarchy of work activities

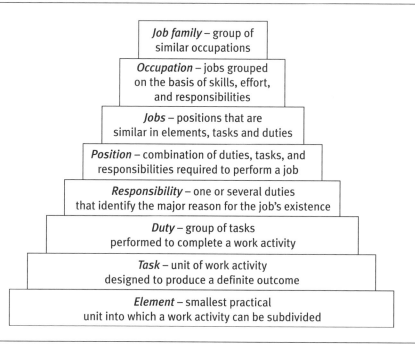

*Job family* – group of
similar occupations

*Occupation* – jobs grouped
on the basis of skills, effort,
and responsibilities

*Jobs* – positions that are
similar in elements, tasks and duties

*Position* – combination of duties, tasks, and
responsibilities required to perform a job

*Responsibility* – one or several duties
that identify the major reason for the job's existence

*Duty* – group of tasks
performed to complete a work activity

*Task* – unit of work activity
designed to produce a definite outcome

*Element* – smallest practical
unit into which a work activity can be subdivided

the opportunity to 'buy-into' and support the process.

The easiest way of ensuring consultation is to enlist the services of a job analysis committee, which normally includes representatives from trade unions, the major departments in the organisation, and members of professional bodies such as engineering, financial, and human resources associations. The latter would be representative of the jobs to be analysed.

- *Step 2: Investigate how all jobs fit into the organisation.* The existing organisation chart offers an overall picture of how all the jobs combine to form the organisation's structure.
- *Step 3: Determine the reason for conducting job analysis.* Job analysis should only be conducted for a specific reason. Is this reason for restructuring purposes? Or training and development? Or perhaps for determining compensation structures? Or a combination of some of these, and

possibly some of the other purposes of job analysis?

- *Step 4: Select the job(s) to be analysed.* It is often expensive and time-consuming to analyse every job in an organisation. To overcome these problems, a representative sample of jobs is chosen.
- *Step 5: Determine the method(s) of data collection.* The method, or methods, of data collection will depend on whether a job-orientated, worker-orientated, or combination approach to job analysis is chosen. The advantages and disadvantages of the methods available are then weighed against each other, before a final choice is made.
- *Step 6: Collect job information.* Job data is obtained through the chosen collection method, or methods. This information is reviewed with employees and the job analysis committee to ensure that it is objective, factual, and easily comparable with analyses of other jobs.

**Figure 7.4** The systematic process of job analysis

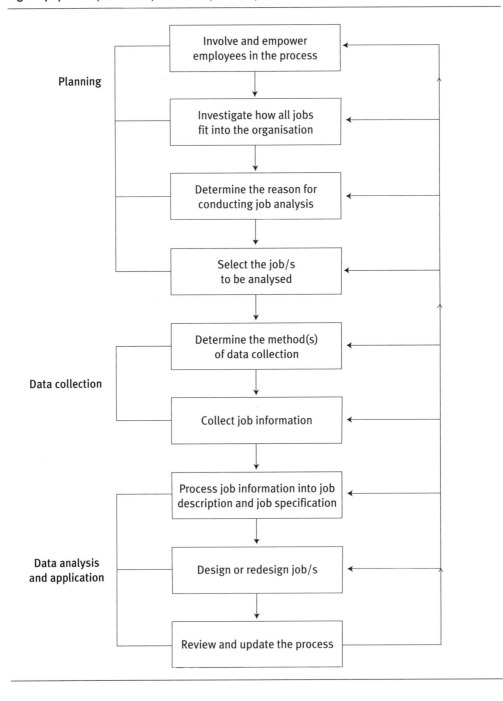

- *Step 7: Process job information into job description and job specification.* The information obtained is refined and used to compile job descriptions and job specifications. These documents are then used to accomplish the purpose of the job analysis exercise, as decided in step three of the process.
- *Step 8: Design or redesign jobs.* Existing job descriptions and job specifications are compared to the revised documents. If there are extreme differences, the new documents are used to design a totally new job; smaller differences can result in redesigning the current job into a more up-to-date form. Where there is no existing job documentation, the newly processed job description and job specification are adopted as official company documents.
- *Step 9: Review and update the process.* After the job analysis is undertaken and the resulting documentation used for the stated purpose, the value of the exercise must be assessed. For example, did the chosen data collection method yield adequate information, or might another method have been preferable?

### 7.4.2  Strategic job analysis

Recognising the changing nature of work, many researchers and HR practitioners conduct 'work' analysis, focusing on tasks and cross-functional skills of workers as required by the National Qualifications Framework (NQF), rather than 'job' analysis with its focus on static jobs. The business environment is changing so rapidly that jobs are unlikely to remain static for any period of time. As information on work (such as knowledge, skills, interests, and motivation) changes, the scope and nature of a job analysis should respond to an equal change in its database. To obviate having to undertake job analysis too frequently on one specific job, strategic job analysis is needed.

Strategic job analysis is the specification of tasks to be performed and the knowledge, skills and abilities required for effective performance in a job *as it is predicted to exist in the future.* Strategic job analysis implies that most of the data collection methods referred to in Section 7.5 are inadequate if used in their present form, as they focus only on actual information which is currently available. Strategic job analysis also requires a process of brainstorming in which job experts make predictions regarding the kinds of issues in the job, the company, and/or the environment that may affect the job in the future (Lundy and Cowling 1996:231).

Periodic organisation assessments are necessary, whether a company is large or small. Stern (2002) states that business requirements should be the key driver when a job analysis is used strategically. By using the systematic process discussed in Section 7.4.1, the analyst can create a strategic pathway for job analysis, as shown in Figure 7.5.

## 7.5   Job analysis methods

Schultz and Schultz (1994:80) divide the approaches to job analysis into the *job-orientated approach and the worker-orientated approach.*

The job-orientated approach directs attention to the specific tasks and outcomes, or level of productivity required for a job. In the worker-orientated approach, worker behaviours in the form of specific skills, abilities, and personal traits needed to perform the job, are the focus of analysis.

### 7.5.1  Job-orientated methods of data collection

The following general methods of data collection follow the job-orientated approach, and are frequently used in South Africa (Ivancevich 2001:158–162):

#### Questionnaires

Most firms use the questionnaire method because, once the initial questionnaire has been compiled, it is the least time-consuming and cheapest of the methods. It usually provides standardised, specific information about the jobs in an organisation, but sometimes requires clarification by means of a follow-up interview. An unstructured questionnaire requires the job incumbent to describe the job in his/her own words. A structured questionnaire uses brief, unambiguous questions that can be answered in a minimum amount of time with the least disruption to the job-holder. Appendix 7.1 to this chapter offers an example of a job analysis questionnaire that can be used by organisations in various sectors.

### Interviews

The interview is the second most frequently used method of job data collection. It is used with individual job-holders, or with groups of people who carry out similar tasks, functions, duties and responsibilities. In many jobs it is simply not possible for the analyst actually to perform the job (such as an airline pilot), or where observation is impractical (such as an architect). Direct communication allows the job analyst to probe for clarity when answers are vague. It also allows the job incumbent to offer information which s/he believes is relevant, and which the job analyst may have overlooked. The interviewer normally uses a structured set of questions.

### Direct observation

People often behave differently when they know they are being watched, so it is necessary for job analysts to remain as unobtrusive as possible when using the observation method. They also need to take into account changes in job behaviour caused by external factors such as fatigue. A variation of on-site observation is work sampling in which a job analyst randomly samples the content of a job, instead of observing all job behaviours. The sample must be representative of the entire domain of tasks, and not isolated acts. Jobs that are normally done by hand, that are standardised and have a short activity cycle, are best suited for analysis through observation.

### Systematic activity logs

Also known as a job-holder's diary, this method of data collection requires the job incumbent to keep a diary of work activities, which registers the content and frequency of duties. Although this method is cost-effective and offers the job-holder 'ownership' of the analysis process, it is the least reliable method. Employees may be negligent in completing diaries due to forgetfulness, reluctance, or organisational obstacles, such as working conditions that make the recording of the information difficult. Sometimes employees try to maximise the importance of their jobs by adding more tasks and responsibilities than are required by the job.

### Job performance

The job analyst can do repetitive jobs that are easily learned, and in this way obtains first-hand information of the job requirements.

Usually, an analyst does not use one job analysis method exclusively. A combination of methods is often more appropriate. In analysing clerical and administrative jobs, for example, the analyst might use questionnaires, interviews and limited observation. In studying production jobs, interviews might be supported by extensive observation. The choice of methods thus depends on the nature of the job to be analysed.

The advantages and disadvantages of the most popular methods of job analysis are illustrated in Table 7.1. This knowledge assists the job analyst in choosing the most appropriate method of data collection.

### 7.5.2 Worker-orientated methods of data collection

Although worker-orientated job analysis methods concentrate on behaviours, skills and abilities, they tend to be subjective. Some of these methods require special training and considerable time in learning how to apply and interpret them (Ivancevich 2001: 161–7; Mondy and Noe 1996:103–8).

**Figure 7.5** The strategic job analysis process

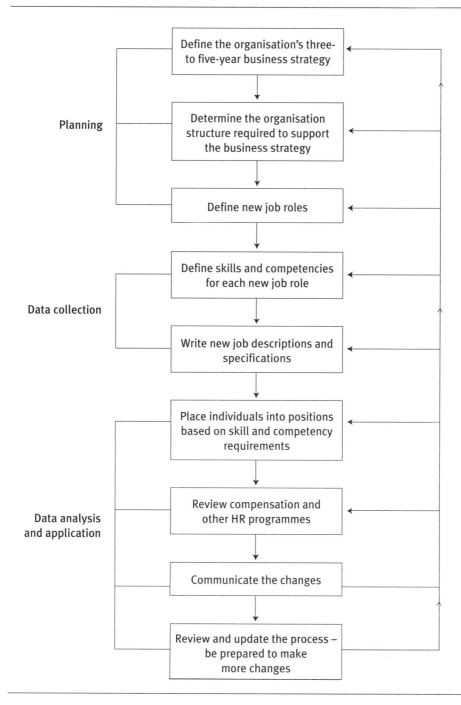

## Critical Incident Technique (CIT)

This technique is based on the identification of those incidents or behaviours that are necessary for successful job performance. Subject matter experts indicate the behaviours that differentiate good from poor workers. A single critical incident is of little value, but hundreds of critical incidents can effectively describe a job in terms of the unique behaviours required to perform it well.

## Position Analysis Questionnaire (PAQ)

The PAQ is a behaviour-orientated questionnaire consisting of 194 items that fall into 27 job dimensions. These dimensions are further grouped into six general job categories,

namely information input, mental processes, work output, relationships, work situation and job context, and other job characteristics. A computer program scores each job in relation to the job dimensions, and the final score represents a profile of the job relative to standard profiles of jobs of a similar nature. The PAQ is a quantitative system that is widely used and produces consistent results when different analysts analyse the same job (McCormick et al. 1972:347–68).

## Functional Job Analysis (FJA)

The FJA is commonly used to describe the nature of jobs and to compile job descriptions and job specifications. Jobs are analysed in three work domains:

**Table 7.1** Advantages and disadvantages of popular job analysis methods

| Job analysis method | Advantages | Disadvantages |
|---|---|---|
| Job performance | Exposure to actual job tasks. Appropriate for jobs that can be learned in a short time. | Inappropriate for jobs that require extensive training or are dangerous. |
| Observation | Provides a richer, deeper understanding of job requirements. | Observations may reveal little useful information. |
| Interviews | Provides information about standard and non-standard activities, and physical and mental work. Worker can provide verbal information. | Workers may be suspicious of interviewer's motives. Interviewer may ask ambiguous questions. Information may be distorted. |
| Critical incidents | Focuses directly on what people do. | Takes time to gather, abstract, and categorise. May be difficult to develop a profile of average behaviour. |
| Structured questionnaires | Cheaper and quicker to administer than other methods. Can be completed off the job, saving productive time. Provides large breadth of coverage. | Time-consuming and expensive to develop. Impersonal approach between analyst and respondent may have adverse effects on cooperation and motivation. |

SOURCE: Adapted from Cascio (1995:137)

- Data – such as working with information.
- People – such as in communicating.
- Things – such as working with machines, tools and equipment.

The FJA is designed to measure the complexity of data, people and things within each task in a job. The main drawback of the FJA is that it takes considerable time to learn to use, is time-consuming and is costly to the organisation.

### Management Position Description Questionnaire (MPDQ)

The analysis of managerial jobs presents a significant challenge because of inequality between positions, different levels in the organisational hierarchy, and the type of industry in which the jobs are positioned. The MPDQ is a list of 208 items that relate to the concerns and responsibilities of managers. The latest version of the MPDQ consists of items grouped in fifteen sections in order to reduce the time it requires to complete and to help with the interpretation of responses. Other methods of job analysis have been developed for a specific purpose, such as the Task Inventory Analysis (TIA), which is a collection of methods that are branches of the US Air Force task inventory method. The technique is used to determine the knowledge, skills and abilities needed to perform a job successfully. Methods Analysis is a systematic means of job analysis for determining the standard time for various tasks through the use of motion study.

## 7.6   Problems in job analysis

The different approaches to job analysis vary in their effectiveness. Unfortunately most job analyses are undertaken without specific goals in mind. Without a definite objective, much of the data collected in interviews, questionnaires, and other methods of job analysis is wasted. In addition, unless the purpose of the job analysis is clear, the company cannot take informed decisions about which data collection technique to use or what kind of information to seek (Schultz and Schultz 1994:83).

Byars and Rue (1997:94–7) discuss some of the problems resulting from natural human behaviour and the nature of the job analysis process:

- *Top management support is missing.* Without communication from top management that they support and encourage the job analysis exercise, full and honest participation might not be forthcoming from the employees.
- *Only a single means and source are used for gathering data.* Very often a job analyst uses only one method of data collection, when a combination of methods could provide better data.
- *The supervisor and the job-holder do not participate in the design of job analysis.* When a job analyst assumes exclusive responsibility for a project and excludes the supervisor and job-holder, distrust, suspicion, and a lack of cooperation are probable consequences.
- *No training or motivation exists for job-holders.* While job-holders are potentially a great source of job information and are called upon to share this information during job analysis, they are seldom trained to generate quality data. They are also almost never rewarded for providing good data.
- *Employees are not allowed sufficient time to complete the analysis.* Supervisors and managers often view the job analysis as a waste of time. The process is rushed through, and inadequate or inaccurate information is produced.
- *Activities may be distorted.* Without proper training and communication, employees may submit distorted data, either intentionally or not.
- *There is a failure to critique the job.* A common mistake made by job analysts is to accept reported job data without investigating whether the job is being done correctly or whether improvements can be made.

In addition, Carrell et al. (1997:89–90) mention the following problems associated with job analysis:

- *Employee fear.* In the past, job analysis was commonly used to expand jobs while reducing the total number of employees, to increase production rates and decrease employees' pay, and to determine minimum numbers of employees required when embarking on a downsizing programme. Employee involvement and representation will help overcome employee fears.
- *The need to update the information gathered.* As job content changes, it is necessary to keep track of those jobs that are affected by these changes. If this is not done, the job analysis information quickly becomes outdated and could result in undue costs for the company if incorrect and obsolete information is used in strategic organisational activities.
- *Only one or two employees hold the job.* This situation often results in an analysis of the person's performance and not of the job itself. The analyst must look at what the job should entail, not at how well or how poorly one employee performs the job.

## 7.7   Job descriptions

### 7.7.1   The job description debate

The traditional job description has been the subject of much debate, especially during the final years of the 20th century. Risher (1997:13–14) believes that it was the principles of scientific management formulated by Frederick W Taylor nearly a century ago, that led to the development of job analysis and documentation practices 'that result in ten-page job descriptions'. It takes about 10 hours for a trained job analyst to develop a traditional job description, which usually sets the parameters for a narrowly defined job, with specific duties and limited expectations of a worker's contributions.

'The end of jobs' and 'a jobless society' have become euphemisms for new methods of organising work, geared to meet the business challenges of global competition and technological change. Modernists feel that there is no longer a place in our organisations for the rigid type of job that only requires specified work to be done and does not 'add value'. The demise of the traditional 'job' would thus also mean the end of the job description.

Holloway (2001) believes that the job description debate should be founded on the reasons why job descriptions have been popular in our organisations. They provide:
- Guidance to people as to what to do and how to do it.
- Information that could be used in staffing the job – not only technical skill requirements, but also information about the nature of the person best suited for the work.
- A basis for the directories that enable people in the organisation to know who does what and who knows what.

Traditional job descriptions should be expanded in order to include multiple roles, responsibilities and areas of expertise. Job descriptions should focus on the relationship between the job and the people who carry out the job. Another belief is that the job-holder should compile the job description, allowing the description to develop as the job itself develops.

However, there are many human resources and business experts who believe that employees cannot contribute to organisational success without an awareness of the structures and limits imposed on a job by a specific job description. Figure 7.6 offers an example of a specific job description. This type of job description, with its detailed tasks, duties and responsibilities, best fits a bureaucratic organisational structure with well-defined boundaries, and allows the practitioner to undertake all the tasks previously discussed in Section 7.2 (Gómez-Mejía et al. 1998:68).

## Encounter 7.1

THE QUESTION OF JOB DESCRIPTIONS

Human resources practitioners continue to struggle with the problem of whether job descriptions are really essential, and useful, for an organisation. During March 2001, this matter prompted an on-line discussion between members of the South African Board for Personnel Practitioners (SABPP). Various thoughts were offered, such as the opinion of Norman Kemp. He wrote:

The question of job descriptions is a vexed one. It depends on what the job description is going to be used for. It appears that many practitioners are suggesting that job descriptions should be performance-based, which makes sense. However, traditionally, the job description was used for job evaluation purposes in order to attach a grading to a job and a salary for the relevant grade. This happens to this day, and annually we get the FSA and PE Corporate salary surveys showing the going rates for the respective grades, be it Hay, Paterson or Peromnes. Most organisations subscribe to one or the other and use the survey to guide them in determining salaries per grade.

I have recently had first hand experience of writing a job description for a certain position in an organisation which employs approximately 40 people in the position for which the JD [Job Description] was written. My argument is that each incumbent should have had their individual job description evaluated as, although they all have the same job title, there are differences. However, the consultant from the organisation that currently holds the Peromnes franchise insisted that there should be a generic job description. The result is a job description that is of very little value, and of course the job description was evaluated by this consultant at the level of the

lowest common denominator, so those who offer more or can offer a lot more than the lowest common denominator, are not receiving a fair deal. But that is what happens when generic descriptions are used.

This is what makes the whole question of job descriptions a vexed issue, and should they become verbal JDs, it could result in people being treated even more unfairly.

SOURCE: Prof. Norman Kemp: Head of Department (Business Management) Port Elizabeth Technikon, personal communication

Not many companies are able to function entirely without job descriptions. Many companies use their own terminology (such as 'job profile'), and design their own format of the written document. The need for greater flexibility has resulted in a number of organisations replacing the traditional job description with a general job description – a concise list of bullet points or accountability statements, often limited to one sheet of paper. Figure 7.7 shows an example of a general job description. This type of job description suits a flat or boundaryless organisational structure, where workflow strategies emphasise innovation, flexibility, and loose work planning. In this way, the fluidity of job content is catered for, and is, perhaps, the way of the future (Dessler 1997:110; Wright and Storey 1997:213).

### 7.7.2 Developing a job description

No matter what it is called, or what it looks like, a job description is a statement of the data collected in the job analysis process. A specific job description usually contains the following information:

**Identification information**

The first part of the job description offers:
- The job title.
- The location of the job (department, branch, etc.).
- The reporting structure.

**Figure 7.6** Specific job description

Job Title:        Senior computer sales assistant
Location:         Durban
Compiled by:   J Sibisi
Verified by:     P Jonas
Date:              January 2004

**Reporting structure**

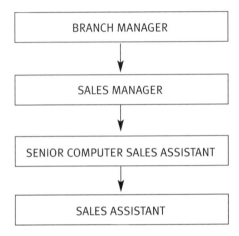

**Job summary**
To assist and advise customers in the selection of computer hardware and software.

**Job duties and responsibilities**
1  Demonstrate equipment and software, and advise customers on different payment methods in order to meet sales target of R400 000 over a six-month period. Advise potential customers of additional software packages that can enhance their purchases and increase organisational sales.
2  Organise delivery of equipment sales to meet the customer's needs. Ensure that equipment is installed to the customer's satisfaction within 12 hours of delivery.
3  Answer after-sales customer queries immediately and provide technical care. Provide telephonic advice and, in an emergency, ensure that a technician provides personal service.
4  Develop and maintain a computerised stock control system. Control stock accurately, and interact with the Sales Manager regarding strategic requirements.
5  Monitor performance of junior sales assistant. Train, mentor, and assess the development of subordinate.

## Figure 7.7  General job description

Job Title:        Senior computer sales assistant
Location:        Durban
Compiled by:   J Sibisi
Verified by:    P Jonas
Date:            January 2004

**Reporting structure:**
Reports to Sales Manager; 1 subordinate (Sales Assistant)

**Accountabilities:**
- equipment and software sales
- sales deliveries and installations
- after-sales service
- stock control system
- performance of sales assistant

---

- The compiler of the job description.
- The date of the job analysis.
- Verification (name of the person authorising, or approving the job description).

**Notes for the compiler of a job description:**
- Do not refer to a specific gender in the job title. For example, use 'Sales Person' rather than 'Salesman'.
- Update job descriptions regularly. A job description reflecting a date that is more than two years old has low credibility and may provide obsolete information.
- Insist that the supervisor, or department manager, verifies the job descriptions of jobs in his/her department. This will ensure that there is no misrepresentation of actual duties and responsibilities.

**Job summary**

This is a short written statement that concisely summarises the purpose of the job.

**Job duties and responsibilities**

This section must be comprehensive and accurate as it influences all other parts of the job description. Job duties and responsibilities explain what is done, how it is done, and why it is done.

**Notes for the compiler of a job description:**
- List the three to five most important responsibilities of the job, beginning with an action verb.
- List one, or more, important job duties associated with each responsibility, also starting each with an action verb.
- Write clearly, unambiguously, and concisely but do not omit any important responsibilities or duties.
- Any job performance standards, time limits, and abnormal working conditions are identified in this section of the job description.

Some organisations, especially those that have a pay-for-skills compensation structure, combine the job description and job specification, and list the skills required to do the job successfully, instead of the responsibilities and duties. The resulting document is not a job description in the true sense of the word, but becomes more a 'skills profile'.

## 7.8   Job specifications

Dessler (1997:107) states that the job specification takes the job description and answers the question: What human traits and experience are required to do this job well?

### 7.8.1  Developing the job specification

The Knowledge, Skills, and Abilities (KSAs) associated with a particular job can be obtained by allowing the present job incumbent to complete a form, such as the one in Figure 7.8. As it is very easy for the employee to 'inflate' the personal requirements, different workers doing similar jobs should all be requested to complete the document without access to each other. A knowledgeable supervisor or manager must also provide information for the specification. These different inputs and perspectives should provide a job specification which is as close to accurate as possible.

Knowledge, skills and abilities that the incumbent possesses, but are not related to the job, must be excluded. In terms of the Employment Equity Act, the job specification must only contain information regarding the essential personal requirements. Also, stating the desirable requirements would exclude certain future job applicants and could amount to an unfair labour practice.

Job experience, job training and qualifications can be included in the job specification, but one must always be careful not to be too rigid in stating these requirements. We feel that the word 'well' should be deleted from Dessler's question quoted at the beginning of this section, and that it should read: 'What human traits and experience are required to do this job?' The emphasis should be placed on collecting information that specifies how the job should be done and should not refer to the level of performance.

## 7.9   A glimpse of ergonomics

We have studied the phenomenon of a job in detail in this chapter but we have not looked at the important area of the relationship between men and women, and the environment. A small section in a chapter such as this one cannot even begin to cover all the aspects of ergonomics in which we, as human resources practitioners, would be interested. However, we cannot close this chapter without providing an introduction to ergonomics.

Ergonomics is defined as the relationship between humans and the environment. The environment referred to is not only one environment – we usually think of nature when we talk about the environment. We live in and interact in many different environments, such as the natural environment (trees, plants, flowers, and water that offer us peace and relaxation). We use the transport environment (cars, busses, taxis and trains) to get to work, to shopping areas, to church and so on. The fittest amongst us make use of the sport environment (the different sports in which we participate such as soccer, rugby, cricket, and swimming). There are many other environments, but the one in which we are interested is the work environment, more specifically the relationship between humans and the work environment.

The objective of the human resources practitioner is to remove anything that is causing an imbalance or disequilibrium in the work environment and to add what is necessary to promote equilibrium or a balanced relationship.

By removing unsafe items from the working environment it is made more pleasant. Balance is restored and the relationship is now balanced and harmonised.

Every person in a work environment strives to establish a comfort zone, an area surrounding his- or herself, either physically or psycho-

---

**Figure 7.8** A sample job specification

| Job Title: | Senior computer sales assistant |
|---|---|
| Location: | Durban |
| Job specification compiled by: | J Sibisi |
| Job specification verified by: | P Jonas |
| Date: | January 2004 |

**Knowledge**
All Microsoft Windows programs; Internet; DVD functions
**Skills**
Installation, set-up, trouble-shooting
**Abilities**
Problem-solving
**Qualifications**
Three-year tertiary qualification in Information Technology or four years' relevant experience
**Training**
No special training required
**Experience**
Four years' relevant experience or three year tertiary qualification in Information Technology

logically, in which the balance of relationships is undisturbed. To create and maintain this balance, there must be zero tolerance for mistakes, obstacles or defects. This means that mistakes, obstacles and defects are unacceptable, otherwise we will find ourselves in an unbalanced environment, causing problems that must be solved ergonomically in order to bring about equilibrium and a state of tolerance in the comfort zone.

Readers or learners might wonder how this links up to the topic of job analysis. We know by now that the job description and job specification are the physical manifestations of job analysis in the form of valuable company documentation. The ergonomic principle is drawn into the nature of these documents by ensuring that the duties, tasks, responsibilities and KSAs that a job requires do not bring about a state of imbalance and do not spoil the comfort zone of the job-holder. According to Gorkin (2002), some of the components of a dysfunctional or imbalanced work environment are:

- A work environment that is driven by crises.
- Rapid and unpredictable change during downsizing or an expansionary mode.
- Destructive communication style that is excessively aggressive, condescending, explosive or defensive.
- Authoritarian leadership.
- A dismissive attitude with little interest in people and policy evaluation.
- Double standards that suggest that there are different policies and procedures for management and employees.
- Unresolved grievances.
- Emotionally troubled personnel.
- Repetitive, boring work.
- Faulty equipment and deficient training.
- Hazardous working conditions.
- A culture of violence.

## 7.10 Job analysis and quality assurance

At the 1995 IPM (Institute of People Management) annual convention there were a number of debates regarding the nature and content of job analysis. These discussions brought to light the different modes of thinking of unionists and managers, and indicated a need for quality assurance and consistency in this area. Although the discussion in this chapter has indicated that job analysis offers a starting point for all human resources activities, it is important to take a holistic view of people-related functions in an organisation. Van Wyk (1996:19–22) states that remuneration, industrial relations and HR development form more of a functional whole today than ever before. Policy decisions on one aspect impact on another. It follows that job analysis efforts must contain the highest levels of quality throughout the process, starting with the involvement of employees, to the development of job descriptions and job specifications, and culminating with evaluation of the success of the process.

## 7.11 Conclusion

In a world where the only thing that is certain is change, job analysis is an anchor that steadies the fast-moving organisational ship. It is clear from this chapter that all our dealings with people in the workplace are based on the jobs that they do, even if these jobs are continuously metabolising. Job analysis provides a platform from which we can manipulate the organisation through its jobs and in so doing, strive for effectiveness and success.

## Summary

- Although many jobs have become defunct over the past few years, new jobs have been created and existing jobs have been adapted to conform to the new technological order. Job analysis allows the practitioner to stay abreast of these changes in order to achieve success in the management of workforce planning, job evaluation and compensation, recruitment, selection, and placement, orientation, training and development, performance management, career planning, ergonomics, safety, organisational restructuring, and labour relations.

- Job analysis is a systematic process involving information collection by means of job-orientated or worker-orientated methods. Job-orientated methods include the use of questionnaires, interviews, observations, and workers' diaries. Worker-orientated methods include collecting information regarding critical incidents, and using the PAQ or the FJA. There are certain advantages and disadvantages to each of these data-collection methods.

- The rapidly changing business environment necessitates that job analysis is conducted from a strategic point of view.

- Job analysis is an indispensable organisational tool, but the job analyst must be aware of the possible problems that can occur during the process.

- Although the job description debate continues, most organisations cannot function without this document. The typical job description contains information on reporting structures, duties and responsibilities, standards of performance and working conditions. Job specifications usually centre around the KSAs required to perform the job adequately.

- Ergonomics is the relationship between humans and the environment. Ergonomists strive to attain a balanced environment in which there is zero tolerance for mistakes and obstacles in the comfort zone.

- Quality assurance is a non-negotiable requirement as job analysis impacts on every other HR function in the organisation.

## Case study
## Giving health-care workers a helping hand

St Marks is a small rural hospital with a ratio of 20 surgical patients to one (each) nursing sister. There has always been a shortage of staff, particularly in the laundry room. The nurses help the laundry staff by loading dirty linen into the washing machines and folding the clean laundry. All the nurses are involved in laundry duties, and this appears to have become part of their job. They usually perform these duties on their free days, but do not complain as they are paid at overtime rates when working in the laundry.

There are usually no empty hospital beds, and the 10 nursing sisters are kept very busy while attending to their patients. Recently there has been an increasing incidence of back injuries among the nurses and a considerable amount of lost-time hours. The medical superintendent realised that this situation had to be rectified and he formed a task team, with himself as the leader, in order to ascertain why the nursing staff were repeatedly succumbing to back injuries. The other four members of the task team comprised two laboratory assistants, the matron, and a visiting doctor.

The task team interviewed all the nurses and the cleaning staff and discovered that the nurses were lifting heavy patients as well as loads of laundry that could weigh up to 20 kilograms. Many nurses complained of lower back problems and an inability to perform standard physical tasks. They assumed awkward postures while performing their tasks and very often the matron inspected the wards during their tea-breaks, which dissuaded the nurses from leaving the wards while the matron was there. Consequently, they worked long hours without a break. Much of the equipment, such as the portable X-ray machines, was old and heavy and required a strong force to be manoeuvered into position.

After the task team had gathered all the information, they held a meeting at which they discussed the problems that had become apparent as a result of their investigation. They agreed that the situation could not continue, as the service they provided to the patients was their highest priority. They realised that these problems were curtailing the quality of nursing care that they offered at St Marks. Their biggest problem was that they did not know how to proceed in their search for solutions.

## Questions

1 What course of action would you prescribe in order to standardise the information that the task team had obtained?
2 What method, or methods, would you have used to collect job data?
3 Would you have developed job descriptions for the nursing staff? Motivate your answer.
4 Indicate the problems that are causing an imbalance in the environment and suggest solutions to the hospital's problems based on ergonomic principles.

## Experiential exercise No. 1

PURPOSE  To investigate whether organisations use job analysis as the basis of their human resources functions.

INTRODUCTION  Often managers are too busy to become involved in undertaking personnel duties. If the organisation does not have a human resources department, HR activities usually take the last place in their order of priorities.

TASK  In groups of four to five students, undertake a survey of at least five companies. It would be interesting to survey a cross-section of different sizes of companies and different industries. Develop a questionnaire that will produce enough information for a report to be written regarding the status of job analysis in each company. Use questions such as: Does the company use a specific job analysis method? What do they use job analysis for? Who in the organisation has the responsibility for carrying out job analysis? Do they feel it is necessary to carry out job analysis? Conclude the report with recommendations for improvement, if necessary.

## Experiential exercise No. 2

PURPOSE  To produce a job description and job specification from job analysis data.

INTRODUCTION  Many companies do not develop or maintain job descriptions or job specifications, as the nature of jobs changes so rapidly. However, other organisations believe that these documents are essential for the maintenance of performance levels.

TASK  Develop a specific job description and job specification for any job you choose. Use one or more of the job analysis methods to collect your information. Use the guidelines contained in this chapter to ensure that the documents comply with all requirements.

## Chapter questions

1 How can you make use of the information provided by a job analysis?
2 Which job analysis method, or methods, would you recommend for developing a job description of a computer programmer, and why?
3 Discuss the problems associated with job analysis.
4 Are there some business situations in which it is better to not use any job descriptions? Discuss.
5 The production department at ABC Foods Ltd. is experiencing a high percentage of absenteeism. The production manager is convinced that this factor is the cause of the department's inability to meet deadlines. Using an ergonomic approach, discuss how a HR practitioner would attempt to solve this problem.

## Bibliography

BYARS, L.L. & RUE, L.W. 1997. *Human resource management, 5th edition.* Irwin, Chicago.

CARRELL, M.R., ELBERT, N.F., HATFIELD, R.D., GROBLER, P.A., MARX, M. & VAN DER SCHYF, S. 1997. *Human resources management in South Africa.* Pearson Education, Cape

Town.

CASCIO, W.F. 1995. *Managing human resources: Productivity, quality of work life, profits.* McGraw-Hill Companies, New York.

DESSLER, G. 1997. *Human resource management, 7th edition.* (Prentice-Hall), Pearson Education Inc.

GÓMEZ-MEJÍA, L.R., BALKIN, D.B., & CARDY, R.L. 1998. *Managing human resources, 2nd edition.* (Prentice-Hall), Pearson Education Inc.

GORKIN, M. 2002. 'Key components of a dangerously dysfunctional work environment'. *Workforce* (www.workforce.com). Reprinted with permission of Copyright Clearance Center.

HOLLOWAY, P. 2001. 'Is it time for a new look at job descriptions?' *Workforce* (www.workforce.com). Reprinted with permission of Copyright Clearance Center.

IVANCEVICH, J.M. 2001. *Human resource management, 8th edition.* McGraw-Hill Companies, New York.

LUNDY, O. & COWLING, A. 1996. *Strategic human resource management.* Routledge, London.

MCCORMICK, E.J., JEANNERET, P.R. & MECHAM, R.C. 1972. 'A study of job characteristics and job dimensions as based on the Position Analysis Questionnaire (PAQ)'. *Journal of Applied Psychology,* 56:347–368.

MONDY, R.W. & NOE, R.M. 1996. *Human resource management, 6th edition.* (Prentice-Hall), Pearson Education Inc.

RISHER, H. 1997. 'The end of jobs: Planning and managing rewards in the new work paradigm'. *Compensations and Benefits Review,* 29(1):13–17.

SCHULTZ, D.P. & SCHULTZ, S.E. 1994. *Psychology and work today: An introduction to industrial and organizational psychology, 6th edition.* Macmillan, Englewood Cliffs.

STERN, M. 2002. 'What are the key items to include in an audit plan?' *Workforce,* March (www.workforce.com). Reprinted with permission of Copyright Clearance Center.

VAN WYK, S. 1996. 'Levelheaded approach to job evaluation'. *People Dynamics,* 14(2):19–22. Reprinted with permission of Copyright Clearance Center.

WRIGHT, M., & STOREY, J. 1997. 'Recruitment and selection'. In Beardwell, I. & Holden, L. (eds.) *Human resource management: A contemporary perspective, 2nd edition.* (Pitman), Pearson Education (UK).

## Websites

The Ergonomics Society: www.ergonomics.org.uk

Occupational information Network: www.onet-center.org

HR Today (Canada): www.hrtoday.com

The Center for Office Technology: www.cot.org

Innovative Practices labs: www.iplabs.com/hr/index/htm

Research and practice in human resources management (Singapore): www.fba.nus.edu.sg/rphr/Astart.htm

# Appendix 7.1

**A job analysis questionnaire**

JOB TITLE: _____   Date completed: _____

Name and job title of person completing this form: _____

1   Complete the following reporting structure:

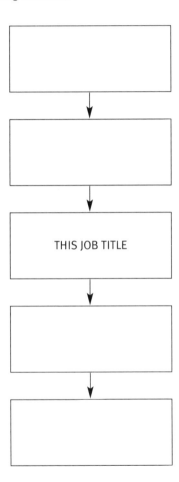

2   What are the main duties and responsibilities carried out in this job?

| Duties/responsibilities | Percentage of time spent | Daily/weekly/monthly |
|---|---|---|
| | | |
| | | |
| | | |
| | | |
| | | |
| | | |
| | | |
| | | |
| | | |
| | | |

3   What machines or equipment are operated during the course of the above duties?

| Machines/equipment operated | Percentage of time spent | Daily/weekly/monthly |
|---|---|---|
| | | |
| | | |
| | | |
| | | |
| | | |
| | | |
| | | |
| | | |
| | | |

4   Are there any extreme or abnormal working conditions associated with this job (e.g. extreme heat or cold, noise levels, etc.)?

5   What decisions are involved in carrying out the duties and responsibilities of this job?

| Decisions | Percentage of time spent | Daily/weekly/monthly |
|---|---|---|
|  |  |  |
|  |  |  |
|  |  |  |
|  |  |  |
|  |  |  |
|  |  |  |
|  |  |  |
|  |  |  |
|  |  |  |
|  |  |  |

6   What level of education is required to perform this job adequately?

7   What type of job training is required to perform this job adequately?

8   What special skills and/or experiences are required to perform this job adequately?

9   What unusual aspects about the job have not been covered in the previous questions?

THANK YOU FOR COMPLETING THIS JOB ANALYSIS QUESTIONNAIRE

# 8

# Workforce planning and recruitment

## HB Schultz

## Learning outcomes

At the end of this chapter the learner should be able to:

- Explain how workforce planning forms part of strategic organisational planning.
- Examine the internal and external factors that influence workforce planning.
- Assist a HR practitioner to carry out the steps in the workforce planning process.
- Describe the role of various staff members in workforce planning.
- Compile a recruitment policy for an organisation.
- Discuss the factors that influence recruitment.
- Decide whether internal or external recruitment sources and methods would be preferable under specific circumstances.
- Consider and make proposals on the use of current and future trends in recruitment.
- Offer some legal considerations in recruitment and explain the impact of quality assurance on workforce planning and recruitment.

## Key words and concepts

- compressed work-weeks
- contingent workers
- employee leasing
- flexi-time
- forecasting techniques
- job-sharing
- labour demand
- labour supply
- long-range, middle-range, and short-range planning
- Management Information System (MIS)
- skills inventory
- telecommuting
- workforce planning

### Illustrative case
### A broken heart

One of the wonders of modern medical science is the ability to give someone a new heart. Heart transplants give new life to recipients who need them. Through their own deaths, donors provide new life to those who are dying. The renowned heart surgeon Christiaan Neethling Barnard was the pioneer of heart transplants. Professor Barnard made medical history on 3 December 1967, when, with a 'gigantic leap of faith and skill', he and his medical team at Groote Schuur Hospital transplanted Denise Darvall's heart into Louis Washkansky.

It was this momentous transplant that was to send Chris Barnard on a trajectory that few medical pioneers were to experience. He captured the imagination and interest of the public worldwide. Described once by a journalist as an 'indefatigable person, carried by a remarkable spirit of adventure', Barnard came from humble beginnings as a missionary's son in Beaufort West. It is said that his family's poverty inspired him to enroll at the University of Cape Town (UCT) to become a doctor. He was well known for his high intelligence and outstanding surgical skills. His results at the Red Cross Children's Hospital for correcting congenital disorders of the heart were remarkable.

In an article in the *South African Medical Journal* (Volume 72, Issue 5, December 1987) to celebrate the 20th anniversary of the first human heart transplant, Chris Barnard reflected on this accomplishment.

> Dr Terry O' Donovan removed the (donor's) heart from the chest and carried it to the adjacent recipient operating room, to which I had returned. Louis Washkansky's heart was then similarly removed, and, for the first time in my life, I stared into an empty chest. At that moment, the full impact of what I was attempting became abundantly clear to me.

Louis Washkansky lived another 18 days but many more heart transplants followed and became a standard form of cardiac treatment.

The first heart transplant could not have been achieved without the skill and support of a large team – cardiolo-gists, radiologists, anaesthetists, technicians, nurses, immunologists, pathologists, and in particular, Professor Val Schrire, head of the Cardiac Clinic. In the course of his work Dr Barnard became famous as a practical surgeon and teacher. He inspired and taught many surgeons from all over the world. Thus he has left a legacy of skills and techniques for helping those with heart disease. Barnard held the Chair of Cardiothoracic Surgery in the Faculty until 1983, when severe arthritis forced his early retirement. He spent the ensuing years providing international advice about cardiac matters, on research, and maintaining the Austrian-based Chris Barnard Foundation for children. He wrote several books, including his autobiographical *One Life* and the last, *Fifty Ways to a Healthy Heart*. Chris Barnard's achievements were based on the same perfectionist foundations in planning and recruiting the specialists and experts that were necessary for the supreme functioning of his medical team.

## 8.1   Introduction

Workforce planning is one of the most important issues in which human resources professionals are involved. But the task of actually implementing workforce planning is daunting because it is so difficult to define. Every organisation must be able to attract a sufficient number of job candidates who have the abilities and aptitudes needed to add value to the company. Recruitment supplies a pool of suitable applicants who can enter the selection process. Recruiting activities occur when someone in the organisation decides what kind of employees are needed and how many. If proactive planning has taken place, filling vacant positions is not a daunting task.

An integrated and holistic resourcing and workforce planning process ensures that the right people are in the right roles to meet the current organisational profit plan.

We commence this chapter by introducing the reader or learner to the concept of workforce planning as part of the strategic planning of an organisation. We explain the factors that influence workforce planning and the steps in the workforce planning process. We take a brief look at the role of staff members in workforce planning before moving on to investigate the basics of recruitment policy and factors that influence recruitment. Internal and external recruitment sources and methods are examined and an overview of current and future recruitment trends is provided. We conclude the chapter by discussing some legal considerations and the impact of quality assurance on workforce planning and recruitment.

## 8.2.  Workforce planning as part of strategic organisational planning

Sullivan (2002:46–50) explains that workforce planning is a systematic, fully integrated organisational process that involves proactively planning ahead to avoid talent surpluses or shortages. It is based on the premise that a company can be staffed more efficiently if it forecasts its talent needs as well as the actual supply of talent that is, or will be, available. By planning ahead, the human resources function can provide managers with the right number of people, with the right skills, in the right place, and at the right time. Workforce planning might more accurately be called talent planning, because it integrates the forecasting elements of all of the functions that relate to talent – recruiting, retention, redeployment, and leadership and employee development.

Human resources practitioners need to operate within the business cycle if they wish to become strategic business partners. It is crucial that the 'talent inventory' (or skilled employees) is maintained at the right levels in order to comply with the requirements of hiring and retention issues.

### 8.2.1  The impact of good workforce planning

Effective workforce planning influences the state of the business in the following ways:
- *It eliminates surprises.* Good workforce planning allows rapid skills replacement so that departments can continue to function smoothly.
- *It smooths out business cycles.* There are no delays in meeting production goals, employees have the required skills, and employees have been developed to meet project needs.
- *It identifies problems early.* Human resources practitioners can warn managers of minor problems before they turn into major ones.
- *It prevents problems.* Efficient workforce planning results in lower turnover rates, lower labour costs, and no layoffs.
- *It takes advantages of opportunities.* One of the objectives of workforce planning should be to identify skilled workers before they are needed, and to ensure that the company retains them until the time that their skills are required.
- *It improves the image of the HR department.* Good workforce planning means that HR professionals build their credibility and inspire confidence in their ability to maintain an effective workforce.

## 8.3  Key areas of workforce planning

Workforce planning systems can be categorised into three basic focus areas.

### 8.3.1  The talent forecast

Talent forecasting is a process for predicting changes in the demand for, and the supply of, talent. Forecasts are broken down into the following areas:
- Estimated increases or decreases in company growth, output, and revenue.

- Estimated changes in talent needs that result from organisational growth.
- Projections of future vacancies.
- Estimates of the internal and external availability of the talent needed to meet forecasts.

### 8.3.2 Talent action plans

Talent action plans outline which specific actions all managers have to take in terms of talent management. These plans aim to attract, retain, redeploy, and develop the talent a company needs in order to meet the forecasted quantity and quality of employees. Talent action plans comprise three general activities:

- Sourcing and recruiting an adequate supply of leaders and key talent.
- Identifying and grooming internal development and the supply of qualified leaders and key talent.
- Forecasting the gap between talent needs and its availability.

### 8.3.3 The integration plan

If a company is to meet its forecasted staffing needs, action plans must be fully implemented. They must be integrated into every aspect of workforce management, including communication and the identification of potential supporters and resisters.

## 8.4 Steps in the workforce planning process

We have already seen how important it is to integrate the plans of the human resources department with the strategic business plans of the organisation. Knowledge of where the company is heading is very important for planners, as firms that do not conduct workforce planning may not be able to meet their future labour needs (a labour shortage) or may have to resort to layoffs (in the case of a labour surplus). Armed with this strategic knowledge, the workforce planning process can begin.

### 8.4.1 Forecasting labour demand

The first activity in workforce planning entails forecasting labour demand, that is, predicting the estimated number of workers the organisation will need in the future. Gómez-Mejía et al. (1998:149) state that in the past, many companies avoided planning the workforce, or developed superficial plans, because HR staff were too busy doing administrative work, or they believed that planning is always a 'hit and miss affair', or they were not trained to use forecasting techniques. These days many computer companies offer sophisticated and powerful software packages that large and small companies can easily use.

Even if a company opts to use computer-forecasting techniques, the planners and users of these programmes should have a basic working knowledge of forecasting methods.

**Forecasting techniques**

Forecasting techniques can be categorised as quantitative and qualitative. Quantitative methods are used more often, probably because it is believed that forecasting is more accurate if one has figures to work with. However, quantitative forecasting models have two main limitations: first, they rely heavily on past data or previous relationships between staffing levels and other organisational variables, and second, most of the quantitative techniques were created between 1950 and the early 1970s, when the large firms of that era had stable environments and workforces.

Quantitative techniques are less appropriate today, when relationships that held in the past may not hold in the future, and when firms are struggling with rapid technological change and intense global competition.

Qualitative techniques rely on the qualitative judgments of experts or the subjective estimates of labour demand or supply. These experts are usually top managers, who are involved in the strategic planning of the organisation and who are also familiar with the demands and requirements of the plant floor. They are flexible enough to incorporate any factors or conditions the expert feels should be considered. However, these subjective methods may be less accurate than those obtained through quantitative techniques.

Quantitative and qualitative techniques are outlined in Figure 8.1.

### 8.4.2 Estimating labour supply

This activity entails estimating the availability of workers with the required skills to meet the company's labour needs in the future. The labour supply may come from existing employees (the internal labour market) or from outside the organisation (the external labour market). Estimations begin inside the organisation because the labour information is readily available and is more accurate than information obtained externally. Skills inventories and Management Information Systems (MISs) are normally used to provide this information.

#### Skills inventories and management information systems

In both large and small organisations, workforce information is often computerised. In addition to storing data, software packages can supply answers to many queries, such as 'Which of our current staff members are due to retire within the next five years, in which departments are they currently employed, and what qualifications, experience, training, and competencies do they possess?'

Typical information found in a skills inventory or a MIS is:
- Personal, or bibliographical data.
- Education and qualifications (including degrees, licences, certifications).
- Service record (including significant work experience).
- Results of performance assessments.
- Language skills.
- Training and development programmes attended.
- Community and industry leadership responsibilities.

---

**Figure 8.1** Quantitative and qualitative techniques of labour forecasting

**Quantitative techniques**
- moving average
- exponential smoothing
- trends projections
- regression
- linear programming
- actuarial models
- simulations
- probability matrixes
- first-order Markov model
- semi-Markov model

**Qualitative Techniques**
- delphi technique
- nominal group technique

SOURCE: Gómez-Mejía et al. (1998)

---

- Disciplinary actions.
- Awards received.
- Career prospects.

The Department of Labour also publishes initiatives for the provision of skilled workers, and these can assist the employer when the organisation cannot completely provide the labour supply.

### 8.4.3 Implementation of the workforce plan

The results of the labour demand forecast and labour supply estimation determine the actions that must be planned. Gómez-Mejía et al. (1998:147) offer three scenarios and the responses the organisation can make to each scenario. These responses are listed in Figure 8.2.

### 8.4.4 Control and evaluation of the workforce planning system

Exercising control and carrying out evaluation of workforce planning systems guides human resources activities that identify devi-

## Figure 8.2 Ways of implementing the workforce plan

**Labour demand exceeds labour supply**
Response
- training or retraining
- succession planning
- promotion from within
- recruitment from outside
- subcontracting
- use of part-timers or temporary workers
- use of overtime

**Labour supply exceeds labour demand**
Response
- pay cuts
- reduced hours
- work sharing
- voluntary early retirements
- inducements to quit
- layoffs

**Labour demand equals labour supply**
Response
- replacement of quits from inside or outside
- internal transfers and redeployment

---

ations from the plan, and their causes. Quantitative objectives make the control and evaluation process more objective and measure deviations from the plan more precisely. Quantitative measures are used more frequently in established planning systems, where key comparisons might include the following:

- Actual staffing levels against forecast staffing requirements.
- Actual levels of labour productivity against anticipated levels of productivity.
- Actual personnel flow rates against desired rates.
- Action programmes implemented against action programmes planned.
- Actual results of action programmes implemented against expected results.
- Labour and action programme costs against budgets.

- Ratios of action programme benefits to action programme costs.

In newly instituted planning systems, evaluation is more likely to be qualitative, because supply-and-demand forecasts are more often based on 'hunches' and subjective opinions (Cascio 1995:157).

## 8.5   Pre-need hiring

When a person resigns, usually a hiring requisition is created and, after a space of time, another person is hired. If the new hire requires initial training, or if there is a long learning curve before s/he becomes productive, managers probably accept this as 'the way it is'. Sometimes the vacant position is frozen for a time, in order to save money. However, these delays can cost an organisation a great deal of money in lost margins and market share, especially if the vacancy is in a key position. Sullivan (2000) suggests that to solve this problem, high growth businesses should use pre-need hiring, which is a strategy that is designed to ensure that there is no significant delay in the product development or delivery cycle as a result of a shortage of talent. Some of the approaches to pre-need hiring are as follows:

- *Yield Model,* which is a forecasting model that indicates how many people a manager will need to hire in order to reach the projected amount of revenue growth.
- *Pre-need hiring,* results in hiring an employee for a particular job a month or more before the person is actually needed.
- *Designating evergreen jobs,* forces a recruiter to become aware of jobs that are particularly hard to fill. A continuous search and hire mode is used for these jobs.
- *'Ramp-up' time hire,* which specifies certain jobs that have a significant learning curve and thus a long delay between the hire date and when the employee normally reaches the minimum levels of productivity.

- *Rapid growth jobs,* which are jobs that are projected to grow rapidly in number within the next 12 to 18 months.
- *Cyclical jobs,* which are the result of seasonal fluctuations and product cycles, and not necessarily the result of a long-term need.
- *'Prepare for promotion' jobs,* which can be the result of promoting people in the position(s) just below a vacancy in the job structure, resulting in having to hire people in advance of the promotions in order to ensure a smooth transition and no loss in productivity.
- *Pre-qualifying candidates,* the result of potential hires between those sourced and those identified, and whose names are kept in a database for retrieval until such time as a suitable job actually becomes open.

Most of the above approaches in pre-need hiring would result in 'over-hiring', and no practitioner would use all these tools at once. However, their availability provides the HR professional with the opportunity of enforcing workforce planning strategically.

---

## Encounter 8.1

AROUND THE WORLD IN HR WAYS

A diverse group of HR professionals is bringing staff and organisational development issues to the top of the United Nations' list of concerns. A worldwide organisation with a staff of 8 500, representing the interests of more than 5.7 billion people in 188 nations presents unique challenges. But the United Nations Office of Human Resources Management (OHRM) has spearheaded a revolution in HR and planning practices.

In 1996, OHRM set up three new full-time posts to embody its HR priorities, one of which was to lead the workforce planning initiative. An HR Task Force Reform was established, consisting of experts from the public and private sectors around the world. The Task Force identified various shortcomings in the personnel system of the UN. Inadequate human resources planning had impaired the UN's ability to identify short- and longer-term staffing needs, and complicated rules

and procedures had discouraged the recruitment, advancement, and mobility of staff. This had affected the UN's capacity to move the right person into the right job at the right time – an essential requirement for a global organisation.

Since October 1997, Kofi Annan, the seventh secretary-general of the United Nations, and Rafiah Salim, the assistant secretary-general for OHRM have emphasised empowerment, responsibility, and accountability within the department. Part of the workforce plan is to have representatives from each member state employed somewhere in the UN Secretariat. Today, a South African representative might be an administrative officer at his/her embassy in Paris, next year s/he might be the cultural attaché in Bangladesh.

In 1998, the workforce plan of the centralised office of the OHRM predicted that 11 per cent of the Secretariat staff would retire by 2003. Everyone in offices around the world was asked to complete a detailed on-line survey of their skills and experience setting up a new skills inventory. This skills inventory will assist in HR planning throughout the Secretariat, providing a clear analysis of what skills are being lost and helping to guide future recruitment. This doesn't mean that external recruitment is being ignored, but the many stakeholders in the organisation are now part of strategic workforce planning.

OHRM champions eight core competencies through the workforce plan. Communication, planning, organisation, teamwork, accountability, creativity, client orientation, commitment to continuous learning, and technological awareness are built into recruitment tactics developed as a result of HR planning. These strategies are all revolutionary for the United Nations, where even such core values as 'integrity' can be questioned by under-developed countries whose values are more likely to reflect those of basic survival.

The OHRM of the United Nations has been transformed into an organisation that prides itself on its new-found ability to plan strategically for the future.

Source: Sunoo (2000:54–8)

## 8.6  Recruitment policy

Cherrington (1995:192) defines recruiting as the process of attracting potential job applicants from the available labour force. Every organisation must be able to attract a sufficient number of job candidates who have the abilities and aptitudes that will help the organisation achieve its objectives.

Recruitment policy reflects the organisation's general business strategy. Usually, a company's recruitment policy includes information on the following aspects:
- Whether internal or external recruitment will take place.
- If relatives of existing employees may be hired.
- If part-time, or any type of flexi-time workers will be considered.
- If people over retirement age may be employed.

According to Brewster et al. (2000:150), the ultimate goal of an organisation striving towards obtaining and retaining a sustained competitive advantage is to have a workforce that possesses a unique knowledge base. This objective should be written into any recruitment policy, as the fulfilment of the intellectual capital requirement of the company is to obtain the right people. This can take place by means of external recruitment, but strategic policy making demands that recruiters now first look within the organisation for those people who have a broad competency base as well as those who have the potential to create and expand their competency base.

Munetsi (1998:52) believes that recruitment policy must take into account the corporate philosophy, organisational mission, strengths and weaknesses. Corporate philosophy should be to promote from within and give chances to existing staff, while at the same time creating employment in the community. An example of a company recruitment policy is offered in Figure 8.3.

## 8.7  Factors that influence recruitment

A number of factors, which may be internal or external, influence the way in which recruitment is carried out:

---

**Figure 8.3** An example of a recruitment policy

---

RECRUITMENT POLICY OF DELHALL TYRE MANUFACTURING COMPANY (PTY) LTD.

It is the intention of this company to develop a learning organisation by building a workforce of knowledge workers. Knowledge workers are defined as those who have a broad competency base, and those who have the potential to create and expand their competency base.

All permanent employees who have completed their probationary period are eligible to apply for any advertised positions, whether it would mean a lateral or a vertical move.

Recruitment will always begin from within the company, providing the opportunity for internal promotions, before recruitment initiatives are expanded to include the external environment.

The following statements of intent have been agreed between management and the majority trade union:
- Relatives of existing employees may be hired, except where there could be a conflict of interests, such as in the financial department.
- Part-time workers may be hired in all areas.
- Flexi-time workers may be employed in administrative departments, provided that staff members are on duty between the core times of 10h00 and 15h00.
- The principles of affirmative action will be taken into consideration in all recruitment efforts.

### 8.7.1 External factors

#### Government or trade union restrictions

Government policy plays an increasing role in recruitment practice. The Labour Relations Act, and the Employment Equity Act in particular, govern the way in which organisations employ new staff (see Chapter 6, this volume). Trade unions are also seeking greater inclusion in the recruitment process, and in many organisations trade union representatives participate in developing recruitment policy.

#### Labour market

Labour market conditions affect the availability of staff. If there is a surplus of skills, many applicants will be available; if there is a shortage of skills, few applicants will be available.

### 8.7.2 Internal factors

#### Organisational policy

The content of the organisation's recruitment policy determines the way in which this factor influences the recruitment process. The statements of intent in the policy dictate the parameters of the recruitment effort.

#### Image of the company

Many organisations are well known in the community, and the way in which the work-seeker perceives the company influences the calibre of potential staff. These days, companies cannot hide behind established names, or the length of time they have been in existence – the ease with which work-seekers can obtain background information, particularly by means of the Internet, means that the company image must be able to withstand a multitude of tests.

## 8.8 Recruitment sources and methods

In the rush to fill a position, organisations sometimes lose sight of the fact that it may not be necessary to find a replacement or fill a new position at all. There may be other ways of dealing with the vacancy. It is important that other options are considered before the decision is taken to proceed with recruitment (Sullivan 2001; Torrington and Hall 1995). Some of the options are:

- Re-organise the work so that the remaining employees do the total amount of work in a section without replacing the leaver.
- Use overtime if there is a short-term problem.
- Mechanise the work if the time has arrived to introduce new equipment.
- Stagger the hours if flexible working arrangements can get the job done.
- Make the job part-time by introducing job-sharing.
- Sub-contract the work if possible.
- Use an agency to provide temporary personnel.
- Increase worker productivity.
- Update the equipment and tools.
- Outsource, or hire consultants for short-term work.
- Increase sales through website ordering, and without increasing the sales staff.
- Benchmark those firms that successfully handle recruitment issues.

A number of the above options are becoming more prominent and are discussed in detail in section 8.9.

### 8.8.1 Internal and external recruitment sources

If none of the above options are feasible and the decision is taken to proceed with recruitment, the recruiter has various sources available. Internal recruitment takes place when current employees of the organisation are considered for a vacancy. External recruitment occurs when the employer uses a source outside of the company. The advantages and disadvantages of internal and external recruitment sources are compared Table 8.1.

**Table 8.1** The advantages and disadvantages of internal and external recruitment

| Internal recruitment | |
| --- | --- |
| **Advantages** | **Disadvantages** |
| Provides greater motivation for good performance | Creates 'inbreeding' and stale ideas |
| | Creates political infighting and pressures |
| Provides greater promotion opportunities for present employees | to compete |
| | Requires a strong management development |
| Provides better opportunity to assess abilities | programme |
| | Creates a homogeneous workforce |
| Improves morale and organisational loyalty | |
| Enables employee to perform the new job with little lost time | |
| **External recruitment** | |
| **Advantages** | **Disadvantages** |
| Provides new ideas and insights | Loss of time due to adjustment |
| The existing organisational hierarchy remains relatively unchanged | Present employees cease to strive for promotions |
| Provides greater diversity | Individual may not be able to fit with the rest of the organisation |

## 8.8.2 Internal recruitment methods

According to Gómez-Mejía et al. (1998:153), the most prominent internal recruitment methods are:

### Current employees

Internal job postings allow current employees to apply for more desirable jobs. The HR department can also undertake computerised searches to identify existing employees who may possess the required job knowledge and competencies. However, an internal promotion automatically creates another vacancy that has to be filled.

### Referrals from current employees

Referred employees tend to stay with the organisation longer and display greater loyalty and job satisfaction than other categories of new-hires. However, current employees tend to refer people who are demographically similar to themselves, which can lead to complex-

ities, especially if the organisation has an affirmative action hiring policy.

### Former employees

People who were laid off during economic downturns, or those who have worked seasonally, are easily recruited and become productive quickly. They tend to be very safe hires, because the employer already has experience with these people.

## 8.8.3 External recruitment methods

Gómez-Mejía et al. (1998:148) also discuss the following external recruitment methods:

### Advertisements

Advertisements can be used for local, regional, national, or international searches. Certain occupations, such as engineering and health care, are becoming increasingly specialised and difficult to fill. In such cases, the employer is targeting not the unemployed, but the currently employed person who will be tempted to change his/her job.

A non-discriminatory advertisement is a prerequisite. An advertisement must reach desirable candidates and supply enough information to unsuitable candidates to allow them to exclude themselves from the process. Other requirements are that the advertisement must enhance the image of the company and ensure demographic representation within the media that is chosen. The key selection criteria must be job relevant, factual and not arbitrary (Damoyi and Tissiman 1997:33).

Experienced advertisers use the AIDA principle to construct their advertising copy:

- First, they attract *attention*, sometimes by using wide borders, or a great deal of empty space.
- Next, they develop *interest* in the job by using aspects such as the nature of the job itself, its location, or challenges.
- Thirdly, they create *desire* by amplifying the job's interest factors plus other details such as job satisfaction, career development, and travel opportunities.
- Finally, they prompt *action*, encouraging the potential recruit to apply immediately.

Figure 8.4 provides an example of an advertisement created according to AIDA principles.

## Employment agencies

Organisations often use employment agencies to recruit and screen applicants for a position. Typically, agencies are used when the company is too small to have its own human resources department that can carry out the recruiting process, or when the vacant position is one that will attract many applicants, resulting in a time-consuming selection process. Employment agencies also sometimes 'head-hunt' talented candidates who are presently employed and are not looking for a new job. Most agencies also assist with the recruitment of temporary workers.

## Campus recruiting

Pre-screening programmes in universities, technikons, and colleges are designed to identify top students who are completing their final year of study and to introduce them to the organisation. Often these students will be offered a place on the company's graduate programme, which allows the organisation to fill vacant positions and mould the new recruit into a 'company employee' while exposing the graduate to a number of different areas.

## Customers

One area that organisations often neglect to use in recruitment is the organisation's customers, who are already familiar with the organisation and what it offers. If these people have been satisfied with the company's products and service in the past, they will usually bring more enthusiasm to the workplace than other applicants who are less familiar with the organisation. Customers who may not wish to apply for vacant positions themselves, could offer valuable referrals for consideration.

## Direct mail

Direct mail recruitment is aimed at gaining the attention of professionals who are generally employed and who would not normally be seeking employment through other media. Attractive advertisements can be included as loose-leaf flyers in professional journals, such as *People Dynamics,* the monthly publication of the Institute of People Management in South Africa (IPM). Alternatively, flyers can be handed out at conferences and trade fairs.

## e-Recruitment

Internet recruitment is growing exceptionally fast as more and more members of the population gain access to technology. Even those who do not possess their own personal computers are able to utilise this means of job searching by using cyber-cafes. Organisations and employment agencies can display their

**Figure 8.4** A recruitment advertisement

COMMERCIAL BANKER
• Ceres • Vredendal
• Caledon

**BoE**
BANK

THE GENERATION OF WEALTH.
FOR GENERATIONS.

INNOVATION – PROFESSIONALISM – COMMERCIAL BANKING – BUSINESS
SOLUTIONS – CLIENT FOCUS

BoE Bank is in the process of targeting the financial world with an entirely new approach towards business and banking. This, then, is the reason why we need to appoint a dynamic, self-motivated professional to complement our team.

The incumbent will primarily be responsible for the development of the commercial market share of the Bank. This involves the procurement of new business and the sustained servicing of existing clients with regard to all banking products and services. In order to identify clients' needs and proactively manage their portfolios, the Commercial Banker must be thoroughly skilled in the analysis of financial statements.

This appointment requires possession of a tertiary qualification in Commercial Science, such as a B.Comm (or equivalent) in Sales or Marketing Management, and at least two years' marketing or sales experience. If you are an assertive person who thrives on challenges and can communicate effectively in English as well as Afrikaans and who focuses on professional service at all times, we would like to hear from you! A distinct negotiating flair is an asset for success in this position.

Your experience in relationship banking, preferably gained within the commercial or agriculture environment, will be a recommendation.

In return for your services, we offer a remuneration package that includes the normal large-company fringe benefits and could be structured to suit your personal needs.

If you would like to join our winning team, forward your latest CV, accompanied by a covering letter in which you motivate your application to Dirk Heydenrych on fax (021) 807-1816 or e-mail: dheydenr@boebank.co.za. Applications close on 1 December 2000.

Commencement of duties: January 2001

**www.boebank.co.za**  The business division of BoE Bank Limited. Reg No 1951/000847/06

SAATCHI & SAATCHI 70298

vacancies and work-seekers can get their CV's on the World Wide Web at a relatively inexpensive price.

Fontyn (2001:32) states that on-line recruitment is becoming more attractive as traditional companies create their own web sites and form strategic partnerships with on-line job boards. An example of this is www.career-junction.com, which is part of the Johnnic group, and which consequently benefits from liaising with Times Media.

When applying on-line, applicants immediately enter their details into the database, and can then apply for as many jobs as they would like. Electronic recruitment provides the automation and efficiency of information management, reduces costs to recruiters, and increases the choice of jobs to candidates.

### Case-in-point
*Outsourced or insourced?*

Outsourcing the recruiting function isn't for every company, but advocates say it reduces costs while maintaining quality. It is a resource available on a project basis, or it can take over a company's entire staffing function.

In the case of Kellogg's, the international cereal manufacturer, the company's entire staffing process was outsourced three years ago. Issues that led to the decision to outsource included reducing the headcount and obtaining better candidates than those who were being sourced through newspaper advertisements and 'walk-ins'. Cydney Kilduff, the director of recruiting and staff says, 'We own and drive the strategy. Only delivery is managed outside.'

The result of the outsourcing strategy is a huge reduction in outside agency fees, reduced cost-per-hire, and almost 50 per cent reduction in the time it takes to fill vacant positions. Kellogg doesn't even contemplate returning to the previous ways of recruiting.

SOURCE: Institute of Management and Administration (2002)

## 8.9   Current and future trends in recruitment

Brewster et al. (2000:80) state that in recent years, factors such as increasing economic volatility, competitiveness and new technology have forced organisations to look for more efficient and effective ways of utilising their resources. The search for competitive advantage demands that management has the ability to flexibly adjust the available internal and external labour market resources in line with the supply and demand of the market. This new flexibility has resulted in a change of mindset for both employers and employees, and although South Africa lags far behind in the development of new work patterns, the time is rapidly approaching when flexible practices will become the norm.

For workers, flexible patterns of work mean:

- A wider range of tasks and abilities and a willingness to offer them to a variety of purchasers (employers).
- A greater variety in the time periods of employment.
- A greater capacity to be deployed, necessitating changed attitudes for all, and skills and time-management change for some.

The flexi-worker has become integral to many organisations' success. The Institute of Management (2001) conducted a survey of 684 managers regarding the use of flexible working practices. The majority (70 per cent) of these managers agree that flexi-time helps organisations to recruit skilled people who are unavailable for traditional full-time work.

Dessler (1997:141) and Leap and Crino (1993:194) discuss trends in recruitment that are currently finding favour in the United States and elsewhere, and which South Africa can accept as possibilities for the future.

### 8.9.1   Contingent workers

Contingent workers are also known as temporary workers, part-time workers, and just-in-time employees. They are broadly defined as workers who do not have permanent jobs. Many companies hire contingency workers when they have absentee or turnover problems, or when there are specific projects to complete. Although contingents are usually flexible and adaptable, they experience real concerns in the way they are employed:

- They are often discouraged by the dehumanising and impersonal way that they are treated on the job.
- They feel insecure about their employment and are pessimistic about the future.
- They worry about their lack of insurance and pension benefits.
- They claim that employers fail to provide an accurate picture of their job assignments.
- They feel under-employed and express feelings of alienation and disenchantment towards the corporate world.

According to Corwin et al. (2001), contingent workers can make their employment a success by:

- Making their work-life priorities, their schedules, and their plans for the future, transparent to the organisation.
- Ensuring that senior managers know that they have an impact on results.
- Establishing routines to protect their time at work and rituals to protect their time at home.
- Cultivating champions in senior management who protect them from those who do not support their working arrangements.
- Reminding their colleagues that they are valuable workers and cannot be ignored.

Employers can strengthen the relationship between themselves and contingency workers by:

- Providing honest information about the length of the job assignment.
- Implementing personnel policies that ensure fair and respectful treatment of temporary workers.
- Using independent contractors and permanent part-time employees to complement the conventional temporary agency workforce.
- Considering the potential impact of part-time workers on full-time employees.
- Providing the necessary training and orientation for temporary workers.

Hiring contingent workers may be appropriate under the following circumstances:

- When full-time employees experience downtimes.
- Whenever there is a peak demand for labour.
- If qualified contingent workers are available.
- Where jobs require minimum training.
- When quick service to customers is a priority.

### 8.9.2  Employee leasing

Rather than employ workers themselves, some companies lease employees from a leasing company. The leasing company is responsible for hiring, record keeping, disciplining, paying, and terminating the employees. Leasing allows a company to adjust the size of its workforce with greater ease and avoid the many responsibilities associated with hiring and terminating employees. The organisation pays a management fee to the leasing company and expects the employee to carry out his/her duties as if s/he were part of the permanent workforce. Leasing is a method of reconciling supply and demand as a company has more planning flexibility and is better able to manage the size and skill composition of its workforce. This type of recruitment is often used in so-called 'support services', such as catering, security, and health-care, and allows a company to get on with its core business.

### 8.9.3  Other recruitment trends

Other programmes that bring flexibility to the workplace are flexi-time, job-sharing, compressed work-weeks, and telecommuting.

### Flexi-time

Flexi-time provides an alternative work schedule for employees who prefer to create their own starting and ending times on the job. The employer establishes a core time when all employees must be on duty. It is particularly beneficial to those employees who wish to schedule leisure activities and family responsibilities, and take care of personal business during working hours. Organisations report improved morale, increased productivity, and decreased absenteeism and turnover. The administrative implications can, however, produce a heavy workload.

### Job-sharing

Job-sharing is a process of dividing a full-time job into two or more part-time positions. Two or more employees hold a position together and are either jointly responsible or, as individuals, only responsible for the part of the job that they carry out. Job-sharing can provide the organisation with increased productivity and a greater pool of qualified applicants and reduced costs. However, job-sharing can cause communication problems between the job-sharing partners and it is often difficult to assign responsibility to a particular individual.

### Compressed work-weeks

A compressed work-week is a schedule with less than the traditional five working days per week. An employee works an increased number of hours per day so that the total number of hours remains the same as it would have been, had the employee worked five days. Usually there are reduced transport costs for the employee and sometimes better utilisation of equipment. The Basic Conditions of Employment Act must be adhered to when an employer considers changing an employee's working hours.

### Telecommuting

Telecommuting refers to the new trend for many employees to maintain an office at their homes and carry out all their normal duties while linked to the head office of their company by means of telephone, fax, personal computer and electronic mail. Many people say that this is the office of the future, and that it will especially benefit working mothers who can be on hand when children return from school. There are, however, certain problems that are inherent in such a work method. Employees have to be particularly disciplined to be able to work on their own without any supervision, and managers will find it difficult to evaluate performance if there are no objective factors that can be measured. Employees themselves may feel that they are not able to develop company loyalty if they are away from the organisational climate. In addition, they might feel cut off from their colleagues and even passed over for promotion if they are out of sight of the rest of the workforce.

## 8.10  Legal considerations in recruitment

The organisation's recruitment policy must reflect diversity issues and provide guidelines for the recruiter. Damoyi and Tissiman (1997:33) mention that the policy should state that job definitions must follow factual, job relevant information. In order to comply with legislation the policy should require the recruiter to make use of key issues such as:

- The purpose of the job.
- How it fits into the organisation.
- Outputs required from the job.
- How these outputs are measured.
- Levels of authority.
- Details of some of the activities performed to meet the outputs.

## 8.11  Workforce planning, recruitment, and quality assurance

For an organisation to be truly effective, each part of it must work properly together and seek continuous improvement of products and processes to satisfy customer requirements. Planning the workforce must be geared towards the skills and behaviours that support Total Quality Management (TQM), and recruitment methods should be designed to ensure that people understand the true nature of the job for which they are applying. Wright and Storey (1997:261) offer the example of Diamond Star Motors (a Chrysler Mitsubishi company) which uses 'a realistic preview video that warns applicants that they must learn several jobs, change shifts, work overtime, make and take constructive criticisms and submit a constant stream of suggestions in improving efficiency.'

The conventional way of recruiting and selecting employees has involved identifying and choosing from a pool of candidates the most competent individual to perform a certain job. The end result is that many skilled individuals are employed who perform reasonably well but are not necessarily contributing directly to attaining organisational goals. Meyer (1998:34) states that people who are well suited to perform in a quality environment will require additional competencies and characteristics over and above just the skills required to perform a certain job, if they are to be expected to add value to the organisation. Quality enforcement thus depends on the ability of the recruiter to seek and find those employees who already have the competencies of quality values, or who have the potential to cultivate them easily and readily.

## 8.12  Conclusion

The primary reason for doing workforce planning is economics. If done well, workforce planning will increase productivity, cut labour costs and dramatically cut production time, because the organisation will have the right number of people, with the right skills, in the right places, at the right time. Workforce planning works because it forces everyone to begin looking towards the future and it prevents surprises. It requires managers to plan ahead and to consider all eventualities. Effective workforce planning is an integrated talent

management system that can make an indelible impression on the functioning of a company.

Although line managers are often involved in the recruitment process, most of the recruitment process is the responsibility of professionals in the human resources department. Recruiters must be aware of the constraints and challenges offered in the organisation's recruitment policy. They must also be familiar with human resources and affirmative action plans, environmental conditions, job requirements, costs, and possible incentives that can be used to induce recruits to become applicants.

## Summary

- An organisation must have the proper number and mix of employees with the required knowledge, skills and abilities, to be able to reach its long-term goals. Effective workforce planning is an effort to find a possible or probable future scenario, rather than an attempt to provide definitive forecasts. The eventual size of an organisation's workforce depends upon its business plans.
- Workforce planning is influenced by a number of internal and external factors. Internal factors are the goals of the organisation, the organisational style, the nature of the task, the work group, and the style and experience of the leaders. External factors are the intervention of trade unions, government requirements and regulations, and economic conditions.
- The steps in the workforce planning process are:
  - Forecasting labour demand by means of various quantitative and qualitative techniques.
  - Estimating labour supply.
  - Implementing the workforce plan.
  - Controlling and evaluating the workforce plan.
- Recruitment policy reflects the organisation's general business strategy. The ulti-

mate goal of an organisation should be to have a workforce that possesses a unique knowledge base while promoting the principles of affirmative action.

- External factors that may influence recruitment are government or trade union restrictions, and the state of the labour market. Internal factors are organisational policy, and the image of the company.
- Various advantages and disadvantages of using internal and external recruitment sources can be distinguished. Internal recruitment methods are job postings among current employees, referrals from current employees and applications and referrals from former employees. External recruitment methods include the use of advertisements, employment agencies, campus recruiting, customers, direct mail, radio/TV, and the Internet.
- Contingent workers, employee leasing, flexi-time, job-sharing, compressed work-weeks, and telecommuting are all either current or predicted future trends in recruitment.
- The organisation's recruitment policy must reflect diversity issues and provide guidelines for the recruiter. Planning the workforce must be geared towards the skills and behaviours that support Total Quality Management (TQM), and recruitment methods should be designed to ensure that people understand the true nature of the job for which they are applying if quality standards are to be upheld in the organisation.

## Case study
## Hello Dolly!

Hello Dollies is the nation's largest combined top store and online toy retailer, operating more that 300 stores in South Africa, Namibia, Zimbabwe, Botswana and Mauritius. The company created a 'Career Opportunities' link on its corporate web site to attract applicants.

Candidates were able to view jobs that were available at their network of stores.

To make their web-based recruitment policy work more effectively, it was necessary to change the method of marketing open positions, including the way in which candidates were screened. This also entailed managing responses in a fast and flexible way. They created a new career centre, complete with a job database, an 'Apply On-line' form with screening questions created by recruiters, and candidate tools, such as 'Job cart' and 'Refer-a-friend'. The system also helped to classify and manage incoming résumés.

However, after the on-line method of recruiting had been up and running for about six months, a company audit showed a high turnover of new recruits, lack of motivation, and reduced profits. The group HR director did a brief assessment and decided that perhaps the company had tried to implement the system too quickly without proper preparation. Hello Dollies' recruitment policy had not been revised when on-line recruitment was started and numerous other factors were also not taken into consideration.

## Questions

1   How should a revised recruitment policy have been designed for Hello Dollies?
2   In your opinion, what other factors were not considered?

## Experiential exercise No. 1

PURPOSE  To assess and use on-line web postings as a recruitment source.

INTRODUCTION  Five years ago, on-line recruiting was only good for filling specialised technical positions. Today it is an integral part of the recruiting strategy for companies of all sizes and many industries. It is a fast, convenient way to find potential candidates, and it is cheaper than using newspaper advertisements or employment agencies.

TASK Access three different job-placement web sites and search each of them for the one job that would interest you. Make notes of the employers, detailed information about the job, benefits information, your expectations of the companies and the job, and how you would be expected to complete an application.

## Experiential exercise No. 2

PURPOSE  To evaluate a recruitment advertisement in terms of AIDA principles.

TASK  Obtain four recruitment advertisements, preferably from a weekend newspaper. Scrutinise these advertisements and evaluate them in terms of the AIDA principles discussed in this chapter. Use the following rating scale to rate each of the principles:

| | |
|---|---|
| 1 = very poor | 4 = very good |
| 2 = below average | 5 = excellent |
| 3 = average | |

| AIDA principle | Advertisement | | | | |
|---|---|---|---|---|---|
| | 1 | 2 | 3 | 4 | 5 |
| Attract *attention* | | | | | |
| Develop *interest* | | | | | |
| Create *desire* | | | | | |
| Prompt *action* | | | | | |
| TOTAL | | | | | |

Which advertisement rates the highest? Do you feel that the rating is a good indication of the best advertisement?

## Chapter questions

1  Between the years 1946 and 1964 there was a noteworthy increase in the number of births worldwide. This phenomenon, known as the baby boom, was due, in part, to expressions of relief after the end of the Second World War. How does such a change in the birthrate influence workforce planning?

2  This chapter concentrates on how an organisation should plan and recruit its workforce. Look at the topic from the other side of the fence. You have just been retrenched from your middle management position in an advertising agency. How will you look for a new job?

3  'As organisations become more global, workforce planning becomes more important and complex.' Discuss this statement.

4  Suppose you manage a restaurant in a holiday town, such as Plettenberg Bay. During the winter months it is profitable to keep the business open, but you need only half the cooks, table servers, and bartenders. Debate various flexible work practices you could utilise in order to ensure that the business remains effective.

5  In small businesses, managers usually handle their own recruiting. You own a small engineering firm in Gauteng. What recruitment methods would you use for the following situations? Motivate your choices.

- Your caretaker is going on holiday for three weeks.
- Your secretary has the flu.
- You need two more full-time salespersons: one to service local customers, and one to open a small sales office in Cape Town.
- You only have one engineer, who is due to retire in three months' time. He must be replaced with a highly skilled individual.

## Bibliography

BREWSTER, C., DOWLING, P. GROBLER, P. HOLLAND, P. & WÄRNICH S. 2000. *Contemporary issues in human resource management: Gaining a competitive advantage.* Oxford University Press, Cape Town.

CASCIO, W.F. 1995. *Managing human resources: Productivity, quality of work life, profits.* McGraw-Hill Companies, New York.

CHERRINGTON, D.J. 1995. *The management of human resources, 4th edition.* (Prentice-Hall), Pearson Education Inc.

CORWIN, V., LAWRENCE, T.B. & FROST, P.J.

2001. 'Five strategies of successful part-time work'. *Harvard Business Review,* (July–August).

DAMOYI, T. & TISSIMAN, C. 1997. 'Structuring your recruitment, selection and placement process'. *People Dynamics,* 15(3):30–34. Reprinted with permission of Copyright Clearance Center.

DESSLER, G. 1997. *Human resource management, 7th edition.* (Prentice-Hall), Pearson Education Inc.

FONTYN, Y. 2001. 'Clicks can work with bricks'. *People Dynamics,* 19(3). Reprinted with permission of Copyright Clearance Center.

GÓMEZ-MEJÍA, L.R., BALKIN, D.B., & CARDY, R.L. 1998. *Managing human resources, 2nd edition.* (Prentice-Hall), Pearson Education Inc.

INSTITUTE OF MANAGEMENT. 2001. 'Flexible working: A revolution in the offing?' (www.managementfirst.com).

INSTITUTE OF MANAGEMENT AND ADMINIS-TRATION. 2002. 'How outsourced recruiting, saves time and money – and gets quality hires'. *HR Focus,* 79(9). ©IOMA Inc.

LEAP, T.L. & CRINO, M.D. 1993. *Personnel or human resource management, 2nd edition.* Macmillan, New York.

MEYER, M. 1998. 'Quality management: The essential component is teamwork'. *People Dynamics,* 16(4):30–35. Reprinted with permission of Copyright Clearance Center.

MUNETSI, W. 1998. 'Importance of the staffing process'. *People Dynamics,* 18(5):52. Reprinted with permission of Copyright Clearance Center.

SULLIVAN J. 2000. 'Pre-need hiring and work-force planning'. *Electronic Recruiting Exchange,* www.erexchange.com (accessed 18 February 2000).

SULLIVAN, J. 2001. 'Alternatives to hiring more people: Tips for managers'. *Electronic Recruiting Exchange,* www.erexchange.com (accessed 23 July 2001).

SULLIVAN, J. 2002. 'Why you need workforce planning'. *Workforce,* November:46–50 (www.workforce.com). Reprinted with permission of Copyright Clearance Center.

SUNOO, B.P. 2000. 'Around the world in HR ways'. *Workforce,* 79(March):54–58 (www.workforce.com). Reprinted with permission of Copyright Clearance Center.

SWANEPOEL, B.J., ERASMUS, B.J., VAN WYK, M.W. & SCHENK, H.W. 1998. *South African human resources management.* Juta, Cape Town.

TEXAS INSTRUMENTS: GENERAL EXCELLENCE OPTIMAS® AWARD PROFILE. Feb 1998, 77(2): 30–35.

TORRINGTON, D. & HALL, L. 1995. *Personnel management: Human resource management in action, 3rd edition.* (Prentice-Hall), Pearson Education (UK).

WRIGHT, M. & STOREY, J. 1997. 'Recruitment and selection'. In Beardwell, I. & Holden, L. (eds.) *Human resource management: A contemporary perspective, 2nd edition,* pp. 210–276. (Pitman), Pearson Education (UK).

## Websites

Texas Instruments' recruiting page: www.ti.com/recruit
Career Mosaic: www.careermosaic.com
Icarian Employment: www.icarian.com
Monster.com: www.occ.com
Workforce Dynamics: www.workdyn.com.au

# 9

# Selection

## HB Schultz

## Learning outcomes

At the end of this chapter the learner should
be able to:
- Explain the internal and external factors
  that influence the selection decision.
- Construct a competency model for carrying out the selection process in a specific
  company.
- Develop application blanks for various
  types of organisations.
- Conduct a structured employment interview.
- Make decisions as to which types of
  employment tests should be used in specific selection situations.
- Discuss the responsibility for making the
  final selection decision.
- Comment on the role of quality assurance in the selection process.

## Key words and concepts

- competence-based employment interview
- Employment Equity Act
- employment test
- group interview
- panel interview
- reference check
- selection decision
- semi-structured interview
- standard application blank
- stress interview
- structured interview
- test reliability
- test validity
- unstructured interview

## Illustrative case

### A life force of its own

'Our brand has a life force of its own,' says the
founder and chairman of Spur Steak Ranches,
Allen Ambor. He has travelled a long road over
the last 35 years since he opened his first
Spur in Newlands, Cape Town. Many great
companies have gone through moments
when they may have closed, before going on
to success. But the Spur brand has never
stumbled. As with all remarkable entrepreneurs, for Allen Ambor the company is every-

thing. Although his own role is now in the area of long-term strategy planning, he delights in taking an active part in many of the daily operations of the chain.

Although the posts of waiters, grillers, and cleaners are usually filled externally, all those who are selected by the franchisees receive the necessary training and commit themselves to becoming loyal Spur employees, 'with a taste for life'. In common with all forward-looking businesses, the Spur leadership is always on the look-out for bright young people to take up senior positions. When posts have to be filled, the company looks for a suitable candidate among its own people first. No outsider is considered for any permanent post in the company unless the company leadership is sure that s/he will fit the company culture.

The result of this selection policy is that they have more than their share of talented managers and executives in their late twenties and early to middle thirties. This policy has also resulted in real loyalty within the company; two of the senior executives have been with the Spur group for more than 20 years.

SOURCE: A life force of its own (2002)

## 9.1    Introduction

Finding and hiring the best person for a job is a complex process of data gathering and decision-making that does not occur through a flash of insight. How do you determine which of the job applicants is the best to hire? This question is the major concern of selection specialists, and is crucial to the organisation because selection decisions can cost or save enormous amounts of money. The problem in selection is to accurately predict who in the applicant pool will become capable, productive, and loyal employees. If the right applicants are identified, there is a savings; if not, there is a cost to the organisation. As can be seen from the following definition, by Swane-

poel et al. (2003:280), there is no guarantee in making a selection; we can only attempt to make it as successfully as possible by utilising all the tools at our disposal.

Selection can be defined as the process of trying to determine which individuals will best match particular jobs in the organisational context, taking into account individual differences, the requirements of the job and the organisation's internal and external environments.

A large number of tools are available to those making these selection decisions. The tools differ mainly in the amount and type of information they provide. Some, such as application blanks, collect information about an applicant's past. Such tools are based on the assumption that past behaviour predicts future behaviour. Others, such as tests, provide behavioural information about the present and are based on the assumption that present behaviour predicts future behaviour.

The selection process should not be undertaken without an awareness of the factors that influence the selection decision. The chapter commences with an overview of these factors before examining the steps of the selection process in detail. Various thoughts are expressed on who should take part in the selection decision, before we examine the importance of quality assurance in the entire process.

## 9.2    Factors that influence the selection decision

Before discussing the actual process of selection, it is important to note that certain factors that are internal and external to the organisation, can have an impact both on the success of the selection decision, and the level of difficulty involved in working through the entire process. Various authors (Mondy and Noe 1996:181–2; Torrington and Hall 1995: 233–4) suggest specific factors that may influence the selection decision. These are discussed below and summarised in Table 9.1.

**Table 9.1** The factors that influence selection

| External factors | Internal factors |
| --- | --- |
| • legislation | • size of the organisation |
| • the labour market | • type of organisation |
| | • speed of decision-making |
| | • applicant pool |
| | • selection methods |

## 9.2.1 Factors in the external environment

### Legal considerations in selection

South Africa has a legacy of discrimination in relation to race, gender and disability that has denied access to opportunities for education, employment, promotion and wealth creation to the majority of South Africans. The Employment Equity Act was passed to address this legacy and has two main objectives:
• To ensure that our workplaces are free of discrimination.
• To ensure that employers take active steps to promote employment equity.

Having a workforce that reflects the demographics of the country can improve market share, understanding of markets, and the ability to service all current or prospective clients.

In order to achieve employment equity, employers have to take the following measures in terms of Chapter 3 of the Act:
• Employers must consult with unions and employees in order to make sure everybody accepts the organisation's employment equity plan.
• Employers must analyse all employment policies, practices and procedures, and prepare a profile of their workforce in order to identify any problems relating to employment equity.
• Employers must prepare and implement an employment equity plan setting out the affirmative action measures they intend taking to achieve employment equity goals.
• Employers must report to the Department of Labour on the implementation of their plan in order for the Department to monitor their compliance.
• Employers must also display a summary of the provisions of the Act in all languages relevant to their workforce. The Government Printer will make these summaries available.

### The nature of the labour market

The labour market from which the enterprise recruits its employees for vacancies is influenced by labour market conditions that affect the whole country. Labour market conditions in the city or district in which the company is situated also play an important part. The labour market is in turn influenced by labour conditions offered by the organisation, the content of the job itself and the general image of the company.

## 9.2.2 Factors in the internal environment

### The size of the organisation

The size of the company usually determines the level of formality of the selection process. In addition, different approaches to selection are generally taken for filling positions at different levels in the organisation. Extensive background checks and interviews are conducted when hiring someone for an executive position, while an applicant for a clerical position normally proceeds through the selection process quite quickly.

### The type of organisation

The sector of the economy in which individuals are to be employed can also affect the selection process. Prospective employees in the private sector are screened with regard to how they can help achieve profit goals. In the public sector, it is commonplace to allow a manager to select only from among the top three applicants for a position. Non-profit organisations may not be able to compete on the same salary levels as private or public sector companies. Therefore, a person who fills one of these positions must not only be qualified, but also dedicated to this type of work.

### Speed of decision-making

The time available to make the selection decision can also have a major effect on the selection process. Sometimes speed is crucial in the selection process, especially where production may come to a standstill if there is no one qualified to do a certain job. On the other hand, selecting a CEO may take a few months, with considerable attention being devoted to careful study of resumes, intensive reference checking, and hours of interviews.

### Applicant pool

The number of applicants for a particular job can influence the selection process. The process can be truly selective only if there are several qualified applicants for a job. However, if there are only a few people available with the required skills, it becomes a matter of choosing whoever is at hand.

### Selection methods

The selection methods chosen can also affect the entire process. The choice of methods depends on a number of factors:
- The selection criteria, such as group selection methods and assessment centres.
- The acceptability and appropriateness of the methods.
- The abilities of the staff involved in the selection process.
- The complexities of administration.
- The cost of selection methods chosen, for example, tests are expensive, as are assessment centres; interviews are much cheaper.

## 9.3   The selection process

Before embarking on the selection process,

the person in charge of the process should develop a competency model which relates to the vacant position. A competency model is worker-focused and has the objective of matching the right person to a specific job. Figure 9.1 provides the outline of a competency selection model.

The selection process is a series of steps through which applicants pass. These steps represent the 'tools', or methods of selection. The steps are essentially a number of eliminators; as applicants drop out of the process at each step, so the applicant pool becomes smaller. A typical set of steps is suggested in Figure 9.2. Although the sequence of steps may vary from firm to firm, with some steps even taking place simultaneously, the process is designed to determine those candidates who are likely to be successful and eliminate those likely to fail. Within each step, multiple approaches help distinguish between performance-related and non-performance-related issues. The selection decision must focus on competency-related issues if the selection process is to contribute to the organisation's success (Werther and Davis 1993: 231).

### 9.3.1  Initial screening

The first step in the selection process is a preliminary screening interview. Individuals who are not qualified for the job opening should be immediately eliminated from the applicant pool. However, the criteria for deciding that someone is not sufficiently qualified, need to be established carefully, especially in terms of South African legislation. Standards that have no relationship to an individual's ability to perform the job should not be used to disqualify an applicant. Lack of education, training, and job experience are legitimate qualifications, only if they relate to job performance. These factors may not be used to disqualify an applicant if s/he provides evidence of ability to perform the job (Cherrington 1995:226).

In most cases of initial screening, the applicant's first encounter with the organisation is via the telephone, or a personal appearance in

**Figure 9.1** A competency selection model

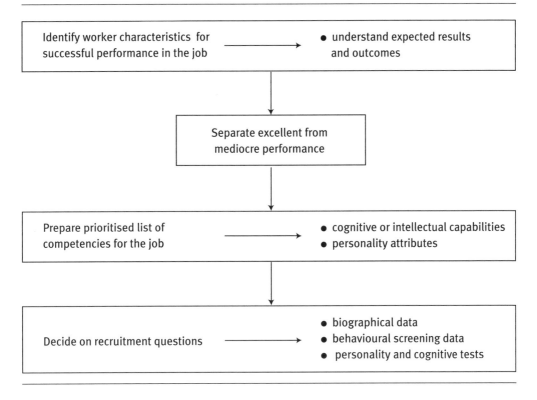

**Figure 9.2** The steps in the selection process

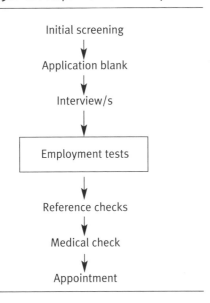

response to a newspaper advertisement, hearsay, or information regarding a vacant position obtained from the company web site. It is thus quite easy for the company representative, for example, the human resources officer, to reject the application immediately, if the minimum requirements are not met.

## 9.3.2 Application form

The standard application form has traditionally been used to evaluate the education and work experience of job applicants. In an effort to answer questions about the validity of the standard application form, industrial psychologists have developed other techniques such as the weighted application form, and biographical inventories.

Because most businesses develop and use their own application forms without the expertise of industrial psychologists, only the standard application form will be discussed.

The standard application form is used to gather routine information. Personal details of the job applicant are obtained from this document, including biographical information such as education completed, work experience, and general issues concerning the applicant's state of health. The questions on application forms must comply with the requirements of the Employment Equity Act, No. 55 of 1998. Any questions about the applicant's race, nationality, religion, age, marital status, and any criminal record that may be regarded as discriminatory must be excluded. In fact, a general rule of thumb should be: if the question on the application form is not relevant in terms of the position for which the applicant is applying, then it could be discriminatory, and should be removed from the form.

Application forms are used to screen applicants for minimum job requirements. This screening can be economical, as applicants who clearly are not acceptable are disqualified early. The expense and time involved in administering tests and conducting interviews can be saved in this way. Application forms must be interpreted with care. Serumula (1999:32) states that certain 'red flags' should be watched and investigated. These include:
- Time gaps in employment.
- Vague reasons for leaving previous jobs.
- All employers listed are out of business.

Applicants who are rejected must be informed, either telephonically or in writing, that their applications will not be taken further. Candidates whose application forms or CVs closely match the requirements of the job are invited to the company for an interview.

## Encounter 9.1

WHEN THINGS AREN'T WHAT THEY SEEM

According to recent figures, 69 per cent of organisations in America claim to perform some sort of background check on potential employees, yet there are continuous reports of bogus directors and fraudulent CEOs.

In February 2001 Pinpoint Networks Inc. decided to recruit a new Chief Executive Office (CEO) to bring age and wisdom to the company, which was created by two teenagers. On paper, Anthony Blake looked ideal. He was currently the CEO of his own company, called ObjectStream Inc. and claimed he wanted this new position so that he could sell his company to a major Internet start-up organisation. He had experience in developing key Internet programmes and it looked like the decision to hire him could not fail.

Unfortunately, Blake had played little part in the implementation of the stated Internet projects; his company was under a bankruptcy ruling, and he was six years older than his CV stated. A few simple checks would have revealed these inconsistencies, but in their haste to recruit, Pinpoint deviated from the normal selection procedure and ignored the reference checking stage.

This isn't the only story of its kind. The newly appointed Medical Director for Becton Dickinson, Seymour Schlager, had served six years in prison for the attempted murder of his wife, and Al Dunlap, the CEO of Sunbeam Corporation was fired by Sunbeam for dubious accounting practices; it was something he had done before.

SOURCE: How to effectively check references and perform background investigations of job applicants (2000)

Advances in technology have meant that application forms and CVs can also be faxed or e-mailed to companies to save time. Organisations are able to widen their recruitment search by downloading CVs from relevant career web sites on the Internet and responding electronically to these applicants.

## Encounter 9.2

JOB-HUNTING IN JAPAN

The Internet is supposed to help Japanese college students simplify their hunt for jobs in this country's complex labour market. But graduates wanting to apply for positions at Sapporo Breweries Ltd. are telling a different story. Going on-line, they have to crawl through a program called the 'Passion-filled Sapporo Drama'. The 'drama' takes them into the lives of actual employees (a beer salesman, wine marketer, and brewery manager) and asks the applicant what s/he thinks of them. Then they answer a number of questions, including 'How do you deal with a customer angry about finding a scratch on his beer can?' Three hours later, an application form finally pops up on the screen.

Japanese companies are hiring fewer graduates in a weak economy, but the most popular companies are flooded with applications. To fight back, they are setting up web roadblocks to make it more difficult to apply. They believe that graduates who have the patience to work through the maze of links, on-line exercises and questions just to get to the application form, are the kind of employees they encourage to apply. However, many students are trading information with others on how to shortcut the on-line recruiting systems of dozens of companies. At Sapporo, Mr Akahane, a human resources official, says the company has to periodically change questions it asks during the on-line application process, because students tend to rush out and 'spill the beans' to others.

Source: 'Job-hunting in Japan means battling employers', *Wall Street Journal* on-line, 2000:
www.207.46.148.249/news/394285.asp

## 9.3.3 Interviews

As Berry (1998:106) states, hardly anyone is ever hired for work without being interviewed at least once. A new employee may have been interviewed several times – by employment agency staff, company recruiters, human resources department interviewers, and the immediate supervisor of the job – before finally being hired.

The selection interview has two purposes: to get information from the applicant, and to judge the applicant on the basis of this information. The evaluation of the interview can also be combined with other assessments of the applicant and used later to make a hiring decision. Interviews can be used to assess the applicant's social ease and confidence, speaking ability, and manner of interacting. However, many jobs are not reliant on interper-

sonal skills such as these, and in such a case, the selection interview is normally used to expand the information obtained from the application blank, particularly if any of the details supplied need further probing. Cherrington (1995:244) adds that interviews provide an opportunity to sell the company and promote a good image by supplying information regarding the company's services, policies, and job opportunities. If nothing else, the interview should be a friendly, interpersonal exchange.

## Traditional versus competence-based employment interviewing

The traditional view of organisations is built around the concept of a job for which the best-qualified individual is selected. Berman (1997:6) states that this works well in a traditional organisation. But the new organisational model is based on open communication and participation of all members. In the past, a job description was the basic document for ascertaining what dimensions were job-related. Now an employee may be expected to perform a wide range of roles as a member of a team. Role description has replaced job description in many organisations. By adopting the concept of competences (such as the ability to make rational decisions when under pressure), the HRM function assesses a job applicant not only on his/her ability to perform certain tasks, but also on the ability to take on changes in work as they occur.

## Types of interviews

The interaction that takes place during an interview can occur in several different ways. The nature of the job vacancy usually determines the type of interview that will take place (Cherrington 1995:245–8).

- *Structured behavioural interview:* In a highly structured interview, the interviewer prepares a list of predetermined questions and does not deviate from it during the course of the interview. This is the best type of interview to use if the interviewer is inexperienced and if the answers to the questions will probably not need further elaboration. However, it does not allow the interviewer to explore incidental remarks that may be passed by the applicant, and which may have a bearing on his/her application.

Gómez-Mejía et al. (1998:163) offer examples of the three types of questions commonly used in structured interviews:

- Situational questions try to elicit from candidates how they would respond to particular work situations.
- Job-knowledge questions assess whether candidates have the basic knowledge needed to perform the job.
- Worker-requirements questions assess candidates' willingness to perform under prevailing job conditions.

Behavioural questioning, however, is more flexible than situational questioning. It allows candidates to explain their skills in real events from their own experience rather than having to imagine a hypothetical situation. By way of a two-way social exchange between the interviewer and job applicant, the advantages of focusing on the behaviour of the applicant are highlighted. Barclay (2001) describes the advantages of behavioural interviewing as:

- *Flexibility.* Interviewers can pattern their questions to each candidate.
- *Equal opportunities.* Good interviews focus on job-related criteria and reduce the likelihood of bias due to superficial and personal characteristic, and increase fairness in selection.
- *Avoid faking by candidates.* Questions that are based on past behaviour are more likely to elicit truthful responses because detailed explanations, which are verifiable, are required from the candidate.
- *Evidence for decisions.* When interviewers are asked to justify their decisions or give feedback to an unsuccessful candidate, behavioural interviews provide the evidence (or lack of evidence) of whatever skills are required for effective job performance.
- *Cost.* Rather than using assessment centres, where the assessor observes the behaviour of the candidate, in a behavioural interview the candidate describes the behaviour required for a job. This type of interview is less time-consuming to develop and conduct, and so presents a quicker and cheaper option.

In Figure 9.3, some of the common interviewing mistakes that inexperienced interviewers often make are summarised.

- *Semi-structured interview:* In the semi-structured interview, only the major questions are prepared in advance. Although these questions are used to guide the interview, the interviewer also can probe into areas that seem to merit further investigation. This approach combines enough structure to facilitate the

---

**Figure 9.3** Common interviewing mistakes

---

Inexperienced interviewers must not:

- Make snap judgments or jump to conclusions during the first few minutes of the interview.
- Allow negative information to influence the outcome of the interview.
- Neglect to obtain proper knowledge of the job, thus erroneously matching interviewees with incorrect stereotypes.
- Make an appointment under pressure to hire someone/anyone.
- Rate candidates in the order in which they are interviewed.
- Allow the applicant's non-verbal behaviour to influence assessment
- Communicate an expected answer by offering clues regarding the answer being sought by the interviewer.
- Talk too much or too little.
- Play the role of a psychologist by probing for hidden meanings in everything the applicants say.

SOURCE: Gómez-Mejía et al. (1998)

exchange of factual information with adequate freedom to develop insights. Semi-structured interviews are easily used by interviewers who are more experienced, as they have a planned framework to work from, but can allow the applicant to digress from the plan if necessary.

- *Unstructured or non-directive interview:* A non-directive interview is also known as an unstructured interview because the interviewer does not plan the questions or the course of the interview in advance. The interviewer may prepare a few general questions to get the interview started, but the applicant is allowed to determine the course of discussion. The process is built on the assumption that an individual will talk about things that are personally important if given the opportunity and encouragement to do so.

To conduct a successful non-directive interview, the interviewer should listen carefully and not argue, interrupt, or change the subject abruptly. The interviewer should ask questions sparingly, allow pauses in the conversation, and occasionally rephrase responses to encourage the individual to say more.

Only highly experienced interviewers, who have the ability to control the interview with a minimum of intervention, yet eliciting as much information of importance as possible, should use unstructured interviews. One of the important requirements of any type of interview is that the interviewer should make brief notes during the course of the interview, which are expanded as soon as the candidate has left. This is even more important in the case of an unstructured interview.

- *Stress interview:* Although most interview situations involve a certain amount of stress, certain jobs are performed under a great deal of pressure, and some interviewers believe that stressful conditions should be simulated in order to assess the candidate's reaction. However, stress interviews are mostly avoided because it is believed they are invalid, unpleasant, and unethical.

- *Group interview:* A group interview allows an interviewer to collect information from several applicants simultaneously and obviates having to repeat the same information about the company to each individual applicant.

- *Panel interview:* A panel interview involves the use of a panel or board of interviewers to question and observe a single candidate. The technique is especially useful in situations where an applicant's appointment depends on the approval of several people.

Whichever type of interview is used, it is at this stage of the selection process that only the top few candidates survive and proceed to the next step. A sample letter of rejection for those applicants who are rejected at this stage is shown in Figure 9.4.

### 9.3.4 Employment tests

According to Dessler (1997:169), a test is basically a sample of a person's behaviour. The use of tests in South Africa is carefully regulated by the government, the Professional Board for Psychology, and the Test Commission of South Africa. Tests are classified by the Test Commission in terms of their legal requirements as follows:

- C Tests – examples of which are intelligence and personality tests, and which can only be used by registered psychologists.
- B Tests – examples of which are aptitude tests, and which can only be used by registered psychologists and psychometrists.
- A Tests – examples of which are elementary aptitude and skills tests, and which can be used by registered psychologists, psychometrists, and psychotechnicians.

Certain concepts are extremely important when considering the use of tests. Test validity is the accuracy with which a test measures what it is supposed to measure. Test reliability is the characteristic that refers to the consistency of scores obtained by the same person when retested with the identical or equivalent tests.

## Types of employment tests

During the 1980s, tests were widely used in the workplace to measure everything from personality to interests. However, during the 1990s, the use of tests, especially psychological tests, fell out of favour in South Africa mainly because many of the tests that were used did not incorporate the norms of the South African population as a whole. During the last few years tests have regained a great deal of popularity because numerous new tests that are fair and unbiased have been developed for the South African workforce.

Mondy and Noe (1996:198–9) discuss some of the types of employment tests that are used to measure individual differences in characteristics related to job performance:

- Cognitive aptitude tests measure an individual's ability to learn and to perform a job.
- Psychomotor tests measure strength, coordination and dexterity.
- Job knowledge tests are designed to measure a candidate's knowledge of the duties of the position for which s/he is applying.
- Work-sample tests require an applicant to perform a task or set of tasks representative of the job.
- Vocational interest tests indicate the occupation in which the person is most interested.
- Personality tests must be administered by a qualified psychologist. Due to their low reliability and low validity, they are not very useful as employment tests.

---

**Figure 9.4** Sample letter of rejection at the interview stage

12 August 2003

Rick Young
678 Chelsea Street
Coega
6100

Dear Mr Young

APPLICATION FOR EMPLOYMENT

Thank you for your application for the position of Sales Manager, and for taking the time to attend an interview at our company. It was very interesting meeting you and getting to know you a bit better.

I regret to advise that your application was not successful. Your qualifications are very impressive, but it was decided that the company needs someone who has more experience in the field than you presently have.

I shall keep your application on file for the next six months and advise you immediately if another position arises for which you would qualify. In the meantime, I wish you every success for the future and hope that you found our meeting as stimulating as I did.

Yours faithfully

Karen Burns
Human Resources Manager

---

### 9.3.5  Reference checks

There are two key reasons for conducting pre-employment background investigations: to verify the accuracy of factual information previously provided by the applicant, and to uncover any damaging background information such as criminal records and suspended driver's licences. The actual reference check can take many forms. Most employers at least try to verify an applicant's current position and salary if s/he has agreed to this. Others call the applicant's current and previous supervisors in an attempt to discover more about the person's motivation, technical competence, and ability to work with others (see Figure 9.5). Handled correctly, the background check can be useful. It is an inexpensive and straightforward way of verifying factual information about the applicant (Dessler 1997:186). An example of a reference checklist appears in Appendix 9.1.

Letters of recommendation are not highly related to job performance because most are highly positive. For this reason, most human resources managers do not have a great deal of faith in letters of recommendation. However, a poor letter of recommendation may be very predictive and should not be ignored. Cambern (2003) says that the three areas in which applicants are most likely to falsify information are education, criminal record, and salary. Each of these areas impinges on the future performance of the applicant; discrepancies should not be overlooked as the consequences could be serious.

### 9.3.6  Medical checks

In order to save money, usually only the person to whom a job offer has been made, is required to undergo a medical examination. There are five main reasons for making a physical examination a pre-employment condition:

- To ensure that the applicant qualifies for the physical requirements of the position.
- To discover any medical limitations of the applicant.

- To establish a record and baseline of the applicant's health.
- To reduce absenteeism and accidents by identifying health problems.
- To detect communicable diseases that may be unknown to the applicant.

Verster (1997:21) explains that unlike other grounds of unlawful discrimination, including race and sex, the disability or health status of an applicant may directly determine whether that applicant would be able to perform at least the essential functions of a particular position. It is apparent therefore that an employer is not required to compromise the integrity of the work in order to employ a person who is physically incapable of carrying out the duties of the job. It is also necessary to ensure that the safety of other workers is not compromised by the disability or ill health of others.

According to Sagall (2003), the pre-placement medical examination should be designed to determine if the person can safely perform the job without putting his- or herself, or others, at undue risk of injury. It is also designed to determine if the person will need space to perform the job. Companies also need to decide:

- If all new hires must undergo medical screening.
- What information is required.
- What should be checked.
- The contents of the physical examination.

---

**Figure 9.5** How to check an applicant's current employer

---

- Ask the applicant for permission.
- Ask the applicant for the name of someone who was associated with him/her at his/her current company, but who has left the company.
- Ask the applicant if s/he is willing to accept a job offer on the condition that a satisfactory reference will be forthcoming after the applicant has tendered her/his resignation.

### 9.3.7 Offer of employment and appointment

If a candidate makes it all the way through the above steps, s/he has a very good chance of receiving a job offer. Job offers are usually made verbally and then backed up with a written job offer. A typical letter of appointment is shown in Figure 9.7.

## 9.4   The selection decision

Having discussed the steps in the selection process, it is pertinent that we turn our attention to the issue of who should make the final decision in choosing a new hire. In many organisations, the HR department routinely makes staffing decisions, particularly for entry-level jobs. There are two good reasons for this: the organisation must ensure that its employment practices comply with legal requirements, and it makes good sense to allow the HR department to follow through the entire selection process from start to finish (Gómez-Mejía et al. 1998:152).

On the other hand, Torrington and Hall (1995:230) point out that employment decisions have long been regarded as a management prerogative for the following reasons:

- They appeal to managers because they underline their authority.
- They are supported by academic research, which provides evidence that line managers make sound judgments about candidates.
- Job applicants believe that they have no influence in the selection decision, and put their faith in the choice made by management.

However, all the above authors advocate a more reciprocal approach to the selection

---

**Figure 9.6** Common types of assessment tools

| | |
|---|---|
| Qualifications screens | Questionnaires that determine if candidates possess specific characteristic needed to perform a job |
| Structured interviews | Managers, recruiters, or trained assessors systematically evaluate candidates on the basis of answers to questions set around key job competencies |
| Job simulations | Evaluate how candidates respond to situations simulating actual job tasks |
| Knowledge and skills tests | Assess knowledge and skills in specific subject areas |
| Talent measures | Measure 'natural' personal characteristics associated with success in certain jobs |
| Culture fit and values inventories | Help to determine how well an applicant will fit into a particular work environment |
| Background investigations | Gather information about a candidate from sources other than the candidate |
| Integrity tests | Written tests that predict whether an applicant will engage in theft or other counterproductive activities |
| Physical ability tests | Have candidates complete physical exercises to assess talents and capabilities such as strength, endurance, dexterity, vision |

SOURCE: Handler and Hunt (2002)

decision. The human resources department should play both an active and directing part in the whole process, sharing its expertise and supporting decisions made by line employees. But the general feeling is that an organisation can decide to involve more employees than just departmental managers. In addition, the new hire's co-workers and, where applicable, her/his subordinates can take part in interviews and work sampling procedures. Offering all three sets of employees part ownership in the hiring process substantiates the final decision, and is probably more effective than a decision made by the human resources department alone. After all, the newly appointed staff member will spend his/her working days with co-workers and subordinates, not with HR staff.

Making personnel decisions from a large number of applicants can be difficult and costly. Many companies make use of external consultants, such as Saville and Holdsworth (SHL) South Africa (Pty) Ltd., to assist them with the selection decision. SHL is part of a worldwide group, and they have designed three systems to aid organisations with their decision-making. These systems are briefly discussed below.

---

## Encounter 9.3

SELECTION STRATEGIES FROM SHL

Based on inherent job/role requirements, and the candidate's selection data, these systems automatically match the applicant's potential to perform in the job/role.
- Person-job match software, which is attribute-based, and competency-based.
- Decision-making models which use scores from selection data that are summarised and weighted according to job relevance and criticality scores derived from the SHL Work Profiling System (WPS).
- Decision maker software, which enables users to match small and large numbers of candidates against the three competency models of Management Competencies, Customer Contact and Sales Competencies, and Graduate Competencies.

These systems generate reports that can be used by line management to make quick and effective selection decisions.

SOURCE: Saville and Holdsworth South Africa (Pty) Ltd. Publicity Brochure, n.d.

---

O'Connell (1999) states that various criteria should be examined when evaluating a company's selection system:
- How difficult is it to administer?
- How difficult is it to interpret the results?
- How many job positions are covered in testing for potential?
- Are interpersonal skills, problem-solving, and work ethic being tested for?
- How would the results generated stand up in court?
- Is the selection system cost effective?
- Is the selection system reliable and consistent?
- Are the tests used fair and unbiased?

## 9.5  Selection and quality assurance

Many companies have successfully used the various selection tools to hire above-average employees who have made a significant contribution to the firm's bottom line. However, for companies emphasising Total Quality Management (TQM), it is important that employees are able to perform effectively in a continuous-improvement, high-involvement environment. It is widely agreed that organisations that do not adopt the objective of seeking a competitive advantage will not survive in the new millennium. This competitive advantage cannot be achieved without embracing the philosophy of a learning organisation, staffed with knowledge workers who add value to the company through the way that they perform. Quality issues are therefore exceptionally important throughout the selection process – decisions made in haste will be repented at leisure.

---

**Figure 9.7** Letter of appointment

---

5 September 2003

Eric Ntuli
20 Harebell Avenue
Coega
6100

Dear Mr Ntuli

APPLICATION FOR EMPLOYMENT

Welcome to Joyful Jumpers CC. This letter confirms the verbal employment offer for the position of Sales Manager at our company. You will commence your duties on 1 October 2003. There is a six-month probationary period, and during your first year of employment, interim performance reviews will be conducted every three months. Your first month with us includes a structured orientation programme focusing on the managerial function and overall business of the company.

Your annual salary, including a flexible benefits plan, amounts to R150 000. You will be allowed to compile your own benefits package within the financial and planned structure offered by Joyful Jumpers CC. You are entitled to 15 working days annual leave after completing 12 months' service, and all statutory public holidays will be paid in full.

The attached booklet tells you more about the benefits plan of the company. This should assist you in your choice of benefits. You will also receive a handbook during orientation, which will offer you additional information on company policies, rules and regulations.

This letter serves as an official contract of appointment. Its termination is conditional on 30 days' notice from either party, except in the case where company policy has been infringed.

You have made an excellent choice in selecting this job, and we are looking forward to having you on the staff. Please sign one copy of this letter and return it to me as soon as possible, to indicate your acceptance of your terms of employment.

Yours sincerely                                          Employment offer accepted

                                                        Name _____

                                                        Date _____

Karen Burns
Human Resources Manager

---

## 9.6   Conclusion

We have seen that the hiring process is filled with challenges: Determining which characteristics are most important to performance, measuring these characteristics, evaluating applicants' motivation, and deciding who should make the hiring decision, all play a part in determining the quality of the choice of a new hire. Because choosing the right person for a job can make a tremendous positive difference to productivity and customer satisfaction, it is important that each step of the hiring process be managed carefully. The key challenge that underlies the entire selection process is to ensure the validity of each step, taking into consideration the needs of the company, co-workers, and the new employee, and also complying with all legal requirements.

## Summary

- Certain internal and external factors influence the selection process. These are: legal considerations, the nature of the labour market, the size and type of organisation, the speed of decision-making, the applicant pool, and the selection methods used by the company.
- The selection process is a series of steps through which applicants pass. The first step in the selection process is a preliminary screening interview, followed by an evaluation of the application form or CV. The questions on application blanks must conform to the requirements of the Employment Equity Act. Application blanks are used to screen applicants for minimum job requirements.
- The selection interview has two purposes: to get information from the applicant, and to judge the applicant on the basis of this information. The traditional selection interview assesses the applicant on the basis of his/her ability to perform certain tasks. Competence-based employment interviewing assesses the ability to take on changes in the work as they occur.
- Various types of employment interviews can be conducted, depending on the nature of the vacant position. These are: the structured or patterned interview, the semi-structured interview, the unstructured or non-directive interview, the stress interview, the group interview, and the panel interview.
- The use of tests in South Africa is carefully regulated. Test validity and test reliability is very important. Employment tests include cognitive aptitude tests, psychomotor tests, job knowledge tests, work-sample tests, and vocational interest tests. Personality tests are not very useful as employment tests.

- Reference checks are carried out to verify the accuracy of factual information previously provided by the applicant, and to uncover any damaging background information. Medical checks ensure that the new hire is physically capable of carrying out the duties of the job and that the safety of other workers is not compromised by the disability or ill health of others.
- Ideally, the responsibility for the selection process should be jointly that of the human resources department and line employees, particularly line management. The line manager should make the final decision, after which a letter of appointment confirms the job offer.

## Case study
### Patient care at Carenet

Carenet Clinic is located in the heart of Johannesburg. It is one of five major private clinics in the area, and has recently built a new wing for treating wealthy and influential patients, such as top company executives and visiting and local celebrities. Carenet Clinic employs about 40 patient escorts. The job of patient escort is a rather simple one, requiring only minimal training and no special physical talents. When patients need to be moved from one location to another, patient escorts are summoned to assist in the move. Patient escorts almost always take patients who are being discharged from their hospital room to the front door of the hospital. A wheelchair is always used, even if the patient is able to walk unassisted. The escort will carry the patient's belongings and accompany him/her to a waiting vehicle in the parking lot, before returning to the workstation.

The job of patient escort is critical to the hospital since the escort is always the last hospital representative the patient sees and therefore has a considerable influence on the patient's perception of the hospital. The hospital follows a standard procedure when hiring patient escorts. When a vacancy occurs, the human resources officer reviews the file of applications on hand. This file usually contains at least 20 applications because the pay is good, the work easy, and few skills are required. The top two or three applicants are asked to come to the hospital for interviews. The majority of those interviewed know some other employees of the hospital, so the only reference check is a call to these employees. Before being hired, applicants are required to take physical examinations given by hospital doctors.

During the last year the hospital has experienced a number of problems with patient escorts that have had an adverse effect on the hospital's image. Several patients have complained that they have been treated rudely, or roughly, by one or more of the patient escorts. Some escorts keep patients waiting for long periods in their rooms, and there have been reports of escorts who carelessly bump patients when wheeling them down corridors, around corners, and in and out of rooms. It is difficult to identify who the culprits are because, although the escorts wear name tags, the patients don't always remember their names.

The hospital administrator knows that he needs to arrange 'courtesy' training for the existing patient escorts, but he feels that in the future, the selection procedure must be improved to ensure that the hospital employs escorts who have the right disposition and motives for dealing with patients. At his request, the human resources manager asked the chief supervisor, the recruitment manager, and the head matron, to meet and discuss the entire process. During the meeting a number of suggestions were made and criticisms of the present system were also voiced. The chief supervisor argued that the application blank is void of any really useful information. He also suggested that each applicant be asked to submit three letters of recommendation from people who know the applicant well. He wanted these letters to focus on personal-

ity, particularly the applicant's ability to remain friendly and polite at all times. The recruitment manager felt that the interviewing procedure should be modified. He observed that during the typical interview little attempt is made to determine how the applicant reacts under stress and with irritable people. The head matron felt that an 'attitude' test was the answer so that the applicant's predisposition towards being friendly and polite could be measured. It was left to the human resources manager to formulate some final recommendations to the hospital administrator.

## Questions

1  Critique each of the alternative approaches suggested for solving the problem of selecting patient escorts.
2  If you were the human resources manager what recommendations would you make to the hospital administrator?

## Experiential exercise No. 1

PURPOSE  To investigate how the selection process is undertaken for a job (such as a call-centre representative).

INTRODUCTION  For many organisations, call-centre representatives are the only human contact that customers ever have with the company. These reps need training far beyond product knowledge and basic telephone skills. Customer relationship management forms a large part of their job.

TASK  Search a newspaper's recruitment pages, or go on-line, to find an advertisement for a call-centre representative. Use the information obtained in this way to prepare a competency selection model that the recruiting company could use for the selection of the right candidate for this job.

## Experiential exercise No. 2

PURPOSE  To experience the roles various participants in the selection process play, namely the job applicant and the interviewer. In this case, the interviewer is a member of the HR department, and the interview is the candidate's first meeting with a company employee.

INTRODUCTION  The interviewer needs to achieve several basic objectives during the employment interview. It is important that at least the following objectives be successfully attained:

- Create an appropriate environment by making the candidate comfortable and ensuring that there is a climate of mutual trust and confidence.
- Obtain behavioural, job-related information from the applicant, clarify vague points on the application form, and uncover additional information.
- Provide information about the job and the company by presenting a realistic summary of job requirements, company policies, products and services.
- Determine whether the candidate is suitable for the vacant position. If the conclusion is positive, the process continues, otherwise the candidate is eliminated from consideration.

TASK  Team up with a partner and obtain a job description for any job in any organisation. Both partners receive a copy of the job description. Assume that this position is vacant in a company. One partner plays the role of a job applicant. This partner fills in an application blank and hands it to the other partner, who will play the role of the interviewer.

The 'interviewer' must scrutinise the application blank and make preparations for a semi-structured interview. The 'job applicant' must try to anticipate the questions that will be asked, and prepare the answers.

The role-play is presented in front of the class. It should not last longer than five to seven minutes, and will be video-taped, if possible. The class will give feedback on both roles, facilitated by the lecturer. If the role-play has been videotaped, the tape will be made available for the role players to review and analyse.

## Chapter questions

1  Some people believe that the human resources department should have the authority to decide who is hired because the department contains the experts on hiring. Others say that the immediate supervisor is responsible for employee performance and should have the final authority. Support one argument or the other and explain your reasoning.
2  If the employment manager of a banking institution asked you to develop a selection process for identifying and selecting internal candidates for job openings, how would you arrange the steps in the selection process?
3  Why is it important to conduct pre-employment background investigations? How would you go about doing so?
4  What type of interview would you recommend in the following scenarios? Motivate your answer in each case:
   - A lawyer interviewed by the senior partner in a law firm, who is an inexperienced interviewer.
   - A sales representative interviewed by the Sales Manager, who has some experience in conducting interviews.
   - An applicant for the position of chief executive officer, to be interviewed by the board of directors.
   - Twenty applicants for 10 vacant positions as seasonal apple packers on a farm.
   - A heart surgeon, applying for a position as head of the cardiac unit at a large hospital, interviewed by the experienced hospital administrator.
5  Some organisations videotape selection interviews (with the permission of the

applicants). This allows multiple assessors to view the videos afterwards and assist in evaluating the application. These video confrontations can also be useful if the interviewer is assessed at the same time. What would you look for in an interviewer if you were evaluating one on videotape?

## Bibliography

A LIFE FORCE OF ITS OWN. 2002. *Succeed.* October.

BARCLAY. J. M. 2001. 'Improving selection interviews with structure: Organisations' use of "behavioural" interviews'. *Personnel Review,* 30(1):81–101.

BERMAN, J.A. 1997. *Competence-based employment interviewing.* Quorum Books, Westport.

BERRY, L.M. 1998. *Psychology at work: An introduction to industrial and organizational psychology, 2nd edition.* McGraw-Hill Companies, New York.

CAMBERN, J. 2003. 'Background screening pays off' (www.workindex.xom/editorial).

CHERRINGTON, D. J. 1995. *The management of human resources, 4th edition.* (Prentice-Hall), Pearson Education Inc.

DEPARTMENT OF LABOUR. n.d. *Preparing an Employment Equity Plan: A user's guide.* Department of Labour, Pretoria.

DESSLER, G. 1997. *Human resource management, 7th ed.* (Prentice-Hall), Pearson Education Inc.

DYSART, J. 1999. 'HR recruiters build interactivity into web sites'. *HR Magazine* (www.shrm.org/hrmagazine/articles/0399hrs.htm).*

GÓMEZ-MEJÍA, L.R., BALKIN, D.B., & CARDY, R.L. 1998. *Managing human resources, 2nd edition.* (Prentice-Hall), Pearson Education Inc.

HANDLER, C. & HUNT, S. 2002. 'Using assessment tools for better hiring'. *Workforce,* December (www.workforce.com).*

'How to effectively check references and perform background investigations of job applicants'. 2000. *Management Research News,* 23(7/8). Barmarick Publications, UK.

MONDY, R.W. & NOE, R.M. 1996. *Human resource management, 6th edition.* (Prentice-Hall), Pearson Education Inc.

O'CONNELL, M. 1999. *Recruiting and hiring in a tight labor market: New practices in recruitment and selection.* Conference paper.

SAGALL, R.J. 2003 'The benefits of post-job-offer medical exams'. *Workforce,* January (www.workforce.com).*

SERUMULA, C. 1999. 'Employee selection needn't be a game of chance'. *People Dynamics,* 17(10):32–37.*

STROSS, R.E. 1996. 'Microsoft's big advantage – hiring only the supersmart'. *Fortune,* November:159–162.

SWANEPOEL, B.J., ERASMUS, E., VAN WYK, M. & SCHENK, H. 2003. *South African human resources management: Theory and practice, 3rd edition.* Juta, Cape Town.

TORRINGTON, D. & HALL, L. 1995. *Personnel management: Human resource management in action, 3rd edition.* (Prentice-Hall), Pearson Education (UK).

VERSTER, J.D. 1997. 'Medical screening of job applicants'. *People Dynamics,* 15(10):18–21.*

WERTHER, W.B. & DAVIS, K. 1993. *Human resources and personnel management, 4th edition.* McGraw-Hill Companies, New York.

* Reprinted with permission of Copyright Clearance Center.

## Websites

SHL website for students: www.shldirect.com/shldirect-forstudents/SHL-Direct-2.asp

Society for human resources management: Links to –

Employment Interviewing Training Course

Discriminatory Effects of the Face-to-Face Selection Interview

The Interview Coach

Interviewer's Edge

www.shrm.org/hrlinks/recruit.htm

Queendom testing center: www.queendom.com

Strategies and insights for HRM: www.pfeiffer.com

The psychological corporation: www.psychcorp.com

# Appendix 9.1
### Reference Checklist

NAME OF APPLICANT _____

POSITION APPLIED FOR _____

PERSON CONDUCTING REFERENCE CHECK _____

COMPANY _____

PERSON CONTACTED _____

POSITION _____

COMPANY _____

TELEPHONE NUMBER _____

FAX NUMBER _____

EMAIL ADDRESS_____

VERIFICATION OF JOB DETAILS

Dates of employment: From _____to _____

Summary of work duties _____

_____

_____

_____

Salary package (Basic compensation and benefits) _____

_____

Reason for leaving _____

Strong points _____

Weak points _____

Details of any supervisory duties _____

Overall job performance: Excellent _____Satisfactory_____Below average _____

Relationships with others _____

DEVELOPMENTAL ISSUES

Is the applicant in the right job/career?_____

How does the applicant behave in times of conflict? _____

What motivates this person?_____

Other comments from the referee_____

_____

PROCEED WITH APPLICATION: Yes _____No _____

# 10

# Induction and staffing decisions

## HB Schultz

## Learning outcomes

At the end of this chapter the learner should be able to:

- Distinguish between the concepts of induction, orientation, and socialisation.
- Explain the objectives and benefits of induction.
- Develop a short training course that explains the responsibility for carrying out the two levels of orientation.
- Write a manual of HR policies for an organisation.
- Describe the stages of induction and discuss how the process of acculturation can be fostered.
- Plan, design, implement and evaluate an induction programme.
- Compare and evaluate various staffing strategies.
- Suggest various approaches to internal staffing in specific situations.
- Briefly describe the influence of quality assurance in induction and staffing decisions.

## Key words and concepts

- acculturation
- anticipatory stage
- buddy
- demotion
- dismissal
- employee handbook
- encounter stage
- induction
- induction kit
- internal, external, and workforce pool staffing strategies
- layoff
- orientation
- promotion
- Realistic Job Preview (RJP)
- Realistic Orientation Programmes for new Employee Stress (ROPES)
- resignation
- retirement
- retrenchment
- settling-in stage
- socialisation
- transfer

## Illustrative case

**What on earth (or in the organisation) is MEHNGO?**

MEHNGO stands for 'my eyes have now glazed over,' says Monica Kirgan, vice-president of Participant Communications, in Des Moines, Iowa, USA. She points out that, although most companies think about, and probably do something about inducting a new employee at the start of his/her career with a company, a much smaller percentage turn their attention to the retirement phase of a staff member's career – the time when s/he starts thinking of leaving the company, and the workforce, for good.

MEHNGO is the result of companies trying to communicate too much information about retirement plans in too short a space of time, because they have not made a timely start to this important aspect of caring for organisational workers. Kirgan says that what all companies need to communicate to potential retirees is 'The Three Commandments': Know thyself, know thy plan, and diversify.

'Know thyself' challenges employees to ask themselves tough questions, such as 'How long do you have until retirement? What do you want retirement to look like? Will you have enough money?'

'Know thy plan' urges employers to highlight financial areas in the retiree's life, and 'diversify' dares employees to confront the fact that they will be jobless after retirement and that they should diversify their interests and hobbies to keep themselves busy and perhaps even provide an additional income.

Companies must encourage their employees not to be short-term thinkers, when it comes to planning for retirement – after all, most workers plan for the start of their careers; it's even more important to plan for the end.

SOURCE: Cornell (2003)

## 10.1   Introduction

'Place them and forget them' is a common approach to recruiting. But it is equally important to ensure that the right people are placed in the right positions, so that top performers can optimise their learning and growth. Unfortunately, many managers take a casual approach to placing and inducting workers, and as a result they have top performers working in non-essential jobs, with a less than perfect knowledge of what is expected of them. In addition to impacting on their morale and to remaining with the firm, it also affects the firm's productivity, as well as its ability to maintain a competitive edge.

Starting a new job is considered to be one of the most stressful life experiences and a proper induction process that is sensitive to the anxieties, uncertainties, and needs of a new employee is of the utmost importance. The impact of diversity in terms of age, language, and cultural background on South African organisations also makes it critical that proper attention be paid to induction.

At this point it is appropriate that we pause and take a look at some relevant terminology. Although induction means to introduce, or to initiate, it is only part of the process that endeavours to absorb an employee into the organisation and turn him/her into a productive worker.

Orientation means to become familiar with, or adjusted to facts or circumstances. It is the process of informing new employees about what is expected of them in the job and helping them cope with the stresses of transition. Employees receive orientation from their co-workers, and from the organisation. The orientation received from co-workers is usually unplanned and unofficial, and it often provides the new employee with misleading and inaccurate information. This is one of the reasons why the official orientation provided by the organisation is so important.

Socialisation means to adapt to life in society. In the organisation, socialisation is the process of instilling in all employees the prevailing attitudes, standards, values, and patterns of behaviour expected by the organisation and its departments. Socialisation really begins with induction, and is often informal. Unfortunately, informal can mean poorly planned and haphazard.

It is clear from the above that the process is actually one of socialisation, incorporating induction and orientation. However, because most organisations refer to the entire process as 'induction', this term will be used throughout the chapter.

The start of this chapter focuses on the objectives and benefits of induction, and the responsibility for carrying out the induction programme. A comprehensive discussion of an induction model follows before an overview of the planning, design, implementation, and evaluation stages of the induction programme is offered. The debate proceeds to examine various staffing strategies and approaches to internal staffing before the chapter concludes with some thoughts on the relationship between induction, staffing decisions, and quality assurance.

## 10.2 The objectives and benefits of induction

The main purpose of induction is to assist the new employee in his/her integration into the organisation. Werther and Davis (1993:281) state that the induction programme helps the individual to understand the social, technical, and cultural aspects of the workplace, and speeds up the socialisation process.

According to Sullivan (2001a) the goals of an induction programme should be to:

- Help the employee understand the 'big picture'.
- Make the new employee part of the team.
- Develop plans and goals for the new employee.
- Gather information from the new hire.
- Anticipate and answer their questions.
- Celebrate the new employee's arrival.

Various authors (Cascio 1995:239; Cherrington 1995:367; Dessler 1997:247; Werther and Davis 1993:273) agree that the following are the main benefits of a successful induction programme. It:

- Reduces reality shock and cognitive dissonance. Dissonance occurs when there is a psychological gap between what newcomers expect and what they actually find.
- Increases job satisfaction and lowers turnover and absenteeism. When employees meet their personal objectives, satisfaction tends to improve, which lowers turnover and absenteeism costs.
- Alleviates employee anxieties. Proper induction results in less hazing by peers and criticism from supervisors, as well-integrated newcomers need less attention from co-workers and supervisors, and perform better.
- Creates positive work values and reduces start-up costs. Fostering a sense of belonging in the organisation allows the new employee to become productive much more quickly.
- Improves relations between managers and subordinates. Improved relationships are the result of new employees settling-in to the new environment as quickly as possible, without becoming too much of a burden on their managers and co-workers.

## 10.3 Responsibility for induction

The two broad categories of an induction programme are:

- General topics of interest to most new employees.
- Specific, job-related issues of concern only to specific job-holders.

Figure 10.1 shows some of the common topics of induction, categorised into two tiers.

These two distinct levels of induction are shared between the human resources department and the new employee's immediate manager (Byars and Rue 1997:206; Werther and Davis 1993:278).

### 10.3.1 The human resources department

- Coordinates both levels of induction.
- Trains line managers in conducting departmental and job induction.
- Conducts general company induction.
- Follows up the initial induction with the employee.

### 10.3.2 The new employee's manager

- Conducts departmental and job induction.

A 'buddy' or co-worker who has been carefully selected and trained to carry out this responsibility sometimes conducts job induction.

## 10.4   Writing human resources policies

For induction to be successful, a company must have its statements of intent in the form of a policy manual which can be handed to new employees and updated with existing employees as policies are amended or new ones are approved.

Managing a workforce is a time-consuming and complicated task. Human resources policies are a tool that can make this task easier and reduce the possibility for misunderstandings between the employer and employee. While the majority of large companies already have an established set of human resources policies, many smaller companies do not. Typically, managers of small companies focus more on expanding the business than on establishing specific human resources policies and procedures. As a result, serious problems can arise. Therefore, it is of the utmost importance that human resources policies be established when the business is founded.

Ellerman and Kleiner (2000:95–8) provide reasons why a company needs human resources policies:

- They help to ensure that the company is in compliance with legal requirements.
- They give management the opportunity to thoroughly evaluate the basic needs of the organisation and the needs of the individual employee.
- Updated policies help to eliminate discrimination in the workplace and differences in management ethics between managers.
- Human resources policies define a standard of performance and conduct.
- They help to build employee enthusiasm and loyalty.

Policies should be written by the person in charge of the human resources function and approved by the board of directors, or senior management. There are five principal sources for determining the content of policies:

- Past practices in the organisation.
- Prevailing practices among other organisations locally and nationally in the same industry.
- The attitudes and philosophy of top management.
- The attitudes and philosophy of middle and lower management.
- The knowledge and experience gained from handling countless personnel problems.

Policies must also be developed in consultation with representatives from trade unions and, after completion of the human resources policies, the company attorney should review the document to ensure compliance with current and relevant legislation, and provide advice regarding potential problems. Once approval has been received, the policies should be assembled in a handbook, preferably a ring binder, so that amendments and new policies can be added with ease, and outdated policies can be removed.

Some of the most common and frequent mistakes employers make in preparing employee handbooks are related to legal issues. A recognised risk in having an employee handbook is that a court may interpret it as a contract of employment. While it is critical for

**Figure 10.1** Some topics often covered in employee induction programmes

**General topics**
- company history
- company structure
- layout of physical facilities
- products/services
- company policies and procedures
- disciplinary regulations
- safety procedures
- pay scales and paydays
- holidays
- employee benefits.

**Job-related issues**
- introductions to supervisor and co-workers
- job location
- job tasks
- job objectives
- relationship to other jobs.

employees to understand that the handbook is not a contract, supervisors need to be taught the importance of treating the handbook as though it were a contract.

## 10.5 An induction model

### 10.5.1 The stages of induction

According to Wanous in Gómez-Mejía et al. (1998:170, 259), the entire process of induction can be divided into three stages:
- Anticipatory, or the induction stage.
- Encounter, or the orientation stage.
- Settling-in, which is the socialisation stage.

The basic ideas in this induction model are presented in Figure 10.2.

At the anticipatory stage, applicants generally have a variety of expectations about the organisation and the job, based on accounts

**Figure 10.2** An induction model

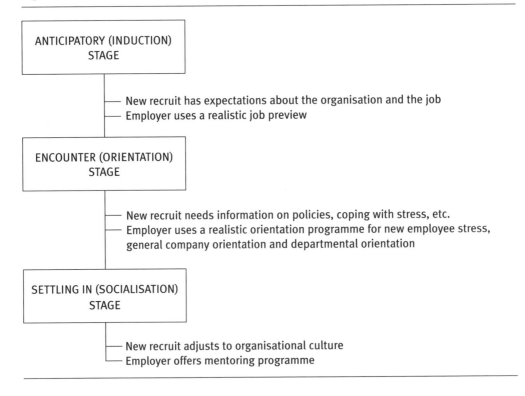

ANTICIPATORY (INDUCTION) STAGE

— New recruit has expectations about the organisation and the job
— Employer uses a realistic job preview

ENCOUNTER (ORIENTATION) STAGE

— New recruit needs information on policies, coping with stress, etc.
— Employer uses a realistic orientation programme for new employee stress, general company orientation and departmental orientation

SETTLING IN (SOCIALISATION) STAGE

— New recruit adjusts to organisational culture
— Employer offers mentoring programme

provided by newspapers and other media, word of mouth, public relations, and so on. A number of these expectations may be unrealistic, and, if unmet, can lead to dissatisfaction, poor performance, and high turnover.

A Realistic Job Preview (RJP) is probably the best method of creating appropriate expectations about the job. For instance, at most Toyota manufacturing plants, job simulations and work samples are used to demonstrate to applicants the repetitive nature of manufacturing work and the need for teamwork.

In the encounter stage, the new hire has started work and is facing the reality of the job. Even if an RJP was provided, new hires need information about policies and procedures, reporting relationships, rules, and so on.

An important function of orientation during the encounter stage is to provide new workers with the tools to manage and control stress. Companies can use an orientation approach called Realistic Orientation Programmes for new Employee Stress, or ROPES. A good ROPES does the following:

- Provides realistic information about the job and the organisation.
- Offers general support and reassurance, informing employees that the stress they are experiencing is normal, and training managers to support their new employees.
- Demonstrates coping skills in how to deal with the stresses of the new job.
- Identifies specific potential stressors that new employees might face.

During the settling-in stage, new workers begin to feel like part of the organisation. An employee mentoring programme, in which an established worker, or 'buddy', serves as an adviser to the new employee, may help ensure that settling-in is a success.

Even the most extensive socialisation programme will not make new hires feel at ease if their immediate supervisors are not supportive during their settling-in period. Although there is no universally effective set of practices for promoting the integration of new workers,

---

**Figure 10.3** Supportive actions for new recruits

- Offer constructive criticism laced with praise.
- Show confidence in the new recruit.
- Listen to self-doubts and share personal experiences.
- Acknowledge the value of past experience.
- Emphasise the new recruit's potential.

---

certain actions that can be used with most people and in most situations are offered in Figure 10.3.

## 10.5.2 Fostering company culture

Induction initiates the whole process of integrating employees into the organisation. Organisational values, beliefs and traditions (commonly known as the organisational culture) are slowly absorbed as a person is exposed to orientation, training and the peer group. Anfuso (1995:70–7) calls this process 'acculturation'. The success of the induction process depends on the degree to which the new employee understands, absorbs and accepts the culture of the organisation. Long-serving employees often forget that the new incumbent has to deal with outside-life conflicts, intergroup role conflicts, the definition of his/her own role within the group, learning new tasks, establishing new interpersonal relationships and learning group norms. Managers must be aware of these conflicts and offer support in resolving conflicting interests.

Open-door policies, group and individual discussions, will assist new employees in understanding corporate culture. Individuals expect a hierarchical structure that emphasises status differences between subordinates and superiors. They also need to know the degree to which the company values personal goals, autonomy, and privacy over group loyalty, commitment to group norms, involvement in collective activities, and social cohesiveness.

Organisations operate efficiently when employees share values. The transmittal of values, assumptions and attitudes occurs from older to younger employees. Every organisation has its own personal symbols, language, ideologies, rituals and myths, which form the basis of its culture. These are often alien to the new employee – organisations even develop their own jargon, or 'slang', which is incomprehensible to strangers.

A common failing of orientation programmes is to ignore this part of the socialisation process, concentrating instead on compliance with rules and regulations, benefits offered by the company, and what the organisation expects from the new employee. In this area, the 'buddy' system can achieve what individual managers often ignore or do not have time to offer. After all, the peer group is closer to the new employee than supervisors or managers.

Fostering company culture is an ongoing process that is strengthened by the involvement of both co-workers and managers. South African managers must be made aware of the challenges demanded by an ethnically diverse workforce. The traditions and values of non-English speaking employees in particular, make it imperative that individual cultures are aligned, and not erased, in an attempt to make new employees conform to organisational culture.

## 10.6 Planning, designing, and implementing the induction programme

### 10.6.1 Planning the induction programme

Research has shown that in many organisations, 50 per cent of voluntary resignations occur within the first six months after organisational entry, often because employee expectations are not met (Boase 1997:50). Most companies base their induction programmes on what the company believes the new employee needs to know. However, the most common questions that new employees have should form the basis of induction. According to Cascio (1995:240) these questions are usually:

- What are the expectations of this company regarding the services I can offer?
- Who is my boss, and what is s/he like?
- What kind of social behaviour is regarded as the norm in this company?
- Will I be able to carry out the technical aspects of my job?
- What is my future in this company?

If one accepts the improvement and promotion of productivity as an ultimate goal of the induction process, it is important to note that there are other categories of employees who will benefit from an induction, or re-induction programme, namely:

- Transferred or promoted employees, especially if the transfer or promotion involves a significant change of environment.
- All current employees, particularly if restructuring changes or mergers have taken place.

Based on these considerations, induction programmes are usually planned in accordance with common employee questions, targeted employees, and budget limitations.

### 10.6.2 Designing the induction programme

Byars and Rue (1997:207) believe that the induction programme must be based on a good balance between the company's and the new employee's needs. With this in mind, the designer must compile an induction programme that is both comprehensive and concise or to-the-point. This is achieved by reviewing the following items:

- The target audience (current or transferred employees may require less information than new recruits).
- Essential and desirable information (essential information cannot be omitted; desirable information can be summarised).

- The literacy level of the employees (in South Africa, the large number of illiterate workers demands a visual rather than a written media of imparting information).

### 10.6.3 Implementing the induction programme

Byars and Rue (1997:207) state that it is desirable for each new employee to receive an induction kit, or packet of information, to supplement the verbal and visual induction programme. This kit can provide a wide variety of materials. Care should be taken not only to ensure that essential information is provided, but also that not too much information is offered. Materials that might be included are:
- Company organisation chart.
- Map of the company's facilities.
- Copy of policy and procedures handbook.
- List of holidays and fringe benefits.
- Copies of performance appraisal forms, dates, and procedures.
- Emergency and accident prevention procedures.
- Sample copy of company newsletter or magazine.
- Telephone numbers and locations of key company personnel (for example, security).

Some organisations even provide a T-shirt and pen with the company logo, as part of the welcoming pack.

Many organisations require employees to sign a form indicating they have received and read the documents in the induction kit. This is commonly required in unionised organisations so as to protect the company if a grievance arises and the employee alleges s/he was not aware of certain company policies and procedures. On the other hand, it is equally important that a form be signed in non-unionised organisations, particularly in light of an increase in wrongful discharge litigation. Whether signing a document actually encourages new employees to read the induction kit is questionable.

### The employee handbook

The handbook should offer coverage of fringe benefits, and not specific information related to particular benefits. The handbook should say explicitly that all statements of coverage are subject to the terms, conditions, restrictions and other eligibility requirements set forth in plan documents. The employer should reserve its right to modify, amend or terminate any benefit plan at any time and for any reason (Segal 1993).

The contents page of a typical employee handbook is shown in Table 10.1.

### Conducting the induction programme

Dessler (1997:247) believes that the actual implementation of the induction programme hinges around three considerations:
- The stage of induction.
- The information that needs to be delivered during the relevant stage.
- The person, or persons, responsible for the relevant stage.

The parameters of implementation are summarised in Table 10.1.

## 10.7 Follow-up and evaluation of the induction programme

Many companies make the mistake of believing that once a new employee has 'attended the induction programme', nothing more is needed from the supervisor or manager. This is almost as bad as an informal policy of 'come and see me if you have any questions'. Instead, regular checks should be initiated and conducted by the line manager after the new employee has been on the job one day and again after one week, and by the HR representative, after one month (Cascio 1995:242). A typical manager's checklist is shown in Figure 10.5.

**Table 10.1** Contents page of a typical employee handbook

### Bakewell Biscuit Company Staff Handbook for Salaried Employees

| Contents | Page | Contents | Page |
|---|---|---|---|
| Introduction | 1 | Study leave | 4 |
| Conditions of service | 1 | Refund of costs of study courses | 4 |
| Hours of work | 2 | Maternity leave | 5 |
| Occasional absence | 2 | Public holidays | 5 |
| Absence due to ill health | 2 | Religious holidays | 5 |
| Accumulated sick leave | 2 | Payment of salary | 6 |
| Absence without permission | 2 | Annual bonus | 6 |
| Medical aid | 3 | Long service bonus | 6 |
| Medical services | 3 | Social club | 7 |
| Compensation for accidental injury | | Smoking | 7 |
| or death | 3 | Safety | 7 |
| Annual leave | 4 | Cleanliness | 7 |
| Unpaid leave | 4 | Communication | 7 |

**Table 10.2** Implementing the induction programme

| Stage of induction | Information | Responsible person(s) |
|---|---|---|
| 1  Induction (anticipatory) | Basic organisational details and brief overview of benefits during recruitment and selection. | HR Officer |
| | Letter of appointment with job description, starting salary, job grade, terms and conditions of employment, probationary period, medical checks, etc. | HR department |
| | First day instructions. | HR department |
| 2  Orientation (encounter) | Induction kit, tour of the workplace. | HR department |
| | Meeting new manager and co-workers. | HR department |
| | Basic job information, departmental goals and expectations. | Line manager |
| 3  Socialisation (settling in) | Advanced job information, social activities. | Mentor or 'buddy' |

Very often, new employees have questions that remain unanswered because they do not wish to disturb the supervisor with something that they may regard as trivial. Werther and Davis (1993:281) suggest that the human resources department schedule a face-to-face meeting where the employee is asked to critique the weaknesses of the induction programme. Weaknesses are presumed to be topics about which the employee needs more information. This type of follow-up not only reinforces the content of the induction programme for the new recruit, but also serves to provide information for the HR department regarding the strong and weak areas of the induction programme. Revision can then take place where necessary. Byars and Rue (1997:210) state that using the following methods can strengthen evaluation:

● Unsigned questionnaires completed by all new employees.
● In-depth interviews of randomly selected new employees.
● Group discussion sessions with new employees who have settled comfortably into their jobs.

## 10.8  The importance of good staffing decisions

Managers must calculate the costs of hiring a new employee who will possibly bring new ideas and enthusiasm into the organisation, but who will require an extensive induction programme before becoming productive. Filling a position with an existing employee might be less costly and might save time, but a current employee will have no new ideas and might not fulfil the hiring goals of an affirmative action programme. Sullivan (2001a) believes that managers must consider the under-utilisation of talent when placing top performers into inconsequential jobs. A placement error occurs if a manager:

● Fails to identify a company's critical positions.
● Fails to identify top performers.
● Allows a critical position to be left vacant.
● Allows a critical position to be filled by a mediocre performer.
● Allows a top performer to remain in a non-critical position.
● Allows a top performer to have a mediocre manager.
● Allows a 'bottom performer' to remain on the same team as a top performer.

## 10.9  Staffing strategies

A staffing strategy is the technique used by an organisation to place the right person in the right position. In their purest form, these

---

**Figure 10.4** A manager's induction checklist

Employee name ................................................................................................

Date attended to

Welcome from supervisors and co-workers _____

Prepping co-workers for start of new employee _____

Introduction to co-workers _____

Introduction to other selected employees _____

Overview of job setting and company tour _____

Mentor or 'buddy' assigned _____

Employee handbook provided _____

Specific job requirements discussed _____

Outline of facilities: rest room, telephone regulations, eating arrangements, parking, day care centre, working hours, breaks, first aid facilities _____ strategies are categorised as either internal or external. A modification of an internal strategy is the workforce pool. These strategies will now be examined.

## 10.9.1 Internal staffing strategy

The internal staffing strategy only recruits new employees for entry-level positions. Existing employees fill all other vacancies in the organisation, whether through a transfer or a promotion. This means that current employees are assured of being considered for promotional opportunities and it is assumed that they will offer increased loyalty, dedication and career orientation. The major disadvantage of this strategy is that individuals are expected to progress through all the levels of a job tree, even if they have the skills and ability to undertake a job at a higher level. Also, the company cannot consider using the services of an external applicant, even if highly recommended, except at entry-level.

## 10.9.2 External staffing strategy

External applicants fill all positions, at all organisational levels, and no provision is made for promotion opportunities. This ensures a constant flow of applicants with new ideas, but because there is no career planning, loyalty and dedication is low and turnover is high.

## 10.9.3 Workforce pool strategy

The pool strategy appoints individuals to a pool of entry-level posts on a temporary basis, from where they are allocated to different positions as required. When a permanent position becomes available, the organisation will already have had the opportunity of observing the employee's performance and can more easily make a staffing decision. A pool strategy offers a company a ready-made staffing source in times of high labour turnover or absenteeism. However, the workforce pool is costly to maintain, as theoretic-

ally, the organisation is then over-staffed.

Organisations very seldom use any of these strategies on their own, and are more likely to use a combination determined by situational variables such as the supply of and demand for labour in various occupations, government legislation and requirements (such as the Employment Equity Act and affirmative action), and the economic situation.

---

## Encounter 10.1

Fruit and Veg City is a franchise concept that has taken off phenomenally within South Africa. The idea of selling only fresh fruit and vegetables appeals to those entrepreneurs who do not want to become involved in a production environment, and who wish to cash in on the 'healthy way of living' idea. The franchise has a novel way of filling open positions – they use the idea of 'intraplacement'. Intraplacement is a dynamic process that uses the tools and strategies of external search and applies them to internal candidates, who are superior to external candidates because they usually have a much higher success rate in their new jobs than external applicants. However, the onus in intraplacement is on the employer to act and keep top performers' careers moving.

Intraplacement differs from the more traditional staffing strategies in a variety of ways:

- It is a shared partnership where the company assists candidates by increasing their opportunities to learn and grow within the firm.
- It focuses on corporate needs as well as employee wants.
- It is a flexible approach that seeks out project assignments, part-time job rotations, and promotions and transfers to increase the opportunities for employees to grow.
- It excites current employees.
- It actively uses internal recruiting specialists, 're-deployers', and their tools to identify potential candidates for growth opportunities.
- It assists the candidate in assessing opportunities and in marketing and selling themselves to internal managers.

---

## 10.10  Approaches to internal staffing

Internal staffing decisions are applied mainly by way of promotions, transfers, demotions, and 'exits' (such as resignations, layoffs, retrenchments, dismissals, and retirements). Werther and Davis (1993:284–5) and Torrington and Hall (1995:260, 267) discuss these staffing approaches.

### Promotions

A promotion occurs when an employee is moved from one job to another that is higher in pay, responsibility, and/or organisational level. Promotions are usually based on merit or seniority. Merit-based promotions occur because of an employee's superior performance in his/her present job. Very often the promotion is a 'reward' for past efforts, and two problems may be encountered. Firstly, 'superior performance' must be objectively distinguished from other grades of performance and those employees who are regarded as 'superior performers' must be treated consistently when it comes to promotional opportunities. Secondly, the Peter Principle states that people tend to rise to their level of incompetence in a hierarchy. Although this is not always true, the Peter Principle suggests that good performance in one job does not guarantee good performance in another. For example, an organisation might promote an engineer identified as being a superior performer, to the job of engineering supervisor. The company might gain an ineffective supervisor and lose a superior engineer.

Seniority-based promotions are given to the employee with the longest length of service. This approach is objective, and one needs only to compare the seniority records of the candidates to determine who should be promoted. This approach can be used quite easily in blue-collar jobs, but is more difficult to implement when promoting from blue-collar to white-collar, or between white-collar jobs at different hierarchical levels. Again, the question of competency might arise in a sen-iority-based promotion decision. Usually, a combination of both approaches to promotion is considered to be most fair.

### Transfers

Decision makers must be able to reallocate their human resources to meet internal and external challenges. Reallocation often takes place through transfer. A transfer takes place when an employee is moved from one job to another that is relatively equal in pay, responsibility, and organisational level. Transfers can thus improve the utilisation of human resources and provide a person with new skills and a different perspective. Often a transfer results in an increase in motivation and job satisfaction, particularly if there was little challenge in the employee's previous job. Technical and personal challenges in the new job can provide growth opportunities, and at the least offer variety and a change in routine.

### Demotions

Demotions occur when an employee is moved from one job to another that is lower in pay, responsibility, and organisational level. There are two main reasons for the use of demotions: in the case of an employee who is punished for an offence, and when an organisation offers redeployment to an employee in the form of a demotion instead of a retrenchment. Demotions are negative solutions to problems and can hold serious motivation and performance problems. They should be used as a last resort and, if possible, other methods of discipline or redeployment should be sought.

### Resignations

Resignations represent an outward movement of staff and take place for various reasons. When there are no promotional opportunities, or better opportunities elsewhere, many employees take the option of leaving the company. Sometimes employees just do not fit into the company culture, or they find themselves in conflict situations from which they decide to withdraw. In the case of female employees, a resignation is sometimes the result of a decision to start a family, or spend more time with children. In the majority of cases, resignations are healthy events and allow the organisation to introduce new blood.

## Retrenchments

A downturn in the economy or business reasons, such as the closure of a branch of a company, dictate that employers are forced to ask employees to seek other work. One of the most difficult aspects of retrenchment for the employer is the selection of who should go. A long-standing convention is that of LIFO, or Last-In First-Out, as this provides a justice that is difficult to dispute, and that satisfies labour unions.

According to Sullivan (2001a), certain action steps can be taken if an organisation is undertaking or considering retrenchments:

- Improve morale and productivity during the retrenchment process.
- Squash rumours and communicate the truth.
- Work with managers to keep their performance from declining.
- Offer counselling to those who have been retrenched and those who are being retained.
- Identify the issues and concerns of employees.

The following text box suggests how retrenchment can be used to start a new career.

---

## Encounter 10.2

RETRENCHMENT CAN BE A NEW BEGINNING

The first response to being retrenched is often self-doubt and a feeling of rejection, emotions that are aggravated by the stigma attached to retrenchment. Often retrenched people are viewed with suspicion, probably because the underlying feeling is that they would not have been retrenched if they were valuable employees. The result of retrenchments in South Africa is a body of unemployed people who are highly skilled in specialist fields, but who are perfectly positioned for the growing industry of coaching and mentoring.

Denise Bjorkman, CEO of Knowledge Universe Group SA, says that many retrenched people have a solid base of knowledge, which is regarded in the business world as knowledge capital. Bjorkman says, 'This knowledge capital can be turned into a good business with clients who need what you know.'

While their knowledge about running a business is limited, they are often perfectly qualified to become life coaches who help people to deal with career choices, the acquisition of new skills, and setting realistic life goals. Starting a coaching or mentoring practice has extremely low entry costs, but the rewards can be tremendous. A coaching practice can be run from a home office with little more than a telephone and a computer. Trained coaches can become global members of the International Federation of Professional Coaches and Mentors (IFPCM) programme. Some of the benefits are national advertising and client referrals. From June 2003, every coach must be registered with the SA Coaching Council (SACC) to regulate academic and behaviour standards.

SOURCE: Bjorkman (2002)

---

## Layoffs

Layoffs take place for the same reasons as retrenchments, but are not as harsh as the latter because the employees are called back as soon as the economy improves. The psychological effects of a layoff can be severe, as the employee is not sure if, and when s/he will be offered her/his position again, and s/he has to take the decision of whether to start a job search in the interim. As in the case of retrenchments, employers try to use other strategies such as cutting back on overtime, dismissing part-time workers, and not hiring new employees.

## Dismissals

Dismissals are the result of employee misbehaviour, and proper procedures must be followed when the employer takes this drastic action. Dismissals cause movement outside the organisation and invariably lead to an unplanned vacancy. Dismissals represent extreme disciplinary action and must not be taken lightly. (Readers or learners should see Chapters 5 and 6 of this book for more information in this regard.)

## Retirements

Retirement has the advantage for the employer that there is usually plenty of notice, so that succession arrangements can be planned. Phased withdrawal from the organisation is encouraged so that the retiree adjusts gradually to the new state of being without stimulating employment and with a lower level of income. Retirees may continue to work part-time after retirement, especially professional employees who can offer consulting services to the organisation.

## 10.11  Induction, staffing decisions, and quality assurance

The effectiveness of all staffing decisions, including the entrance of new employees into the organisation, depends on a minimum of disruption to the employer and the employee. Appropriate induction procedures and relevant staffing decisions can help in relieving the pressures caused by these staff movements. Given the pace of change in modern society and with regard to technology, superior induction programmes and staffing decisions are necessary to achieve a high level of quality in the people who staff our organisations. Cascio (1995:223) believes that the evaluation of induction programmes and employer-initiated staff movements is crucial if one is to measure the impact on productivity, quality of work-life, and the bottom line.

## 10.12  Conclusion

Traditionally, induction programmes were rigid, generic, and completed over a limited period. However, as organisations begin to restructure their overall HR practices to ensure continual growth and competitiveness, they need to refocus on the impact that initial employment experiences with an organisation have on a new employee. Induction can ease the entry process into an organisation, with positive results both for new and repositioned employees, and for the company. Induction deals with change – technological and social – and trends such as leased employees, disposable managers, and free-agent workers will make induction programmes even more important in the future.

Movement within and outside an organisation is healthy and challenging, provided that decision makers have the knowledge to be able to stimulate and control these changes. It is clear that all managers must come to accept the fact that organisational effectiveness depends to a large degree on the quality of these decisions.

## Summary

- Induction is only part of the process that endeavours to absorb an employee into the organisation and turn him/her into a productive worker. Orientation is the process of informing new employees about what is expected of them in the job and helping them cope with the stresses of transition. In the organisation, socialisation is the process of instilling in all employees the prevailing attitudes, standards, values, and patterns of behaviour expected by the organisation and its departments.
- The main purpose of induction is to assist the new employee in his/her integration into the organisation. The two distinct levels of induction are shared between the human resources department and the new employee's immediate manager. Sometimes a 'buddy' or co-worker conducts job induction.

- For induction to be successful, a company must have its statements of intent in the form of a policy manual.
- The entire process of induction can be divided into three stages: 1) anticipatory, or the induction stage; 2) encounter, or the orientation stage; and 3) settling-in, which is the socialisation stage. Planning, designing and implementing the induction programme must be done methodically, and follow-up and evaluation of the programme is essential.
- The allocation of people to jobs in an organisation is the result of new appointments and the redeployment of employees. Staffing strategies can be internal, external, or workforce pool, and these strategies are put into practice by means of promotions, transfers, demotions, and 'exits', such as resignations, layoffs, retrenchments, dismissals, and retirements. Well planned induction programmes and staffing decisions contribute greatly to organisational effectiveness.

## Case study
## Cold as ice at Ibiza Refrigerators

Ibiza Refrigeration Company builds refrigerators for other large refrigerator companies in South Africa. It employs about 300 people, mostly assembly line workers, and is located in a small rural town in Mpumalanga. The company builds chest-type freezers and small bar-type refrigerators. The owner and managing director of the company is a former engineer, as are most of the other executives. They are very knowledgeable about engineering, but have received little training in the basic principles of management.

During the summer months, volume at the factory increases a great deal, and the company hires about 50 casual employees to handle the heavy workload. Most of these are studying engineering diplomas or degrees at a technikon or university. When a new employee is hired, the company asks him/her to complete an application blank and then report for duty at the plant gate on the day specified by the Plant Manager. Employees receive no orientation. The worker is shown to a workstation and after a minimum period of on-the-job training, the new employee is expected to start performing a job. Typical jobs are screwing assorted screws into the sides of a freezer and placing strips of insulation into the freezer lid.

This procedure has worked well in the past, but recently the company experienced an abnormally high number of injuries to its employees (both permanent and casual workers). The managing director felt they should conduct a series of short training programmes on safe material-handling techniques. He was at a loss as to who should conduct the training. The human resources manager was a 64-year-old former engineer who was about to retire and was a poor speaker. The only other employee in the human resources department was a young secretary who knew nothing about proper handling techniques. Out of desperation, the managing director finally asked the first-line supervisor of the 'lid-line' to conduct the training.

At the first training session, this supervisor nervously stood up in front of 30 employees and read his presentation in a monotone voice. His entire speech lasted about one minute and consisted of some thoughts on how to pick up a heavy load. Afterwards everyone returned to their workstations, but by the end of the day everyone was laughing about the so-called 'training course'.

## Questions

1   Comment on the way that employees are introduced to the company.
2   What should the company be doing to prevent injuries in the future?

# Experiential exercise

PURPOSE: To act as a consultant and develop or revise an induction programme for a small company.

INTRODUCTION: Very often, small companies, with less than 30 employees, do not have a formal induction programme, usually because there is no-one appointed to take charge of this aspect of human resources management, or because they are just too busy. This chapter will have taught you about the benefits of having a programme and the disadvantages of ignoring the need for a good orientation process.

TASK: Working in a group of four or five students, make contact with a small organisation that needs to develop or revise its induction programme. Offer to perform this function for the company, and use as much of the theory in this chapter as is necessary to provide a good quality programme.

# Chapter questions

1  'All new employees, whether permanent or part-time staff members, should attend an induction programme.' Explain why you agree or disagree with this statement.

2  You must design an orientation programme for part-time sales assistants at Woolworths. Describe the issues that would be covered by the human resources department and the issues that would be covered by the first-level supervisor. Bear in mind the target audience, essential and desirable information, and the literacy level of the employees.

3  If you were a new first-year student at your institution, what information would you want to learn in an induction or orientation programme?

4  Compare and evaluate the staffing strategies at the disposal of South African managers. Bearing in mind issues such as unemployment, skills shortages, and global competitiveness, which of these strategies do you believe is situationally best for South Africa at the beginning of the 21st century?

5  Discuss the three stages of the socialisation process. Explain which of these stages (if any) contribute to the development of high-performing employees.

# Bibliography

ANFUSO, D. 1995. 'Creating a culture of caring pays off'. *Personnel Journal,* 74(8):70–77. Reprinted with permission of Copyright Clearance Center.

BJORKMAN, D. 2002. 'Retrenchment can be a new beginning'. *Succeed.* 30. September/October.

BOASE, N. 1997. 'Induction – introducing new employees to the organisation'. *People Dynamics,* 15(8):50. Reprinted with permission of Copyright Clearance Center.

BYARS, L.L. & RUE, L.W. 1997. *Human resource management, 5th edition.* Irwin, Chicago.

CASCIO, W.F. 1995. *Managing human resources: Productivity, quality of work life, profits, 4th edition.* McGraw-Hill Companies, New York.

CHERRINGTON, D.J. 1995. *The management of human resources, 4th edition.* (Prentice-Hall), Pearson Education Inc.

CORNELL, C. 2003. 'Keep talking to employees about retirement'. *HR Magazine* (www.workindex.com/editorial/benefit/). Reprinted with permission of Copyright Clearance Center.

DESSLER, G. 1997. *Human resources management, 7th edition.* (Prentice-Hall), Pearson Education Inc.

ELLERMAN, J.S. & KLEINER, B.H. 2000. 'How to write excellent human resource policies'. *Management Research News,* 23 (7/8).

GÓMEZ-MEJÍA, L.R., BALKIN, D.B. & CARDY, R.L. 1998. *Managing human resources, 2nd edition.* (Prentice-Hall), Pearson Education Inc.

KLEIN, C.S. & TAYLOR, J. 1994. 'Employee orientation is an ongoing process at the DuPont Merck Pharmaceutical Co.' *Personnel Journal,* 73(5):64–67. Reprinted with permission of Copyright Clearance Center.

LAABS, J. 2000. 'Mixing business with passion'. *Workforce*, 79(3): 80–86. Reprinted with permission of Copyright Clearance Center.

RUBIS, L. 1998. 'Disney show and tell'. *HR Magazine* (www.shrm.org). Reprinted with permission of Copyright Clearance Center.

SEGAL, J. 1993. 'Is your employee handbook a time bomb?' *HR Magazine* (www. shrm.org). Reprinted with permission of Copyright Clearance Center.

SULLIVAN, J. 2001a. 'A manager's guide to orientation'. *Electronic Recruiting Exchange*, www.erexchange.com (accessed 13 August 2001).

SULLIVAN J. 2001b. 'Maintaining morale and productivity during layoffs'. *Electronic Recruiting Exchange*, www.erexchange.com (accessed 29 October 2001).

TORRINGTON, D. & HALL, L. 1995. *Personnel management: Human resource management in action, 3rd edition.* (Prentice-Hall), Pearson Education (UK).

WERTHER, W.B. & DAVIS, K.D. 1993. *Human resources and personnel management, 4th edition.* McGraw-Hill Companies, New York.

## Websites

Disney World: www.disney.com
HR Magazine:
    www.shrm.org/docs/Hrmagazine.html
Retirement Planning Associates, Inc.:
    www.insworld.com/Newsletter/index.html
Workforce: www.workforceonline.com/research-center/

# 11

# Compensation management

## HB Schultz

## Learning outcomes

At the end of this chapter the learner should be able to:
- Discuss the objectives of a compensation system.
- Investigate the elements of total compensation and describe the rationale behind value-chain compensation.
- Use the steps of the theoretical model to design and implement a new compensation system for an organisation.
- Describe the steps in a job-based compensation plan.
- Debate the pay-for-knowledge and skills, pay-for-competencies, pay-for-performance, and incentive compensation plans.
- Provide a brief overview of the concept of broadbanding.
- Explain the circumstances in which mandatory and voluntary benefits are used.
- Compile a flexible benefits plan for a blue-collar, and a white-collar employee.
- Calculate the costs of employee benefits.
- Describe the impact of quality assurance on compensation systems.

## Key words and concepts
- broadbanding
- cafeteria benefit plans
- compensation survey
- incentive pay systems
- job evaluation
- job hierarchy
- mandatory benefits
- pay for competencies
- pay for knowledge and skills
- performance-based pay
- reward systems
- total compensation
- value-chain compensation
- voluntary benefits

### Illustrative case

### Inflation, salaries – what else is climbing?

On 20 March 2003, the Reserve Bank Governor, Tito Mboweni, announced that the key repo rate was to be left unchanged at 13.5 per cent. The man in the street probably did not regard this announcement as very important, but it could have far-reaching repercussions in the area of remuneration for the next year. Governor Mboweni said that although South Africa's inflation outlook had improved, it still hovered around eleven per cent, very far above the six per cent regarded as the target range for 2003. The recent high rates of increase in the average nominal remuneration per worker in the formal non-agricultural sectors of the economy, combined with a slowdown in labour productivity growth, were very disconcerting. High rates of increase in unit labour costs invariably lead to an acceleration in domestic inflation.

The rate of inflation is largely used as a basis for negotiating wage and salary increases each year. This figure usually determines the starting point for trade unions when they request a mandate for negotiations from their members. And many employees do not understand why their final increases are consistently nothing like the starting point. Will the man in the street ever understand why a 'high' salary increase is not a good thing for the economy of the country, or for inflation?

SOURCE: 'No interest rate cut for SA', *The Herald*, 21 March 2003

## 11.1   Introduction

An organisation's payroll can involve enormous sums of money. This is a major reason why pay systems must be part of organisational business strategy. The whole subject of pay has become increasingly complex; the impressive and sometimes confusing proliferation of compensation systems and trends of the 21st century can have a profound effect on new occupation structures and employee relationships. The pay debate – that is, the argument regarding the best way of rewarding people for their services – is far from settled. Some aspects of this pay debate are covered in this chapter.

The objectives of a compensation system

introduce our studies in this chapter on compensation management. We proceed to discuss the design of compensation systems with an emphasis on the concept of value-adding designs. Conventional job evaluation methods and emerging pay systems are debated before we take a brief look at employee benefits and services in an organisation. We close the chapter with some thoughts on the influence of quality assurance on compensation systems.

## 11.2   The objectives of a compensation system

Companies spend a very large proportion of their gross income on paying the people who work for them, and a large amount of this goes to the senior people who direct the business. It is an accepted fact that people must be rewarded for the services they provide for organisations, and it is also accepted that the majority of these rewards are monetary. Every company must be aware that the design of its rewards system rests on the objectives of compensation management – what must the compensation system achieve?

Firstly, the system must attract good employees by structuring salary packages that tempt people to apply for the job in the first place. The system must also be able to retain good workers, because if they are good, many other employers in the marketplace will be seeking their services as well. Once in the job, the compensation system must provide all the support needed to keep the employee motivated to perform at his/her best (McClune 1997:76).

Boase (1997:61) points out that the achievement of these objectives is influenced by several external factors:
- Labour market forces.
- Collective bargaining.
- Government legislation.
- Top management's philosophy regarding pay and benefits.
- Top management's willingness to recognise individual ability and effort.

## 11.3 The design of a compensation system

According to Risher (1997:14–5), our wage and salary programmes have been designed to reinforce bureaucratic structures. Traditional pay systems have focused on each job in isolation, ignoring the interaction of organisational members and buying employees' time by the hour. There have rarely been any incentives to provide for rewards above the hourly wage. The new work paradigm argues that people are the only sustainable source of competitive advantage and they really do want to contribute to the organisation's success. Risher has proposed this hypothesis: Employees who work in a rewarding environment often work very hard. What he is actually saying is that when people are rewarded for old behaviours they are less likely to adopt new behaviours. The reward environment is thus the starting point for adding value to the organisation. The reward environment should provide the opportunities to ask questions such as:

- How does this practice benefit the organisation?
- Does the benefit offset the administrative costs?
- If we discontinued this practice, would that adversely affect the organisation's performance?

When companies turn to the development of innovative compensation approaches, some basic caveats should be considered. First, companies must not assume that the latest and most popular compensation fad is the answer to their problems. Second, a holistic approach to implementing a new compensation design must be followed, not a piecemeal approach (Hackett and McDermott 1999:37). McClune (1997:98) states that whatever type of compensation design is decided upon, the concept of total compensation must always be addressed. Total compensation is the sum of all the cash items and the annualised value of non-cash benefits provided to the employee. The elements of total compensation are shown in Figure 11.1.

### 11.3.1 The elements of total compensation

Direct compensation is the fixed pay an employee receives on a regular basis, either in the form of a salary or as an hourly wage. These days, direct compensation has expanded to include cash incentives and various share offers from employers, but the defining factor of direct compensation is that it has a cash value.

Incentives are programmes designed to reward employees for good performance.

**Figure 11.1** The elements of total compensation

**Direct compensation**
- cash compensation
- basic salary
- deferred cash

**Other direct compensation**
- share options
- share ownership
- restricted shares

**Incentives**
- bonuses
- profit-sharing
- recognition

**Employee benefits**
- retirement benefits
- death benefits
- disability benefits
- medical benefits
- other

**Perquisites/fringe benefits**
- cars
- holidays, loans
- other

SOURCE: McClune (1997:73–101)

They come in many forms and can be monetary or non-monetary.

Benefits encompass a wide variety of programmes, such as medical aids, pension schemes or provident funds, unemployment insurance, and many others. Perquisites, or perks, are a special category of benefits and are available only to employees with some special status, such as upper-level managers.

## 11.3.2 The principles of value-chain compensation

Newman and Krzystofiak (1998:60) maintain that companies must look at compensation as a value-creating function in the organisation. There are two basic principles of this compensation approach:

- Value-chain compensation creates value for both the organisation and the employee.
- Value-chain compensation balances the four major compensation objectives of sustaining membership, motivating performance, building employee commitment, and encouraging growth in employees' skills.

A compensation system becomes value-adding when the system designers take into account the employees' priorities as well. The way in which the latter rank rewards at any given time in history determines the basis of the compensation structure. Rewards are ranked differently at different times, for example, job security ranks highly as a reward during times of high unemployment.

According to Hale and Bailey (1998:72–7), human capital gives a company its sustainable competitive advantage. Successful companies recognise seven principles of reward strategy that lead to superior business results:

1 Pay for performance and ensure that performance is tied to the successful achievement of critical business goals.
2 Link rewards to other levers of organisational change, such as providing recognition when deserved, offering career development, and providing challenging opportunities.
3 Reward measurable competencies.
4 Match incentives to the company culture.
5 Keep group incentives clear and simple.
6 Over-communicate the reward strategy for best results.
7 The greatest incentive is the work itself; employees want to be recognised for the work they do and the contribution they make.

## 11.3.3 A model for designing and implementing a new compensation system

Figure 11.2 shows the steps required to design and implement a new compensation system.

The first step requires a thorough analysis of the present compensation structure, current remuneration policies, pay procedures and salary problems. Thereafter, the compensation system designer formulates new salary policies based on the business strategy of the organisation and incorporating the value chain.

The choice of a new compensation system follows. The nature of the business and its strategic plans will influence this decision. The new system could be skills- or knowledge-based, competency-based, performance-related, variable-based incorporating incentives, and broadbanding could be used as a pay base. If the organisation has decided to investigate the feasibility of a new compensation system, it probably means that it has become dissatisfied with the existing one. In many cases this will be a job-based system. The organisation must not discard this system completely, as there is always the possibility that it might still be the best system if improvements are looked at.

The next step is to develop the implementation plan, working closely with remuneration experts, consulting with trade unions, and communicating with all employees. Once the new system is in place, evaluation and monitoring should be carried out on an ongoing basis.

**Figure 11.2** A model for a new compensation system

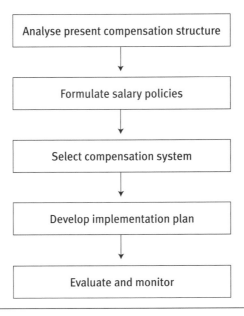

**Figure 11.3** The job-based compensation plan route

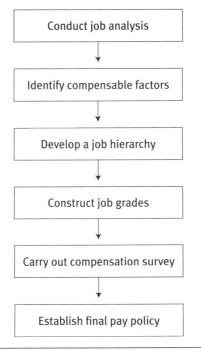

## 11.4 Conventional job evaluation methods

Gómez-Mejía et al. (1998:307) state that job-based approaches to compensation assume that work gets done by people who are paid to perform well-defined jobs. Because all jobs are not equally important to the organisation, and the labour market places a greater value on some jobs than others, the job-based compensation system aims to allocate pay so that the most important jobs are paid the most.

Most job-based plans follow a similar route in determining the value of jobs within the organisation, and the range in which the job should be paid. This route is depicted in Figure 11.3.

### 11.4.1 Conduct job analysis

The concept of job analysis was discussed in Chapter 7 and you will recall that it includes the gathering and organising of information concerning the tasks, duties and responsibilities of specific jobs. In a job-based compensation system, the initial step of conducting a job analysis produces job descriptions and job specifications for the specific jobs of the organisation.

### 11.4.2 Identify compensable factors

Job descriptions allow the identification of factors that are deemed necessary for acceptable job performance. These factors could be certain mental processes such as decision-making, reasoning and planning, or know-how, which is the sum total of every kind of skill required to do the job. The practice of identifying compensable factors is known as job evaluation.

Job evaluation is a process of systematically analysing jobs to determine the relative worth of jobs within the organisation. This analysis is the basis of a job hierarchy and pay ranges. Job evaluation does not assess the value of the employees within a position, but rather determines the worth of the job to the organisation. Popular job evaluation methods include job ranking, the classification method, the factor comparison method, and the point method. The job ranking and classification methods are simple to use and do not need much prior training. They call for subjective decisions, usually with a benchmarked job as a starting point, and are often used by very small companies that do not possess the expertise to undertake more complex job evaluation methods.

Because it is impossible for one person to have a comprehensive knowledge of all jobs in an organisation, especially in a large company, a trained job evaluation committee usually carries out the factor comparison and points methods of job evaluation. The committee members should have an adequate knowledge of all work areas in the organisation, and should have received basic training in the way that job evaluation is carried out. Job evaluation committee members typically consist of a:

- Departmental head from the area in which the job to be evaluated is performed.
- Departmental head from another, neutral area in the organisation.
- Trade union representative.
- Representative from the human resources department who keeps the process moving forward and on track.

In some cases an external compensation consultant may join the committee as an unbiased 'third party'.

In South Africa, popular forms of the factor comparison and points job evaluation methods are the Patterson method – based on decision-making; the Hay method – based on factors such as know-how, problem-solving, and accountability; and the Peromnes method – based on the eight factors of problem solving, consequences of judgment, pressure of work, knowledge required, job impact, educational qualifications, training, and experience. Computerised software packages have made the utilisation of these job evaluation methods much simpler and more accurate than they once were.

### 11.4.3 Develop a job hierarchy

Once jobs have been evaluated by means of one or other of the job evaluation methods, the value that has been established for each job allows it to be slotted into a hierarchy that will eventually paint a picture of the importance of each job to the organisation. In this way, the value of certain jobs can be compared to the value of other jobs in the company. A typical job hierarchy is depicted in Figure 11.4.

### 11.4.4 Construct job grades

A job hierarchy allows an organisation to classify the jobs into grades. All the jobs in a given grade are judged to be essentially the same in terms of importance and therefore it is logical that all the jobs in a specific grade would be paid relative to each other, and to other jobs in the organisation. Job evaluation does not take into account the wage rates in the marketplace and organisations use compensation surveys to determine and fix pay rates to specific jobs.

### 11.4.5 Carry out compensation survey

Nearly all compensation professionals use surveys to determine data for creating, adjust-ing, or updating a firm's pay system. Compensation surveys may be purchased from companies that specialise in collecting and interpreting pay data, outsourced to a consulting firm, or conducted by a company itself. Accurate data is extremely important because inaccuracies can result in high labour costs and an increase in undesirable employee behaviours. Compensation surveys generally yield ranges of data for different salary grades. It must be borne in mind that this information refers to the value of the job to the specific organisation, not to the value of the person doing the job.

Werner et al. (1999:56) state that the data obtained from compensation surveys should be assessed in terms of the answers to the following questions, before it is used by an organisation:

- How well does the survey describe the job being measured?
- If the job in the survey is a multi-level job, are all levels represented?
- What is the effective date of the data?
- What is the labour market for the job to be priced (geographic or industry-specific)?
- Who participated in the survey?
- Does the survey describe the methodology used to process the data?

**Figure 11.4** A job hierarchy

| General manager | | |
|---|---|---|
| Production manager | Sales manager | Financial manager |
| Production supervisor | Sales supervisors | Accounts supervisors |
| Artisans | Sales representatives | |
| Machine operators | Creditors clerks Receptionist | Debtors clerks |
| Cleaners | Security assistants | |

- What was the methodology used to collect the data?
- How do the average, median, and 25th and 75th percentiles relate to each other?
- Does the survey provide non-weighted as well as weighted averages?
- Do the survey participants vary significantly from year to year?

Dickmeyer (2002) describes the advantages of customised surveys as follows:
- They can be targeted directly at the companies with the closest match for the position you are surveying.
- Current salary data can be collected, rather than obsolete data.
- Specific information can be targeted, rather than using general information in broad salary surveys.

One must also take into account the disadvantages of using customised salary surveys:
- They can be costly to administer in terms of time and money. However, these costs must be compared to purchasing expensive and general salary surveys.
- They can come under legal scrutiny with regard to pay discrimination.
- It is challenging and time-consuming to develop a good survey instrument.

## 11.4.6 Establish final pay policy

Because wages and salaries vary widely in the marketplace, the company must decide whether to take the lead, lag behind or pay the same as the majority of companies in the industry. The company's pay policy is therefore determined by how it chooses to position itself in the pay market. A number of factors will influence this decision, among them the wages and salaries it can afford to pay, and whether it wishes to attract above-average or mediocre workers. Those organisations that position themselves around the midpoint of the wage and salary distribution are said to follow the going rate.

## 11.5 Emerging pay systems

Traditionally, people were paid primarily through base salaries, determined by the specific job, the need to maintain a certain level of internal pay equity, and the need to pay externally competitive salaries. Employees were not encouraged to develop skills other than those required by the job, nor were they rewarded for attributes such as flexibility, practical judgment, and the ability to work with others. While such programmes work well in functional organisations, they do little to advance many of the values of the newer work cultures. Base pay does not motivate employees in a flatter, leaner organisation, where individual and organisational success hinges on performance and the lateral growth of the workforce (Flannery et al. 1996:83).

In many organisations, individuals have not changed as rapidly as the cultures in which they are expected to work. Many employees cling to the belief that they are entitled to ever-increasing salaries, punctual and substantial raises, and luxurious benefits packages.

But old habits can be broken, old behaviours changed, old expectations replaced with more attractive new ones. The knowledge of new cultures and compensation strategies must not be the sole property of the compensation professional. Line managers must have a clear understanding of pay strategies and the pay process must be made clear to both supervisors and employees. To be successful, pay strategies must add value to the organisation, but one must understand how they work, what values and behaviours they support, how they must be administered and communicated, and what their limitations are.

## 11.5.1 Pay for knowledge and skills

As employees acquire more skills, they become more flexible resources, developing a broader understanding of the work processes and of their contribution to the organisation.

Various critical issues manifest themselves within a knowledge- and skill-based pay system:

- A scheme must be created for training employees and helping them develop the required new skills.
- The organisation must also address what skills and knowledge they will pay for, and the scope of development that will be rewarded.
- The organisation must decide whether it is going to design a programme that works within a single job family, or whether it will utilise a plan that encourages true cross-training, or multi-skilling.

Lee (1999) states that the increase in the adoption of skills-based pay plans is due to the expected benefits in worker productivity, motivation, work team effectiveness, and workforce flexibility to adapt to changing production needs. Because people can rotate into different positions as needed, the impact of absenteeism and turnover on organisational effectiveness is minimised.

In terms of employee-related outcomes, skills-based pay results in higher pay rates, increasing satisfaction, higher skills growth, commitment, and capacity for self-management or problem-solving. There is greater teamwork among individuals and better career opportunities. Other potential benefits include higher product quality, decreased labour costs and increased productivity.

A potential disadvantage of a skills-based pay plan is its effect on higher average pay rates. Since training is critical in skills-based pay programmes, higher costs are associated with training. Production losses and problems may result while the more experienced employees are being trained. However, in the long run, training results in a more flexible and productive workforce.

## Case-in-point
### *Environment for success*

It will take time before South African companies decide to offer the more unusual perks that are becoming more common in first-world countries – providing tee-pees where employees can take a nap, and allowing staff to bring pets to work. The 2001 South African Deloitte and Touche Human Capital Corporation survey found job satisfaction to be the most important requirement for South African employees, above career development and remuneration. The Escher Group – rated number one of the survey in terms of employee happiness – bears out the philosophy that job satisfaction comes from a culture of equality and a whole lot of personal freedom for individual staff members.

Escher's remuneration policy is becoming legendary. Tracey van der Heijden, managing director of the group, says that everyone is paid well. They pay according to pay surveys, and the way salaries are determined is transparent. Everyone knows everyone else's salary. Everyone is a shareholder, and thus has a stake in the company. There is not much staff turnover in this company, where all employees are allocated a share option equal to three times their annual package. Staff have an equal vote on all issues – including salary increases. Escher listed on the Johannesburg Securities Exchange in 2001, and the share price has remained steady in a fluctuating market. Something about this system must be creating an environment for success.

SOURCE: Fontyn (2001:26–8)

## 11.5.2 Pay for competencies

Many organisations are discovering that they want to reward more than just the skills or knowledge necessary for a new role. Employees are needed who are not only skilled, but also energetic, service-conscious, and problem-solvers. The answer lies in the development of less obvious competencies – the ability to work in teams, to accomplish specific goals, to solve problems rapidly, and to understand the customer's perspectives and meet their needs in a way that really adds value.

Competencies are the sets of skills, knowledge, abilities, behavioural characteristics, and other attributes that predict superior performance. True competencies are those that add value and help predict success – these are the ones that should be rewarded, which involves identifying those competencies that are needed to support an organisation's strategy.

Certain problems manifest themselves when a company considers adopting a competency-based pay model. Firstly, how does one define a competency, and secondly, what competencies are appropriate in a specific organisation? Cira and Benjamin (1998: 22–5) state that more than 25 years ago David McClelland, the renowned psychologist, defined competencies as those underlying characteristics or behaviours that excellent performers exhibit more consistently and more effectively than average performers. The actual selection of competencies depends on the nature of the business, and the nature of the job – competencies could include leadership, flexibility, initiative, and so on. Organisations can establish a competency model as a basis for determining competencies. These models are:

- The core competency model, which is used to capture the competencies required in the organisation as a whole and is often closely aligned with the organisation's mission, visions, and values.
- The functional competency model, which is built around key business functions, such as finance, marketing, information technology, or manufacturing.
- The role competency model, which applies to the specific role that the individual plays in the organisation – technician, manager, and so on.
- The job competency model is the narrowest of the four models, it only applies to a single job, and its relevance to pay applications is limited.

What sets superior performers apart from the more mediocre workers, what do the best performers do and what behaviour characteristics predict outstanding performance? Every organisation will find different answers to these questions. The decision to be made is how to find the answers. In the following text box, we read about how two large American organisations handled this issue.

---

### Encounter 11.1

THE HOLIDAY INN AND LEGO SYSTEMS INC. EXPERIENCE

When Holiday Inn and LEGO Systems Inc. decided to implement competency-based pay systems, they took the route of using their employees to identify top performers and their competencies. They made sure that employees were trained to utilise only distinguishing competencies, that is, those competencies that not only set the best performers apart from the rest, but also added value to the results of the organisation. If this was not done they could land up paying for new behaviours, but not necessarily new results.

These organisations found that tying the competencies to the base salary programme in the initial stages of the new system was the least painful way of achieving acceptance. Managers also ensured that their competency-based pay system was incorporated into the processes for selecting new employees and assessing employee performance. They realised that a 360 degree performance evaluation was the best way of assessing performance based on competencies.

SOURCE: Flannery et al. (1996)

---

Competency-based pay should be implemented only as part of a broader competency-based human resources programme, and it must follow successful implementation of competency-based performance management.

### 11.5.3 Performance-based pay

The pay strategies described thus far focus on two primary issues critical to organisational success – people, and how they perform. Yet this alone does not drive the organisation forward. In searching for answers to the fundamental changes in business, organisations rediscovered the value of variable, performance-based pay strategies.

Empowerment has followed the moving of incentive programmes beyond the executive suites, and has allowed employees to share in the organisation's risks and rewards. These pay strategies have slowly found favour, particularly in the United States, but it is extremely important that employees are told not only how the programme works, but what they must do to make it work.

Some of the following strategies have been used in South Africa for a number of years, but normally only in the domain of white-collar employees. The difference between international companies and South African companies, is that our colleagues abroad are involving blue-collar workers as well in performance-based incentive schemes.

## 11.5.4 Incentive pay systems

Incentive pay systems may be either individual or group plans, and they are usually geared to measurable performance results, such as units of production, sales volume, cost savings, or profitability. A common type of individual incentive programme is the piecework plan in which the employee is paid for each unit produced. The more an employee produces, the more s/he receives. Sales commissions represent a common individual incentive, as do managerial and executive bonuses, and stock option plans. All these incentive pay systems are usually built upon a minimum base pay that remains standard no matter what the measured performance results are. Individual incentives are gaining popularity lower in the organisation, and are used to drive not only traditional financial goals, but also more contemporary values of productivity, customer satisfaction, service, and quality.

Group incentive plans include profit-sharing, which involves all or certain groups of employees sharing in a non-deferred pool created by a percentage of the profits.

Gainsharing is another type of group incentive, and is usually tied to achievement of very specific goals for productivity, quality improvement, and cost effectiveness. A difficulty is how to measure the gains, and how to determine the role employees have had in achieving those gains (Leap and Crino 1993: 424–7).

Small group incentives are often paid to specific career groups, project groups, or teams. They tend to be temporary, lasting only until the project is finished.

Long-term incentives and lump-sum payments are also used as part of variable pay programmes.

Whether the emphasis is on teams or individuals, it is clear that pay strategies, like the business strategies they support, are changing dramatically. Managers and leaders must understand five basic tenets of dynamic compensation:

1 Pay is first and foremost a people issue. It is about motivating them, reshaping and refocusing their behaviours and accepting new values.
2 Pay is a major organisational communication tool.
3 No single pay strategy is right for everyone. Even different employee groups in the same organisation may require different strategies.
4 Pay must support – not lead – the organisation's vision, values, and business strategies.
5 To achieve the first four points, pay must be aligned with the organisation's work culture.

Taking the step to change a company's compensation strategies is not an overnight decision. What strategies have international companies selected, and what is the success factor? Two examples of American companies that changed their compensation policies are offered in the text box below.

## Encounter 11.2

WHIRLPOOL AND OWENS-CORNING REROUTE
THEIR PAY STRUCTURES

Whirlpool Corporation, one of the world's largest automatic washer manufacturers, opted to institute a performance-based compensation system. The cornerstone of their gain-sharing programme is an approach that provides workers, especially those on the line, with the incentives and motivation to treat their work as if they're an owner of the company. Whirlpool places the money from all cost savings, business improvements and productivity gains into a fund for each specific facility, and workers receive a quarterly payout for their efforts.

Total cost savings for the company's Ohio plant recently measured $36.4 million, with payouts of $19.2 million. Managers say that employees are more knowledgeable, there is greater cooperation and involvement, and financial and quality-control benchmarks have reached all-time highs. The programme has helped narrow the culture gap between hourly and salaried employees, and payouts have alleviated pressure for base-wage increases.

Owens-Corning, a construction material manufacturer, scrapped its existing compensation and benefits programmes and created a variable compensation and flexible benefits programme that is tied to performance.

Their Rewards and Resources programme is linked to company performance. Base rewards, such as salary and variable rewards, depend on performance. Resources incorporate a global stock plan, where each employee receives an annual bonus in stock; savings and profit sharing; a cash balance plan, which converts retirement benefits to an opening cash balance; and choice making – handing over benefits choices to individuals to encourage employee ownership and decision-making.

source: Greengard (1995:100); Solomon (1998:78–81)

## 11.6  Broadbanding

If an organisation has reduced staff and cut management levels it must look for new ways to move people through the organisation. But, when there is not much of a pyramid left to climb, how will people get their kicks – their bucks, their psychic compensation?

Even the few organisations that remain fatter rather than flatter are adopting new organisational values and changing cultures. Their traditional pay strategies and delivery systems have become obsolete. The vertical system of grading is out of synch with the flatter, flexible, team-orientated cultures that many organisations are moving towards. To counter this mal-alignment, some are adopting the strategy known as broadbanding, in which a few relatively broad bands replace numerous grades.

Broadbanding is not another pay-for strategy. It is a new pay platform on which a compensation strategy, such as skill- or competency-based pay can be built and effectively operated.

Rather than climb up through a series of grades, employees might spend most, if not all their careers in a single band, moving laterally and getting more pay as they gain new skills, competencies, or responsibilities, or as they improve their performance. Unlike traditional pay grades, bands can be designed to overlap, adding flexibility to an already flexible pay programme. This overlap allows employees to continue to progress within the organisation without the elevation to another pay range or job title.

Broadbanding can be especially useful in the new 'boundaryless' organisations and in those team-based organisations that emphasise less specialised jobs and processes that cross departments and require more skills and individual or team authority. It also facilitates the growth and development of alternate career tracks.

Collapsing the old grading system without first changing the culture, or deciding how people will move through the bands, can only lead to failure in a broadbanding system.

However, it can be very effective when tailored to an organisation's individual culture, values, and business strategy (Flannery et al. 1996: 99).

## 11.7 Employee benefits

Employee benefits are items in the total package offered to employees over and above salary which increase their wealth or well-being at some cost to the employer. Benefits can frequently add up to around one third of payroll costs. Items such as pensions, sick pay, holidays and a varying range of other benefits, are an integral part of every employer's conditions of employment.

Many benefits are interdependent and an effective benefits policy generally depends on careful evaluation of the pattern and balance of benefit entitlements throughout the organisation. Many of the problems that arise over benefits occur because the effect of new or improved benefits on employee attitudes has not been properly assessed. Many benefits are linked with status, and this can often be the source of discontent. No organisation should have to waste valuable time sorting out problems of this nature. They can usually be prevented by careful benefits policy planning and effective and detailed communication of entitlements to employees (Armstrong and Murlis 1994:140). Readers or learners are referred to Chapters 5 and 6 of this book for more information in this regard.

### 11.7.1 Types of benefits

Some employee benefits and services are regulated by the government, and employers are compelled to make these benefits available to their employees. These are called mandatory benefits. Other benefits are offered to the employees voluntarily.

### 11.7.2 Mandatory benefits

Benefits that must be provided by law include:

### Unemployment insurance

The Unemployment Insurance Act, No. 63 of 2001, makes provision for the establishment of a central fund to be utilised for the payment of unemployment, maternity, death, and sick benefits. The fund makes provision for the insurance of employees contributing to the fund, against the risk of loss of income through the termination of their services, illness or pregnancy. In addition, provision is made for the payment of benefits to dependants of deceased contributors. The main purpose of the fund is to insure contributors against temporary loss of employment, and not to provide for those who leave the labour market.

### Compensation for injuries and diseases

The Compensation for Occupational Injuries and Diseases Act, No. 130 of 1993, regulates the payment of compensation to persons who are injured or who contract a disease during the execution of their duties. All persons who employ one or more employees are required to register and to pay annual assessments to the Compensation Fund. The revenue of this Fund comprises mainly the annual assessments paid by the registered employers. Employees do not contribute to the Fund.

### 11.7.3 Voluntary benefits

Employees can rely on a number of benefits, which are non-mandatory or voluntary on the part of the employer. It should be noted, however, that a number of the benefits discussed below do have certain legislated minimums, such as the number of days vacation leave, the number of paid public holidays, the number of days sick leave, and maternity leave benefits. In South Africa, these minimums are legislated in the Basic Conditions of Employment Act, No. 75 of 1997.

### Vacation leave

Vacation leave serves primarily to improve employees' health, personal development, and morale. Most companies offer their employees vacation leave with pay after a set minimum period of service, usually one year. Employees are entitled to three weeks' fully paid leave after every 12 months' continuous employment.

## Paid public holidays

South Africans currently enjoy 12 paid public holidays per year as follows:

| | |
|---|---|
| New Years Day | 1 January |
| Human Rights Day | 21 March |
| Good Friday | |
| Family Day | |
| Freedom Day | 27 April |
| Worker's Day | 1 May |
| Youth Day | 16 June |
| National Women's Day | 9 August |
| Heritage Day | 24 September |
| Day of Reconciliation | 16 December |
| Christmas Day | 25 December |
| Day of Goodwill | 26 December |

Whenever one of the above public holidays falls on a Sunday, the following Monday is proclaimed a public holiday.

## Time for personal matters

Employees may receive full pay for a number of personal absences, such as sorting out business matters, attending funerals, dental appointments, and weddings.

## Sick leave

The number of days sick leave to which an employee is entitled depends on company policy regarding seniority and period of service. The minimum entitlement is six weeks' paid sick leave for every 36 months of continuous employment.

## Maternity leave

Under the Basic Conditions of Employment Act, a pregnant employee is entitled to four months' maternity leave, which may be taken on full, partial, or no pay, according to the rules and regulations laid down and negotiated by the company. It must be noted that where there is only partial or no pay, the Unemployment Insurance Fund makes up the difference to an amount of 45 per cent of the worker's rate of pay, provided that certain requirements have been met.

## Health and life insurance

Many employers provide insurance benefits as part of a group life insurance plan, which covers employees while they are in the employ of the company. Group life insurance allows the company and the employee to benefit from lower premium rates and these insurances are often subsidised or paid in full by the employer. These insurances also cover episodes such as trauma experienced due to a life-threatening disease, disability of the employee, and death of a spouse.

## Medical aid schemes

Medical aid schemes are highly valued by employees because they provide medical coverage for both themselves and their dependents, especially with the high cost of medical care in South Africa, and the perception that services at state run hospitals and clinics leave a lot to be desired. Basic medical plans usually make provision for a restricted number of hospital, surgical and medical services, or offer full services with a percentage levy paid by members, while general plans provide for the cost of prolonged treatment for more serious conditions in full. A number of companies in South Africa also make provision for funding towards the costs of consulting traditional healers.

## Pension Funds

Although company pension funds have been around since the 1950s, many organisations have never taken the time to impress upon their employees the importance of managing their investment in retirement. As people have moved from one company to another they have drawn their pension contributions and then started contributing to a new fund as they enter new employment. If this trend continues throughout a person's working life, it is obvious that the provision for retirement will be totally inadequate. Moreover, since the notion of permanent employment for long periods of time in one company, is becoming globally outdated, this trend towards spending retirement funds is likely to continue unless companies take it upon themselves to do a great deal more counselling, or unless some kind of legislation is passed.

Be that as it may, most organisations provide a pension, or a provident fund to which employees contribute a percentage of their wages, a portion of which is usually subsidised by the employer. There is usually a waiting period before an employee can join a pension fund, after which membership is compulsory.

### Employee services

Employee services include the provision of various facilities that are non-mandatory but offered by employers because these additional services to employees are thought to have a positive impact on employee loyalty, and to decrease absenteeism and turnover. These services include cafeteria facilities, relocation expenses, social and recreational facilities, financial and legal services, educational facilities, childcare programmes, transportation programmes, and housing subsidies or allowances.

## 11.8   Benefit planning and flexible benefit plans

Research shows that employees prefer employee benefits that reflect the dynamic labour market. More than 75 per cent of all workers prefer health benefits, young workers state a second preference for a savings plan, older workers for a pension. The vast majority of all workers state a preference for the ability to make choices in order to shape the ben-

efits package to their special needs (Salisbury 1997:74–5). In the past, most large private employers adopted a paternalistic approach in managing employee benefits. Today, although the tendency in bureaucratic-style organisations is still to dictate the terms of benefits packages, employers are starting to realise that the new deal in the employer-employee relationship demands much more flexibility. Figure 11.5 suggests a framework for comprehensive benefit planning.

Dessler (1997:530) states that the terms 'flexible benefits plan' and 'cafeteria benefits plan' are generally used synonymously. The idea of cafeteria benefits allows the employee to put together his/her own benefits package, subject to two constraints: the employers must limit the total cost for each total benefits package, and each benefit plan must include certain non-optional items, such as the mandatory benefits mentioned above. The philosophy behind flexible benefit plans is that no one knows the employee's needs better than the employee him- or herself, and his/her needs change through the years, so s/he can alter his/her benefits. Software packages are avail-

---

**Figure 11.5** A framework for comprehensive benefit planning

---

1  Establish objectives.
2  Collect complete descriptive data on the current workforce.
3  Determine how much money is available in the budget.
4  Determine what programmes fit your objectives, your workforce, and your budget.
5  Determine what your employees need and want.
6  Decide what you will provide and what you will actually spend in total.
7  Determine options, and costs, of administration, management, and communication.
8  Plan how the above will be accomplished.
9  Implement all the above.

SOURCE: Salisbury (1997:74–80)

---

**Figure 11.6** Advantages and disadvantages of flexible benefits programmes

---

Advantages
- The company can set the sum total of benefits for each employee.
- The changing needs of the workforce are catered for.
- Employees take ownership of their choice of benefits by satisfying their own unique needs.
- It is less costly for the organisation when an employee adds a new benefit.

Disadvantages
- Without proper assistance employees can make bad choices and find themselves not covered for emergencies.
- Company administrative costs increase.
- The cost of some benefits may increase as a result of a majority of employees choosing the benefit.

---

able to assist employees in making wise choices under a flexible benefits programme. The advantages and disadvantages of flexible benefit programmes are summarised in Figure 11.6.

The assessment of proposed alterations or improvements to benefit provisions can be developed around the following questions suggested in an *HR Executive* survey (2002):
- How do you anticipate benefits at your organisation to change?
- What benefits do you anticipate decreasing in the next year?
- What benefits do you anticipate will increase in the next year?
- Does your organisation plan on changing the current employee contribution for benefit plans?
- Does your organisation offer benefits to dependents?
- Does your organisation contribute towards the cost of dependent coverage?
- Will your organisation make changes in the coming year to the contribution currently provided for dependent coverage?

- Has the economy influenced the change expected in benefit plans?

## 11.9   Calculating the costs of employee benefits

There are four bases on which employers can calculate the costs of benefits and services, namely:
- The total annual costs of benefits for all employees.
- Costs of benefits per employee per annum (total costs divided by number of employees).
- Percentage of the payroll (total costs of benefits divided by annual wages).
- Costs per employee per hour (costs per employee per annum divided by number of hours worked).

It is important to note that when management makes certain decisions in respect of incurring costs for benefits and services, it has to take into account the following considerations:
- There is little evidence that benefits and services really encourage improved performance, or increase employees' job satisfaction.
- Costs of employee benefits and services have increased dramatically.
- Employers are required by law to introduce certain programmes.
- So-called voluntary programmes are constantly under pressure from labour unions, competitors and the industry to improve on employee benefits and services.

Calculating the costs of the benefits and services the company offers to its employees allows management to decide which benefits strategy the company will follow:
- The pace-setter strategy, which means that the organisation is the first to introduce the benefits employees want.
- The comparable benefits strategy, which means that the organisation puts its

benefits on a par with those offered by other similar organisations.

- The minimum benefits strategy, which means that the organisation offers only those benefits required by law and demanded by employees.

## 11.10 Compensation systems and quality assurance

According to Boase (1997:61), certain future trends are likely to manifest themselves in South Africa:

- Compensation practices will shift towards base rates with top-up incentives based on performance, such as gain share, profit share, etc.
- Increased flexibility will become evident in remuneration packages.
- Remuneration packages will become more tax-effective.
- Remuneration will be linked to teams, rather than to individuals.

The whole question of whether an organisation's compensation plan is adequate or not, depends on the quality of compensation planning, design and implementation. The external customers of the company are the ultimate winners in this game; well-designed benefits inspire motivated employees, who in turn, contribute towards the satisfaction of the customer.

## 11.11 Conclusion

Whatever the future holds in store for the way people are remunerated in an organisation, one thing which appears certain is that effective, well-motivated and appropriately rewarded employees are pivotal to a successful business. The technicalities of a compensation system are important because pay determination creates the climate of trust that is essential to building a sense of fairness and equity. Without this, it is difficult to see how a performance management system could be maintained.

## Summary

- The compensation system must attract good employees, it must also be able to retain good workers, and it must provide all the support needed to keep the employee motivated to perform at his/her best.
- The reward environment is the starting point for adding value to the organisation. A holistic approach to implementing a new compensation design must be followed. Total compensation is the sum of all the cash items and the annualised value of non-cash benefits provided to the employee.
- Direct compensation is the fixed pay an employee receives on a regular basis, either in the form of a salary or as an hourly wage. Incentives are programmes designed to reward employees for good performance. Benefits encompass a wide variety of programmes such as medical aids, pension schemes or provident funds, unemployment insurance, and many others.
- Value-chain compensation creates value for both the organisation and the employee and balances the four major compensation objectives of sustaining membership, motivating performance, building employee commitment, and encouraging growth in employees' skills.
- Seven principles of reward strategy lead to superior business results. A new compensation system could be skills- or knowledge-based, competency-based, performance-related, variable-based incorporating incentives, and broadbanding could be used as a pay base. Job-based compensation systems aim to allocate pay so that the most important jobs are paid the most. Most job-based systems determine the value of jobs within the organisation, and the range in which the job should be paid.
- Pay strategies must add value to the organisation, but one must understand how they work, what values and behav-

iours they support, how they must be administered and communicated, and what their limitations are. Emerging pay trends include pay for knowledge and skills, pay for competencies and incentive, variable-based pay systems. Broadbanding is not another pay-for strategy. It is a new pay platform on which a compensation strategy such as skill- or competency-based pay can be built and effectively operated.

- Employee benefits are items in the total package offered to employees over and above salary, which increase their wealth or well-being at some cost to the employer. Mandatory benefits are regulated by the government and other benefits are offered voluntarily by employers. A cafeteria benefits plan allows the employee to put together her/his own benefits package.

- There are four bases on which employers can calculate the costs of benefits and services: the total annual costs, costs of benefits per employee per annum, percentage of the payroll, and costs per employee per hour. Benefits strategies include the pace-setter strategy, the comparable benefits strategy, and the minimum benefits strategy.

## Case study
## Cutting the costs of the cloth

Cathy Tate is the owner and chief executive officer of Quantum Linens, a textile manufacturer situated near Durban. Cathy's father started the business in 1962, and she took over the reins in 1994 when he retired. Revenues and profits increased slowly but surely during her father's term of office, but during the latter part of the last decade, Cathy has had to face many financial problems as a result of foreign competition, mounting raw material costs, and the increasing burden of providing employee benefits.

Local newspapers reported that delegates at the 13th International AIDS Conference, held in Durban in July 2000, agreed that health care costs have grown faster than overall inflation and faster than any other segment of the economy since 1990. Besides the AIDS crisis, many of the delegates at the conference cited large catastrophic-illness claims, increased use of mental health and substance abuse services, increased use of medical services, high-technology medicine, and the demographics of blue-collar workers – a higher percentage of older employees requiring medical treatment for ageing conditions, and an increasing percentage of younger employees requiring medical treatment for AIDS-related diseases.

Cathy knows that she must do something about managing the benefits programme in her small company of 80 employees. There is currently no structure to the benefits programme and she doesn't know where to start. Cathy has decided to procure the services of a benefits consultant.

## Question

Assume that you have been hired as the benefits consultant. Evaluate the situation and write a report containing recommendations regarding the employee benefits programme at Quantum Linens.

## Experiential exercise

PURPOSE: To act as a compensation consultant and to carry out a remuneration project.

INTRODUCTION: The outline overleaf was used for a remuneration project.

TASK: Form a group of at least four people and make contact with an organisation that requires an evaluation of its compensation system. Use the outline to compile a report to its top managers.

| | Actions | Requirements |
|---|---|---|
| 1 Analyse present compensation structure and determine whether current pay system will be retained | 1 Investigate basis of current compensation policies (job evaluation, or alternative systems?)<br>2 Study current pay procedures (what elements of total compensation are included in the pay system?)<br>3 Explore existing compensation problems and compile profile of current remuneration packages (Reasons for this study – equity? Structure?) | 1 Relevant company policy documents<br>2 Personal and telephonic discussions |
| 2 Job profiling | 1 Explore the validity of existing job profiles/descriptions/specifications<br>2 Communicate the rationale for the study to relevant employees<br>3 Starting from a zero-base, develop an applicable job analysis questionnaire for relevant jobs<br>4 Administer questionnaires<br>5 Analyse completed questionnaires<br>6 Follow-up with interviews to clarify points on questionnaires<br>7 Prepare job profiles | 1 Existing company documents |
| 3 Remuneration benchmarking | 1 Determine base-line organisations<br>2 Analyse and interpret data and market-related remuneration packages of targeted organisations<br>3 Prepare schedule of remuneration scales<br>4 Match proposed salary packages to job profiles<br>5 Arrange and compare hierarchical positions in accordance with job profiling and remuneration data<br>6 Prepare final report for company | |

## Chapter questions

1  You have been asked to evaluate whether your organisation's current pay structure competes with the pay structure of similar organisations. How would you go about conducting this comparison and what criteria would you use to determine if your data is valid and reliable?

2  The decision makers in your organisation have agreed that the company is too bureaucratic and has too many layers of jobs to compete effectively. The company has decided to flatten the structure to not more than five levels and you have been asked to suggest innovative alternatives to the traditional job-based approach to employee compensation. Discuss and compare your suggestions in detail.

3  The Port of Nqira (Coega) is currently

being built north east of Port Elizabeth. This deep-water harbour is offering thousands of workers the opportunity to participate in this exciting scheme. If you had to make recommendations for the type of pay plans that should be used here, what would your recommendations be?

4   Although there are a number of innovative pay systems available, many companies believe that the traditional job-based pay system is still the best choice. Discuss the job-based compensation model and indicate which type of organisational structure it would match the best.

5   Why is communication so important in the area of employee benefits? What methods can be used to communicate new and existing details regarding benefits to employees, and what are the positive consequences of effective benefits communication?

# Bibliography

ARMSTRONG, M. & MURLIS, H. 1994. *A handbook of salary administration, 2nd edition.* Kogan Page, London.

BOASE. 1997. 'Strategising the remuneration policy'. *People Dynamics,* 15(9):61. Reprinted with permission of Copyright Clearance Center.

CIRA, D.J. & BENJAMIN, E.R. 1998. 'Competency-based pay: A concept in evolution'. *Compensation & Benefits Review,* 30(5):21–28.

DESSLER, G. 1997. *Human resource management, 7th edition.* (Prentice-Hall), Pearson Education Inc.

DICKMEYER, W. 2002. 'How to conduct an effective pay survey'. *Workforce* (www.workforce.com). Reprinted with permission of Copyright Clearance Center.

FLANNERY, T.P., HOFRICHTER, D.A. & PLATTEN, P.E. 1996. *People, performance, and pay: Dynamic compensation for changing organizations.* The Free Press, New York.

FONTYN, Y. 2001. 'Gow Escher creates an environment for success'. *People Dynamics,* 19(3):26–28. Reprinted with permission of Copyright Clearance Center.

GÓMEZ-MEJÍA, L.R., BALKIN, D.B., & CARDY, R.L. 1998. *Managing human resources,* 2nd edition. (Prentice-Hall), Pearson Education Inc.

GREENGARD, S. 1995. 'Whirlpool build a performance-based strategy'. *Personnel Journal,* 74(1):100. Reprinted with permission of Copyright Clearance Center.

HACKETT, T.J. & MCDERMOTT, D.G. 1999. 'Integrating compensation strategies: A holistic approach to compensation design'. *Compensation and Benefits Review,* 31(5):36–43. Sage Publications.

HALE, J. & BAILEY, G. 1998. 'Seven dimensions of successful reward plans'. *Compensation & Benefits Review,* 30(4):71–77. Sage Publications.

LEAP, T.L. & CRINO, M.D. 1993. *Personnel/human resource management,* 2nd edition. Macmillan, New York.

LEE, C. 1999. 'The importance of justice perceptions on pay effectiveness: A two-year study of a skill-based pay plan'. *Journal of Management,* November:1–24.

MCCLUNE, D. 1997. 'Managing reward strategy'. In Tyson, S. (ed.) *The practice of human resource strategy,* pp. 73–101. (Pitman), Pearson Education (UK).

NEWMAN, J.M. & KRYSTOFIAK, F.J. 1998. 'Value-chain compensation'. *Compensation & Benefits Review,* 30(3):60–66. Sage Publications.

RISHER, H. 1997. 'The end of jobs: Planning and managing rewards in the new work paradigm'. *Compensation & Benefits Review,* 29(1):13–17. Sage Publications.

SALISBURY, D.L. 1997. 'Benefit planning and management in a changing, dynamic labor market'. *Compensation & Benefits Review,* 29(1):74–80. Sage Publications.

SOLOMON, C.M. 1998. 'Owens-Corning: Optimas ® Award Profile'. *Workforce,* 77(2):78–81. Reprinted with permission of Copyright Clearance Center.

WERNER, S., KONOPASKE, R. & TOUHEY, C. 1999. 'Ten questions to ask yourself about compensation surveys'. *Compensation & Benefits Review,* 31(3):54–59. Sage Publications.

ZINGHEIM, P.K. & SCHUSTER, J.R. 2000. *Pay people right!* Jossey-Bass, San Francisco.

# Websites

American Compensation Association:
www.acaonline.org

Benefits Link: www.ifebp.org

Equity Compensation Strategies:
www.fed.org/library.html

Retirement Planning Associates, Inc.:
www.insworld.com/Newsletter/index.html

Kryslyn Corporation:
www.krislyn.com/sites/hr/htm

Benefits and Compensation Solutions Magazine
Online: www.bcsolutionsmag.com

# 12

# Health and safety management

## HB Schultz

## Learning outcomes

At the end of this chapter the learner should be able to:
- Explain the job and personal stress factors that can have a detrimental effect on an employee.
- Diagnose burnout and workaholism in the workforce.
- Develop a programme for reducing job stress.
- Explain the idea of spirituality in the workplace.
- Propose a holistic approach to health care for an organisation.
- Investigate the causes of accidents in the workplace.
- Discuss ways in which unsafe acts can be reduced.
- Develop an ergonomic approach to eliminating accidents in the workplace.
- Offer a brief overview of the legal requirements in health and safety management.
- Understand the work of the National Occupational Safety Association (NOSA).
- Discuss the impact of health and safety issues on quality assurance.

## Key words and concepts
- burnout
- Employee Assistance Programmes (EAPs)
- HIV/AIDS
- holistic healthcare
- job stress
- National Occupational Safety Association (NOSA)
- Occupational Health and Safety Act
- smoking policy
- spirituality
- substance abuse
- unsafe conditions and unsafe acts
- wellness
- work overload and work under-load
- workaholism

### Illustrative case
### The grim toll of travel
To South Africa's shame and loss, more than 1 200 people died on its roads between

1 December 2002 and 7 January 2003. This is a grim figure which represents a huge cost to the nation. But Transport Minister Dullah Omar said that measures taken by provincial traffic departments had been a success – without a zero-tolerance approach on traffic violations, the number of deaths would have been far worse.

Holiday seasons always put massive pressure on safety resources as national highways fill with high-speed traffic and drivers feel the urgency of getting to their destinations. In holiday resorts, too, there are wild parties, often leading to accidents and crime when alcohol is a factor. The waste of so many lives annually is an intolerable and costly toll in insurance pay-outs, in the loss of breadwinners, and in the maiming and injury of many others.

When we think of maintaining the health and safety of employees in organisations, we seldom equate this with preserving the health and safety of everyone who uses our country's roads. But the Department of Transport has just as difficult, if not a more complicated task, as the managers in the workforce. All the factors that impinge on organisational health and safety – stress, burnout, work overload, substance abuse, unsafe acts (such as road rage) and unsafe conditions – contribute to the grim toll of road casualties. Every member of the population can play a part in reducing this carnage.

## 12.1  Introduction

Stress means different things to different people. Feeling tense, anxious, or worried are all manifestations of the stress experience. Most people can endure short periods of stress without serious consequences. However, when this acute type of stress becomes chronic or long duration stress, the consequences can be devastating. But managing stress is only one aspect of the entire spectrum of health considerations in an organisation. The maintenance of good physical health

standards in the workforce is of utmost importance.

Safety issues are also critical both from the point of view of the employee and of the employer. The employee has a right to expect a work environment that is free from unnecessary hazards, and the employer has the right to expect the employee to maintain a safe working area.

This chapter commences with a discussion of job and personal stress factors, including references to the modern phenomena of burnout and workaholism. Some thoughts are presented on the reduction of job stress and the idea of spirituality in the organisation. Organisational healthcare programmes are investigated before the discussion proceeds to the causes of accidents and ways in which they can be reduced. Health and safety legislation in South Africa is examined briefly, and an opinion is offered on the impact of health and safety programmes on quality assurance.

## 12.2  Job and personal stress

Job-related stress factors can put an employee under such stress that a pathological reaction occurs. Cherrington (1997:640) states that the two main sources of job stress are environmental and personal.

### 12.2.1 Environmental stress factors

Environmental stress factors are external and include work schedules, revised work procedures, new workplace facilities, pace of work, job security, route to and from work, and the number and nature of customers or clients. A number of other environmental stress factors are discussed below.

#### Work overload and work under-load

Schultz and Schultz (1994:413) indicate that both work overload and work under-load can lead to a stressful condition.

Quantitative overload involves having too much work to do in the time available, and has been related to stress-related ailments such as coronary heart disease. It appears that the key factor is the degree of control workers have over the rate at which they work, rather than the amount of work they are required to do. Qualitative overload involves work that is too difficult. Many employees have found themselves in a position of having insufficient ability to perform a job. The threat of discipline and embarrassment caused by failure to be able to perform, can lead to a high degree of stress.

Work under-load, or having work that is too simple or insufficient to fill one's time and challenge one's abilities, is stressful, and demotivating. A lack of stimulation leads to boredom, and can also result in mental health problems. This discussion suggests that somewhere between under-load and overload, an area of optimal stress must exist – an area where workers should be able to perform at their peak. Figure 12.1 represents this assumption on an under-load/overload continuum.

## Change

Change can be exciting and challenging to some workers while others view change as a threat. Those who see change as a challenge are less vulnerable to stress consequences, but those who resist change succumb more easily to stress because they prefer familiar situations where they know what to expect.

## The changing mix of the workforce

Many older workers find the growing number of younger workers, more females (and female managers), and a culture of transformation and diversity stressful. In South Africa this is a particular problem amongst older, white, male workers.

## Organisational requirements

The 21st century demands that workers take up new roles in the organisation. Changing structures lead to role ambiguity and role conflict as employees grapple to come to terms with the multi-skilling requirements of a learning organisation. Problems of career development, taking responsibility for subordinates, uncomfortable physical working conditions, and repetitive pacing of work, all contribute to rising stress levels. Even rapid advances in technology have not succeeded in diminishing organisational stress – everyone has experienced the consequences of computers going 'offline'.

**Figure 12.1** The under-load/overload continuum

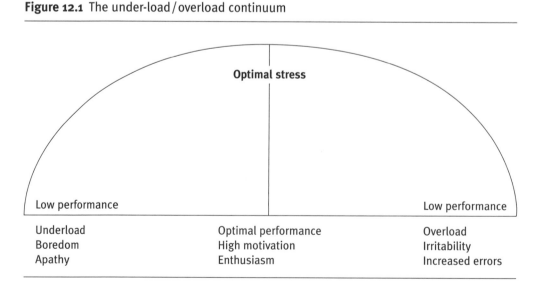

| Underload | Optimal performance | Overload |
| Boredom | High motivation | Irritability |
| Apathy | Enthusiasm | Increased errors |

## 12.2.2 Personal stress factors

No two people react to the same job in the same way, because personal factors also influence stress. Type A personalities, who feel driven to always be on time and meet deadlines, often place themselves under greater stress than do others. Tolerance for ambiguity, patience, self-esteem, health and exercise, work and sleep patterns also affect a person's reaction to stress. Non-job problems such as financial troubles, divorce, and sickness, intensify the susceptibility to succumb to stress.

## 12.2.3 Consequences of stress

Stress is not necessarily dysfunctional. A modest amount of stress may encourage a person to perform better, especially when working towards a deadline; it may lead to more creativity in a competitive situation and generate new ideas as a matter of necessity. However, when stress turns into distress it leads to negative consequences.

Human consequences of stress include anxiety, depression, and anger. Physical consequences can manifest themselves as cardiovascular disease, headaches, accidents, drug abuse, eating disorders, and poor interpersonal relations.

Organisational consequences of stress include reduction in the quality and quantity of job performance, increased absenteeism and turnover, increased disciplinary offences, and grievances (Dessler 1997:640).

## 12.3   Burnout

Dessler (1997:642) defines burnout as the total exhaustion of physical and mental resources as a result of excessive striving to reach an unrealistic work-related goal, combined with an overload of job stress. The signs of burnout are shown in Figure 12.2.

### 12.3.1 The victims of burnout

Persons who are prone to burnout include those who are over-dedicated to achieving

---

**Figure 12.2** The signs of burnout

- Unable to relax, emotionally exhausted, and bored.
- Less energetic and less interested in your job.
- Identify so closely with your activities that when they fall apart you do too.
- Positions you worked so hard to attain often seem meaningless now.
- Doing more work, but enjoying it less.
- Constantly irritable, apathetic and depressed.
- Strive to achieve work-related goals but exclude almost all outside interests.

SOURCE: Dessler (1997:642)

---

their goals. They don't lead well-balanced lives, often casting aside family and social involvement because they are so focused and intent on their work performance. It is not only executives that suffer from burnout. Workers at lower levels in the hierarchy, and even social-work counsellors are often burnout victims.

Victims of burnout can do a number of things to relieve a potential burnout situation:

- They can break their patterns by trying a variety of new activities instead of doing the same things over and over.
- They should make time for occasional periods of reflection, preferably alone, in order to gain a perspective on the direction their lives is taking.
- They should reassess their goals in terms of whether they are really worth the sacrifices that are being made.
- They must consider whether they could perform as efficiently if they allowed time for pursuit of outside interests.
- They must reduce stress by organising time effectively, building better relationships, developing realistic deadlines, and making time for relaxation.

### 12.3.2 Workaholism

Workaholism is sometimes confused with burnout, although there is a subtle difference between the two concepts. Not all workaholics strive to perform well because they are driven by anxiety and insecurity. Very often workaholics are happy, well-adjusted, and committed people who enjoy the satisfaction derived from putting more into their jobs than is required. They are likely to have supportive families and are able to balance the demands of their jobs with the demands of society.

## 12.4    Mechanisms for stress reduction

Berry (1998:442) states that although some stressors can be removed, it is not likely that we will ever live in a stress-free world. The results of uncontrolled stress are serious and costly to the individual and the organisation. It is therefore necessary that we learn how to cope effectively with the stress we experience. Ivancevich and Matteson (1999:277) agree that stress management seeks ways of coping with stress while stress prevention focuses on controlling or eliminating stressors.

### 12.4.1 Reducing job stress

Making use of personal and organisational interventions can alleviate job stress. Simple commonsense remedies such as getting more sleep, improving one's eating habits, using relaxation techniques, changing one's job, getting counselling, and planning and organising daily activities, all contribute to the reduction of stress. In the organisation, HR specialists and supervisors can also play a role in identifying and monitoring symptoms of stress. The HR professional can make use of attitude surveys to identify organisational sources of stress, ensure an effective person/job match in the selection and career-planning processes, and together with supervisors, can recommend job transfers or counselling (Cherrington 1997:649).

Research suggests that gender-related issues such as the threat of sexual harassment and the 'glass ceiling' phenomenon are distinct stressors for women. Although there is no general remedy for relieving stress caused by the threat of sexual harassment, certain factors can contribute towards achieving a balanced job state. The amount of control an employee has in the job, and the opportunity to discuss anxieties with managers without fear of victimisation assist in managing workplace stress.

In the first reported case on sexual harassment, the Industrial Court stated that an employer has a duty to ensure that employees are not subjected to sexual harassment within the workplace. There is no common ground for a definition of sexual harassment. Some perceive subtle, unwelcome sexual attention as harassment; for others it is suggestive remarks, blackmail (such as promotion as a reward for sexual favours), or violent behaviour (such as attempted or actual rape). Sexual harassment can take several forms, such as verbal and non-verbal, visual, and physical gestures (Boase 1996:88).

### 12.4.2 Spirituality in the workplace

Spirituality at work attempts to make corporations friendlier, and to develop a more creative environment by tapping into the spiritual side of employees. Many people believe the primary reason for the emerging trend of insecurity is the widespread feeling that workplaces have become vulnerable environments. The downsizing, re-engineering and layoffs of the past several years have transformed company cultures into bases of uncertainty. Survivors who are left are emotionally scarred by retrenchments of their friends and co-workers. There are less support staff and more difficult technology to master.

Many business people are growing away from the idea that science and technology can solve every business problem. Spirituality is seen as a mainstay for integrating and cementing corporate and employee values. Spirituality is not a religion. Its goal is greater personal awareness of universal values, helping an individual live and work better and more joyfully.

## 12.5 Holistic healthcare programmes

Occupational health practitioners are starting to adopt a proactive approach to managing employee health matters. Besides realising that prevention is better than cure, a holistic focus requires that what needs to be taken care of is the broader social and domestic dynamics of employees – a focus that aims at achieving a well balanced work and family life.

### Case-in-point
### The business of South Africa's healthcare future

Thirty five South African healthcare practitioners and authorities participated in a national conference from 28 to 30 January 2003, at the VW Conference Centre in Midrand, Gauteng. The focus of this conference, entitled 'Health Care Structure™', was to assess the present state of the healthcare industry from both local and international perspectives and to establish the future of the industry up to 2010. Health Care Structure™ is a strategic annual conference dealing with the business of improving healthcare systems in terms of costs, quality and continuous innovation. The primary goal is to provide delegates with the opportunity to hear about the many reforms, policies and initiatives taking place throughout South Africa.

That such a conference takes place annually is a clear indication of the importance of healthcare programmes in the country. Topics ranged from the future of private and managed healthcare, the sustainability of health care for the low income group, empowering health providers, and the latest legislative and regulatory changes in the Medical Schemes Act.

A highlight of the conference was a presentation of the current philosophies of leading governmental health professionals. The question 'What are the key issues in healthcare for the next five years?' was put to Dr Manto Tshabala-Misimang, Minister of Health, Dr Ayanda Ntsaluba, Director General of the Department of Health, and Dr Kammy Chetty and Mrs Nthari Matsau, Deputy Directors General, of the Department of Health. And the issue of HIV/AIDS was not at the top of everyone's list!

### 12.5.1 Wellness

Wellness programmes focus on the employee's overall physical and mental health. These programmes concentrate on preventing or correcting specific health problems, health hazards, or negative health habits. They include not only disease identification but also lifestyle modification, such as hypertension identification and control, smoking cessation, physical fitness and exercise, nutrition and diet control, and job and personal stress management (Ivancevich and Matteson 1999:280). As Cascio (1995:55) states, the objective of wellness programmes is not to eliminate symptoms and disease; it is to help employees build lifestyles that will enable them to achieve their full physical and mental potential through health awareness.

Gómez-Mejía et al. (1998:508) point out that wellness programmes can be as simple and inexpensive as providing information about stop-smoking clinics and weight-loss programmes, or as comprehensive and expensive as providing professional health screening and multi-million Rand fitness facilities. According to Matlala (1999:24), South African organisations can promote wellness by:

- Incorporating employee wellness or health promotion into the overall strategy of the organisation.
- Adopting employee wellness into the culture of the organisation.
- Encouraging involvement and support from all the role-players such as labour representatives, management, and others.
- Developing and implementing health promotion policies such as employee assistance programmes, smoking policy, HIV/AIDS policy and programmes.

Managers should be equipped to identify symptoms of diseases such as alcoholism, drug abuse and HIV/AIDS, and must provide lines of referral to professionals who can assist with treatment. Whatever action is planned, the rights of employees must be taken into consideration (*Sunday Times,* Business Times, 10 January 1999).

## 12.5.2 Employee Assistance Programmes (EAPs)

Malatji (2001:34) explains that EAPs are designed to enable management to build the productive capacity of each individual in the organisation. EAPs prevent the impact of political, social and economic problems on the individual, the organisation and the economy. These difficulties can cause a decline in employee performance and productivity and ultimately result in excessive absenteeism, damage to equipment, safety problems, attitude and behaviour difficulties, family problems, higher recruitment and training costs, loss of skilled people, potential labour relations breakdowns and high litigation costs.

Some of the basic guidelines for EAPs are:
- Creating a neutral space between management and labour.
- Making assistance and services accessible and available to employees.
- Keeping all employee information confidential.
- Removing the chances of victimisation or unfair dismissal.
- Allowing employees to use the programmes voluntarily.
- Using the EAP referral system rather than terminating an employee's service.
- Collectively agreeing on a policy statement that guarantees survival of the EAP.
- Ensuring quality service delivery.

Although EAPs tend to take on different forms in different organisations, they are broadly used to:
- Deal with the HIV/AIDS pandemic.
- Reduce excessive substance abuse.

- Eliminate all forms of harassment, including sexual and racial harassment.
- Avoid situations where there is a propensity for violence, conflict and rage.

Statistical data from the International Labour Organisation (ILO) indicates that absenteeism is four times higher due to substance abuse, five to seven times higher due to family problems, and five times higher due to mental illness. Through the EAP process, an average of 71 per cent of employee problems are solved and increases in productivity are significant.

---

## Encounter 12.1

### THE EAP CHALLENGE

Annually, the Employee Assistance Professionals Association of South Africa (EAPA-SA) presents a conference that aims at addressing topical issues and problems. The EAPA-SA is a non-profit making organisation for practitioners and people related to the field of Employee Assistance Programmes. This association has been at the forefront of the EAP profession in South Africa. EAPA helps employers to retain skilled workers and enhance workplace performance – directly and indirectly saving the company money.

HR managers, Corporate Health managers, Industrial Relations (IR) managers, EAP coordinators, Occupational Health practitioners, Nursing Sisters, and Organisational Development practitioners are just some of the delegates that benefit from attending the annual conference. In the past decade, the employee assistance field has considered Behavioural Risk Management (BRM) for the new millennium. Employee Assistance professionals contribute to the risk assessment processes of companies. Human resources professionals are apt to see EAPs in general and HIV/AIDS as part of risk management as well. EAP practitioners can position themselves as BRM leaders and providers. The skills, knowledge and interventions for successful behaviour risk management are already within the EAP professional repertoire. With the liability of employment practices rapidly becoming a major risk factor, the need for practices and interventions that control and reduce the cost of human risk is growing exponentially. EAPA-SA challenges all stakeholders to make a difference through the superior management of their EAP programmes.

SOURCE: SABPP (2002)

## 12.5.3 Sexual harassment

Burke (2003) relates that in California, a jury awarded $30 million in damages against the 450-store Ralphs supermarket chain for failing to stop sexual harassment by a store manager. During the trial, the jury heard of repeated incidents of abuse from six female employees, including foul language, racial slurs, fondling them, and throwing everything from pens to telephones at them. Although it seems amazing that such incidents could be allowed, it is evident that many such occurrences regularly take place in South Africa.

Examples of hostile environment aggravation, such as sexual harassment, include unwelcome touching, leering, sexually orientated jokes or cartoons, sexually orientated comments and epithets, and even staring at an employee's body. Hostile environment harassment can also occur based on racial or religious jokes, ethnic insults, offensive emails, and similar inappropriate workplace behaviour.

Employers can be liable for hostile environment harassment engaged in by their supervisors and fellow employees. Employers can be liable for compensatory damages and punitive damages. It can also be used in support of other discriminatory treatment claims to show that the employer is insensitive to workplace behaviour that denigrates others (Kern 2002).

To stop sexual harassment employers must:
- Have a clear, comprehensive, HR policy on sexual harassment.
- Investigate harassment complaints.
- Educate the workforce in all aspects of sexual harassment.

## 12.5.4 Substance abuse

Alcoholism is a serious and widespread disease. The effects of alcoholism on the worker and his/her work are severe. The quality and quantity of work decline sharply and the morale of other workers is affected as they are called upon to do the work of their alcoholic peer. On-the-job accidents do not increase significantly, because the alcoholic becomes more cautious, but off-the-job accidents can be three to four times higher than those in which non-alcoholics are involved. Turnover is not unusually high.

Recognising the alcoholic on the job can be difficult. It often takes a medical expert to be able to attribute early symptoms, such as tardiness, to alcoholism, as they could easily be related to other problems. Often, alcoholism is not detected until it has reached a problematic stage. However, once diagnosis has taken place, it is important that the organisation is able to deal with the problem in a systematic way.

A formal written policy on substance abuse must be developed. This document should state management's philosophy and position on the use and possession of illegal drugs and alcohol, it should set standards for appropriate conduct both on and off the job, it should list the methods that might be used to determine the causes of poor performance, and state the company's views on rehabilitation, including specific penalties for policy violations. The policy must be communicated to all employees.

Traditional techniques for dealing with substance abuse problems include: disciplining, discharge, in-house counselling, and referral to an outside agency. Often discipline is used in conjunction with counselling or referral. Most companies acknowledge that addiction is an illness, but are strict when it comes to giving the employee an opportunity to rehabilitate him- or herself (Ivancevich and Matteson 1999:280).

## 12.5.5 Smoking

Smoking has long been an issue in the workplace. 'Passive smoking', or smoke inhalation by non-smokers is becoming more of a matter for concern as employers become aware of evidence of measurable health effects and possible legal implications. An increasing number of public places have demarcated areas for 'smoking' and 'non-smoking', and most employers in South Africa have either introduced or have considered developing a smoking policy. Araujo (1996:39) suggests some general principles for formulating a smoking policy:

- Establish a working party to develop basic guidelines.
- Consult the workforce.
- Develop the policy as part of the total company health policy, and not as a management/subordinate issue.

Introducing a smoking policy in stages is most practical. The first stage could forbid smoking in certain areas (such as canteens, lifts, designated offices, and conference rooms). The next stage reinforces and extends the above, and the final stage implements a total smoking ban, with the possible exception of a few areas allocated to die-hards for this purpose. When considering whether or not to introduce a smoking policy, companies should consider the following:

- Smoking leads to increased absenteeism, higher cleaning costs, medical retirements, premature deaths, and various other liabilities. If these figures could be quantified, employees may see the desirability of introducing the policy.
- Smoking bans provide considerable health benefits for both smokers and non-smokers in the workforce, the organisation as a whole, and the community. It is a relatively inexpensive way of making a good health investment.

## 12.5.6 Depression

Alan Engelberg, the managing director of the American College of Occupational and Environmental Medicine (ACOEM n.d.), says: 'Depression is a common disorder that can

wreak havoc with the health and productivity of workers and their families.' Depression is the result of unsolved problems, and can manifest itself in physical and organisational troubles. A depression-screening programme is an effective and inexpensive way to identify some of the most emotionally distressed employees. With proper diagnosis and treatment following screening, workers suffering from depressive states are likely to experience significant clinical improvement and, as a result, become more productive at work.

There are many depression screening instruments available. There is even an effective yet simple approach, such as asking the two questions: Over the past two weeks have you felt down, depressed or hopeless? And: Over the past two weeks have you felt little interest or pleasure in doing things? These may be useful in identifying employees who should be referred for a diagnostic procedure (see: www.workindex.com).

## 12.5.7 HIV/AIDS

The high incidence of ignorance and prejudice that still surrounds the issue of Acquired Immune Deficiency Syndrome (AIDS) indicates that attempts to educate the general population have not been altogether successful. Managers must accept the burden of informing their workforces about the disease, although in Africa deep-seated tribal customs very often prevent a complete understanding of the social reality of AIDS.

Numerous issues present themselves for consideration: organisations must make decisions and formulate policies on whether to use pre-employment testing for AIDS, exclusions from medical funds, termination of employment due to HIV/AIDS, and confidentiality. Bracks and Van Wyk in Swanepoel et al. (1998:593) maintain that employers can play an important part in sponsoring AIDS awareness programmes and providing informative training.

The South African Business Council on HIV/AIDS was formed in February 2000 in an effort to fight the AIDS pandemic. The council aims to create universal strategies for fighting the disease in the workplace; experts predict that one in five South African workers may have HIV by the year 2005. In a statement, the business council noted that the pandemic has already taken its toll, with a loss of skilled workers, more absenteeism, higher health care costs, and higher labour turnover.

## Encounter 12.2

DISEASE WARNING AS COEGA SET TO BEGIN

Local authorities are bracing themselves to deal with a possible increase in AIDS in the Port Elizabeth metro, with the construction of the Coega deep-water harbour project. A report compiled by Acer Africa for Aluminium Pechiney (proponents of an aluminium smelter at Coega), warns that with several thousand construction workers due to start work at the Coega project during 2003, there are potential risks looming such as an increased incidence of communicable diseases resulting from an increase in local population due to induced migration, occupational health risks associated with work on a construction site, and an increased risk of the spread of HIV/AIDS.

The report states: 'Construction camps are renowned for activities such as prostitution and varying levels of promiscuity. This could lead to scenarios where an infected construction worker coming into the area spreads the disease through contact with sex trade workers or local individuals, who, in turn, will spread it locally.'

SOURCE: *The Herald* (2003)

## 12.5.8 Conflict and violence in the workplace

South African workers are faced with continual and rapid change, economic uncertainty, unrealised expectations and a general feeling of disempowerment (Burton 2001:24–6). It is predictable, then, that workplace bullying is widespread and costs a great deal of money. People who are being bullied develop depression and psychosomatic illnesses, and are prone to absenteeism. According to Martino (2001:21–2), bullying in the workplace is one of the fastest growing forms of violence plaguing the world today. Workplace bullying is everything from offensive behaviour to vindictive, cruel, malicious or humiliating attempts to undermine an individual or groups of employees. It includes refusing to delegate because the bully feels no one else can be trusted, shouting at staff to get things done, punishing others by constant criticism, or removing responsibilities from those who threaten the bully by being too competent.

Changes in the way we work have contributed to violence against workers. Workers who are left alone in small shops, gas stations, and kiosks, are often seen as easy targets by aggressors. Cleaners, maintenance or repair staff and others who work alone outside of normal hours are at risk of suffering physical and sexual attacks, and taxi drivers are at the greatest risk of violence (Chavez 2003).

Intervention measures that can produce more permanent results include:
- Disseminating information about innovative legislation, guidance and practice.
- Encouraging anti-violence programmes, specifically addressed to combating violence at work.
- Assisting government, employers' and workers' organisations to develop effective policies against violence at work.
- Assisting in the elaboration of training programmes for managers, workers and officials exposed to violent situations.
- Assisting in the explanation of procedures to enhance the reporting of violent incidents.
- Assisting in coordinating different anti-violence initiatives at different levels into organised strategies and plans.
- Understanding the mind-set of the potentially violent person.
- Establishing an atmosphere of cooperation.
- Listening to the aggrieved party and allowing a total airing of the grievance without comment or judgment.

- Allowing the aggrieved party to suggest a solution.
- Moving towards a win-win resolution for all parties.

## 12.6  The causes of accidents

According to Dessler (1997:628) there are three basic causes of workplace accidents: chance occurrences, unsafe conditions, and unsafe acts. Chance occurrences are more commonly referred to as 'freak accidents', and are usually beyond the control of employees and the employer. Unsafe conditions and unsafe acts can be controlled.

### 12.6.1 Unsafe conditions

Unsafe conditions include factors such as:
- Improperly guarded equipment, or the lack of protective equipment.
- Defective equipment.
- Hazardous procedures in, on, or around, machines or equipment.
- Unsafe storage – congestion, overloading.
- Improper illumination – glare, insufficient light.
- Improper ventilation – insufficient air change, impure air source.
- Excessive noise, heat, or cold.

The correction and elimination of unsafe conditions is catered for in the Occupational Health and Safety Act, No. 85 of 1993, and through the operational activities of NOSA (National Occupational Safety Association). Both are discussed in a later section.

Other accident-causing factors may also be present in the workplace. The job itself may be inherently dangerous; overloaded work schedules, night shifts, fatigue, and a psychological climate of hostility caused by dissatisfaction among workers tend to increase employees' susceptibility to work accidents.

### 12.6.2 Unsafe acts

People cause accidents by continuing to take part in unsafe acts such as:

- Throwing material indiscriminately.
- Operating or working at unsafe speeds.
- Making safety devices inoperative.
- Using unsafe equipment or displaying a disregard for safety rules.
- Using unsafe procedures in loading, placing, mixing, and combining.
- Taking unsafe positions under suspended loads.
- Lifting improperly.
- Distracting, teasing, abusing, startling, quarrelling, horseplay, and fighting.
- Alcohol or drug intoxication or abuse.
- Failure by supervisors to enforce safety rules.

What causes people to take part in unsafe acts? Dessler (1997:630–1) believes that a number of factors contribute to the problem. Certain personal characteristics serve as the basis for unsafe behaviour, such as the tendency to take risks, and undesirable attitudes. The debate on 'accident-prone' people has not yet been resolved, but it appears that certain personality traits, coupled with specific job situations and a lack of motor skills also result in unsafe acts. Poor vision, young employees (between the ages of 17 and 28), and employees with a low perception level, have also been identified as contributing factors.

## 12.7  Promoting safety

Neither the presence of unsafe conditions nor unsafe employee behaviours necessarily mean that an accident will occur. Employees may manage to survive dangerous conditions or unsafe behaviours for months or even years without an accident. Even if an accident does occur, the employee may escape without injury. When an injury is sustained, its severity may range from minor abrasion to death.

According to Leap and Crino (1993: 527–9) the severity of an accident can be assessed in a number of ways:
- Totalling the medical expenses incurred.
- Work time lost.
- Costs associated with hiring and training

new employees to replace those who are injured.

- The costs of decreased output of the injured worker after s/he returns to work.
- Cost of damage to material or equipment.
- Increased workers' compensation and health insurance costs.
- Pain, suffering, and mental anguish.

Reducing unsafe conditions is an employer's first line of defence. Safety engineers should use ergonomic principles to design jobs in such a way that physical hazards are removed or reduced. Supervisors and managers must develop a self-awareness of potential hazards and the promotion of safe working areas, even though legislation requires this.

Reducing the incidence of unsafe acts is more difficult because the human element always comes into play. A number of activities can be undertaken:

### 12.7.1 Reducing unsafe acts through selection and placement

Identifying the human traits that might be related to accidents on the specific job can screen out so-called 'accident prone' individuals. Emotional stability and personality tests, measures of muscular coordination, tests of visual skills, and employee reliability tests, although not foolproof, can assist in making placement decisions. In terms of South African legislation one should be cautious in allowing the results of any of these tests to exclude a potential employee from a job.

### 12.7.2 Reducing unsafe acts through publicity

Safety posters, although not a substitute for a comprehensive safety programme, can be combined with other techniques to reduce the occurrence of unsafe acts. They serve as a visual reminder that safety rules must be obeyed, and must be changed often to stimulate interest in safety.

### 12.7.3 Reducing unsafe acts through training

Safety training is especially appropriate with new employees, although current employees should receive regular refresher training courses. Specialist safety organisations, such as NOSA, provide such training, and a number of pioneering organisations even have their employees engage in exercises such as callisthenics before starting work.

### 12.7.4 Reducing unsafe acts through positive reinforcement

Pictorial graphs showing assigned safety goals, current performance and previous performance of departmental groups, coupled with supervisory praise for performing selected incidents safely, are a continuous reinforcement to maintain safety levels.

### 12.7.5 Reducing unsafe acts through top-management commitment

Successful programmes require a strong management commitment to safety. Top managers must become personally involved in safety activities on a routine basis. They must give safety matters high priority in company meetings and production scheduling and the company safety officer must have a high rank and respected status within the organisation.

## 12.8 An ergonomic approach to combating occupational injuries

### 12.8.1 Situational and individual variables in accident occurrence

The principles of ergonomics dictate that imbalances between the person and her/his environment must be eliminated, and the balance maintained. This is known as person-environment (P-E) fit. This approach to combating occupational injuries and illnesses focuses on two dimensions of fit. One is the extent to which work provides formal and informal rewards that meet or match the person's needs. The other type of fit deals with the extent to which the employee's skills, abilities, and experience match the demands and requirements of the employer. Neglecting these two aspects of P-E fit leads to an increase in occupational injuries (Ivancevich and Matteson 1999:277).

Accidents are caused by situational and/or individual variables. Situational factors include the failure to remove physical hazards, resulting in unsafe working conditions. This implies that a 'zero defect' situation is necessary in the general administration of the workplace. Other situational factors include inadequate job design, work schedules and atmospheric conditions that are less than optimal.

Unsafe behaviours can be attributed to individual differences. Repeated investiga-

tions have been conducted into the reasons why people behave in an unsafe manner. The ergonomist's view is that it is a matter of user error. Each person experiences a comfort zone as a feature of interaction between his/her job and the job environment. When the tolerance limits of the comfort zone are exceeded, the individual functions less effectively and this sets the scene for possible unsafe behaviour (Blignaut 1988).

## 12.8.2 Stress as a source of accident behaviour

The last decade of the 20th century was a time of rapid technological change and increasing pressure on employees in the form of obscure and conflicting demands, limited guidance, unrealistic deadlines, unclear responsibility, and information overload. Many employees perceive these demands and pressures as a threat, and this results in stress which manifests itself in lack of concentration and physi-

**Figure 12.3** A flow diagram of the accident process

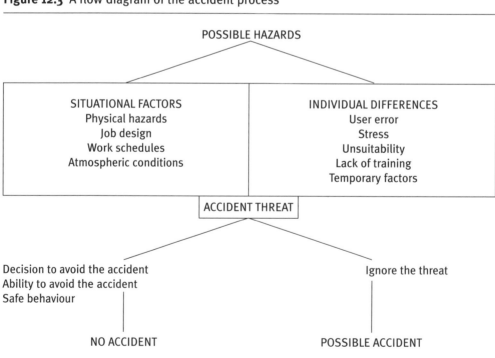

cal and mental ill-health. This scenario leads the worker to place less emphasis on his/her job behaviour, resulting in a situation where accidents are likely to occur. Figure 12.3 offers a model in the form of a flow diagram, indicating how accidents are caused, and how they can be avoided.

## 12.9 Legal requirements in health and safety management

The two main pieces of legislation concerning employee health and safety are the Occupational Health and Safety Act (OHSA), No. 85 of 1993, and the Mine Health and Safety Act, No. 29 of 1996.

### 12.9.1 The Occupational Health and Safety Act, No. 85 of 1993

The OHSA provides for the health and safety of persons at work and for the health and safety of persons in connection with the use of plant and machinery. The following is a summary of some of the measures provided for in the Act in order to achieve its objectives:

- The establishment of an Advisory Council for Occupational Health and Safety.
- Every employer must provide and maintain a working environment that is safe and without risk to the health of employees and other people affected by business operations.
- Suppliers and manufacturers must ensure that their products do not pose a safety or health risk in the workplace.
- Every employer must inform her/his workforce of workplace hazards.
- Every employee must take reasonable care of his/her own health and safety and of those persons who may be affected by his/her acts or omissions; s/he must carry out any lawful order given to him/her regarding workplace health and safety; s/he must report any unsafe or unhealthy situations or incidents that affect his/her health.

- The appointment of health and safety representatives.
- The establishment of health and safety committees.
- Certain incidents must be reported to an inspector.
- Wide powers of inspection, entry, enquiry and seizure are conferred on inspectors.
- A wide range of acts of omission and commission are declared offences and can incur criminal penalties.

It must be remembered that legislation lays the foundation for the enforcement of good health and safety habits in an organisation. However, employers should take a proactive stance in the implementation of a holistic approach to wellness. Such an approach goes beyond being bound by the law, and if achieved, will ensure that optimal states of health and safety are maintained.

### 12.9.2 The Mine Health and Safety Act, No. 29 of 1996

The Mine Health and Safety Act provides for the health and safety of all persons employed in the mining industry through regulations governing the reporting of incidents and accidents, and for the appointment of health and safety representatives and committees. Mining is a very hazardous occupation, yet the South African economy is reliant to a great extent on the activities of local mines. For this reason, the Mine Health and Safety Act is an extremely important part of the statute book.

### 12.9.3 Safety and first aid training

The majority of organisations provide some sort of orientation to safety regulations and procedures in their induction programmes. Regular refresher training is vital so that safety practices can be applied consistently.

The Occupational Health and Safety Act, No. 85 of 1993, requires that one in every 50 people employed in industry must be in possession of a Level O First Aid Certificate. The syllabus of this course is laid down by the

Department of Labour. The Act also defines the minimum content of First Aid boxes.

Many organisations make use of the St John's Ambulance First Aid Training for Industry (St John Ambulance Home Page: www.stjohn.org.za). Regular training programmes are offered at St John's twelve centres around the country and on-site at many companies. The Emergency First Aid Safety Oriented Course (EFASO) is a modular course of basic First Aid skills and other subjects needed to sustain life and manage the scene of injury. It meets industry, business and legislative requirements. The minimum compulsory content of the EFASO Level 1 course covers the following areas:

- Principles of first aid and safety; emergency scene management.
- Artificial respiration.
- One-rescuer CPR.
- Choking.
- Wounds and bleeding.

- Shock, unconsciousness and fainting.
- Fractures.
- Burns.
- Head and spinal injuries.

## 12.10 National Occupational Safety Association of South Africa (NOSA)

The website of The National Occupational Safety Association of South Africa (NOSA) is an informative source on the details of the organisation (see www.nosa.co.za). NOSA is a non-profit organisation that plays a prominent role in supporting quality health and safety standards in the workplace. Since its inception, on 11 April 1951, NOSA has provided an exceptional service in educating, training and motivating employees in the mining sector, industry and commerce. NOSA aims to foster among workers and

---

**Figure 12.4** The NOSA Five Star System

The NOSA Five Star System can be divided into three distinct phases of activity:

### 1  The Preparation Phase
Once a company has confirmed its full participation in the NOSA system the following actions are undertaken:
- Formulation of a policy statement signifying the importance of health, safety and environmental management in the business.
- Development of an implementation plan emphasising employee participation, defining responsibilities and accountabilities.
- Establishing organisational health, safety and environmental management needs.
- Determining priority elements and establishing appropriate standards.
- Establishing a health, safety and environmental training programme for the company.

### 2  The implementation phase
The following aspects are now implemented:
- Identification and priority standards.
- Furthering awareness and recommended training.

NOSA officials conduct a baseline audit to identify strengths and weaknesses in the development of element standards. The programme then commences using self-audits and external NOSA audits.

### 3  The sustaining phase
All additional elements and standards are developed and implemented during this phase. Self-audits and grading audits are conducted. Follow-up audits could follow dependant on the needs of the client. The concept of continuous improvement ensures that the process maintains its momentum and new innovations and further improvements are added.

SOURCE: NOSA information brochure: www.nosa.co.za

management alike an awareness of the need for safety in all work operations in order to prevent industrial accidents and occupational diseases. NOSA's thrust for the 21st century is the promotion of new attitudes and approaches to occupational safety, health and environmental risk management, a programme known as SHE. These issues were the focus of NOSA's 1999 national conference.

The training services of NOSA include in-house or on-site training, the NOSA Training Academy (NTA) and Occupational Hygiene Technologies (OHTEC). NOSA also offers consulting services in the form of baseline safety audits, legal compliance audits, occupational hygiene surveys, and environmental services.

Perhaps the most widely known aspect of NOSA's services is the Five Star Grading System. The system is based on the continuous application of the ISSMEC process, namely:

- **I** – identify possible causes of incidents.
- **S** – set standards of practice and procedures.
- **S** – set standards of accountability.
- **M** – measure performance against standards.
- **E** – evaluate compliance with standards.
- **C** – control deficiencies and deviations.

An overview of the NOSA Five Star System is offered in Figure 12.4.

## 12.11 Health and safety issues and quality assurance

Given the amounts of time and money invested in employees, especially highly skilled knowledge workers, many firms try to rehabilitate those with substance abuse and stress-related problems. Safety programmes target an accident-free and productive workplace. But the competitive society and quality requirements of the 21st century demand that employers take a proactive stance in managing health and safety issues. Environmental issues also necessitate that strategic precau-

tions are taken to safeguard communities from chemical spills, pollution, hazardous gases, and so on. Yet in many of the less developed countries around the world where labour unions are weak and corruption is often endemic, safety and health matters are at the bottom of the agenda. South African organisations must make a concerted effort not to allow this to happen.

## 12.12 Conclusion

Employee safety, health, and wellness are important issues. Managers have the responsibility of ensuring that workers are not unnecessarily endangered, and that they are fully aware of and properly trained and prepared for unusual workplace risks. As society has experienced such problems as chemical substance abuse, AIDS, and the ever-increasing stresses on the individual, so too have employees. There is growing recognition that work is an important part of life, and that organisations, by providing more than simply a safe place to work, can have a positive impact on the physical and psychological well-being of employees.

## Summary

- Environmental job stress factors include work schedules, revised work procedures, new workplace facilities, pace of work, job security, route to and from work, and the number and nature of customers or clients, work overload and under-load, and changing organisational circumstances and personal factors.
- Burnout is the total exhaustion of physical and mental resources as a result of excessive striving to reach an unrealistic work-related goal, combined with an overload of job stress. Workaholics do not always manifest abnormal behaviour patterns.
- Personal and organisational interventions can alleviate job stress. HR specialists and supervisors can also play a role in identifying and monitoring symptoms of stress.

- An employer has a duty to ensure that employees are not subjected to sexual harassment within the workplace.
- Spirituality is seen as a mainstay for integrating and cementing corporate and employee values. Its goal is greater personal awareness of universal values, helping an individual live and work better and more joyfully. Wellness programmes focus on the employee's overall physical and mental health. They include Employee Assistance Programmes (EAPs) that are designed to deal with a wide range of stress-related problems.
- Unsafe conditions and unsafe acts cause accidents. Certain personal characteristics serve as the basis for behaviour such as the tendency to take risks, and undesirable attitudes. Reducing unsafe conditions is an employer's first line of defense. The incidence of unsafe acts can be reduced through proper selection and placement methods, the use of safety posters, training, positive reinforcement, and top-management commitment.
- Accidents are caused by situational and/or individual variables. Many employees perceive the demands and pressures of the workplace as a threat and this results in stress. This leads the worker to place less emphasis on his/her job behaviour, resulting in a situation where accidents are likely to occur.
- The two main pieces of legislation concerning employee health and safety are the Occupational Health and Safety Act (OHSA), No. 85 of 1993, and the Mine Health and Safety Act, No. 29 of 1996. Safety and first-aid training are also legal requirements.
- The National Occupational Safety Association of South Africa (NOSA) plays a prominent role in supporting quality health and safety standards in the workplace. The training services of NOSA include in-house or on-site training, the NOSA Training Academy (NTA) and Occupational Hygiene Technologies (OHTEC). NOSA also offers consulting services and the Five Star Grading System.

## Case study
## Landmark suicide overwork ruling in Japan

The *Evening Post* of 26 June 2000 reported that Japan's top advertiser, Dentsu Inc., agreed to pay 168m yen (R11.2m) in damages for an employee's suicide. The case of Ichiro Oshima was a milestone in this workaholic nation, where death and suicide from overwork are a serious problem. Oshima was only 24 years old when he killed himself in 1991 after working 17 months without a single day off, averaging 30 minutes to two hours of sleep a night. Dentsu Inc. had denied that it ordered the extra overtime and argued that personal problems led to the suicide.

More Japanese are coming to value leisure and family, but pressures to conform and work hard remain. Many work unpaid overtime and fear they won't be promoted if they take vacations. An overwork hotline dealt with 206 calls in just one day in June 2000. In the case of Oshima, it was reported that he often worked late, sometimes until dawn, arranging radio ads and coordinating publicity events, even running around getting drinks for guests. He was back early every morning, dusting desks and answering telephones.

There are about a dozen similar pending court cases in Japan, and the outcome of this case is likely to have a positive impact on their settlement.

## Questions

1 Do you think Dentsu Inc. was entirely to blame for Oshima's suicide? Explain your reasoning.
2 How do you think Oshima's suicide, and many others in Japan, could have been prevented? Do you think that a similar state of affairs exists in South Africa?

# Experiential exercise No. 1

PURPOSE: To advertise the importance of maintaining a healthy and/or safe working place.

INTRODUCTION: It is unfortunate that many of our blue-collar workers are unable to read or write. However, pictures tell a story, and often this is the best, and only, way to communicate an organisational policy.

TASK: Prepare a large, colourful poster that is based on any of the topics discussed in this chapter. Develop a brief verbal presentation using the poster as the basis for the presentation. Remember that posters should:

- Depict clearly the subject under discussion.
- Be built around large upper, or lower case letters.
- Have between three and four colours (no more, no less).
- Not contain too much information.
- Encourage the viewer to want to learn more about the topic.

# Experiential exercise No. 2

PURPOSE: To assist a subordinate in diffusing a stressful situation.

INTRODUCTION: Read the following background information and prepare to role-play the part assigned to you.

ROLE PLAY (SUBORDINATE): You are Phumeza, secretary to Siseko, the Marketing Manager of your company. Although you love your job, your relationship with Siseko has been worrying you lately. In your opinion, he has sexually harassed you. Some of the things that have bothered you are:

- Siseko jokes about women's breasts in front of you. It makes you feel uncomfortable.
- Siseko has told you that you should wear mini-skirts when he is entertaining clients, as it makes male clients 'feel good'.

- On at least three occasions Siseko has suggested that he will give you a lift home from work if you stay behind in the office after the rest of the staff have left. You have declined each time. Now Siseko is dropping hints that there may not be much of an increase for you this year.

You have decided to talk to Jane, the Human Resources Manager, about your problem. You are very shy and embarrassed about the matter, and you are not sure how much you will be able to tell her.

ROLE PLAY (HUMAN RESOURCES MANAGER): You are Jane, the HR Manager. Phumeza has asked to speak to you about a personal problem. Although you are not sure what it is about, you have an idea that it might have something to do with Siseko, her boss. Two other ladies who work in the Marketing Department have already approached you for advice on what they call the 'sexual harassment problem' in their office. You know that Phumeza is very shy. If this is indeed the problem she wants to discuss, she is going to find it very difficult.

However, you are aware that you must get to the bottom of the matter. If Siseko's behaviour is out of place, you must be able to build up a case before you can confront him with any accusations. To do this you will need as much specific information as possible.

TASK: Prepare for your discussion with Phumeza.

# Chapter questions

1 Besides work overload, a number of other environmental and personal stress factors can contribute to a pathological reaction in workers. Discuss these factors, and include any other stress factors that you or a colleague may have experienced.

2 Explain how spirituality and wellness

programmes can contribute to a holistic approach to health care in the workplace.

3 Discuss how an ergonomic approach to safety can be used in combating occupational injuries.

4 Sir Winston Churchill was a great statesman, who led Britain to victory in the Second World War. He made the following comment: 'Most of the world's work is done by people who do not feel very well all of the time.' Do you agree or disagree with his statement?

5 Port Elizabeth recently won the 'Cleanest Town Competition' commissioned by the Department of Environment and Tourism. How do you think that a competition such as this one can contribute to the health and safety of the nation?

# Bibliography

ACOEM (American College of Occupational and Environmental Medicine) n.d. 'ACOEM recommends depression screening' (www.workindex.com/).

ARAUJO, J.P. 1996. The introduction of a no-smoking policy. *People Dynamics.* 16(1):39–40.*

BERRY, L.M. 1998. *Psychology at work, 2nd edition.* McGraw-Hill Companies, New York.

BLIGNAUT, C.J.H. 1988. *Ergonomics for behavioural scientists.* RAU, Johannesburg.

BOASE, N. 1996. 'Dealing with sexual harassment in the workplace'. *People Dynamics,* 14(11):88.*

BRANDT, E. 1996. 'Corporate pioneers explore spirituality'. *HR Magazine,* April (www.shrm.org).*

BURKE, K.T. 2003. 'Stop sexual harassment in its tracks' (www.workindex.com/editorial/hre).

BURTON, L. 2001. 'Violence at work in South Africa'. *People Dynamics,* 19(3):24–26.*

CASCIO, W.F. 1995. *Managing human resources: Productivity, quality of work life, profits.* McGraw-Hill Companies, New York.

CHAVEZ, L. 2003. 'Defuse workplace violence' (www.workindex.com/editorial).

CHERRINGTON, D.J. 1997. *The management of human resources, 5th edition.* (Prentice-Hall), Pearson Education Inc.

DESSLER, G. 1997. *Human resource management,* 7th ed. (Prentice-Hall), Pearson Education Inc.

GÓMEZ-MEJÍA, L.R., BALKIN, D.B., & CARDY, R.L. 1998. *Managing human resources, 2nd ed.* (Prentice-Hall), Pearson Education Inc.

IVANCEVICH, J.M. & MATTESON, M.T. 1999. *Organizational behavior and management, 5th edition.* McGraw-Hill Companies, New York.

KERN, D. 2002. 'Hostile environment harassment – Dual perspectives' (www.bernsteincom.com/docs/).

LEAP, T.L. & CRINO, M.D. 1993. *Personnel/human resource management, 2nd edition.* Macmillan, New York.

MALATJI, S.M. 2001. 'Get with the programme'. *People Dynamics,* 19(3):34.*

MARTINO. V.D. 2001. 'Human wrongs'. *People Dynamics,* 19(3):21–22.*

MATLALA, S. 1999. 'Prioritising health promotion and employee wellness'. *People Dynamics,* 17(6):22–25.*

NATIONAL OCCUPATIONAL SAFETY ASSOCIATION (www.nosa.co.za).

SABPP (South African Board for Personnel Practices). 2002. *EAP Association Annual Conference,* e-mail, 30 Aug. ©P. Bhoodram, EAP.

SCHULTZ, D.P. & SCHULTZ, S.E. 1994. *Psychology and work today: An introduction to industrial and organizational psychology, 6th edition.* Macmillan, Englewood Cliffs.

SWANEPOEL, B.J., ERASMUS, B.J., VAN WYK, M.W. & SCHENK, H.W. 1998. *South African human resources management.* Juta, Cape Town.

*The Herald.* 'Disease warning as Coega set to begin', 7 January 2003.

* Reprinted with permission of Copyright Clearance Center.

# Websites

National Occupational Safety Association: www.nosa.co.za

St John's Ambulance: www.stjohn.org.za

AIDS Conference 2000: www.aids2000.com

CDC National Prevention Information Network: www.cdcpnin.org

AIDS in South Africa: www.redribbon.co.za

FAMSA: www.famsa.co.za

Healthy culture: www.healthyculture.com

# part four

Behavioural aspects
of human resources
management

# 13

# Motivation

## A Werner

## Learning outcomes

At the end of this chapter the learner should be able to:
- Explain the concept of motivation.
- Discuss the content theories of motivation and their application to the work context.
- Discuss the process theories of motivation and their application to the work context.
- Explain how goal-setting serves as a motivational tool.
- Discuss money as a motivator.
- Analyse the motivational levels of employees in various situations.
- Discuss new developments in the study of motivation.
- Indicate the relevance of quality assurance in motivation.

## Key words and concepts

- creativity
- equity
- expectancy
- hygiene factors
- instrumentality
- meaningfulness
- motivators
- self-actualisation

## Illustrative case

### A will to succeed

Thembi Mogoai, CEO of the Johannesburg Zoo, is at work on a public holiday. But this is not surprising. This young woman (not yet 40) is driven to succeed, determined to take the latest challenge that has presented itself to her and turn it around into something spectacular.

Thembi was born at Baragwanath, grew up in Soweto and studied at Fort Hare, where she obtained a BA in Communications. Her first jobs were at SA Perm and Ogilvy and Mather, an advertising agency. She was then appointed the first black female airport manager in South Africa at George Airport, and went on to become assistant GM of Durban International Airport.

> Thembi got where she is today through hard work, determination and a willingness to learn. Thembi says she has achieved her success and stayed motivated by constantly looking beyond where she's standing. 'I'm not an administrator, I'm a builder. I hate doing the same thing over and over again, and I'm very afraid of stagnating.'
>
> SOURCE: Collins (2001: 20)

## 13.1    Introduction

Motivating employees is one of the most important managerial functions. Success in this endeavour is essential in the quest to utilise the full potential of people so as to ensure quality products and service. Motivation is a very complex issue due to the uniqueness of people and the wide range of internal and external factors that impact on it. Motivation can also not be separated from leadership, which is the ability to inspire people to voluntarily and enthusiastically work towards the attainment of organisational goals. But what is motivation? And how does one motivate people?

The purpose of this chapter is to provide a holistic approach to the question of employee motivation. Firstly, we explore the meaning of motivation. We investigate the practical application of various content and process theories in the workplace. The role of goal-setting in motivation is examined, and the power of money as a motivator is considered. We also consider new developments in the study of motivation.

## 13.2    The meaning of motivation

Employees function at one of three basic levels (Mol 1990:42):
- *Minimum level:* doing less than what is required.
- *Expected level:* doing what is required.

- *Maximum level:* doing more than what is required.

The employee who does less than what is required of him/her makes more errors, is tardier, delivers poor quality work, and is disciplined more often. Employees at the in-between level do what is expected of them – nothing more, nothing less. They do enough not to get into trouble, but nothing more. The third group of employees performs at the maximum level. They are prepared to walk the extra mile, use their initiative, apply their skills where needed, and put in an extra effort to achieve goals. Employees who voluntarily and enthusiastically do more than what is required of them, are motivated.

Mol (1990:39) distinguishes between the words 'motivation' and 'movement'. When a person carries out a task just for the sake of being remunerated, the person is being moved rather than being motivated. Mol does not denounce the movement of employees. According to him, it has always been used as a strategy to get people to achieve goals. Yet, it cannot be considered as motivation. Only when a person carries out a task because s/he is enjoying it or totally involved in it, is s/he being motivated.

Motivation can be described as intentional and directional. The word 'intentional' refers to personal choice and persistence of action. The word 'directional' indicates the presence of a driving force aimed at attaining a specific goal. A motivated person is always aware of the fact that a specific goal must be achieved, and continuously direct his/her efforts at achieving that goal, even in the face of adversity. Motivation is affected by both internal (for example, personal needs and expectations) and external forces (for example, organisational reward systems).

Richard McKenna offers an interesting alternative view of motivation. He believes that managers do not and cannot motivate their employees, but that constructive employee-organisation relations (and therefore excellence) are a product of an employee's self-identity (McKenna in Wiesner and

Millet 2000:35–44). According to him, employees (and people in general) are at all times already motivated 'to become who they want to be' (McKenna in Wiesner and Millet 2000:44). When a situation is congruent to the development of self-identity, a person will be motivated. This view relates to the concept of job involvement, which Bergh and Theron (2003:172) describe as the degree to which an employee psychologically identifies with his/her job and considers his/her performance important to self-worth. The challenge for managers is to help employees find an identity within the organisational context so that, through their individual motivation, employees will channel their efforts towards the attainment of organisational goals. McKenna predicts that the current concern for motivation will be replaced by a mutual investment approach, and recognition of the importance of individual identity in relation to the psychological contract.

The general belief is that all people can be motivated. However, people are not motivated by the same things, at the same time, for the same reasons, or with the same intensity. For this reason it is important for managers to understand the different motivational theories.

## 13.3  Motivational theories

The motivational theories that we are going to discuss in this chapter can be divided into content and process theories. Content theories focus on the needs and factors that motivate behaviour, the 'what' of motivation, while process theories focus on the origin of behaviour and the factors that influence the strength and direction of the behaviour, in other words the 'how' of motivation.

### 13.3.1 Maslow's needs hierarchy

Maslow's (1954) theory is based on the following: People continuously want things. People always want more, and what they want depends on what they already have. As soon as one need is satisfied, another takes its place.

People can therefore never be fully satisfied, and they behave in a particular way to satisfy a need or a combination of needs. A satisfied need cannot act as a motivator of behaviour. Much of this will become clearer once you have worked through the self-assessment exercise at the end of this chapter and identified your position on the need hierarchy.

People's needs are arranged in order of importance. Maslow divides human needs into five main categories according to importance. Human needs may be placed in a hierarchy according to their importance for human survival. The lowest level contains the most basic human needs, which must be satisfied before higher-order needs emerge and become motivators of behaviour. The levels of needs in Maslow's hierarchy are as follows:

- *Physiological needs.* The satisfaction of these needs is essential for a human being's biological functioning and survival (for example, the need for food, water and warmth). These are the most prominent needs; if they are not satisfied, human behaviour will be mainly directed at satisfying them. If you are really hungry, you will risk your safety in order to find food.
- *Safety needs.* As soon as physiological needs are reasonably satisfied, needs on the next level emerge, and the importance of the previous level of needs diminishes. Humans now use energy to satisfy the need for safety, which also has a direct bearing on their survival.
- *Social needs.* Once a person feels safe and in control of possible threats, social needs are activated. These include the need for love, acceptance and friendship.
- *Ego needs.* These needs may be divided into two groups: self-respect and self-esteem, and respect and approval from others. They include the need for self-confidence, independence, freedom, recognition, appreciation and achievement.
- *Self-actualisation needs.* If all the above-mentioned needs are largely satisfied or can readily be satisfied, people then spend

their time in search of opportunities to apply their skills to the best of their ability. Self-actualisation needs now become uppermost. Maslow (1954:92) describes these needs as 'the desire to become more and more what one is and to become everything one is capable of becoming'. Self-actualisation is the uninhibited expression of your true self and your talents.

Figure 13.1 illustrates Maslow's needs hierarchy.

This theory has many implications for individual performance. The most common strategy used by management to motivate people (among other things, by means of money, service benefits and job security), is aimed at the continued satisfaction of needs on the physiological and safety levels. For most people, these needs have been satisfied, either by themselves or through the country's social systems. Once satisfied, a need no longer acts as a motivator, so this strategy is not an incentive to perform. Performance bonuses often do not have the desired result.

Social needs may be satisfied to a large extent in the work situation, but it is difficult to develop a strategy that will translate these needs into an incentive for improved individual performance. The work people do, and the work environment, may be designed in a way

**Figure 13.1** Maslow's needs hierarchy

Self-actualisation needs

Ego needs

Social needs

Safety needs

Physiological needs

that increases interaction between employees. However, the disadvantage is that excessive socialisation may have a negative effect on employees' work output.

The needs that probably provide the best opportunities for employee motivation are the fourth- and fifth-level needs of Maslow's hierarchy, i.e. the ego and self-actualisation needs. Self-esteem and self-respect (as well as the esteem and respect of others) are functions of the type of work people do rather than of working conditions, such as free interaction and good remuneration. Interesting, challenging and meaningful work provides a solid foundation for the improvement of performance.

A further implication of Maslow's theory concerns the control function. People need to control their environment in order to manipulate it according to their needs. If, however, people are controlled by the environment and thwarted in the satisfaction of their needs, they become frustrated and tense. If prevailing needs cannot be satisfied, the result is undesirable employee behaviour, such as aggression, frustration and resignations, which can hardly be described as healthy or productive.

If a person's work is in itself a source of need satisfaction, that person becomes self-regulating and the roles of external incentives, such as remuneration or punishment, become much less prominent as motivators. Systems relying on external mechanisms to motivate people usually also require a control system to ensure continued employee performance. The maintenance of mechanisms such as strict supervision, policy, rules and regulations requires a great deal of effort on the part of the organisation. When people are motivated by challenging, interesting and meaningful work, however, such control mechanisms are superfluous.

Maslow's theory provides a useful framework for the understanding of needs and expectations. It has had a significant influence on management approaches to motivation and can be related to Herzberg's two-factor theory of motivation.

### 13.3.2 McClelland's achievement motivation theory

McClelland's motivational theory, dating back to 1962, considers three needs, namely a need for affiliation (nAff), a need for power (nPow) and a need for achievement (nAch). People with a strong need for affiliation will aim their behaviour at fostering interpersonal relations, while people with a strong need for power try to influence the behaviour of others. McClelland distinguished between two types of power, namely social power and personalised power. Social power is aimed at inspiring and influencing employees to achieve goals, while personalised power is exercised to control and exploit people.

It is, however, McClelland's achievement motivation theory that attracts the most attention and research. People with a high need for achievement are often the top performers in an organisation, and frequently demonstrate the following characteristics:

- They set challenging, yet attainable goals.
- They require regular and immediate feedback.
- They take calculated risks.
- They are problem solvers.
- They seek autonomy and freedom.
- They perceive money as an indication of their success rather than for its material value only.

McClelland perceived the level of need achievement among members of a specific population as important to the economic success of that specific population. He believed that it is a need that can be learned, which has positive implications for a country such as South Africa in which entrepreneurship is being encouraged.

McClelland also proposed that top managers should have a high need for power coupled with a low need for affiliation. He believed that top managers should not have a high need for achievement. This view has been supported by other studies (see, for example, Kreitner and Kinicki 2001:213).

## Case-in-point

CONTROLLING A CONTROL FREAK

The following question was posed on the Internet:

We have a team composed of a highly motivated subordinate and a supervisor who tends to micro-manage. The subordinate feels restrained and controlled, and as such is losing motivation. Both see the potential of their working together, but there is friction. How can we get them to function more cooperatively?

An expert in the field answered as follows: Highly motivated workers tend to be people with a high achievement drive – a need for personal mastery and a drive for self-improvement. Such people function best when:

- They are given a mission that rationally ties in with the big picture.
- The expected outcomes are well defined.
- They are given ownership over the task and the outcome.
- They receive feedback or rewards based on how well they do.

SOURCE: Tredwell (2002)

### 13.3.3 Herzberg's two-factor motivation theory

As far back as 1954, Herzberg used the critical incident technique to identify factors that made employees feel exceptionally good or exceptionally bad about their jobs. Responses were generally consistent, and based on them, Herzberg developed the two-factor theory of motivation. Herzberg identified two sets of factors that influenced motivation and job satisfaction, and he called the one set of factors hygiene factors and the other motivators.

Hygiene factors are closely related to the working environment. They include:

- Organisational policy and administration.
- Equipment.
- Supervision.
- Interpersonal relationships with colleagues, superiors and subordinates.
- Salary.
- Status.
- Working conditions.
- Work security.

Hygiene factors, also called maintenance factors, do not motivate. If they are inadequately met, they cause dissatisfaction. If they are adequately met, the employee is neither dissatisfied, nor satisfied (not motivated), but feels neutral about his/her job. The opposite of dissatisfaction is not satisfaction, but no dissatisfaction. A dissatisfied employee cannot be motivated. It is therefore important that management first give attention to hygiene factors before introducing motivators into the employee's job. If a secretary's computer is out of order, s/he becomes dissatisfied and complains. However, you don't hear secretaries say: 'I really love my job, my computer is working well and not giving any problems.' Good work equipment is taken for granted. So are fair pay, equitable benefits, good and safe working conditions, and so on.

Only motivators can motivate people. Motivated people exert a bigger effort than what is expected of them in achieving goals. Motivators, also called growth factors, are closely related to the nature and content of the work done.

Motivators include:

- Achievement (for example, successful execution of tasks).
- Recognition for what has been achieved.
- The job itself (how interesting, meaningful and challenging it is).
- Progress or growth (learning and developing).
- Responsibility.
- Feedback.

According to Herzberg, the answer to the motivation problem lies in the design of the work itself. Job enrichment is based on the application of Herzberg's ideas. Job enrichment is the vertical loading of an employee's job to make it more challenging, interesting and to provide opportunities for responsibility, growth and recognition. Job enrichment is an alternative to scientific management, also called Taylorism, where specialised and standardised jobs lead to monotony, boredom, and psychological stagnancy.

Herzberg's theory can be linked to the needs hierarchy of Maslow. The hygiene factors are similar to the lower level needs in the hierarchy, while the motivators are similar to the higher level needs. Figure 13.2 illustrates the relation between these two theories.

Although Herzberg's theory has elicited much criticism, his view that job satisfaction lies in the task itself is of value. According to Mol (1990:21), employees enjoy their work when they take pride in attaining a goal. If the work itself is not a source of pride for the employee, s/he will never be motivated, but will only be moved. This statement is based on the assumption that most workers have a basic need for self-actualisation and personal pride.

There are, however, a number of theories that question this assumption. These so-called contingency theories emphasise the individual differences between employees and the necessity for managers to focus their approach to motivation on the individual characteristics of each employee. A supporter of these theories might reason that some employees are maintenance-seekers and others motivator-seekers. According to Mol (1990:15), the danger in holding this belief is that managers might have low expectations of some employees, and therefore not create opportunities for them to learn and grow. By over-emphasising hygiene factors in the workplace, employees are reinforced to become maintenance-seekers.

Mol (1990:12) says that his experience in South African organisations indicates that a large number of managers are very successful in motivating their subordinates, particularly at the lower levels. They do this by concentrating on the task or job itself. One of the greatest mistakes made by management and trade unions is to think that fair treatment, pleasant working conditions, above-average remuneration, and outstanding fringe benefits will motivate employees. There is no doubt that these aspects are important, but they seldom give rise to an increase in productivity – for the simple reason that they do not contribute towards an employee's enjoyment of the job.

### 13.3.4 The job characteristics model

The job characteristics model, proposed by Hackman and Oldham (in Kreitner and Kinicki 2001:220) – see Figure 13.4 – is based on the idea that the task itself is the key to employee motivation. It provides a framework by which jobs can be redesigned to make the incumbents feel that they are doing mean-

**Figure 13.2** A comparison of Maslow's needs hierarchy and Herzberg's two-factor theory

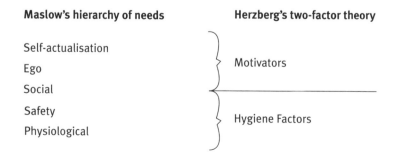

| Maslow's hierarchy of needs | Herzberg's two-factor theory |
| --- | --- |
| Self-actualisation | |
| Ego | Motivators |
| Social | |
| Safety | Hygiene Factors |
| Physiological | |

ingful and valuable work. Enriching certain elements of the job leads to altered psychological states in employees that influence both their work performance and satisfaction positively.

The five critical job dimensions are skill variety, task identity, task significance, autonomy and feedback. The first three dimensions impact on the meaningfulness of the work, autonomy impacts on the responsibility experienced for outcomes, and feedback impacts on the employee's knowledge of the actual results of work activities:

- *Skill variety:* The extent to which a job requires a person to do a variety of tasks that require different skills and talents. Instead of just feeding a machine with raw material, a typical machine operator can also become responsible for routine maintenance on the machine, calculating wastage, safety checks on the machine, and quality and quantity of production.
- *Task identity:* The extent to which a person is responsible for a completely identifiable piece of work. A person who designs a piece of furniture, buys the raw material, and does all the carpentry has high task identity.
- *Task significance:* The extent to which the job impacts on other people. Employees who really understand how their jobs impact on customer satisfaction, experience task significance. A computer technician who is responsible for maintaining the organisation's computer network experiences task significance.
- *Autonomy:* The extent to which the job allows the person to experience freedom and discretion to plan, schedule and execute the task. A mechanic who decides

independently what repairs need to be done, who schedules his/her own day and decides how to do repairs, is working autonomously.
- *Feedback:* The extent to which the person receives factual information on how effectively the job is done. A credit controller who receives information on the amount of bad debts, number of 'bad' customers, average time it takes to respond on a credit application and number of queries outstanding, knows exactly how well the job is done.

The critical psychological factors influenced by the core job dimensions are the following:
- *Experienced meaningfulness:* A meaningful job is one that is perceived by the employee as highly important, worthwhile and valuable.
- *Experienced responsibility:* The employee feels that s/he is personally responsible for the successful completion of the job.
- *Knowledge of results:* Effective feedback helps an employee to understand the level of performance and serves as a basis for goal-setting and improved performance.

## Applying the job characteristics model

The job characteristics model can be applied in three steps (Kreitner and Kinicki 2001:222). The first step is a diagnosis of the work environment to determine whether a problem exists. This is done through a self-report instrument called the Job Diagnostic Survey (JDS), which is completed by the employee. The Motivating Potential Score (MPS) is then calculated. This index represents the extent to which the job characteristics foster internal

---

**Figure 13.3** Computing the motivating potential score (MPS)

$$MPS = \frac{Skill\ variety + Task\ variety + Task\ significance}{3} \times Autonomy \times Feedback$$

**Figure 13.4** The job characteristics model

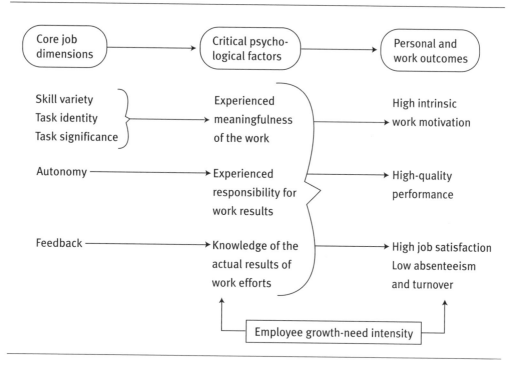

work motivation. Low scores indicate a low motivating potential and that job redesign should be considered. The MPS is computed as shown in Figure 13.3.

If the MPS is high and the employee is under-performing, the problem does not lie with the job itself, but with contextual factors, such as the condition of equipment, inability, stress, and conflict (Herzberg's hygiene factors). If the MPS is low, determine what aspects of the job are inadequate.

Step two involves determining whether job redesign is appropriate for a given group of employees. According to Kreitner and Kinicki (2001:222), job redesign is more suited to a participative work environment where employees have the necessary skills. Greenberg and Baron (1995:150) reason that job redesign will work better when employees have a strong growth need. Mol (1990) argues that all jobs can be redesigned, that training

forms an integral part of the job enrichment intervention, and that most employees can develop a growth need through effective goal-setting.

The third step involves the redesign of the job, starting with those job characteristics that are lower than the national norm. Including employees in the redesign of the job will lead to greater commitment.

According to Greenberg and Baron (1995:150), a South African study found that job enrichment led to significant improvements in internal motivation and job satisfaction. It also led to lower rates of absenteeism and labour turnover. An interesting fact is that no significant changes were found in job performance; employees in unenriched jobs performed just as well as those in enriched jobs. This is ascribed to the complexity of job motivation and job performance as explained by the expectancy theories.

## 13.3.5 The expectancy theories

Two expectancy theories will be introduced and examined in this section: Vroom's expectancy theory and Porter and Lawler's expectancy theory. Both theories hold that people are only motivated to act in a specific way if they believe that a desired outcome will be attained. Expectancy theories view behaviour and motivation as a function of beliefs, expectation, perceptions, values and other mental cognitions.

### Vroom's expectancy theory

According to Vroom's theory (see Luthans, 2002), a person will exert a high effort if s/he believes that there is a reasonable probability that the effort will lead to the attainment of an organisational goal, and that the attainment of the organisational goal will become an instrument through which the person will attain his/her own personal goals. If an employee desires a promotion, and believes that through meeting certain organisational criteria s/he will get a promotion, the person will put in greater effort. The opposite is also true. If a person believes that no amount of hard work will lead to promotion, s/he will

put in less or no effort. Figure 13.5 illustrates the key concepts of Vroom's expectancy model. Three key concepts in this theory are valence, instrumentality, and expectancy.

Valence refers to how attractive a specific outcome is to an individual. It is the anticipated satisfaction from attaining a goal or object. It differs from value in the sense that a person might desire a specific outcome, and when it is obtained, the person derives less satisfaction from it. Valence is the anticipated satisfaction, and value the actual satisfaction. A person might desire a promotion (valence), and when it is realised, the person might wonder why s/he actually wanted it. Valence can be assessed on a scale ranging from +2 (very desirable) to 0 (neutral) to –2 (very undesirable).

Expectancy refers to an individual's belief that a certain level of effort will lead to a certain level of performance. This represents the effort-performance expectation. If an individual has a zero expectancy that effort will lead to performance, the person will not put in a remarkable effort. If a reward is offered to students who achieve 80 per cent or more for a test, and a student desires the reward (positive valence) and believes that it is an unrealistic goal and cannot be attained, s/he will not put in a big effort. Likewise, if the student expects

**Figure 13.5** Vroom's expectancy theory

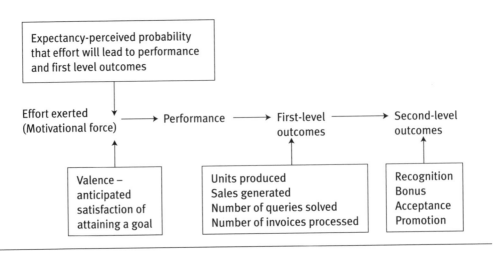

that s/he will be successful at achieving the desired level of performance, s/he will put in a bigger effort in order to perform.

According to Kreitner and Kinicki (2001: 247), the following factors influence a person's expectancy perceptions:

- Self-esteem.
- Self-efficacy.
- Previous success at the task or a similar task.
- Support from others (supervisor, subordinates, colleagues).
- Access to relevant information.
- Sufficient material and equipment.

Instrumentality is the perception that performance will lead to the desired outcome. Performance is instrumental when it leads to a specific outcome or outcomes. The first-level outcomes are performance-related and the second-level outcomes are need-related. People normally do not receive rewards for their efforts, but for achieving actual results. Instrumentalities range from +1.0 to –1.0. An instrumentality of 1.0 indicates that the attainment of an outcome is totally dependent on performance, an instrumentality of zero indicates no relationship between perform-

ance and an outcome, while an instrumentality of –1.0 indicates that high performance reduces the chance of obtaining an outcome while low performance increases the chance. For example, the more time you spend at work to get a promotion (high performance), the less time you will have for your family. The less time you spend working for a promotion (low performance) the more time you have for your family.

## The expectancy theory of Porter and Lawler

Lyman Porter and Edward Lawler III extended Vroom's theory into an expectancy model of motivation. This model, presented in Figure 13.6, attempted to:

- Identify the origin of people's valences and expectancies.
- Link effort with performance and job satisfaction.
- Identify factors other than effort that influence performance.
- Emphasise the importance of equitable rewards.

Value of reward is similar to valence in Vroom's theory. People desire a combination

**Figure 13.6** The Porter and Lawler model

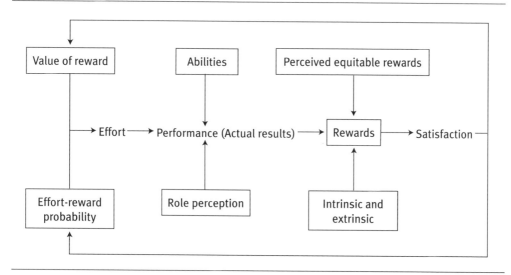

of outcomes or rewards for what they put into their jobs. The content theories of motivation can be used to further explore these values.

The perceived effort-reward probability is the extent to which a person believes that his/her efforts will in fact lead to the reward. This is similar to the concept of expectancy in Vroom's theory. Both the desirability of the reward and the perceived probability that the effort will lead to the reward impact on the effort the person will put into her/his job.

Effort does not lead directly to performance, but is moderated by abilities and traits, and role perception. A sales person can spend hours promoting a product without making a sale. This can be due to using the wrong techniques, an unconvincing manner, or perhaps the sales person believes his/her role is only to demonstrate the product and not to persuade people to buy it.

Satisfaction is influenced by both intrinsic and extrinsic rewards. Intrinsic rewards are self-granted, and consist of intangibles such as a sense of accomplishment and achievement. Extrinsic rewards include bonuses, public recognition, awards and acceptance. Job satisfaction is influenced by an employee's perception about the equity of rewards given. Employees expect rewards that are not only equitable to their own inputs, but also equitable to the rewards that other employees with similar inputs receive. If employees experience inequity, they direct their behaviour towards creating equity.

It is also important that some congruency exists between intrinsic and extrinsic rewards. Consider feeling very good about a job you have done, but nobody else notices your achievement. Also, consider receiving ample praise from others knowing that you do not deserve it.

The traditional organisation paid much attention to extrinsic awards. Organisations do need systems that clearly and closely tie rewards to performance. Lawler (1996:57) uses the term 'line of sight', indicating the extent to which employees see that the extrinsic rewards they receive are a consequence of their performance. In the modern organisation the emphasis is less on individual pay for performance, and more on gain sharing, profit sharing and stock ownership, also linked to performance. Intrinsic rewards have a potent influence on performance and employee behaviour. Although individuals give themselves intrinsic rewards, organisations can influence the likelihood of those rewards being tied to performance by addressing job design. The complexity of the task, how challenging it is, and the kind of feedback people receive about their work, have a huge impact on intrinsic rewards.

Managers can enhance the effort-performance expectancies by helping employees accomplish their performance goals. Specifically managers can:

- Communicate with individuals or groups to determine what personal goals or rewards they value.
- Clearly link rewards to performance goals.
- Train and guide employees to required performance levels.
- Make the individual and group responsible for goal attainment.
- Provide equitable rewards.
- Foster a positive environment for intrinsic rewards through careful job design.

Lastly, employees' future effort-reward probability expectations are influenced by past experience with performance and rewards.

## 13.4 The role of goal-setting in motivation

Any idea that is not translated into specific goals will stay an idea only. Objectives and goals dictate our purpose and direction. Motivation is described as a driving force aimed at attaining a specific goal. The importance of goal-setting and goal attainment in performance management illustrates the role of goals in shaping and reinforcing the behaviour of employees. Management By Objectives (MBO) is a widely used management technique that fosters employee participation in goal-setting, decision-making and feedback. A motivated person is always aware of the fact that s/he is working towards a specific goal, and continuously directs her/his efforts at achieving that goal, even in the face of adversity. The goal-setting approach to motivation is based on the work of Edwin Locke.

## Encounter 13.1

SPECIFIC GOALS MOTIVATE

Les Hewitt, co-author of *The Power of Focus*, writes:

> One of our clients in The Achievers Coaching Programme indicated his goal for better health was to start exercising. He was feeling sluggish and wanted more energy. 'Start exercising' is a very poor definition of this goal. It's too general. There's no way to measure it. So we said, 'Be more specific'. He added, 'I want to exercise thirty minutes a day, four times a week.'
>
> Guess what we said next? 'You're right. Be more specific'. By repeating this question several times his health goal was redefined as follows: To exercise for thirty minutes a day, four times a week, Monday, Wednesday, Friday and Saturday from 7 A.M. to 7:30 A.M. His routine consists of ten minutes stretching and twenty minutes on his exercise bike. What a difference! Now we can easily track his progress. If we show up at the scheduled times to observe, he will either be doing what he says, or not. Now he's accountable for results.

### 13.4.1 Why do goals motivate?

Goal-setting influences behaviour in four different ways:
- *Goals direct attention to what is most important.* The goal of the Ritz-Carlton Hotel Company is to delight their customers. The Ritz credo is to 'fulfil even the unexpected wishes and needs of our guests'. Good customer service is discussed every single day (Hays 1999:1–4).

- *Goals prompt us into action.* At the Ritz-Carlton, employees address the needs of customers immediately. If a waiter overhears a customer complaining about a television's reception, the waiter addresses the issue immediately by reporting it to the engineering department and phoning the customer afterwards to find out if the problem had been resolved satisfactorily.
- *Goals increase our persistence.* An athlete whose goal it is to run the 100 metres in less than 10 seconds will practise more regularly and with more dedication than an athlete who just wants to stay fit.
- *Goals direct strategies and action plans.* The goal of a swimming pool construction company was to attract 25 per cent more customers during the following year. Once this goal was identified, marketing strategies (participation in exhibitions and fairs, sales specials, intensive advertising) were formulated. For each strategy, specific action plans were identified.

### 13.4.2 Practical application of goal-setting

To apply goal-setting, the key performance areas of jobs must first be identified. The Key Performance Area (KPA) of a job refers to those areas in a job in which an employee must perform well in order to be successful. The key performance areas in any position must be aligned with the overall goals and strategies of the organisation. If excellent customer service is an organisational goal, then it should also become the individual employee's goal as well.

In order to facilitate commitment, the manager and employee should set goals together. One of the most important considerations is that the employee must have control over the achievement of results. Goals should be quantifiable and specific.

Many authors accept that goals should be specific and difficult, yet attainable through persistence. Mol (1990:115) prefers to differ here. According to him, low goals are more motivating than high goals. Mol sees a low goal as a realistic goal, where the likelihood of success is very good. A 'sense of achievement' is synonymous with 'an experience of success', and by lowering the goals the likelihood of success provides the motivating force. Mol also states that performance improvements should always be viewed in terms of the original baseline measure, and that the goal posts should not be moved unless conditions change, such as an improvement in machinery. If the historical standard for performance was 50 units per hour, and management found it acceptable, all improvements should be viewed against this acceptable standard of performance. All improvements, regardless of their size, should be regarded as successful attempts. By continuously setting higher goals, while maintaining the baseline as the acceptable rate, quality will be improved in the organisation. Kreitner and Kinicki (2001:239) also acknowledge that different goals may have to be set for employees with different levels of skill and ability. Unfortunately, this practice might lead to perceived inequity among co-workers.

Managers must provide adequate support and feedback for employees to be successful. This includes ensuring that employees have the necessary skills and information to achieve their goals. Managers should also pay attention to employees' perceptions of effort-performance expectancies, self-efficacy and valence of rewards. Feedback on performance should be timely, accurate, objective and aimed at identifying performance areas that need further development. Feedback is an interactive process between an employee and the manager.

---

## Encounter 13.2

SOUTH AFRICAN BREWERIES (NOW CALLED SABMILLER)

According to Norman Adami, MD of South African Breweries Ltd. between 1994 and 2002:

> Three key strategic themes provide a frame of reference for the company going into the new

century: growth, people and corporate reputation. Most growth achievements have more to do with motivation than pure technological performance – which is the relevance of our second key strategic theme, SAB's own people. It is why the company pays so much attention to its organisational culture. It constantly evaluates and reviews the overall effectiveness of the company, including leadership style and management practices such as fostering a culture of performance and reward, increasing employee participation and setting goals for individuals and teams. In SAB we strive to nurture a high-performance, high-involvement culture where there is a low tolerance for mediocrity and an openness to challenge, change and learning. Our Integrated Management Process (IMP) ensures that we align our people processes with our goals, and that our measures, rewards and incentives are effective in driving the right behaviour.

In 2003 Adami took over as chief executive and president of Miller Brewing, the world's second-largest brewer, after it was bought by SABMiller from the tobacco and food group Philip Morris. The previous chief executive was asked to leave after the plant did not perform as expected.

Norman Adami had few illusions about the challenges he faced in the US. SABMiller's plan, when it bought Miller in 2002 for $5.6-billion, was to 'run with the US management and make it work'. But the plan backfired when it became clear to SABMiller management that the performance ethic at the US company was 'not anywhere near our style'.

Adami was frank about the challenges:

'I recognise that, despite one's experience in the brewing industry, there is no single SABMiller formula one can put in place. I don't know enough about the American way, about Miller and its people. It's a big learning curve.' Adami says there is room for energising the Miller business and ensuring that the rights things are done.

Give your opinion on following two issues:
- Is 'work ethic' related to motivation?
- Are the motivational theories discussed in this chapter applicable to all cultural groups?

SOURCES: Adapted from Vaida, G. and Klein, M. www.sunday-times.co.za; *Financial Mail*, Corporate Report, 22 October 1999

## 13.5 Money as a motivator

Whether you perceive money as a motivator or not depends on what you perceive as motivation. Both Frederick Herzberg and Arnold Mol perceive motivation as an internal, inward-directed desire to achieve a primary goal. An employee exerts a high effort to accomplish goals that will make him/her feel good. According to Mol, money does not motivate, but moves a person to achieve a goal in order to obtain the reward. Herzberg's two-factor theory states that extrinsic awards, such as pay, benefits, working conditions or company policies do not motivate people. They merely bring performance to an acceptable level. Motivated people perform at levels that are higher than the acceptable standard. Intrinsic awards, such as responsibility, growth and opportunities motivate an employee to these high levels of performance.

According to Maslow's need hierarchy theory, money can only serve as a motivator if it is a means to satisfy a need. Money can be used to satisfy many needs. People can buy food and clothes with money (physiological need), money provides physical and emotional security, increases your social capacity, gives status, and makes more opportunities for personal realisation accessible.

Lawler (1996:207) reasons that if money as a reward can cause dysfunctional behaviour, it obviously affects behaviour, and therefore also performance. According to him, the effect of money as a motivator depends largely on the pay system used in the organisation. When pay systems are not designed well, they either do not motivate or motivate the wrong behaviour.

### Case-in-point

Robert is a manager at Solar Salt Works. This is what he has to say about a recent promotion:

> I had mixed feelings when I was promoted to a managing position. My first thought was that my friends would be impressed and that I would earn more money. However, I was worried that my previous co-workers, who now became my subordinates, would not accept me. I also saw it as a wonderful new opportunity to develop my skills, and to secure my position in the company.
>
> I was not quite sure how to motivate employees but I spoke to a friend who gave me good advice. What I do now is to set challenging yet realistic goals with each employee. I then give the person the freedom to use his/her creativity to decide how to reach the goals. I am available when my input is needed, but I do not supervise closely. I found that if I identify an employee's needs, whether it is for recognition, guidance, security or more freedom, and address these needs, the person works very hard and shows a positive attitude. If an employee does not achieve the set goals, we discuss the problem and find a solution together.

- Are you able to identify which needs of Robert were satisfied by the promotion?
- Which motivational theories can be used to explain how Robert motivates his employees?

According to Kreitner and Kinicki (2001: 258-9), pay should only be linked to performance goals when:
- Goal attainment is under the control of the employee.
- Goals are quantitative and measurable.
- Payments are frequent and substantial.

The critical point that organisations and their managers should remember from Maslow's theory and related theories, is that human beings are motivated by internal feelings of accomplishment, capability, and competency – not just extrinsic rewards, such as food, water, acceptance and financial well-being. Money is a motivator, but it is not the only or most powerful source of motivation. Organisation designs that do not emphasise the role of intrinsic rewards, fail to tap a very powerful source of motivation that can lead individuals to perform at extraordinary levels (Lawler 1996:55).

---

## Encounter 13.3

PEPSICO

Considering the various motivational theories discussed in this chapter, which ones do you think can be used to explain the strategy used by PepsiCo to motivate their employees?

PepsiCo believes that to meet shareholders' and customers' needs, it has to create a work environment that will attract the very best. Once employed, these employees get the opportunity to develop their skills and talents fully. The company encourages creativity and innovation, and free collaboration with others. Above all, the highest standards of integrity are encouraged.

Pepsi-Co is looking for people who are results-oriented, committed to excellence, willing to engage in lifelong learning, passionate about their jobs, innovative, intelligent, dedicated, and who appreciate diversity. To encourage these types of behaviours, the company offers a wide range of opportunities and benefits, including career challenges, mobility, world-class training and development, excellent compensation, flexible benefits, and a culture of inclusion.

SOURCE:

www.pepsicocareercentre.com/about pepsico/culture.shtml.

---

## 13.6  Motivating contingent employees

Part-time jobs attract a full range of employees – students, retirees, working mothers and fathers needing an extra income, people wanting to earn while searching for 'the right job', and even professionals who prefer the freedom that comes with flexi-time. Downsizing, rightsizing and outsourcing also create fewer opportunities for full-time employment and more for part-time. The ratio of part-timers to full-timers is expected to increase in the next few years.

Organisations need to consider the motivation and performance standards of part-timers. Nelson (1999) suggested the following guidelines for the motivation of part-time employees:

- Appreciate part-time employees for the job they do. Recognition and appreciation is only achieved if goals are set, performance measured, and feedback given.
- Treat part-time employees the way you want them to act. If you want them to have a long-term perspective, talk about their relation with the organisation, their goals, and the skills they need or are interested in learning.
- Provide new challenges through job rotation. Provide a choice of assignments where possible.
- Assign a mentor to the part-timer. This will ensure that the part-timer internalises the values and the attitudes of the organisation.
- Encourage part-timers to take initiative in providing better products and services to customers.
- Provide the right training and resources.
- Provide orientation as well as training related to the successful execution of jobs.
- Communicate. Part-time employees are easily excluded from meetings and discussions that concern their jobs. Allow ample opportunities for communication. Encourage part-timers to initiate communication.

- Make part-timers feel part of the team. Part-timers also have affiliation needs and want to feel accepted in the organisation. Invite part-timers to attend formal and informal meetings.
- Make it fun. Create an enjoyable work environment. Labour turnover is very high under part-time employees. High labour turnover is not only disruptive, but also affects customer satisfaction.

## 13.7 New developments in the study of motivation

Ambrose (1999) analysed and compared the empirical results of more than 200 studies done on work motivation during the last decade. Most of these studies relate to the motivational theories discussed in this chapter. Other motivational research areas that have received increased interest and activity during the last decade include creativity, groups, and culture.

### 13.7.1 Creativity

Creativity is the ability to come up with novel ideas that are useful. In order for organisations to adapt to a changing environment, employees should be encouraged to become more creative. Research has shown that creativity can be developed by carefully construing situational (contextual) variables. Creativity is closely related to motivation, as the same contextual variables that are predicted to foster intrinsic motivation are also associated with creative performance. The implication is that organisations can simultaneously influence motivation and creative performance in an effective way. So far, no studies have attempted to identify the effect of intrinsic motivation on creativity (Ambrose 1999).

Ambrose is of the opinion that goal-setting should include creativity goals. It was found that a controlling environment is likely to inhibit creativity, while supervisory support and trust (high quality relationships) enhanced creativity in employees. It is not yet clear to what extent competition influences

creativity, although it was found that an awareness of possible conflict could boost creativity.

### 13.7.2 Groups and motivation

As organisations continue to move towards group-based systems, research on motivation within groups is increasingly important. Research done in this area was primarily done from the cognitive expectancy theory and goal-setting perspective. Although literature suggests that group membership will affect an individual's perception of expectancies, instrumentalities or valences, as well as their perceptions of these values for the group overall, little is known about how these perceptions are formed.

Studies on work teams revealed that semi-autonomous work teams experienced higher levels of job scope (job characteristics that increase intrinsic motivation) and greater intrinsic satisfaction, extrinsic satisfaction and organisational commitment than traditional work groups (Ambrose 1999). This would imply that employees generally feel more motivated and satisfied when they work in groups that are allowed administrative oversight of their work. However, a few studies, including a study done at a motor manufacturer in the Nelson Mandela Metropole, indicated that higher levels of absenteeism and labour turnover are associated with autonomous work groups. These results highlight the pressure and stress associated with the establishment of autonomous work groups.

### 13.7.3 Culture and motivation

Cross-cultural research in the area of work motivation has increased during the last decade. Research on motivation and other work-related behaviours has often been criticised for focusing almost exclusively on US populations and companies. Most of the cross-cultural comparisons on motivation examine differences in motives, needs, PWE (Protestant Work Ethic), or preferences for job attributes. PWE refers to the extent to which work is perceived as a central life value. Borg and Braun (in Ambrose 1999), for example, found that West Germans put less emphasis on existence and relatedness values than East Germans. (Existence needs are similar to Maslow's lower order needs, while relatedness needs are similar to affiliation needs.) This could imply that there is no universal set of motivators, but that people in different cultures might be motivated by different things (Ambrose 1999).

Bergh and Theron (2003:282) point out that one cannot ignore the effect of cultural differences on work behaviour. The emphasis on collectivism and collective responsibility in African and Asian cultures could, for example, influence the need for affiliation, power and achievement.

Research results on cross-cultural studies have in many cases given varying results (for instance, in the case of work ethic) and should therefore be interpreted with caution.

## 13.8 A holistic approach to motivation

In a holistic approach the assumption is that a human is an organised whole, functioning in totality through the interaction of various needs, expectations, beliefs, personality traits, skills and abilities. Humans are also perceived as unique beings, with a dynamic nature. From this approach the question should not arise as to which motivational theory is the 'best' one, but all the theories in their totality should be used to understand human motivation in the workplace. The different theories on motivation complement each other and provide a framework for the understanding of human behaviour.

When a performance problem arises in the organisation, it should not immediately be ascribed to a lack of motivation. The cause might lie in poor material, machinery or work processes. When a motivational problem is evident, the inter-relatedness of the individual, the job characteristics, the job context and the organisational culture should be considered. The various approaches to motivation should be considered and utilised in analysing and rectifying the situation.

## 13.9 Motivation and quality assurance

Organisations cannot compete successfully without a motivated workforce. Total Quality Management (TQM) implies a continuous improvement in products and services through the active learning and participation of all employees. It is therefore imperative that a culture is established within an organisation where all human potential is realised. Motivating employees should not be an isolated initiative of one or a few managers. Instead, it should become a well-planned and carefully monitored intervention jointly driven by the human resources department/consultant and management. First-line supervisors and managers can only empower their employees if they, themselves, are empowered by their managers. An organisational culture of achievement, self-actualisation and continuous learning is conducive to quality products and service.

## 13.10 Conclusion

Organisations exploit various resources in order to compete successfully. These resources include material, machinery, money, methods and manpower. Few people realise that in comparison to other resources, human resources is the only resource that increases in quality and capacity the more it is utilised. Employees who actively participate in decision-making and problem-solving learn and develop in the process, and are then progressively able to handle more complex and challenging situations. The potential of people is unlimited. Organisations cannot afford to ignore this valuable resource. Motivation is a calculated technique that managers can use to explore human potential and talents. A positive self-enhancing organisational culture is more likely to render higher motivation and commitment than a culture dominated by power, punishment and suspicion.

## Summary

- Motivation is defined as intentional and persistent behaviour aimed at achieving a goal. A motivated employee is one who willingly and enthusiastically works towards achieving the organisational goal.
- The content theories of Maslow and Herzberg attempt to explain specific things that motivate people at work. They identify people's needs and the goals they pursue in order to satisfy these needs.
- The process theories attempt to identify the variables that impact on motivation.

These theories are concerned with how behaviour is initiated, directed and sustained. The emphasis is placed on the actual process of motivation.
- The various motivational theories provide a framework for understanding employee behaviour and performance in the workplace. It is important that a holistic perspective of motivation is taken rather than isolating one theory as the 'best' one.
- New areas in the field of motivational research include creativity, groups and cultural differences.
- Theorists differ on the impact that money has as a motivator. Money only serves as a motivator if it is directly linked to performance. However, it is agreed that

## Self-assessment exercise

### What are your needs?

For each of the items below, circle the number that best describes you at this point in your life. Answer as honestly as possible.

| How often do you | Never | Seldom | Sometimes | Often | Always |
|---|---|---|---|---|---|
| 1  wish you had more intimate friends? | 1 | 2 | 3 | 4 | 5 |
| 2  worry about your financial position? | 1 | 2 | 3 | 4 | 5 |
| 3  identify potential learning opportunities? | 1 | 2 | 3 | 4 | 5 |
| 4  feel your life is not worth much? | 1 | 2 | 3 | 4 | 5 |
| 5  think about your safety? | 1 | 2 | 3 | 4 | 5 |
| 6  feel lonely and unloved? | 1 | 2 | 3 | 4 | 5 |
| 7  feel good about yourself? | 5 | 4 | 3 | 2 | 1 |
| 8  experience personal growth? | 5 | 4 | 3 | 2 | 1 |
| 9  think others appreciate your skills? | 5 | 4 | 3 | 2 | 1 |
| 10  compare your income and expenses? | 1 | 2 | 3 | 4 | 5 |
| 11  feel you are in physical danger? | 1 | 2 | 3 | 4 | 5 |
| 12  feel that you are making progress in your life? | 5 | 4 | 3 | 2 | 1 |
| 13  feel perfectly safe and secure from personal harm? | 5 | 4 | 3 | 2 | 1 |
| 14  worry about how you are going to pay your bills? | 1 | 2 | 3 | 4 | 5 |
| 15  feel well accepted by others? | 5 | 4 | 3 | 2 | 1 |

intrinsic rewards have a powerful impact on motivation.
- Managers should also consider the motivation of part-time employees, as they will increasingly form a significant part of the future workforce.
- Quality cannot be separated from motivation. By building quality into the job context and job environment, employees will be enabled to produce quality products and services.

## Self-Assessment application

This self-assessment is based on Maslow's needs hierarchy and indicates what needs are important to you at this present time.

| | |
|---|---|
| Physiological needs | Add up the total for items 2, 10 and 14 |
| Security needs | Items 5, 11 and 13 |
| Social needs | Items 1, 6 and 15 |
| Esteem needs | Items 4, 7 and 9 |
| Self-actualisation needs | Items 3, 8 and 12 |

Which needs are the most important to you? Which needs are the least important to you? Compare your need profile to that of another learner. Do you have similar needs? If you do have similar needs, is the strength of these needs the same? In which ways do you try to satisfy your most important needs in your own life? Considering the need profile of your fellow learner, what would you suggest s/he does to satisfy her/his needs?

## Case study
## A mismatch?

Andile Jones is employed as a clerk in the purchasing department of a huge company in the food industry. He started working at the company four years ago. At first he was quite excited about his job and tried to learn as much as possible. Recently his feelings about his job have changed and he has become dissatisfied.

It all started when he met an old school pal, Johnny, several years after they had last seen each other. Johnny was a salesperson for a pharmaceutical company and responsible for sales in the whole metropolitan area. He earned a handsome commission, on top of a basic salary. And he had so many experiences to share. Andile earned much less, which to him was understandable, because he had lower qualifications than Johnny, and his work was more routine and structured. What really irritated Andile was that his manager did not consider individual performance, and if something went wrong, everybody got into trouble. His manager was also not a good listener, because he ignored all suggestions on how the work could have been done better, and forced them to stick to old-fashioned procedures. Andile felt that the work they did could be done by the secretaries anyway. Every morning he just dealt with whatever landed on his desk. He had no say in the allocation of work. It felt to him as if he had no direction at all.

As Andile became more and more dissatisfied in his job situation he approached you, the human resources practitioner, for some guidance. First of all, you gave him a questionnaire to complete to determine his needs. The results were as follows:

| | |
|---|---|
| Achievement | Very High |
| Affiliation | Low |
| Power | Low |
| Autonomy | Moderately High |

Secondly, you asked Andile to complete a questionnaire to determine the motivational potential of his current job. The results were as follows:

| | | | |
|---|---|---|---|
| Skill variety | 4 | Autonomy | 3 |
| Task identity | 5 | Feedback | 3 |
| Task significance | 3 | | |

The normal Motivating Potential Score (MPS) (norm) for clerical jobs is 106. Anything above this score would imply that the job has high motivational potential and anything lower indicates that the job has low motivational potential.

## Questions

1  Calculate the MPS for Andile's job.
2  Analyse Andile's needs using McClelland's theory.
3  Use both McClelland's theory and the job characteristics model to recommend ways for improving Andile's job.

## Experiential exercise No. 1

PURPOSE: To evaluate the extent to which employees in diverse jobs are motivated. To recommend ways in which the motivation levels of employees can be improved.

INTRODUCTION: The various motivational theories provide a framework for the understanding of motivation in the workplace. It is shortsighted to believe that one theory will provide all the answers to motivational problems.

TASK: STEP 1 (1 hour)
Form groups of five learners each. Each group will be allocated a specific motivation theory (excluding Maslow's need hierarchy). In your groups, compile a questionnaire based on the allocated theory that can be used to determine how motivated an employee is. Make provision for a short job description.
STEP 2 (done outside scheduled periods)
In your own time, ask three diversely employed people to complete the questionnaire as honestly as possible. Your study facilitator will provide advice on how to conduct this task in a professional manner.
STEP 3 (30 minutes)
Analyse and compare the completed questionnaires. How motivated would you say each person is? What would you recommend should be done to increase their motivational levels?
STEP 4 (5 minutes per group)
The groups get the opportunity to share their findings and recommendations with everybody.

## Experiential Exercise No. 2

PURPOSE: To debate the impact money has on the motivation of South African employees.

INTRODUCTION: Well-known theorists disagree about the impact of money on the motivation of employees. Most management theories originate from America and their application in the South African context is not conclusive. Many organisations use financial incentives to increase productivity.

TASK: STEP 1 (30 minutes)
Form groups of five learners each. Half of the groups will prepare an argument for, and the other groups will prepare an argument against the use of money as a motivator in the South African workplace.
STEP 2 (3 minutes per group)
Each group offers their argument in a debate presentation.
STEP 3 (5 minutes)
The facilitator (or designated person) summarises the main arguments and draws conclusions.

(To make this exercise more meaningful, the groups could be granted an opportunity to do additional research and also interview managers and employees on their experiences with financial incentives before presenting their arguments.)

## Chapter questions

1  Whose responsibility is it to motivate employees?
2  What behaviours distinguish a motivated employee from one who is not motivated?
3  How does self-identity tie in with motivation?
4  How will you respond to a person who says that it is impossible to motivate employees in certain jobs, such as machine operators, mechanics, cleaners or security officers?
5  Use the concepts in Vroom's expectancy

theory to explain how motivated you are in terms of your studies.

6    Considering all motivation theories discussed in this chapter, what general guidelines will you provide to managers for motivating their employees?

7    Discuss the new developments in the study of motivation.

# Bibliography

AMBROSE, M.L. 1999. 'Old friends, new faces: Motivation research in the 1990s'. *Journal of Management* (www.findarticles.com).

BERGH, Z.C. & THERON, A.L. 2003. *Psychology in the work context*. Thomson, Johannesburg.

COLLINS, M. 2001. 'Breaking new ground'. *Motivation of Champions*, 2(1).

GREENBERG, J & BARON, R.A. 1995. *Behavior in organizations. Understanding and managing the human side of work, 5th edition*. (Prentice-Hall), Pearson Education Inc.

HAYS, S. 1999. 'Exceptional customer service takes the "Ritz" touch'. *Workforce Journal* (www.workforceonline.com). Reprinted with permission of Copyright Clearance Center.

IVANCEVICH, J.M. & MATTESON, M.T. 1999. *Organizational behavior and management, 5th edition*. McGraw-Hill Companies, New York.

KREITNER, R. & KINICKI, A. 2001. *Organizational behavior, 5th edition*. McGraw-Hill, Irwin.

LAWLER, E.E. 1996. *From the ground up*. Jossey-Bass, San Francisco.

LUTHANS, F. 2002. *Organizational Behavior, 9th edition*. McGraw-Hill Companies, New York.

MASLOW, A.H. 1954. *Motivation and personality*. Harper & Row, New York.

MOL. A. 1990. *Help! I'm a manager*. (Tafelberg), NB Publishers, Cape Town.

MULLINS, L.J. 1996. *Management and organizational behaviour, 4th edition*. (Pitman), Pearson Education (UK).

NELSON, B. 1999. 'Top 10 ways to motivate part-time employees' (www.workforceonline.com/00/04/13/005284.html). Reprinted with permission of Copyright Clearance Center.

PLUNKET, W.R. 1996. *Supervision: Diversity and teams in the workplace, 8th edition*. (Prentice-Hall), Pearson Education Inc.

ROBBINS, S.P. 1989. *Organizational behavior: Concepts, controversies and applications*. (Prentice-Hall), Pearson Education Inc.

ROBBINS, S.P. 1998. *Organizational Behavior, 8th edition*. (Prentice-Hall), Pearson Education Inc.

TREDWELL, B. 2002. 'Controlling a control freak' (www.workforce.com). Reprinted with permission of Copyright Clearance Center.

WIESNER, R. & MILLET, B. 2000. *Management and organizational behavior*. John Wiley & Sons, Brisbane.

# Websites

South Africa:
www.microsoft.com/southafrica/
South African Breweries: www.SAB.co.za
Ritz Carlton Group: www.workforceonline.com
PepsiCo: www.pepsico.com
Various articles on motivation:
www.accel-team.com

# 14

# Leadership

## A Werner

## Learning outcomes

At the end of this chapter the learner should be able to:

- Define leadership.
- Compare and contrast leadership and management.
- Discuss the task and people dimensions of leadership.
- Explain how power and authority influence leadership.
- Discuss and apply various leadership theories to organisational situations.
- Provide an overview of transformational leadership.
- Discuss leadership challenges in a virtual workplace.
- Indicate the importance of quality assurance in leadership.

## Key words and concepts

- emotional intelligence
- empowerment
- quantum change
- self-fulfilling prophecy
- situational leadership
- transformation
- virtual leadership

## Illustrative case

### MADIBA, the icon of transformational leadership

The Black Management Forum (BMF) chose to dedicate its annual conference, in October 2002, as a tribute to previous president, Nelson Mandela. In the words of Bheki Sibiya, national president of the BMF:

We chose the topic of Transformational Leadership for this conference for a purpose. The English Oxford Dictionary describes transformation as a thorough or dramatic change in form, outward appearance or character. Leadership, on the other hand, is a process of envisioning a different and better future for an aspect of life, then persuading and galvanizing people to work diligently and tirelessly for its achievement. This conference is a tribute to Madiba. It goes without saying that Madiba is the greatest icon of transformational leadership who is alive today. There is no debate at all about that.

SOURCE: Sibiya (2002)

## 14.1 Introduction

In a world that is becoming more and more complex through the accelerated development and application of information technology, organisations have to respond much quicker to challenges. Bill Gates of Microsoft urges that it is now necessary to 'operate at the speed of thought'. Globalisation is forcing organisations to become competitive and to operate at international standards. These challenges require quantum leap change from organisations rather than adaptive change. Quantum leap change becomes necessary when environmental changes make traditional ways of operating organisations redundant and thus demand fundamentally different approaches to ensure ongoing survival and future success. In order to cope in a new world a new breed of leader is required. What the leaders of today have learnt in the past may not be applicable to the future. The way in which organisations respond to new challenges is unmistakably tied to the values, attitudes, styles and responses of their leaders. It is therefore imperative for leaders to unlearn old habits and beliefs, and engage in ongoing learning and personal development.

Maritz (2002:44) mentions that some leaders believe the performance of an organisation depends on the quality of its personnel. However, it is rather the quality of the leadership that determines whether the talents, potential and commitment of employees will be expressed as competency and creativity for the benefit of the organisation.

In this chapter we will explore what leadership is, dimensions of leadership, power and authority in leadership, and different approaches to leadership. We will also discuss contemporary leadership approaches, namely transformational and charismatic leadership. We will consider the leadership challenges in a virtual workplace and the importance of quality assurance in leadership.

## 14.2 What is leadership?

A general accepted definition of leadership is: the process whereby one individual influences others to willingly and enthusiastically direct their efforts and abilities towards attaining defined group or organisational goals. This definition suggests that leadership involves the exercise of influence and not coercion. The leader attempts to change the attitudes and actions of people which are related to specific goals, and not attitudes or actions that are not related to the goal. Leadership is very much a two-way relationship; not only does the leader influence the followers, but the followers also exert influence over the leader.

## 14.3 Leadership versus management

In everyday speech, the terms leader and manager are often used interchangeably. There is, however, a clear distinction between the two. Figure 14.1 demonstrates some of the important differences between leadership and management. Leadership focuses on vision, strategic development and initiative, whereas management deals with the implementation of the vision. Humphrey Walters (1999:10), co-founder and chief executive of Mast International Organisation, writes the following: 'Most people realize that the art of leadership is a learned craft. Management, on the other hand, is a science.' Managers are more concerned with short-term problems in the organisation, whereas leaders take a much broader perspective and concern themselves with the environment internal and external to the organisation. Leaders have a long-term perspective and anticipate the future needs of the organisation. It is often said that leaders do the right things, while managers do things right. Leadership in an organisation, unlike management, is not restricted to people in specific positions or roles, but related to all people with the ability to influence and inspire others to attain a goal. To enhance innovation and teamwork in the organisation, leadership must be present at all levels. Managers will also become much more effective if their leadership skills are developed and utilised. The fact that South Africa maintains a very low position in the World Competitive Survey (www.btimes.co.za/97/0330/news/news.htm), indicates a need to identify and develop more leaders, and to create an organisational culture that encourages and supports leader initiative.

Ken Parry is of the opinion that management and leadership are not comparable entities, but that managership and leadership are two styles of management that work together to attain organisational success. Management can thus be perceived as managership plus leadership. These two styles are, for example, reflected in Hersey and Blanchard's matrix of 'leadership styles', which progresses from a strongly managership style to a strongly leadership style (Wiesner and Millet 2001:167–8). This theory is discussed in section 14.11.

## 14.4 The qualities or traits approach to leadership

A question often asked is whether leaders are born or not. Many studies have been done to identify common characteristics of leaders. Although some of these studies have found common characteristics in leaders, no universal set of characteristics has been confirmed. However, these studies underline the fact that leaders are different to other people and that they possess outstanding characteristics. Leadership is a very demanding, unrelenting job, with enormous pressures and grave responsibilities.

Humphrey Walters (1999:10) identified the following characteristics of leaders:

- Leaders have the ability to create a vision and excite people to achieve the impossible.
- Great leaders have an external energy and an inner strength that see them through tough times.
- Leaders have a mental agility that enables them to make effective decisions much faster than most other people.
- Leaders allow their team members to grow and carry out tasks without interruption. They relinquish power to others.
- Leaders have the ability to tap into people's souls. They are emotionally intelligent and enhance people's confidence by understanding and dealing appropriately with their emotions and concerns. It reflects the ability to adapt one's style to the needs of the situation and people.

One leadership characteristic that receives a lot of attention these days is integrity. In a world where corruption and the pursuing of self-interest are commonplace, integrity is perceived as a scarce attribute that gives a competitive advantage. Kotter (2003:6), a leadership expert at Harvard University, is

**Figure 14.1** Leadership versus management

| Criteria | Leadership | Management |
|---|---|---|
| Change | Provide a vision and initiate change | Implement changes as suggested by leader |
| People | Inspire and develop | Control |
| Power derived from | Ability to influence others | Authority |
| Task | Do the right things | Do things right |
| Commitment to goal | Passionate | Impersonal |

contemptuous of many fallen heroes, and says: 'I've yet to find a great leader who has done something illegal.'

In the end one has to accept that even if a person has certain inborn characteristics that provide the potential for good leadership, these natural talents need to be encouraged and developed.

---

### Encounter 14.1

IN MARCH 2003, the University of Port Elizabeth hosted a satellite linked presentation featuring Rudy Giuliani, who became a symbol of leadership under fire in the aftermath of the September 11 attacks in New York. As mayor of New York, Giuliani provided incredible strength and stability at a time of great confusion and fear.

Although the September 11 events pushed Giuliani into the international public eye, his leadership at this time is not perceived as a once off achievement. Giuliani is also credited with:

- Reducing crime by 57 per cent.
- Cutting welfare rolls in half.
- Reducing taxes by $2.5 billion.
- Creating a record number of new jobs.

Read more about this remarkable man, who was named the *TIME Magazine's* Person of the Year for 2001, by searching the following website: www.time.com/time/poy2001/poyprofile.html

---

## 14.5  Participative versus autocratic leadership behaviours

In the late 1940s, researchers began to explore the idea that a leader's behaviour determined effectiveness. One of these studies, the Ohio State Leadership Studies, identified two clusters of behaviour:

- *Consideration*, including behaviours such as helping subordinates, communicating, listening and explaining things. Consideration involves creating mutual respect and trust, and having a concern for group members' needs and desires.
- *Initiating structure*, such as clarifying rules and procedures, maintaining per-

formance standards, and explaining to employees what their roles are. Initiating structure focuses on what the group should do to achieve results.

Consequent studies have delivered the concepts of employee-centred and job-centred behaviours that are parallel to consideration and initiating structure. The original idea of these studies was to determine which behavioural approach was more effective.

Contemporary leadership theories such as the leadership grid and the situational leadership theory of Hersey and Blanchard also distinguish between task behaviour and people behaviour. However, these theories do not suggest that there is one best leadership style. Rather, they argue that the effectiveness of a given leadership style depends on situational factors. These theories are discussed later on.

## 14.6  Power and authority

Every leader possesses a certain influence and power over others. Managers, on the other hand, have the ability to influence subordinates due to the authority vested in them. Leaders are not always associated with a specific position, yet still have the ability to influence people towards the attainment of organisational goals. Power to influence is awarded to the leader by the followers. The exercise of power is a social process that helps to explain how different people can influence the behaviour of others. The ability to influence people is based on various sources of power:

- *Reward power:* the extent to which the follower believes that the leader has the ability and resources to provide rewards for behaviour that meet the expectations of the leader. Examples of rewards are recognition, praise, money, privileges and allocation of challenging tasks.
- *Coercive power:* the extent to which the follower believes that the leader has the ability to punish or disadvantage followers. Examples of punishment include withholding information, privileges or growth opportunities; withdrawal of

emotional support, formal reprimands or ostracism.

- *Legitimate power:* the extent to which the follower believes that the leader has the right to influence due to the leader's role or position in the organisation. Legitimate power is based on authority.
- *Referent power:* the extent to which a follower identifies with the leader and has respect for the leader. The leader attracts followers due to perceived attractiveness, charisma or reputation.
- *Expert power:* the extent to which the follower believes that the leader is an expert in a specific field, is competent and has special abilities.

Leaders may have more than one source of power. These sources of power are based on the perceptions of the followers, and may not be based on objective evaluation of the leader's ability or strengths.

## 14.7 McGregor's X and Y theory

McGregor's X and Y theory is based on the following self-fulfilling prophecy: A manager's assumptions about the nature of human beings impact on the manager's behaviour towards employees. The manager's behaviour then influences the employees' behaviour, which again serves to reconfirm the manager's assumptions.

We wish to first explore the different assumptions managers could have about employees and then consider how these assumptions influence the manager's and employees' behaviour.

McGregor identified two sets of assumptions (beliefs) managers have about employees, and he called these Theory X and Theory Y. Theory X assumptions are negative, and include the perception that people are lazy, dislike work, require close supervision, do not want responsibility, and have little ambition. Since people act according to what they believe, a manager with these outdated beliefs will give detailed instructions, supervise employees closely and use threats of punishment to control behaviour. Employees treated in such a way tend to do just what is required of them to stay out of trouble, abuse sick leave and stay uncommitted to the organisation or its goals. The X-leader will observe the behaviour of employees and allow them to reconfirm his/her original beliefs about people. A vicious circle of negativity is created. South Africa is notorious for its low levels of productivity. Is the answer to this problem to be found in McGregor's theory? Why do some companies, such as South African Breweries, manage to compete successfully despite tough international competition?

Theory Y is a modern and positive set of assumptions about people. Theory Y leaders believe that employees are hard-working, want to make a positive contribution, seek responsibility, and can control their own performance. They view employees as self-energised, committed, responsible, and creative. Managers with Y-beliefs provide employees with opportunities, positive guidance and recognition. Employees working under such a leader feel respected, acknowledged, and proud. They become responsible and hardworking. The subsequent performance of the employees reconfirms the original beliefs of the leader. Figure 14.2 illustrates leaders' assumptions about people according to McGregor's theory.

McGregor's theory exerts a major influence on modern-day management, especially since it underlines a humanistic perspective.

## 14.8 Schein's theory of human assumptions

The human assumptions identified by Schein (1980:53) reflect the historical course of human assumptions. Each assumption is briefly discussed below.

### 14.8.1 The rational-economic assumption

The rational-economic assumption is underpinned by hedonism, which claims that people's behaviour is aimed at obtaining the greatest advantage for themselves.

**Figure 14.2** Leaders' assumptions about people

| X beliefs | Y beliefs |
| --- | --- |
| People are inherently lazy and avoid work whenever they can. | People perceive work as natural as play. |
| Most people are only interested in money. | People want to make a worthwhile contribution. |
| People do not want responsibility. | Most people are keen to demonstrate their ability. |
| The average person does not have much ambition. | People are creative and strive for self-actualisation. |
| Most people are not capable of solving problems. | People are problem-solvers by nature. |

Assumptions of the rational-economic approach can be summarised as follows:

- People are motivated mainly by economic incentives, such as money and bonuses and their behaviour is directed towards actions that will result in the greatest economic gain.
- Since economic incentives are controlled by the organisation, people are a passive factor that can be manipulated, activated, and controlled by the organisation.
- People's feelings are irrational, therefore an attempt must be made to prevent these irrational emotions from interfering with people's work.
- Organisations must be designed in such a way that people's feelings are controlled.
- A supervisor who holds rational-economic assumptions will exercise control over subordinates by means of direct authority. The rational-economic assumption relates to McGregor's X-theory.

## 14.8.2 The social assumption

The social assumption is a result of the well-known Hawthorne experiments done by Elton Mayo and his colleagues. Mayo found that work negates people's social needs. In this respect, Schein (1980:59) says that 'industrial life had taken the meaning out of work and had frustrated man's (*sic*) basic social needs.'

The following assumptions are typical of this approach:

- People are motivated by social needs and acquire their basic identity in relationships with others.
- The meaning of work has been reduced by the Industrial Revolution and the rationalisation of work. Therefore people must find meaning in their social relationships at work.
- People will react to the social influence of their immediate colleagues (peer group) rather than to incentives and control from management.
- Subordinates will only react to management influence to the extent that a supervisor can satisfy their social needs.
- The conduct and attitude of a supervisor with a social assumption towards subordinates will differ considerably from that of one with a rational-economic approach. Such a supervisor will pay much more attention to meeting the needs of subordinates, especially the need for social acceptance.

## 14.8.3 The self-actualisation assumption

The self-actualisation assumption supports the view of several searchers, including Argyris, McGregor and Maslow, that the meaning of work is lost in organisational life:

> ... many jobs in modern industry have become so specialised or fragmented that they neither permit workers to use their capacities nor enable them to see the relationship between what they are doing and the total organisational mission (Schein 1980:68).

Schein emphasises the role of self-actualisation (1980:76): 'Even the lowliest untalented man seeks self-actualisation, a sense of meaning and accomplishment in his work, if his other needs are more or less fulfilled.'

Maslow' hierarchy of needs (discussed in Chapter 13) is representative of this approach.

People strive towards maturity in their work and they can experience growth in the context of their work. This implies that they have to have independence and autonomy, accept long-term perspectives, and develop special skills and greater adaptability. People are primarily self-motivated and can exercise self-control. External control measures and strict supervision are likely to make them feel threatened and reduce their maturity level in their work.

There is no inherent conflict between self-actualisation and effective organisational performance. If an individual is given the opportunity, s/he will voluntarily integrate her/his own needs and goals with those of the organisation.

A supervisor who follows the self-actualisation approach will act in the same way as one who follows the social approach, except for a few important differences. According to the self-actualisation assumption, the supervisor will concentrate on making the work intrinsically more meaningful and challenging, rather than considering the social needs of subordinates.

### 14.8.4 The complex person assumption

The complex person assumption postulates that humans are much more complex than assumed by past organisational theories. Schein (1980:80) states: 'Not only is he more complex within himself, being possessed of many needs and potentials, but he is also likely to differ from his neighbour in the patterns of his complexity.'

The complex person assumption may be summarised as follows:
- People are not only complex, they are also highly changeable.
- Employees can develop new needs as a result of their experience in an organisation.
- Employees' needs may differ from one organisation to the next, and even in different departments of the same organisation.
- People may productively join in the activities of an organisation to satisfy different needs; ultimate need satisfaction and the ultimate effectiveness of the organisation are only partially dependent on the nature of employees' motivation.
- People may react positively to different management strategies (or leadership styles), depending on their own needs, goals, abilities and the nature of their work; in other words, there is no one correct managerial strategy that will work for all people at all times (see Schein 1980:80).

The most important implication of the complex person assumption for managers is that they must first be good diagnosticians, and second be adaptable.

## 14.9 The leadership grid of Blake and Mouton

The leadership grid of Blake and Mouton was first published as the Managerial Grid in 1964 and republished in 1991 as the Leadership Grid (Mullins 1996:439). The Grid is illustrated in Figure 14.3. The Grid provides a basis to compare different leadership styles in terms of two dimensions:
1   A concern for production.
2   A concern for people.

*Concern for production* is the extent to which the manager emphasises production, profit, deadlines, task completion, and results. This is represented on the horizontal axis of the Grid.

*Concern for people* is the extent to which the leader emphasises the needs and expectations of employees, and fosters employee satisfaction. This is represented on the vertical axis of the Grid.

'Concern for' is not a specific term that indicates the amount of actual production of actual behaviour towards people. Rather, it indicates the character and strength of assumptions present behind any given managerial style (Blake and Mouton 1978:9).

Both dimensions of leadership behaviour are presented on the managerial grid in nine-point scales from low (point 1) through average (point 5) to high (point 9). The different scale points do not allocate absolute values to leadership behaviour, but merely indicate varying degrees of concern for people and for production.

The following leadership styles are identified:

- *The authority-compliance leader* (9.1 rating) shows maximum concern for production (scale point 9) and minimum concern for people (scale point 1). Production is achieved by means of formal authority, and subordinates are controlled by enforcing submissiveness. Decisions are made unilaterally and communication is mainly one-way.
- *The country club leader* (1.9 rating) is a democratic leader who will show minimum concern for production (scale point 1) and maximum concern for people (scale point 9).

Cultivating and maintaining sound interpersonal relationships with colleagues and subordinates will therefore be most important. This leader maintains that the job will be done automatically if interpersonal relationships are sound. Conflict is avoided at all cost.

**Figure 14.3** Blake and Mouton's Leadership Grid

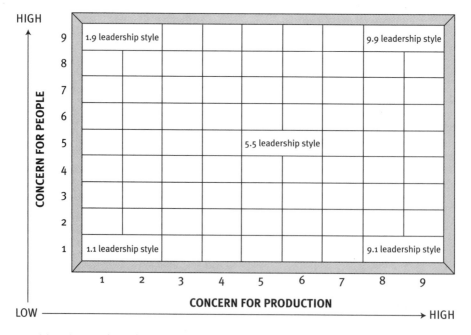

SOURCE: Blake and Mouton (1978:11)

Communication is aimed at maintaining a pleasant working atmosphere.

- *The impoverished leader* (1.1 rating) has a laissez-faire approach. This person shows little concern for production and little concern for people (both at scale point 1). A laissez-faire leader does the absolute minimum required, in both the job and interpersonal relationships, to stay on as a member of the organisation. The impoverished leader avoids commitment to decisions. This style is often associated with managers who are close to retirement or managers who have emotionally withdrawn from the organisation.
- *The middle-of-the-road leader* (5.5 rating) tries to maintain a balance between production and interpersonal relationships. Blake and Mouton (1978:12) describe this style as:

> ... the 'go-along-to-get-along' assumptions which are revealed in conformity to the status quo. Such leaders try half-heartedly to pay attention to both aspects (both at scale point 5) but do not succeed. They assume that it is impossible to integrate the needs of employees with organisational goals.

- *The team leader* (rating 9.9) integrates concern for production and concern for people at a high level (both at scale point 9). This style emphasises teamwork, is goal-orientated and strives for excellent results through participative management, involvement with people, and conflict management. The 9.9 style provides the 'ideal' leaders should strive for.

In the 1991 edition of the Grid (Mullins 1996:441), two additional styles were added: 9+9 paternalistic leadership, and opportunistic leadership.

- *9+9 paternalistic leadership.* Here, reward and approval are exchanged for loyalty and obedience, and punishment is threatened for failure to comply. It is also called 'father knows best' leadership.

- *Opportunistic leadership.* Here, the leader will utilise a style that will return him/her the most benefit. It is also called the 'What's in it for me?' management.

By knowing the styles of other leaders and their own leadership style, leaders will be better equipped to appraise themselves and others more objectively, communicate better, understand where differences originate, and assist and lead others in being more productive. Blake and Mouton (1978:6) describe the usefulness of their approach as follows:

> Learning grid management not only makes people aware of the assumptions under which they operate but also helps them to learn and to embrace scientifically verified principles for effectiveness in production under circumstances that promise mentally healthy behaviour.

## 14.10 The leadership continuum of Tannenbaum and Schmidt

Tannenbaum and Schmidt (1958) advocate a leadership continuum that illustrates the situational and varying nature of leadership. Figure 14.4 illustrates this continuum. This approach identifies four main styles of leadership: tells, sells, consults, and joins.

- *Tells:* The leader identifies a goal, decides how the goal should be achieved, and instructs employees without providing an opportunity for participation.
- *Sells:* The leader still decides what should be done and how it should be done, but expects resistance and therefore convinces employees of the validity of the decision.
- *Consults:* The leader chooses a decision only after the views and proposals of employees are considered.
- *Joins:* The leader defines the problem and the decision parameters, and leaves the decision to the group, with the leader acting as a group member of equal status.

**Figure 14.4** The leadership continuum of Tannenbaum and Schmidt

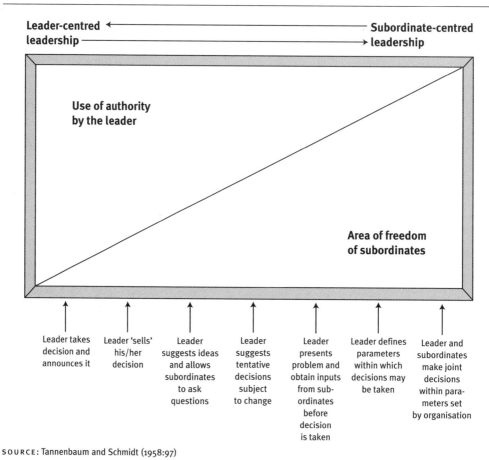

SOURCE: Tannenbaum and Schmidt (1958:97)

The continuum illustrates that leadership varies according to the distribution of influence among the leader and his/her subordinates. The leadership style changes from left to right from leader-centred to subordinate-centred as the leader exercises less control (authority) and allows subordinates more influence and freedom to take decisions on their own. Leadership behaviour and the leadership style used by a leader will therefore depend on how much authority s/he delegates to subordinates.

Three types of forces determine which style is practical and desirable: forces in the leader, forces in the subordinates, and forces in the situation. An effective leader is aware of these forces and acts according to them.

- *Forces in the leader:* A leader's behaviour is influenced by his/her personality, background, knowledge and experience. Other internal forces are:
  - The leader's value system.
  - The leader's confidence in subordinates.
  - The leader's own leadership philosophy.
  - The leader's feeling of security in an uncertain situation, especially when s/he is operating towards the right of the continuum.

- *Forces in the subordinates:* Before a leader can decide how to guide subordinates, s/he must consider the forces affecting these subordinates. Each subordinate is affected by personality variables and expectations of how the leader will act towards him/her. A leader can allow subordinates more freedom and involvement in decision-making if they:
  - Have a relatively high need for independence.
  - Are prepared to accept responsibility for decision-making.
  - Are interested in the problem and feel that it is important.
  - Understand the goals of the organisation and can identify with them.
  - Have the knowledge and experience required to deal with the problem.
  - Understand that they are expected to share in decision-making.
- *Forces in the situation:* Apart from the forces present in the leader and the subordinates, the general situation may also affect a leader's behaviour. Important factors include:
  - The type of organisation, and the people's values and traditions.
  - Group effectiveness, including previous experience, group cohesion, mutual acceptance and commonality of purpose.
  - The complexity of the problem.
  - Time pressure which may result in others not being involved in decision-making.

Although the leadership continuum is a logical concept with practical application value, it does have some shortcomings, the most important of which is the lack of instructions on exactly how a situation is to be diagnosed. Furthermore it is not clear how leadership behaviour must be judged. Little empirical research has been conducted about the leadership continuum.

## 14.11 The situational leadership theory of Hersey and Blanchard

Hersey and Blanchard devised a leadership model based on the maturity or readiness level of employees. Four leadership styles, based on a combination of task and relationship behaviour, are possible. This theory is represented in Figure 14.5.

- *Task behaviour,* according to Hersey and Blanchard (1982:96), implies the degree to which leaders are likely to organise and spell out the tasks of group members by indicating who should do what, when, where, and how. Task behaviour is also characterised by a leader instituting well-defined organisational patterns, channels of communication and procedures for the execution of tasks.
- *Relationship behaviour* implies the degree to which leaders are likely to maintain interpersonal relationships between themselves and group members by providing open channels of communication, socio-emotional support, psychological stroking, and facilitating of subordinates' behaviour.

Hersey and Blanchard (1982) identify four maturity levels:

- M1 – (low maturity) refers to subordinates who are unwilling or unsure how to execute a task, and do not have the necessary ability to do it.
- M2 – (low to average maturity) refers to subordinates who do not have the ability to execute a task although they are willing and confident enough to do it.
- M3 – (average to high maturity) refers to subordinates who have the ability to execute the task, but are unwilling or unsure how to do it.
- M4 – (high maturity) refers to subordinates who have the ability and confidence to execute the task and are willing to do it.

**Figure 14.5**  Hersey and Blanchard's situational leadership theory

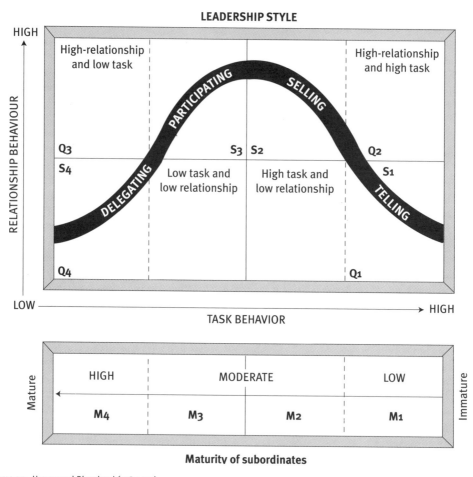

SOURCE: Hersey and Blanchard (1982:152)

Hersey and Blanchard (1982) also identify four leadership styles, derived from the combination of task and relationship behaviour:

- S1 – *telling:* involves high task behaviour combined with low relationship behaviour by the leader. The leader explains by means of task behaviour to his/her subordinates what to do, how, where, and when. Such a leader describes his/her subordinates' tasks thoroughly, without explaining to them why a task has to be done or why certain procedures are to be followed. Communication is mainly one-way only.
- S2 – *selling:* involves high task behaviour with high relationship behaviour. The leader provides guidance to subordinates and tries by means of two-way communication and socio-emotional support to persuade his/her subordinates to accept decisions.
- S3 – *participating:* is characterised by high relationship behaviour with low task behaviour, which means that the leader

and subordinate take decisions together by means of two-way communication. Subordinates can participate in decision-making because they have the required abilities and are encouraged to participate by means of high relationship behaviour.

- S4 – *delegating:* is characterised by low relationship behaviour with low task behaviour, which implies that the leader allows subordinates to take completely independent decisions by delegating authority to them. Therefore supervision is of a general nature, which means that subordinates' work is not checked continuously as they are fully capable of executing their tasks, they have the necessary confidence and are willing to do so.

According to Hersey and Blanchard, leadership behaviour is a function of subordinates' maturity. The leader first determines the maturity level of the subordinates, either individually or as a group, with regard to the particular task to be carried out, and then assumes the appropriate leadership style. The appropriate leadership style can easily be determined by drawing a perpendicular on the continuum from the identified maturity level to where it crosses the bell-shaped curve in Figure 14.5. The appropriate leadership style is indicated by the quadrant in which the lines cross.

According to Hersey and Blanchard's situational leadership theory, a leader whose subordinates have a low maturity level (M1) should maintain a high level of task behaviour and a low level of relationship behaviour (the S1 leadership style: telling). As the maturity level of the individual subordinate or group of subordinates increases (to level M2), the leader should reduce task behaviour and increase relationship behaviour (the S2 leadership style: selling). When subordinates become even more mature (M3), both task behaviour and relationship behaviour must be reduced (the S3 leadership style: participating). When the individual subordinate or group of subordinates reaches a high level of maturity (M4), the leader should maintain a

low level of both task behaviour and relationship behaviour (the S4 leadership style: delegating). An effective leader is one who is able to adjust his/her style accurately according to the maturity level of the employee.

A subordinate does not have a fixed maturity level; it depends on the task at hand and the experience and confidence of the employee in relation to the specific task. A person might have a high maturity level in terms of one task, and a low maturity level in terms of another task. Leaders should, however, at all times keep the development of subordinates in mind, and help them to increase their maturity levels.

## 14.12 Nicholls' revised model of situational leadership

The validity of Hersey and Blanchard's basic model has been challenged by Nicholls (1985:60), who claims that the model violates three logical principles:

- *Consistency:* It is inconsistent in the way it connects concern for task or relationships with ability or willingness.
- *Continuity:* The development level continuum lacks continuity since it requires willingness to appear, disappear, and reappear as the development level increases.
- *Conformity:* It runs counter to conformity in that it does not start with a style of high task and high relationship for a group which is simultaneously unable and unwilling.

Nicholls suggests a corrected model (Figure 14.6), which no longer violates the principles of consistency, continuity and conformity, and which presents a completely new model for situational leadership.

Mullins (1996:273–4) explains Nicholls' situational leadership model as follows:

> For groups at a low development level, that are both unable and unwilling, the leader acts in the same role as a parent

**Figure 14.6** Nicholls' revised model of situational leadership

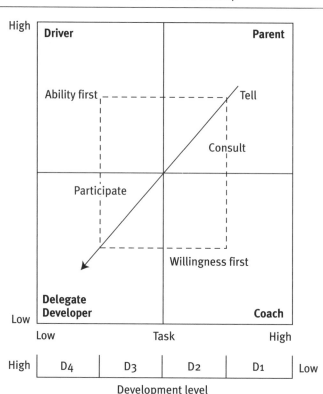

SOURCE: Mullins (1996:273)

who wishes to develop simultaneously the ability and the social skills of a child. As both ability and willingness increase, activity connected with both task and relationships can be reduced. This allows progression from 'tell', through 'consult' to the role of a developer (bottom left quadrant).

The developer role of leadership continues with a light touch to use 'participation' and 'delegation' in order to develop further the ability and willingness of the group. However, if willingness develops more quickly than ability, the leader will have the opportunity to act more in the role of a coach who is anxious to improve ability. If, however, ability develops more quickly than willingness, the leader may

have to revert to the role of driver in order to push the group to achieve results up to its potential, and to prevent unwillingness causing a shortfall in performance.

To summarise, the model requires a smooth progression of the leader from parent, using a high task and high relationship leadership style (following the usual progression 'tell-sell' or consult-participate-delegate) to the leader as developer (and using a low task and low relationship leadership style). But if ability and willingness do not develop in harmony, the leader may find it appropriate to act more like a coach to develop ability, or more like a driver to overcome unwillingness.

In the latest edition of their work, Hersey and Blanchard appear to make reference to the points raised by Nicholls (see Mullins 1996:

273–4). Some people have difficulty understanding the development of followers from M1 to M2 to M3 (see Figure 14.5). How can one go from being insecure to confident and then become insecure again? The important thing to remember is that at the lower levels of readiness, the leader is providing the direction – the what, where, when, and how. Therefore, the decisions are leader-directed. At the higher levels of readiness, followers become responsible for task direction, and the decisions are follower-directed. This transition from leader-directed to self-directed may result in apprehension or insecurity. As followers move from low levels of readiness to higher levels, the combinations of task and relationship behaviour appropriate to the situation begin to change.

The situational leadership theory provides for contingency and flexibility. The leader is not restricted to one specific leadership style, but adjusts his/her style after a careful evaluation of the situation. The leader and follower can jointly determine the follower's maturity or readiness level and the most appropriate leadership style. This will provide a greater chance that the follower will respond positively to the leader's style and expectations.

## 14.13 Transformational leadership

Various macro- and micro-environmental factors have made it necessary for South African organisations to adapt or renew their basic structures, systems, organisational culture and management practices. These factors include international competition, emphasis on information technology, and socio-political and socio-economic changes.

Transformation is a difficult and long-term process. It is only possible to institute meaningful change if credible and capable leaders lead the process. Unless top management support and guide change, it is likely to be fragmented. Strategic leadership is required for systematic, planned, and controlled change. The change leaders help define the vision of the organisation and establish the link between that vision and the type of management and organisational principles that are introduced. A 'vision' is the ability to perceive something not actually visible. It is an impossible dream which the transformational leader or leaders communicate to others. Transformational leaders influence others to believe that the dream can become reality. Even though change in certain organisations is associated with a single 'transformational hero', change is normally led by a group of leaders who provide ongoing leadership and direction. The transformational leader acts as a coach, role model and inspirational figure to create conditions under which employees and all other stakeholders enthusiastically contribute towards achieving the stated organisational goals.

What do transformational leaders do? They:
- Establish a sense of understanding of the need and urgency for change to take place.
- Build a team that will guide change.
- Articulate a dream or vision for the organisation.
- Provide a systematic plan and clear objectives for attaining the vision.
- Formulate structures to foster the full participation and buy-in of everybody involved in the organisation.
- Remove constraints that hinder the accomplishment of the new vision and provide capacity for successful goal attainment.
- Evaluate the process on a periodic basis.
- Sustain and reinforce the new culture continuously.

The following characteristics are associated with transformational leaders:
- Credibility, ability to foster trust by acting fairly and honestly in all relationships.
- Sense of mission and purpose.
- Ability to communicate a vision.
- Ability to perform at high levels.
- Result orientation.
- Ability to inspire others.
- Emotional intelligence.
- Ability to participate fully with people on all levels.

- Strength to resist peer pressure and confidence to stand up for what is right.
- Ability to detect positive qualities in others, and the willingness to share responsibility in a measure appropriate to those qualities.
- Willingness to learn, adapt and grow since change is often a step into the unknown.

Since leaders provide a model of attitude, direction and action, which is usually reflected in the workforce, success or failure of transformation rests squarely on the shoulders of those who lead the process.

## 14.14  Charismatic leadership

There are numerous examples of charismatic leaders who, through their unique and charismatic personal characteristics, have reached high positions in organisations and societies. This view of leadership gives rise to the question of 'born' or 'natural' leaders. Charismatic leaders have very strong referent power. They always have a very strong vision, and an exceptional ability to communicate that vision with passion and conviction. According to Bergh and Theron (2003:210), a charismatic leader is characterised by behaviour that is out of the ordinary, novel, unconventional and counter to norms. They are also perceived as mavericks who initiate and support radical change. In an organisation, charismatic leaders are useful in the sense that they can convince and inspire people to support changes. Charismatic leaders instill trust and reduce resistance to change. According to Francesco and Gold (1998:150), charismatic leadership is more appropriate in situations that require drastic change, while other leadership styles are more appropriate in situations where gradual change is required.

## 14.15  Leadership in a virtual workplace

With the new paradigm of a virtual business environment, the need to define and redefine leadership is becoming more important. Leadership lessons learnt in the past may not apply to the future. Leaders of the present and future need to become receptive to new ideas on how to improve the effectiveness of virtual teams who operate in an environment that constantly changes.

Virtual leadership gives rise to the following questions:
- Can inspirational leadership be attained in a situation where physical contact is minimal?
- What communication processes and tools can be used in an atmosphere of constant change?
- How are teams formed and maintained in cyberspace?

In a virtual environment, where the leader cannot keep visual tabs on team members, motivation cannot be sustained through verbal encouragement and personal attention. The leader of the virtual team mostly influences the behaviour of group members by the way the work is designed and allocated, and by monitoring the group's functioning. Fundamental to the virtual working environment is a workforce that is dynamic and knowledgeable and able to function relatively independently. Virtual team systems and work designs enable individuals to act anywhere any time. The success of the virtual team depends to a large extent on the design of the organisation, the team and the job, as well as the state and use of technology. The work design in the new knowledge-based and results-orientated organisation encourages high involvement, provides job enrichment, is process-based and allows individuals to control how the work is being done. The virtual era is an era of partnerships, where work and work relationships are based on equality and competence. Leaders in this environment do not fear that they will lose control, and they allow high levels of participation in decision-making.

In a virtual team, one of the leader's main functions is to proactively manage potential problems that can harm the effectiveness of the team. Specific issues that need the leader's attention are:

- *Trust:* Employees from different locations, cultures and technical backgrounds may mistrust the way their information will be used, presented or valued. They may also doubt the quality of other members' contributions.
- *Expectations:* A virtual team is not continuously exposed to the organisational culture and may not know exactly what is expected of them or what behaviours are allowed. The leader must explicitly discuss norms and expectations.
- *Cultural differences:* Virtual team members often represent different organisations, or departments, each with its own distinctive culture. These cultures may represent different views on commitment, participation, or values, which may cause conflict in the virtual team.
- *Work coordination:* Virtual team members cannot collaborate or react timeously if they are not equipped with up-to-date computer and communication technology, or do not have access to adequate technical support.
- *Group dynamics:* It can be difficult to build good relationships among group members who are not in face-to-face interaction. Some members may easily feel neglected or isolated. It is suggested that virtual teams do spend some time together in order to establish a working relationship (see Jarvenpaa and Leidner 1998).

Virtual teams add a whole new dimension to organisational structure, performance, and customer satisfaction. The effectiveness of the virtual team depends to a large extent on how well it is composed and managed.

## 14.16 Quality assurance in leadership

The success of outstanding organisations is almost always associated with the efforts of one or more unique individuals who are iden-

tified as leaders. These leaders did not achieve fame through their own efforts, but through their ability to inspire others to work towards the attainment of organisational goals. Leaders have a tremendous influence on the behaviour and attitudes of others. Leaders articulate the vision of the organisation and inspire others to direct their efforts and skills at realising the vision. Without quality leadership, an organisation cannot become a significant role-player in the economy or in society. Leadership is not restricted to specific positions or roles in the organisation, and different people can serve as leaders in different situations. Quality in leadership is only achieved if potential leaders on all organisational levels are identified, developed and provided with opportunities to exercise their skills. The human resources manager has a vital role to play in the development of organisational leaders.

## 14.17 Conclusion

Many South African organisations have delivered leaders of outstanding quality who have made a name for themselves and their organisations. However, when we consider South Africa's poor rating in the World Competitive Survey, it remains an indisputable fact that we do not have sufficient quality leadership in our organisations. It is therefore imperative that people with leadership potential are continuously identified, trained, and developed to become effective leaders. The dynamic environment in which organisations operate necessitates the ongoing development of all leaders. It is also imperative that a culture within the organisation is established where employees from all levels are encouraged to take initiative and assume leadership when the situation arises.

## Summary

- Leadership is the ability to influence others to enthusiastically work towards organisational goals. Leaders derive their ability to influence from a variety of sources of power.

- Leadership differs from management. Leaders are visionary, and concerned with the organisations' long-term success. Managers are more concerned with every-day problems and decisions.
- The quality or trait approach to leadership assumes that leaders are born, not made. However, no common set of leadership characteristics or traits has been agreed upon.
- Two important dimensions of leadership behaviour have been identified: initiating structure (task dimension) and considera-tion (people dimension). The extent to which the leader exercises these dimensions gives rise to autocratic or participative leadership.
- According to McGregor, a leader's assump-tions about the nature of human beings in-fluence the leader's as well as the employee's behaviour.
- Schein provided a historical perspective of the different assumptions about human nature.
- Blake and Mouton developed the Managerial Grid which identifies five lead-ership styles based on the amount of con-cern the leader has for the task and people.
- Both Tannenbaum and Schmidt, and Hersey and Blanchard proposed a situa-tional approach to leadership. Hersey and Blanchard's theory was adjusted by Nicholls to provide for continuity, consis-tency and conformity.
- Transformational leadership is imperative in a changing and dynamic business envi-ronment. Charismatic leaders have a unique ability to influence people to accept a new order and support changes.
- The virtual work environment provides new challenges for leadership. Leaders must carefully consider the composition of the virtual team and its job design, and also monitor the virtual team's effectiveness by anticipating potential problems.
- Quality leadership cannot be compromised in a competitive business world.

## Case study
## Management by walkabout

'I used to be an avid reader of management books, but the problem is they are all the same now. Everybody is on this leadership trip. You don't need that many leaders, but you need some really good managers. Just being a very good manager in my book is right up there. The difference between the average and the excel-lent manager is that great managers get things done through other people, willingly and well.'

Alan Leighton is chairman of Royal Mail in the UK. It is his mission to turn the loss-making company around. He is also director of nine other companies, and deputy chairman of Leeds United Football Club. According to Leighton, the biggest influence in his life was the 18 years he spent at Mars, where he learned the importance of talking directly to employees and customers. Leighton perceives himself as a person who does not manage time, but issues. He is ener-getic and highly focused. He says he does not manage the top management team, but that he is responsible for everybody. Leighton is proud that he manages to visit all post offices, mail centres, delivery offices and other relevant sites on his way. He says that sometimes you just have to pop in for ten minutes to ask how every-body is doing and what issues they are con-fronting. Leighton gets 300 to 400 e-mails a week from people in the company. Sometimes he phones them while in his car. To him a leader has to be accessible, yet in control.

Read more on www.royalmailgroup.com

source: *Financial Times*, UK, 20 February 2003

## Questions

1  How does Leighton perceive the differ-ence between leadership and manage-ment?
2  Analyse Leighton's leadership approach by means of the behavioural leadership perspective.
3  Would you describe Leighton as a trans-formational leader?

# Experiential exercise No. 1

PURPOSE: To demonstrate all the leadership styles as presented by the various leadership theories.

INTRODUCTION: Leaders act on a continuum ranging from autocratic to participative behaviours. Different leadership styles are associated with specific leadership behaviours.

TASK: Step 1 (30 minutes). Form groups of approximately five members each. Each group is assigned a specific leadership style from a specific leadership theory without the other groups knowing which style it is. Each group prepares a role play to demonstrate their assigned leadership style. Carefully consider ways in which to demonstrate specific behaviours that are associated with the specific leadership style.

TASK: Step 2 (3 to 5 minutes per group). Each group gets the opportunity to demonstrate their assigned leadership style. The facilitator will introduce each group by indicating which leadership theory the group represents. The other groups must try to identify the exact leadership style in accordance with the identified leadership theory.

# Experiential exercise No. 2

PURPOSE: To identify the outstanding characteristics and behaviours demonstrated by successful leaders.

INTRODUCTION: Researchers who investigated the specific qualities or traits of successful leaders were not able to identify one common set of shared qualities or traits. However, we all know that leaders, especially transformational or charismatic leaders, are different from other people.

TASK: Step 1 (30 minutes). Form groups of three to five members. Each group selects a leader of their choice and writes a memo to explain why the selected leader is considered as exceptional.

Step 2 (2 or 3 minutes per group). An assigned member of each group reads the memo to the whole class.

Step 3 (5 minutes). The class identifies the most common characteristics of qualities mentioned and lists them on a flip chart or white board.

## Self-assessment exercise

### Are you an X or Y person? Answer TRUE or FALSE:

1 Most people will do less if the supervisor is not present.
2 The average person can be trusted with the valuables of an organisation.
3 Employees want to improve themselves.
4 Punishment is the best way to ensure that employees do not disobey rules.
5 Most people work only for payday.
6 Employees will work hard if they set their own goals.
7 People don't like to be told how to do things.
8 Employees are willing to accept responsibility for a task.
9 Employees feel motivated if they receive detailed instructions on how to do their jobs.
10 Most people will disobey rules when nobody is watching.
11 If a person had a choice, s/he would choose the easiest task.
12 Punishment is an ineffective way to control employees.
13 Most employees prefer the manager to make decisions.
14 People are only interested in how much they get at the end of the month.
15 Employees feel proud when managers show trust in them by giving them moderately difficult tasks.
16 Most people are willing to learn new things.
17 People want to show others how well they can do things.
18 People are lazy by nature.
19 Knowledge of progress (feedback) motivates employees.
20 Employees will always complain about management.

This self-assessment is based on McGregor's X and Y theory. Decide whether your answer to each statement reflects a positive or negative assumption about the nature of people. If your answer reflects a positive assumption, write a Y next to your answer. If your answer reflects a negative assumption, write an X next to your answer. How many Ys and how many Xs did you get? Do you want to compare your responses to those of a fellow learner? What advice will you offer to a person who has predominantly X assumptions?

## Chapter questions

1   How will you respond to a person who says: 'You are either a leader, or not'?
2   In your opinion, what type of leadership is most appropriate in South African organisations today? Substantiate your answer.
3   'There is no one effective leadership style in organisations'. Discuss this statement.
4   According to Blake and Mouton, the 9.9 leadership style (team leader) is the most appropriate. Hersey and Blanchard, on the other hand, suggest that there is no one best style of leadership. How can these two theories be reconciled?
5   What advice will you offer to a person who has to monitor the performance of a project team of which the members are physically dispersed and communicate mainly through e-mail and telephone?

## Bibliography

BERGH, Z.C. & THERON, A.L. 2003. *Psychology in the work context*. Thomson, Johannesburg.

BLAKE, R.R. & MOUTON, J.S. 1978. *The managerial grid*. Gulf, Houston.

CANTU, C. 1999. 'Virtual teams'. *CSWT Reports*, (www.workteams.unt.edu/reports/Cantu/html).

FRANCESCO, A.M. & GOLD, B.A. 1998. *International organizational behavior: Text, readings, cases and skills*. (Prentice-Hall), Pearson Education Inc.

GREENBERG, J. & BARON, R.A. 1995. *Behavior in organizations: Understanding and managing the human side of work, 5th edition*. (Prentice-Hall), Pearson Education Inc.

HERSEY, P. & BLANCHARD, K. 1982. *Management and organizational behavior: Utilizing human resources*. (Prentice-Hall), Pearson Education Inc.

JARVENPAA, S.L. & LEIDNER, D.E. 1998. 'Communication and trust in global virtual teams', (www.ascusc.org/icmc/vol3/issue4/jarvenpaa.html).

KOTTER, J. 2003. 'Leaping into the future'. *Management Today*, 19(1):4–6.

KREITNER, R. & KINICKI, A. 1998. *Organizational behaviour, 4th edition*. McGraw-Hill Companies, New York.

LAWLER, E.E. 1996. *From the ground up*. Jossey-Bass, San Francisco.

MARITZ, F. 2002. 'Team creativity: Relationships with human potential'. *Management Today*, 18(9):42–44.

MCGREGOR, D. 1960. *The human side of enterprise*. (Prentice-Hall), Pearson Education Inc.

MULLINS, L.J. 1996. *Management and organizational behavior, 4th edition*. (Pitman), Pearson Education (UK).

NICHOLLS, J.R. 1985. 'A new approach to situational leadership'. *Leadership and Organizational Development Journal*, 6(4):2–7.

SCHEIN, E.H. 1980. *Organizational psychology*. (Prentice-Hall), Pearson Education Inc.

SIBIYA, B. 2002. 'Transformational leadership – A tribute to Madiba'. *The Black Management Forum Conference*, 2002. Essential Publishing, Johannesburg.

TANNENBAUM, R. & SCHMIDT, W.H. 1958. 'How to choose a leadership pattern'. *Harvard Business Review*, 2(36):95-101. HBSP.

WALTERS, H. 1999. 'Leadership and teamwork in a hostile environment: A true inspirational challenge'. *Management Today*, 15(7):10.

WEISNER, R. & MILLET, B. 2001. *Management and organizational behavior*. John Wiley & Sons, Brisbane.

## Websites

SA Breweries: www.sab.co.za
Leadership: www.leadershipmanagement.com
         www.lessonsinleadership.co.za

# 15

# Groups and teamwork

## A Werner

## Learning outcomes

At the end of this chapter the learner should be able to:

- Explain the importance of groups in South African organisations.
- Evaluate the extent to which a given group reflects the defining characteristics of a group.
- Contrast and compare formal and informal groups.
- Determine the extent to which a given group's development follows the progressive steps of the five-stage model and the punctuated equilibrium model.
- Outline aspects that contribute to effective group functioning.
- Explain the utilisation of quality circles and self-managed work teams in organisations.
- Provide guidelines for effective teamwork.
- Discuss various types of work teams.
- Highlight criteria for successful virtual teams.
- Relate groups and teams to quality assurance.

## Key words and concepts

- conformity
- grapevine
- gestalt
- group development
- group dynamics
- inertia
- networking
- norms
- role conflict
- status
- teambuilding
- teams

## Illustrative case

### Success through self-managed work teams

When Yannick Lakhnati took over Rainbow Chicken in 1998 the company was in deep trouble. Rainbow Chicken showed a three-year loss of R657-million rand. The share price dropped by 90 per cent to 35 cents a share. The processing plants produced 300 000 chickens a week in comparison to the one-million-a-week international standard. For weeks Lakhnati agonised about whether the business could be saved. He then decided on a plan of action.

Lakhnati initiated a complete change in the organisational structure by adopting a totally different management style to the previous one. The company was divided into 300 mini-businesses (self-managed work teams), each with its own team leader. These teams became responsible for the daily operations within the company. Each team identified customers and suppliers and recorded volumes, attendance and performance. Each team had its own board displaying the team name and photograph as well as the record for daily, weekly and monthly targets and general information. The system was custom-designed for Rainbow after an in-house survey that established specific requirements. Extensive, company-wide staff training highlighted the natural leaders and boosted the management development programme.

The introduction of these self-managed teams had a positive effect on organisational goal attainment.

Compare the share price of 35c in 1998 with the current share price by searching the website www.sharenet.co.za

## 15.1  Introduction

According to the Gestalt principle, the whole is worth more than its separate parts. In a very competitive environment organisations realise that they can only achieve their goals through the combined efforts of everybody involved in the organisation. Previously organisations relied on hierarchical, functionally-orientated, command-and-control systems. Today the adoption of a team-based work arrangement creates a flat, focused, flexible, and adaptive organisation capable of rapid responses to change. Group and teamwork allow for greater participation, increased performance, and ultimately influence the motivation and satisfaction of employees.

However, changing to a team-based struc-

ture does not guarantee success. Some groups tend to be more successful than others, and for this reason it is essential to investigate the factors that contribute to effective group functioning. The introduction of virtual teams into the workplace also offers new challenges for the way in which people are managed.

In this chapter we will explore the nature of groups, how they develop, and the factors that contribute to effective group functioning. We will examine the difference between groups and teams, and give special attention to the utilisation of teams in the workplace.

## 15.2  What is a group?

According to Kreitner and Kinicki (2001:379), a group can be defined as two or more individuals interacting with each other to achieve particular goals, and who share a common identity and have common norms.

We can derive from this definition that a group consists of individuals who:
- Have a mutual goal or objective.
- Consciously work towards achieving this goal or objective.
- Relate to each other.
- Have behavioural expectations of each other.

As the interaction between group members increases, the group becomes closer (cohesion increases) because the members of the group realise that they can help and support each other in achieving their common goal. The members of the group then begin to speak of 'us'. In other words, they develop a feeling of belonging to the group. Figure 15.1 illustrates the four sociological criteria of a group.

## 15.3  Comparing and contrasting formal and informal groups

A formal group is one established through the formal organisation, and whose goals and activities are directly related to the achievement of the declared organisational goals. Formal groups are part of the structure of an organisation, and are formed during the organisational process. Formal groups may be departments, sections, task groups, committees, and so on. A group of employees investigating cost saving measures in the organisation is an example of a formal group.

An informal group is one that, as a result of the daily activities, interactions and feelings of its members, develops spontaneously so that it can satisfy their needs. The main goal of the informal group is social satisfaction. A group of employees working in close proximity and who develop affection for each other, is an example of an informal group. The informal group also serves as a source of identification, motivation, status, power, communication and security for its members. Any deficiency in the formal organisation is catered for by the informal organisation. If, for example, the formal organisation does not provide adequate and timely information, employees create

information through the informal communication network, the grapevine. Although this information spreads very quickly, it is often distorted, especially when the content is more emotional in nature.

The formal and informal groups have a reciprocal relationship, which can either be positive or negative. The formal organisation often exerts a great influence on the formation and functioning of informal groups (for example, because of the physical layout of the work, leadership practices of the manager, or security offered in the organisation). At the same time, informal groups can also exert a great influence on the formal organisation. It often happens that employees discuss work-related problems during a social get together outside working hours, and come up with useful solutions. On the other hand, if, for example, the manager's leadership style is unacceptable to the employees, the informal group can offer resistance to him/her by its members agreeing amongst themselves to

**Figure 15.1** Sociological criteria of a group

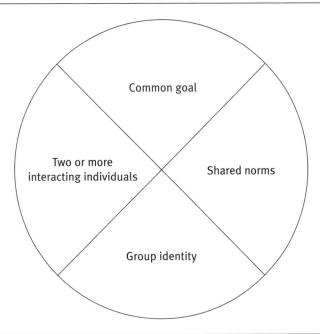

---

**Table 15.1** Comparison between the formal and informal group

|  | **Formal group** | **Informal group** |
|---|---|---|
| Goal | Profit/organisational goal | Satisfaction of needs |
| Structure | Planned | Develop spontaneously |
| Basis for interaction | Task or position | Personality |
| Communication | Formal channels | Grapevine |
| Individual power base | Authority | Influence |
| Behaviour control mechanism | Rules and procedures | Norms |
| Position identification | Job/Task | Role |
| Behavioural control mechanism | Progressive discipline | Rejection from group |
| Representation of relationships | Organogram | Sociogram |

---

lower their work output. Table 15.1 illustrates some of the differences between formal and informal groups.

Robbins (2001:217–18) classifies groups as command, task, interest, or friendship groups:

- *The command group.* This group is usually characterised by a formal organogram and a line of authority. Almost all businesses are formally organised into command groups, as the activities are carried out at the command of a manager. The 'command' may take the form of a request, but it still remains a command due to the line of authority within the group. The training manager and her/his subordinates, consisting of two trainers, one course developer, one training administrator and one secretary form a command group.
- *The task group.* This group is created for a specific task or project. It is also a formal group. As soon as the specific project has been completed, the group disbands. A group commissioned to investigate alternative administrative systems, is a task group.
- *The interest group.* This group may be either formal or informal. The emphasis is on the needs of the group itself. There may be a line of authority, and the group may have a task to fulfil, but the reason for the existence of the group is that the members all have the same interests. In a

specific school, five teachers have shown a special interest in children with learning problems. When they are requested to explore creative methods for teaching these children, and do a presentation on their findings, a formal interest group is formed. On the other hand, if these teachers do some reading on the topic in their own time, and discuss their findings and ideas during tea time, an informal interest group has developed.
- *The friendship group.* This group develops because the members have common characteristics. The group may be based on similar age, ethnic heritage, support for a particular sport, or any other shared attribute.

## 15.4   Group development

Knowledge about the development of groups is very useful to assist groups in progressing towards goal attainment. Work groups are only effective if a spirit of cooperation and combined action towards achieving goals exists. In a dynamic working environment, where quick action is required, groups cannot afford to waste time on unproductive conflict and behaviour.

Different opinions exist in terms of how groups develop. We will discuss the five-stage model of group development and the punctuated-equilibrium model.

## 15.4.1 The five-stage model of group development

Bruce W Tuckman proposed the five-stage model of group formation in 1965 (Kreitner and Kinicki 2001:382–4). The five stages of group development are: forming, storming, norming, performing, and adjourning. Figure 15.2 illustrates these five stages and some of the behaviours that are associated with each stage. During each stage certain group developmental tasks must be completed successfully for the group to be effective. The development of groups does not necessarily take place in a specific order. Sometimes a group might experience two stages at once, or regress to a previous stage.

- *Forming* is characterised by uncertainty. Members do not know what is expected of them, and they are often scared that they will not measure up or will not be accepted by other group members. They are also unsure of the structure, leadership, and roles in the group. Groups progress successfully through this stage once members perceive themselves as part of the group.
- *Storming* reminds one of the way in which animals in the animal kingdom fight each other to establish leadership and subordination. Human beings engage in a more psychological contest, where things such as skill, experience, authority, popularity, personality and even the cell

**Figure 15.2** The five-stage model of group development

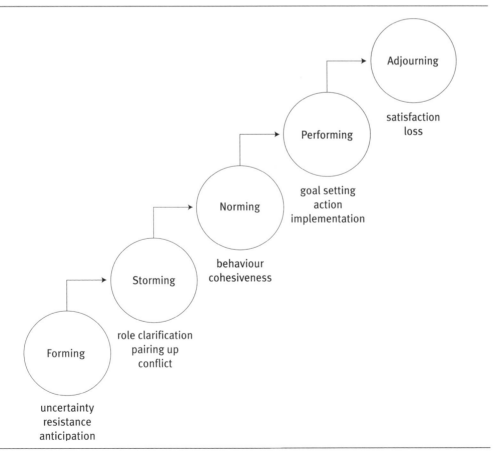

phone you have are assessed and compared. This stage is characterised by interpersonal conflict, in the form of fighting or physical or emotional withdrawal. Groups progress successfully through this stage when a leader has been chosen and accepted, members become aware of and accept their roles, and a relatively clear hierarchy exists.

- *Norming* is marked by cooperation and collaboration. During this stage members become aware of what behaviour is acceptable or not. Members share information openly and are willing to listen to others. Close relationships develop and cohesiveness increases. The group progresses successfully through this stage when the group structure is relatively established, behavioural expectations are clear, and the group is ready to function fully.
- *Performing* is characterised by full participation of all group members. Energy and efforts are spent on the task at hand. In some groups performance is maintained at a constant level, while in other groups, through the process of learning and development, higher levels of effectiveness and creativity are reached continuously. The success of this stage is marked by goal attainment.
- *Adjourning* marks the end of the group's existence. Members look back at what they have achieved and assess their experiences in the group. Emotions vary from satisfaction with achievements to a feeling of loss of friendship.

According to Kreitner and Kinicki (2001:384), groups could shift into decay after they have reached the performing stage. De-norming occurs when a natural decline in standards takes place; de-storming, when an undercurrent of discontent surfaces; and de-forming, when group members abandon the group.

In a strong organisational context, where goals, structure, norms and information are provided, groups can move faster to the performing stage, and then the five-stage model might have limited applicability. However, in the modern era, where piece work and project work become more and more common, group members might find themselves in a less familiar environment with less clear goals and undefined norms. Group members will have to establish a common ground before they will be able to function effectively.

## 15.4.2 The punctuated-equilibrium model

The punctuated-equilibrium model highlights a consistent time-frame within which groups change during their existence. More specifically, the following has been found (Bergh and Theron 2003:237):

- The first meeting sets the group's direction. Behavioural patterns and norms are firmly established during this meeting. For example, when a group meets the first time, the behaviour of members at this first meeting will set the tone for their future interaction and behaviour. If members socialise instead of concentrating on the task, a clear message is sent out to members that relations are much more important than the task. A behavioural pattern for the future is established. If during this meeting the group strongly speaks out against a member who is not present, everyone will know that attendance is a crucial requirement.
- The first phase of group activity is one of inertia. Group members often feel that they have achieved a lot by having a first meeting, and they then relax, as there is no immediate pressure to perform.
- A transition takes place at the end of the first phase, when the group has used up half of its allotted time. Exactly halfway between the first meeting and the official deadline, members of the group realise that they have used up half their time, and that they have either done very little constructive work or taken the wrong course of action. Members tend to criticise each other, and open conflict can occur.

- Major changes are made with the transition. The group experience heightened levels of energy and activity. New expectations are determined. Goals are reviewed, new perspectives adopted, and alternative actions taken.
- Phase two is a new equilibrium or period of inertia. During this phase, plans adopted during the transition phase are carried out. The group is once again locked in a fixed course of action.
- The group's last meeting is characterised by a burst of energy. Consider a group of students just before they have to hand in their project. Final changes have to be negotiated, separate parts need to be integrated and everyone is anxious that the project must be completed and handed in. Figure 15.3 provides a schematic representation of the punctuated-equilibrium model.

When comparing the five-stage model with the punctuated-equilibrium model we can say that the group goes though forming, norming and storming during the first meeting, followed by a stage of low performance, then through another phase of storming and norming, followed by a stage of high performance before finally adjourning.

## Case-in-point
## Sentry Laboratories

Sentry Laboratories is a private organisation in the medical industry that specialises in the testing of blood and tissue samples for cancer detection, development of pharmaceutical products and research. The management of Sentry Laboratories consists of five people who are respectively responsible for daily operations, marketing, finances, technology and administration/personnel. Once a year the team books into a remote holiday resort for three days. This breakaway serves more than one purpose. Firstly, it allows the group to interact in a more relaxing atmosphere, away from the daily work pressures. This is a great booster for interpersonal relations and group cohesion. The group will typically engage in a physical exercise that requires teamwork, skill and strength, such as playing soccer, snorkeling, or net fishing. Secondly, the group uses this opportunity to re-evaluate and review the business environment and strategic goals for the organisation. The group decides on ways in which to achieve these objectives and work out a schedule for implementation.

The organisation employs 160 people and prides itself on having a well-skilled and diverse group of employees. Once a year, over a weekend, all employees, together with management, gather at a local holiday resort. This breakaway takes a similar shape to the one discussed above. Employees get an opportunity to interact in an informal way and have fun. They also divide into their natural work teams and set their own strategic goals for the next year. A number of very creative ideas have flowed from these breakaway sessions. Right at the beginning, a management consultant was contracted to facilitate these sessions, but employees became so skilled in

**Figure 15.3** The punctuated-equilibrium model

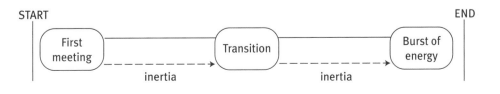

strategic planning and goal-setting that they are now able to appoint facilitators among themselves. It is not surprising, then, that a number of 'organisational successes' can be directly linked to ideas originating from these weekend breakaways.

## 15.5 Effective group functioning

Not every collection of people satisfies the definition of a group or function effectively. The internal functioning of a group (i.e., its goals, patterns of interaction, etc.) develops over time and largely determines the success of the group in achieving its goals and satisfying the needs of its members. Use the self-assessment exercise at the end of the chapter to evaluate your team's effectiveness. Compare your responses to those of the other team members. Do you have any suggestions for improving the way in which your team functions?

Effective groups have the following characteristics:

- The group knows the reason for its existence.
- There are guidelines or procedures for decision-making.
- There is communication between the group members.
- The members receive and render mutual assistance.
- The members handle conflict within the group in a constructive manner.
- The members diagnose their processes and improve their own functioning.

Various factors that influence the effectiveness and performance of a group will be discussed below.

### 15.5.1 Group leadership

A leader is someone who has the ability to inspire group members to achieve group goals voluntarily and enthusiastically. Leadership influence depends on the type of power that a leader can exercise over followers. This power varies from reward-, coercive-, legitimate-, and referent- to expert power. The most important point here is that each group has a leader at any given time, and that the person who is formally appointed is not necessarily the leader.

Effective leaders have a concern for the task, as well as for the members of the group. Task behaviours expected from leaders include planning, decision-making, organising and monitoring. People functions include individual functions, such as meeting the needs of individual members, giving recognition, developing skills, providing opportunities; and group functions, such as building group cohesiveness, communication, resolving conflict, and training.

Although most of us would assume that a democratic leader is more preferable and desirable, most authors and researchers suggest that the effectiveness of a leadership style depends on the characteristics of the followers and the task. A democratic approach is more effective when followers are ready to participate in the decision-making processes and can make a reasonable contribution. An autocratic approach is more effective when the followers lack knowledge and experience, and don't feel confident to participate. One important function of a leader is to facilitate the developmental process of group members so that they can make a meaningful contribution to the attainment of group goals, and experience satisfaction.

### 15.5.2 Roles

A role refers to a set of expected behaviour patterns associated with someone in a given position in a group. Each role has associated attitudes and behaviours which create role identity. People find it relatively easy to learn new roles, and to shift from one role to another. Consider the change in behaviour and attitude of a machine operator who has been promoted to supervisory level. Most of the time such a person will adopt a pro-management attitude and orientation.

Understanding roles is complicated by the difference between role expectation and role perception. Role expectations are defined as how others believe an individual should act in a given role. Most of us have stereotyped conceptions about how certain roles should be acted out. We expect different behaviours and attitudes from a minister, manager, professor, prison warden, waitress, and soccer coach. Role perception refers to how we believe we should act out our roles. Many women experience a discrepancy between traditional role expectations and their own perceptions of how they should fulfil their roles. This discrepancy can cause a lot of frustration and tension, both in the workplace and at home. When we compare the traditional employment contract to the new employment contract, we see vast differences between what were expected of employees before and what is expected of them today. Previously employees were expected to be at work and deliver a decent amount of work. Today employees are expected to make a meaningful contribution to the organisation and manage their own careers. Employees' role perception should change accordingly. Conflict in groups occurs when members perceive their roles differently to what is expected of them. It is therefore important that roles are clarified through open discussion.

Role conflict occurs when a person performs multiple roles, with contradictory role expectations. A human resources manager trying to satisfy the needs of both managers and employees might experience role conflict. Managers might emphasise cost-cutting measures while employees demand higher wages. When we belong to more than one group, which places different demands on our time and perspectives, tension occurs.

Roles can also be divided into task roles and maintenance roles. Task roles include: initiator, information seeker, information giver, procedural technician, evaluator, and recorder. Maintenance roles ensure the well-being of the group and foster supportive and constructive interpersonal relations. Maintenance roles include: encourager, peacemaker, and follower.

### 15.5.3 Group norms and conformity

Over time, the interaction within the group leads to the development of group norms. A norm is a generally accepted standard of behaviour that each member of the group is supposed to maintain. The strongest norms apply to the forms of behaviour that the group members regard as the most important.

Norms can be defined as acceptable standards of behaviour within a group that are shared by the group's members (Robbins 2001:230).

**comment**

Cell phones are still a novelty for South Africans, and norms for the use of cell phones have not been firmly established. For example, is it acceptable to let a cell phone ring or answer a phone call during a meeting? Is it acceptable to talk on a cell phone in the presence of others, or should one move away in order not to disrupt the conversation?

Norms may be formal, and explicitly stated by the group leader, for example: 'Membership cards will be produced at each meeting'. Norms can also be informal and based on interaction between group members, for example, when a cell phone rang during the first meeting and sounds of irritation were uttered, everybody knew that they had to keep their cell phones switched off during meetings. Certain norms are valued more highly than others, and members of the group must adhere to them. These norms are called obligatory norms, and are unlikely to change. A student who does not attend the compulsory classes will quickly find out that s/he is not granted admission to the examination: an obligatory norm.

There are also peripheral norms, and although it is not obligatory for members to adhere to them, they are regarded as sound and worth the effort. A member of a soccer team, for example, will not gain the approval of his/her team-mates if s/he misbehaves during the reception held after the match. A norm that is regarded as important by one group may be unimportant to another. A social club, for example, might prescribe that men who dine there should wear a tie and jacket, while another club might well regard this as a peripheral norm and permit its members to wear what they like.

The success and continued existence of a group may depend on whether the members adhere to the group norms. Groups that lack strong norms are unlikely to be as stable, long-lived or satisfying for their members as groups with well-developed norms that are strongly supported by the members.

Conformity refers to the acceptance of group norms by its members. There is consensus in the literature that a group member can react to group norms in three different ways: s/he may reject them, conform to them, or only accept the important ones and ignore the peripheral norms. When a group member rebels against the group's norms, s/he will experience considerable pressure to conform, as noticeable nonconformity constitutes a threat to the group's standards, stability, and survival. This type of pressure may be particularly strong. It has happened in organisations where employees are paid according to a piece wage system, in other words according to the production of each individual. In such instances, employees have a well-founded fear that if some of them were to perform at a very high level, management would reduce the work tariff. The result is strong pressure on employees not to exceed the group norms for work carried out.

The extent to which people conform to norms depends on a number of factors such as their values, personalities, status and needs. Individuals with low status in the group, for example, will tend to adhere strictly to all the group's norms so that the other group members will accept them. People with little self-confidence also tend to conform to a greater extent, because they regard the group's decisions to be better than their own. Individuals who feel that the group's goals coincide with their own also tend to conform to a greater extent.

Is conformity to norms good or bad? As said already, norms preserve a group's existence and survival. However, blind conformity, on the other hand, may counteract innovation, as the creative ability of a member will be lost to group conformity. Groupthink, the tendency of a group to make a premature decision based on limited information, is the result of conformity. This happens when everyone in the group supports a decision, without considering alternatives, in order to preserve group solidarity. The ideal is probably that certain basic norms are supported, such as showing respect to other group members, but that members are encouraged to be divergent and creative.

### 15.5.4 Status

Status refers to the relative social position a person has in comparison to others in the group. Status is important because it is a motivational factor and also influences the behaviour of those who experience disparity between what they believe their status is, and what they believe others perceive their status to be. Status can be formal or informal, and is awarded as follows:

- *Scalar* status refers to status obtained through an individual's formal position in a group. A supervisor has status due to the authority associated with her/his position.
- *Functional* status is earned through the task a person has to fulfil in the group. A computer technician, who is on a lower level in the organisational hierarchy, might have more status than a manager due to his/her ability to solve everyone's computer problems.
- *Achieved* status is earned through hard work and effort, and based on the individual's qualifications and achievements. We are all impressed when there is a professor in our midst!
- *Ascribed* status refers to inborn characteristics over which we have limited or no control, such as attractiveness, gender, build, and age.

Status differences can either facilitate or hinder group interaction. It facilitates interaction when members perceive status differences as equitable, that is, they believe those with higher status rightfully deserve more status. Lower status members in this case are more willing to follow the directives of high status members. Consider the training department as a (command) group, where the training manager has more status due to his/her authority, expertise, and skill. On the other hand, status differences might be inappropriately emphasised in a group where members are supposed to work as equals. It happens far too often that when a group meets to brainstorm ideas, those with lower status hesitate to share ideas, and ultimately, criticise the ideas of others.

### 15.5.5 Group size and composition

*Size* influences a group's overall performance, depending on the purpose of the group. Larger groups (15 or more members) are generally preferred when a group has to produce divergent ideas or alternatives. A large group offers greater combined experience and ideas. One negative aspect of a bigger group is social loafing, namely when some individuals lessen their input knowing or hoping that others will unwittingly stand in for them. This has an important implication for organisations that utilise groups as a means to improve employee satisfaction and productivity. Even though an individual works in a team, his/her individual efforts must be identifiable and measurable. Smaller groups are more effective with the execution of tasks. Smaller groups work faster and responsibility is more explicitly given to individuals.

According to Bergh and Theron (2003: 242), research has shown that groups of five to seven members are preferable. An odd number prevents a tie with voting. Groups made up of five to seven members combine the best of small and bigger groups, with the group small enough to avoid domination, the formation of cliques and inhibited participation, and large enough to allow for diverse input.

*Group composition* relates to the extent to which group members are alike. A homogenous group shares a number of similar characteristics, such as race, gender socio-economic background, education, age, work experience, or cultural orientation. A heterogeneous group, on the other hand, is composed of individuals who have few or no similar characteristics.

In South Africa, work groups are more likely to be heterogeneous than homogeneous. A heterogeneous group will most likely be able to perform at a higher level in terms of creativity. However, in order to synergise the group to high levels of effectiveness, the group has to manage conflict constructively.

We should also consider the group demographics – the degree to which members of a group share the same demographic attribute such as age, gender, race, tenure, or qualification. This becomes important when most individuals in the group share the same characteristics, with the exception of one or two. Imagine being the only male/female in a group, or the only person without a remarkable qualification. People are more likely to leave a group if they are different to others in terms of any attribute that they perceive as relevant to them feeling comfortable.

### 15.5.6 Decision-making in groups

Groups are formed to make decisions. There are, however, advantages and disadvantages to group decision-making.

Advantages of group decision-making:
- More knowledge and experience are put into decision analysis and alternative design.
- Individuals participating in decision-making will rather support the decision and take responsibility for its implementation.
- It stimulates communication and discussion in the organisation.
- It is in line with social and political changes, and therefore perceived as more legitimate.
- It serves as a developmental tool by exposing people to each other's ideas.

Disadvantages of group decision-making:

- It is a time-consuming process and places more demands on the leader's ability to facilitate a meeting and to manage behaviour.
- Pressure to seek conformity may lead to less than optimal decisions.
- The formation of cliques and pre-meeting agreements can negate the virtue of group decision-making.
- People often act impetuously during group meetings, and decline to take responsibility for implementations of ideas.

In order to get the most out of group decision-making, appropriate decision-making techniques should be utilised. The following techniques are very useful to stimulate creative thinking while preventing domination by individuals.

- *Brainstorming.* This process is frequently used to provide the maximum number of ideas in a short period of time. A group comes together and is presented with a problem. Members are then encouraged to generate as many ideas as possible to solve the problem. The emphasis is on quantity and not quality, and members refrain from making any remarks about the presented ideas. Weird ideas are welcomed as a way to stimulate the thoughts of others. Once a satisfactory number of ideas has been presented, the ideas are analysed and evaluated systematically.
- *Nominal Group Technique.* This technique is excellent for ensuring full participation without individual domination. Individuals meet as a group, and they silently generate ideas in writing. This silent period is followed by a round-robin procedure in which each group member presents an idea to the group, which is then recorded on a flip chart. Once all the ideas are presented, each idea is discussed for clarification and evaluation. Finally, the group members conclude the meeting by silently and independently recording their rank ordering of the ideas. The scores are tallied and the idea with the highest ranking is chosen. It is called a nominal group due to the limited interaction among group members.
- *Delphi technique.* This technique is used with group members being physically dispersed. Participants never meet face to face. A facilitator presents members with a carefully designed questionnaire to provide potential solutions to a well-defined problem. The questionnaires are completed independently and returned to the facilitator, who summarises the results. These results are circulated back to the members who will offer a second round of input. This process is then continued until members reach consensus. The Delphi technique can be conducted electronically though sophisticated computer technology to save time and expenses.

## 15.5.7 Communication

The only way through which we can establish and maintain relationships with other people, is through communication. The more easily people in a group communicate with each other, the more cohesion will be experienced. Cohesiveness refers to the extent to which group members are attracted to each other and vote to stay in the group.

Communication is clearly a social process. A variety of social influences affect the accuracy with which we perceive information. These include differences in status, language, frame of reference, and expectations as well as selective listening, premature judgements and source credibility.

Most people assume that they are good communicators. Yet, most interpersonal problems stem from misunderstandings. People do not formulate their messages accurately, and do not listen attentively to what others say. Should it become evident that communication is a problem in a group, it should not be ignored, but addressed through training.

The following can serve as guidelines for effective communication in groups (adapted from Ivancevich and Matteson 1999:490):

- Follow up to determine how a message was received. A friendly gesture, such as suggesting that a person does not take on added responsibility, might be interpreted as a perceived inability that s/he cannot handle multiple tasks.
- Regulate information flow in terms of quality and quantity. To prevent overload, ensure that only matters of importance are discussed in the group. Prevent repetitive arguing around one specific point.
- Use feedback to check whether a message was understood as intended.
- Show empathy towards others, especially when backgrounds and experiences differ considerably.
- Encourage mutual trust so that all members will feel confident in expressing their opinions and feelings.
- Time communication effectively to prevent barriers that result in distortions and value judgements.
- Use simplified language to convey meaning and not to impress people, especially in diverse groups.
- Listen effectively to others by reflecting on the content and feeling conveyed by the message.
- Use the grapevine. The grapevine is the informal network of communication that bypasses the formal communication network. It is known for its speed, but also its inaccuracy. The grapevine is a useful tool to distribute information rapidly and to determine the prevailing mood and needs of a group. Ensure that information spread through the grapevine is accurate and that all group members are exposed to it.
- Promote ethical communication. Group members must be respected, treated justly and exposed to all relevant information.

## 15.5.8 Conflict

In all groups some conflict is inevitable. Conflict can be defined as the process in which individuals feel that other individuals have frustrated their ability to achieve their goals.

### Conflict – good or bad?

Conflict in groups can be positive or negative, depending on its consequences. Positive conflict is an energising force that spurs members to better alternatives and higher goals. It stimulates creative thinking and innovation. Members agree on the goal to achieve, but disagree on how to achieve it. Debating the alternatives helps with the evaluation process, and a combination of ideas might prove to be the best course of action. In groups where there is no or very little conflict due to high levels of cohesion and conformity, performance tends to be low. The status quo is seldom challenged. Negative conflict, on the other hand, occurs when goal attainment is frustrated because energy is spent on highlighting or resolving interpersonal differences rather than on goal attainment. This can lead to chaos and a negative attitude that hinders constructive problem solving. Figure 15.4 illustrates the effect of various levels of conflict on performance.

### Managing the different levels of conflict

Levels of conflict that are either too low or too high lead to low performance. A moderate level of conflict leads to an optimum level of performance. Conflict (if it is too low) can be stimulated through the dialectic technique (where individuals in the group are requested to take an opposing perspective on an issue), or the devil's advocate technique (where an individual is asked to critically evaluate any proposed action). It is also useful to introduce new, diverse members to the group to offer fresh ideas and different perspectives.

When conflict levels are too high, various methods can be adopted to reduce it. These vary from setting superordinate goals, identifying a common enemy, smoothing differences, and compromising, to using authoritative command. Interpersonal conflict is best resolved through levelling, a process through which members of a group are totally open and honest with each other about their feelings and concerns.

**Figure 15.4** The effect of various levels of conflict on performance

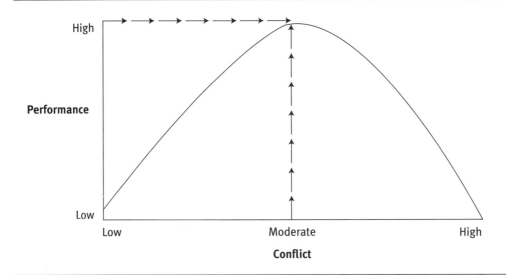

## 15.6  **Work teams**

What is the difference between a group and a team? A team can be defined as a small number of people with complementary skills who are committed to a common purpose, performance goals, and a work strategy for which they feel mutually accountable. We referred earlier to the five-stage model of group development. A team is considered as a group that has matured to the performing stage. Due to conflicts over leadership and member roles during the storming and norming phases, many groups never reach this stage. Gordon (2002: 178) states that teams are created for specific purposes, often, but not always, with a short-term scope. Teams differ from groups in the intensity with which they work on specific tasks or projects.

### 15.6.1 **Characteristics of successful work teams**

The following characteristics describe a high-performing work team:

- The group has a clear vision and goal, which are internalised by each member.
- The group consists of a diverse group of individuals who, due to their unique characteristics, make unique contributions to the group's success.
- Disagreement is considered as constructive, and members are willing to consider all ideas with an open mind.
- Interpersonal relations are relaxed, with ample open communication and mutual support.
- Group members identify strongly with the group, and feel proud of the way the group functions as well as its achievements.
- Change is not feared, but initiated.
- Networking with outside individuals and groups is used to achieve excellence and to build credibility.
- Even though the group might have a formal leader, leadership shifts from member to member depending on the task at hand.
- Group members evaluate their own development and performance, and seek opportunities for continuous learning.

## 15.6.2 Types of work teams

Examples of work teams are problem-solving teams, cross-functional teams, self-managed work teams, virtual teams, and multicultural teams. These teams differ in terms of their nature and purpose.

### Problem-solving teams

Problem-solving teams comprise employees who meet on a weekly basis to discuss ways of improving the quality of products, efficiency of work methods, and work environment. The supervisor usually leads these groups. Members identify problems, brainstorm alternative solutions, and present their suggestions to management. These groups seldom have the direct authority to implement their ideas. According to Lawler (1996:147), a problem is that these groups are normally not informed of financial and capacity constraints, and therefore they often suggest unrealistic and impractical interventions. If group members feel bulldozed into proposing ideas that fall within the thinking of management, they see no purpose for the group's existence, and will withdraw emotionally, if not physically, from the team. However, if these groups are well managed and their ideas seriously considered and implemented, they can make a valuable contribution to quality assurance in the organisation. Problem-solving groups are sometimes called quality circles and green areas.

### Cross-functional teams

Cross-functional teams are very popular in the motor manufacturing industry, where project teams comprise representatives from a cross-section of the organisation: manufacturing, engineering, marketing, research, development, and traders. The cross-functional team has a specific task to accomplish, such as to develop a new product.

These teams allow people from diverse areas to analyse problems, exchange information, develop creative ideas, solve problems and coordinate complex projects. It is a chal-

lenging task to build trust and cohesion in such a complex team. The group leaders should have a clear understanding of group processes and provide a sense of direction for the group.

### Self-managed work teams

Self-managed work teams are formed to take accountability for a complete work process, which was previously perceived to consist of separate jobs, often performed by separate departments. The ideal design for a work team allows it to take a product through the entire production process. The team manages an entire mini-business, where the process starts from buying raw material from an external vendor and ends with delivering a finished product or service to an external customer. The team enjoys autonomy over how it meets the customer's demands. An example of how a team-based design differs from the traditional functional approach can be illustrated with a shoe factory. Previously a work team designed, planned and controlled the whole manufacturing process, the purchasing department obtained the raw material, and separate groups of employees cut and dyed the leather, sewed the shoes, attached fittings, packed the shoes and delivered the finished product. Different levels of supervisors and managers managed the process, staff specialists took care of human resources, finance and scheduling and quality controllers checked the final product. The plant manager took responsibility for quality, costs, and productivity. In the team-based design, a team takes responsibility for the entire process and becomes accountable for cost, quality and rate of production. In the shoe factory, teams were given responsibility for a specific product, such as slippers, ladies' court shoes, or sport shoes, and had to take the product through the entire process, from raw material to a finished and packed product. This has led to improvements in cost, speed, and quality.

Various studies highlight a few crucial points for a team-based system to be successful (Lawler 1996:167; Schultz 2003:98):

- The core work done by the team must be interdependent and relatively complex.
- The team must share a common vision and goals which are aligned to organisational goals.
- The team must be able to accomplish tasks and solve problems without supervision.
- Team members must be multi-skilled.
- A high level of trust must exist in the group.
- The team must have autonomy to make important decisions about work, people and the internal allocation of tasks through a process of consensus.
- The team must decide on recruitment and disciplinary issues.
- Team leaders must understand group processes and provide direction.
- HRM reward and information systems need to provide the right kind of training, feedback and recognition for teams.
- The location of the members of a team, and its size are crucial to its effectiveness.
- Teams must take responsibility for satisfying their customers.

## Virtual teams

Global competition, information technology, and excessive travel expenses have given rise to virtual teams that transcend distance, time zones and organisational boundaries. To the uninformed, the perception remains that virtual team members are in one location, and that they operate in the same time zone. Examples of virtual teams are groups of individuals in different locations who develop and manage new products such as an electronic advertising board, a new financial package for women, an internet company, or gymnasium equipment. The possibilities are endless. The members of a virtual team might not even belong to a specific organisation, but are contracted to a specific project. Virtual team members communicate mainly through electronic media. The success of the virtual team, however, depends a lot on the structure and management of the team.

The following potential problems make the management of virtual work teams more challenging:

- *Trust:* Members could mistrust each other due to the perception that their contributions might not be adequately valued and presented by others.
- *Expectations:* Members might be unsure of what is expected of them and what they are allowed to do and not do.
- *Cultural differences:* These differences can inhibit cohesion, participation and open communication.
- *Work coordination:* A real danger for virtual teams is a slow response time in dealing with each other and environmental demands. Members might become despondent if they feel that no progress it made.
- *Group dynamics:* Virtual teams do not have the same opportunities as other teams to build rapport.
- *Leadership:* The leader is not in physical contact with members to influence them on a daily or weekly basis. The leader must be aware of the above-mentioned factors and manage them proactively.

As said before, planning and design are key factors to the virtual team's success. The following should be considered when establishing virtual teams:

- *Organisational design:* The virtual team's goals must be aligned with the overall organisational goals. Behavioural norms should be developed that allow for multi-cultural and multi-functional work, yet support basic organisational values. Infrastructure must be created to support the involvement of team members with each other and with the host organisation. The virtual team could manage their own design and support systems as a way to establish ownership for their success.
- *Job design:* A realistic description of how the member will spend his/her time as well as the negative aspects of the job will help the member to cope better in the virtual environment. Every member

should know what s/he is accountable for and how it links up with the responsibilities of other members. The team must have authority to make decisions. Compensation must be clarified. In virtual teams, compensation is linked to contributions and end-results. Performance feedback remains an inherent part of managing a virtual team.

- *Team design:* Members are only selected after a careful study is done of the purpose of the team and the skills needed to achieve the goals. An identity for the team is created through a team name that is descriptive and that expresses the mission, such as the 'X-Generation Gym Equipment Team' for a team that designs gymnasium apparatus. The team must go through the exercise of creating a vision or mission statement. The value lies more in the exercise than in the framed version. The goals of the team must be clearly stated and the team must be organised around the goals. Contact between virtual team members is enhanced if contact and location information is formally supplied. This should include names, office locations, traditional postal addresses, phone numbers, fax numbers, e-mail addresses, web page addresses and meeting places.
- *Coordination of work through technology:* Some face-to-face interaction is absolutely essential for the success of the team, especially during the establishment phase. All members should be present during these interactions. Electronic technology that assists the interaction of virtual group members includes video conferencing, desktop-conferencing, group software, newsgroups, bulletin boards, and electronic mail linked to Internet as well as intranet systems.

Virtual teams have the ability to revolutionise the workplace by pooling expertise in an incredibly short time to achieve organisational goals of quality products/services and excellent customer satisfaction.

## Multicultural teams

International business strategies necessitate the establishment of multicultural teams. These teams can be very challenging, as language and behavioural differences could compromise excellence. Typical problems encountered in diverse teams are increased ambiguity, complexity, confusion, mistrust, miscommunication, difficulty in reaching agreements, difficulty in reconciling diverse perspectives, difficulty in reaching consensus and decreased cohesion. Diversity can, however, also enhances a team's performance due to increased perspectives, multiple interpretations, greater openness to ideas, increased flexibility, increased creativity, improved problem solving, and improved understanding of foreign employees or customers (Gordon 2002:201).

Building an effective multicultural team often starts with diversity training. Group members should acknowledge cultural differences and minimise stereotyping. Following Gordon (2002:202), the effectiveness of a multicultural team can be increased by:

- A clear sense of a common purpose.
- A common language or procedure.
- Identifying and building on successes.
- Openly addressing issues flowing from cultural differences.
- Understanding one's own cultural programming and its impact on individual and group behaviour.
- Having fun.

## 15.7 Groups and teams and quality assurance

One of the cornerstones of Total Quality Management (TQM) is teamwork. Teamwork is increasingly being introduced into the structures of South African organisations to increase performance levels and employee and customer satisfaction. These goals can only be achieved if attention is first focused on the internal functioning of groups and teams. Quality within the team must first be achieved before quality in the organisation can be achieved. This can be done through team-building exercises that focus on goal-setting, interpersonal relations, conflict management and trust building, and through continuously monitoring the performance of the group.

## 15.8 Conclusion

The introduction of groups and teams in the South African workplace is not only in line with political and social changes, but also with the dominant African cultural value of collectivism. However, group and teamwork do not guarantee higher performance levels. Many factors influence the effectiveness of groups. These factors should be identified and managed continuously. When groups are well managed, they do contribute to greater employee commitment and organisational effectiveness.

## Summary

- Groups are defined as a collection of individuals who interact with each other to achieve a common goal, whose behaviour is directed by a common set of norms, and who share a common identity.
- Groups and teams have become a prominent feature in organisations in the form of self-managed work teams and problem-solving teams. Many organisations have switched from a traditional assembly line to a team-based work arrangement that allows for greater employee participation and satisfaction. Virtual teams are groups of people who are physically dispersed but work towards a common goal. Virtual team members interact mostly through advanced computer technology. Leading and motivating virtual teams and

---

## Self-assessment exercise
### Assess your team's effectiveness

Indicate on a scale from 1 to 5 to what extent your group meets the following requirements:

1 Team members work towards achieving a clearly stated vision.

| Seldom | 1 | 2 | 3 | 4 | 5 | Usually |
|---|---|---|---|---|---|---|

2 Team members adhere to the agreed behavioural norms.

| Seldom | 1 | 2 | 3 | 4 | 5 | Usually |
|---|---|---|---|---|---|---|

3 All team members participate in the decision-making process.

| Seldom | 1 | 2 | 3 | 4 | 5 | Usually |
|---|---|---|---|---|---|---|

4 Communication is open and uninhibited.

| Seldom | 1 | 2 | 3 | 4 | 5 | Usually |
|---|---|---|---|---|---|---|

5 A spirit of cooperation and collaboration prevails in the group.

| Seldom | 1 | 2 | 3 | 4 | 5 | Usually |
|---|---|---|---|---|---|---|

6 Every team member makes a special contribution to the team.

| Seldom | 1 | 2 | 3 | 4 | 5 | Usually |
|---|---|---|---|---|---|---|

7 Members provide honest feedback to each other.

| Seldom | 1 | 2 | 3 | 4 | 5 | Usually |
|---|---|---|---|---|---|---|

8 Members are encouraged to express diverse opinions.

| Seldom | 1 | 2 | 3 | 4 | 5 | Usually |
|---|---|---|---|---|---|---|

9 Differences are discussed in a mature and constructive way.

| Seldom | 1 | 2 | 3 | 4 | 5 | Usually |
|---|---|---|---|---|---|---|

10 Team members assume rotating roles to foster multi-skilling and personal development.

| Seldom | 1 | 2 | 3 | 4 | 5 | Usually |
|---|---|---|---|---|---|---|

team members pose a new challenge to management. Multicultural teams are becoming a norm in a global environment but pose many challenges to management and team members.

- Many factors, such as leadership and conflict management, can influence a group's effectiveness. The internal functioning of groups as well as their performance should be monitored continuously to identify and address problems. Moderate levels of conflict increase a group's performance when aimed at finding the best course of action, and not focused on personal differences.
- Quality assurance in both the inputs and outputs of groups and teams will add value to the organisation and its quest to deliver top quality products and services.

## Case study
### Teamwork

You are the purchasing manager of a medium-sized paper distributor. The organisation expects every department to set aside one day a year for the purpose of strategic planning. Your department's strategic meeting is next Friday. The meeting will take place at the conference centre of a local holiday resort and include lunch at the resort's restaurant. While preparing for the meeting the following issues cross your mind:

- Employees hate strategic planning and perceive it as a waste of time.
- Some employees perceive it as a social outing.
- Year after year the same issues and problems are discussed yet few new ideas are eventually implemented.
- There are always complaints about a lack of capacity (time and money) to implement ideas, but you think these are just excuses not to get involved.
- Employees decide beforehand not to raise certain issues.

- It has been mentioned that employees are afraid to raise ideas in case they will be held responsible for the implementation of their ideas, which might also affect their performance appraisal.
- Some employees have resorted to withdrawing while others tend to dominate meetings.
- There are always employees who excuse themselves during meetings to attend to 'important company business'.

## Questions

1 What type of group is evident in the above situation?
2 Discuss the five stages through which groups develop and indicate to which stage each of the above problems could relate.
3 Discuss various factors that influence the effectiveness of a group and indicate how these could explain the problems encountered by the above group. What will you do to address each problem?

## Experiential exercise No. 1

PURPOSE: To identify shared values within a group.

INTRODUCTION: When groups are formed, individuals often feel that they do not have much in common with other group members, and therefore reserve their participation. This exercise demonstrates that regardless of how diverse the group is, group members can still find common ground.

TASK: Step 1 (10 minutes).

INDIVIDUAL TASK: Each individual learner lists the five people s/he admires most for what they have done or stand for. It can be a family member, community leader, political leader, teacher or lecturer or sports person. After compiling the list, the learner describes the characteristics of each person on the list.

Step 2 (20 minutes). Form groups of five to seven people. In the group each person gets the opportunity to share his/her list with the rest of the group. Once everybody has had a chance to do this, the group reaches consensus on the five characteristics that appear most often on the individual learners' lists. A new single list is compiled of the five characteristics most often mentioned. These characteristics represent the values that are most important to the group and which should be used to guide their behaviour as group members.

Step 3 (10 minutes). Each group shares their list with the rest of the class.

## Experiential exercise No. 2

PURPOSE: To experience group interaction and performance. If the weather allows, this exercise can be performed outside.

INTRODUCTION: A variety of factors influence the effectiveness and performance of groups. This exercise requires groups consisting of five to seven members to construct an object and then to present the symbolism behind the construction to the class or entire group.

MATERIAL: Each group is supplied with a variety of material which could include newspapers, spaghetti, plastic discs, string, masking tape, match boxes, cool drink straws, plastic bags, wire, nails or any other unused objects, and some tools such as scissors, pliers or hammers.

TASK: Step 1 (40 minutes). Groups of five to seven people are formed. Each group receives, in a bag, a variety of material and tools. Each group is required to construct an object of symbolic nature. Groups may negotiate and barter with each other for tools or material not included in their bags. After approximately 40 minutes each group gets an opportunity to present their construction to the class or entire group.

Step 2 (15 minutes). During this stage the groups are requested to complete a questionnaire provided by the facilitator. The questionnaire covers various aspects of group functioning.

Step 3 (15 minutes). Groups report back to the class or entire group on their experiences.

## Chapter questions

1   What, in your opinion, is the difference between a group and team?
2   Consider a group that you were part of that did not function well. How could this group have become more successful?
3.   Are group norms and conformity to group norms a positive or negative aspect of groups? Discuss.
4.   Which two characteristics of successful work teams do you consider as most important?
5.   What are the positive aspects of belonging to a virtual team? What are the negative aspects?
6.   Would you say that the information studied in this chapter is more useful for managers and leaders, or should team members also be exposed to it? Explain your answer.

## Bibliography

BERGH, Z.C. & THERON, A.L. 2003. *Psychology in the work context.* Thomson, Johannesburg.

CANTU, C. 1999. 'Virtual Teams'. *CSWT Reports*, (www.workteams.unt.edu/reports/Cantu.html).

GORDON, J.R. 2002. *Organizational behavior.* (Prentice-Hall), Pearson Education Inc.

HOLPP, L. 1999. *Managing teams.* McGraw-Hill Companies, New York.

IVANCEVICH, J.M. & MATTESON, M.T. 1999. *Organizational behavior and management, 5th edition.* McGraw-Hill Companies, New York.

JENVEY, N. 1998. 'Rainbow comes out of hiding'. *Business Day*, 23 July (www.bday.co.za).

KREITNER, R. & KINICKI, A. 2001. *Organizational behavior, 4th edition.*

McGraw-Hill Companies, New York.

LAWLER, E.E. 1996. *From the ground up.* Jossey-Bass, San Francisco.

MULLINS, L.J. 1996. *Management and organizational behavior, 4th edition.* (Pitman), Pearson Education (UK).

PLUNKET, W.R. 1996. *Supervision: Diversity and teams in the workplace, 8th edition.* (Prentice-Hall), Pearson Education Inc.

ROBBINS, S.P. 1989. *Organizational behavior: Concepts, controversies and applications.* (Prentice-Hall), Pearson Education Inc.

ROBBINS, S.P. 2001. *Organizational Behavior, 8th edition.* Prentice-Hall, Upper Saddle River.

SCHULTZ, H.B. 2003. *Organisational Behaviour.* Van Schaik, Pretoria.

## Websites

HR Magazine:
www.shrm.org/docs/Hrmagazine.html
Workforce:
www.workforceonline.com/researchcenter/
CSWT Reports: www.workteams.unt.edu/reports
Rainbow Chicken: www.rainbowchicken.co.za

# part five

# Employee, group and organisational empowerment through human resources management interventions

# 16

# Job and organisational design

HB Schultz

## Learning outcomes

At the end of this chapter the learner should be able to:

- Explain the difference between the aspects of job range and job depth.
- Evaluate the merits of specialisation as an approach to job design in South Africa.
- Make decisions on the use of job range, job depth, and team-based designs as a means of improving the design of specialised jobs.
- Briefly discuss the bureaucracy and differences between mechanistic and organic organisational designs.
- Explain the context in which new organisational designs develop.
- Describe shamrock, doughnut and horizontal organisational designs and consider the situations in which these designs would be appropriate.
- Explain the characteristics of the virtual organisation and make proposals as to when the implementation of a virtual office would be conducive to organisational success.
- Describe the benefits of using good organisational designs.
- Discuss the necessity for quality assurance in job and organisational design.

## Key words and concepts

- bureaucratic structure
- doughnut organisation
- horizontal structure
- job depth
- job enlargement
- job enrichment
- job range
- job rotation
- job specialisation, or job simplification
- mechanistic structure
- organic structure
- shamrock organisation
- team-based job design
- virtual organisation

## Illustrative case

### Rolling Beedis

Rolling Beedis (beedis are an indigenous, hand-made cigarette), has provided employment for millions of Indians, most of them women, over the centuries. Now the anti-tobacco movement is cutting the demand and, in the process, threatening their economic well-being. While decline in smoking habits is seen as a way to improve public health, the women rolling the little brown tendu leaves into slim cigarettes and tying them with filaments of bright red cotton thread, worry that an industry that once sustained them may soon 'go up in smoke'. Most of the women are illiterate, in poor health, and socially marginalised. They have no assets of any kind and are concerned that their under-age children may be pushed into hazardous labour to make ends meet. However, the International Labour Organisation (ILO) is offering these impoverished women new and better ways of earning a living.

Arun Kumar, the National Coordinator of a new ILO project established to help the beedi rollers find other jobs, is cooperating with workers' unions to launch a new programme under the auspices of the ILO's Gender Promotion Programme and the government of the Netherlands, to promote decent work for women in the beedi industry. Through group meetings and activities, they are able to receive basic education, become aware of their legal rights, and are taught alternative skills, including entrepreneurship development, health, and family, and child welfare.

Jalala is a beedi group spokesperson who has benefited by getting a loan from the ILO's programme, and with this micro-credit arrangement, is setting up her own laundry business in an area where there is no facility for washing clothes. She has used the specialised job design to create employment for a number of other women as well, by simplifying the job of laundering clothes into stain removal, washing, ironing, and delivering the finished service. A close friend of Jalala's used a micro-credit loan to buy a small plot, grow vegetables, and sell them in a nearby market. She, on the other hand, has used a primitive version of job enlargement, by combining the tasks of tending the vegetable garden and selling her produce on market days.

These sustainable and socially empowering interventions by the ILO have focused on improving the livelihoods of the beedi rollers, and have shown that basic examples of job design can create employment and teach new skills to a previously disadvantaged group of workers.

SOURCE: *World of Work*. ILO, Geneva.

## 16.1 Introduction

Globalised competition and technological innovation are changing the way companies are managed. Organisations wrestle with revolutionary trends such as accelerating product change, deregulation, demographic changes, a service society, and the so-called 'information age'. Companies that have successfully responded to these challenges have recognised the need to examine their job and organisational structures. They have not been content to retain the status quo; instead they have tested new job and organisational designs, and have acknowledged the need to accept changes that are sometimes drastic and radical.

Job design determines the content of work, how the job is performed, and the depth of responsibility associated with the job. The objective of a well-designed job is to provide job satisfaction for the job-holder, and to achieve the strategic goals of the organisation. Although a number of job designs have been around for decades, the mere fact that we now live in a 'competency-based' world necessitates that all job-holders have the opportunity to test different job designs.

Traditionally, an organisation's structure was hierarchical and based on physical location. But technology has made that obsolete, and we are quickly moving to a new model that sees organisations as flatter and less linked to geography, with more dependence on networking and personal empowerment.

This chapter commences with a discussion of the differences between job range and job depth. Various approaches to job design are examined, including the specialised approach and team-based designs, before proceeding to investigate the bureaucratic organisation and its mechanistic form. Organic organisations and the impact of change on organisational design are discussed, and the chapter closes with some thoughts on the benefits of good job and organisational design and the impact of maintaining quality assurance in designing new structures.

## 16.2  Job range and job depth

According to Swanepoel et al. (1998:237), job design refers to the way in which the different tasks and responsibilities needed to carry out a job, structure the work activities of that job. For the sake of strategy, work should be organised in some specific way to obtain the required performance from the employee.

Job range is the number of different tasks that make up a particular job, and job depth refers to the extent to which a job-holder is able to influence the activities and outcomes of that job. Swanepoel et al. (1998:238) state that the greater the job depth, the more autonomy the job-holder will have; the greater the job range, the larger the variety of activities and tasks a job-holder will be expected to undertake.

Job range and depth distinguish one job from another not only within the same organisation, but also among different organisations. Highly specialised jobs are those having only a few tasks to accomplish by prescribed means. These jobs are routine and they tend to be controlled by specified rules and procedures, resulting in low depth. A job with high range has many tasks to be accomplished within its framework; a job with high depth requires a great deal of autonomous decision-making.

There are usually great differences among jobs, in both range and depth, within an organisation. When consideration is given to the design or redesign of jobs, the focus point is usually on the amount of range or depth associated with the job (Ivancevich and Matteson 1999:236).

## 16.3  The specialised approach to job design

Carrell et al. (1998:110) discuss specialisation-intensive jobs as those that are characterised by very few, repetitive tasks, and that require few skills and little mental ability. These jobs display the characteristics of low range and low depth. The job specialisation approach, which is also known as job simplification, produces jobs that are designed for people with very few skills or little experience. Specialisation is a method of job creation but over-specialisation can cause a number of problems:

- Routine tasks, repeated many times during a work shift, cause employees to become bored.
- The mechanically paced speed of an assembly or production line causes those employees who find the pace too slow, to divert their attention away from the task at hand.
- Employees are not part of the entire process and, because they are not able to identify with the end product, have little pride in or enthusiasm for the work.
- Specialisation-intensive jobs are not conducive to social interaction among employees.
- Employees do not make inputs regarding how the job should be performed, the work procedures, or the tools to be used. This creates a lack of interest, because the employees are unable to change or improve anything.

Werther and Davis (1993:155) propose an interesting theory that could be used by countries with a high unemployment rate, such as South Africa. They state that the potential problem of boredom is more common in advanced industrial countries that have a well-developed workforce. In less developed countries, highly specialised factory jobs may be acceptable because they provide jobs for workers with limited skills. South Africa cannot be truly regarded as a 'less developed country', although in many areas we teeter on the brink of third-world status. The quandary, then, is to perform a balancing act between providing jobs for the unemployed through work simplification or specialisation, and developing a multi-skilled labour force that adds value to organisations and will not find job satisfaction where job specialisation has taken place.

### 16.3.1 Designing job range

Limited, uniform and repetitive tasks yield a narrow job range. The consequences of narrow job range are job discontent, high dissatisfaction, turnover and absenteeism. Various strategies are used in an attempt to increase job range and reverse some of these consequences (Ivancevich and Matteson 1999:239).

#### Job rotation

This practice involves rotating managers and non-managers alike from one job to another, in an attempt to offer more activities to the job-holders, since each job includes different tasks. The job range and perception of variety in the job content is therefore increased. The advantages of enlarged task variety are:

- Increased employee satisfaction.
- Reduced mental overload.
- Decreased number of errors due to fatigue.
- Improved production and efficiency.
- Reduced on-the-job injuries.

Many companies have had great success in using job rotation. Where there are teams, team members rotate jobs with other team members to provide task variety and cross training. Team members are also trained to do routine maintenance and repairs of their equipment, and not to depend on a separate maintenance team for that support. These companies aim to give individuals as much control as possible of the conditions that govern work pace and quality. Some thoughts on job rotation are offered in Figure 16.1.

Although some critics state that job rotation often involves nothing more than having people perform several boring and monotonous jobs rather than one dull and tedious job, the case in point provides research data indicating that rotating people from job to job can be a good corporate strategy.

---

**Figure 16.1** Eight points you need to consider about job rotation

1   Manage job rotation as part of the company's training and career-development system.
2   Ensure that there is a clear understanding of which skills will be enhanced by placing an employee in a job rotation process.
3   Use job rotation for developing employees in all types of jobs – managerial and non-managerial.
4   Plan to use job rotation with early-career, later-career, and plateaued employees.
5   Job rotation provides opportunities to develop and motivate employees without necessarily granting promotions.
6   Female and previously disadvantaged employees can receive special attention through job rotation plans.
7   Ensure that job rotation is perceived as voluntary, that the assignment is linked to predetermined outcomes, and employees know the developmental needs addressed by each job assignment.
8   Manage the timing of rotations and operating procedures to maximise benefits and minimise costs of rotation.

SOURCE: Cheraskin and Campion (1996)

---

## Job enlargement

An alternative design strategy to job rotation is job enlargement. Job enlargement strategies are directed at increasing the number of tasks that an employee performs, but effective job enlargement involves more than simply increasing task variety. Other aspects of job range, such as worker-paced, rather than machine-paced control are also taken into consideration. Job satisfaction usually increases because boredom is reduced.

Not all employees can cope with enlarged jobs because they cannot comprehend complexity. They may also not have a sufficiently long attention span to complete an enlarged set of tasks. However, if employees are open to job enlargement and have the required ability, job enlargement should increase satisfaction and product quality, and decrease absenteeism and turnover.

## 16.3.2 Designing job depth

Creating opportunities for employees to gain more control in their jobs, make more decisions themselves, and solve problems on their own increases job depth. One can then say that job enrichment has taken place.

The application of job enrichment is based on Herzberg's two-factor theory. The basis of this theory is that factors that meet individuals' need for psychological growth (especially responsibility, job challenge, and achievement) must be characteristic of their jobs. Job enrichment is brought about through direct changes in job depth. Job depth can be expanded in the following ways:

- Through timely and direct feedback in the evaluation of performance.
- By providing opportunities to learn while in the job.
- By allowing employees to schedule at least some part of their own work.
- By ensuring that each job possesses some unique qualities or features.
- By allowing individuals to have some control over their job tasks.
- By forming natural work groups, combining tasks, and establishing client relationships.
- By providing employees with the opportunity to be accountable for the job.

Managers have become aware that job enrichment requires numerous changes in how work is done. Employees must be given greater authority to participate in decisions, to set their own goals, and to evaluate their own and their work group's performance. Managers must also be willing to delegate authority. Ivancevich and Matteson (1999:242) believe that if these conditions are met, gains in performance can be expected, provided that the work environment is supportive.

## 16.3.3 Team-based job designs

Team-based job designs aim at providing a team, rather than an individual, with a whole and meaningful piece of work to do. The onus is on team members to decide among themselves how to accomplish their tasks. They are cross-trained in different skills, and rotated within the team.

A self-managed team (SMT) represents a job enrichment approach to redesigning jobs at the group level. SMT members are empowered to perform certain activities based on procedures established and decisions made within the group, with minimum or no outside direction. SMTs include task groups, project teams, quality circles, and new venture teams. Team members are typically responsible for an entire process from inception to completion. They often select their own members and evaluate their own performance (Ivancevich and Matteson 1999:245). Worldwide, the automotive industry has been particularly interested in the use of SMTs. Varying degrees of success have been experienced, based predominantly on workers' acceptance of the team concept.

There is no one best approach to job design. However, with the different approaches at our fingertips, we possess the tools for making an informed choice. The various approaches to job design are displayed in Figure 16.2.

## 16.4 Organisations as bureaucracies

The organisational structure known as a bureaucracy was originally formulated by the German sociologist Max Weber, who believed that a bureaucracy was the best way to organise work efficiently in all situations. Modern approaches to organisational design recognise that different forms of organisational structure may be appropriate under different conditions. Weber's characteristics of a bureaucracy are:

- Each position has fixed official duties.
- Conduct is governed by impersonal rules and regulations.
- Effort is coordinated through a hierarchy of levels of authority.
- Order and reliability are maintained through written communication and files.
- Employment is a full-time occupation for members of the organisation.
- Appointment to office is made by superiors.
- Promotion is based upon merit.

When these characteristics become extreme or dysfunctional, practical and ethical problems can arise. Lundy and Cowling (1996:144) believe that this type of structure provides us with an orderly, well-regulated organisation, where there are clear career configurations, and where top management has a transparent overview of the whole structure. However, Schultz et al. (2003:230) state that organisations with excessive or dysfunctional bureaucratic tendencies have become rigid, inflexible and resistant to environmental demands and influences, and unable to respond timeously to current organisational conditions. Consequently, a bureaucracy does not allow organisational flexibility and adaptability, and Weber's model of efficiency has become a synonym for inefficiency in the 21st century.

## 16.5 Mechanistic versus organic structures

Mechanistic organisations are reliant on a lack of change in both the external and the work environments. They support a high degree of specialisation, but impose many rules, narrowly defined tasks, and direct, top-down communication.

In contrast to mechanistic designs, organic

**Figure 16.2** The approaches to job design

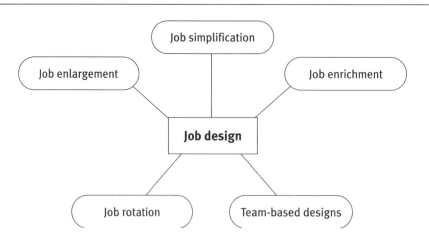

organisations are flexible networks of multi-talented individuals who perform a variety of tasks. The organic organisation is the opposite of a bureaucracy. Organic structures are flexible and change-orientated, and they foster creativity. In the organic structure:

- Knowledge and ability determine participation in decision-making and problem-solving rather than position titles.
- Decision-making is decentralised, and there is an attempt to involve lower-level participants in decision-making whenever possible.
- Communication channels operate vertically and horizontally. Information is shared throughout the organisation, including across areas of expertise and status.

The start-up of many 'dot-com' companies on the Internet has introduced the need for elec-tronic organisational design. Dot-coms rely on an e-commerce product and venture capital to support them. An example of a well-known dot-com company is Amazon.com, the world's largest virtual bookshop. Most dot-com, global organisations introduce highly organic, flexible organisational structures that allow them to be compliant and adaptable and to grow rapidly and responsively.

The characteristics of mechanistic and organic organisations are compared in Table 16.1.

## 16.6 The impact of change on organisational design

When successful companies face big changes in their environments, they often fail to respond effectively, leaving themselves open to a downward spiral into a decrease in the

**Table 16.1** The characteristics of mechanistic and organic organisations

| Characteristic | Mechanistic Organisation | Organic Organisation |
|---|---|---|
| Specialisation | Many specialists | Many generalists |
| Task definition and knowledge | Narrow, technical | Broad, general |
| Task flexibility | Rigid, routine | Flexible, varies |
| Authority | Centralised in a few top people | Decentralised, diffused throughout the organisation |
| Degree of hierarchical control | High | Low |
| Primary decision-making style | Authoritarian | Democratic, participative |
| Primary communication pattern | Top-down | Lateral |
| Formal rules | Rigid rules | Considerable flexibility |
| Specification of techniques, obligations, and rights | Specific | General |
| Emphasis on obedience and loyalty | High | Low |

organisation's resource base. Decline is almost unavoidable unless deliberate steps are taken to prevent it. Schultz et al. (2003:231) express the early warning signs of decline as:

- Excess personnel.
- Tolerance of incompetence.
- Cumbersome administrative procedures.
- Disproportionate staff power.
- Attributing more importance to a process than to the results achieved.
- Scarcity of clear goals and decision benchmarks.
- Fear of embarrassment and conflict.
- Loss of effective communication.
- Outdated organisational structure.
- Increased scapegoating by leaders.
- Resistance to change.
- Low morale.
- Special interest groups are more vocal.
- Decreased innovation.

In order to stop decline, organisations must react positively and specifically by redesigning their structures. While we accept that organisational design is the macroscopic term that includes an organisation's structure and its processes for decision-making, communication, and performance management, we need to take a broad look at the reasons why organisational designs take on new forms.

In Figure 16.3, the context in which organisational designs alter and develop is displayed. Some research indicates that social and environmental forces produce current organisational designs. Changing levels of individual aspirations and loyalty, evolving family systems (such as the increase in single parents), the aging workforce, and diversity in the workplace account for the impact of society on organisations.

External environmental forces such as increased competition, changing expectations of shareholders and technological development combine with the internal forces of modernisation of plant and equipment, joint ventures, contracting, mergers, and strategic

**Figure 16.3** The context in which organisational designs develop

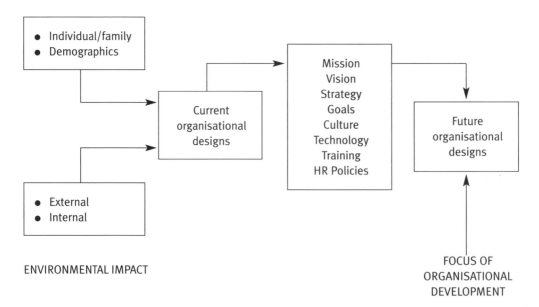

SOCIAL IMPACT

ENVIRONMENTAL IMPACT

FOCUS OF
ORGANISATIONAL
DEVELOPMENT

reorientation to create current organisational designs.

If the current design copes inadequately with the symptoms of decline, the organisation is forced to concentrate on organisational development through the application of its organisation's mission, vision, strategy, goals, culture, technology, training, and HR policies. The product of this focus reveals itself in a relevant future design for the organisation.

## Encounter 16.1

THE MAVERICK

In 1981, Ricardo Semler became president of Semco SA, the Brazilian marine and food processing machinery manufacturer. He is internationally famous for creating the world's most unusual workplace, something, he says, which was forced upon him by the circumstances of an organisation in serious decline. Semler's management philosophy of empowering employees and looking at corporate structures in new ways is a serious challenge to the ingrained model of the corporate pyramid.

At Semco, workers choose their bosses; financial information is shared with everyone; thirty per cent of the employees determine their own salaries. And self-managed teams replace a traditional bureaucratic hierarchy and procedures. Semler's simple belief is:

- Generate success through unconventional wisdom.
- Motivate employees by involving them.
- Run your company in a more humane, enthusiastic and enlightened way.

Many CEOs have used Semler's viewpoints, which he originally set out in his book entitled *Maverick: The success story behind the world's most unusual workplace.* In his book he described how he powered his company to 900 per cent growth in ten years and increased Semco's industry ranking from 58th to 4th, despite extremely severe economic conditions. His new book, *The seven day weekend,* will be published in 2003 and will probably enjoy as much success as his book describing his man-

agement philosophy, *Turning the tables,* which provoked intense discussion among senior managers worldwide.

## 16.7 Shamrocks, doughnuts and horizontal organisations

New organisational designs have become more the exception than the norm during the last decade. Some of these designs have a great deal of merit, and we shall examine some of the more feasible designs, starting with Charles Handy's shamrocks and doughnuts.

In an interview on the Australian Broadcasting Corporation's programme 'Lateline', Charles Handy, the British human resources philosopher and author, stated:

> In the future your working life will span 25 years, not 45 years; most of your education will take place outside the classroom; corporate retirement funds will become a thing of the past; and half of all jobs available will be part-time, not full-time.

Is this fact or fantasy? You can listen to Handy's entire interview, lasting 35 minutes, at www.morganbanks.com.au/handy.htm and decide for yourself.

### 16.7.1 The shamrock organisation

Handy's metaphor of a shamrock, or four-leaf clover, which he used to illustrate his predicted organisational structure, is depicted in Figure 16.4, together with Handy's doughnut organisation. The first leaf of the shamrock contains core workers who are essential to the existence of the firm – qualified professionals, technicians, and managers. The second leaf contains contract workers who carry out non-essential, but specialised work at low cost. The third leaf contains the flexible workforce – part-time and temporary workers who are contracted and terminated according to customer requirements. The fourth leaf features the external customers. This radical departure from traditional structure views the customer as an integral part of the organisation and not a separate entity.

It is only the professional core that will be relatively permanent. The other 'leaves of the shamrock' will be adaptive and flexible. The new worker will have a 'work portfolio' made up of wage or fee work, homework, gift work, and study work. Portfolio people will continually contract their skills where there is the greatest demand and will move on when the assignment is finished.

**Figure 16.4** The shamrock and doughnut organisations

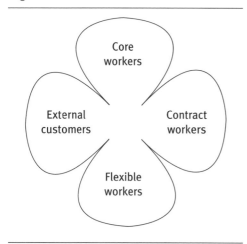

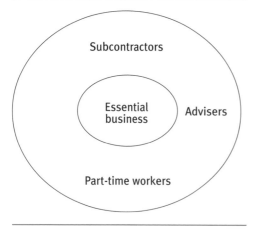

## 16.7.2 The doughnut organisation

In 1994, Handy identified three concepts crucial to the survival of organisations in the future. He believes that organisations must consider the doughnut principle as a future organisational design, they must be aware of and react to the sigmoid, or S-shaped curve, and Chinese contracts must become part of organisational systems. Each one of these concepts will be discussed.

### The doughnut principle

Handy's doughnut organisation is an inside-out one, in as much as the usual hole one would find in the middle of a doughnut has become a solid core surrounded by an empty but bounded space. The core of the doughnut represents the place for essential business and offers scope for initiative. The space around the core is filled by a flexible band of subcontractors, advisers, and part-time workers.

In the past, jobs were tightly designed, leaving little room for discretion. Handy proposes that jobs should also be designed in the form of his inside-out doughnut, with a specified essential core having outer limits of discretionary and expandable authority.

Handy goes on to describe organisations as comprising groups of doughnuts, for example, a doughnut group responsible for the development and marketing of a particular product. This group would have its essential core of permanent 'community members' (Handy does not call them employees any more), with an outer space providing flexible support in the way of researchers, suppliers, and service contractors. Doughnut groups are continuously evolving and declining as their life span comes to an end, but the sigmoid curve (discussed in the next section) should be brought into play before the curve starts to dip.

### The sigmoid curve

The sigmoid curve plots the path of every successful human system, including organisations. A period of experimentation is followed by one of growth and development, before the curve reverses its trajectory and enters a declining phase. To be successful, organisations must develop and initiate a new curve before the old one starts its downward slope. This very often entails a complete turnaround in mindsets, culture, product development, and strategy. Many organisations fail to start a new curve because top managers see the company in a period of growth and success, and are afraid to change the status quo before it is entirely necessary. They really only wake up when it is too late.

Change on the curve results in great confusion, represented by the shaded areas (Figure 16.5). This is due to the two contrasting, and often competing cultures existing side-by-side. However, continued success and survival depend on the development of new curves, which will provide the foundation for a learning organisation. The sigmoid curve is depicted in Figure 16.5.

**The Chinese contract**

Handy maintains that partnerships must be based on a win-win situation, where both sides benefit equally, reinforcing trust rather than enforcing legal agreements. True partnerships prefer to support each other rather than to compete, and they look for shared benefits. Parties should know each other well enough to share information, common goals, and ambitions for the enterprise. This philosophy is contrary to Western traditions where the principle of competition has always been foremost. However, Handy believes that a successful future for our organisations, and society as a whole, depends on the adoption of Chinese contracts.

### 16.7.3 The horizontal organisation

A horizontal organisation has a flat structure and is built around core processes instead of tasks. Employees are close to both internal and external customers, they ask questions, receive feedback, and they jointly solve problems. Cross-functional teams are the norm, and lateral transfers are more common than traditional vertical promotions. The horizontal structure has the following elements:

- Process owners take responsibility for an entire core process.
- It flattens the hierarchy as a result of empowering workers and eliminating non-value-added work.
- It uses teams to manage everything.
- It uses information technology to help reach performance objectives and deliver value to customers.
- It lets customers' satisfaction drive performance.
- It rewards workers for their team-related performance.

**Figure 16.5** The sigmoid curve

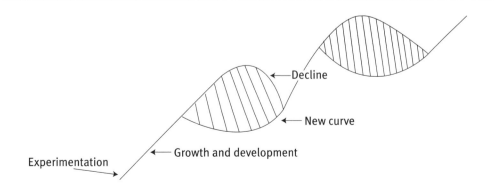

Decline

New curve

Growth and development

Experimentation

- It maximises contact with suppliers and customers.
- Top management continuously informs and trains all employees to help develop multiple competencies.
- It measures end-of-process performance objectives.
- It builds a culture of cooperation, collaboration, and openness.

Unfortunately, the horizontal organisation has little scope for upward moves, and constant change results in interpersonal conflict, personal stress, and burnout.

## 16.8  The virtual organisation

Schultz et al. (2003:238) describe a virtual organisation as a network of independent suppliers, customers, and competitors, linked by computer technology. This network is continually evolving and capitalises on skills, access to markets, and common objectives. Each participating company contributes only its core competencies, or areas of greatest strength, thus creating something better than any single company could have produced alone.

Virtual organisations have the following characteristics:

- *Technology.* Partnerships are based on electronic contracts.
- *Excellence.* Each partner brings its best competencies to the corporation.
- *Opportunism.* Partnerships are less permanent, less formal, and more opportunistic.
- *Trust.* Members of the virtual organisation must trust each other in order to achieve their goals.
- *No borders.* Traditional company boundaries are redefined. Cooperation among competitors, suppliers, and customers makes it difficult to determine borders.

Sometimes the virtual workplace combines the efforts of people in diverse venues or different corporate entities. Crandall and Wallace (1997:27) believe that survival will depend increasingly on people from two or more companies working together in a virtual environment. They identify three successive stages in the development of the virtual workplace:

- The telecommuting model, in which individual employees work from remote locations and commute most of the time on an electronic basis.
- The front-line model, which involves placing sales and service locations in the field and close to the customer.
- The cyber link model, which represents the greatest level of 'virtuality' an organisation can hope to achieve. Teams of employees and customers work together in a flexible, virtual environment, remaining virtually linked, sometimes never even meeting face-to-face, until business opportunities have been fully realised.

### Case-in-point
*Surfing the virtual wave*

Jeffreys Bay is the surfing 'paradise' of South African and international surfers. It is probably the greatest wish of all surfers to be able to 'ride the tube' at the 'J-Bay pipes'. Be that as it may, Johan and Susie Esterhuysen have been married for twelve years, having met while both were studying Industrial Psychology at Stellenbosch University. After they had both graduated with honours degrees, they were lucky enough to both find jobs in Cape Town and they settled down in the 'mother city'. Seven years and two children later, Johan was becoming more and more discontented with their life-style. He and Susie both had well-paid jobs, but Johan's desire to make a life for his family in Jeffreys Bay, where he could 'ride the waves' virtually every day, was becoming obsessive.

Susie knew about his ambition – he had voiced it already back in their university days, and she encouraged him to take the plunge and make a new life for themselves. Five years ago they moved to Jeffreys Bay, bought a small cottage and quickly got used to their new 'laid-back' life-style. But how were they going to support themselves? There were no companies in this over-grown 'village' where they could do the work they loved and for which they were both trained. But Johan knew that they could easily ply their trade from the comfort of their own homes via electronic means.

They set themselves up as consultants and visited numerous companies in the Eastern Cape area who could use their services. And now they freelance in the field of HRM and Industrial Relations, communicating with their customers through the magic of e-mail, cell-phones, the fax machine, and the Internet. Johan even sometimes takes his laptop computer to the beach and gets some work done in between surfing the waves.

It sounds idyllic, and it is. But it could never have worked and Johan would never have been able to pursue his dream without the reality of a virtual office.

A major concern of a virtual organisation is how managers should evaluate their workers. Many managers believe that only face-to-face interaction is meaningful and may pass over mobile workers for promotions. Performance reviews in a virtual environment should be conducted informally every quarter, and for-

mally every six months. The final analysis of performance can no longer measure good citizenship and attendance, but how much work people actually get done, and how well they do it. Figure 16.6 offers the attributes of a successful remote employee.

According to Wright and Oldford (1995), several elements must be present if the virtual organisation is to stand a chance of success:
- Top-level management support.
- Careful choice of management and subordinates.
- No forfeiture of benefits, training, and career advancement opportunities.
- Employee evaluation based on output or results.
- Good communication links.
- Fixed commuting days to the main office.

Proponents of virtual organisations list a wide range of benefits:
- Personal scheduling of hours.
- Less commuting time.
- Fewer interruptions.
- Less absenteeism.
- Retirees can continue to contribute to the organisation.

## 16.9 The benefits of using good organisational designs

George and Jones (2002:563–9) believe that relevant organisational designs can offer the following benefits for an organisation:
- *Increase efficiency.* Many levels of managers can cost a company millions annually. By trimming hierarchical layers, operating costs can be reduced.
- *Increase quality.* High quality differentiates one organisation's goods and services from another's. An improvement in quality can allow an organisation to pursue a strategy of differentiation in its design.
- *Increase innovation and creativity.* Organisations that select a differentiation strategy produce superior skills through innovation, which is often a source of competitive advantage.

---

**Figure 16.6** The attributes of a successful remote employee

- Familiar and comfortable with the job.
- A strong work ethic and self-motivated.
- Discipline and skills for self-management.
- Effective communication skills.
- Adaptable and able to compromise.
- Knowledgeable about organisation procedures.
- Technical self-sufficiency.
- Results-orientated.

SOURCE: O'Connell (1996)

- *Increase responsiveness to customers.* Relevant organisational designs can build a competitive advantage by adjusting to customer needs and developing techniques to provide customers with the best possible service.

Garnant (2001:283–7) adds the following benefits in redesigning organisational structure:

- An optimal structure complements the organisational vision and strategy, and needs to be fluid in order to respond to continual changes.
- A revised organisational structure can complement both formal and informal modes of communication.
- Structural changes can assist in capitalising on each individual's personal style and motivational focus, which provides the ability to optimise diversity within a group setting.
- Organisational structure can produce a return on investment in the form of reduced personnel costs and improved productivity.

## 16.10　Job and organisational design and quality assurance

Job design strategy focuses on jobs in the context of individuals' needs for economic well-being and personal growth. But Ivancevich and Matteson (1999:247) state that the issue of quality in job design cannot be separated from the technical demands of jobs and the social demands of people doing the jobs. They maintain that too great an emphasis on the technical system or too great an emphasis on human relations will lead to poor job design. This socio-technical approach to job design is compatible with total quality management (TQM), and designers must take both issues into account for the sake of quality assurance.

In the field of organisational design, organisations must be aware that quality losses are inevitable when implementing a new model.

For this reason it is imperative that decision makers investigate very thoroughly the implications of proposed changes before finalising radical departures from established structure.

## 16.11　Conclusion

Playing around with job designs and organisational structures is of no use without consideration of the purpose of the organisation, the nature of the demands being placed on it from outside, the types of operation it carries out, and the people available. The bottom line is that organisations of the 21st century must be adaptable and flexible enough to consider departure from established structures in order to maintain equilibrium in the future.

## Summary

- Job design is the way in which the different tasks and responsibilities required to carry out a job structure the work activities of that job. Job range is the number of different tasks that make up a particular job. Job depth is the extent to which a job-holder is able to influence the activities and outcomes of that job.
- The greater the job depth, the more autonomy the job-holder will have; the greater the job range, the larger the variety of activities and tasks a job-holder will be expected to undertake.
- Specialisation-intensive jobs are those that are characterised by very few, repetitive tasks, and which require few skills and little mental ability. Over-specialisation can cause a number of problems.
- The consequences of narrow job range are: job discontent and high dissatisfaction, turnover, and absenteeism. Strategies that are used to increase job range and reverse some of these consequences are: job rotation, job enlargement, job enrichment, and team-based job designs.
- Bureaucracies have many layers of management and huge amounts of red tape that frustrate creativity. They encourage stability, rigidity, and permanence, and do

not adapt quickly or well to changing social conditions and technological innovations. Mechanistic organisations are typical of a bureaucracy. Organic organisations are flexible networks of multitalented individuals who perform a variety of tasks. Organic structures are flexible, change-orientated, and foster creativity.

- Decline in an organisation's resource base necessitates response in the form of organisational development.
- Newer organisational designs are the shamrock, doughnut, and horizontal organisations. The virtual workplace creates tremendous opportunities, but also generates a great deal of stress and difficulty as there are many organisational changes required to make it work.
- The application of relevant organisational designs can lead to increased efficiency, quality, innovation, creativity, and responsiveness, but quality losses must be anticipated when changing job or organisational designs.

## Case study
## Behind the scenes at
## Pick 'n Pay

BEHIND THE SCENES AT PICK 'N PAY

Raymond Ackerman, the 68 year-old CEO of South Africa's Pick 'n Pay Group, knows he cannot remain the company leader forever. When he does leave, which he says will probably be during the next eighteen months, he wants to stay on as executive chairman. His son, Gareth Ackerman, is MD of Group Enterprises, and manages the strategic investments made locally and internationally by his division, which includes the 7-Eleven convenience store chain, Boardmans, Score's Rite Valu franchise supermarkets, PNA stationers, and a significant interest in TM Supermarkets in Zimbabwe, and Pick 'n Pay's franchised outlets.

'I have been examining top structures around the world and there are many solutions which don't conform to the obvious,' says Raymond Ackerman. The MD of the Pick 'n Pay core business, Sean Summers, agrees. Sean is in charge of all Pick 'n Pay supermarkets, hypermarkets, superstores, family stores, and Price Rites.

Raymond Ackerman's dilemma is to design a structure in which Gareth Ackerman and Sean Summers complement each other. The most obvious scenario, and one which Ackerman is looking at, would be for Gareth to become CEO and Summers to be made Group MD overseeing a number of divisions each run by their own MDs.

Before the restructuring of the group into the above two divisions in 1995, Pick 'n Pay was not growing. Ackerman appointed Bain International Consultants to analyse the company and identify issues needing attention for the group to regain its upward profit path. Their solution was to focus the business and redefine organisational structures. The aim was to give more power to the younger executives. The most significant change was to separate the group into the core business and non-core business.

SOURCE: www.suntimes.co.za/97/0216/

## Questions

1   Based on the above information, explain the type of organisational design that Pick 'n Pay has been following since 1995.
2   What do you think Raymond Ackerman should do with the organisational design when he retires?

## Experiential exercise No. 1

PURPOSE: To develop an organisational design for a new company.

INTRODUCTION: The current economy has forced many school-leavers and graduates to become entrepreneurial when they discover that finding employment is not an easy proposition. Business graduates usually have a great deal of exposure to marketing and sales principles, but they do not always learn how to set up and design a new company.

TASK: In a group of four to six members decide what type of business you would enter into if you were forced to become an entrepreneur. Compile a list of the types of jobs you would find in the company and describe the profile of all stakeholders (internal and external). Discuss the optional organisational designs that could be applied to this organisation.

## Experiential exercise No. 2

PURPOSE: To investigate the viewpoints of employees in various types of organisations regarding the most feasible designs for their own jobs.

TASK: Make contact with at least five people who are employed in the following jobs:

● nurse
● librarian
● lecturer
● shop assistant
● teacher
● receptionist
● trade unionist
● manufacturing manager
● administration clerk

Present a short overview of the job designs discussed in this chapter and ask your contacts which of the designs are used in their organisations. Are they satisfied with their own job designs?

## Chapter questions

1   Explain the difference between job enlargement and job enrichment. Under what circumstances would an organisation not wish to enlarge or enrich a job?

2   How could the range and depth of the following jobs be increased: a kindergarten teacher, laboratory assistant, credit controller, plumber?

3   If you were responsible for the daily man-

agement of a university campus, which of the following activities would you locate in the core and which on the periphery of your business?

● campus security
● lecturing duties
● catering
● technical services
● printing
● campus information
● car park attendance
● maintenance of equipment
● administrative duties
● cleaning

4   Discuss how changing forces impact on the design of organisations.

5   In which organisational structure would you prefer to work – a bureaucratic organisation, one of the new, modern designs, or a virtual organisation? Motivate your answer.

## Bibliography

BENTON, D.A. 1995. *Applied human relations: An organizational approach, 5th edition.* (Prentice-Hall), Pearson Education Inc.

CARRELL, M.R., ELBERT, N.F., HATFIELD, R.D. GROBLER, P.A., MARX, M. & VAN DER SCHYF, S. 1998. *Human resources management in South Africa.* Pearson Education, Cape Town.

CHERASKIN, L. & CAMPIO, M.Z. 1996. 'Study clarifies job-rotation benefits'. *Personnel Journal,* 75(11):31–38. Reprinted with permission of Copyright Clearance Center.

CRANDALL, N.F. & WALLACE, M.J. 1997. 'Inside the virtual workplace: Forging a new deal for work and rewards'. *Compensation and Benefits Review,* 29(1):27–36.

DESSLER, G. 1997. *Human resource management, 7th edition.* (Prentice-Hall), Pearson Education Inc.

GARNANT, C.W. 2001. 'Who re-moved my cheese? Responding to staff reductions'. *Tax Executive,* 53(4):283–287.

GEORGE, J.M. & JONES, G.R. 2002. *Organizational behavior, 3rd edition.* (Prentice-Hall), Pearson Education Inc.

GÓMEZ-MEJÍA, L.R., BALKIN, D.B., & CARDY, R.L. 1998. *Managing human resources, 2nd edition*. (Prentice-Hall), Pearson Education Inc.

GREENGARD, S. 1994. 'Making the virtual office a reality'. *Personnel Journal,* 73(9):66–79.

HAMMER, M. & CHAMPY, J. 1993. *Reengineering the corporation: A manifesto for business revolution*. Nicholas Brealey Publishing, London.

HANDY, C. 1994. *The Doughnut organization. A management resource on video*. Melrose Film Productions, London.

IVANCEVICH, J.M. & MATTESON, M.T. 1999. *Organizational behavior and management, 5th edition*. McGraw-Hill Companies, New York.

LUNDY, O. & COWLING, A.1996. *Strategic human resource management*. Routledge, London.

O'CONNELL, S.E. 1996. 'The virtual workplace moves at warp speed'. *HR Magazine,* March. Reprinted with permission of Copyright Clearance Center.

SCHULTZ, H., BAGRAIM, J., POTGIETER, T., VIEDGE, C. & WERNER, A. 2003. *Organisational behaviour*. Van Schaik, Pretoria.

SWANEPOEL, B.J., ERASMUS, B.J., VAN WYK, M.W. & SCHENK, H.W. 1998. *South African human resources management*. Juta, Cape Town.

TORRINGTON, D. & HALL, L. 1995. *Personnel management, 3rd edition*. (Prentice-Hall), Pearson Education (UK)

WERTHER, W.B. & DAVIS, K. 1993. *Human resources and personnel management, 4th edition*. McGraw-Hill Companies, New York.

WRIGHT, P.C. & OLDFORD, A. 1995. 'Telecommuting and employee effectiveness: Career and managerial issues'. Reading from the *International Journal of Career Management, Internet Conference*, 15 May– 15 August.

*World of Work.* 2002. 'In India, beedi rollers seek new ways of earning a living' (www.ilo.org/public/english/bureau/inf/ magazine.htm).

## Websites

Interview with Charles Handy: www.morgan-banks.com.au/handy.htm

Strategy and Business – Thought Leaders: Charles Handy: www.strategy-business.com/thoughtleaders

What will HR look like in 2020? www.work-forceonline.com/archive/article/000/79/64

Four key forces shaping the future: www.work-forceonline.com/archive/article/000/64/68

The future calls for change: www.workforceonline.com/feature/00/00/68/index

Do you understand the new workforce? www.workforceonline.com/archive/article/000/16/26

Job rotation system: www.danmacleod.com

# 17

# National level skills development issues

GD Haasbroek

## Learning outcomes

At the end of this chapter the learner should be able to:

- Explain the macro-economic context within which training policies are developed.
- Critique the education and training challenges faced by South Africa.
- Explain the role of governments in shaping training policies.
- Express an opinion on the relevance of certain universal training principles for South Africa.

## Key words and concepts

- certification of training
- cost and benefit of training
- demand for labour
- Education and Training Quality Assurance (ETQA) bodies
- funding mechanism for training
- global markets
- learnerships
- National Qualifications Framework (NQF)
- National Skills Authority
- National Skills Fund
- National Standards Bodies (NSBs)
- new world economy
- Sector Education and Training Authorities (SETAs)
- Skills Development Act
- Skills Development Levies Act
- South African Qualifications Authority (SAQA)
- South African Qualifications Authority Act
- Standard Generating Bodies (SGBs)
- supply of labour
- training levy-grant scheme
- unemployment
- vocational education and training

## Illustrative case

Midlands Engineering started as a small enterprise with a workforce consisting of Peter, a qualified engineer, two artisans and three unskilled workers. Peter, the founder of the company, did not regard training of his workforce as a high priority, and failed to recognise the competitive edge he could gain on his competitors by investing in a competent and satisfied workforce. Over time Midlands Engineering grew from a small business to become a medium size business with a workforce of 200 employees. Peter was still in charge of the company and had not yet changed his view that training does not pay. His policy was rather to recruit skilled workers instead of training his own workforce. During 1998, the company was experiencing financial problems and unrest amongst the employees – managers as well as unskilled workers. Peter appointed X-Consulting, a financial and human resources development consulting firm, to advise on how the company's problems could be addressed.

X-Consulting's report revealed, inter alia, a lack of loyalty and dissatisfaction amongst the workforce, mainly due to the fact that workers do not perceive the company to offer them any career development prospects. Absenteeism was the order of the day, and the more experienced and competent employees were taking up jobs with the competitors. Peter requested X-Consulting to submit a plan of action on how to turn the situation around. The plan revolved around a company policy which made provision for the training and development of the company's workforce. The plan further suggested that Peter work in close collaboration with the Sector Education and Training Authority of the engineering industry with the view to capatilising on the benefits arising from the levy-grant system, the learnership system, and the National Qualifications Framework (which makes provision for employees of companies to obtain recognised qualifications). Peter eventually decided to implement X-Consulting's plan of action. Within one year there were already visible signs that things were changing for the better at Midland Engineering. After two years, 40 learnerships were registered, managers were given development opportunities and the company managed to recoup almost

60 per cent of the training expenses through the levy-grant system. At a recent seminar on skills development in the engineering industry, Peter acknowledged that the development of the workforce of Midland Engineering, over the last four years, turned the company into a profitable organisation that not only cares for its people but that also contributes to the well-being of society at large.

## 17.1   Introduction

Skills development through education and training has always been the most powerful lever for improving both individual opportunity and institutional competitiveness of companies worldwide. Governments and employers recognise the critical role a skilled and knowledgeable workforce can play in securing competitive advantages in international markets. There is consensus amongst the forward-looking countries and organisations that the quality of their human resources will be the determining factor for its continuing progress and prosperity.

National vocational education and training systems form an integral part of the socio-economic environment of most countries, particularly advanced industrial countries. Vocational education and training is in the first place a political issue because of its relationships to economic growth, levels of unemployment, productivity and industry competencies, and should therefore not be approached in the narrow context of being only an economic or human resources issue.

The South African Government's human resources strategy has two roles to play. One is to ensure that the various components of the state work together in a coordinated way to deliver opportunities for human development. The second is to ensure that those people who have suffered from discrimination in the past are put in the front of the queue in terms of the identified national priorities (RSA 2001).

The Australian government's national strategy for vocational education and training for 1998 to 2003 recognises a number of forces arising from complex economic, technological and social changes, which they believe will influence the education and training environment (Australian National Training Authority 1998). Some of these forces are:

- The growth in global markets accompanied by intensified international competition and the lowering of tariffs in Australia.
- The emergence of service and knowledge-based industries as important sources of employment.
- Changes in the geographical and regional distribution of employment opportunities.
- The impact of new information and communication technologies on the community in general, and on Australian enterprises in particular.
- The growth in small business and changes in working arrangements, such as increasing part time and casual employment, and the use of outsourcing arrangements and labour hire firms.
- Changes in the ways in which work is organised within enterprises, such as the use of flatter business structures and an emphasis on teamwork and multi-skilling.
- Demographic changes, such as the ageing of the Australian population, the ethnic diversity of the population and the feminisation of the labour force.
- Social changes, such as those brought on by changes in family structures, lifestyles, sources of income, and personal aspirations.
- Community expectations that all Australians, including those who are most disadvantaged, should have the opportunity to realise their full potential, for example, through education and employment opportunities.
- The continuing needs to reduce the level of unemployment.
- Increasingly sophisticated consumer expectations about the range and quality of products and services.
- Changes in the role of government, away

from direct service provision to the purchasing of services, with an increased focus on competitive processes and purchasing output.

The approach of the Australian government is indicative of many industrially developed or newly industrialised countries that address the challenge of skills development from a strategic point of view. This chapter explores a number of macro-strategic issues impacting on skills development policies, gives a national perspective on the policy environment influencing skills development, provides an overview of the funding and certification of training, touches on the legislative framework regulating and facilitating skills development and training (the National Skills Development Strategy introduced by the Minister of Labour), and examines some universal principles underpinning training and skills development strategies.

## 17.2    Macro-economic context

To be successful and to yield the necessary returns requires education and training policies shaped within the prevailing macro-social and economic circumstances as well as the national strategic vision of a particular country. In the following sections a number of macro-issues impacting directly or indirectly on the formation of training policies are discussed.

### 17.2.1 New world economy

The world economy finds itself on a rapid path of globalisation. The new world economic environment is changing the structure of labour markets by increasing the level of competitiveness and thereby creating a need for improved labour productivity and a more flexible workforce. In this environment of rapid and fundamental change, the education and training of human resources has become the driving force for meeting the demand for highly skilled workers and technical staff needed to manage the new social and economic challenges.

## 17.2.2 The changing working environment

The working world is currently undergoing radical change. The impact of economic, technological, social and political factors is transforming it fundamentally. The movement of technology, goods, capital, the location of production, and labour (albeit to a lesser extent) across national borders, is leading to the rapid globalisation of the world economy. The result is that national economies are becoming interdependent and integrated. The liberalisation of trade and the development and universal availability of rapidly evolving information technologies are among the major driving forces behind the globalisation of the economy. International trade is also becoming more market-orientated as a result of deregulation and the transition of former socialist economies to market economies. In the process, labour markets are being restructured to meet the challenge of being competitive, thereby creating a need for increased productivity and continuous innovation in the business environment. This leads in turn to restructuring, privatisation, the relocation of production, the redeployment of workers and change in job content, work processes, and organisation (which eventually affects skill requirements).

New technologies are being developed and introduced across all industry sectors and areas of work, boosting productivity and creating demands for new and different skills. Electronic commerce is creating more business opportunities and is expected to sustain economic and employment growth. It is expected that online technology will create a major shift from people employed by large organisations to people working for themselves (see Chapter 16 regarding the virtual workplace).

## 17.2.3 Productivity and flexibility

Both common sense and economic research support the idea that the quality of a nation's workforce is important to economic growth and social development. Two factors are generally considered to be prime determinants of the quality of a workforce. One is labour productivity, and the other is the flexibility of the workforce. These two factors become increasingly significant in countries seeking to expand their economies and improve the welfare of their citizens in a highly competitive and rapidly changing world economy. The higher a country's labour productivity and the more flexible its workforce, the better that country is able to acquire and adapt the technology needed to produce better quality goods and services at lower costs, and to shift the structure of production to new markets and products. Productivity and flexibility depend on a number of factors, such as the level of capital investment, the technology of production, and the quality of management. All these factors are, however, dependent on the skills of workers at all levels, from senior level to semi-skilled operators. Sound management alone is not enough for improved productivity and flexibility. Of equal importance is the competence of skilled workers and technicians who occupy the middle level of the workforce. In modern economies, these workers facilitate the adaptation and use of new technologies, enhance the efficiency and quality of production and maintenance, and supervise and train workers with lesser skills (Middleton et al. 1993).

## 17.2.4 Investment in training

Improving the job skills of the workforce has attracted considerable amounts of funds (either from governments or from donors) in developing and developed countries. Unfortunately, and according to Middleton et al. (1993), the results of much of the investment in skills training have been disappointing. The causes of poor returns in training investment are complex and vary from country to country. In some cases expectations regarding the power of training programmes, especially those aimed at young people making the transition from school to work, have been unrealistic, largely because of the slow growth in skilled wage employment. In other cases inefficient administration has reduced the returns in public training investments, and governments are not always mindful of economic policies that distort the incentives for firms and individuals to invest in skills.

A hard but important lesson countries have learned over the years, is that economically and socially disadvantaged citizens do not benefit from training unless the skills learnt improve their productivity in employment. The effectiveness of investment in training is highly dependent on the nature of employment in society.

### 17.2.5 Economic and social policies

A nation's economic and social policies not only affect patterns of economic and employment growth, but also determine the market signals and incentives that guide individuals, employers, and trainers in making decisions about investments in training. It is therefore important for policy makers to understand the relationship between the economic environment and the incentive structure for skills development that individuals and enterprises face. The record suggests that training policies are more effective if they are adapted to the nature of the economy, and that these policies should evolve as economies change. Governments' role in vocational and technical education and training can be made more effective through more dynamic planning, encouragement of employer and private training, and improved responsiveness and efficiency in public training programmes.

### 17.2.6 State intervention

Middleton et al. (1993) address the fundamental question of why and when should governments intervene in skills training. They argue that traditional private training markets proved too limited in meeting the broad skills needs associated with economic development and growth. The result was that governments started to emerge as the leading actors in the training market. There are two main justifications for government intervention in training markets. First there is the issue of external benefits. The focus of individuals and enterprises is on higher productivity, profits, and wage earnings, which come from training and which affect them directly. Government, on the other hand (and representing society at large), is likely to capture the largest share in tax from a flexible and competitive economy, which may accrue from a better-trained workforce. Second, there is the issue of social equity. Public subsidisation on equity grounds for the disadvantaged, women, and marginalised youth is justified, provided it is carefully targeted to ensure that only those in need benefit.

## 17.3 A national perspective

### 17.3.1 The broad political, social and economic scene

With the advent of the new democratic and socio-economic dispensation, besides the challenge of bringing about peace and political stability, the government of the day has the enormous task of developing policies aimed at the promotion of economic growth and social development.

Much of the debate in South Africa today is about policies and programmes to facilitate job creation, to narrow income differentials, and to redress inequalities in access to wealth. General consensus exists between the main role-players that South Africa's future hinges on a sound and vibrant economy that can fulfil all the needs and aspirations of its people. Political stability, a policy that encourages economic growth largely through private initiative, fiscal discipline, exposure to foreign competition, and sound labour relations are seen by experts as prerequisites for sustainable growth and for tackling the problems associated with unemployment, poverty, and socio-economic backlogs.

Great emphasis is placed on a supply-side approach in the new economic order to be adopted in South Africa, including supply-side measures such as education and training and job creation through national public works programmes. Reconstruction and development are currently high on the national agenda and are seen as a process of empowerment through which each and every citizen is entitled to active participation in the economy, not only to help create wealth and prosperity, but also to share in its fruits.

## 17.3.2 Human resources development

South Africa's human resources hold the key to many of its economic and social problems. The challenge is to provide its people with a solid educational foundation and to equip its workforce with relevant and marketable skills. The socio-economic history of South Africa, however, requires that the country's education and skills development strategies prepare and empower its citizens to fully participate in society and achieve self-sufficiency, self-expression, and full citizenship. Not only does the workforce have to be able to make a meaningful contribution towards economic growth and eventually wealth creation, but it must also be able to share in the wealth created by participating in the economy.

For South Africans to meaningfully participate in economic and social development, as well as their own advancement, they need not only general capabilities, such as the ability to read and write, to communicate effectively, and to solve problems in their homes, communities and workplace. Given the demands of a complex and changing economy, characterised by increasing use of information and the general rise in the quantity and quality of the skills required for jobs, people must also have rising levels of applied competence (Department of Labour 1997).

The Human Resources Development (HRD) strategy of South Africa has, as its key mission 'to maximise the potential of the people of South Africa, through the acquisition of knowledge and skills, to work productively and competitively in order to achieve a rising quality of life for all, and to set in place

an operational plan, together with necessary institutional arrangements, to achieve this' (RSA 2001). The HRD strategy consists of five strategic objectives, namely:

- Improving the foundation for human development.
- Improving the supply of high-quality skills which are more responsive to societal economic needs.
- Increasing employer participation in life-long learning.
- Supporting employment growth through industrial policies, innovation, research and development.
- Ensuring that the four strategic objectives of the HRD strategy are linked.

The HRD strategy covers twenty-two strategic indicators, ranging from early childhood development, to the role and responsibilities of the private sector. A number of the salient indicators are discussed below.

### Adult basic education and general literacy

Illiteracy is highly prevalent in South Africa. It is estimated that three million South Africans cannot read or write at all, and many more are semi-literate. This has devastating negative consequences on their ability to participate fully in the political, economic, and social spheres of life. The government actively encourages adult education programmes, and has established the South African National Literacy Initiative to mobilise three million participants into literacy programmes.

### General education

The Department of Education reports a decrease in the numbers of learners of inappropriate age – those who are either too young or too old to sit in primary school classrooms – within the schooling system. This, and the fact that the primary enrolment has increased sharply to 93 per cent, in the last five years, is an indication of an improvement in the efficiency of the education system.

## Learning in science, engineering and technology

In general, mathematical and scientific education is extremely poor in the entire schooling system. This has a detrimental effect on the number of students enrolling for studies in Science, Engineering and Technology (SET). There has been a gradual shift in enrolment away from the humanities, between 1993 and 1999, to business and commerce and SET. Although the movement is in the right direction, it is still insufficient to meet national priorities. The HRD strategy comprises a number of actions by government and the private sector to correct the situation.

## Changing labour market structure and employer responsiveness to new skill requirements

Structural changes to the labour market have resulted in employers seeking skills different to those required three decades ago. The fact that the South African economy is becoming more service- and knowledge-based each year, has far-reaching implications for the unskilled and low-skilled workforce. The HRD strategy emphasises the role of the private sector in seeking solutions to this problem which does not only impact on the labour market's ability to function properly, but also on society in general.

## Skills development for the Small to Medium Micro-Enterprise sector

The Small, Medium and Micro-Enterprise (SMME) sector is seen by Government as key to addressing many of the unemployment and socio-economic problems of the country. Surveys examining the employment of the economically active population indicate that in the order of 1.7 million persons were involved in 1995 in the informal sector of the economy (accounting for seven per cent of the gross domestic product and 18 per cent of employment). The HRD strategy emphasises skills development in terms of the SMME

sector as a key issue in order to enhance its employment-creating potential.

## 17.3.3 The labour market

### Supply of labour

The Economically Active Population (EAP) comprises the number of people, over the age of 15 years, who present their labour for remuneration on the labour market for the production of economic goods and services, whether employed or not. Barker's (2002) estimates show that the South African economically active population was in the order of 18 million in 2001. More than 70 per cent of the EAP are African and about 50 per cent are women. According to Barker (2002) 400 000 persons are entering the labour market annually looking for work. Standing et al. (1996:63) found that the size of the African working age population and overall population have been growing much faster than the size of the African employed labour force. This apparently implies that a substantial portion of those entering the labour market will not find work.

The supply of labour will be negatively affected by HIV/AIDS seeing that the overwhelming majority of persons affected by HIV/AIDS are between the key productive ages of 20 to 40 years. Barker (2002) reports that the total labour force is likely to be 21 per cent lower in 2015 than it would have been in the absence of AIDS. (See chapters 1 and 24 for more detail.)

### Demand for labour

The demand for labour is dependant on the demand for a product or service in the market. According to Barker (2002), the low demand for labour is due to low economic growth rates, the high supply of labour, and high population growth rates. These are the most important reasons for the high unemployment that South Africa is experiencing. The Survey of Employment and Earnings of Statistics South Africa shows that formal employment in non-agricultural sectors has declined by about 200 000 between September 1999 and September 2001, from 4.8 million to 4.6 million. This represents an annual decline of 1.6 per cent (Barker 2002).

## Level of literacy education of the labour force

From the point of view of economic growth and development, and of material standards of living, it is the quality of the labour force, and not just its size, that really counts. There are indications that the education level of the labour force has improved substantially over the last two decades, but that there are still a large number of illiterate people in the country. Three million South Africans cannot read or write at all, and millions more are semi-literate (RSA 2001). Barker (2002) reports that the South African Institute of Race Relations estimated that in 2000 there were 7.5 million people aged 20 years and older who were illiterate. Nearly 3 million were totally unschooled, and another 4.5 million had so little primary education that they were 'barely literate'. These figures represent an adult illiteracy rate of 29 per cent.

## 17.3.4 Supply of skills

South Africa's economy has gone through a stage of structural transformation away from activities based in the primary sectors of agriculture and mining towards more secondary and tertiary activities. This has far-reaching implications for employment patterns and the type of skills that the economy demands. This structural change in the economy, together with the low level of educational attainment among the economically active population, puts a constraint on economic development.

As far as educational attainment is concerned, among the 18 million working people 7.2 per cent had no educational qualifications in 2001; 24.4 per cent had completed education up to grade 7; 23.7 per cent had completed between grade 8 and 10; 22.3 per cent had completed grade 11 or 12 of schooling; and

6.1 per cent had a university degree or higher qualification. A further significant issue is the fact that the fields of study students follow at universities are skewed towards the humanities (opposed to science and business studies) (Department of Labour 2002).

The Department of Labour (2002) further reports that 14.9 per cent of the economically active population had received training in skills useful for work, and that 17 per cent of the employed persons have received some training in skills that are related to their work. A promising factor is that there is an indication that occupations associated with lower qualification levels, such as labourers and related workers, are receiving at least the same volume of training as those workers in higher-level occupations. This is contrary to those with higher-level qualifications, who tend to receive more training than those with lower-level qualifications.

Besides the throughput of the formal education system, which is not sufficient to fulfil the skills needs of the country, there are also poverty-related diseases, as well as migration, which impact significantly on the working age population. This represents one of most serious threats to the creation of a skilled and well-trained workforce (Department of Labour 2002).

## 17.3.5 Vocational education and training

The school-to-work transition in South Africa is not up to standard with its trade partners. There is very little linkage between school-based vocational training and in-company training. The level of enterprise-based training is low by international standards. The apprenticeship system has been declining for over a decade, and technical college education and training has, on average, produced poor outcomes. The training of unemployed persons through special training programmes is limited, and has failed to provide meaningful work opportunities. Although the private training market is relatively well developed, it specialises mainly in short courses tailored to very narrow industry demands, or focuses on communication and service-related skills (Department of Labour 1997). The new training legislation introduced by the Department of Labour is an attempt by Government to correct these and other deficiencies in the South African training market.

## 17.4   Funding of training

### 17.4.1 Who is responsible?

Historically, the role of governments, worldwide, in training has been a limited one. Private training markets were far more important. It was the small enterprises that assumed the dominant role in skill creation. Informal apprenticeships in craft trades were the primary training venue (Middleton et al. 1993).

It has always been, in general terms, the view of the government in South Africa that employers are responsible for the funding of the training of their employees, while government should be responsible for the funding of education. During the 1980s, however, government did make a significant contribution to the funding of training through the tax concession scheme for approved training. But the scheme was phased out in 1990. During the nineties the government's financial contribution to training was mainly in the areas of training of unemployed persons and the subsidisation of trade tests. The introduction of payroll levies in 1999, in terms of the Skills Development Levies Act, emphasises the responsibility of employers for the funding of the training of their employees.

Against this background the question is: What kind of policies should be introduced that would, on the one hand, place an obligation on employers and, on the other hand, encourage employers to contribute to the country's workforce? The notions of training as an investment in human capital and that it should be a key part of an enterprise's human resources development strategy, should ideally be strengthened by national economic and training policies. Policies on funding mechanisms should also be based on fundamental principles ensuring the most productive application of scarce funds.

### 17.4.2 Cost and benefit of training

#### Economic policies and incentives for skills development

There is a direct relationship between the economic environment and skills development. Quite often this relationship is overlooked in planning and policy development.

It is important for policy makers to understand the relationship between the economic environment and the incentive structure for skills development that individuals and enterprises face. Education planners and policy makers should take this incentive structure into account in anticipating the mix of public and private funding in skills development and the demand for training places. Economic planners and policy makers, on the other hand, should also consider the market signals a country's economic policies send to individuals and enterprises with regard to training and skills development, and the consequences of these signals for labour supply, economic growth, and wage and price stability.

In the following sections an outline is given of the influence of the economic environment on the cost and benefit of training.

#### Individuals, enterprises and government

The cost and benefit of training applies to individuals, enterprises and the government.

- *Individuals.* For individuals, training is at the cost of lower earnings, but could also be regarded as an investment in the sense of higher future earnings, career opportunities, and personal fulfilment. Resources used for schooling and training yield net benefits of greater value than alternative uses. Economic policies that would alter this stream of benefits and its value in relation to the value of alternative uses are expected to change an individual's incentives to acquire skills. If no jobs are available, for example, the incentive to acquire skills is reduced. Economic policies that distort relative capital and labour costs affect employment growth and eventually the pace of skills development.

- *Enterprises.* Training is perceived by enterprises as an investment but also as a cost that must be measured against potential profitability and productivity gains. The fact that training competes for an enterprise's resources with other investments, including capital investment, means that it needs to offer a greater productivity improvement than alternative uses of those resources. Like any other form of investment, training can only be seen as a nett contributor to improved efficiency if it leads to the enhancement of an enterprise's performance to the extent that the cost of training is outweighed.

The economic environment not only influences the incentive to acquire skills but also the incentive to provide training. Government interventions that distort competitive markets can also affect the willingness of enterprises to train. Because enterprises are the most efficient providers of skills training, economic policy makers must guard against policies that are detrimental to skills development by enterprises. According to Middleton et al. (1993), general economic policies, such as a minimum wage, may actually discourage enterprises from skills training. The requirement to pay minimum wages may restrict the ability of an enterprise to shift the cost of general skills training to the worker in the form of lower wages. Enterprises are quite often also reluctant to invest in general skills training because of the risk that their investment will be lost through labour turnover. The individual worker can capture all the benefits of investment in training but still leave the employer for higher wages elsewhere.

For enterprises, however, benefits of training should not be viewed strictly in mechanistic terms. Research consistently shows that those production systems that treat management, capital investment, workplace consultation, and training as an integrated whole, lead to more superior outcomes than a piecemeal approach to these issues.

Swanson (2001) emphasises the point that the outcomes of HRD programmes are valuable only to the extent that they are connected to specific organisational performance requirements. HRD programmes must further also have integrity and quality or they will not deliver the expected benefits.

- *Government.* Governments in many developing countries are faced with pressure to stabilise spending on social programmes, including education and training. At the same time, rapid population and labour force growth are increasing the demand for these services.

The question may arise: Why should governments be involved in the financing of training? According to Middleton et al. (1993), there are two main conditions that justify government intervention in the financing of training: external market benefits and striving for social equity:

  - *External market benefits:* The focus of individuals and enterprises is on higher productivity, profits and wage earnings that come from training and which affect them directly. Government, on the other hand, and representing society at large, is likely to capture the largest share from a flexible and competitive economy, which may accrue from a better-trained workforce.

  - *Social equity:* Public subsidisation of training on equity grounds for the disadvantaged, women, and marginalised youth, is justified when carefully targeted to ensure that only those in need benefit.

## Regulation and certification of training

A cost/benefit analysis with regard to training should not only be applied in the case of the provisioning of training, but also in the case of regulation and certification of training. Care should be taken to ensure that the development and implementation of qualification structures do not become cumbersome and expensive processes that eat too deeply into funds that are actually earmarked for the provision of work-place education and training. The investment made in certification systems must eventually be offset by the benefits, which government, employers and individuals eventually gain from the certification of training.

## 17.4.3 Sources and application of training funds

Funds earmarked for training usually come from four sources: government, enterprises, individuals and donors, and are usually applied in three areas, namely:
● Regulation and quality assurance.
● Training of employees.
● Training of unemployed persons and those in pre-employment programmes.

### Government

Government's involvement in the funding of training can take a variety of forms, such as:
● Vocationally-orientated education and training through the technical college system, for example, apprentice training.
● Tax credits for approved training.
● Assistance to industry through incentives encouraging employers to employ, for example, apprentices.
● Grants for training innovation and infra-structure.
● Offset of interest in terms of loans granted to individuals.
● Training of unemployed persons and other labour market programmes.
● Pre-employment training programmes.
● Cost of the regulation of training and measures to ensure quality of training.

### Enterprises

Training funded by enterprises can be divided into two broad categories:

● Enterprise-specific training that is offered by individual enterprises to its employees. This training can either be conducted according to a structured plan and format designed to develop job-related skills and competence, or unstructured on-the-job training, whereby employees are shown how to do things as the need arises and learn by doing a job.
● Industry-specific training that could either be funded through sectoral payroll levy schemes or through a national levy scheme.

### Individuals

Training expenditures by individuals include:
● Fees payable to training providers.
● Loans that have to be paid back.
● Indirect contributions made through acceptance of lower income during the period of training.

### Donors

The contribution of donors should be guided by the national human resources develop-ment targets of a country, and not by the ini-tiatives of the donors themselves, as these may not necessarily respond effectively to national goals and needs. Donors are likely to focus their contributions on research, policy design and the implementation of training and skills development systems.

### Mix of funding sources and the application of funds

The mix of sources of funding and areas of application of funds earmarked for workforce education and training is outlined in Table 17.1.

The different levels of contributions indi-cated in the matrix are arbitrary and do not necessarily reflect our views. Ideally such con-tributions should be established through negotiation, on the one hand, and the meeting of national targets, on the other hand.

**Table 17.1** Mix of sources of funding and areas of application of funds earmarked for workplace education and training

| Source of funds →<br>Areas of application ↓ | Government | Industry | Donors | Individuals |
|---|---|---|---|---|
| Regulation and quality assurance | High | Low | Medium (R&D) | Low to zero |
| Training of employees | Low | High | Low to zero | Low |
| Training of unemployed persons and pre-employment | High | Low | Medium to high | Zero |

## 17.4.4 Alternatives for generating training funds

In the discussion above, reference was made to government intervention in training as a means of obtaining external benefits which come from producing a skilled workforce that is able to adapt quickly to changing economic conditions in a global economy. Reference was also made to government intervention in order to address social disparities in access to training.

How can stable funding be secured for vocational education and training? According to Middleton et al. (1993:125), the three main sources of revenue that could be applied in this regard are as follows:

### General taxation

The generation of training funds through general taxation constitutes a vulnerable source of finance due to budgetary constraints as well as other social concerns that need to be addressed. Funds raised through general taxation are mainly for the training of the unemployed and less is used for the funding of training for the employed.

### Levies on payroll or turnover

The principle that those who benefit should be those who pay implies that the financing of entry-level training and skills upgrading for the employed should come from employers and the workers themselves.

Payroll levies, if not planned and applied correctly, may increase the cost of labour and possibly discourage employment creation. Where this occurs, employers quite often respond by substituting capital for labour, or engage in informal sector activities outside the scope of government regulations and taxes. If the training is, however, productivity-orientated, there is less reason for resistance to such a levy on the grounds of its possible negative effects on employment. Not only can improved labour productivity help to lower the unit costs of goods produced, but it can also expand output and employment as well as wages.

There are basically three types of levy systems:
- Levy-exemptions allow enterprises to prove that they have paid for approved training and avoid paying the levy.
- Levy-grant systems require payments of levies, but funds may be returned to enterprises to pay the cost of approved forms of training.
- The levy income is turned over to state-recognised organisations to provide training. Labour and business are usually part of the governance structure of these organisations.

### Private expenditure

Governments can also intervene via the tax system by introducing tax exemptions or credits for enterprises' and individuals' training expenditure. However, experience shows that for small enterprises and low-income populations, cash transfers in the form of tax rebates are more effective instruments for expanding private spending on skills training. Other alternatives are vouchers that entitle individuals to purchase approved training or loans that are either subsidised or not.

## 17.4.5 Funding mechanisms in South Africa

### Background

Funding mechanisms for training in South Africa took on various forms during the last three decades. A national tax incentive scheme for employers was in place from 1974 to 1990. The Manpower Training Act, which was introduced in 1982, provided for industries to establish a training levy scheme. Approximately 15 industry-based levy schemes were registered up to the time that new legislation was introduced in 1999, namely the Skills Development Levies Act, making provision for the funding of training. Some of the serious deficiencies of the industry-based training levy schemes were inefficient collection of levies, the inadequate coverage of the workforce, and a weak linkage between training and labour market skills needs.

A study into the funding mechanisms for training in South Africa (Department of Labour 1995) was conducted under the auspices of the then National Training Board and the National Economic and Development Labour Council (NEDLAC). Seven main conclusions were drawn from the findings, which served as the bases for subsequent policy proposals for funding mechanisms to be considered by government, namely:

- The training system is not well coordinated – there are no agreed national targets and priorities for training in South Africa, formal sector funding mechanisms do not cover all sectors, and training programmes rarely link the unemployed (and the youth) with employers.
- Employer expenditure on training is low, and there is limited external pressure to

train – mechanisms need to be found to increase the activities of individuals (and their trade unions) to pressurise employers to train and to provide portable qualifications, and government may wish to intervene with financial incentives to increase employer investment in training.

- Individual attitudes to training are restricting investment – individuals need to change their attitudes regarding their contribution towards the investment in training beyond obtaining their initial pre-employment qualifications (especially if portable qualifications are provided by employers), and government could encourage cost sharing arrangements through suitable incentive programmes.
- There are gaps in the provision of training – significant gaps exist in the provision of training for school leavers, rural people, the long-term unemployed and emerging businesses, and mechanisms are needed to encourage greater provision of technical skills training.
- The introduction of a qualification and accreditation framework is required – mechanisms are needed to encourage portability of training and for government to link the provision of public funds for training to a proper qualifications framework.
- Competition in the training supply market is constrained – many issues are currently adversely affecting the supply market. In many cases government and donors often determine demand based on insufficient information or research regarding market demand, rural areas are under-provided, and industry training boards have a 'control' over certain sectors of the market. Also, government policy needs to address   these issues.
- Barriers prevent suppliers entering the market – in addition to the above issues, investment costs for technical vocational training are high and restrict the entry of new suppliers, and the shifting allocation of government funds also creates uncer-

tainty and consequently a lack of investment.

In terms of the formal sector, the following policy options were eventually identified by the above-mentioned study:

- Option 1:
  Retain voluntary system of Industry Training Boards (ITBs).
  Retain industry based levies.
  No central coordinating body.
- Option 2:
  Introduce compulsory ITBs.
  Introduce compulsory industry-based levies.
  Allow escape clauses for certain industries.
  Consider a national tri-partite coordinating body with limited funding from ITB levies.
- Option 3:
  Introduce a national training levy.
  Establish a national coordinating body to collect and disburse funds.
- Option 4:
  Introduce a national tax incentive scheme for employers.
  Establish a national collection agency.

### Levy-grant scheme

The government eventually opted for a national levy-grant scheme when it introduced the Skills Development Levies Act (RSA 1999). The Act establishes a compulsory levy scheme for the purpose of funding education and training as envisaged in the Skills Development Act (RSA 1998).

The government decided on the levy-grant scheme because it is easier to monitor, and because the levy-grant relationship establishes a closer link between the cost and benefit of training. This improves the market discipline acting on the training undertaken by firms, which is not present in either tax incentive or subsidy schemes. In short the levy-grant scheme provides the following benefits:

- *Ensure core levels of training.* The levy-grant scheme serves as a platform for revenue allocated to training, as an active labour market policy, to enable the provision of a core level of training to be consistent with the skill requirements of the labour market. It locates the funds for training directly with the main beneficiaries, namely, the employers and unions. It will also require from employers that they consider their training needs more seriously, and that providers offer training that meets the needs of the workplace.
- *Alleviate the free-rider problem.* The levy will ensure that all firms contribute to the cost of training and therefore successfully address the free-rider problem.
- *Improve collection efficiency.* The collection of the levy by the South African Revenue Service will improve compliance and reduce administrative costs for collection.
- *Balance development and equity.* The levy scheme serves as a mechanism to redeploy resources consistent with economic needs. Training resources will be shifted to expanding sectors and sectors that are targeted for strategic development. It will further also balance regional and social needs within the country and redistribute training resources within established parameters to respond to strategic development needs and social equity.
- *Promoting training effectiveness and efficiency.* Resources, assembled on the demand side of the labour market, will be assembled to promote effectiveness and efficiency from training providers in the market system. Grants will be linked to the National Qualifications Framework which will allow for the purchase of outcomes, in the form of skills acquisition, rather than the cost of inputs.
- *Ensure multipartite participation.* The responsibility of employers and workers in the governance of training funds changes the psychology of funding in the sense that it develops a culture amongst employers and workers to accept the necessary accountability for the productive utilisation of training funds.

- *Allocate revenue to address social equity needs.* The levy-grant scheme will also allow for the training of unemployed persons and groups in the informal sector and allocations for the purpose of social equity.
- *Emphasise competitive procurement.* Training will be moved from a supply-driven to a demand-driven system. This will be achieved by awarding training grants to providers on a competitive basis.
- *Ensure proper monitoring and evaluation.* The levy-grant scheme further also has the potential for the establishment of monitorable performance indicators to evaluate the performance of the various role-players in the system.
- *Advantages of a payroll levy.* There is general consensus amongst stakeholders that a payroll levy is in the interest of equipping the country's workforce with the required skills, because (Department of Labour 2001):
  - The employers who benefit pay.
  - The payment is fair because it is based on payroll. Payroll measures workers and it is workers who must be trained.
  - The levy is one per cent of monthly payroll, which is relatively small and will not cause employers to employ fewer workers.

### Sector Education and Training Authorities

Sector Education and Training Authorities (SETAs), established in terms of the Skills Development Act, play a significant role in the collection and disbursement of levy funds. The Skills Development Levies Act stipulates that employers must pay the levy to the Commissioner for the South African Revenue Services. However, the Act also makes provision for SETAs, if they are able to meet certain criteria, to collect levies.

Of all levy funds collected, 80 per cent is paid into the bank accounts of SETAs and 20 per cent into the National Skills Fund. The levy funds paid over to SETAs are utilised to defray their administrative cost within prescribed limits and to allocate grants to employers who meet the eligibility for grant recovery.

## 17.5 Certification of training

### 17.5.1 A qualification structure

Certification of training brings with it the notion of a qualification structure. A qualification structure could be regarded as the driving force behind a Vocational Education and Training (VET) system. Besides the general objective of providing training that leads to recognised qualifications, it also facilitates accessibility towards further learning experiences. A qualification structure is therefore not aimed exclusively at obtaining a qualification at the end of a training programme, but also aims to promote admission to courses that are already under way as well as to make it easier for candidates to switch over to other education programmes, if they so wish. Besides access to training opportunities a qualification structure will also allow, for example, for different learning pathways leading to the same qualification.

Stewart (1999) refers to five key principles that should inform and guide the design and operation of any national system of education and training, namely:
- Removing barriers to access to development opportunities and qualifications.
- Recognising current ability achieved through means other than formal education and training.
- Being flexible in practice in terms both of development and assessment.
- Responding to the different needs of occupations at different levels, from foundation to professional.
- Being relevant to vocational practice.

The lack of uniformity between qualifications offered in the VET market is usually due to the absence of a national approach. Various bodies, including education departments, industry-training organisations, employers and private providers, develop occupational profiles and standards according to their own needs and insights. This method results in a wide variety of content that is of limited use in educating the country's workforce in a coherent way, and is considered to be aimless and inefficient.

Such a situation gives cause for several shortcomings:

- A wide discrepancy exists between the standards of the various courses offered in the VET market.
- Harmonisation problems occur between initial training and further training.
- The plethora of training courses and pathways that are available make it increasingly difficult for employers to determine the value of the qualifications achieved by trainees.
- Trainees find it difficult or even impossible to continue with further learning based on the results they have already achieved.
- Those who leave the education system before completion of the whole course or programme cannot show any proof of a marketable qualification.

## 17.5.2 Certification in South Africa

### National Qualifications Framework

Studies conducted during the nineties into the education and training systems in South Africa, revealed three major challenges:

- The introduction of an equitable system of education and training which serves all South Africans well. Such a system will need to accommodate those people who are in conventional schools, colleges and training programmes. It will also need to find ways to include the learning needs of the many South Africans who have not been exposed to formal education and training in the past.
- The quality of education and training is inadequate for meeting the following needs:

  - Achieving significant levels of economic growth.
  - Becoming internationally competitive.
- The perception has to be removed that education and training are not linked. Education and training have been separated, both by the way they are organised and by the way society thinks about them. For example, academic study is generally perceived to be more valuable than training for useful occupations.

These challenges prompted interested parties to find solutions that would enable the country's education and training systems to provide a productive and skilled workforce matched to the needs of employment. The answer was found in an approach that makes education and training more flexible, efficient and accessible. Eventually this led to the National Qualifications Framework (NQF).

The NQF is a framework on which standards and qualifications, agreed to by education and training stakeholders throughout the country, are registered. Registered unit standards and qualifications are structured in such a manner that learners are able, on successful completion of accredited prerequisites, to move between components of the delivery system. It further also allows for multiple pathways to the same learning end. The NQF is essentially a quality assurance system with the development and registration of standards and qualifications as the first important step in implementing a quality education and training system in South Africa. The NQF system makes provision for bodies responsible for the generation and recommendation of qualifications and standards, namely Standard Generating Bodies and National Standards Bodies respectively. The bodies responsible for quality assurance are called Education and Training Quality Assurance Bodies. The principles underlying the NQF are cited in Table 17.2.

The objectives of the NQF are as follows:

- Create an integrated national framework for learning achievements.
- Facilitate access to, and mobility and pro-

**Table 17.2** Principles underlying the NQF

| Principle | Definition – Education and training should: |
|---|---|
| Integration | form part of a system of human resources development which provides for the establishment of an integrated approach to education and training |
| Relevance | be and remain responsive and appropriate to national development needs |
| Credibility | have national and international value and acceptance |
| Coherence | work within a consistent framework of principles and certification |
| Flexibility | allow for multiple pathways to the same learning ends |
| Standards | be expressed in terms of a nationally agreed framework and internationally acceptable outcomes |
| Legitimacy | provide for the participation of all national stakeholders in the planning and coordination of standard and qualifications |
| Access | provide access to appropriate levels of education and training for all prospective learners in a manner which facilitates progression |
| Articulation | provide for learners, on successful completion of accredited prerequisites, to move between components of the delivery system |
| Progression | ensure that the framework of qualifications permits individuals to move through the levels of national qualifications via different appropriate combinations of the components of the delivery system |
| Portability | enable learners to transfer their credits or qualifications from one learning institution or employer to another |
| Recognition of prior learning | through assessment give credit to learning which has already been acquired in different ways, for example, through life experience |
| Guidance of learners | provide for the counselling of learners by specially trained individuals who meet nationally recognised standards for educator and trainers |

gression within, education, training and career paths.
- Enhance the quality of education and training.
- Accelerate the redress of past unfair discrimination in education, training and employment opportunities.
- Contribute to the full personal develop-

ment of each learner and the social and economic development of the nation at large.

The NQF consists of eight levels providing for General, Further and Higher Education and Training bands. The NQF structure is outlined in Table 17.3.

**Table 17.3** The NQF structure

| NQF Level | Band | Qualification type |
|---|---|---|
| 8 | Higher Education and Training | • Post-doctoral research degrees<br>• Doctorates |
| 7 | | • Masters degrees<br>• Professional qualifications |
| 6 | | • Honours degrees<br>• National first degrees |
| 5 | | • Higher diplomas<br>• National diplomas<br>• National certificate |
| **Further Education and Training Certificate (FETC)** | | |
| 4 | Further Education and Training | National certificates |
| 3 | | |
| 2 | | |
| **General Education and Training Certificate (GETC)** | | |
| 1 | General Education and Training | Grade 9 ABET Level 4 |

SOURCE: South African Qualifications Authority (2000a)

## Development and Implementation of the NQF

The South African Qualifications Authority, (SAQA) which came into being through the SAQA Act of 1995, is responsible for overseeing the development and implementation of the NQF.

All learning in terms of the NQF is organised into twelve areas of learning. These are called fields (see Figure 17.1). A National Standards Body (NSB) exists for each field. Members of an NSB are drawn from six constituencies, namely state departments, organised labour, organised business, providers of education and training, interest groups and community or learner organisations. The prime task of NSBs is to recommend standards and qualifications for registration on the NQF to SAQA and to ensure that all standards and qualifications fit into the NQF.

The SAQA Act requires training standards to be developed and signed off in a democratic way. This is achieved by getting everyone with a direct interest in a standard together in a Standards Generating Body (SGB) and reaching consensus as to what the learning outcomes should be. SGBs submit qualifications and standards to the relevant National Standards Body for registration on the National Qualifications Framework. SGBs are established according to sub-fields within a specific learning area, and members are drawn from the sub-field in question. The SGB for Teacher Education, for example, is made up of school teachers, professional teacher bodies, and university, college and technikon teaching staff.

To ensure that the education and training that are offered in terms of the NQF, are of high quality and in accordance with the regis-

**Figure 17.1** Fields of the NQF

- Agriculture and Nature Conservation
- Culture and Arts
- Business, Commerce and Management Studies
- Communication Studies and Language
- Education, Training and Development
- Manufacturing, Engineering and Technology
- Human and Social Studies
- Law, Military Science and Security
- Health Science and Social Services
- Physical, Mathematical, Computer and Life Sciences
- Services
- Physical Planning and Construction

SOURCE: South African Qualifications Authority (2000a)

tered standards and qualifications, SAQA accredits Education and Training Quality Assurance (ETQA) bodies. ETQAs do not set standards, but are primarily responsible for accrediting education and training providers and to certify learners. In doing so they assure the quality delivery and assessment of registered standards and qualifications. In seeking accreditation from ETQAs, providers need to fulfil *inter alia* the following criteria:

- Be registered as providers in terms of the applicable legislation.
- Have a quality management system.
- Be able to develop, deliver and evaluate learning programmes which culminate in NQF qualifications or standards.
- Have the necessary financial, administrative and physical resources.
- Have the ability to achieve the desired outcomes using available resources and procedures (South African Qualifications Authority 2000a).

### Compliance and quality assurance

The NQF is a qualification system that makes provision for the hallmarking of qualifications. In essence it means assuring employers, learners and providers that learning outcomes are relevant, market related, and in terms of nationally recognised standards.

It further also makes provision for a recognised assessment process through which learners are certified to be competent in terms of recognised standards, which serves as an assurance for the employers and the learner that a qualification earned in terms of the NQF system is valid and nationally recognised.

To ensure general acceptance of and confidence in the NQF, a comprehensive quality assurance process has been put in place. The development and registration of qualifications and standards on the NQF are, for instance, subjected to the participatory and representative structures and processes of the NSBs and SGBs. The quality of provision of education and learning, and the legitimacy of certification of learners, are ensured through the ETQA system. In essence the NQF is a system of assuring and continually re-assuring learners and other users of the education and training systems that credits, awards or certificates, issued during the learning process, adhere to the standards registered on the framework, and that all forms of provision are geared to deliver learning to the same standards for accreditation purposes. The inclusive nature of the quality assurance cycle ensures that the responsibility for setting standards and for delivery of quality education and training rests with the education and training stakeholders who participate in the SAQA processes (South African Qualifications Authority 2000b).

### NQF Qualifications

In terms of the SAQA Act a qualification is defined as the achievement of a certain number of credits embodied in a coherent number of unit standards. A qualification is a nationally agreed statement of learning achievements. The achievement of a qualification serves as proof that a learner has achieved an outcome on one of the eight levels, irrespective of when, how and where it was achieved.

**Figure 17.2** The NQF process

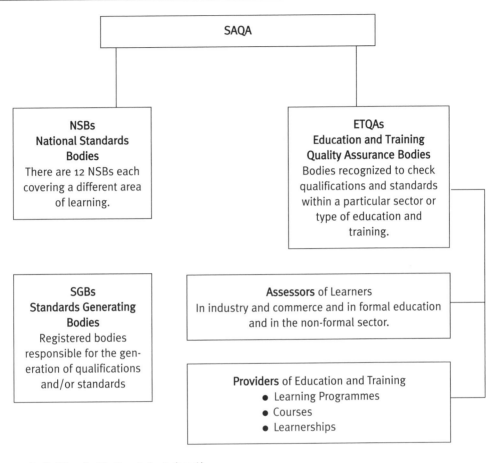

SOURCE: South African Qualifications Authority (2000b)

Qualifications are made up from unit standards which are clustered in a systematic and coherent way. Unit standards are nationally agreed and comparable statements supported by specific outcomes and assessment criteria. Unit standards are packaged according to specific criteria to establish a qualification.

All qualifications are made up by three elements:

- Fundamental elements being competencies needed to successfully undertake the learning contained in the qualification, for instance functional literacy and numeracy.

- Core elements being the contextual elements to the relevant qualification.

- Elective elements being optional elements from which learners may choose.

The minimum requirements a qualification must comply with, are as follows:

- Represent a planned combination of learning outcomes which has a defined purpose and which is intended to provide qualifying learners with applied competence and a basis for further learning.

- Add value to the qualifying learner by

providing status, recognition, enhancing marketability and employability.

- Provide benefits to society and the economy.
- Comply with the objectives of the NQF by enhancing access to learning, mobility and progression and national recognition.
- Embody specific and critical cross-field outcomes that promote life-long learning.
- Be internationally comparable, where applicable.

Through an accreditation process, learners and other users of the NQF system are assured that a learner who has achieved a qualification has demonstrated the required learning outcomes in terms of the NQF framework (South African Qualifications Framework 2000b).

## 17.6   Training legislation

### 17.6.1 Introduction

The training environment, as emphasised in previous chapters, should not be viewed in isolation but against the background of current economic, technological, social and political factors that are in the process of transforming the working world. In Section 17.2 and 17.3 it was shown that the responsibility of reforming the training system in response to changing demands rests with the state. In fulfilling this core function the state is faced with the dilemma of increasing the relevance, effectiveness, efficiency, equality and sustainability of the training system to meet new requirements at a time of reduction in public spending. The training system in South Africa, as in many other countries, is receiving severe criticism for lacking relevance to market demands. It is a universal problem of training systems being trapped in tradition and bureaucracy and unable to respond to rapidly changing labour markets. The government in South Africa is faced with the challenge of balancing the demand for a skilled and flexible labour force to make industries in the country more competitive, on the one hand, and, on the other hand, to ensure equal

access for all citizens to training opportunities as well as to redress disadvantages faced by particular groups.

To influence the training system and bring about the necessary changes to meet new challenges, the state is compelled to take the lead in developing policy that is supportive of the economic and social changes the country is facing. Hand in hand with policy goes legislation that should make provision for enabling mechanisms but that will also regulate the actions and inputs of those involved in the training market.

In this section, the focus falls on the legislation, governing training and skills development in South Africa.

### 17.6.2 The background to the current training legislation

The South African training legislation went through different stages, each being characterised by the political climate of the day. Prior to 1981, racial discrimination was still entrenched in training legislation, making it illegal for blacks to be indentured as apprentices. Arising from the Wiehahn Commission's report in which it was recommended that industrial relations be de-racialised, the Manpower Training Act was passed in 1981. For the first time training legislation did not particularly refer to racial categories. The Act also introduced for the first time a tripartite forum, namely the National Training Board, to advise the relevant Minister on training matters. In 1991, the Manpower Training Act was amended to make provision for the establishment of Industry Training Boards (ITBs). ITBs were made responsible for the training of all workers in their respective industries, including the management of apprenticeships and trade testing.

The foundation for the current training legislation was laid by the work of a representative Task Team (under the auspices of the then National Training Board), consisting of four constituencies, namely business, trade unions, the state, and providers of education and training. The Task Team conducted its work in accordance with the following vision: 'A human resources system in which there is an integrated approach to education and training and which meets the economic and social needs of the country and the development needs of individuals.'

Arising from the Task Team's report, three totally new pieces of training legislation were developed and enacted by Parliament, namely the Skills Development Act, Skills Development Levies Act and the South African Qualifications Authority Act.

## 17.6.3 Skills Development Act

### Rationale for the Skills Development Act

South Africa has a poor skills profile as a result of the poor quality of general education for the majority of South Africans, the low relevance of much publicly funded training, and the low level of investment by companies in training. This poor profile inhibits productivity growth in companies, new investment prospects, and employability of the young and unemployed. The sustainability of small and medium-sized enterprises is similarly impaired.

The Skills Development Act seeks to develop the skills of the South African workforce and thereby increase the quality of working life for workers, improve the productivity of the workplace, and promote self-employment and the delivery of social services. The Act also seeks to encourage employers to use the workplace as an active learning environment and to provide opportunities for new entrants to the labour market to gain work experience.

A special focus in the Act is to improve the employment prospects of previously disadvantaged persons through education and training. The employment services are to focus on helping work-seekers to find work, retrenched workers to re-enter the labour market, and employers to find qualified employees.

Alignment of the Skills Development Act and the South African Qualifications Authority Act is ensured so as to promote the quality of learning in and for the labour market. The Act also gives organised employers and workers greater responsibility for ensuring the relevance of training, which will enhance quality (RSA 1998).

### Objectives of the Skills Development Act

The objectives of the Act, as well as the Skills Development Levies Act, are to be achieved by establishing a stronger institutional and financial framework than previously existed under the Manpower Training Act. The National Training Board is replaced by a National Skills Authority (NSA). The NSA is an advisory body to the Minister of Labour with responsibility for ensuring that national skills development strategies, plans, priorities, and targets are set and adhered to. Industry training boards are replaced by sector education and training authorities (SETAs), responsible for developing sector skills plans that correspond to the national skills strategies and targets. The sector skills plans will be presented to the National Skills Authority and approved by the Minister of Labour.

The functions of the National Skills Authority are:
- To advise the Minister of Labour on:
  - A national skills development policy.
  - A National Skills Development Strategy.
  - Guidelines on the implementation of the National Skills Development Strategy.
  - Allocation of subsidies from the National Skills Fund.
  - Any regulations to be made.
- To liaise with Sector Education and Training Authorities (SETAs) on:
  - The national skills development policy.
  - The National Skills Development Strategy.
- To report to the Minister on progress made in the implementation of the National Skills Development Strategy.
- To conduct investigations arising out of the Skills Development Act.

Two learning programmes are identified in the Act: learnerships and skills programmes. Learnerships have replaced traditional apprenticeships. They include structured learning and work experiences that lead to nationally registered, occupationally linked qualifications in areas of skill, need or opportunity in the labour market. Skills programmes assist young unemployed people to enter employment, as well as existing workers to improve their skill levels. Skills programmes are not learnerships, but should also meet quality and relevance criteria to qualify for grant payments from SETAs or the National Skills Fund.

A learnership is a mechanism to facilitate the linkage between structured learning and work experience in order to obtain a registered qualification that signifies work readiness.

The decline in traditional apprenticeships over the last decade has prompted the relevant role-players to seek a new mechanism to facilitate more flexible learning arrangements that are linked to the NQF.

A learnership consists of combined structured learning and work experience components. The structured learning component includes fundamental learning, core learning, and specialisation. The work experience component relates to the structured learning, and prepares the learner for competence assessment.

The functions of SETAs are:
- To develop a sector skills plan within the framework of the National Skills Development Strategy.
- To implement its sector skills plan by:
  - Establishing learnerships.
  - Approving workplace skills plans.
  - Allocating grants to employers, education and training providers and workers.
  - Monitoring education and training in the sector.
- To promote learnerships by:
  - Identifying workplaces for practical work experience.
  - Supporting the development of learn-

ing materials.
  - Improving the facilitation of learning.
  - Assisting in the conclusion of learnership agreements.
- To register learnership agreements.
- To collect and disburse the skills development levies in its sector.
- To liaise with the National Skills Authority on:
  - The national skills development policy.
  - The National Skills Development Strategy.
  - Its sector skills plan.
- To liaise with the employment services of the Department of Labour and any education body to improve information:
  - About employment opportunities.
  - Between education and training providers and the labour market.

## 17.6.4 Skills Development Levies Act

### Rationale for the Skills Development Levies Act

The rationale for a national levy scheme for skills development is premised on the assumption that effective skills formation requires a strong link between occupationally based education and training and the workplace. The Skills Development Levies Act provides a regulatory framework to address the current low level of investment by companies in training. The Act establishes a compulsory levy scheme for the purpose of funding education and training as envisaged in the Skills Development Act (RSA 1998).

### Objectives of the Act

The Act introduces a levy equivalent to one per cent of employers' payroll per month.

Employers must pay the levy to the Commissioner for the South African Revenue Service. However, where the Minister of Labour and Minister of Finance are satisfied that sufficient grounds exist, and where certain criteria are met, they may grant permission for employers within the jurisdiction of a particular SETA to pay their levies directly to that particular SETA. Twenty per cent of the funds collected will be allocated to the National Skills Fund established by the Skills Development Act. Together with the money received from the fiscus, this money is used to fund national skills priorities. The remaining 80 per cent of the levies must be paid into the bank accounts of the various SETAs to fund the performance of their functions and pay for their administration within the prescribed limit. Where there is not a SETA, funds for that sector are  paid into the National Skills Fund. The Skills Development Act requires national and provincial government departments to budget at least one per cent of personnel costs for skills development. The same applies to national and provincial public entities, where 80 per cent or more of their expenditure is defrayed directly or indirectly from funds voted by Parliament. All public service employers in the national and provincial spheres of government and the said national and provincial public entities are, therefore, exempted from the payment of the levy. Those employers not required to register for employees' tax purposes in terms of the Fourth Schedule to the Income Tax Act, No. 58 of 1962, and whose total annual wage bill is less than R250 000, are also exempted. The Bill makes provision that the levy is not payable by:

- Any religious or charitable institution contemplated in section 10(1)(f) of the Income Tax Act of 1962, or any fund contemplated in section 10(1)(a) of the Act, established to provide funds to any such institution.
- Any national or provincial public entity where 80 per cent or more of its expenditure is defrayed directly or indirectly from funds voted by Parliament (RSA 1999).

## 17.6.5 South African Qualifications Authority Act

### Rationale for the South African Qualifications Authority Act

The plethora of training qualifications and pathways that are available on the training market make it increasingly difficult for learners to judge the credibility and market value of a course and for employers to determine the value of the qualifications achieved by trainees. The South African Qualifications Authority Act successfully addresses this problem by providing a regulatory framework for a comprehensive national recognition framework consisting of national standards to improve the quality and relevance of training. The object of the Act establishes the South African Qualifications Authority (SAQA), whose function it is to oversee the development and implementation of the National Qualifications Framework. The NQF serves as a vehicle to create an integrated national framework for learning achievements and to enhance access to and mobility and quality within the components of the education and training delivery system (RSA 1995).

The vision of the South African Qualifications Authority is to develop an education and training system that reflects the objectives of the National Qualifications Framework. The mission, on the other hand, is to ensure the development and implementation of a National Qualifications Framework which contributes to the full development of each learner and to the social and economic development of the nation at large (South African Qualifications Authority 2000a).

## 17.7 National Skills Development Strategy

The Skills Development  Act and the Skills Development Levies Act , discussed in the former sections, charged the Minister of Labour to prepare a National Skills Development

Strategy, covering the period April 2001 to March 2005. The Strategy is designed to support economic and employment growth and social development.

The title of the Strategy document, 'Skills for productive citizenship for all', summarises the vision for the future. The vision includes the following:

- *Skills:* Skills development is about empowering and enabling individuals to acquire skills and competencies that are in demand. Skills must be linked to qualifications that are part of the National Qualifications Framework.
- *Productive citizenship:* Citizenship includes the right to actively contribute to and participate in making decisions that affect investment and work. Skills development needs to enable individuals to engage in decisions regarding productivity, the organisation of work and technology, entrepreneurship, sustainability and growth.
- *For all:* The strategy provides opportunities for those in work as well as for the unemployed, for new entrants to the world of work as well as for older people, for women as well as men, and for people with disabilities.

The vision is underpinned by six guiding principles:

- *Life-long learning:* The ongoing changes in communities and the workplace require that individuals continuously upgrade and improve their skills.
- *Promotion of equity:* Skills development needs to provide not only opportunities for disadvantaged groups but also encouragement of effective collaboration amongst people from diverse backgrounds.
- *Demand-led:* The emphasis will be on skills and competencies required to support productivity, international competitiveness, the mobility of workers, self-employment, and meeting community needs.
- *Flexibility and decentralisation:* The role

of Government is to provide the framework, direction and coordination, and to monitor implementation. Employers and workers need to make judgements about priorities and determine the most effective providers to meet their needs.
- *Partnership and cooperation:* The implementation of the strategy should be based on partnerships between and amongst social constituencies.
- *Efficiency and effectiveness:* The delivery of skills development programmes and initiatives must be characterised by cost-efficiency and should lead to positive outcomes.

The mission statement, to encapsulate the goals of the National Skills Development Strategy, reads as follows: 'To equip South Africa with the skills to succeed in the global market and to offer opportunities to individuals and communities for self-advancement to enable them to play a productive role in society.'

In fulfilling this mission, five objectives have been identified to drive the National Skills Development Strategy:
- To develop a culture of high quality life-long learning.
- To foster skills development in small businesses.
- To stimulate and support skills development in small business.
- To promote skills development for employability and sustainable livelihoods through social initiatives.
- To assist new entrants into employment.

These objectives will frame the work of the Department of Labour and the Sector Education and Training Authorities. They also define the uses of the National Skills Fund and the skills development levies. The objectives offer priorities around which government, employers, trade unions, and the wider community can unite to achieve the skills revolution South Africa so badly requires.

To monitor the roll-out of the National Skills Development Strategy, success indicators have been defined in terms of national targets to be met at predetermined target dates.

The National Skills Development Strategy charts the ways in which South Africa can build its skills to enable it to compete more successfully in the global economy, attract investments, enable individuals and communities to grow to eradicate poverty, and to build a more inclusive and equal society. It is based on the conviction that South Africa has the means and the will to make progress to ensure a better life for all (Department of Labour 2001).

## 17.8 Universal principles underpinning training and skills development policies

The nature and the pace of development of economies varies from country to country. The one single factor that is critical for a country to secure the competitive advantages offered by international markets in growing its economy, is the quality of its workforce. In designing its education and training policies, a country needs to take into account factors unique to its political, social and economic environment, at a specific point in time. There are, however, a number of universal principles any country should consider in the design and implementation of human resources development policies.

South Africa's future economic and social challenges will inevitably influence national and sectoral policies and strategies in the medium to long term. The country's economic challenges will come from a competitive global economy requiring a world-class workforce. Its social challenges, on the other hand, will come from the quest to build a democratic, non-racial, non-sexist future. The quality of South Africa's human resources is central to both challenges, and is the prime factor in determining the country's continuing progress and prosperity.

The advent of the new political era opened a window of opportunity, from a strategic management point of view, which provides excellent opportunities to create a policy environment with the potential of steering the country, within the next 20 to 30 years, towards becoming one of the world's developed nations. Judging from various policy documents and initiatives, human resources development has shifted to the centre stage of the strategic management environment. Conceptually, this is a major victory for the country on its road to prosperity and social equity. However, the vital question is: What type of investments in the country's human resources will eventually yield the returns that are vital for sustainable growth and development?

This section will concentrate on a number of universal principles underpinning training and skills development policies, which many of the more progressive countries apply with great success. The following areas will be touched on briefly: strategic partnerships between stakeholders; an education system that is supportive of economic growth; a vocational education and training system that is flexible and responsive to market demands; interventions in the informal sector to stimulate employment creation, and provide public training programmes for the unemployed.

- *Principle 1.* Align human resources development policies with economic and social development policies to ensure that:
  - The education and training systems are responsive to the skill needs of the economy and society.
  - Education and training initiatives are supportive of business activity and the improvement of the national quality of life.
  - In the face of global competition, South Africa's industries are competitive.

The lessons from the successful newly industrialised economies indicate that there is no quick-fix solution to achieving sustainable growth and development that would enable the country to provide for the basic needs of its citizens. A long-term vision, supported by effective growth and development policies, is needed to achieve the desired results. The prerequisite for growth and development is empowered people who are skilled and motivated to create wealth as well as to share in it by means of the participation in the economy and society. Against this background, it is essential for South Africa to align its human resources policies with policies that are aimed at the stimulation of industrial and economic growth.

- *Principle 2.* Introduce measures to turn around the current enrolment ratio of universities to career institutions (technical colleges and technikons), to ensure:
  - Education institutions provide for the envisaged needs of the economy.
  - The science and engineering workforce is improved quantitatively and qualitatively.

From international comparisons it is apparent that South Africa is sadly lacking in engineers and scientists, and would be faced with a dilemma were the economy to improve substantially. Add to this the unfavourable enrolment ratio of universities to technikons, and it becomes evident that market-orientated education and training policies are vital for South Africa in its quest to achieve higher economic growth rates and greater social equity. Policy makers in the field of tertiary and further education and training should seriously consider implementing policies that would stimulate growth in the science and engineering workforce by turning around the current enrolment ratio of universities to career institutions.

- *Principle 3.* Establish strategic partnerships between the state and enterprises that are based on mutual trust, co-determination and sharing of responsibility.

Public-private collaboration takes place at both the macro- and micro-levels in a wide range of areas. The value of these partnerships lies not only on the opera-

tional level but in that they could also be directed towards priority areas for national and local development which have a strategic impact on functional areas such as the provision of skilled human resources for the economy. Critical areas for collaboration in skills development are the following:

- *Training policy development.* Policies give specific signals to different stakeholders. They also influence decisions and can be instrumental in building commitment among enterprises to invest in skills development. Policies could also influence decisions made by individuals to acquire skills and the provision of training by private providers. One of the values of public-private partnerships in the training policy environment is that policies stand a better chance to be market-driven. Another benefit, from the state's point of view, is the commitment of enterprises and private providers to actively support the implementation of training policies. From the private sector's point of view, the value of a partnership is that it could influence policy to suit or benefit their own interests provided they are aligned with the national interest.

- *Financing.* Collaboration in this area includes the exploitation of new sources of financing from the various stakeholders, incentives for investment in training with a view to encouraging voluntary initiatives, and the joint management of funds by social partners.

- *Delivery of training services.* Collective arrangements between the state and the private training market for the delivery of training have a benefit in that it leads to the improvement of the performance of public training institutions in terms of relevance, effectiveness and efficiency of training when enterprises are involved in its design, delivery and quality control. A further value is that it encourages the private sector, particularly enterprises, to share their experience and infrastructure with a view to increasing the training capacity of the country in the most cost-effective way.

- *Principle 4.* Institute a world-class education system that has the potential to:
  - Instil a culture of learning and a sense of discipline.
  - Provide for the basic learning needs of all citizens.
  - Respond to the needs of the economy.
  - Equip students with the desired knowledge, understanding and attitudes.

There is no doubt that the current deficiencies in South Africa's education system constitute a major threat for future growth and development. The system not only lacks a culture of learning and a sense of discipline but also struggles to prove its relevance. The education system seems unable to meet the requirements that employers expect from their employees. Education also seems to trail behind the technological developments experienced by industry. The end result is wide discrepancies between the competence of workers and the requirements necessary to fulfil certain functions within the employment system.

- *Principle 5.* Ensure that the vocational education and training system is able to:
  - Respond quickly to changing skill needs.
  - Provide the critical interface between the general education system and the working world.
  - Create opportunities for workers to upgrade their skills on a continuous basis.

A dynamic Vocational Education and Training (VET) system not only serves as the critical interface between the general education system and the working world, but is also regarded as the decisive factor determining the competitive strength of South Africa's economy. The following essentials are fundamental to a VET system that would respond sufficiently to the needs of individuals, the community, and the economy:

- It should be based on sound initial education. Employers and training providers expect trainees to at least possess basic literacy and numeracy skills in order to be able to react positively to education and training programmes.
- It should be able to respond quickly to market demands. Critical in this regard is who is in control of policy design and implementation. International experience proves that VET systems that are mainly teacher-controlled tend to have a very strong supply-driven character. In an attempt to move the centre of gravity of the VET system from a supply-driven to a demand-driven system, South Africa should take the option of the full involvement of industry (social partners) in the designing and execution of VET programmes.
- It should be underpinned by a national qualification structure. A qualification structure should not serve exclusively as a mechanism to award a qualification at the end of a training programme, but should also promote admission to courses that are already under way, and make it easier for candidates to switch over to other education and training programmes if they so wish.
- It should provide for key actors in the labour market to be involved. The active role to be played by the social partners in designing policy and training specifications establishes the notion of co-responsibility for a skilled and flexible workforce – one of the essentials for competitive industries.
- It should provide for a broad-to-specific approach. Within similar

learnerships, training should start with vocational foundation training which is the same for all trainees. In the second stage, learnerships within similar trades should be grouped together before the training becomes highly specialised in the final stage.

- It should provide for initial work-based training. As there is currently very little linkage to school-based vocational training, consideration should be given to bringing work-based training, provided by enterprises, into the ambit of the VET system.
- It should complement occupational skills with transferable life skills. Besides occupational competence, emphasis should be placed on personal and social competence as well as methodological competence. The ability to plan, execute and monitor one's work in a self-reliant manner should serve as a guideline in the structuring of the training curriculum. Personal and social competence consists of skills related to motivation, decision-making and the ability to work in a team. Methodological competence consists of abstract and logical reasoning and problem-solving strategies.

- *Principle 6.* Target the informal sector as an area for intervention by using training as an instrument to transfer knowledge, skills and attitudes by focusing on:
  - Areas in the informal sector that have the potential for sustainable growth.
  - The real needs and problems of the target group.
  - The possibility of integrating training with other interventions.

There is a growing awareness of the SMME sector's potential for job creation. It is generally accepted among planners that the formal economy will not generate sufficient employment for the expanding labour force in South Africa. Those that cannot be absorbed by the formal economy turn to the informal sector as a means of survival. The records show that more than three-quarters of the working population in developing countries eke out a meagre living in the informal sector. Training is an intervention that has stood the test of viability and cost effectiveness worldwide, and is seen as an instrument to transfer knowledge, skills and attitudes to ensure that business activities in the informal sector are more than just a means of subsistence. In order to yield returns, training must, however, ensure greater efficiency, and minimise the risk of informal sector operators ignoring the most basic business principles. There are a number of prerequisites in order for training to be successful as an intervention in the informal sector:

- Training should not be seen as a means to create jobs, apart from those for trainers and support staff, and should therefore not be designed and implemented in isolation, but should be integrated with other interventions.
- Training interventions should be based on knowledge of the people, their environment and their major problems and aspirations.
- Training should not be offered as a social service but rather as a response to market stimuli. It should correspond to national training policies and fit in with national training practices and the prevailing labour market situation.

- *Principle 7.* Training provided to the unemployed should form an integral part of active labour market policies by ensuring a linkage between training and job placement, unemployment benefits and growth industries. Active labour market policies portray a progressive shift of resources from passive income support for the unemployed to active measures. Training should not be a goal in itself but should improve access to jobs, develop job-related skills and promote efficient labour markets by establishing an inter-face between the supply and demand of qualified labour. The training of the unemployed is justified from a social equity point of view, as well as in terms of the government's commitment to fight unemployment. To improve cost-effectiveness, policy makers should seri-ously consider linking the current train-ing programme with other measures, such as job placement and employment benefits, in order to minimise the risk of trainees not accessing the labour market. Although training of the unemployed is regarded as of great importance, broad training programmes, aimed at large groups have proved not to be cost-effective. To ensure that training pays dividends, the following policy issues should be considered:

- Target and diversify training pro-grammes for the unemployed based on thorough assessment of labour market needs.
- Purchase training for the unemployed on a competitive basis in the private and public training markets.
- Involve all key players at local level – employees, trade unions, education institutions, provincial and local gov-ernments – in a combined effort to develop training programmes that respond to local needs.

## 17.9  Conclusion

The new world economy, characterised by global markets and fierce competition by countries in an attempt to secure maximum market share, gave cause to the emergence of service and knowledge-based industries as an important source of employment. This forces countries to approach education and training from a strategic point of view in order to be able to respond to the need for improved labour productivity and a more flexible work-force. The notion of training as an investment in human capital raises the question of who should be responsible for training and what

are the respective roles of governments, employers and individuals in this regard. This chapter addresses the cost and benefit of training, alternatives for generating training funds and the funding mechanism adapted by the South African government. Fundamental to recognized and quality training is the issue of certification. The South African Quali-fications Authority (SAQA) is responsible for the development and implementation of the National Qualifications Framework (NQF) which makes provision for national standards and qualifications. The role and functions of SAQA and its supporting structures are dis-cussed and explained in this chapter. Atten-tion is also given to the legislative framework governing training in general, the funding of training and the certification of training. The chapter concludes with a reflection on univer-sal principles underpinning successful train-ing and skills development policies against the background of the challenges facing a country in the face of global competition.

## Summary

- A variety of factors in the contemporary workplace demand a strategic corporate approach to, as well as a formal and organised state programme that addresses and assists with, ongoing education and training. We can only deal in generalisa-tions and broad-brush strokes here: the majority of the national workforce is illit-erate, the labour market has a poor skills base, and the economy is marked by low productivity and poor quality produc-tion. There is also a real need to ensure socio-economic equality (present same-ness of conditions on the basis of a dis-criminatory past) and equity (future-ori-entated sameness in opportunities and life-chances). More broadly, there is a demand for global and international competence and success.
- It is clear that corporate and organisa-tional prosperity is inseperable from social responsibility and investment in human capital, two issues of particular

pertinence in South Africa given its divided past and shortcomings in the present global knowledge economy. Human resources development is at the centre of efforts to meet and manage these demands.

- There is a need for a comprehensive and coherent national skills development and qualifications framework. Training and education programmes need to be implemented with rigid and meticulous standards, quality assurance mechanisms, monitoring and regulatory structures, and certification procedures. In this regard, learnerships are increasingly offered to workers and employees so as to ensure professionalism and progress in the market.
- The state is now able to forge new alliances in the name of economic improvement and human development: individuals, enterprises and government are now inter-related in seeking an empowered workforce. The state facilitates learnerships and vocational education and training, through Sector Education and Training Authorities, who act in turn in accordance with the National Qualifications Framework under the South African Qualifications Act, by incentivising skills development (corresponding to the Skills Development Act) through the Skills Development Levy. Here the individual is assisted by the state, as is the organisation in which the individual is employed.
- Fundamental to recognised and quality training is the issue of certification. Remember: quality assurance is the very core of HRD. The South African Qualifications Authority is responsible for the development and implementation of the National Qualifications Framework , which makes provision for national standards and qualifications.

## Case study

Skills Vision is a consultancy firm advising multinational companies on skills development strategies and how to maximise investments in human resources development. Western Enterprises, an international mining company, commissioned Skills Vision to advise them on South African training legislation and to develop a strategy and a plan of action that is not only in compliance with South Africa's laws and socio-economic challenges, but that would also guarantee an acceptable return on the investment in developing their workforce.

Skills Vision embarked on a process of liaising with the relevant government authorities and the statutory bodies entrusted with skills development in the mining industry. Their point of departure was to develop a strategy that would balance the skills development needs and requirements of Western Enterprises with that of the country in general. They successfully managed to obtain the necessary approval for importing workers with specialised skills and to convince Western Enterprises to register 2 000 learnerships with the Sector Education and Training Authority of the mining industry. The National Skills Development Strategy designed by Skills Vision made provision for Western Enterprise to fully capitalise on the returns the levy-grant system, a statutory obligation, offers. This enabled Western Enterprises to recoup a large amount of the funds they invest in training annually. Western Enterprises has been singled out, through a survey on skills development initiatives in the mining industry, as a company that fully embraces the Government's skills development strategies with the added benefit of sufficiently providing in their skills and human resources development needs.

# Chapter questions

1   Identify the macro economic issues that impact on training policies worldwide.
2   The question is: Does South Africa have a sufficient skills base in the face of global competition? Express an opinion on this question by motivating your view.
3   Discuss the cost and benefit of training from the employer's and government's point of view.
4   Critique the levy-grant system from a commercial as well as a socio-economic point of view.
5   What benefits could employers and workers derive from the certification of training qualifications? Address this question from a general education point of view as well as from a commercial point of view.
6   Do you believe the state should regulate skills development to a greater extent? Motivate your answer by referring specifically to the responsibilities of the various social partners.
7   Critique the universal principles underpinning training and skills development listed in this chapter.

# Bibliography

AUSTRALIAN NATIONAL TRAINING AUTHORITY (ANTA). 1998. *A bridge to the future – Australia's National Strategy for Vocational Education and Training, 1998–2003*. ANTA, Brisbane.

BARKER. F. 2002. *The South African labour market, 4th edition*. Van Schaik, Pretoria.

DEPARTMENT OF LABOUR. 1995. *South African funding mechanism research, industry training – Supply and competition*. Department of Labour, Pretoria.

DEPARTMENT OF LABOUR. 1997. *Green Paper: Skills development strategy for economic and employment growth in South Africa*. Department of Labour, Pretoria.

DEPARTMENT OF LABOUR. 2001. *The National Skills Development Strategy*. Department of Labout, Pretoria.

DEPARTMENT OF LABOUR. 2002. *The state of skills in South Africa*. Pretoria. Department of Labour, Pretoria.

MIDDLETON, J., ZIDERMAN, A. & ADAMS, A.V. 1993. *Skills for productivity*. Oxford University Press, New York.

RSA (REPUBLIC OF SOUTH AFRICA). 1995. *South African Qualifications Authority Act*, No. 58 of 1995. Government Gazette, No. 16725. Government Printer, Pretoria.

RSA (REPUBLIC OF SOUTH AFRICA). 1998. *Skills Development Act*, No. 97 of 1998 Government Gazette, No. 19420. Government Printer, Pretoria.

RSA (REPUBLIC OF SOUTH AFRICA). 1999. *Skills Development Levies Act*, No. 9 of 1999. Government Gazette, No. 19984. Government Printer, Pretoria.

RSA (REPUBLIC OF SOUTH AFRICA). 2001. *Human resources development strategy for South Africa*. Government Printer, Pretoria.

SOUTH AFRICAN QUALIFICATIONS AUTHORITY (SAQA). 2000a. *The National Qualifications Framework and standards setting*. SAQA, Pretoria.

SOUTH AFRICAN QUALIFICATIONS AUTHORITY (SAQA). 2000b. *The National Qualifications Framework and quality assurance*. SAQA, Pretoria.

STANDING, G., SENDER, J. & WEEKS, J. 1996. *Restructuring the labour market: The South African challenge*. International Labour Organisation, Geneva.

STEWART, J. 1999. *Employee development practice*. Financial Times Management, London.

SWANSON, R.A. 2001. *Assessing the financial benefits of human resource development*. Persues Publishing, Cambridge.

# Websites

South African government: www.gov.za
Department of Labour: www.labour.gov.za
Department of Education: www.education.pwv.gov.za

# 18

# Training and development of employees and career management at organisational level

PS Nel

## Learning outcomes

At the end of this chapter the learner should be able to:

- Explain the difference between education, training, and development.
- Compile his/her own strategic training and development model for his/her organisation.
- Explain the different elements of a training programme you identified or designed and the contribution it can make towards effective training and development.
- Be able to identify and apply training methods relevant to a particular training situation.
- Be able to design and apply an evaluation model for the training and development employees have undergone.
- Explain the difference between training, development, and career management.
- Be able to distinguish between career planning and career development.
- Draw up a programme to establish a career path for an employee.

## Key words and concepts

- apprentice training
- adult learning
- brainstorming
- career management
- career stages
- case study method
- coaching
- competency
- development
- diversity training
- education
- Human Resources Development (HRD)
- in-basket exercises
- job analysis
- job rotation
- management development
- management games
- managerial obsolescence
- needs assessment
- On-the-Job Training (OJT)
- Outcomes-based education and training
- performance gap
- programmed instruction
- promotion
- recognition of prior learning

- roleplaying
- sensitivity training
- training and development models
- training and development evaluation
- vestibule training

## Illustrative case

### The Training Seemed Irrelevant

Samuel Mokena is a regional manager for an organisation called Nation Profin Inc., and operates in the financial sector. The organisation runs office operations to service clients in various regions based on the provinces throughout Southern Africa including Botswana, which is regarded as one comprehensive region. Within these regions there are branches that are run by a branch manager, assisted by a resource manager. The senior management team for the organisation is based in Johannesburg and has the responsibility of providing resource and training for all the regions. As a regional manager in Cape Town responsible for the whole of the Western Cape, Samuel, along with two other regional managers, had been asked by senior management to do training in their management software, which incorporates human resources, financial, and accounts management. Samuel naturally accepted the opportunity for training, but wondered how it would benefit him when he was not expected to use the software, as it was the resource manager's responsibility. The resource managers had been using the management software for sometime and clearly did not require any assistance.

It was later found that the resource managers did not want Samuel or other branch managers to be trained in the use of the software as they did not want them to have access to the accounts and financial information that explicitly showed how resources and finances were allocated. It was proven that the training acquired by the regional or for that matter branch managers (who have seniority over the resource managers), would

enable them to reveal inconsistencies within financial statements and maintain control of the leadership of a branch without compromising their position by having wayward claims through allocation of resources and finance. Ultimately, the mere suggestion from the senior managers that Samuel and his colleagues would be doing the training was uncomfortable for the resource managers who had autonomy with the finance and resources for the Cape Town regional office and all other branches. This strategy highlighted that training was not only for those who would use the software as a day-to-day tool, but also for those in authority who had the ultimate responsibility for the output of the branch.

This case clearly shows that even innocent endeavours to enhance training in an organisation can have repercussions. All training and development should therefore be approached with sensitivity and awareness of its possible implications.

## 18.1  Introduction

In the previous chapter the macro-environment regarding human resources training and development was discussed. Aspects such as the macro-economic context, training legislation, funding of training, certification of training, the South African Qualifications Authority (SAQA) and the National Qualifications Framework (NQF) were focused on. The national training strategy was also outlined to provide the context within which the development of employees at organisational level takes place.

This chapter focuses on operational issues relating to training and development at organisational level that are of vital importance for the human resources staff to foster a learning culture that will eventually contribute meaningfully to the bottom line of the organisation. The chapter is concluded with a focus on career management as an additional intervention to develop employees and to prepare them for their upward mobility in an organisation, once they are adequately skilled in the required facets of business.

## 18.2 Clarification of concepts

### 18.2.1 The concept of 'education'

The concept of education refers to activities directed at providing the knowledge, skills, moral values, and understanding required in the normal course of life. The approach thus focuses on a wide range of activities rather than on providing knowledge and skills for a limited field or activity. Education is therefore concerned with the development of sound-reasoning processes to enhance one's ability to understand and interpret knowledge. De Cenzo and Robbins (1994:265) define it as the deliberate, systematic and sustained effort to transmit, evoke or acquire knowledge, attitudes, values, skills and sensibilities, and any learning that results from such effort, whether intended or unintended. Education therefore refers to a process of deliberately and purposefully influencing and shaping the behaviour of people.

Education in essence creates a general base that prepares the individual for life without any specific job-related skills being developed. The concepts training and development, however, guide an individual, and prepare him/her to perform specific activities as directed by the job they occupy or aspire to. These concepts are elucidated below.

### 18.2.2 The concept of 'training'

According to De Cenzo and Robbins (1994: 255), 'training is a learning experience in that it seeks a relatively permanent change in an individual that will improve his or her ability to perform on the job.' Training can therefore be regarded as a planned process to modify attitude, knowledge or skilled behaviour through learning experience, so as to achieve effective performance in an activity or range of activities. Its purpose, in the work situation, is to develop the abilities of the individ-

ual and to satisfy the current and future needs of the organisation. Training brings about behaviour changes required to meet management's goals for the organisation. It is thus a major management tool to develop the full effectiveness of the organisation's most important resource: its people.

Training is executed to ensure that a task is performed correctly, and therefore the behaviour change brought about by training must be measurable in terms of an organisation's requirements. Consequently, training must be result-orientated, it must focus on enhancing those specific skills and abilities to perform the job, it must be measurable, and it must make a real contribution to improving both goal achievement and the internal efficiency of an organisation.

The training standards for a specific job are primarily derived from the job description or task requirements of a particular job. Training is therefore directed at improving the employees' job performance in an organisation. Training is executed when current work standards are not maintained, and when this situation can be ascribed to a lack of knowledge and/or skills, and/or poor attitudes among individual employees or groups in an organisation. Training is also essential when there is technological innovation in an organisation. (See Chapter 7 in this regard.)

### 18.2.3 The concept of 'development'

Development is aimed at employees serving in a managerial capacity or preparing for managerial posts within an organisation. It is essentially directed towards preparing supervisory and managerial staff for subsequent levels of management. It can be seen as a process whereby managers obtain the necessary experience, skills, and attitudes to become or remain successful leaders in their organisation.

De Cenzo and Robbins (1994:255) maintain that development focuses on future jobs in an organisation. As the individual's career progresses, new skills and abilities are required, for instance, for management positions. Development thus refers to development possibilities within a job or position for a specific employee, with reference to the employee's personal growth and personal goals.

Should every manager be appointed in an organisation solely for aspiring towards its objectives, it might be concluded that considerable demands are made on management. To fulfil this task efficiently, managers must keep abreast of new developments in technological, economic, political, legislative, and social fields, as well as contemporary personnel-management practices. Due to pressure of work, this is not always possible, and management often becomes obsolete in its outlook. This often affects an organisation detrimentally since it pervades the whole organisation and results in stagnation. One of the general objectives of development is the prevention of obsolescence. Obsolescence occurs when the person in a particular post lacks the current skills and knowledge generally considered by other managers as important and vital if the person is to remain effective in performing his/her work (Van Dyk et al. 2001).

For an organisation to survive in a highly competitive and developing market, it is essential to prevent obsolescence and develop managers to keep abreast of new challenges. Management development is therefore an organisational development intervention at the individual level to strategically align an organisation's management potential according to the demands that flow from a proactive business strategy.

## 18.3  Outcomes-based education and training

In terms of the National Qualifications Framework and Skills Development Act, the current national approach followed by the Department of Labour with regard to education and training is outcomes-focused.

The outcomes-based approach therefore differs from the traditional approach to education and training in that it focuses on the mastering of processes to achieve certain outcomes. It therefore focuses on the mastering of knowledge and skills which are required to achieve a certain outcome. Outcomes-based education and training therefore integrates the traditional approaches such as Trainer-Centred, Learner-Centred, Mentor-Centred (Sit-by-Nelly), Criteria Referenced Instruction, and Competency Based Training (Strydom 1998:5–6).

An outcomes-based education and training system has, as its starting point, intended outputs (outcomes), as opposed to inputs of traditional curriculum-driven education and training. An outcome is regarded as what a person can do and understand, whereas a competence is what a person is able to combine regarding the use of skills, information, and understanding necessary to a particular situation. An essential outcome is a competence a learner has acquired at a required level of performance. According to Erasmus and Van Dyk (1999:4):

> An outcome is not simply the name of the learning content, or a concept, or the name of a competence, a grade or score, but an actual demonstration in an authentic context. The basic approach is thus that if learning were based on outcomes, the starting point would be with the intended outcome – the end result. Once this is established, the curriculum processes (learning programmes) such as design, instructional planning, teaching, assessing and the development of learning according to the outcome can commence. Outcomes-Based Education is a results-orientated approach to learning and is learning-centred.

Outcomes-based education and training is therefore a radical departure from the previous system used in South Africa. This is illustrated in Table 18.1, which compares outcomes-based education to the traditional approach.

According to Strydom (1998:10), outcomes-based training methods focus on two

**Table 18.1** Comparison of the outcomes-based approach and the traditional approach

| TRADITIONAL APPROACH | OUTCOMES APPROACH |
|---|---|
| • Rote learning.<br>• Syllabus is content-driven and broken down into subjects.<br>• Textbook- or worksheet-bound.<br>• Teacher-centred.<br>• Syllabus is rigid and non-negotiable.<br>• Emphasis on what teacher hopes to achieve.<br>• Curriculum development process not open to public. | • Critical thinking and reasoning.<br>• Learning is a process and outcome-driven, connected to real life situations.<br>• Learner- and outcome-centred.<br>• Teacher is facilitator.<br>• Learning programmes are seen as guides.<br>• Emphasis on outcomes – what learner achieves.<br>• Wider community involvement if encouraged. |

important aspects: Firstly, the end result of the learning process, where learners must be able to demonstrate that they are competent with regard to prescribed outcomes; and secondly, the learning process and the transfer of information. This must guide the learner to the end result.

Outcomes-based training is a learner-based and result-orientated approach to learning based on the following principles:

- All learners are allowed to be able to learn to their full potential. (Both trainer and learner must therefore have high expectations to be able to learn successfully.)
- Success breeds success. Every success a learner achieves motivates the learner to strive for greater success.
- The environment must be learner friendly.
- The atmosphere should thus be one of encouraging a culture of learning.
- All parties concerned, such as the community, the State, and learners, must share in the responsibilities of learning. In outcomes-based training, all stakeholders should therefore cooperate in their development and implementation of learning processes.
- Learning achieves much more than mere memorising of knowledge and rote learning of skills.

According to Van Der Horst and McDonald (1997:27), the characteristics of outcomes-based training are as follows:

- Active learners.
- Learners are regularly assessed.
- Critical thinking and reasoning are encouraged.
- Integration of knowledge that is relevant and linked to life experience.
- Learner-centred approach; trainers are merely facilitators and group and team-work are important.
- Learning programmes merely provide the guidelines, because creativity in the establishment of learning programmes is encouraged.
- Learners take responsibility for their own learning.
- Regular feedback and recognition of their learning efforts motivate learners.
- The emphasis is shifted to outcomes, which the learner understands and in which s/he is competent.
- Flexible time allocations, because learners work according to their own pace.
- Recommendations and inputs into the process by the community are encouraged.

From this information it is clear that outcomes-based education and training constitutes a radical departure from the traditional approach to training and development in South Africa.

## 18.3.1 Distinguishing between objectives and outcomes

It is essential to distinguish between objectives and outcomes when education and training is being executed. According to Swanepoel et al. (2003:461), the difference between objectives and outcomes is as follows:

- Objectives focus on what the teacher does, whereas outcomes focus on what the learner will do.
- Objectives describe the intent of teaching, and outcomes describe the results of learning.
- Objectives focus on the opportunities provided for learning, and outcomes emphasise how learning is used and can be applied in new areas.
- Objectives estimate how much can be learnt in a given period of time, and outcomes require a flexible allocation of time.

Objectives are viewed as input-driven, whereas outcomes are viewed as output-driven. An argument against the use of objectives is that objectives are knowledge-driven, giving rise to a static form of learning and thus promoting rote learning. The outcomes approach encourages the use of an end result which is a product of a learning process in which knowledge is obtained through participation and transparency. An outcome statement should entail the following:

- Describe the learner's performance in terms of observable, demonstrable, and assessable performance.
- Contain action verbs, be clear and unambiguous.
- Involve more than mere isolated tasks or skills.
- Refer to knowledge, skills and attitudes or values (abilities).

An outcome must indicate:
- Who is to perform.

- What task is to be performed.
- What conditions apply (if any).
- What the minimum response is that will indicate mastery of the task.

In this regard it is logical to clarify what exactly are the outcomes regarding training and development that are to be achieved in an organisation. An organisation's overall aim regarding the outcomes to be achieved with training and development should be to:
- Improve the quality of an enterprise's output.
- Reduce costs incurred through wastage and maintaining machinery and equipment.
- Reduce the number and cost of accidents.
- Restrict labour turnover and absenteeism.
- Promote job satisfaction and motivation.
- Reduce or overcome obsolescence in management.
- Qualify employees for their jobs.
- Provide present employees with further training.
- Rectify poor performance as a result of poor knowledge and skills.
- Reduce learning time and cost.
- Improve job performance.
- Ensure that the right attitudes are fostered.
- Ensure better recruitment and selection.
- Guarantee that manpower needs are met.
- Guarantee increased customer satisfaction.

## 18.4 The place and role of the training function in an organisation

According to Erasmus and Van Dyk (1999:39–41), an organisation consists of various sub-systems that pursue the achievement of organisational objectives by means of different organisational processes. These enterprise sub-systems are organised according to the unique needs of each enterprise, and usually include sub-systems such as the marketing, production, financial, and human resources functions. Each of these sub-systems can again be divided into smaller systems or sub-subsystems, such as the planning, provision, maintenance, training and development of human resources, as well as labour relations.

The training and development function is regarded as a sub-system of the HRM function based on the following assumptions:

- The training function is a processing system that determines training needs, applies training technology and expertise, and transforms untrained employees into trained employees who can make productive contributions to the organisational objectives.
- The primary input into a training system (training needs and untrained employees) is transformed into an output (trained employees) by means of training processes such as analysis, design, development, and the evaluation of training.
- As a sub-system of an enterprise, the training function is exposed to the same influences as the other systems in the enterprise. These influences include politics, the economy, and legislation.

The training function should be viewed as part of the human resources function as a whole, but should function as a separate training department if this is affordable, because training takes place at various levels in an enterprise and provides a support service to the enterprise as a whole. A critical factor is that, to ensure success, training practitioners must continuously monitor the training input that is made available in order to achieve organisational objectives. This will increase the credibility of the training department in the enterprise.

The key roles that should be present in all training departments are:

- Achievement and need analysis.
- Development of curricula.
- Development and obtaining of training resources.
- Training per se.
- Advancement of training efficiency.
- Administrative management of learners.

Training departments often take on the following additional duties:

- Marketing training courses and learner registration systems.
- Supply of training material for on-the-job training.
- Supply and management of training facilities and equipment.
- Organising achievement conferences.
- Representing the enterprise on professional bodies.
- Trading training programmes and training material with other enterprises.

## 18.5  Strategic human resources development

Due to the importance of training and development for an organisation and the costs it incurs, it must be effectively managed. Over and above this, a human resources development manager faces a wide range of challenges, namely:

- The human resources manager must ensure that all programmes must be presented in a purposeful and effective manner. Organisations must therefore ensure that the training and development programmes are not offered for the sake of presenting a programme in an organisation only.
- Imbalances exist between traditionally advantaged managerial personnel and historically disadvantaged personnel, and must be addressed to be rectified via accelerated programmes.
- Management must realise that the attitudes towards employment equity programmes cannot change organisations overnight and must be carefully addressed via training and development programmes.
- Human resources development managers and practitioners ought to be selected since the success of programmes largely depends on their quality and knowledge of training and development.

From this point of view, therefore, it is essential to adopt a strategic approach to human resources development so as to ensure that it has the maximum benefit to an organisation. Strategic human resources development is geared for the strategic business plan and to help implement the human resources strategy by improving the knowledge and skills of employees of the organisation and/or the knowledge and efficiency levels of interest groups outside the organisation. (See Chapter 21 for more detail in this regard.)

The key assumptions in executing Strategic Human Resources Development (SHRD) are as follows:

- There should be an overall purpose statement for the organisation, and the Human Resources Development (HRD) effort should be related to it.
- Every major plan of the organisation should be weighed in terms of the skills available to implement it, and alternative ways of obtaining those skills.
- People at all levels in the organisation's chain of command should share responsibility and accountability for HRD.
- There should be a formal, systematic, and holistic planning process for the corporation, personnel department, and HRD.

## 18.6 A strategic training approach

Arie de Geus (in Swartz 1992) made the observation that learning faster than your competitors is the only sustainable competitive advantage. Every organisation learns – some just learn faster than others, learn more deliberately, and use their new knowledge more rapidly. Nicky Oppenheimer, chairman of Anglo American Corporation, emphasises the strategic role of training when he refers to the contribution of the HR manager as a bottom line issue, because it is only those businesses with human resources policies that are sustainable and that enhance the company's capacity to create wealth and ensure success that will soar in the 21st century.

Strategic training requires an approach in which the primary thrust is to create an environment in which learning for all the members of the organisation is encouraged, rather than seeing the establishment and maintenance of a training department as a major strategy to only influence the development of people in organisations.

When referring to strategic training the concept virtual training in organisations comes to mind. The virtual organisation is the ultimate results-centred enterprise. By using future work principles it is able to produce results that are at least equal to those of its traditional competitor but leveraged from a smaller asset base. The results of the virtual organisation are real and will show up in the bottom line, but if we start searching for the traditional means of achieving these results – massive office buildings, work restricted to fixed times and locations, and the madness of large-scale commuting – we will not find them because they are not there.

According to McIntosh (1995), virtual organisations are becoming a virtual reality. They are organisations that forge alliances with other firms in order to streamline processes, cut costs, and crack new markets. For virtual organisations to evolve, they need support from Virtual Training Organisations (VTOs). VTOs devise flexible structures and systems so that they can respond rapidly to their organisation's needs. Three principles dictate VTO operations:

- Individual employees, and not their organisations, have the primary responsibility for their own personal growth.
- The most powerful learning takes place on the job, not in a classroom.
- Improved preference hinges not on the relationship between a trainer and a class participant, but on the relationship between the manager and the employee.

Table 18.2 illustrates a VTO model that incorporates five competencies: strategic direction, product design, structural versatility, product delivery, and accountability for results. McIntosh (1995) illustrates each of the five

**Table 18.2** Comparing a traditional training department with a virtual training organisation

### Strategic direction

A traditional department:
- leaves objectives unstated or vague
- assumes that class participants are its only customers
- limits offerings to predetermined list
- continues to supply products that are no longer useful
- organises its offerings by courses

A virtual training organisation:
- broadly disseminates a clearly articulated mission
- recognises that its customer base is segmented
- provides customised solutions to its clients' needs
- understands product life cycles
- organises offerings by competencies
- competes for internal customers

### Product design

A traditional department:
- uses rigid and cumbersome design methodologies
- views suppliers as warehouses of materials

A virtual training organisation:
- uses benchmarking and other innovative design strategies to develop products quickly
- involves suppliers strategically

### Structural versatility

A traditional department:
- employs trainers who serve primarily as facilitators and classroom instructors
- operates with a fixed number of staff
- relies solely on training staff to determine the department's offerings

A virtual training organisation:
- employs professionals who serve as products managers and internal consultants
- leverages resources from many areas
- involves line managers in determining direction and contents

### Product delivery

A traditional department:
- distributes a list of courses
- offers courses on a fixed schedule at fixed locations

A virtual training organisation:
- offers a menu of learning options
- delivers training at the work site

### Accountability for results

A traditional department:
- believes that the corporation manages employee development
- ends its involvement with participants when courses end
- considers the instructor the key player in supporting learning
- relies on course critiques as its primary source of feedback
- vaguely describes training outcomes

A virtual training organisation:
- believes individual employees must take responsibility for their personal growth
- provides follow-up on the job to ensure that learning takes place
- considers the manager the key player in supporting learning
- evaluates the strategic effects of training and its bottom-line results
- guarantees that training will improve performance

SOURCE: McIntosh (1995)

competencies in detail, and compares the characteristics of a traditional training organisation with those of a virtual training organisation.

By re-orientating traditional training approaches to enable learners to anticipate the future and prepare for it, training departments will not only justify their existence but also contribute to meaningful growth and development of the organisations.

## 18.7 Training and development policy

A training and development policy is based on certain assumptions and principles which manifest themselves in the form of a philoso-phy. The policy therefore can be described as the managerial attitude (either proactive or reactive) or perception of the importance of the human resources potential to enhance company goal achievements by means of investments in the training and development efforts of the organisation. The policy should reflect, from a strategic as well as an operational point of view, the reasons why an organisation is willing to invest in the development of its employees.

It is essential for an organisation to base its training and development policy on an integration of job content training as well as management skills and leadership training in accordance with the various career levels. A theoretical basis for a training and development policy is depicted in Figure 18.1.

**Figure 18.1** A theoretical basis for a training and development policy

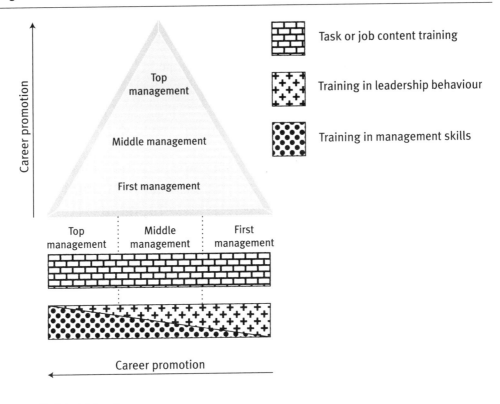

source: Van Dyk et al. (2001)

This conceptualisation indicates that all employees of an organisation should receive job content training throughout their careers. Initially job content training (at a low level) would enable employees to gain basic skills, which are required in the execution of their tasks. Later, job content training would enable employees to know more about their functional area, in order to be promoted in accordance with those newly learned skills and to be promoted above others. Job context training at the highest level implies that senior personnel are kept up to date with the latest technology in their functional areas. This enables them to become better decision makers.

The training in leadership behaviour must be directed at the establishment of a situational diagnostic approach to the practice of leadership. The attitude of an organisation towards the training and development of employees should be reflected in its policy. This policy governs the priorities, standards, and scope of its training activities.

Training policies are developed for four main reasons:
- To define the relationship between the objectives of the organisation and its commitment to the training function.
- To provide operational guidelines for management.
- To provide information for employees.
- To enhance public relations.

## 18.8 Training and development models

Training and development can only take place effectively if it is executed within the context of a logical and systematic process. This can take place via the application of a training model, which would include steps such as determining training needs and job analysis, programme design, presenting training and evaluation of training. In this regard, various models exist in the literature. For example, popular models are:
- *Nadler's (1982) model* views the training process in holistic terms and is regarded

as the critical events model. In this model nine steps are outlined, namely:
  - Step 1: identifying the needs of the enterprise
  - Step 2: evaluation and feedback
  - Step 3: specifying performance
  - Step 4: identifying training needs
  - Step 5: formulating training objectives
  - Step 6: compiling a syllabus
  - Step 7: selecting instructional strategies
  - Step 8: acquiring instructional resources
  - Step 9: presentation of training
- A further model, which has gained popularity due to its simplicity but also effectiveness, is the so-called *high impact model*. This is a six-phase process that focuses on providing effective and targeted training. It was developed by Sparhawk (1994). In this model, each phase of the model moves the training and development effort forward. In other words, the one phase is the input for the next.

The model's use and application can be illustrated in terms of the activities that ought to take place in each phase, and the product that is to be produced as a result thereof (see Table 18.3).

## 18.9 Application of various models to training and development

A sound approach to training and development ought to take cognisance of the models outlined above. It should begin with scanning and assessing the macro-environment (see Chapter 17), and then progress to observing or, if need be, re-evaluating the strategy and policy of the organisation concerning training and development.

It must also be borne in mind that the process of executing training and development requires two major aspects prior to training itself. Firstly, the standards against which job performance must be measured, i.e.

**Table 18.3** Action and product phases of the high impact model

| Phase | Action | Product |
|---|---|---|
| 1 Identify training needs | Gather and analyse appropriate information | A description of the specific training needed to improve job performance |
| 2 Map the approach | Define what needs to be learnt to improve job performance<br>Choose the appropriate training approach | Detailed objectives for the training programme<br>A design plan for the training programme |
| 3 Produce learning tools | Create the actual training materials | Training manuals; Facilitator's guide; Audio-visual aids; Job aids, etc. |
| 4 Apply training techniques | Deliver the training as designed to ensure successful results | Instructor-led training<br>Computer-based training<br>One-on-one coaching, etc. |
| 5 Calculate measurable results | Assess whether your training/ coaching accomplished actual performance improvement; communicate the results, and redesign (if necessary) | An evaluation report<br>A redesigned course, if needed |
| 6 Track ongoing follow-through | Ensure that the impact of the training does not diminish | Ongoing suggestions and ideas that support the training |

SOURCE: Sparhawk (1994:14)

the job content of the post must be clearly defined; and secondly, the performance of the individual (the actual state of affairs) must be measurable. The difference between the standard and the current performance forms the performance gap and therefore represents the training need to be executed to achieve the desired outcome.

The job content must also be analysed before the training needs determination can commence. A process of job analysis to determine training standards and improve job performance must therefore be undertaken (see Chapters 8 and 19).

## 18.9.1 Identify training needs

According Swanepoel et al. (2003:456–8), whenever a comprehensive needs analysis is undertaken, it will usually address one or more of the following three key areas, namely the organisation, the job, and the individual concerned.

### Organisational assessment

Consider the proposed training within the context of the rest of the organisation.
- What are the training implications of the organisation's strategy?
- What will the result be if training is not undertaken?
- How does this training programme fit in with the organisation's future plans and goals?
- Where in the organisation is training needed?
- How are various departments performing in relation to expectations or goals?
- In which departments is training most likely to succeed?

- Which departments should be trained first?
- Can the organisation afford this training?
- Which training programmes should have priority?
- Will this training adversely affect untrained people or departments?
- Is this training consistent with the organisation's culture?
- Will this training be accepted and reinforced by others in the organisation, such as the trainees' superiors, subordinates, and clients?

It must also be borne in mind whether or not the training is commensurate with the organisation's mission, strategy, goals, and culture. Today, corporate culture in particular is important when training and development is to be executed in an organisation.

### The job

Conduct a thorough task analysis of an incumbent. The purpose is to find out if an individual's task is of importance to the organisation, and whether training is to be executed.

### The individual

Training can only be executed if it has been determined which employees should receive training and what their current levels, knowledge, and skills are. The assessment of the individual will indicate the range of skills and knowledge that is to be acquired. Note that the difference between actual performance and required performance will ultimately form the training gap, and therefore indicate the extent to which training need occur.

Training is thus based on one or more needs. Training addresses gaps or discrepancies between an ideal and an optimal stage. Needs, on the other hand, arise from the job, from a comparison between desired and actual work methods, or between desired and actual work results. Rothwell and Kazanas (1994) refer to three methods of identifying

needs: the generic method, performance analysis, and competency assessment. Where performance analysis focuses on deficiencies or problems, competency assessment focuses on opportunity for improvement. Trainers identify how they believe people should perform and then design the training programme to give the workers the skills they need.

## 18.9.2 Devise instructional objectives

An instructional objective is a description of a performance learners must be able to exhibit before they can be considered competent. It describes an intended result of instruction, rather than the process of instruction itself.

Rothwell and Kazanas (1994) categorise objectives by type and by scope. They distinguish between three types of objectives:

- *Cognitive*, which has to do with knowledge and information.
- *Affective*, which has to do with feelings and beliefs.
- *Psychomotor*, which has to do with the ability to manipulate objectives.

There are also two ways of thinking of the scope of objectives, namely:

- *Terminal*: what learners will be able to do upon the completion of a course or programme.
- *Enabling*: behaviours that contribute to mastery of terminal objectives.

## 18.9.3 Prepare test items based on the objectives and desired outcomes

Test items enable the trainer to establish whether the learner has mastered behaviours that a training programme has been designed to teach. There are generally two types of test items, namely:

- *Norm referenced*. Achievement is assessed relative to other learners and each learner is compared to others.

**Figure 18.2** Algorithm for deciding whether to produce your own instructional material

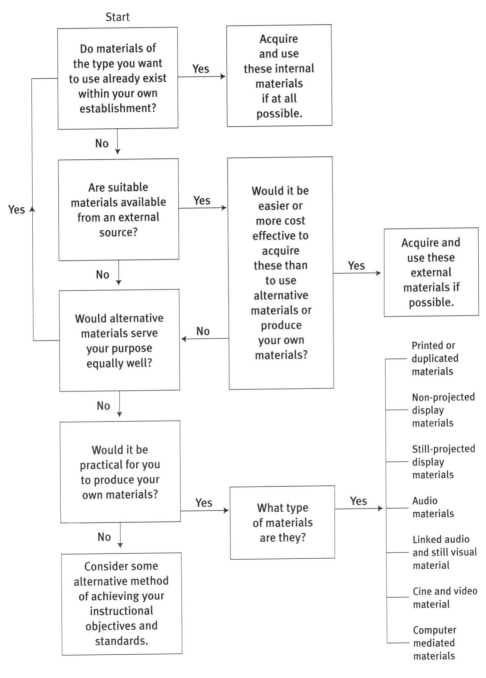

- Criterion referenced. Achievement is assessed relative to individual success, and compares a learner's progress to pre-established measures.

### 18.9.4 Select or design instructional content

The selection or design, in other words, the decision what to teach, is based on the test items and instruction objectives. In this process it is important to consider whether the content should be obtained from existing sources, such as textbooks, other training courses or published articles, tailor-made for the purpose at hand, or prepared from a combination of externally available and internally generated content. Figure 18.2 provides a useful algorithm for making this decision.

### 18.9.5 Choosing delivery methods

The method of teaching is dependent on what to teach. Teaching methods depend heavily on the preference of the trainer. Table 18.4 provides a list of different delivery methods. (See Section 18.3, where training techniques are discussed in more detail.)

### 18.9.6 Offering instruction

Training can be offered either on the job by the supervisor, off the job by in-house trainers, or outside the organisation. The latter is commonly associated with formal instruction, while on the job is usually informal and rarely distinguishable from regular work activities.

### 18.9.7 Transferring learning back to the job

The main purpose of off the job training is to give employees the knowledge and skills they need to perform effectively on the shop floor. According to Rothwell and Kazanas (1994), there are a number of factors on the job that prevent transfer of learning. They include:

- *The individual (learner).* If learners see no value in applying new skills, believe no rewards will result from doing so, or do not value the rewards, then transfer of learning from classroom to the job will not occur.
- *The job.* If individuals have little or no latitude to change what they do because the job tasks are tightly controlled, then training can never be applied unless the job itself is changed first.
- *The supervisor.* If a learner's supervisor is not in favour of training, then there is little likelihood that a learner will be applying newly acquired skills. Supervisors exert powerful influence over the behaviour of subordinates because they control rewards and punishment.
- *The work group.* If a trainee returns to the shop floor only to find that fellow workers greet new ideas with scepticism, then training will not transfer successfully.

### 18.9.8 Evaluation

Training and development can never be effective if it is not properly assessed. The expression that to measure is to know is acutely apt in this context. It also forms the last link in the loop of the systems approach to training and development, since it determines whether the training need (the difference between the required performance and the actual performance of the trainee) was satisfied. Without measuring what had happened, the training department and its efforts cannot be effectively assessed. It also forms the starting point for the next round of training and development if need be.

The following aspects regarding the evaluation of training and development are of cardinal importance if it is to be successful:

- The evaluation of training is a continuous process and not something that occurs only at the end of the training period.
- Training evaluation must be well planned and objectives must be clearly indicated. Training evaluation is therefore not conducted on an ad hoc basis.

**Table 18.4** Training delivery methods and strategies

| Method | Description | Appropriate for |
|---|---|---|
| Lecture | • A structured presentation, usually lasting an hour or longer | • Group presentations<br>• Orientating employees to policies, introducing topics, providing information |
| Tutorial | • A one-on-one, structured instructional experience | • Individualised presentation<br>• On-the-job training<br>• Building skills, demonstrating how to use equipment |
| Case study | • A narrative description of a situation, real or fictitious, prepared for instruction purposes, usually written | • Stimulating discussion, especially in a small group setting<br>• Identifying problems in realistic situations<br>• Weighing alternative solutions |
| Critical incident | • A very short narrative description of a problem situation, usually only a sentence or paragraph in length | • The same purposes as case study |
| Role-play | • Trainees are assigned parts to play in a dramatised version of a case study or problem situation | • Groups of two or more<br>• Dealing with instruction about interpersonal situations |
| Game | • A ritualised representation of a job duty | • Group instruction<br>• Especially useful for developing cooperation or assessing leadership in a team setting |
| Simulation | • An extended role-play or game | • Same purposes as game |
| Buzz groups | • A small group of people, assembled to identify a problem or problems, consider and select alternative solutions | • Use with case study, critical incident<br>•Taking advantage of the ability of small groups to deal with unstructured problems more effectively than individuals |
| Panel discussion | • A structured or unstructured presentation on a topic, problem or issue by a group of from three to ten people to a larger group | • Stimulating insight<br>• Posing problems<br>• Clarifying issues and problems |
| Computer-based instruction | • The use of a computer, usually a microcomputer, to present instructions | • Communicating information very efficiently but not necessarily cheaply |
| Videotape | • The use of a televised presentation to provide instruction, often in a form that mixes instruction with entertainment | • Demonstrating effective interpersonal skills<br>• Conveying information in an interesting (but not necessarily cheap) manner |

- Accurate and applicable measuring instruments must be used to obtain information for the purposes of decision-making.
- Training evaluation is a form of quality control.
- Evaluation is not directed only at testing learners, but also at testing the entire training system.

The principles of assessment proposed by Meyer (1996:90–1) are as follows:

- Assessment must be reliable and valid. Reliability refers to the consistency of assessment results for equal performance of an individual (which are independent of time or the assessor). Validity refers to whether the assessment method tests the behaviour (which it is supposed to test).
- Assessment must be practical, cost effective, and create a minimum of disruption in the workplace. Access to assessment should not be subjected to artificial barriers, for example, prescribed educational qualifications, prescribed learning times, age restrictions, etc.
- An appeals mechanism should be established for those dissatisfied with their assessment.
- The process of setting assessment criteria and procedures should be open to all stakeholders.
- Those involved in assessment should be competent in both the performance being assessed and in assessment techniques and principles.
- Where practical, multiple assessment methods should be used to gather evidence from a variety of contexts or situations.
- Where it is only practical to assess a sample of required performance, it is essential that the performance measured provide sufficient evidence of competence and the achievement of the required outcome.

Various types of evaluation exist, but the two main types are formative and summative.

*Formative evaluation* implies that a learner's learning performance must be evaluated in order to:

- Determine the extent to which the course content was mastered.
- Provide feedback to learners.
- Assist learners in correcting errors which still occur and improve future learning performance.

*Summative evaluation* means that a human resources training and development practitioner must execute the following in order to be effective:

- Examine all instructional materials after they have been revised in the light of formative evaluation results. Do they appear to do what they are supposed to do?
- Observe an instructor delivering the material. Do learners respond as expected? Does the instructor adequately present the material?
- Administer a post-test to measure trainee achievement of objectives.
- Administer an attitude survey to find out how well participants liked the course and to what extent they felt that it met their needs.
- Compare the subsequent job performance of:
  - Those who received training.
  - Those who did not receive training (or benefited from a different kind of performance improvement strategy).

The evaluation of training can also be executed by bearing in mind why it fails. This can be used to correct training. In this regard Rothwell and Kazanas (1994:475) listed a number of reasons why training failed in the United States of America (see Table 18.5). Their findings are based on empirical research by the American Society for Training and Development. There is little doubt that it probably also applies in South Africa.

The issue of written or oral examinations is of particular importance in South Africa. Where an outcome does not necessarily

**Table 18.5** Why training fails

| Reason for failure | Respondents (%) |
|---|---|
| • No on-the-job rewards for behaviours and skills learnt in training | 58 |
| • Insufficient time to execute training programmes | 55 |
| • Work environment does not support new behaviours learnt in training | 53 |
| • Lack of motivation among employees | 47 |
| • Inaccurate training needs analyses | 40 |
| • Training needs changed after programme had been implemented | 35 |
| • Management does not support training programme | 30 |
| • Insufficient funding for training programme | 21 |

SOURCE: Rothwell and Kazanas (1994:475)

require reading or writing ability, oral assessment should be permitted. It is essential in this case that the assessor records the questions asked and notes the correctness or otherwise of responses. A checklist is an important tool in oral assessment.

## 18.10 Training and development methods

Various methods can be applied which are either off the job or on the job.

### 18.10.1 Off the job training

Off the job training is exactly what it says. It is training that is done in a classroom, vocational school or any other place, except for the shop floor.

Organisations apply off the job training in varied ways and do not only stick to the most obvious method, i.e. for the trainer to give a lecture of the material to be learnt. Besides the lecture method, a number of other ways of applying off the job training are also briefly discussed below.

#### Case studies

The trainees read, study, and analyse a hypothetical business problem that contains elements of a real-life situation. They are then required to choose the best solution and implement it. Learning is best if there is interaction between the learners and the instructor, because the role of the instructor is that of catalyst and facilitator. This method gives learners an opportunity to apply the knowledge and principles they have learnt previously and to test their ability to deal with a simulated real-life situation. It also provides trainees with an opportunity to develop independent thinking and to exchange ideas. The experience is a trial run for business activities in the real world.

#### The incident method

This is a variation on the case study method. In this method, trainees are given the bare outlines of a problem, and are each assigned a role. Each trainee must then view the problem from the perspective of his/her role. Additional information is made available according to the questions they ask.

In this method each student 'solves' the case, and groups based on similarity of solutions are formed. Each group then formulates a strong statement of position, and the groups then debate or role-play their solutions. The instructor may describe what actually happened in the case, and the consequences, and then everyone compares their solutions with the results. The final step is for participants to try to apply this knowledge to their own job situations.

## Role-play

This is another variation on the case study method, in which trainees act out a specific role, applying the theory instead of merely thinking passively about it. It becomes a dynamic learning process, particularly if closed-circuit television, which films the trainees playing their roles, is used to assess them. In role-play there are no rehearsals, since situations must be spontaneously acted out. A realistic representation should be allowed to develop, particularly when the topic deals with human relations. The instructor should first explain the human relations problem in a formal lecture. S/he then stipulates the roles that learners are to play, but not how they should play them. Learners then use their initiative and play the role, as they perceive it ought to be played. The role-play starts with a given passage of dialogue and ends when the stipulated problems have been solved and the situation has been brought to a conclusion. At the end, the instructor comments on the observed actions. Role-play can be effectively used to give learners insight into interpersonal problems. It makes them aware of their attitudes towards others and it creates opportunities for them to improve their ability to deal with human relations issues. It is important for trainees to understand that this method involves serious learning and that each participant needs to be positive towards change, otherwise the exercise will not be successful.

## In-basket training

This is also called the in-tray exercise. The trainee is given a number of letters, messages, reports, and telephone messages that would typically come across a manager's desk. These items range from urgent to routine handling. The trainee must act on the information contained in these items. S/he has to analyse each item and decide how to carry out the tasks. Afterwards the decisions are analysed and evaluated by the instructor. Trainees are normally not allowed to communicate with one another during this type of exercise. They are thus compelled to undertake independent thinking and problem solving.

This method can be effectively used to analyse trainees' decision-making abilities in order to identify further training needs. It can also be used to develop their managerial skills and provide them with practice in decision-making. This method is often used in assessment centre training.

## The Kepner-Tregoe technique

This variation on the in-basket method resembles case studies in that material about an organisation is provided in writing ahead of time. It also involves role-play, and each trainee is assigned one, two or even five roles, which s/he is required to play in the hypothetical organisation. Each trainee plays a role for approximately 90 minutes and then switches roles. Trainees are subsequently evaluated on their performance in each role. Once again, some problems are more urgent than others, and trainees have to distinguish the important from the unimportant in order to make decisions. This method claims to make trainees better aware of the managerial decision-making process, and it also improves problem solving skills if teams work together on the exercises.

## Management games

Management games, also called business games, are a development of the in-basket and role-play methods. Trainees play various roles in an imaginary business situation over a period of time. A business game usually involves two or more hypothetical organisations competing against each other in a given product market, and participants are assigned the roles of managing director, marketing manager, etc. They are required to take decisions on price levels, production volume and inventory levels. Their decisions are manipulated in a computer to give results as in an actual business situation. The participants are then able to see how their decisions affect other groups, and vice versa. A lengthy business phase of five to ten years can be played in three to five hours. There are usually six to eight participants in a group representing a specific organisation. Two to five organisations can compete against each other simultaneously. The groups normally start off by controlling identical shares on the market and they then have to react to various stimuli presented to them.

The feedback session by the trainers is an important aspect of this method because it enables individuals and groups to evaluate their performance. Participants' performance and decision-making abilities are compared with those of other groups representing other hypothetical organisations. The advantage of this training is that if a group makes a mistake that costs their hypothetical organisation a few million rand, they do not lose their jobs. They will, however, learn to exercise caution when making decisions in a real-life situation.

## Syndicate training

This is also a variation on the case study method, and combines lectures and group work in small groups of about five to 10 trainees. Instructors formulate points that should be considered by their groups. After the groups' deliberations, each trainee writes a report which is then criticised and discussed by other members of the group. Finally, group decisions are arrived at and discussed by the instructor and other groups. This method gives each trainee a chance to participate in group discussions, especially about complex tasks. Problem solving ability is improved by deciding what is relevant and what is irrelevant. This form of training can also bring about changes in attitudes and behaviour in individuals and groups.

## Conference method

Group discussions are conducted according to an organised plan in which the trainer seeks to develop knowledge and understanding by obtaining verbal participation from all the trainees. This method has advantages over the lecture method, because each trainee plays an active role. Learning is achieved by building on the ideas contributed by the various participants. Thus one trainee learns from another. Groups should be limited to 15 to 20 participants who should sit facing one another around a conference table, rather than in rows as in a classroom. The responses of trainees are recorded on a chalkboard, and the discussion is summarised by the instructor. Interest tends to be high because this method stimulates talk about problems and issues, which can be examined from different points of view. It can also be used to reduce dogmatism and to modify attitudes, because trainees participate in finding solutions and reaching conclusions, and because many different points of view are heard and expressed.

## Brainstorming

This is also sometimes called 'free wheeling'. Brainstorming seeks creative thinking rather than practical analysis. Small groups of participants meet, with or without conscious knowledge of the subject, and submit any solution or idea that occurs to them, no matter how strange or impossible it may sound. Trainees do not consider the practicality of ideas. They list all ideas generated and place the list where all the participants can see it. Later all the ideas or solutions are examined and assessed to determine how practical or acceptable each might be. The time period for such an exercise is usually five to 20 minutes. Brainstorming is primarily used to develop novel ideas to solve problems, and to encourage creativity and participation among trainees. Note that the number of ideas is more important than their quality, because the prerequisite for this method is the suspension of all judgement and of all evaluative or analytical discussion until the group has drained itself of ideas. To ensure the success of this method, participants should represent a variety of disciplines and management functions in the organisation. Brainstorming is a form of synergism because it produces a result that is better than the members could have achieved had they been working on the project individually.

## University programmes not for degrees

University programmes give managers a new perspective on their organisations, helping them to change their outlook on events around them. Courses of this nature are ideal for middle and top managers with the potential to broaden their perspective and to prepare them for the highest positions in their organisations. Such programmes are aimed at adapting a manager's attitude to changing circumstances and providing him/her with up-to-date information on a broad front. Examples are the Management Development Programme (MDP) and the Senior Management Programme (SMP) of the University of Pretoria's Graduate School of Management. In these programmes the teaching staff act as equals, rather than superiors, and serve as moderators and discussion leaders rather than teachers. In this way executives gain maximum benefit from these courses in an adult teaching environment. Managers expand their knowledge and learn about theories and procedures that they would not encounter on the job. University programmes are also popular for career development.

## Sabbaticals

Sabbaticals provide managers with the opportunity for mind stretching, particularly those who have been in business for a number of years. Managers should be granted one academic year (sabbatical) in every ten years of employment. The sabbatical should be planned well in advance to give an assistant the opportunity to understudy the superior's position and gain experience in it while the superior is away. A variation is to allow top managers who are experts in certain fields to be assigned to academic institutions for a time to teach. This gives such managers an opportunity to refresh their knowledge, update facts in a different environment and advance their own development. It provides students with an opportunity to learn practical know-how from seasoned business people. Such an exchange programme could be of great benefit to South African students who need practical knowledge of the business environment, since many students are rapidly moved into managerial positions because of the dire shortage of managerial personnel the country is experiencing.

## Lectures

Lectures remain an essential method for supervisory and management training and hold considerable advantages, particularly flexibility and economy. A good lecturer can achieve excellent results within a short space of time, provided lectures are carefully structured and presented. Lectures are seldom presented on their own; they are usually accompanied by a variety of audio-visual aids and tools. Some of these can also be used on their own. The most common training aids are:

- *Films and video-tape recordings.* These can be used to good effect in training, in particular to explain principles and theories, and to present case studies, etc. They should, however, be used in combination with other methods. For example, films, slides, tapes, flip charts, and the chalk-board can enhance lectures.
- *Closed-circuit television.* Videotape recordings of role-play situations are often used to give trainees direct feedback on their behaviour. They are often used in interpersonal skills training and team building exercises because they let trainees see a recording of their own behaviour. Trainees can use videotape recordings to make detailed analyses of their skills.
- *Overhead projectors, magnetic boards and flip charts* are other tools that can be used to supplement a lecture.

## 18.10.2 On the job training

On the job training methods usually fit the needs of a particular employee and suit his/her background, knowledge, and skills. Trainees learn by doing; they learn continuously and over a long period. Their immediate superiors extensively influence trainees; superiors are usually directly responsible for the training of their subordinates. On the job methods are regarded as allowing workers to learn by actually performing the tasks of the job. New employees work under the guidance of an experienced employee who can offer advice and suggestions for performing the job efficiently and effectively.

On the job training can, however, prevent trainees from acquiring a broad perspective and can adversely influence their perception of their job and how it fits into the activities of the organisation.

The methods below are generally used for on the job training or development:

## Coaching

According to Stone (2002:331), coaching is planned one-to-one instruction. The coach sets a good example of what is to be done, answers questions and generally offers counsel to the trainee. Coaching takes a work situation and turns it into a learning opportunity. When combined with job rotation, coaching can be a very effective technique of learning by doing.

Caution should, however, be exercised regarding the elements of ethical coaching. These are as follows:
- Adhering to a recognised code of practice.
- Being trained and able to use the core skills of coaching.
- Being careful to take on clients suited to their skills.
- Being willing to make referrals where appropriate.

## Job rotation

Job rotation is a method whereby trainees receive training and gain experience in turn, under close supervision. According to Skinner and Ivancevich (1992:383), job rotation

means that 'managers are transferred from job to job on a systematic basis. Job assignments can last from two weeks to six months.' It is used to develop generalists with wide experience of the organisation to enable them to make high-level decisions later in their careers. By rotating through various jobs, learners cultivate a fresh approach, which will enable them to establish new procedures and make changes in their existing jobs. Trainees are moved into new jobs for short periods of time. They need to be extensively briefed as to what is expected of them, and their progress must be carefully checked. This method enables trainees to acquire specific practical experience quickly, instead of having to wait for opportunities to present themselves over a period of time through transfers and promotions. Job rotation is also an invaluable method of inducting a young graduate.

## Junior boards

This method, also called multiple management, is usually employed to give promising managers experience in analysing the overall problems of the organisation. These managers are given assignments by top management to study problems identified by top managers and to propose solutions. The members of junior boards, mostly promising middle and junior managers, usually rotate to ensure the continuity of the board's work in the organisation. This is an effective development method only if the problems assigned to the junior board are genuinely company-wide and cut across all departmental lines. Junior boards are not usually granted authority to take decisions, but merely to investigate and analyse problems and propose solutions to top management.

## Job instruction training

This is a precise method for teaching a trainee to do a specific job. It compels all trainees to learn in a standard fashion. It is a way of quickly expanding manual and psychomotor skills, and is particularly applicable to lower-level workers. A number of steps are followed. The trainer decides what the employees are to be taught and ensures that the right tools, equipment, supplies and material are ready, and the workplace is properly arranged. Once this is done, trainees are instructed by means of the following four steps: preparing the workers, presentation of the operation, performance try-out, and follow-up.

## Understudy

This method resembles coaching and job rotation in some respects. Understudy is the temporary assignment of a manager to a more senior manager in order to broaden his/her managerial viewpoints by exposing him/her to various aspects of managerial practice. During a short period of time, the subordinate manager closely observes the activities of the senior manager and helps him/her to perform duties, and at the same time is given the opportunity to be coached. This method usually provides a trainee with a broader perspective because the senior manager normally carries out the work s/he does during training. Giving junior managers understudy assignments provides the organisation with a pool of potential managers who have been carefully observed and evaluated and could, if they were successful as understudies, be promoted at a later date to a higher level of authority in the organisation. It is also a popular career development method. It is therefore a practical and fairly quick way of preparing chosen junior managers for greater management responsibility. The motivation to learn is usually high because 'learning by doing' is emphasised.

## Mentoring

According to Carrell et al. (2000:262), mentoring starts in two ways – formally and informally. Because a mentor can 'show the ropes' to the protégé, many organisations have set up formal mentor programmes, often as part of their affirmative action or orientation efforts. Informal mentoring relationships seem to

have always existed, generally based on a judgement by the mentor that the employee has promise and that the mentor's advice and counsel will not be wasted. The effectiveness of formal, somewhat artificial, mentoring programmes has not been established to be the same as in the traditional informal relationships, where the mentor and protégé are perhaps more genuinely committed to each other.

## Learner-controlled instruction

This method allows trainees to decide on the pace at which they choose to learn, as well as the specific methods used and the sequence of learning steps. They also evaluate their own learning. Methods that could be used are, for instance, case studies, simulations, group discussions, books, and films. The instructor only acts as facilitator and offers assistance to the trainees. There are no set lesson plans and no examinations. The instructor sets learning objectives with the learners' participation. The learners themselves are expected to be accountable for meeting these agreed-upon objectives. This method is usually used in conjunction with other methods.

## Behaviour modelling

It is also called 'observational learning' and refers to how people learn from the experience of others. Trainers at IBM, General Electric, and AT&T have found that supervisory, sales, and customer relations skills are learnt faster and more effectively when taught from a modelling base. Stone (2002:333) mentions the following basic steps in behaviour modelling:

- Provide trainees with suitable models by videotape or film. The models should demonstrate effective approaches in handling 'real-world' problems.
- Allow trainees to rehearse and practise the behaviours they have seen demonstrated by models. Use repetition until high levels of skill are evidenced.
- Systematically reinforce trainees by allow-

ing them to see whether their behaviour approximates that of the model. Use videotaping to provide feedback to trainees. This provides reinforcement by demonstrating progress towards skills acquisition.

### 18.10.3 Learnership training (previously apprenticeship training)

This type of training dates back to biblical times. It is used to train workers in technical trades, such as tool making, armature winding, electronics, and as diesel mechanics. The major characteristic is that the apprentice works under the guidance of a skilled artisan. Trainees receive training mainly at two sites – on the shop floor and at vocational schools. One of the main characteristics of apprentice training is its inter-linkage with the production process. Not only is it a more cost-effective way of training, but it also enables the trainee to make contact with the working world right from the start. An apprentice enters into a contract, which can be registered only if the trade has been designated and the conditions of apprenticeship have been prescribed. These designated trades and conditions vary in South Africa, since they depend on the needs of a particular industry. Contract conditions include qualification requirements for apprenticeship, periods of apprenticeship, remuneration, technical studies required, centralised technical training and the use of logbooks, all of which are covered by Chapters 4 and 5 of the Skills Development Act, No. 97 of 1998.

### 18.10.4 Vestibule training

In vestibule training the trainee learns the job in an environment that simulates the real working environment as closely as possible. An example is the simulated cockpit of an aircraft used to train airline pilots in operating a specific type of aircraft.

Vestibule training is especially appropriate when the job to be learnt involves the operation of a new machine, repetitive processes, or is performed in an area too full of distractions to permit effective learning. An advantage of this style of training is that there are none of the production requirements and pressures of the real work situation. The trainee is not under stress to maintain a standard of production from the outset nor is s/he held accountable for high reject rates in the early stages of training. Once employees meet the standards, they move onto the job itself.

## 18.11 The use of computer-based technology in training

This modern development is indispensable in the modern day and age, and cannot be done without in any training and development in an organisation today. Various modes and approaches exist, and that which is selected for training and development purposes will depend on the sophistication of the organisation in terms of its technology, the cost of the method, and whether the necessary computers and other technology are available for use in the organisation. Various writers emphasise the importance of these methods: Abernathy (1999:36–7), Carrell et al (2000:266–7), Noe (2002:252–266), and Swanepoel et al. (2003: 466–9).

Various methods and approaches are briefly outlined below.

### 18.11.1 Computer-Based Training (CBT)

This is an interactive training experience in which the computer provides the learning stimulus, the trainee must respond, and the computer analyses the responses and provides feedback to the trainee. This includes interactive video, CD-Rom and other systems when they are computer-driven. This mode of training has become more sophisticated with the development of laser discs and DVDs and increasing use of the Internet.

CD-Roms and DVDs utilise a laser to read text, graphics, audio and video off an aluminium disc. A laser disc uses a laser to provide high-quality video and sound. A laser disc can be used alone (as a source of video) or as part of a computer-based instruction delivery system.

Computer-Based Training also includes Computer-Managed Instruction (CME) and Computer-Assisted Instruction (CAI), the latter previously being known as programmed instruction. Since trainees need a computer for this training approach it is very expensive, and because there is no interaction between trainees it is not suitable for developing interpersonal skills.

## 18.11.2 Interactive video

This approach combines video and Computer-Based Instruction (CBI), and it provides a one-to-one approach to trainees via a monitor connected to a keyboard. Trainees use the keyboard or touch the monitor to interact with the program. Interactive video is used to teach technical procedures and interpersonal skills.

## 18.11.3 Web-Based Training (WBT)

According to Carrell et al. (2000:267), no educational or training approach has ever exploded onto the scene faster and with as much promise as Web-Based Training (WBT). The Internet offers training opportunities not bound by either time or place. Research reflecting the year 2001, revealed that 66 per cent of all Americans aged 12 or older used the Internet in the relevant year, and half of these users went online daily.

According to Stone (2002:337), this type of training is delivered on public or private computer networks and is displayed by a web browser. Intranet-based training refers to training delivered by a company's own computer network. Internet- and intranet-based training use similar technologies. The major difference is that intranet training is restricted to a company's employees. Internet and intranet training cover simple communications, online referencing and actual delivery of training and storage of the organisation's intellectual capital or knowledge. Internet and intranet training have similar advantages to multimedia training. The disadvantages of web-based training include bandwidth and virus problems, the need to control and bill users, and the difficulties (and costs) of writing (and revising) training programs.

## 18.11.4 Worldwide web (www)

This is a user-friendly service on the Internet. The web provides browser software (such as Mosaic and Netscape) that enables the user to explore the web. Besides browser software, users also need a search engine (for instance, Yahoo, Infoseek, Alta Vista, Excite, and Lycos) to find information on topics of their choice. This can be used for training purposes. The following are examples of Internet resources which are related to training topics:

- www.ast.org: home page for American Society for Training and development
- www.brandon-hall.com: information on web-based training
- www.km.com: portal to knowledge management resources
- www.webbasedtraining.com: sample websites, tips for building websites
- www.avilar.com: tools for creating web learning environments
- www.webct.com: tools to create online learning programs
- www.riskybusiness.com: example of a simulation

## 18.11.5 Internet- and intranet-based training

Internet training refers to training that is delivered on public or private computer networks and displayed by a web browser. Intranet training refers to training delivered using a company's own computer networks. Both types are stored in a computer and accessed by using a computer network.

## 18.11.6  E-learning or online learning

This refers to instruction and delivery of training by computer online through the Internet or the web. E-learning also includes web-based training, distance learning, virtual classrooms, and can even involve CD-Rom. According to Noe (2002:257), e-learning has three important characteristics:

- E-learning involves electronic networks that enable information and instruction to be delivered, shared, and updated instantly.
- E-learning is delivered to the trainee using computers with Internet technology.
- E-learning focuses on learning solutions that go beyond traditional training. E-learning goes beyond training to include the delivery of information and tools that improve performance.

It is clear that e-learning not only provides trainees with content, but also gives learners the ability to control what they learn, the speed at which they work through a program, how much they want to practice, and when they want to learn.

## 18.11.7  Virtual reality

This is a computer-based technology that provides trainees with a three-dimensional learning experience. Using specialised equipment or viewing the virtual model on the computer screen, trainees move through the simulated environment and interact with its components. According to Noe (2002:264), technology is used to stimulate multiple senses of the trainee. Devices relay information from the environment to the senses. For example, audio interfaces, gloves that provide a sense of touch, and treadmills or motion platforms are used to create a realistic, artificial environment. Devices also communicate information about the trainee's movements to a computer. These devices allow the trainee to experience presence of actually being in a particular environment.

## 18.12  Mixed-mode training

There are variations to mixed mode learning with buzzwords such as 'experiential', 'project', and 'self-directed', but there are essentially two distinguished mixed-mode models: action learning and adventure learning. Action

**Table 18.6** Comparing traditional learning, action learning, and adventure learning

| Traditional learning | Action learning | Adventure learning |
|---|---|---|
| Individual-based | Group-based | Group-based |
| Knowledge emphasis | Skills emphasis | Skills/Knowledge emphasis |
| Input-orientated | Output-orientated | Mixed orientation |
| Classroom-based | Work-based | Work-based |
| Passive | Active | Active |
| Memory tested | Competence tested | Attitude tested |
| Focus on past | Focus on present and future | Focus on past, present and future |
| Standard cases | Real cases | Mixed cases |
| One way | Interactive | Interactive |
| Teacher-led | Facilitated/self-facilitated by students | Facilitated/self-facilitated by students |

SOURCE: Adapted from Swanepoel et al. (2003:472) and Mellalieu and Leberman (1996)

learning is clearly demonstrated when it is compared with traditional learning. Mellalieu and Leberman (1996) have indicated differences attributable to adventure learning (see Table 18.6):

### 18.12.1 Action learning

Employee development is important for organisations to remain competitive, since their original training quickly becomes outdated. Action learning is a way to give employees real-life problems and then provide them with solutions, which include systems support to help them learn and provide them with solutions within a real-life environment. Action learning therefore provides challenges and demands the transformation of problems into opportunities for employees. A broader description of action learning would be 'learning by doing'.

Action learning is not a business game, case study, or simulation because it is for 'real' people, tackling 'real' problems, in 'real' time. This can be illustrated through some of the characteristics of action learning:

- Project-based.
- For real.
- Learner-driven.
- A social process.
- High visibility.
- Time-orientated, i.e. typically between four to nine months.

Action learning is usually carried out in small groups of up to 30 people. Noe (2002) points out that there are several types of problems that action learning addresses: to change the business, to better utilise technology, to remove barriers between the customer and the company, and to develop global leaders.

Yorks (2000) suggests that the appropriateness of action learning needs to be considered by asking the following questions:

- What kind of learning occurs during action learning?
- What are some of the advantages and benefits of action learning?
- What kind of programme should I design

(objectives, format, length, resources, and so forth)?
- How is a learning coach different from other types of group facilitators?
- How can I ensure that the learning transfers back to participants' jobs?
- How can I sell action learning to my organisation?

A key to action learning is its flexible framework, which moulds around the objectives that an organisation has, rather than assimilating new objects and models. Larger organisations may even develop their own internal action learning specialist.

According to Noe (2002:236), it must be borne in mind that although action learning has not been formally evaluated, the process appears to maximise learning and transfer of training, because it involves real-time problems employees face. Also, action learning can be useful for identifying dysfunctional team dynamics that can get in the way of effective problem solving.

### 18.12.2 Adventure learning

Smolowe et al. (1999) describe adventure learning by orientating it within a framework called IMMERSION. This acronym stands for:

*Interactive:* Compelling participants to interact with each other, which will highlight how they work together. This is also for accelerating trust development within the group of participants.

*Meaningful:* Adventure activities trigger innovative thinking, re-awaken creativity, and foster a sense of discovery.

*Mirthful:* Challenging the assumption that work should not be fun.

*Experiential:* Engaging all senses for learning, rather than just the traditional sitting and listening.

*Risky:* Taking participants out of their comfort zones and placing them in unfamiliar territory in order to develop emotional and physical risk-taking management.

*Supportive:* Affirming each person's

strengths, and helping people learn the value of input from others.

*Introspective:* Compelling people to look into the mirror by reflecting critically, thus enabling new awareness not only about their own behaviour but also of how it affects others.

*Out-of-the-box:* Removing people from the office and doing activities in a new environment. Debriefing from these adventures will guide the group to seeing and recognising relationships and processes that affect their work environment.

*Natural:* Extracting natural behaviours as a part of exploring human nature.

Human resources managers may engage an adventure consultant to facilitate a group of participants to review situations in a work-based environment. This will help them to solve problems and highlight barriers to risk taking so that limitations to the group's effectiveness can be understood.

## 18.13 Issues intrinsic to training and development in the South African context

Owing to the peculiarities of the South African situation, which are a result of the legacy of the past, a multitude of factors impact on training and development. These need to be borne in mind when executing training.

### 18.13.1 Adult learning

Workplace training and development programmes in South Africa must take particular cognisance that learners are adults (quite often illiterate or semi-illiterate), who require different teaching methods to children. Adults and children learn in fundamentally different ways. Androgogy is the study of how adults learn, as opposed to pedagogy, which investigates how children learn.

While children are more often charac-terised as learning for curiosity's sake or just for the sake of learning, adults are more orientated towards learning for application in the near future. The reasons most frequently mentioned for adult learning episodes are problems on the job, preparing for an occupation, home and personal responsibilities, and improving some area of competence related to recreation or hobbies.

The following are characteristics of adults that facilitate adult learning:

- Adults prefer to plan their own learning projects and to adopt a self-directed approach towards learning. This is derived from a desire to set their own pace, establish their own structure and keep open the option to revise the learning strategy.
- Adults possess a vast reservoir of experience, which can greatly facilitate the learning process. Adults approach learning with a fairly well-defined cognitive map. This map is based on their experience in the world, and the older they are the more detailed their map is likely to be. Adults should therefore be made aware of how the newly acquired knowledge will supplement their existing knowledge and what benefits they stand to derive from it.
- Adults act from internal motivation, which originates from the need to grow and develop to self-realisation. The lecture material should accordingly be meaningful to learners and should relate to their objectives and work situation.
- Adults are problem- and task-orientated in their approach to the learning process. They learn best if learning is built around their practical living and working environment. Instead of presenting subject matter to be memorised the trainer should present it as problems that have to be investigated and solved.

Table 18.7 is a summary of the difference between the child and adult in the learning situation.

**Table 18.7** Summary of learning characteristics

| Characteristic | Child | Adult |
|---|---|---|
| 1  Need to know | Need determined by teacher | Needs to know why before learning |
| 2  Learner's experience | Little or no experience | Great volume and quality of experience |
| 3  Concept of learner | Dependent on teacher | Self-directing |
| 4  Readiness to learn | Ready when told to learn | Ready when need is experienced |
| 5  Orientation to learning | Activities are subject-centred | Activities are life- or task-centred |
| 6  Motivation to learn | Largely extrinsic | Largely intrinsic |
| 7  Authority | Dependent on teacher | Self-dependent and self-responsible |
| 8  Responsibility | Little or no responsibility | Co-responsibility |

SOURCE: Van Dyk et al. (2001)

## 18.13.2 Diversity Training

The changing demographics and socio-political scene in South Africa are having a significant impact on communities, organisations, society, and the nation. Employee morale, productivity, and success will depend on the way organisations manage the changing demographics of their current and future workers. (Also see chapter 6 of this volume.)

Theories on training usually assume that the workforce is homogeneous. In South Africa, this may be counterproductive if they do not take into account the diverse composition of the South African workforce. Diversity training has become one solution to assist organisations in their efforts to retain productive workers, maintain high employee morale, and foster understanding and harmony among culturally diverse workers.

To be effective, diversity training must be designed to change the myths of diversity (such as affirmative action training), to educate participants about the realities of diversity, and to offer ways to respond to the challenge of valuing and managing diversity in the workplace.

## 18.13.3 Recognition of Prior Learning

The identification of training needs should, however, take cognisance of the realities that exist in South Africa, and should include the Recognition of Prior Learning (RPL), although it often has no documented or certificated proof. The RPL approach has become popular in South Africa over the last number of years due to its informal evolution and restrictions regarding access to education and training for historically disadvantaged groups. The high profile RPL enjoys is because it brings hope for many people, especially those from historically disadvantaged communities, who have acquired capabilities outside the formal learning system and for which they receive no formal recognition.

According to Coetzee (2002:153), RPL is a process that enables people of all ages, backgrounds, and attitudes to receive formal recognition for experience, skills, and knowledge they already possess. Recognition of prior learning attempts to put a value on all learning, irrespective of how achieved, through an open and transparent approach to assessment. Recognition of prior learning must be managed according to certain principles, namely:

- Sound assessment principles must be applied.
- Competence should be evaluated against defined unit standards.
- A variety of assessment methods should be used.

- A procedure should be applied enabling a learner or employer to have access to RPL evaluation processes.

## 18.13.4 The training of supervisors in South Africa

Supervisors control the activities of lower-level employees, and through those employees in their charge they are responsible for carrying out the policy and achieving the objectives of management. Supervisors not only act as a model and example to subordinates, but also form the link between higher-level management and lower-level employees. For this reason it is essential that supervisors fulfil their role effectively.

Supervisors' jobs can be divided into two parts: supervisory work, which deals with planning, organising, directing, and controlling a subordinate's work; and technical work, which covers everything else in the job. For the technical part of the job, the supervisor will need on-going technical training for which s/he was initially employed. Technical training, however, falls outside the scope of supervisory training, which is concerned only with the non-technical or supervisory part of a supervisor's job.

The Institute of People Management (IPM Fact Sheet 14) suggests the following questions to check whether a supervisor is doing his/her job effectively. The supervisor requires assistance if the answer to any of these questions is 'yes', and s/he should receive training in the identified area.

- Does the supervisor fail to get the best out of the workers?
- Has s/he failed to tell them what they are doing and why they are doing it?
- Is absenteeism among people under his/her supervision high?
- Is discipline poor?
- Are workers often late?
- Is the labour turnover in his/her department high compared with other departments?
- Do new employees working under the supervisor leave within the first three months?
- Is the accident rate high?
- Does it happen regularly that management hears of accidents under his/her supervision too late to take effective action?
- Is the supervisor often overloaded with work while his/her subordinates are under-utilised?

According to Wood and Spicer (1995), the three most common weaknesses of existing supervisory staff are: a lack of assertiveness, unwillingness to make decisions, and a lack of planning skills. Against this background the question can be asked whether the successful supervisor displays attributes that distinguish him/her from the unsuccessful supervisor. Wood and Spicer (1995) detected the following attributes among successful supervisors in the footwear industry:

- A willingness to teach others.
- Self-control.
- Advice-seeking skill.
- Understanding of individual psychology.
- Self-planning skill.
- Motivation skill.
- Quality orientation.
- Positive expectations.
- Assertiveness.
- Productivity.
- Self-organising skill.
- Accurate self-perception.
- Manager-assisting skill.
- Loyalty to the company.
- Idea-generation skill.
- Role understanding.
- Conceptualising skill.

Wood and Spicer's (1995) analysis of the traits in those individuals who were promoted to supervisors, found that the majority of the attributes are related to self-management and describe the behaviour of the individual before promotion.

Building on the personal attributes that are vital for any supervisor to be effective, a training programme for supervisors should also concentrate on the knowledge and skills that supervisors need to manage their job success-fully. The Institute for People Management (IPM Fact Sheet 217) lists a number of knowl-edge and skills areas for supervisory training:

- An understanding of their role in the organisation.
- Problem solving and decision-making.
- Planning.
- Organisation.
- Time management (their own time and that of others).
- Delegation.
- Giving instructions.
- The empowerment of subordinates.
- Control.
- Leadership.
- Effective communication (both verbal and written).
- The bridging of communication barriers.
- Teamwork and the initiation of team leader strategies.
- The effective chairing of meetings.
- The management of change.
- An understanding of how the organisa-tion functions.
- Understanding employee behaviour.
- Handling conflict.
- Implementing quality procedures.
- Giving effective feedback.
- Effective cooperation with workers, peers, and managers.
- Carrying out recruitment and making appointments.

These aspects will give supervisors an overall grasp of their work, which means that they will have a holistic understanding of their job. There are also broad organisational and socio-economic factors that directly influence supervisors in their work environment, and that should also be covered in training:

- *Understanding and implementation of the organisation's policies and rules.*
  Supervisors may be expected to know and understand the policies and practices relating to, for example, job evaluation, job grading, and wage deductions. However, many supervisors lack a basic understanding of policies, practices, and

structures. Training should therefore focus on these issues.
- *Human resources policy.* Concepts such as the NQF and RPL should also be explained as part of a training pro-gramme. This should be done not only as a matter of interest but also so as to demonstrate how they can benefit super-visors as well as the employees working under them.
- *Employment relations.* The recognition of trade unions through legislation has brought about changes in the power and authority of supervisors. Their authority has been modified, and often even erod-ed. Supervisors need to be trained to deal with trade union officials and shop stew-ards as well as with workers who are trade union members. Unacceptable behaviour on the part of the supervisor in dealing with these workers cannot be tolerated, as the consequences for the organisation are too great. Therefore training in employ-ment relations is of great importance in South Africa's work environment. (See Chapter 4 in this regard.)
- *Intergroup conflict in the work situation.* Supervisors have long been recognised as key figures in socio-political problems and with difficulties related to cultural diversity in South Africa. This is because the relationship between themselves and their subordinates is so significant. Supervisors' values and attitudes often shape the attitudes and behaviour of their co-workers and subordinates. Therefore, if supervisors received interpersonal rela-tions training at this level, they could contribute significantly to peace and sta-bility in the workplace. The effectiveness of a supervisor in minimising intergroup conflict depends on his/her values and knowledge of company policy and of other management aspects (see chapter 5, this volume).
- *Interpersonal contact and social interac-tion.* It is well known that intergroup stereotyping and prejudice can be allevi-ated by contact between members of the

different groups. Frequent informal social events should be organised within the organisation. Diversity training to develop an understanding between different race groups and training to develop interpersonal skills could promote better relations in the working environment.

Various challenges face illiterate supervisors in South Africa in order to do their job well, as discussed in the text box below.

---

## Encounter 18.1

Once organisations are convinced that immediate training is vital and agree to go ahead, they discover a critical obstacle. In order to participate in supervisory-level workshops and training programmes, supervisors must be literate.

Out of a population of 43 million, English is the mother tongue of only 8.7 per cent of South Africans, while 43 per cent can speak it as a second or third language, yet it is the most common language for supervisory training.

Three forms of literacy can be identified:
- Traditional literacy, the ability to read and write in an academic setting;
- Functional literacy, the ability to comprehend and use information that people need to participate effectively in society; and
- Workplace literacy, encompassing basic communication and computation skills required to successfully perform the day-to-day operations of a job. This is the form of literacy that employees are most concerned with, because of its direct connection to work, to quality, and to job performance.

With the advent of new thinking, many organisations embarked on training programmes for their workers, including supervisors. The typical question that came to the fore was, 'How am I expected to teach these people when they can't read?' Possible solutions to this problem are to:
- Minimise the written work by designing exercises for small-group discussion.
- Simplify the language by rewriting text books to make them easier to read, use short simple questions, short paragraphs,

lots of white space, and replace difficult words with easier to read synonyms.
- Build into the programme the major principles of adult learning, such as:
  - participants should see the immediate practical value of what they are learning;
  - the curriculum should include materials and tasks that apply to the specific needs of supervisors;
  - experimental learning situations should be created with exercises relating to on-the-job uses;
  - participants should be given ample opportunity to succeed and be treated as intelligent adults, learners should be addressed and the learning process should be enjoyable; and
  - the programme should be highly interactive, with participants realising that the focus of the training is not directed at the trainer but that the students are leading the training themselves.
- Use competent trainers who can 'switch gears' between the literate and illiterate supervisors.
- Select a highly visual format for transferring knowledge and skill. Rely on the old adage 'a picture is worth more than a thousand words'.

SOURCE: Katz (1994). Adapted by the authors.

---

## 18.13.5 Benefits of training and development to an organisation

Now that training and education has been discussed, it should be easy for a reader or learner to identify with the following benefits training and development has for an organisation. Training and development:
- Leads to improved profitability and/or more positive attitudes toward profit orientation.
- Improves the job knowledge and skills at all levels of the organisation.
- Helps people identify with organisation goals.

- Helps create a better corporate image.
- Fosters authenticity, openness, and trust.
- Improves the relationship between boss and subordinate.
- Aids in organisational development.
- Helps prepare guidelines for work.
- Aids in understanding and carrying out organisational policies.
- Provides information for future needs in all areas of the organisation.
- Leads to more effective decision-making and problem solving.
- Aids in development for promotion from within.
- Aids in developing leadership skill, motivation, loyalty, better attitudes, and other aspects that successful workers and managers usually display.
- Aids in increasing productivity and/or quality of work.
- Helps keep costs down in many areas, for example, production, personnel administration, etc.
- Develops a sense of responsibility to the organisation for being competent and knowledgeable.
- Improves labour-management relations.
- Reduces outside consulting costs by utilising competent internal consulting.
- Stimulates preventative management as opposed to putting out fires.
- Eliminates suboptimal behaviour (such as hiding tools).
- Creates an appropriate climate for growth.
- Aids in improving organisational communication.
- Helps employees adjust to change.
- Aids in handling conflict, thereby helping to prevent stress and tension.

Benefits to the individual, in turn, should benefit the organisation. Here, training and development:
- Helps the individual in making better decisions and effective problem solving.
- Internalises and operationalises the motivational variables of recognition, achievement, growth, responsibility, and advancement.

- Aids in encouraging and achieving self-development and self-confidence.
- Helps a person handle stress, tension, frustration, and conflict.
- Provides information for improving leadership, knowledge, communication skills, and attitudes.
- Increases job satisfaction and recognition.
- Moves a person towards personal goals while improving interaction skills.
- Satisfies the personal needs of the trainer and the trainee.
- Provides the trainee with an avenue for growth and a say in his/her own future.
- Develops a sense of growth in learning.
- Helps a person develop speaking and listening skills.
- Helps eliminate fear in attempting new tasks.

Benefits in personnel and human relations, intra- and inter-group relations, and policy implementation impact positively on the organisation. Training and development:
- Improves communication between groups and individuals.
- Assists in the orientation of new employees and those taking new jobs through transfer or promotion.
- Provides information on equal opportunity and affirmative action.
- Provides information on other governmental laws and administrative policies.
- Improves interpersonal skills.
- Makes organisational policies, rules, and regulations viable.
- Improves morale.
- Builds cohesiveness in groups.
- Provides a good climate for learning, growth, and coordination.
- Makes the organisation a better place to work and live.

## 18.14  Career management

Career management is part of the throughput process and occurs in the job context environment. The interaction of career management and the various environments has a direct influence on the development, status, and recognition of workers in the job content environment. In the job context environment, it has an influence on management philosophy, leadership, working conditions, and intra- and inter-group relations.

It is to the advantage of any organisation to retain productive employees for as long as possible. Training and development to make employees more productive in an organisation was discussed earlier in this chapter. A further means, closely linked to training and development, is for the organisation to invite employees to treat their relationship with their employer as a career. Ideally there should be sufficient opportunities and promotion possibilities to enable employees to remain with their employer for the duration of their working lives.

## Encounter 18.2

WHERE EXACTLY, IS YOUR HR CAREER HEADED?

As aware as we are of these realities, many HR professionals haven't fully grasped how our own careers are being affected. However, we are just like professionals in any other function. We no longer have only one option – to climb the corporate ladder. Our career paths have come to resemble chessboards, with movements up, down, and sideways with a number of employers. In addition, the same counsel we give others, also applies to us: It's up to us to create our own careers.

SOURCE: Mengel (2002:27)

The long-term interests of employees should be protected by the organisation, and employees should be encouraged to grow and realise their full potential for the benefit of the organisation. If the career planning and development of employees is effective, they will realise their full potential and will probably be prepared to remain with their present employer till retirement. However, this trend is decreasing, and more and more employees change jobs more frequently than before, not only in their own country, but also literally from country to country. The world is really starting to become a global village in terms of the international job market, as international barriers fall away and the mobility of professionals in particular increases rapidly.

Succession planning in an organisation is essential to ensure that suitably qualified and experienced employees are available when vacancies arise, and to fill human resources needs that result from the growth and re-orientation of the organisation in the economic environment in which it operates. Employee succession and filling of new jobs, particularly management jobs, are therefore essential for the survival of any organisation.

Career management has become a crucial issue in South Africa, and one reason is that many organisations are controlled by their founders or the families of the founders. The success of a number of organisations listed on the Johannesburg Securities Exchange is attributed, at least in the public mind, to the continued good health and leadership of a single founder-owner. However, with the rapid development of the South African economy, organisations of this nature will jeopardise their position if they do not implement career planning and development or succession in posts.

Scores of small and medium-sized organisations in South Africa are in this position, and they will suffer losses if the founder-owner should die suddenly.

In South Africa, it is more important than ever before that large organisations draw up five-year career management plans, medium-sized organisations draw up three-year plans, and small organisations plan to implement career management within a year to meet changed market demands for human resources.

*A career* can be defined as a series of jobs that follow a hierarchy of levels or degrees of difficulty, responsibility, and status. *Career planning* may be defined as the process by which an individual analyses his/her work situation, specifies his/her career goals, and plans various means to achieve these goals.

To plan a career, an employee must set certain career priorities, evaluate the behaviour and attitude of other people who have successfully achieved such a career, choose a type of work that makes use of his/her strong points, undergo the necessary training, and where possible get a good mentor to guide him/her. The individual must then regularly monitor his/her progress against the goals that have been set, investigate shortcomings and, where necessary, re-plan. A *career path* is regarded, from the organisation's point of view, as flexible lines of progression through which an employee typically moves in his/her career. By following an established career path, the employee participates in career development with the assistance of the organisation. Career development is defined as a formal approach taken by the organisation to ensure that employees with proper qualifications and experience are available when they are needed by the organisation.

An important question is who is responsible for career planning and development. The answer is that it normally requires effort from three sources – the organisation itself, the employee's immediate manager, and the employee.

- *The organisation's responsibilities.* An organisation cannot and should not bear the sole responsibility for planning and developing an employee's career. The organisation has to furnish career opportunities for its employees and advise employees about the various career paths that are available in that organisation to enable them to achieve their career goals. The human resources department is generally responsible for relaying this information to employees and informing staff when new jobs are created and old ones are phased out. The human resources department therefore needs to work closely with individual employees and their superiors to ensure that their career goals are realistic and are followed within the constraints of the organisation.
- *The employee's immediate superior.* This person, although s/he is not expected to be a professional counsellor, can and should take part in facilitating his/her

immediate subordinate's career planning. The superior should act as communicator, counsellor, appraiser, coach and mentor, ensuring that the subordinate employee gets the information necessary for furthering his/her career. It is unfortunate that many superiors do not see it as part of their duties to assist in the career development of their subordinates. Either they do not know how to go about it, or they see every subordinate as a potential threat to their own position, so they give no assistance, and may even exert a negative influence.

- *The individual employee.* The final responsibility for career planning and development rests with individual employees because they know what they want from their career and how hard they are prepared to work.

## Encounter 18.3

SHOULD I STAY OR GO?

Terry Meyer of Deloitte & Touche's Human Capital Corporation lists the top five factors affecting an employee's decision to stay or leave. They are:

1  Quality of relationship with supervisor or manager.
2  Ability to balance work and home life.
3  Amount of meaningful work – feeling of making a difference.
4  Level of cooperation with co-workers.
5  Level of trust in the workplace.

On the employer's side, Meyer cites the five retention interventions that were found to be most valuable in a global benchmarking study. They are:

1  Conducting internal studies (surveys and focus groups).
2  Improving selection practices – don't oversell the job.
3  Conducting exit interviews.
4  Improving the openness of communication between management and employees.
5  Enhancing training and development opportunities.

SOURCE: Morgan (2003:18)

Successful career planning and development is therefore a joint effort by the individual employee, his/her immediate superior and the organisation: the employee does the planning, the immediate superior provides the resources, and the organisation provides the means and structure for development.

The rest of this section is devoted to the importance of career management, career choices employees should make, the various career stages of employees, legislation that assists employers with career choices for employees in South Africa, a more detailed analysis of career planning and development itself, and a practical five-step approach that employers and employees can use for career management.

## 18.14.1 The importance of career management to employers and employees

For the organisation, the major purpose of career management is to match the employee's needs, abilities, and goals with the current or future needs of the organisation. This is intended to ensure that the organisation places the right employee in the right place at the right time and thus offers the employee the opportunity of achieving personal fulfilment in the job. Matching the employee with the job is the first step, which entails matching the employee's potential with the requirements of the job, and the employee's needs with the job reward, as discussed in Chapters 8 and 9.

There are a number of reasons for implementing career management in organisations:

- To cope with global competition and the threats of highly increased mobility of professional employees in particular.
- Employees wish to have control over their own careers, and the new generation of younger employees wants greater job satisfaction and more career options. Being given the ability to advance increases the quality of work life of employees.
- It is necessary today for organisations to avoid obsolescence by encouraging

employees to learn new skills. This is because rapid changes in technology and changes in consumer demand cause skills to become outdated. With career development programmes, employees can gain new skills when their old skills are no longer in demand.

- Career management reduces staff turnover in the organisation. Employees experience less frustration and greater job satisfaction because they know they can advance in the organisation.
- When employees' specific talents have been identified, they are given the opportunity through career planning to perform better and to be placed in jobs that fit their ambitions and personal talents.

Career management integrates the objectives of the individual and the organisation in such a way that both will gain. The employee will experience satisfaction and personal development, while there will be increased productivity and creativity within the organisation.

The end result of career management is an organisation staffed by committed employees who are well trained and productive.

## 18.14.2 Career stages and choices

South Africa has a vast unskilled and semi-skilled population and small numbers of qualified personnel. Organisations therefore need to identify skills and talents quickly and embark on effective career development programmes, so that employees can contribute to the productivity of the organisation. The Human Sciences Research Council does research into the aptitudes, career choices, personalities, and so on, of employees. The various needs and the career and life stages of employees need to be taken into account when career planning and development programmes are being designed. Employees also need to analyse how a career choice should be made and developed.

Figure 18.3 shows that all people go through different but inter-related stages in their lives and careers. Depending on the state they have reached in their lives and their careers, they have different needs. This should be borne in mind when careers are planned and developed. Most people prepare for an occupation in some formal educational institution like a high school, and then take their first job. They will eventually move to other jobs within the same organisation or join other organisations. Although the stages may vary, most employees go through all the stages indicated in Figure 18.3.

Analysis of the various career and life stages of people shows that the most important decision a person makes is what career to follow. It is generally accepted that what employees accomplish and derive from their career will depend on the congruence between their personality and the job environment. Each individual resembles one of six personality types to some extent, and people choose their occupations in accordance with their personality, in order to follow a career that generally matches it. People sometimes have a combi-

nation of these personality characteristics. The personality types are:

- *Realistic:* individuals who prefer activities involving the use of machinery or tools; for example artisans, tool and die makers, farmers, engineers, and carpenters.
- *Investigative:* individuals who are analytical, curious, methodical and precise; for example, medical technologists, teachers, biologists, and astronomers.
- *Artistic:* people, who strive for self-expression, are non-conformist, original and introspective; for example, artists, musicians, photographers, sculptors, and actors.
- *Social:* individuals who enjoy helping and working with others and who avoid systematic activities such as working with tools or machinery; for example, police officers, social workers, and guidance counsellors.
- *Enterprising:* individuals who enjoy activities that permit them to influence others

**Figure 18.3** The relationship between people's most important needs and their career and life stages

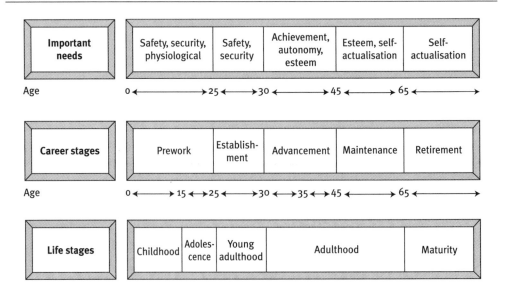

SOURCE: Adapted from Ivancevich (1995:494)

to accomplish their goals; for example, computer salespeople, life assurance agents, estate agents, business managers, and lawyers.

- *Conventional:* individuals who enjoy the systematic use of data or reproduction of material; for example, credit managers, office workers, accountants, and supermarket managers.

Depending on the personality type alternatively referred to as 'career anchors' by some writers, an employee could find an occupation that suits his/her personality or combination of characteristics, and it would be a satisfactory career. Organisations should be flexible enough to provide alternatives for satisfying employees' varying career needs. Organisations should also recognise that not every employee is or wants to be the enterprising type.

## 18.14.3 Career planning

### Career planning by the individual

We have stated that career planning is a process whereby an individual sets career goals and identifies the means to achieve them. The responsibility for career planning rests primarily with the individual, but s/he will need support from superiors and the organisation in general. Career planning begins with understanding oneself. Each individual needs to identify his/her personality characteristics, as described above. Career planning is as important to a new job seeker as it is to an adult worker already in employment. Adult workers planning their careers need to establish their present life stage and career stage (Figure 18.3). As a person progresses through life, his/her priorities usually change. People also have different priorities in different life and career stages.

By introspection, individuals should decide what kind of person they are, what skills they possess, their values and interests, likes and dislikes, and strengths and weaknesses. They should draw up a balance sheet listing their strengths on the left-hand side and weaknesses on the right. It may be necessary to make several lists because such repetition forces a person to discover more about his/her characteristics. On the basis of these lists a person might decide on a career in, say, a technical field instead of in the arts or management.

An employee should identify job opportunities in his/her organisation by asking:

- What are my prospects for promotion and transfer from my present job?
- What positions have my peers reached within the last year or two?
- What is the compensation range for various jobs in the organisation?
- Which division in the organisation has the fastest growth and therefore provides the best promotion opportunities?

The employee might even consider changing jobs and accepting a lower-grade job in the organisation to obtain a position that is an avenue for moving up faster in the organisation.

Employees should also study trends in the economy, for example, where there are human resources shortages in various skills, what technology developments are taking place and how government policy could shape the future job market. In South Africa, there is a particular shortage of managerial talent and technically competent artisans, as discussed elsewhere in the book, particularly in Chapter 17. These issues should be taken into consideration when career decisions are made and opportunities investigated.

The next step, after job trends and specific opportunities in the employment market have been analysed, is to set goals in terms of the personal strengths, weaknesses, interests, and values identified. Then short-, medium-, and long-term goals must be set in order to monitor growth in the chosen career. Goals should be consistent with a person's capabilities and compatible with his/her self-image, because unrealistic goals lead to frustration and disillusionment.

Once the goals have been set, the employee needs to prepare a plan to meet them. In drawing up this plan the employee needs to have discussions with superiors in the organisation and with members of the human resources department. They will assist him/her to implement the plan.

## Career planning by the organisation

If an organisation is to be successful, it needs to ensure that sufficient numbers of qualified employees are available when vacancies occur or expansion takes place. Recruitment and selection is one means of ensuring this. On the other hand, an organisation can implement training and development and have recourse to promotion from within to achieve this goal. What is essential is that people must be groomed for posts, and planning must be instituted so that the right people are available for vacant positions when other people retire or resign or when the organisation expands. This process is a technique that outlines specific progression from one job to another by employees according to the goals and needs of the organisation. It includes plans for a sequence of development activities, which will give an individual job experience enabling him/her to step into more advanced jobs in the future. The major aim of career planning programmes, therefore, is to ensure that the goals of the organisation are smoothly achieved through the utilisation of human resources.

To help employees with their career planning, employers should make information available about jobs and should create career options; they should help employees to set realistic career goals and to plan their careers.

Employers traditionally developed career paths for upward mobility because if a person could not move upward s/he had to leave the organisation. Today, enlightened organisations recognise that not everybody wants to follow a vertical career path and become a top executive; career paths can be developed with lateral, diagonal and even downward career progression (for example, as a person nears retirement). In other words, when an employee's career is planned, the career path can be built in accordance with his/her goals, ensuring that the employee's job satisfaction remains of paramount importance. If the organisation synchronises its career planning activities with the career planning of the individual, the result is bound to be a positive response on the part of employees, and the organisation will have sufficiently qualified and motivated staff when vacancies occur.

In the modern era, organisations have also come to the realisation that careers per se are not sufficient to retain employees, since a plateau can often jeopardise an employee's future career development. Consequently, the idea of a two-career ladder approach has evolved: one hand being the traditional managerial ladder and, the other hand, a professional ladder. The latter implies that an employee who has not had the opportunity to move up the managerial ladder can actually move along a different technical or professional job ladder (for instance, engineers, advisors, legal specialists, etc.). This can be substituted for the steps in the managerial career and retain the employee's services instead of resigning in order to move up in her/his job elsewhere in her/his career. This approach has also been followed in various semi-governmental organisations such as military service, police, correctional services, etc. where doctors, lawyers, social workers, and so on can follow their own professional ladder instead of the rank-orientated managerial structures. Such staff often attain remuneration and fringe benefit levels which would be at higher rank levels than the rank they would occupy in the managerial structure.

## 18.14.4 Career development

As we have mentioned, career development is a formal approach by the organisation to ensure that employees with proper qualifications and experience are available when needed. To realise this goal, the organisation needs to support career development and be committed to it. The immediate superior of the employee is of cardinal importance in providing support, advice, and feedback, but the employee is ultimately responsible for his/her own career development. Employees proceed from one job to another in a certain sequence. It is generally accepted that the right sequence of jobs contributes materially to career development. In the first place, career development starts with the job itself. Each day the employee faces different challenges and different tasks to be mastered. What is learned at work often has a greater influence than formally planned development activities. Second, different jobs demand different skills: a supervisor needs human relations skills, and a training specialist needs teaching skills and technical knowledge. Development can take place when a person is assigned a job for which s/he has not yet developed the necessary skills and s/he would learn the skills while doing the job. Third, a transfer might help an employee to acquire the skills and knowledge needed for a further promotion. Fourth, a rational sequence of job assignments can reduce the time required for an employee to develop the necessary skills for a chosen target job. If particular jobs teach particular skills, a series of job assignments should be selected that will provide the best means of development over the course of an employee's career.

Career development programmes can use both formal and informal means. Informal means would, for example, be on the job training or off the job training, but within the organisation. Alternatively, the trainee can participate in off the job programmes away from the organisation, for example, seminars and short courses provided by technikons, universities, and the Institute of People Management. If employees want to be successful in their careers, they must be on the constant lookout for the best career opportunities. In addition, they must keep their options open, not waste time working for a manager who procrastinates, ensure that they are vital subordinates to a proactive superior, strive for exposure and visibility in the organisation, be prepared to present themselves when jobs become vacant, leave the organisation if their career development slows down too much, be ready to resign if necessary, and not let success in their present job jeopardise

their career plan, because it would reduce their upward mobility.

## Career development methods

The most important methods used in carrying out career developments are outlined below:

- *Performance appraisal.* The organisation can use performance appraisal as a valuable tool for career development, because the strengths and weaknesses of employees are assessed.
- *Workshops.* Through workshops lasting two or three days, employees can be actively assisted with the planning and development of their careers.
- *Career counselling.* The human resources department or outsiders can assist employees by counselling them on their careers.
- *Tailor-made materials.* Some organisations provide material that has been specifically developed to assist employees in their career development planning, for example, company brochures showing future plans and expansion. Assessment-centre material is devised which portrays a specific organisation's activities and needs.
- *Management by objectives.* This could be an excellent means of assisting employees with career development, because superior and subordinates jointly agree on ways to achieve the organisation's goals, while also taking employees' personal goals into account. When goals are not achieved, new development needs may be identified and included in employees' career development.

## Career development for retirement

Career development for retirement is the last logical step in the career management process.

Employers should not retrench or dismiss staff lightly, but rather focus on re-training employees for a new career. Retirement via retrenchment has become so widespread in South Africa during the last few years that employees under the age of 40 are given the option to retire voluntarily. This means that a second or even a third career will have to be embarked upon before an employee reaches genuine maturity and retirement, which normally occurs at age 65 or older. Organisations therefore have a wider responsibility not only to retire employees, but if they are younger, to assist them with career development for a new and sometimes vastly different career to that they presently occupy.

For numerous employees, retirement is a bitter experience because many organisations do not prepare employees for it, particularly if they are retrenched for operational reasons. Some employees look forward to retirement as the culmination of their career, providing an opportunity to relax. Yet, often it is a disappointment and a bore. Where life was once busy and full of incident it has become dull and unexciting. Furthermore, retirees sometimes struggle to maintain their sense of identity and self-worth without a fulfilling job. This is particularly the case when an employee is retired before the normal retirement age due to restructuring, unbundling, retrenchment, and so on. Organisations therefore need to devote attention to this stage of career development for employees, and start by asking the following questions:

- When does the employee plan to retire?
- Who is considering early retirement?
- What does the employee plan to do during retirement?
- Will s/he attempt a second career outside the organisation?
- Can the organisation assist him/her in preparing for such a career?
- Can the retiree be approached by the organisation to help new employees learn the job?

The human resources department, in particular, should provide counselling for those about to retire, helping them to accept their reduced role, to live a less structured life, and to make adaptations in their family and community life. Other subjects for counselling are how the pension scheme operates and how lump sum payments will be made, how leisure time can be spent, health issues, accommodation arrangements, financial arrangements, and investments.

## Career management for dual career couples

Career management has evolved dramatically over the last three decades. It is a fact of life today that with many couples, both parties actively pursue careers. Sometimes both work for the same organisation, which requires even more fine-tuning between the two spouses than would otherwise be the case. It is also in the interests of the organisation employing them to view them jointly with regard to career development.

In general, however, where both spouses pursue a career, working for different organisations, it is in their interests to synchronise their career-pathing and personal lives in conjunction with the organisations' human resources departments. The result will be enhanced relationships in their private and business lives, since conflict can easily arise out of their employment activities. The human resources department must focus on this aspect as part of its human resources development activities.

According to Stone (2002:370), a dual career is defined as a situation where both spouses and partners have career responsibilities and aspirations. Dual career couples often experience work and family conflict, which does not occur where only one member of a family works.

Swanepoel et al. (2003:413) make the statement that conflict does exist between work and family roles, which can be created by the following work-related factors:

- Number of hours worked.
- Lack of control over the decision to work overtime.
- An inflexible work schedule.
- Irregular starting time.
- Psychologically demanding work.

Carrell et al. (2000:298) point out that the following are workplace *aspects and programmes*

that dual career couples regard as helpful to them:
- Tools (like laptops and cell phones).
- Corporate climate and managerial support.
- Emphasis on results (rather than a time card).
- Informal flexibility based on the nature of work.
- Having managers with kids or who are also dual career couples.

There are also *needs* of dual career couples, and organisations must take note of the following needs:
- Flexible hours.
- Formal flexible work programmes.
- Family leave time.
- Company-supported childcare.
- Helping relocating the trailing spouse.

Schreuder and Theron (1997:152), however, suggest the following action to balance family and work needs:
- More organisational sensitivity for home life.
- The introduction of flexible benefits to assist employees with family needs, such as child care and the care of sick children.
- The introduction of flexible work hours and work-at-home programmes.
- The revision of relocation policies to make provision for the needs of the modern worker.
- The introduction of alternative career paths – not all employees want to climb the corporate ladder.

Should an approach of this nature be followed, it will also have a positive effect on the organisation.

## 18.14.5 A practical approach to career management

As already stated, employee career development is the joint responsibility of the employee and employer. According to Carrell et al.

(2000:295), career management is defined as 'the process of designing and implementing goals, plans, and strategies that enable HR professionals and managers to satisfy workforce needs and allow individuals to achieve their career objectives. If there is to be sound employee career development, a structured strategy should be followed.' A practical five-step strategy those employers can use to ensure effective career development in their organisations is given below:
- *Step 1: Match the goals of the individual with those of the organisation.* It is essential that each employee involve him- or herself in a career planning exercise to determine what s/he wants to do now and in the future. This means that the organisation must also have very clearly defined strategic and tactical plans, i.e. careful organisational planning is undertaken.

In addition, the employer should undertake human resources planning, which will indicate exactly what the demand will be for particular employees in the organisation at any particular time, and whether there will be sufficient people to meet the demand. Job analysis is also important, because it indicates what the personal requirements are for a job and what the job entails. It is then easy to determine whether a specific employee is capable of doing a particular job. Recruitment and selection are also easier if career planning is done because employers are able to fill specific vacancies internally. Career development will identify internal staff when capable outside employees cannot be recruited. The reward system could motivate employees to develop themselves in a particular direction. It can also gauge how successful an employee's career development programme has been. Performance appraisal also plays a role in employee career development in that it can be used to determine an employee's development potential.

An individual who is already in the employ of the organisation must go through a specific procedure related to his/her career before s/he can participate in career development. The steps are as follows, and the employer should help the employee with each step:

- Self-assessment by the employee.
- Crystallisation of work values in the organisation as the employee sees it.
- Advice on how the employee can decide on a career.
- A connection workshop, where employee and employer are sensitised to future labour needs and the availability thereof.
- A discussion between the employee and the relevant supervisor or manager to ensure understanding exists regarding jobs to be performed.
- Supervisors and managers should be trained to counsel subordinates about their future career opportunities.
- The writing of an individual development plan based on the information obtained in conjunction with his/her superior and the human resources department.

## Case-in-point
### Turning a job into a career

Career management, then, is an ongoing process whereby a person obtains self-knowledge (interests, values, abilities, personality, and career anchor); obtains knowledge of the working environment (job and organisation); develops career goals; and develops a strategy and obtains feedback on the effectiveness of the strategy and the relevance of goals.

South African organisations tend to fix the boundaries of job roles and actively discourage people from moving beyond them. But career management should be the shared responsibility of the employer and employee. Companies that fail to assist employees in advancing their careers will find themselves the losers.

Daimler Chrysler's philosophy is that the company needs to 'build people to build world-class cars'. They achieve this by having a 'Fit for Profession' framework in place, which maps out the route employees can follow to achieve their career goals. For example, an employee within the logistics environment will have built up numerous career skills, such as job-specific, generic ('soft skills') and management training.

SOURCE: Abrahams (2003:6)

- *Step 2: Link career development with the human resources department and with management.* Management, and particularly the human resources department, needs to ensure that all key supervisors and managers are fully conversant with the career development programmes in the organisation, and must actively support them. Top management could circulate a letter expressing support for career development and praising supervisors and managers who direct such programmes. Such support is essential if career development programmes are to succeed in an organisation.

Career development should fit in with the organisation's management system to ensure that career development programmes do not clash with the organisation's long-term philosophy, strategy and goals.

According to Abrahams (2003:7), the following should be borne in mind in developing a career strategy: 'The strategy that the individual has in mind to realise his/her career is a sequence of activities, which assists the individual in reaching a career goal. There are many strategies, namely working long hours to show loyalty to the company, taking advantage of opportunities by increasing one's visibility, strengthening one's image to gain positive feedback by being perceived as "fitting in" and networking with others for best practice.'

- *Step 3: Link career development with environmental trends and values.* The whole process of career development needs to be refined in terms of future trends. The organisation's goals, production methods, and demographic shifts should be considered.

It is commonly accepted that technological changes occur so rapidly today that an employee's skills should be comprehensively updated every five years if s/he is to remain abreast of technological developments. These factors should be taken into account in career development. Employees should start working on a bridging qualification long before it is actually required, so that they can adjust their career and move to a more suitable job if necessary. It may be necessary, for example, to put some employees on flexitime so that they can undertake part-time study in case they need to change their job.

- *Step 4: Have regular communication between the employer and employees.* All affected parties should communicate regularly on the drawing up of career development plans, and should be kept up to date on the actual progress made.

These parties are the human resources department, heads of sections and departments, trade union representatives, and the affected employees. Interactive meetings should be held where career development plans are updated, and employees should receive feedback on their progress.

Should employees discover that their career development takes place at a faster pace than their actual progress in the organisation, consideration should be given to lateral moves within the organisation. If upward movement is out of the question and the employee insists on it, s/he should be assisted by the employer to find alternative employment either in another plant or in a different organisa-

tion. This is important since a major impediment in the career development path of an employee could lead to frustration and a decrease in productivity.

- *Step 5: The employer's responsibilities in effective career development for employees.* The employer's commitment to career development should be evident in the creation of opportunities and provision of the means required by an employee to carry out his/her career development. The participation of employers should be apparent in the following areas:
  - Periodic review of employees' progress.
  - Opportunity for self-study.
  - Establishment of support teams.
  - Provision of counselling by the employer.

## 18.15 Conclusion

In the fast-moving world of the new millennium, factors such as global competition and the socio-economic challenges to enterprises have brought a new dimension to workplace training and development. The days are gone when enterprises could regard the equipping of their workers as a 'nice to have' or an add-on activity just because everybody else was doing it.

For enterprises to survive in a highly competitive market place, the decision to invest in the development of their human resources must be a business decision. To maximise their investment, enterprises will have to adopt a strategic training approach, and in so doing, move away from the notion that training is an activity run by trainers somewhere in a lecture room. This chapter gave training as well as operational managers insight in how to adapt traditional training approaches to a much more strategic approach.

## Summary

- Education is an extremely broad concept, encompassing basic competencies and the use of reason and rational thought.

Training is job- or task-specific learning and skill acquisition. Development is management-level and leadership training – the advancement of existing managers or leaders, or the grooming of aspirant managers or leaders, through learning and instruction.

- In the present, with the importance of knowledge as a resource and the centrality of the knowledge economy, the workplace must be understood as a nurturing environment marked by a culture of learning. The dynamics of the contemporary work environment demand formal training and development programmes.
- There are various training delivery approaches and methods available for the transfer of knowledge and skills in the workplace. Action learning, mixed-mode training, and e-learning are prominent aspects today which trainers should utilise in sharpening the skills of their workforce so as to foster optimal work.
- Effective training requires much more than an instructor, a lecture room, and learning material. To become managers of learning, training people must be informed on the broad contextual issues related to workplace training and development. Key contextual issues include: competency-based training, recognition of prior learning, adult learning, diversity training, and the National Qualifications Framework.
- There is a close relationship between training and development and career development, since training and development are means that enable employees to achieve their own career goals. It is also of cardinal importance, however, that employees know what they want and how they want to spend their working lives. They need to plan their career in terms of their own talents and limitations.
- Career planning and development need to be painstaking if an employee is to gain the maximum benefit from his/her endeavours. Career management by organisations should be broad enough to meet the specific career needs of individuals, yet specific enough to afford employees flexible job experience.

## Case study
## Mod Clothing Fashion Stylists (Pty) Ltd.

This clothing manufacturing concern was established as a family business in the 1950s, in the Mobeni area south of Durban. As a consequence of various initiatives and incentives, it decided to relocate in Hammersdale, Kwazulu-Natal (in 1982), and to convert itself into a company and float its shares on the Johannesburg Securities Exchange. This was done very successfully. It grew from strength to strength, and utilised the surrounding textile companies' products to create advantage in clothing fabrics that others could not do quickly due to locations elsewhere in South Africa. Since it specialised in more boutique-type clothing with short production runs, it capitalised very well on the availability of new fabrics and special materials, which were developed for Mod Clothing in the adjacent textile manufacturing concerns. Products were, and are, distributed throughout South Africa to various boutique chains like Chick Lady and Charming Gents outlet groups, with whom they have sale agreements for men's and woman's clothing.

Mod CFS, as it is generally known in the trade, employs 390 employees, and includes a range of stylists, cutters, and designers who are specialist in modern male and female clothing tastes. Due to its recent growth, which has catapulted it into a major role-player in the clothing industry, Mod Clothing has experienced various problems. The management do, however, regard staff as their competitive edge and try to do training wherever they can. The company's senior management recently made a decision to seriously consider their commitment to training and development and to really intensify the skills of staff at all levels.

The business previously contracted various organisations to assist with training and development. These organisations were private sector as well as tertiary educational sector enterprises, and were sourced for particular skills which could be provided to the clothing-manufacturing sector. General training and development is now also sought, as the company has expanded into areas that are not really serviced by these providers. Programmes they have used in the past are as follows:

- The IPM training courses.
- Online world clothing training association courses based in London.
- The Kwazulu-Natal Clothing Manufacturers Association training courses.
- Specialist training courses in fashion design and cutting provided by the Mangusotho College in Durban.
- Tailor-made courses from consultants in training, for example, Full Need Analysts cc. (headed by a prominent trainer Dr Asoka Naidoo).

Most of the training and development programmes are either on a distance learning basis or attendance over two consecutive weekends, which run from Friday lunchtime to Sunday lunchtime, and which are presented on an in-house basis by Dr Naidoo and his team. The company does not believe in sending employees to any full-time courses, as this is too expensive and loss of production cannot be tolerated in this highly competitive clothing manufacturing industry.

Profit margins have been less than expected and the share price has gone down by 30 per cent over the last 18 months. This is primarily due to imports of similar products from Botswana and Kenyan-based companies who have recently made great strides in specialist clothing manufacturing. The fact that their cost structure is also very low makes it very difficult to compete effectively.

The training manager, John Soloman, has been requested by the managing director,

Ravi Reynolds, to review the business' strategy drastically and to compile courses to be conducted in-house to save costs. He also believes that some of the managers should be skilled in issues that are unique to the business and which could not be effectively learned at the available off the job courses. Tailor-made programmes should therefore be compiled in some areas.

Mod CFS recently expanded the production plant and employed a further 30 staff who also need training in their systems.

# Question

John was requested by the managing director to provide guidelines as to the compilation of programmes to suit the business' purposes and particularly the methods to be used in training and development for supervisory and middle management staff in the administrative and manufacturing sections of Mod CFS. These programmes should be of a two-weekend in-house duration. Design these programmes in detail.

# Experiential exercise

PURPOSE: To demonstrate the inadequacies of poor planning for a training course.

INTRODUCTION: Time management is an important element of any business' activities and employees must be made aware of the effective utilisation thereof.

TASK: Form groups of five members each. Discuss the approach that could have been followed, and how to correct it for the effective management of the following training course attended by Dawn, where the underlying personal and environmental characteristics in everyday practice preclude people from optimal learning:

NO GOOD TIME MANAGEMENT: Dawn attended time management training because she found herself persistently missing deadlines. The techniques she learnt on the course were simple and practical and could certainly help if she put them into practice. Dawn returned to work feeling cheerful, empowered, and confident.

Three months later, Dawn's filing trays are certainly more smartly labelled than they were before. However, she still misses most deadlines despite knowing in theory what she should do to address this. Her manager blames the training course. 'Just proves what a waste of time and money all this training stuff is', and Dawn feels despondent that she still seems so unable to correctly work out her priorities.

We believe Dawn's problem was not necessarily that the training was of poor quality in its own right. The real problem for Dawn was that the course did not tackle those underlying personal and environmental characteristics that, in everyday practice, inhibit her willingness or ability to implement what she had learned. Perhaps it is unrealistic for short courses to address these kinds of issues in any real depth, but that does raise the question of where they could be tackled instead.

Do you agree?

## Chapter questions

1  Explain, in one page, the difference between strategic and traditional training approaches.
2  Assume the human resources manager provides you with a challenge to draft a training programme aimed specifically at achieving the organisation's strategic objectives. Concentrate on issues such as a training and development philosophy, training policy, training intent, and the various steps in the training process.
3  Explain the difference between norm and criteria-referenced test items. Elaborate on the latter with special reference to competency-based training.
4  Write an essay on adult learning.
5  List the various methods that could be

used to equip a worker on the shop floor with the necessary knowledge and skills and refer specifically to e-learning methods.
6  Express a view on the challenges faced by enterprises with regard to supervisory training and discuss how these challenges can be met.
7  Describe the relationship between training and development and career development.
8  What benefits do you see from managing your own career? Discuss.
9  Who should be responsible for managing an employee's career – the individual or the organisation? Discuss critically.
10  What are your career goals? Draw up a balance sheet of your strengths and weaknesses and decide whether you are in the right job at present.

## Bibliography

ABERNATHY, D.J. 1999. *Training and Development*, 53(9):36–37 (www.online.learning).

ABRAHAMS, I. 2003. 'Job or career?' *People Dynamics*, 21(2):6–7. Reprinted with permission of Copyright Clearance Center.

ARMSTRONG, M. 1984. *A handbook of personnel management practice, 2nd edition.* Kogan Page, London.

CARRELL, M.R., ELBERT, N.F. & HATFIELD, R.D. 2000. *Human resource management. Strategies for managing a diverse and global workforce, 6th edition.* Dryden Press, San Diego.

COETZEE, M. 2002. *Getting and keeping your accreditation.* Van Schaik, Pretoria.

DE CENZO, D.A. & ROBBINS, S.P. 1994. *Human resource management concepts and practices.* John Wiley & Sons, New York.

DEPARTMENT OF LABOUR. 1995. *1994 Annual Report.* RP 136–1995. Government Printer, Pretoria.

DEPARTMENT OF LABOUR. 1999. *Career guide.* Government Printer, Pretoria.

DUBOIS, D.D. 1993. *Competency based performance improvement.* HRD Press, Amherst.

ELLINGTON, H. 1985. *Teaching materials: A*

*handbook for teachers and trainers.* Nichols Publishing, New York.

ERASMUS, B.J. & VAN DYK, P.S. 1999. *Training management in South Africa, 2nd edition.* International Thomson Publishing, Halfway House.

IPM (INSTITUTE FOR PERSONNEL MANAGEMENT). n.d. *Fact sheet No. 14.* IPM Journal, IPM, Rivonia (www.ipm.co.za).

IPM (INSTITUTE FOR PERSONNEL MANAGEMENT). 1992. *Fact sheet No. 217.* IPM Journal, IPM, Rivonia (www.ipm.co.za).

FIRER, S. & SAUNDERS, S. 2003. 'Human capital measurement'. *People Dynamics,* 21(3):17–19. Reprinted with permission of Copyright Clearance Center.

IVANCEVICH, J.M. 1995. *Human resource management.* McGraw-Hill Companies, New York.

KATZ, M. 1994. 'Illiterate supervisors: A home-grown solution'. *People Dynamics,* 13(4):27–30. Reprinted with permission of Copyright Clearance Center.

KINLAW, D. 1996. *The ASTD trainer's sourcebook: Coaching.* McGraw-Hill Companies, New York.

KINLAW, D. 1996. *The ASTD trainer's sourcebook: Facilitation skills.* McGraw-Hill, New York.

MAGER, R. 1975. *Preparing instructional objectives, 2nd edition.* Fearon-Pitman, California.

MCINTOSH, S.S. ©1995. 'Envisaging virtual training organisations'. *Training and Development,* 49(5):27–38. American Society for Training and Development.

MELLALIEU, P.J. & LEBERMAN, S.I. 1996. 'A Trojan Horse for moving from Mystery to Mastery: ALP-DevCo and the Action Learning Programme', *Outdoor Education Conference.* MindSurferS Limited, Auckland.

MENGEL, D. 2002. 'Where, exactly, is your HR career headed?' *People Dynamics,* 20(2):27. Reprinted with permission of Copyright Clearance Center.

MEYER, T. 1996. *Creating competitiveness through competencies.* Knowledge Resources, Randburg.

MORGAN, P. 2003. 'Get them young'. *People Dynamics,* 21(2):18. Reprinted with permission of Copyright Clearance Center.

MUCHINSKY, P.M., KRIEK, H.J. & SCHREUDER,

A.M.G. 1998. *Personnel psychology.* International Thomsons Publishing, Halfway House.

NADLER, L. 1982. *Designing training programs. The critical events model.* (Addison Wesley), Pearson Education (UK).

NOE, R.A. 2002. *Employee training and development, 2nd edition.* McGraw-Hill Companies, New York.

OLIVIER, C. 1998. *Outcomes-based education and training programmes.* Van Schaik, Pretoria.

REID, M.A. & BARRINGTON, H. 1997. *Training interventions managing employee development, 5th edition.* IPD, London.

RSA (REPUBLIC OF SOUTH AFRICA). 1995. South African Qualifications Authority Act, No. 58 of 1995. Government Gazette, No. 16725. Government Printer, Pretoria.

ROTHWELL, W.J. & KAZANAS, H.C. 1994. *Human resources development: A strategic approach.* Massachusetts HRD Press, Amherst.

SCHREUDER, A.M.G. & THERON, A.L. 1997. *Careers: An organisational perspective.* Juta, Cape Town.

SILBEMAN, M. 1995. *101 ways to make training active.* Pfeiffer & Company, San Diego.

SKINNER, M.S.J. & IVANCEVICH, W.F. 1992. *Business for the 21st century.* Irwin, Chicago.

SMOLOWE, A., BUTLER, S., & MURRAY, M. (1999). *Adventure in Business – An I.M.M.E.R.S.I.O.N Approach to Training and Consulting.* Pearson Custom Publishing, Needham Heights.

SPARHAWK, D. 1994. *Identifying targeted training needs: A practical guide to beginning an effective training strategy.* Richard Chang Associates, California.

STONE, R.J. 2002. *Human resource management, 4th edition.* John Wiley & Sons, Australia.

STRYDOM, J.D. 1998. *'n Kritiese evaluering van 'n bevoegdheidsgebaseerde ontwikkelings en opleidingsproses vir Sappi.* Unpublished MBA script. University of Pretoria, Pretoria.

SWANEPOEL, B.J., ERASMUS, B.J., VAN WYK, M. & SCHENK, H. 2003. *South African human resources management. Theory and practice, 3rd edition.* Juta, Cape Town.

SWARTZ, P. 1992. 'Peter Swartz' long view'. *People Dynamics,* 11(1):11–14. Reprinted with permission of Copyright Clearance Center.

VAN DER HORST, H. & MCDONALD, R. 1997. *Outcomes-based education. A teachers manual, 1st edition.* (Kagiso Publishers), Pearson Education (SA).

VAN DYK, P.S., NEL, P.S., VAN Z. LOEDOLFF, P. & HAASBROEK, G.D. 2001. *Training Management. A multidisciplinary approach to human resources development in Southern Africa, 3rd edition.* Oxford University Press, Cape Town.

WOOD, A. & SPICER, K. 1995. 'Supervisors: Flopped promotions'. *Productivity SA,* 21(3):18–25.

WRIGHT, N. 2003. 'Down to earth: An introduction to applied learning'. *Training Journal,* January:24–26.

YORKS, L. 2000. 'The emergence of action learning'. *Training & Development,* 54(1):56.

## Websites

www.workforceonline.com

www.careertrainer.com

www.careeremag.com

www.cweb.com

www.careers.com

www.hbs.harvard.edu

# 19

# Performance management

HB Schultz

## Learning outcomes

At the end of this chapter the learner should be able to:

- Discuss how performance management has become the initiator of knowledge management.
- Develop a performance management system for an organisation, based on launching the process, coaching for improvement, and evaluating performance.
- Make decisions as to who should perform the evaluation.
- Compare and apply relative and absolute performance evaluation techniques.
- Explain common rater errors.
- Conduct an effective feedback interview.
- Consider the influence of legislation on performance management systems.
- Discuss how effective performance management contributes to the development of a high-performance organisation.
- Discuss the necessity for quality assurance in managing employee performance.

## Key words and concepts

- 360° appraisals
- absolute and relative evaluation methods
- actor or observer bias
- added value
- Behaviourally-Anchored Rating Scales (BARS)
- bias
- central tendency
- critical incidents
- customer appraisal
- essay method
- forced choice
- forced distribution
- graphic rating scales
- halo effect
- leniency and strictness
- Management By Objectives (MBO)
- paired comparisons
- peer review
- ranking
- rational and political perspectives
- recency
- reverse appraisals
- self-appraisal
- team appraisals

## Illustrative case

### How effective is performance management

Lisa D Sprenkle is a manager in Andersen Consulting's Human Capital Practice division. She says that one could argue that some form of performance appraisal has been in existence since the time of the Roman Empire. But it wasn't until after World War II that formal approaches began to appear. Finally, in the 1980s, performance appraisal gradually became performance management, and the process started to become more than just a once-a-year event. It began to involve feedback, goal-setting, and self-reviews. But, Lisa asks, 'Does performance management work?'

Numerous industry surveys indicate that it does not. Lisa quotes the results of a survey conducted by her company, Andersen Consulting. Less than five percent of managers and employees are satisfied with the way in which the performance management process was conducted in their companies. Some of the reasons why so many people are dissatisfied include:

- Managers have no training.
- Managers want to be liked.
- Setting goals is tough and imprecise.
- There are few consequences for not conducting performance reviews.
- Ratings are not consistent among raters.
- Leaders don't set the example.

Almost half of the HR professionals who participated in the survey said that their performance management systems were set up more than six year ago. And perhaps this fact gives an indication as to why performance management, in general, does not work – it hasn't kept up with changes in the workplace.

SOURCE: Sprenkle (2002)

## 19.1 Introduction

Today's business environment and the shortcomings of existing processes are prompting companies to rethink performance management. Now, more than ever, it is critical to identify the top performers and distinguish them from the under-performers. Individual performance in organisations has traditionally centred on the evaluation of performance and allocation of rewards. Organisations are increasingly recognising that planning and enabling individual performance have a critical effect on organisational performance. However, comparatively few companies have overhauled their outdated performance management systems. Strategic success lies in focusing attention at all levels on key business imperatives, which can be achieved through effective performance management (Bennett and Minty 1999:58).

This discussion commences with some thoughts on how performance management has become the forerunner of knowledge management. The performance management process is introduced in detail; the debate covers the inception of the process, coaching the employee to better performance, and the evaluation of performance. Possible rater errors are described, and the feedback interview is examined. Guidelines are offered for the avoidance of legal problems, and some thoughts on the characteristics of a high-performance company are presented. The chapter closes with an overview of the link between performance management and quality assurance.

## 19.2 From performance management to knowledge management

The 1980s saw the growth of performance appraisal systems into the fully-fledged performance management systems of the 90s. Most successful companies have accepted the necessity of managing employees' performance in order to manage the organisation's performance.

The main thrust of this chapter is aimed at the implementation and maintenance of effective performance management systems. However, learning organisations are beginning to look past the notion of just managing a subordinate's performance. The driving force behind some of the world's largest and most successful corporations, almost halfway through the first decade of the new millennium, is that performance leadership, not just performance management, enables a company to integrate knowledge management into its corporate strategy.

Holtshouse (2002) believes that the systematic capture, re-use and retention of knowledge through voluntary sharing remain the primary organisational challenge. Organisations must focus on creating a work environment with a culture and incentives that are conducive to sharing, and should support that environment with improved work processes and strong technology. The best performers are proactive sharers, while the lowest performers are hoarders, who equate the sharing of knowledge with the loss of power. High performers talk about 'knowledge' while the lower performers speak in terms of 'information'. This indicates that the correlation between effective knowledge sharing and high performance is very real.

According to Davenport (2002), in the first phase of managing organisational knowledge, employees were encouraged to consult various types of storehouses (such as real and virtual libraries, policy manuals, and employee handbooks) for the knowledge they needed. Unfortunately, people today are too busy to consult and contribute to knowledge storehouses on a frequent basis. So, in the second phase of knowledge management, practitioners have to fathom out how to embed knowledge and knowledge management into the jobs of knowledge workers.

The reasoning behind this discussion is that performance management cannot be successful unless the management of knowledge is integrated into the process. One of the ways in which the consequences of effective performance management are put to use in a knowledge environment is through the use of e-learning portals. An e-learning portal is a virtual setting developed by an organisation to give users access to knowledge. It advises users, through electronic means, what skills and experience they need to advance, and provides competency maps and assessment. Portals recognise what the user knows, certifications earned, experience gained, and the user's ideal learning style. There is evidence that an e-portal is an essential requirement of successful knowledge management (Brockbank 2003).

In the following section, an attempt is made to provide a holistic approach to managing performance, incorporating some traditional processes and offering some newer approaches and trends for consideration.

## 19.3 The performance management process

Bennet and Minty (1999:59–60) state that there are generally three major purposes of performance management:

- It is a process for strategy implementation.
- It is a vehicle for culture change.
- It provides input to other HR systems such as development and remuneration.

According to Sloman (1997:167), performance management systems are considered to be operating when the following conditions are met:

- A vision of objectives is communicated to employees.
- Departmental and individual performance targets are set within wider objectives.
- A formal review of progress towards targets is conducted.
- The whole process is evaluated to improve effectiveness.

Figure 19.1 places the performance management process in perspective.

**Figure 19.1** The performance management process

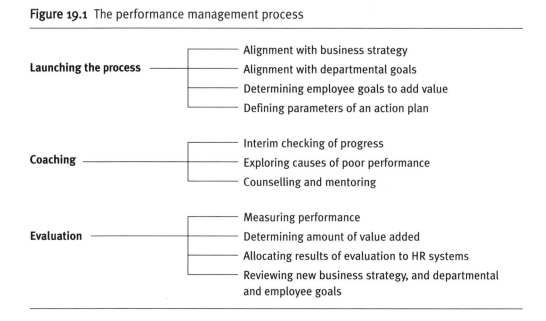

### 19.3.1 Launching the process

A new paradigm is emerging in the way that performance is managed in an organisation. The trend is away from the prescriptive mode towards collaboration in the workplace. What is evolving is the management of performance through the amount of value the subordinate's performance adds to the overall organisational performance. The traditional way of managing performance, by measuring whether the employee has achieved prescribed objectives, is no longer adequate. Crossley and Taylor (1995:11) state that managers are being pressurised to rediscover competitive advantage and the only way to achieve this is by developing the core competency of becoming a 'knowledge worker' and encouraging subordinates to become knowledge workers as well. Knowledge workers are those who can use their hands and minds to organise and deal in information and technology. They possess the skills to analyse and problem-solve complex issues and tasks, and they are far more independent than employees of the past.

Organisations must still set strategic goals, which must be filtered down to departments and individuals. But the new paradigm goes further. Top managers must decide how much value will be added to the organisation if the goals are achieved. Value can be financial, developmental, competitive, or knowledge. The individual can add value in the form of knowledge, skills, abilities, competencies, and innovation.

The first stage of the performance management process therefore involves the following steps:

- *Step 1.* Manager and subordinate meet to jointly discuss how the organisation's strategic goals must be adopted and adapted by the department and the individual.
- *Step 2.* Manager and subordinate jointly decide on an action plan to achieve the individual's goals.
- *Step 3.* Manager and subordinate agree specific times for formal checks to be made on progress towards the goals.
- *Step 4.* Manager and subordinate agree to the type of value, and the amount of value that will be added if the goals are achieved.

If the outcomes of the above four steps are incorporated into a written document, signed by both the manager and the subordinate, it becomes a contract that should encourage the participation of both parties. It is also useful in checking the progress made towards the achievement of added value.

### 19.3.2 Coaching and mentoring

The astute manager is always aware of the level of his/her subordinate's performance. Whether the organisation's objective in managing performance is to achieve goals or to add value, performance problems must be noticed and analysed at an early stage. Informal day-to-day performance management is much more important than an annual review. When a team member is not performing adequately, the desire to avoid conflict can lead team leaders to waste time and personal energy trying to rationalise, rather than correct, the problem. The result is that the problem is not attended to and the under-performer does not improve his/her performance. McKenna and Maister (2002) list the reasons why employees can have performance problems:

- Personal problems such as divorce, alcoholism, and depression.
- No longer finding the work interesting or challenging (loss of enthusiasm).
- Lack of competency.
- Fear of failure.
- Lack of desire to contribute more energy or time to the job.
- Externally-driven reasons such as loss of a client or a downturn in the sector.
- Failure to revise knowledge in the job.
- Poor time management.
- Uncertain of what to do to succeed.
- Poor management.
- Job insecurity due to issues such as pending mergers.

Katz (1995:38) states that interim progress reviews and coaching meetings are key elements in monitoring an employee's performance. The manager uses coaching skills to help the employee to improve, offers advice on changing behaviours and approaches, and encourages progress towards achieving goals and adding value. According to Gómez-Mejía et al. (1998:219–223), supervisors who manage performance effectively generally share four characteristics:

- They explore the causes of performance problems.
- They direct attention to the causes of problems.
- They develop an action plan and empower workers to reach a solution.
- They direct communication at performance and emphasise non-threatening communication.

### 19.3.3 Performance evaluation

Employee performance can be measured on the basis of whether the type of judgment called for is relative or absolute.

Relative judgments require supervisors to compare an employee's performance to the performance of other employees doing the same job. Relative judgments force supervisors to differentiate among their workers. However, relative judgments do not make it clear how great or small the differences between employees are. Relative systems do not provide any absolute information so managers cannot determine how good or bad the performance of workers is.

Absolute judgments ask supervisors to make judgments about an employee's performance based solely on performance standards. Feedback to the employee can be more specific and helpful because ratings are made on separate dimensions of performance. Absolute rating systems also have their disadvantages. All workers in a group can receive the same evaluation if the supervisor is reluctant to differentiate among workers. Also, different supervisors can have different evaluation standards. Nevertheless, absolute rating systems avoid creating conflict among workers, and are generally harder to defend when legal issues arise (Gómez-Mejía et al. 1998: 205).

## The objectives of performance evaluation

There are two perspectives that can be taken when evaluating an employee's performance: the rational perspective and the political perspective. The rational perspective assumes that the value of each worker's performance can be estimated. The political perspective assumes that the value of a worker's performance depends on the agenda, or goals, of the supervisor. The political approach holds that performance measurement is a goal-orientated activity and that the goal is seldom accuracy (Gómez-Mejía et al. 1998:215). The distinction between the rational and political approaches is depicted in Table 19.1.

## 19.4   Methods of performance evaluation

The success of performance evaluation depends on two decisions: the person, or persons, designated to carry out the evaluation, and the method or technique chosen to measure the performance.

### 19.4.1  Who should evaluate performance?

Cascio (1995:290) states that the fundamental requirement for any rater is that an adequate opportunity is made available for performance to be observed over a reasonable period of time. This offers the possibility of several different choices of raters.

### The immediate supervisor

This is the most popular and easiest choice for a rater. The supervisor is probably most familiar with the subordinate's performance and has the best opportunity to observe actual job performance on a daily basis. The disadvantage in using the immediate supervisor as a rater is that s/he may be too lenient in rating an employee in an attempt to curry favour.

### Peers

Logistics preclude that the immediate supervisor rates some jobs, such as outside sales, law enforcement, and teaching. Although objective criteria could be used in these cases, the judgment of peers often provides a perspective on performance that is different from that of immediate supervisors. However, the potential of friendship bias to skew the feedback value of the information provided is always present and it is important to specify exactly what the peers are to evaluate. Even when peer evaluations are done well, it is best

---

**Table 19.1** The difference between the rational and the political approaches to performance evaluation

---

**Rational approach**
- The goal of appraisal is accuracy.
- Supervisors and workers are passive participants in the process.
- The focus of appraisal is measurement.
- A worker's performance should be clearly defined.
- Supervisors make dimensional and overall assessments based on specific behaviours they have observed.

**Political approach**
- The goal of appraisal is utility.
- Supervisors and workers are motivated participants in the measurement process.
- The focus of appraisal is management.
- What is being assessed is left ambiguous.

- Appropriate assessment of specifics follows the overall assessment.

SOURCE: Gómez-Mejía et al. (1998:215)

to consider them as part of a system that includes input from other raters as well.

## Subordinates

So-called 'reverse appraisals' can be a useful input to the immediate supervisor's development. Subordinates know how well a supervisor delegates, communicates, plans, and organises. Considerable trust and openness is a prerequisite if subordinate appraisals are to be valuable. They can work well in a large organisation where a manager may have a large number of subordinates and anonymity of the subordinate is assured.

## Self-appraisal

Cascio (1995:291) believes that the opportunity to participate in the performance management process, particularly if appraisal is combined with goal-setting and the chance to add value to the organisation, improves the ratee's motivation and reduces defensiveness during the evaluation interview. However, self-appraisals tend to be more lenient, less variable, and more biased, and are probably more appropriate for counselling and development than for employment decisions.

## Customer appraisals

In many situations, an individual's internal customers, or the organisation's external customers, can provide a unique perspective on job performance. Although the customer's objectives cannot be expected to correspond entirely with those of the individual or the organisation, the information that customers provide can serve as useful input for promotion, transfer, and training decisions.

## 360° feedback

Over the past decade, 360° feedback, or the multi-rater system of carrying out employee evaluation, has revolutionised performance management. It is a questionnaire that asks many people (superiors, subordinates, peers,

and internal and external customers) to respond to questions on how well a specific individual performs in a number of behavioural areas. An example of the statements found in a 360° questionnaire is offered in Figure 19.2.

The combination of these multiple perspectives offers a more balanced point of view on the employee's overall performance. 360° feedback can be valuable if it complies with the following requirements. It should:
- Be thoroughly tested for reliability and consistency.
- Measure what it says it measures.
- Be easy to use, straightforward and simple.
- Be clearly focused on a specific set of skills, competencies or behaviours.
- Generate clear, detailed and personalised feedback.
- Guarantee confidentiality.

It would seem that more and more HR professionals are moving beyond the initial isolated view that 360° evaluations are only useful for developmental purposes, and are linking multi-rater feedback to other HR initiatives such as coaching, promotions, and salary increments. The 360° system has been linked to organisational competency models, so that the feedback is focused directly on the employee's competency areas. Although they are conducive to candidness and discussion, negative feedback could result in:
- The employee completely neglecting the feedback.

---

**Figure 19.2** Typical statements found in a 360° feedback questionnaire

S/he is someone who is open to questions.
S/he tries new ideas first with his/her employees.
S/he keeps firm in difficult matters.
S/he tries to be as independent as possible.
S/he has a large social network.
S/he is easy to understand.

Source: Jansen and Vloeberghs (1999:455–476)

---

- The employee only taking positive feedback into account.
- The employee being motivated by negative feedback.
- The employee only taking an interest in feedback that is given by someone who is considered 'really important' (such as a supervisor).

Peiperl (2001) believes that if managers can overcome the four paradoxes inherent to 360° feedback, the system provides an excellent way of improving individual and organisational performance. The paradoxes are:

- The paradox of roles, in which colleagues juggle being both peer and judge.
- The paradox of group performance, which steers between assessing individuals, and the reality that much of today's work is done by groups.
- The paradox of measurement, which arises because simple, straightforward, quantitative rating systems do not always produce the most useful appraisals.
- The paradox of rewards, which reveals that most people focus almost exclusively on reward outcomes during evaluations, neglecting developmental issues.

Nevertheless, there have been many successes in the 360° system of performance evaluation. The evolution of the system at the World Bank is reported in the text box below.

## Case-in-point
## Alleviating world poverty through 360° feedback

The Washington-based World Bank is a non-profit organisation devoted to supporting developing nations financially, and alleviating world poverty. Initially, the World Bank used a 360° questionnaire comprising more than 100 items, and used only for its executive leadership. When the Bank decided to extend the process to its entire staff, it began using a 25-item questionnaire for its non-managerial staff. The feedback for those staff members was for development purposes only. While the original lengthy survey offered valuable feedback, it had to be reduced so that it wouldn't over-burden the raters when it expanded the system to the rest of the workforce.

As part of the expansion to managers below the executive level, the bank also initially used the same 25-item questionnaire that had been designed for the rest of the workforce, but decided to develop a nine-item feedback instrument that places more emphasis on written commentary than ratings. The rationale behind this decision was that written comments are often more valuable and enriching than quantitative ratings.

The World Bank offers anonymity to feedback providers, but it differs from many organisations in that the employees being reviewed are responsible for nominating those who give feedback. That makes it more difficult for an employee to disregard the feedback comments. And the Bank's philosophy is 'Each employee owns his/her performance and owns his/her career as well,' thus leaving it up to the employees to make use of, or ignore, the feedback.

## Team appraisals

The growth of self-directed work teams has created a need for a new way of managing and appraising group performance. Team evaluations require a combination of two approaches: a measure of how well each member contributes to the team, and a measure of how well the team accomplishes its goals. Individual member contributions are usually measured through peer evaluation. The focus of this appraisal is usually developmental. Team performance is most often measured against specific team objectives. Cherrington (1995:300) states that teams are usually created to increase organisational flexibility. Members often rotate assignments, and therefore a team must be evaluated as a unit and rewarded as a unit with team incentives. The team evaluation process is relatively easy if specific and measurable objectives are in place.

## 19.4.2 Performance rating techniques

In section 19.3.3 performance evaluation was categorised into relative and absolute judgments. Rating techniques can be categorised in a similar manner (Swanepoel et al. 1998: 415–422).

### Relative rating techniques

- *Forced ranking.* Sprenkle (2002) defines forced ranking (also called peer ranking) as a system that ranks employee performance from best to worst. It is a person-to-person comparison, for example, Susan is 1, Tuli is 2, Joe is 14. Gary (2001) states that a potential disadvantage of this technique is that it does not assess an employee's progress in mastering certain job-critical skills.
- *Forced distribution.* This aligns employees in accordance with pre-assigned performance-distribution fields. It is a person-to-standard comparison, for example: exceeds expectations, meets expectations, or does not meet expectations.

Disadvantages of these techniques are that they may:
- Be detrimental to morale.
- Emphasise individual performance at the expense of team performance.
- Promote competition.
- Invite legal action.

However, many organisations are using forced ranking and forced distribution rating techniques because they:
- Create and sustain high performance by eliminating weak performers and retaining strong performers.
- Establish well-defined consequences such as larger salary rewards.

- Make performance management a corporate priority.
- Inform employees about their standard of performance.

- *Paired comparisons.* In this technique each worker is compared with every other worker in a selected group. The final placement of each individual is then determined by the number of times s/he was judged to be better than the others. This measurement instrument becomes cumbersome when large numbers of employees are involved. The disadvantages are similar to those of the ranking technique. Figure 19.3 compares four employees by means of the paired comparison rating method.

### Absolute rating techniques

- *Essay method.* The essay method requires the rater to write a report in the form of an essay, describing the strengths and weaknesses of the employee. It is a time-consuming method, dependent on the

---

**Figure 19.3** The paired comparison rating method

| | |
|---|---|
| Nomfuso | Harrison √ |
| Nomfuso | Thanduxolo √ |
| Nomfuso | Lisolomzi √ |
| Harrison | Thanduxolo √ |
| Harrison √ | Lisolomzi |
| Thanduxolo √ | Lisolomzi |

NUMBER OF FAVOURABLE COMPARISONS

| | |
|---|---|
| Nomfuso | 0 |
| Harrison | 2 |
| Thanduxolo | 3 |
| Lisolomzi | 1 |

RANKING

| | |
|---|---|
| Thanduxolo | 1 |
| Harrison | 2 |
| Lisolomzi | 3 |
| Nomfuso | 4 |

writing skill of the rater and reliant on comprehensive reporting.

- *Critical incidents.* This technique focuses on the continuous recording of actual job behaviours that are typical of success or failure. Incidents reflecting good and bad performance are noted. It is a time-consuming method and can be influenced by incidents that are recorded towards the end of the review period, or by incidents that may have been forgotten or omitted.
- *Forced choice.* The rater is provided with a list of paired job-related descriptions from which s/he is forced to choose the description that most fits the employee in each case. It is a partly objective method of evaluation, but the rater may be forced into making a choice between two descriptions, neither of which may fully describe the employee's performance.
- *Graphic rating scales.* A rating scale is developed by selecting various characteristics that relate to the specific job. The rater makes a choice across a continuum between two poles, usually ranging from strongly agree to strongly disagree, or from exceptional to poor. Figure 19.4 provides an example of a five-point graphic rating scale. Graphic rating scales are popular because they are easy to understand and apply, they are standardised, acceptable to users, are less time-consuming, and provide a high degree of

consistency (provided that all raters are trained to avoid rater errors). However, it has become evident that some American companies have used rating scales for purposes other than employee development.

---

## Encounter 19.1

DON'T GET HOOKED INTO GRADING

In March 2001, the *New York Times* reported that an increasing number of lawsuits concerning grading systems were being brought into the American courts. One of the results of grading exercises is the allocation of workers into the normal distribution curve, revealing which employees are most and least valuable to organisations, a disclosure which can be potentially unfair and discriminatory. Employees from top companies, such as Microsoft and Ford Motor Company, have turned this issue into a legal one, as evaluations based on grading can be used to decide which employees to terminate during economic slowdowns.

Employees question the validity of rating techniques that use inappropriate statistical models to determine an employee's future. There are possibilities for bias and there is often a lack of scientific basis for many of the criteria used in establishing these rankings and gradings. Microsoft employees, for example, have questioned gradings that are decided on the basis of a so-called 'lifeboat discussion', which requires managers to rate subordinates according to whom

---

**Figure 19.4** A graphic rating scale

| | 5<br>EXCEPTIONAL | 4<br>HIGH | 3<br>AVERAGE | 2<br>LOW | 1<br>POOR |
|---|---|---|---|---|---|
| Reliability | | √ | | | |
| Initiative | | | √ | | |
| Dependability | √ | | | | |
| Accuracy | | | √ | | |
| Interpersonal skills | | | √ | | |
| Quality of work | | √ | | | |

OVERALL RATING: Average

they would most like to have with them in the event of a ship-wreck.

However, the organisational defence of grading systems is founded on managers' insistence that these are less biased means for evaluating employee performance than many others. They call attention to the fact that the intensity of competition in the business environment in which they operate requires them to employ only the highest calibre of staff.

There could be a lesson to be learnt from this problem for South African employers and workers, as the trend seems to indicate a hardening of attitudes in the workplace, increasing competition between co-workers, and an escalation in their sense of insecurity about the status of their employment.

SOURCE: Donaldson-Briggs (2000)

- *Behaviourally-Anchored Rating Scales (BARS).* The BARS technique combines graphic rating scales with examples of critical incidents. These rating scales are job specific and require a high level of participation from supervisors. The complex development procedure of the BARS technique makes it time-consuming and expensive but it could provide a counter argument to the problem discussed in the text box above.
- *Management By Objectives (MBO).* The MBO technique provides for an initial goal-setting phase, based on the formation of long-range organisational objectives that are cascaded through to departmental goals, and finally individual goals. The latter goals are set mutually by the employee and his/her manager. The aspect of joint participation in goal-setting is one of the major strengths of the MBO technique, provided that the goals are measurable and achievable.

The manager pursues an open-door strategy, inviting the employee to discuss performance problems on an informal basis at any time. Periodically, the manager will measure progress towards the goals, and will coach the subordinate if progress is lacking or slow. The final evaluation is carried out at the end of the review period. The regular interaction between subordinate and manager provides opportunities for building good relationships, but the popularity of the MBO method has declined somewhat due to the fact that it only addresses results, and not how the performance should be managed.

## 19.5    Rater errors

Performance evaluations are fraught with danger, mainly because many human agendas can come into play. Managers can unwittingly 'play God', and employees can be overly optimistic or 'put on a good show', knowing that increases, career progress, and peace of mind may well rest on how they are rated. Several issues must be borne in mind by whoever is undertaking the measurement of employee performance (Dessler 1997:360).

### 19.5.1 Unclear standards

Whether performance is evaluated according to goal achievement, or value-added, an ever-present problem is inconsistency of standards between raters. The problem lies in the way that different people define standards. 'Good', 'average', and 'fair' do not mean the same things to everyone. The solution is to develop and include descriptive phrases that define the language the rater is required to use. This specificity results in performance evaluations that are more consistent and more easily explained.

### 19.5.2 Halo effect

The halo effect occurs when a manager's rating of a subordinate on one characteristic biases the way that other characteristics are rated. For example, if the employee has successfully added value to the organisation through the development of higher skills, s/he may be rated satisfactory overall, even if s/he has not added value in other areas that were agreed upon. Likewise, failure in one area may negatively influence an overall rating. This is known as a negative halo, or the 'devil's horns' effect. Being aware of this problem is a major step towards avoiding it.

### 19.5.3 Central tendency

Some raters find it difficult or unpleasant to evaluate individual employees higher or lower than others, even though job performance may reflect substantial differences. In this case, they may tend to rate everyone as average, resulting in a central tendency. This problem also can occur if supervisors are unfamiliar with the work of the subordinate, if they lack supervisory ability, or if they fear a reprimand for rating too leniently or too strictly. The solution to this problem lies in ascertaining the reason for applying the central tendency, and then counselling the supervisor.

### 19.5.4 Leniency or strictness

Inexperienced supervisors often appraise performance too leniently and rate an employee highly because they feel it is the easiest route to follow. In some cases, the employees may not deserve the rating. However, there could be individuals in the department whose performance has been above average and who do deserve a high rating. In addition, some supervisors may feel that they could gain in popularity if they use a lenient approach. This could result in feelings that the evaluation has been unfair.

Strictness is the opposite of leniency, and could occur if the supervisor believes that no one has achieved the standards required. In both the above cases, counselling is probably the best method of dealing with the problem.

### 19.5.5 Recency

Raters can easily be influenced by recent incidents in the employee's performance. This tends to influence the supervisor's overall perception of the individual's performance. One way of combating this would be to hold more frequent and regular performance evaluations

throughout the performance management cycle.

### 19.5.6 Bias

Supervisory bias may occur when the rater is influenced by characteristics such as the age, gender, race, or seniority of the employee. Bias may be conscious or unconscious, and can be difficult to overcome because it is usually hidden. Counselling is the only way that the supervisor can be made aware of this problem.

On the whole, proper rater training and specific development of the appraisal system by means of job analysis can improve performance evaluations. Many rater errors can be dealt with in this way.

## 19.6   The feedback interview

### 19.6.1 The nature of the feedback interview

The appraisal interview should be both evaluative and developmental. Goals that have been met do not warrant long discussion except for the praise that must accompany these achievements. The evaluators should be evaluated against the guidelines contained in Figure 19.5.

Cascio (1995:298) suggests a framework of activities that should be used by the person conducting the feedback interview. These activities should take place before, during, and after the interview.

- *Before the interview.* The rater must:
  - Communicate frequently with employees about their performance.
  - Get training in performance appraisal interviewing.
  - Plan to use a problem-solving approach rather than 'tell-and-sell'.
  - Encourage subordinates to prepare for the interview.
- *During the interview.* The rater must:
  - Encourage ratee participation.
  - Judge performance, not personality.
  - Be specific.

- Be an active listener.
- Set mutually agreeable goals for future improvements.
- Avoid destructive criticism.
- *After the interview.* The rater must:
  - Communicate frequently with ratees about their performance.
  - Periodically assess progress towards goals.
  - Make organisational goals contingent on performance.

---

**Figure 19.5** Guidelines for conducting the feedback interview

---

The evaluator must:
- Strive for internal consistency.
- Treat employees fairly.
- Make meaningful comments.
- Focus on employee behaviour, not on the employee.
- Focus on employee actions, not on intent.
- Focus on deficiencies, not their causes.
- Focus on organisational expectations, not legalisms.

The evaluator must not:
- Make comments that are inconsistent with numerical rankings.
- Criticise indirectly.
- Offer excuses for the subordinate's poor performance.
- Make comments that are either too general or too specific.

SOURCE: Segal (1995)

---

Gómez-Mejía et al. (1998:219) mention the two schools of thought regarding the discussion of salary matters during the feedback interview. In the past, many organisations have believed that if performance and salary discussions are combined, employees don't listen to their performance feedback because their interest is focused on salary decisions. However, human resources practitioners now widely believe that discussion of salary in an evaluation session has a positive impact on the success of the interview. There are a number of reasons for this: managers and employees are much more likely to take the evaluation session seriously when money is at stake, and discussion on salary can energise the performance discussion.

## 19.6.2 Scheduling the feedback interview

It is difficult to prescribe how often feedback interviews should take place. The structure of the performance management system will determine when an interview should be scheduled. However, if the system is cyclical, formal feedback should occur at least twice a year. Often new recruits to an organisation, who are still in training for their jobs, have feedback interviews scheduled more regularly. In addition, the very nature of performance management systems that add value to the organisation, demand continuous feedback, even if it is not on a formal basis.

## 19.7 Legal considerations in performance management

With the enactment of new labour legislation all over the world, and especially in South Africa, human resources professionals and those in charge of performance management programmes must take into consideration how every aspect of such a programme is implemented. Dismissal on the grounds of poor performance is justifiable in terms of the Labour Relations Act, No. 66 of 1995, and the process must also be legally sound with relevance to the Employment Equity Act, No. 55 of 1998, to avoid litigation. Carrell et al. (1998:264) suggest several guidelines that will help protect a company from legal problems in performance management:
- Written appraisals must be conducted at all levels in the organisation and must never be backdated or altered later.
- All raters, whether supervisors, subordinates, peers, or customers must be trained

in evaluation procedures.
- Standards must be job-related and must be consistent, explicit, and objective.
- Rater errors must be guarded against.
- Problem areas must be identified.
- Timetables and specific goals for improvement must be established when substandard performance is identified.
- Employees must be given clear opportunities to respond to negative feedback.
- Written evidence must be provided that the employee received the performance evaluation.
- Access to performance evaluations must be restricted to those with a need to know.
- Past performance evaluations must be checked for evidence of poor performance, especially if there are grounds for dismissal.

Katz (2000) acknowledges that managers often dread appraising their subordinates' performance, but he believes they can be enjoyable, productive and successful if the following steps are followed:
- *Preparation:* The key to success is creating attainable objectives for the performance period.
- *Assessment:* A critical responsibility is assessing and giving timely feedback to staff.
- *Reviewing documents:* This entails reviewing all pertinent documentation for the assessment period, including commendations, memoranda received from other staff members regarding the subordinate's performance and notes from meetings.
- *Appropriate setting:* The manager's office is not the best place for a feedback discussion. Neutral territory, away from interruptions and distractions, such as a conference room, or even a private corner of the cafeteria, outside of mealtimes, is better.
- *Deliver the feedback clearly:* Simple language must be used, without code words, jargon, or abbreviations, and allowing the employee to respond.

- *Encouragement:* The subordinate must be motivated to continue what s/he does well and to improve in the areas where there is room for growth.

## 19.8 The characteristics of high-performance companies

This chapter would be incomplete without some viewpoints on what effective performance management can achieve in an organisation. The product of successful performers is a high-performance company with an unmistakable profile that distinguishes it from the mediocre. Osborne and Cowen (2002) list the key attributes that differentiate the culture of high-performance companies as follows:
- High-performance companies have a *simple, compelling vision* for the future.
- They promote a *'true believer'* mentality (where everyone believes in the vision of the company, certain that it will bring success).
- Three or four *plain values* guide the organisation, such as self-confidence, speed, and simplicity.
- Employees are *proud* of their company, but *dissatisfied* with their current performance, learning from every mistake and every success.
- The urge to earn and maintain *peer respect* is the greatest motivator.
- Employees in a high-performance company expect *that long-term relationships* will foster their careers.
- A single person's *success* is celebrated throughout the company.

### Encounter 19.2
WHAT A TRUE LEADER CAN DO

Before Jack Welch retired from the helm of General Electric, he took the company to the top in profits and performance. Growth became the imperative of every decision and every strategy. High performers, those who delivered growth, were inundated with incentive rewards and, above all, recognition. In Welch's opinion, the following characteristics and values permeated throughout the organisation:

- High-performing companies attract exceptional people.
- Failure is unthinkable.
- High-performers are obsessed with crushing the competition.
- They believe they are 'the best in the business'.
- They do not accept excuses.
- The boss is a colourful character and an excellent role-model.
- The superb execution of solid strategies is complemented by a management system of the highest order.
- The truth is the only acceptable news and communication in all directions is wide open.

SOURCE: Osborne and Cowen (2002)

## 19.9 Performance management and quality assurance

Studies conducted by the Institute of Personnel Management, in the United Kingdom, as reported by Fletcher and Williams (in Lundy and Cowling 1996:308), found that there were four major weaknesses in the manner in which performance management was being conducted. Firstly, there was little indication of a real sense of ownership of performance management among line managers. This resulted in little depth of commitment, as too many managers perceived it as a top-down process with no feedback loop. There was also a widespread perception that performance management systems were 'owned' by the human resources departments. Finally, a lack of thought and imagination had been shown in tackling the issue of rewards. Lundy and Cowling (1996:309) maintain that if these issues are addressed, the quality of performance management systems will be improved and maintained. Although these viewpoints were presented more than a decade ago, they still hold good. South African organisations have no other options – performance management systems must be made to work.

W Edwards Deming, the father of Total Quality Management (TQM), argues that everything in an organisation is done within the framework of a system – if the system itself prevents good work, individuals will not be able to improve their performance, even if they want to. It all boils down to the fact that the quality of a performance management system will only be assured if workers have significant control over the variables that affect their individual performance (Cascio 1995:295). Meyer (1998:32) maintains that the most important criterion in performance management should be a measurement of an individual's contribution towards customer satisfaction. It is thus imperative that performance systems are adapted to support quality management implementation.

## 19.10 Conclusion

This discussion of performance management has seen the introduction of some contemporary viewpoints and also the elaboration of some traditional schools of thought. It is obvious that the performance evaluation process can no longer stand on its own and must become an integral part of a holistic performance management system that adds value to the organisation. Human resources practitioners and senior managers are beginning to realise that the management of employee performance must take place within the pursuit of strategic business goals. This is one of the major reasons why many organisations are starting to favour a multi-rater, or 360° approach to performance evaluation.

## Summary

- When performance management systems are tied into the objectives of the organisation, together with the benefits of knowledge management, the resulting performance is more likely to meet organisational needs. Ownership of performance management systems must be vested in both line managers and subordinates.

- Performance management is a process for strategy implementation, a vehicle for culture change, and it provides input to other HR systems. It involves communicating a vision of objectives to employees, setting departmental and individual performance targets, and conducting a formal review of performance.

- Performance management is evolving around the amount of value the subordinate's performance adds to the overall organisational performance. Managers and subordinates meet to jointly discuss and agree on the adoption and adaptation of organisational goals, an action plan to achieve the individual's goals, specific times for formal checks to be made, and the type and amount of value that will be added if the goals are achieved. The manager uses coaching skills, offers advice on changing behaviours and approaches, and encourages progress towards achieving goals and adding value. Either relative or absolute judgments are made when measuring employee performance. Several different choices of raters can be made.

- Rating techniques can be categorised into relative and absolute methods. There are advantages and disadvantages to all of them, but the use of rating scales and forced ranking is questionable. Rater errors must be eliminated or at least minimised.

- The appraisal interview should be both evaluative and developmental. Certain guidelines must be followed when planning and conducting the feedback interview.

- High-performance companies are the result of effective performance management.

- The performance management process must be legally sound to avoid litigation. The quality of a performance system will only be assured if workers have significant control over the variables that affect their individual performance.

## Case study
## In the dark on 360° feedback

Based on his strong technical background and sound track record as a successful manager, Ed Scott was hired to manage a technical department at Allitech, a company of 850 employees, producing high-fibre optics. After four years at Allitech, Ed's department had accomplished its objectives and he received good performance reviews and bonuses each year. Ed had just completed a major project, when his manager Julian Haynes, suggested that Ed participate in the senior management 360° feedback programme. The multi-rater feedback programme was only used for senior managers, and Ed was unsure whether to feel excited and flattered to be included in the top management's evaluation programme, or whether he should be apprehensive of its possible outcome. He knew that, while under stress, he had been a little hard on a few poor-performing workers. He still believed, however, that he had an excellent reputation, and assumed his feedback would reflect that.

Ed was shocked when he read the feedback from the 19 people who had completed the questionnaire as part of the review. Five of the eight people who reported to him commented that they disliked his management style so much, they would take a transfer out of his department if the chance arose. The remaining reviews emanated from senior managers, internal customers (in the form of other departmental heads), and external clients of the company. Of these, four respondents gave him an excellent review, and the rest were mixed in their responses.

Ed Scott was astonished that some people no longer considered him to be a good manager. He wondered whether he had been subjected to the 360° process because Julian felt threatened by him, or because some of his more competitive colleagues were trying to undermine him. Although there was some truth in the feedback, Ed felt harassed by the experience. However, he agreed to work with a consultant to address some of the problems, which helped him to realise that he would have to work on his management style. For example, he learnt that when he reprimanded a few workers, it affected the morale of the whole team.

Nevertheless, long after the multi-rater feedback issue had been laid to rest, Ed still felt aggrieved by the whole affair. Six months later, he left Allitech for another company. Other factors entered into his decision, but the 360° feedback definitely played a big role.

SOURCE: Wimer (2002)

## Questions

1   Analyse this case and discuss why the 360° feedback process was not a success for Ed Scott.
2   Recommend a performance management technique, or techniques, that could easily have been applied to Ed Scott, instead of a multi-rater review.
3   From the facts of the case it appears that Ed was given the multi-raters' responses without any other intervention from Julian Haynes. Explain how Julian should have given Ed feedback on his performance.

## Experiential exercise

PURPOSE: To carry out routine supervisory duties and role-play a feedback interview.

INTRODUCTION: You are a supervisor in the Parts and Accessories (P&A) warehouse of Pyramid Motor Corporation and are sitting at your desk at 16h00 (you work from 08h00 to 16h30). You are completing an end of shift report that must be handed to your manager before you leave today.

You are in charge of a six-person team, whose main duty is to retrieve parts and accessories from the warehouse shelves according to the information on paper tags that you issue to them. This

operation is called 'picking', and you receive the details from the 'Just-in-time' programme on your computer. You are reflecting back on the day and know that if your team members picked well according to the tags issued, they would pick ±200 items per day. You review the report below and survey the performance of your team.

| Name | No. of items picked today |
|------|---------------------------|
| Robert Jordon | 105 |
| Danie Hugo | 189 |
| Tolo Ngaliswe | 205 |
| Abraham Joseph | 155 |
| Simon Pietersen | 179 |
| Sally Ngcosini | 125 |

As you finish and look up from the report, Robert Jordan is approaching your desk. He says, 'Can I have an authorisation slip to go up to the Pyramid Gear shop? I want to buy some seat covers for my motor car.'

You pause for a moment before you respond.

TASK: The class is divided into two groups: everyone in one group plays the role of the supervisor. Everyone in the other group plays the role of Robert Jordan. Each employee finds a partner from the other group so that pairs are formed comprising Robert and the supervisor. Each employee and each supervisor spend a few minutes getting used to their roles in terms of the information provided.

The students role-playing the supervisor must decide whether they will allow Robert to visit the Pyramid Gear shop. Give him your decision and inform him that you wish to see him tomorrow at 11h00 for an informal performance review. Supervisors have an action list to follow in helping Robert to improve his performance. Use this list during the role-play.

Step 1   Describe the employee's specific performance.
Step 2   Describe the expected standard of performance.
Step 3   Ask the employee to identify the cause of the problem.
Step 4   Ask the employee for his suggestions and discuss each solution with the employee.
Step 5   Decide and agree on specific action to be taken.
Step 6   Agree on a follow-up date.

Everyone then role-plays his/her part. The supervisor should do his/her best to defend the evaluation and at the same time encourage the employee to persevere with future performance. This should take about 15 minutes.

After the role-play the supervisor rates his- or herself by completing Form A. The employee rates the supervisor by completing Form B. Thereafter they compare forms in terms of similarities and differences.

# Chapter questions

1   Many employees dislike performance evaluations, just as many students dislike tests and examinations. What would happen if employers discontinued managing and evaluating their subordinates' performance? What would happen if everyone received the same rating?
2   Is involving someone else besides the immediate supervisor a realistic approach to evaluating performance? Consider the

---

**Form A**
**Supervisor's appraisal of own interview technique**

| | Yes | No |
|---|---|---|
| 1   Did I put the employee at ease | | |
| 2   Did I ask the employee how s/he feels about his/her own performance? | | |
| 3   Did I praise good performance? | | |
| 4   Did I give the employee a chance to ask questions? | | |
| 5   Did I allow the employee to make suggestions? | | |
| 6   Did I help the employee to establish future goals? | | |
| 7   Did we clarify any disagreements? | | |

**Form B**
**Employee's appraisal of the supervisor's interview technique**

| | Yes | No |
|---|---|---|
| 1   Did the supervisor make me feel at ease? | | |
| 2   Did the supervisor ask me how I feel about my own performance? | | |
| 3   Did the supervisor praise my good performance? | | |
| 4   Did the supervisor give me a chance to ask questions? | | |
| 5   Did the supervisor allow me to make suggestions? | | |
| 6   Did the supervisor help me to establish future goals? | | |
| 7   Did we clarify any disagreements? | | |

advantages and disadvantages of input from more than one source in performance evaluation.

3 How would you discuss negative information with an employee if you were a supervisor? How would you want your supervisor to handle negative information if you were the employee?

4 Discuss common rater errors and indicate how these errors can be reduced or minimised.

5 Almost all organisation members will have contact with a variety of internal customers. Contact someone who has a permanent job and ask him/her to identify his/her internal customers. With the help of your contact, design a short questionnaire to collect feedback that would be important in performance evaluation.

6 'My subordinates depend on me for instructions and guidance on how to do their jobs.' Do you think this manager would use the rational or the political approach to performance evaluation? Motivate your answer by comparing the two approaches.

# Bibliography

BENNETT, K. & MINTY, H. 1999. 'Putting performance management on the business map'. *People Dynamics*, 17(11):58–63. Reprinted with permission of Copyright Clearance Center.

BROCKBANK, B.J. 2003. 'Smart e-learning portals'. *HR Executive* www.workindex.com (accessed 18 March 2003).

CARRELL, M.R., ELBERT, N.F., HATFIELD, R.D. GROBLER, P.A., MARX, M. & VAN DER SCHYF, S. 1998. *Human resources management in South Africa*. Pearson Education, Cape Town.

CASCIO, W.F. 1995. *Managing human resources: Productivity, quality of work life, profits*. McGraw-Hill Companies, New York.

CHERRINGTON, D.J. 1995. *The management of human resources, 4th edition*. (Prentice-Hall), Pearson Education Inc.

CROSSLEY, T. & TAYLOR, I. 1995. 'Developing

competitive advantage through 360-degree feedback'. *American Journal of Management Development*, 1(1):11–15.

DAVENPORT. T. 2002. 'Interview with Tom Davenport' (www.kmeurope.com).

DESSLER, G. 1997. *Human resource management, 7th edition*. (Prentice-Hall), Pearson Education Inc.

DONALDSON-BRIGGS, A.L. 2000. 'Why grading your employees is not the same as valuing them' (www.managemenfirst.com/articles/grading.htm). ©Emerald Group Publishing.

GARY, L. 2001. 'The controversial practice of forced ranking'. *Harvard Management Update*, October.

GÓMEZ-MEJÍA, L.R., BALKIN, D.B., & CARDY, R.L. 1998. *Managing human resources, 2nd edition*. (Prentice-Hall), Pearson Education Inc.

HOLTSHOUSE, D. 2002. 'Interview with Dan Holtshouse' (www.kmeurope.com).

JANSEN, P. & VLOEBERGHS, D. 1999. 'Multirater feedback methods: Personal and organizational implications'. *Journal of Managerial Psychology*, 14(6):455–476.

KATZ M. 1995. 'Performance management'. *People Dynamics*, 38, January. Reprinted with permission of Copyright Clearance Center.

KATZ, R.M. 2000. 'Six steps to successful performance appraisals'. *Workforce*, September (www.workforce.com). Reprinted with permission of Copyright Clearance Center.

LUNDY, O. & COWLING, A. 1996: *Strategic human resource management*. Routledge, London.

MCKENNA, P.J. & MAISTER, D.H. 2002. 'How to help under-performers'. *HR Voice* www.workindex.com (accessed 23 October 2002).

MEYER, M. 1998. 'Quality management: The essential component is teamwork'. *People Dynamics*, 16(4):30–35. Reprinted with permission of Copyright Clearance Center.

OSBORNE, R.L. & COWEN, S.S. 2002. 'High-performance companies: The distinguishing profile'. *Management Decision*, 40(3). ©Emerald Group Publishing.

PEIPERL, N.A. 2001. *Getting 360-degree feedback right*. Harvard Business School Publishers,

Boston.

SCHULTZ, D.P. & SCHULTZ, S.E. 1994. *Psychology and work today: An introduction to industrial and organizational psychology, 6th edition.* Macmillan, Englewood Cliffs.

SEGAL, J. 1995. 'Evaluating the evaluators'. *HR Magazine,* October. Reprinted with permission of Copyright Clearance Center.

SLOMAN, M. 1997. 'Relating human resource activities to business strategy'. In Tyson, S. (ed). *The practice of human resource strategy,* pp.155–173. (Pitman), Pearson Education (UK).

SPRENKLE, L.D. 2002. 'Forced ranking: A good thing for business?' *Workforce,* September (www.workforce.com). Reprinted with permission of Copyright Clearance Center.

SWANEPOEL, B.J., ERASMUS, B.J., VAN WYK, M.W. & SCHENK, H.W. 1998. *South African human resources management.* Juta, Cape Town.

TORRINGTON, D. & HALL, L. 1995. *Personnel Management: Human Resource Management in action, 3rd edition.* (Prentice-Hall), Pearson Education (UK).

WIMER, S. 2002. 'The dark side of 360-degree feedback: The popular HR intervention has an ugly side'. *Training and Development,* 56(9), September. Reprinted with permission of American Society for Training and Development.

## Websites

Knowledge Management Conference: www.kmeurope.com

The father of knowledge management: www.sveiby.com

Performance Management Associates, Inc.: www.pmassoc.com

Performance-by-design: www.performance-by-design.com/human

Performance Management Resources: www.zigonperf.com/performance.htm

360-Degree Feedback: www.360-DegreeFeedback.com

## 20

# Organisational renewal and change management

T Sono and PS Nel

## Learning outcomes

At the end of this chapter the learner should be able to:
- Understand the distinctions between organisation renewal, organisational development, and organisational change.
- Discuss critical factors for organisational renewal.
- Explain Waterman's key corporate renewal factors.
- Distinguish the relationship between environmental factors and organisational renewal.
- Know the role of globalisation in organisational renewal.
- Discuss the role of technology in organisation renewal.
- Discuss change and change management.
- Outline the impact of disengagement, dis-identification, disenchantment and disorientation in the workforce as reaction to change.
- Distinguish between managing change and managing diversity.
- Discuss the impact of quality management on organisation renewal and HRM.

## Key words and concepts

- adaptation or adaptiveness
- co-optation
- corporation or company
- corporate renewal
- goal-directed behaviour
- globalisation
- informal organisation
- informed opportunism
- innovation
- lessons in organisational renewal
- new norms
- Organisational Change(OC)
- Organisational Development (OD)
- Organisational Renewal (OR)
- quality management
- renewal processes
- responsiveness
- stability in motion
- technology
- transformation

## Illustrative case

## Good Hear Phone (GHP) Company Ltd.

GHP was founded by Cyril Ruiters as a small business in 1956, and became a company employing 12 330 employees with branches all over southern Africa (including South Africa, Namibia, Botswana, Swaziland and Zambia) by the end of 2000. The head office has been located in Cape Town ever since the company started doing business. The company is the only one of its kind in South Africa, and enjoys a government supported monopoly in the manufacture of its products. The company changed from traditional equipment and analog products to producing digital products from new digital manufacturing equipment in 1998, after obtaining local manufacturing rights from the Phillips Head Office located in Eindhoven, Holland, in 1995. With the promulgation of the new labour legislation, it was necessary for GHP to change its management and human resources processes. Since its inception, the company has been primarily dependent on government funding and contracts, but did not receive the same funding after 1998 because it did not comply with the Employment Equity Act, No. 55 of 1998, in particular.

John Dlamini was appointed CEO early in 2003, when Cyril Ruiters had a stroke and had to retire as executive chairman and CEO. Cyril clung to these positions and had not yet done a comprehensive environmental scan to determine the company's future direction. Cyril originally earmarked this job for his talented son who had studied Electronic Engineering at the University of Cape Town, and thereafter completed postgraduate management studies with a Rhodes scholarship at Oxford University. In 1998 his son was already one of the general managers of GHP. Cyril's son, however, unfortunately died unexpectedly after a car accident while on holiday in Indonesia.

John realised that he had to execute a thorough investigation into organisation renewal and to reposition the company to remain profitable. He had to make far-reaching decisions, because profits were declining and customers were dissatisfied with the service they received. Radical changes had to be made in a relatively short time to keep GHP in business since international competition had become stiff. There was also gossip in business circles in Johannesburg that a Japanese firm intended locating a plant with high-level digital technology in South Africa. This Japanese company would compete directly with GHP's market share, as government is trying to relax trade restrictions and to move more into a market economy approach for the South African economy.

John had the vision and determination that GHP will survive and that transformation through organisational renewal was the key to survival. He was furthermore advised to do the transformation in different phases. The first phase was to be centralisation, and was apparently more painful and less popular than he anticipated. It meant that he might have to reduce the number of employees in the business. He made it clear in the monthly corporate communication newsletter that no massive job losses would take place, but that downsizing should happen through natural attrition offering voluntary retrenchment, early retirement or outsourcing of non-core services, etc.

John insists that valuing people and their diversity remains one of the core values that guide business decisions and working relationships at GHP.

POINTS FOR DISCUSSION:
- Did John start off with the correct phase? Use the information presented in this chapter to support your point of view.
- What should the next phase of transformation be at GHP?

## 20.1  Introduction

New organisational possibilities have constantly appeared in the late 20th and early 21st centuries. Organisational renewal is a form of change and learning, where improvement processes in the organisation have become widespread and are part of the culture of the workforce and management. In organisational renewal, new norms must be communicated and understood throughout the organisation (Kast and Rosenzwiez 1985:618). In the renewal of the organisation, new approaches become an integral part of the basic planning, control processes, and communication procedures of the organisation. Thus, organisational renewal is a behavioural change by an organisation. That is to say, organisational renewal involves organisational change and development.

Organisational renewal is actually adaptation and development. This requires organisations to invest some resources in activities that will enhance the net worth of the organisation in the future (for instance, R&D investments). Without renewal efforts, an organisation is often threatened by short-term shifts in market demands, etc. Human resources managers are an integral part of renewal processes. In some studies, the terms Organisational Renewal (OR), Organisational Change (OC) and Organisational Development (OD) are inter-changeable. The following definition of OD identifies the three inter-changeable elements of renewal, change, and development:

The term 'organisational development' implies a normative, re-education strategy intended to affect systems of beliefs, values, and attitudes within the organisation so that it can adapt better to the accelerated rate of change in technology in our industrial environment, and in society in general. It also includes formal organisational restructuring, which is frequently initiated, facilitated, and reinforced by normative and behavioural changes.

Organisational development is a long-range effort to improve an organisation's problem solving and renewal processes, particularly through a more effective and collaborative management of organisational culture – with special emphasis on the culture of formal work teams – with the assistance of a change agent, or catalyst, and the use of the theory and technology of applied behavioural science, including action research. But organisational development and organisational renewal are not exactly one and the same thing.

Organisational development is a planned, systematic process of organisational change, based on behavioural science technology, research, and theory. To the extent that organisational development is characterised by the following, it is not different from organisational renewal:

- Seeking to create self-directed change to which people are committed.
- Being a system-wide change effort.
- Placing equal emphasis on solving immediate problems and long-term development of an adaptive organisation.
- Placing emphasis on collaborative efforts of data collection, diagnosis, and action planning.
- Often leading to new organisational structures and relationships.

Thus, both organisational development and organisational renewal involve organisational change. The elements of one are involved in the processes of the other.

Organisations that effectively manage change, continuously adapting their bureaucracies, strategies, systems, products, and cultures so as to survive the shocks and also prosper from the forces that decimate their competition, are masters of renewal. Managers are going to have to become masters of change and renewal to be effective in the future.

Organisations, like individuals, undergo changes in both ends and means, i.e. the goals they strive for and the methods they use. Some goals remain stable, such as survival, profitability, market share, service to clients, and growth. The means to achieve these goals, however, vary from time to time because of various internal and external factors, such as the environment, government regulations, competitive conditions, and technological innovations and advancement.

In some cases, the means stay the same, while the ends are adjusted. In other cases, simultaneous adjustments to both ends and means are made in order to attain, for instance, racial balance in organisations (which is critical in South African businesses today). Introducing diversity in the workforce is to introduce change. It is to renew the organisation. Another example is corporate responsibility for the control of water, ground, or air pollution, which may introduce new and significantly different production processes and management foci and direction. It is these new processes that give impetus to the renewal of organisations. Failing to change when change is required may lead to the demise of the organisation.

For the past decade, businesses and other organisations have been facing the crises of organisational renewal, but also the need to change the composition of the workforce. Diversity and change are also central to today's companies, and both require management. (Readers are referred to Chapter 6 regarding diversity.) Change, however, occurs in many forms, and is necessary to remain competitive. However, as change is thrust upon organisations, human resources managers must also be aware that resistance to change and attempts to manage it are central to human resources management's job.

Renewal and change go hand in hand with managing quality as a focus to remain competitive in the contemporary global market. (This aspect is addressed at the end of the chapter.)

## 20.2  What is an organisation?

The corporation, or company, is the current dominant organisational form in the Western world. When we refer to organisational renewal in this chapter, it should be understood as a reference to the renewal of a corporation. The organisation, however, is a dynamic system, constantly changing and adapting to internal and external pressures, and is in a continual process of evolution.

There are essentially two forms of organisation, the formal and the informal. A formal organisation is a rationally structured system of interrelated activities, processes, and technologies within which human efforts are coordinated to achieve specific objectives. We are accustomed to observing such organisations in business, schools, hospitals, government, etc. Informal organisations, on the other hand, spontaneously develop whenever people interact closely for a period of time. Informal organisations exist in cliques, gangs, and cooperative work groups. Another view sees formal organisation as that part of a corporation that has legitimacy and official recognition, and informal organisation as the unofficial part of the corporation.

Because of overlapping membership of formal and informal organisations, the latter play a significant role in the life of the former. The term organisation should, nevertheless, be understood to mean formal organisation. Organisations may produce goods or deliver services; they may manufacture products such as automobiles, candles, computers, and food, or provide services, such as insurance and banking. Organisations are, thus, open systems. They are also viewed as sub-systems of a broader supra-system – the environment. They have identifiable but permeable boundaries that separate them from their environment. An organisation is thus a consciously coordinated social unit, composed of two or more people, that functions on a relatively continuous basis to achieve a common goal or set of goals.

## 20.3  Critical factors for renewal

Although organisations are not necessarily destined for a life cycle of birth, growth, maturity, decline, and death, many aspects of such a cycle are apparent. Adaptation and innovation are critical for organisational survival, especially if traumatic experiences such as bankruptcy are to be avoided. These factors are also essential for renewal. While stability and continuity are important attributes to the basic function of organisations, other factors that give impetus for renewal continually play upon these attributes.

The importance of organisational renewal cannot be over-emphasised, because it can make the difference between the success and the survival of the organisation. This means that an organisation must continuously adapt to its environment; without renewal, management will not maintain efficiency, excellence and, thus, sustained productivity. Organisational renewal is an on-going process of building innovation and adaptation into the organisation (Eisenhardt in Harvey and Brown 1996:31).

Stability and change often vie with each other in organisational processes, precisely because both are essential in an organisation. Yet, at the same time, they obstruct each other. Effective and successful organisations tend to resist change. They see no need to change what they see as successful. This is the 'if-it-ain't-broke-don't-fix-it' mindset. Organisational renewal, nevertheless, is an approach to preventing organisational ossification. Waterman (1987:8) suggested eight key factors for corporate renewal:

- *Informed opportunism.* Renewing organisations set directions, and do not detail strategy. These companies treat information as their main strategic advantage, and flexibility as their main strategic weapon.
- *Direction and empowerment.* The renewing companies treat everyone as a source of creative input. They give up some control over subordinates to gain what counts, namely results.
- *Friendly facts.* The renewing companies treat facts as friends, and financial controls as liberating. They love facts and information that remove decision-making from mere opinion.
- *A different mirror.* The leaders of renewing organisations seem to get their determination from their singular ability to anticipate crises. This stems from their

willingness to listen to all sources – to look into a different mirror.
- *Teamwork and trust.* Renewers constantly use such words as teamwork and trust. They are relentless at fighting office politics.
- *Stability in motion.* The renewing companies know how to keep things moving. Renewing companies undergo constant change against a base of underlying stability.
- *Attitudes and attention.* In renewing companies, visible management attention gets things done. Action may start with words, but must be backed by behaviours.
- *Causes and commitment.* Renewing organisations seem to run on causes. Commitment results from management's ability to turn grand causes into small actions so that everyone can contribute.

## 20.4 Characteristics of organisational development

Organisational development (OD) shares certain distinguishing characteristics with the renewal process. These are as follows:
- *It is planned.* OD is a databased approach to change that involves all of the ingredients that go into managerial planning. It involves goal setting, action planning, implementation, monitoring, and taking corrective action when and where necessary.
- *It is problem-orientated.* OD attempts to apply theory and research from a number of disciplines to the solution of organisational problems. It is taking problem to method, and not method to problem.
- *It reflects a systems approach.* OD is both systemic and systematic. It is a way of more closely linking the human resources and potential of an organisation to its technology, structure, and management processes.
- *It is an integral part of the management process.* OD is not something that is done to the organisation by outsiders. It

becomes a way of managing organisational change processes.

- *It is not a 'fix-it' strategy.* OD is a continuous and on-going process. It is not a series of ad hoc activities designed to implement a specific change. It takes time for OD to become a way of life in the organisation.
- *It focuses on improvement.* OD's emphasis is on improvement. It is not just for 'sick' organisations or for 'healthy' ones. It is something that can benefit almost any organisation.
- *It is action-orientated.* The focus of OD is on accomplishments and results. Unlike approaches to change that tend to describe how organisational change takes place, the emphasis of OD is on getting things done.
- *It is based on sound theory and practice.* OD is not a gimmick or a fad. It is solidly based on the theory and research of a number of disciplines.

## 20.5 Environmental factors and renewal

Organisational renewal is often stimulated by alterations in the environment. The environment may be both general and specific. The general environment for any organisation includes economic, ecological, demographic, informational, political, and cultural factors. We may also speak of an external or market environment that is made up of customers, competitors, suppliers, government, etc. That is, within the general environment, each organisation has a more specific set of factors (i.e. its task or market environment) that is pertinent to its decision-making processes. Each has an influence on an organisation's goal-directed activities. Change in these spheres has been taking place at an accelerating pace, especially in the last decade of the last century, and will continue to do so in the new century.

Managers of organisations have historically been concerned with reacting to changes in the marketplace. Competitors introduce new products, increase their advertising, reduce their prices, or increase their customer service. In each case, a response is required unless the managers are content to permit the erosion of profit and market share. Simultaneously, changes occur in customer tastes and incomes. The firm's products may no longer have customer appeal; customers may be able to purchase less expensive, higher quality forms of the same product. A human resources manager would, in such an event, be alerted to the dearth of management ability to make the organisation efficient and viable. Intervention would be required to renew the organisation. There is, thus, a correlation between efficiency in organisational productivity and efficient human resources management's responses.

The most important of the general environmental factors are globalisation and technology, and are outlined below.

### 20.5.1 Globalisation

Globalisation implies that the world is free from national boundaries and that ours is really a borderless world. The globalisation phenomenon is a challenge that spurs renewal in organisations. The increased movement across borders of people, products, services, and capital are some of the driving forces behind globalisational processes. All these forces are greatly aided by the rapid evolution of IT (information technology) and other technologies. Just as boundaries between industries are blurring, boundaries among nations are becoming fluid in our globalised era.

The pressure of globalisation has rendered the nation-state less important, and the global organisation ever more important. Countries have become like companies; they are all engaged in competition. Organisations are in search of optimal operating environments. They thus engage in self-renewal. Without renewal, organisations soon become less competitive. Many simply die off.

In the global organisation there are no mental distinctions between domestic and foreign operations. Global organisations are constantly engaged in renewing themselves because they constantly meet new environmental situations and complex cultural demands. Demands for organisational change increase at a rapid pace. Organisations, like their workers, are buffeted by these demands.

Workers, like companies, are of the world. Companies, like their workers, are now competing across nations and across borders. They are involved in a continuum of renewal. They are compelled to become innovative, inasmuch as they renew themselves on a constant basis. In organisational renewal, adaptiveness, flexibility, and responsiveness are critical. These are vital qualities for organisations, especially global companies, to succeed in meeting the competitive challenge that organisations today face. Change and renewal have been the norm in the globalisation era.

It is no longer enough, as it was in the past, for organisational success to be based on excellence in one area, such as quality, reliability or cost (Nelson and Quick 1997:540). To be truly global, organisations must have capability and efficiency in all areas. The concept of customisation is fast becoming a lead indicator in terms of organisations positioning themselves locally and globally. To meet the needs of customers, companies (and other organisations) both locally and globally, are placed on good relationships with customers. Customer intimacy is becoming an important factor in the renewal of global companies. The basic ingredients of globalisation are increased trade and the use of IT, and these demand the global company to continually renew itself in order to stay competitive. The growing power of IT reinforces the idea that we live in a global village.

### 20.5.2 Technology

In a general sense, technology refers to the application of knowledge for the more effective performance of certain tasks or activities. By organisational technology is meant the techniques used in the transformation of inputs into outputs. Both human resources managers and production managers employ technology in the transformation and renewal of their organisations. The effects of technology on organisational structure and behaviour are today more pronounced than ever before. The actions managers take to make some change, improvement, or development in the organisation are referred to as technology impacts. A compatible but broader definition of technology, is that 'technology is the application of knowledge to perform work'. Thus, organisational structures reflect technology in the ways that jobs are designed (the division of labour) and grouped (departmentalisation).

Technology improves the range of choices that managers have in increasing organisational efficiency and renewal. Even though technology can also be constraining in the range of such choices, managers have considerable discretion within those constraints. Technology affects people in organisations in diverse ways. It is now a key factor in determining the tasks and degree of specialisation required, even in human resources management. It often determines the size and composition of the immediate work-group and the range of contacts with other workers and supervisors. Its impact on management systems is even more dramatic than on other organisational sub-systems.

## 20.6 Necessity of organisations to renew themselves

The major failure of a number of tertiary institutions is one of lack of self-renewal and appropriate transformation. Many mistook affirmative action programmes to be the real transformation that was required. These institutions are now gradually ossifying and a few are at risk of becoming peripheral players in the educational arena by 2008 if they do not renew rapidly.

## Encounter 20.1

The South African Parliament warned of an impending collapse of university and technikon education as a result of drastically falling student numbers. The Council on Higher Education also informed Parliament that in the year 2000 there were at least 100 000 fewer students at tertiary education institutions than was predicted in 1995.

Initial calculations in 1995 estimated an annual four per cent increase in student numbers, from 570 000 to 710 000 in the year 2002. Instead, numbers dwindled to 560 000 in 1999. University and technikon institutions fail to undertake renewal strategies that would enhance and sustain their viabilities. Their problems are:

- Large reductions in student enrollments.
- Government grants drying up, and tertiary institutions lacking innovative ways and means to garner replacement funds.
- White students emigrating in larger numbers than anticipated.
- Large numbers of black students being ineligible for entry into higher education.

Of the total half a million students who wrote final examinations in 1999, 272 000 passed, but only 69 000 obtained the exemption that allows entry into higher education.

What the higher education sector failed to fully grasp are the patterns of successful and unsuccessful change.

## 20.6.1 Organisational learning as a renewal strategy

According to Van Dyk et al. (2001:121), organisations must learn faster and adapt to rapid change. 'The need for a culture of learning in organisations has hardly been greater. We have entered the knowledge era and therefore survival in a rapidly changing world depends on adaptability and adaptability depends on the capability to learn ... The learning inside the organisation must be equal or greater than the change outside or the organisation may not survive.'

The two main concepts in organisational learning are organisation and learning. An organisation, as we have seen, is a dynamic system that is constantly changing. It therefore has the capacity to learn as if it were a subject. It processes information and knowledge. It has skills, expertise, and the capacity to store, retrieve, and communicate data and information.

Organisations have a close relationship with the process of learning and, thus, with knowledge and information and its transmission. Since organisations can be seen as systems that learn, learning is intrinsic to organisational renewal. The father of the learning organisation, Senge (1990:5–9) sees five new 'component technologies' of the learning organisation:

- System thinking.
- Personal mastery.
- Mental models.
- Shared vision.
- Team learning.

A learning organisation continuously expands its capacity to create its future; it constantly renews itself to overcome organisational entropy.

## 20.6.2 Organisational renewal strategies

Strategies are not separate and independent of other organisational processes, but are intertwined with organisational development, organisational change, organisational transformation and the learning organisation.

- Organisational development poses the following questions:
  - Where are we?
  - Where do we want to be?
  - What must we do to get there?
- Organisational change is more constant than stability. Change occurs because of external and internal forces impacting on the organisation. Change is constant, or organisations atrophy.
- Organisational transformation is not simply a search for a new organisational

identity, but rather a positioning of the organisation in response to new forces so as to stave off obsolescence.

- Learning organisation. An organisation that does not learn cannot renew itself. Self-renewal of an organisation demands the learning of new approaches, new understandings, and new alignments.

## 20.7   Goals and values

These are a further impetus for renewal and change. Modifications to the goals of the organisation require modifications to the organisation itself. Changes in what is good and desirable (values) are also important because they lead to changes in goals; or, if the goals remain constant, changes in values can lead to changes in what is considered appropriate behaviour.

Organisations depend on the basic values that underlie goal-setting and decision-making. In the renewal of organisations, values and goals therefore play an important role, especially as regards the future operations of the organisation. But what, then, are goals and values?

Goals represent the desired future conditions that individuals or organisations strive to achieve. They thus include missions, purposes, targets, and deadlines. Values are normative views, held by individuals, of what is good and desirable. Value issues affect organisations in a variety of ways, such as group dynamics, organisation, pursuit of goals, and the entire management of the organisation. Values and goals are integral to the process of renewal.

The goals of an organisation influence its interactions with the environment; but goals are themselves shaped by the unique tasks or problems an organisation emphasises, since organisations are contrived goal-seeking systems.

We have seen the environmental influences on organisational renewal, but the environment also has an impact on organisational goal-setting, which is a product of specific interactions, namely competition, bargaining, co-option, and coalition.

Competitive relationships do exist where two organisations are competing for the support of a third party; for instance, companies compete for customers, material resources, and labour inputs, and universities compete for funds, students, and faculties, and hospitals for paying patients. Competition, thus, drives organisations to renew themselves. Competition leads to goal-attainment, which is in turn a renewal agency.

Bargaining involves direct negotiations between organisations. In the bargaining situation, each party must modify its own goals in response to the needs of the other party. In the joint ventures that have occurred in the last decade, bargaining has featured prominently, and companies have modified their goals and, thus, advanced their renewal prospects.

Kast and Rozenzweiz (1985:182) define co-optation as 'the process of absorbing new elements into the leadership or policy-determining structure of an organisation as a means of averting threats to its stability or existence.' This is an action of giving 'outsiders' positions of responsibility in the organisation. For instance, businesses may have representatives of banks on their boards, and university managements may have student representative councils on their councils or administrative boards. Co-optation influences goals in this fashion.

Coalitions between organisations require a further modification of the goals, and the term coalition refers to a combination of two or more organisations for a common purpose. Coalition appears to be the ultimate or extreme form of environmental conditioning of organisational goals. A coalition suggests organisational modification of goals to accommodate other parties or interests.

However, renewal is not the only aspect organisations must contend with to survive some aspects of the organisation change and general change. Management is just as important and is discussed below.

## 20.8   Change management

The need for change becomes evident when there is a gap between organisation, division, function or individual performance objectives and actual performance in the organisation. According to Stone (2002:573), indicators are usually changes to total net profit, sales per employee, labour costs, and accident rates. These factors can be used to identify performance deficiencies. This is supported by Van Dyk et al. (2001), who state that change usually takes place as a result of an adjustment to the environment, workplace, customers, or worker relationships. Furthermore, if a strategic decision is made by management to enter a new business (for example, the move into savouries and chips by a tobacco company – such as United Tobacco did a few years ago) or to exit existing businesses, change will be required. They often require radical organisational change and very strong confrontation by entrenched interest groups.

Change may dramatically shorten the life spans of organisations. This would in turn reflect the organisation's inability to phase out strategies, policies and businesses that are no longer relevant whilst creating new activities, products, services and strategies to sustain performance, relevance and success. Some organisations are more affected than others. The human resources manager will have to improve the balance between the competing demands of managing current performance and letting go of some other activities, attitudes and patterns of thinking to enable an organisation to survive.

Change is now a powerful factor in organisations, much like productivity has been for years. Simply defined, change means to make things different. Change, to be successful, requires unfreezing the status quo, a movement to a new state, and refreezing the new change to make it permanent. Too much change, however, leads to chaos; and too little change leads to stagnation.

Lombard (1998:45) is of the opinion that transformation (change), in an organisational sense, is associated with the restructuring of companies needing to respond to changes in their environments, missions, strategies, and advances in technology.

Structural adjustments are often also made to either enhance the company's competitiveness or for reasons of survival. Restructuring also refers to how a company rearranges its functioning components and the employee relationships between them and the influence on organisational culture. Traditionally, restructuring was used for planned change, but recently to help facilitate strategic changes (also known as change management). A more difficult task in change management is the management of the employee's resistance to change. There are processes involved in the management of change. In most cases they require unfreezing and freezing of attitudes in an effort to establish new patterns of behaviour (Lombard 1998:66).

The change process usually entails four steps, namely: determining the need for change, identifying the obstacles to change, establishing how to implement change, and setting in place the mechanisms to evaluate change.

According to Dawson (2003:15), a range of 'triggers' to organisational change exist, and the main external factors are as follows:

- Laws and regulations (for example, legislation on age discrimination, world agreements and national policies on pollution and the environment, and international agreements on tariffs and trade).
- Globalisation of markets and the internationalisation of business (the need to accommodate new competitive pressures both in the home market and overseas).
- Major political and social events (for example, September 11, the widespread European uptake of the euro in January 2002, and ongoing tensions between countries).
- Advances in technology (computerisation).
- Organisational growth and expansion (as an organisation increases in size so may the complexity of the organisation, requiring the development of appropriate coordinating mechanisms).
- Fluctuations in business cycles (for example, changes in the level of economic activity, both within national economies and within major trading blocks).

## 20.8.1 Forms of change

Two basic forms of change are found in organisations: planned and unplanned change.

- *Planned change.* This occurs when a change results from a deliberate decision to alter the organisation. A company may wish to move from one structure to another and, thus, engage in a carefully constructed or orchestrated approach to alter the structure or functions of the organisation. However, change is not always planned.
- *Unplanned Change.* Alterations may occur as a result of imposed conditions. Such change may be unforeseen. Unplanned changes may be environmental, for instance, natural disasters. Government regulations and economic conditions may lead to abrupt and unexpected changes for organisations.

Whether forced or planned, but especially in the case of the latter, change needs to be managed. Because it can be either disruptive or constructive, change must be managed.

## 20.8.2 Scope of change

Planned change has three facets:

- *Incremental change.* This is change of a relatively small scope, such as making a small modification in a work procedure. It is change involving minor improvements.
- *Strategic change.* This is change of a larger scale, such as the restructuring of an organisation. In strategic change, the organisation moves from an old state to a known new state during a controlled period of time. Strategic change usually involves a series of transitional steps.
- *Transformational change.* This is the most massive scope of change. With this change, the organisation moves to a radically different, and, at times, unknown future state. In this change, the organisation's mission, culture, goals, structure, and leadership may all change dramatically.

Those who introduce or manage change are known as change agents. Managers or employees who oversee the change process are internal change agents. Change agents can also be external, such as outside consultants.

Simply put, change management is managing change. Once a company has made a decision to change, a careful management of the change is imperative if the goals of the desired change are to be attained. Change management is thus a challenge because diverse individuals in the organisation will invariably hold diverse views of change, and their energy will need to be harnessed in order to meet the goals of change.

Change is, thus, its own challenge, and is driven by many factors and forces. It in turn unleashes many reactions among affected individuals. Change is a big challenge that faces many managers in today's companies. Companies continually evolve, and thus change, which in turn makes managing change a complex issue.

---

## Encounter 20.2

AIR TRAVEL CHALLENGES FOR AIRLINES

The terrorist attacks of September 11 acted as a trigger for a dramatic change in the airline industry (which had already been operating on small profit margins), exposing its weak financial position, and threatening its commercial viability ('International airlines emerge from a turbulent year', *The Times*, 12 January 2002). During 2002, the New Zealand government provided Air New Zealand with a NZ$1 billion rescue package, and British Airways experienced a serious decline in premium air traffic.

In an article in *The Times* ('Grounded: The big spenders of business class', 12 January 2002), it was observed that: 'BA is not alone. Sabena of Belgium and Swissair, carriers with histories that stretch back to the start of commercial aviation, have been dragged through the bankruptcy courts. Aer Lingus is teetering on the brink. BA, Air France and Lufthansa will probably survive, but KLM has thrown in the towel, predicting its own assimilation by one of the leaders.'

SOURCE: Dawson (2003:172)

Change has to be managed so as to control it. Managing change, in effect, is also management of the reactions and resistance to change.

## 20.8.3 Resistance to change

Change has to be managed because people generally fear and resist change. They perceive change as a threat to their self-interests. Reactance is a negative reaction that occurs when people feel that their personal freedom is threatened. Swanepoel et al. (2000:755) are of the opinion that if an organisation has a track record of opposing change, more care should be taken to design a gradual, non-threatening participative implementation process for future changes.

According to various writers (Dawson 2003:19 and Harigopal 2001:319), employees often resist change when they do not understand its implications, and perceive that it might cost them much more than the amount they will gain. In most cases, it is lack of trust in management, i.e. there is little or no faith in the change agent and the employees. The chances that the employees will experience some emotional turmoil are very good. Therefore, individuals or even groups can react differently to change. It can take different forms, such as passively resisting change or aggressively undermining it, or sincerely supporting and enhancing it. It may even reduce employee power and career opportunities.

When managers and employees resist change, it is for a reason. They perceive the change as a threat. According to Stone (2002: 579), some of the common reasons why people resist change are as follows:

- *Fear of the unknown:* not understanding what is happening or why.
- *Disrupted habits:* feeling upset when old ways of doing things cannot be followed.
- *Loss of confidence:* feeling incapable of performing well under the new way of doing things.
- *Loss of control:* feeling that things are being done 'to' them rather than 'by'

them or 'with' them.
- *Poor timing:* feeling inadequate or humiliated because the 'old' ways are no longer perceived as 'good' ways.
- *Lack of purpose:* not seeing a reason for the change or not understanding its benefits.
- *Economic loss:* feeling that their pay and benefits may be reduced or that they may lose their jobs.

---

## Encounter 20.3
### THE EFFECT OF COMPUTERISATION

When new user-friendly computer systems are introduced, computer experts, for instance, may feel threatened, as they may feel that their expertise is eroded by the introduction of the new systems. When experts perceive an erosion of their expertise, their status is perceived to be lowered and their jobs, ultimately, felt to be at stake. Computerisation has also led to fewer interpersonal relationships developing in the workplace because it leads to closer person-machine interactions.

---

Some employees fear change because it may introduce new situations in which they may have to deal with new colleagues with different attitudes in the workplace. Conflicts may result as a consequence of a changed workplace situation; this may lead to conflict because employees may feel that their concerns and needs no longer receive the attention they once did. Furthermore, one of the greatest fears of organisational change is the disturbance of the settled balance of power. Those who hold power, or have great influence under the prevailing arrangement, will feel threatened by the prospects of losing their political advantages or influence with the advent of change.

## 20.8.4 Managing resistance to change

Managers planning to implement change must predict the reason why people resist change: usually they do not want to lose something valuable, they misunderstand the change and its implications, the change might not be in the best interests of the company, and a low tolerance for change may exist because they fear they will not have the skills and/or knowledge required of them.

The traditional view, however, treats resistance to change as something to be overcome, but many organisational attempts to reduce resistance have only served to intensify it. The contemporary view holds that resistance is simply a form of feedback, and that this feedback can be used very productively to manage the change process. One key to managing resistance is to plan for it, and to be ready with a variety of strategies to help employees to negotiate the transition.

Management and employee resistance to change is something that is common human behaviour. Human resources managers should therefore treat such an occurrence as an opportunity to re-evaluate a proposed change, and to identify and deal with the real barriers to the change. According to Stone (2002:579), some of the ways managers can overcome employee resistance to change are:

- *Communication:* management should give advance information regarding the reasons for the change, the nature of the change, the planned timing of the change and its possible impact on the organisation and employees.
- *Participation:* whenever possible, management and employee participation should be encouraged to give everyone a sense of ownership and involvement regarding the decision to introduce the change.
- *Guarantee:* management should guarantee that employees will not be disadvantaged. For example, an organisation may guarantee employees a position in the organisation while they undergo any required training.
- *Counselling:* non-directive counselling has proved a useful management tool in change situations.
- *Reward:* managers and employees who contribute to the successful introduction of change should be rewarded. See the comments by Swanepoel et al. (2000) in

this regard when dealing with unions and where negotiation is introduced into the process.

The pressures of changes threaten many traditional and long-held ways of managing and working. Dealing with change is among the greatest challenges facing managers and workers in modern day business management.

Swanepoel et al. (2000:755) indicate that it would be wise, when an organisation is highly unionised, to view the trade union representatives as full stakeholders in any change or transformation. Union representatives have to be involved in order to avoid eventual collective resistance to change by the workforce, because any form of change will have an impact on the employees of the organisation. The degree and nature of such impact will vary from organisation to organisation, among the union representatives, and among the workforce. The impact experienced by employees collectively is one of the most important factors requiring professional attention during any process of change or transformation. According to Swanepoel et al. (2000:759), a six-step process approach to overcoming resistance to change should be implemented sequentially:

- *Step 1.* Mobilise commitment to change through joint diagnosis of business problems. Help all employees to develop a shared diagnosis of what is wrong in an organisation and what can and must be done about it.
- *Step 2.* Develop a shared vision of how to organise for competitiveness. Once commitment is obtained to the analysis of a problem, managers lead employees towards a task-aligned vision of the organisation that defines new roles and responsibilities.
- *Step 3.* Foster not only consensus for the new vision, but also the necessary competence to enact it and required cohesion to move it along. Since employee commitment to change is uneven (some are enthusiastic, others are lukewarm, etc.)

everyone needs to develop competencies to make the changes work, and support mechanisms need to be in place. Managers who cannot adapt to change and transformation issues during this period must be replaced.

- *Step 4.* Spread revitalisation to all departments without pushing it from the top. Use teams to break down resistance by enlisting their feedback about how to organise their department and responsibilities.
- *Step 5.* Institutionalise revitalisation through formal policies, systems and structures. Enact changes in structures and systems that are consistent with change and transformation during this step (not earlier).
- *Step 6.* Monitor and adjust strategies in response to problems in the revitalisation process. Monitoring the change and transformation process needs to be shared by all employees through use of an oversight team – key manager(s), union leaders, secretary, engineer, someone from finance, etc. Regular attitude surveys to monitor behaviour patterns are also essential.

From the above six steps it is apparent that in order to maintain stability when organisational change occurs, the climate must be conducive to the change; employee understanding, participation and support are needed; and some of the changes need to be incremental, step by step, and congruent with the existing culture. Changes must be implemented with the utmost care and sensitivity so as not to demoralise loyal employees.

## 20.9 Typical reactions and interventions

Change can lead to a series of negative reactions, which would, in turn, trigger managerial interventions. Corporate change constantly needs appropriate husbandry. Some of the negative reactions and the managerial interventions they call for are dealt with below:

- *Disengagement.* Disengagement is a psychological withdrawal from change. The employee may appear to lose initiative and interest in the job. Employees who disengage may fear the change, but take on the approach of doing nothing and simply hoping for the best. Disengaged employees are physically present but mentally absent. They lack drive and commitment, and they simply comply without real psychological investment in their work.

  The disengaged are recognised by behaviours such as being hard to find or doing only the basics to get the job done. Typical of their statements include 'no problem' or 'this won't affect me'. The basic managerial strategy for dealing with disengaged individuals is to confront them with their reaction and draw them out so that they can identify the concerns that need to be addressed. Disengaged employees may not be aware of the change in their behaviour, and they need to be assured of organisational intentions and plans. Disengaged people seldom become cheerleaders for change, but they can be brought closer to accepting and working with a change by open communication with an empathetic manager who is willing to listen.

- *Dis-identification.* Those reacting in this way feel that their identity has been threatened by the change, and they feel very vulnerable. They often cling to a past procedure because they had a sense of mastery over it, and it gave them a sense of security. Dis-identified employees often display sadness and worry. They may appear to be sulking and dwelling in the past by reminiscing about the old ways of doing things. Because dis-identified employees are so vulnerable, they often feel like victims in the change process. The dis-identified are characterised by such verbal indications as 'my job is completely changed' and 'I used to …'

As a manager you can help them through the transition by encouraging them to explore their feelings and to transfer their positive feelings into the new situation. One way to do this is to help them identify what they liked in the old situation, and to show them how it is possible to have the same positive experience in the new situation. Show them that work and emotion are separable.

- *Disenchantment.* This is also a common reaction to change. It is usually expressed as negativity or anger. Disenchanted employees realise that the past is gone, and they are angry about it. They may try to enlist the support of other employees by forming coalitions. Destructive behaviours like sabotage and backstabbing may result. It is often difficult to reason with disenchanted employees. Typical verbal signs of disenchantment are 'this will never work' and 'I am getting out of this company as soon as I can'. A particular danger of disenchantment is that it is quite contagious in the workplace. Bad-mouthing and rumour mongering are its chief weapons of sabotage.

The manager should bring these people from their highly negative, emotionally charged state to a more neutral state. To neutralise the reaction does not mean to dismiss it, but rather to allow the individual to let off the necessary steam so that s/he can come to terms with her/his anger. The second part of the strategy is to acknowledge that their anger is normal and that you do not hold it against them. Sometimes disenchantment is a mask for one of the other three reactions, and it must be worked through to get to the core of the employee's reaction.

- *Disorientation.* Disorientation is a final reaction to change. Disoriented employees are lost and confused, and are often unsure of their feelings. They waste energy trying to figure out what to do instead of how to do things. Disoriented individuals ask a lot of questions and become very detail-orientated. They may

appear to need a good deal of guidance and may leave their work undone until all their questions have been answered. The disoriented are characterised by 'analysis paralysis'. They feel that they have lost touch with the priorities of the company, and they may want to analyse issues to death before acting on them. The disoriented employees may ask questions like 'now what do I do?' or 'what do I do first?' Disorientation is a common reaction among people who are used to clear goals and unambiguous directions. When change is introduced, it creates uncertainty and a lack of clarity.

Managers should explain the change in a way that minimises the ambiguity that is present. The information about the change needs to be put into a framework or an overall vision so that the disoriented individual can see where s/he fits into the grand scheme of things. The employee needs a sense of priorities to work on.

Managers need the ability to diagnose these four negative reactions to change.

## 20.10 How to manage change

Human resources managers have a critical role to play to ensure that the change process is run smoothly, as the event in itself causes a high level of turmoil in an organisation. The following are ways to manage change:

- Managers should be able to identify forces of change. These forces come from diverse sources, both external and internal.
- A shared vision for change should be developed and should include participation by all employees in the planning process.
- Top management must be committed to the change and should visibly demonstrate support.
- A comprehensive diagnosis and needs analysis should be conducted.
- There must be adequate resources for carrying out the change.

- Reward systems should reinforce new behaviours, not old ones.
- Participation in the change process should also be recognised and rewarded.
- Change management efforts should be undertaken in an ethical manner and should preserve employees' privacy and freedom of choice.

It is important to note that human resources managers must provide support for employees who have trouble dealing with change. Expression of concerns about the change can provide important feedback that managers can use to improve the change process. Emotional support and encouragement can help an employee deal with the anxiety that is a natural response to change.

## Case-in-point

The following organisations serve as a case in point which reflects the adjustments made by them to be successful: Ford in Australia, General Motors in the United States, and British Airways in the United Kingdom. They used different reasons and methods such as right sizing, restructuring, and Total Quality Management (TQM) to cope with necessary change in order to remain competitive. In retrospect, it is readily apparent that all the changes were done to help these organisations cope with new and challenging environments.

SOURCE: Kotter (1999:75)

## 20.11 Strategic change management

The word 'strategy' comes from the Greek word 'stratego', meaning to plan the destruction of one's enemies through the effective use of resources. Strategic management has the focus on winning market share from compe-

tition. To have effective strategic changes take place, a manager must have creative ideas (plans) and be innovative and original, but should also be practical and reachable. The change in the organisation must meet the demand and this can only be done if management adjusts its management style to meet these new demands. Therefore, management must have the skills to implement change. Management must be able to convince and persuade, even be aggressive where and when necessary, and also be very confident. And management must believe that the change being implemented is right and the best practice for the organisation. Strategic change must be planned well in advance in such a way that the activities integrate to have the best results. A time frame must be part of the manager's plan to change, and s/he must have procedures in place to monitor the changes. (Readers or learners are also referred to Chapter 21, where aspects with regard to strategy are discussed.)

The strategic management perspective suggests that managers are central figures in organisational change. As decision makers, they have a proactive role in anticipating and shaping the environment and in charting the organisation's course. A strategist's primary task is to ensure a good strategic alignment between the organisation and its environment. This alignment process involves two functions: firstly, matching the organisation's competences with the demands of the environment, and secondly, arranging internal structures and processes so that other people can come up with creative strategic alternatives and develop new competencies to meet the challenges of the future.

Strategic management is thus important to change management. Without it, it is not easy both to legitimise change and to assess whether its impact has a positive or negative effective on an organisation. The features regarding strategic management are as follows:

- The full scope of an organisation's activities, including corporate objectives and organisational boundaries.

- Matching the activities of an organisation to the environment in which it operates.
- Ensuring that the internal structures, practices and procedures enable the organisation to achieve its objectives.
- Matching the activities of an organisation to its resource capability, by assessing the extent to which sufficient resources can be provided to take advantage of opportunities or avoid threats in the organisation's environment.
- The acquisition, divestment, and re-allocation of resources.
- Translating the complex and dynamic set of external and internal variables, which an organisation faces, into a structured set of clear future objectives which can be implemented on a day-to-day basis.

### 20.11.1 Strategic planning as part of change management

Whether it is formal or informal, all managers are engaged in planning. It is largely a conceptual function – it requires thinking about the future. Strategic planning is a top management function. A strategy evaluates and develops the organisation's purpose, mission and overall objectives and policies to place the organisation in an advantageous position in its operating environment. A strategic plan involves directing the organisation's activities to achieve overall strategic objectives, consistent with the organisation's mission and policies. Company strategy therefore is the whole pattern of decisions that sets the long-term direction of the organisation.

The screening of information to detect emerging trends and create scenarios can be seen as environmental scanning. By doing this, you cannot predict the future, but certainly reduce the uncertainty by playing out potential situations under different specified conditions. Therefore, an organisation would be better prepared to initiate changes in its strategy to gain and hold competitive advantage.

Environmental scanning creates the foundation for forecasts. Information for thorough scanning is used for predictions of future outcomes such as technological change or revenue generation opportunities. Benchmarking is also used in strategic planning. This includes the search for best practices among competitors or non-competitors that lead to their superior performance. Analysing and then copying methods of the leaders in various fields can improve quality.

The strategic vision for the company is just as important to make a company successful. By setting objectives, the manager converts managers' statements of the business' mission and company direction to specific performance targets.

The reason why organisations fail with their strategic planning is the lack of support from those who are crucial to its success. Strategic planning assures that an organisation can transform itself through words or be forged as a result of the intellectual exercise of top management, who do not obtain the help of the people who need to put the plan into action.

Strategic thinking is an exercise in entrepreneurship and the crafting of a strategy from outside. A manager must keep the strategies closely matched to outside drivers, such as changing buyer preferences, the latest actions of rivals, market opportunities and threats, and newly appearing business conditions.

By studying market trends, listening to customers, enhancing the company's competitiveness, and steering company activities in new directions in a timely manner, company strategies can then be responsive to changes in the business environment. Good business entrepreneurship and strategy making are inseparable.

Decisions are made on the basis of information available about the past, present and future, but with future results in mind. Therefore decisions made in the present will have an impact on the future. Strategic planning is directed towards action and prepares a mode of coping with the future. Nobody can predict the future with accuracy; there are many risks and uncertainties. Some managers deal with the future by ignoring it; others by predicting it, controlling it, and responding to it.

Planning has to do with predicting the future, and it depends on the ability to predict where the environment will be during the execution of the plans.

Effective strategists are people who don't separate themselves from the daily detail of running an organisation, but they are the ones who immerse themselves in it – they determine strategy while running the business.

## Case-in-point
### ICI (Pty) Ltd. Australia

A company's survival depends on its ability to change. ICI is a publicly owned Australian company manufacturing chemicals. Its origins date back to 1874. A total of 40 per cent of the shares are owned by Australia and 60 per cent are owned by the UK parent company. ICI markets a large range of domestic and industrial products.

There are 110 operational sites in Australia, and they employ 9 400 employees. In the mid- to late-1980s, the company's Australian operations faced the following major problems:
- Poor productivity.
- Run down plant and equipment.
- Frequent industrial disputes.
- Increased competition.
- They were losing money.

The company embarked on a massive reorganisation and reform. The first step was to reform the workplace culture, and it took 10 years to complete. The leaders of ICI knew that if they wanted to change the organisation one of the first and most important things to use is HRM as a vehicle to help bring about that change. They asked themselves: What is a workplace culture? The following was addressed and changed over this period of time:
- Vision and mission.
- Communications throughout the organisation.

- Leadership style.
- Decision-making system.
- Pay and reward system.
- Relationships.
- Work practices.

In more detail, ICI did the following:

ICI's tariffs on their products were cut from 40 per cent to five per cent. The company's business environment also changed. To stay internationally competitive, ICI restructured the overall business as well. It closed plants between 1986 and 1991, and had 3 000 jobs declared redundant and the employees either re-deployed or simply not replaced. Thirteen thousand employees stayed in the workforce. This was still not enough; ICI still had to take a quantum leap – it had to use its people effectively to make a significant change. It also looked at new ways of doing things, it reformed its relationship with its employees, and it established new industrial relations agreements. There was strong resistance to changing the old way of doing things in an environment that was previously characterised by conflict, poor communication, and disputes arbitrated by a third party. There were certain counter-productive job demarcations, employees were in jobs not careers, and a degree of adversity existed on occasion. Communication and decision-making needed reform in ICI, as did work practices, management style, award provisions, employee's attitudes to their roles, and quality of communication. Furthermore, the company had to find ways to use its people more effectively and invest time and money.

ICI had to become customer-focused and had to build a bridge with its employees. It wanted commuted, flexible, and skilled employees, and to move them towards careers not jobs. ICI set up a number of consultative committees with representation from union officials, employees, and management. Steering committees oversaw this and monitored the board direction – it took a long period of time to deliver the results that really mattered to the employees. ICI succeeded, and created a sense of purpose and unity in the organisation. Employees received job descriptions, targets were set, performance reviews initiated, and a single-status workforce was established.

Management reform was absolutely necessary to this process. Quality management was introduced, which HRM used to monitor and maintain the new workplace culture. ICI concentrated on planning, doing, measuring, and improving. The HR department executed surveys to measure absenteeism, turnover, etc.

Employees now understand their roles in the organisation, have an improved understanding of what the business is all about, and enjoy a significant level of recognition.

In summary, ICI did the following to renew and change the organisation in order to be modern and competitive:

- *Changed the structure,* i.e. removed the bureaucracies, got decision-making down to where it matters, and got communication open and efficient.
- *Changed the systems,* i.e. gave employees information on the system, explained why the company was doing things and how employees could make changes.
- *Changed the culture,* i.e. created an innovative culture, became risk-takers, and empowered and coached employees.

The above actions resulted in ICI being profitable and competitive as it effectively addressed renewal and change.

There are three types of strategies, namely corporate level, business level and functional level strategies:

- *Corporate level* concerns the direction, composition and coordination of the various businesses and activities that comprise a large and diversified organisation. Corporate level strategy reveals six basic types of strategy, that are outlined below:

- Stability strategy is designed to keep organisations quiet and stable, and is frequently found in successful organisations. Because of their markets and products, such organisations believe they have no need to make sudden changes, and have the time and position to allow events to unfold before making any response.

- Growth strategy is the most common form of all strategies, and involves either concentrating on dominating one industry or growing by diversification across a number of industries.

- Portfolio extension is a variant of growth strategy, but is achieved through mergers, joint ventures or acquisitions, rather than organic growth.

- Retrenchment strategy is usually embarked upon when an organisation is in trouble or, because it sees trouble ahead of adverse market conditions. It usually involves a process of cutting back on numbers employed and activities undertaken. The general aim is to refocus the organisation so as to be able, once again, to attain prosperity.

- Harvesting strategy involves reducing investment in an area of business activity in order to reduce costs, improve cash flow, and capitalise on whatever residual competencies or areas of advantage still remain. This strategy can involve fast or slow harvesting.

- Combination strategy: as the above strategies are not mutually exclusive they can be linked together in whatever combination seems appropriate, given the circumstances of the organisation in question.

- *Business level* strategy relates to the operation and direction of each of the individual businesses within a group of companies.

- *Functional level* strategy concerns individual business functions such as marketing or personnel.

There are different types and levels of change (the individual, the work group, and the organisational levels). Since our focus is on the level of organisational change as process, no matter what theory or approach (and there are many theories and approaches) is applied, the process requires some person or group to intervene in the running of the organisation to effect this change. The people who are the subject of the change process itself could lead the intervention. Successful intervention involves moving an organisation through several distinct states in order to achieve a higher level of performance.

There are various elements that constitute a new approach to manage organisational change and that are proposed by a variety of experts in the field (Dawson 2003; Harigopal 2001; Kotter 1996). The summarised opinions are as follows:

- Creating a vision.
- Developing strategies.
- Creating the conditions for successful change.
- Creating the right culture.
- Assessing the need for and type of change.
- Planning and implementing change.
- Involvement.
- Sustaining the momentum.
- Continuous improvement.

## 20.12 Leadership and change

Effective change and leadership goes hand in hand, and Krieg (2002:25), who is the CEO of HR Africa Labour Solutions, proposes a particular approach to be followed in change leadership. This approach can be summarised as follows:

- *Develop the need to change.* Nobody will change without feeling the need to change, which must be created by management utilising knowledge management.
- *Develop a change vision.* The top leader must have a clear vision and idea where s/he wants to take the organisation.
- *Develop a communication strategy.* Communication is the golden rule to

change process. Staff need to be informed at least once a month about the progress made in change.

- *Communicate the vision.* The vision must be communicated to the organisation in understandable terms to prevent panic.
- *Get worker leaders informed.* It is imperative to consult with union leaders on what is being planned for the future, and the earlier the better. Remember: this is consultation not negotiation.
- *Get the transformation team(s) together.* The transformation team should also receive the necessary power and status to make it acceptable in the organisation.
- *Do an organisational audit.* An organisation must know what it has before it can plan specific changes.
- *Decide on the change process strategy.* The planned process of implementing change needs to be communicated to all stakeholders to test acceptability. Transformations can take up to 10 years to achieve lasting success.
- *Prepare the organisation and also the stakeholders.* Managers need to be developed in handling change, as they must support the staff during the change process.
- *Implement the changes.* Leadership will be meaningless without action. The various plans now need to be implemented. The use of project teams is advisable, but must be selected carefully as they can make or break the change.
- *Remove hindrances.* Any hindrances holding back the process should now come to light and must be removed if the organisation wants its changes to last. Hindrances include policies, organisational structures and/or even managers and employers. The top leader must be ruthless in this case.
- *Mainstreaming the changes.* Changes need to be made part of the mainstream organisational process. Performance management issues need to be implemented. Changes in organisational structure often need to be made at this stage.

Central measures should be implemented to encapsulate the changes.

- *No plans or projects must be cast in stone.* Adjustments will continuously be made as circumstances change.

Readers are also referred to Chapter 15 of this volume, where leadership is discussed.

Kotter (1999:49) provides an approach as to how a manager can improve his/her chances of success in an organisational change effort by doing the following:

- Conducting an organisational analysis that identifies the current situation, problems, and the forces that are possible causes of those problems. The analysis should specify the actual importance of the problems, the speed with which the problems must be addressed if additional problems are to be avoided, and the kinds of changes that are generally needed.

- Conducting an analysis of factors relevant to producing the needed changes. This analysis should focus on questions of who might resist the change, why, and how much; who has information that is needed to design the change, and whose cooperation is essential in implementing it; and what is the position of the initiator vis-à-vis other relevant parties in terms of power, trust, normal modes of interaction, and so forth.

- Selecting a change strategy (on the basis of the previous analysis) that specifies the speed of change, the amount of pre-planning, and the degree of involvement of others; that selects specific tactics for use with various individuals and groups; and that is internally consistent.

- Monitoring the implementation process. No matter how good a job one does of initially selecting a change strategy and tactics, something unexpected will invariably occur during implementation. Only by carefully monitoring the process can we identify the unexpected in a timely fashion and react to it intelligently.

The most difficult and also the most complicated and time-consuming changes to achieve are those at the group and organisational performance levels (Lombard 1998:138). Lombard is also of the opinion that management styles may be modified and altered satisfactorily, but trying to drastically change the behaviour of all levels of management will be time-consuming and emotionally exhausting. Attempting to make behavioural changes is trying to alter the long-standing and cherished customs, norms, values, attitudes, and the traditions of people that have developed over many years.

## 20.13  Change and quality management

According to a number of writers (Dawson 2003:149; Kelemen 2003:43; Stone 2002:580), quality initiatives have been developed and implemented in all areas of business as part of the change process. Worldwide competition sets international standards of performance. Global organisations adopt international best practices to secure a competitive advantage. Organisations that do not change and adapt to the new competitive environment will be defeated in the marketplace and will disappear or be taken over by those that do. The consistent demand for improved performance caused by intense competition, demanding customers, cost pressures and rapid change have made continuous productivity improvement a necessity for survival. One process which has taken center stage in recent years, has been Total Quality Management (TQM) as a means to address change and change management. This approach has also been taken on board by human resources managers to manage human resources from a quality assurance point of view. (The quality assurance approach was discussed in Chapter 3 of this book.)

According to Kelemen (2003:43–4), the human resources management policies used to increase commitment to quality and quality assurance are important, and are outlined below:

- *Rewards.* Such policies attempt to establish a system of rewards and punishments that aligns itself with the ethos of quality management. Rewards refer to both monetary and non-monetary types, including the utility generated by participation in quality management activities (if any), and the benefit of making one's job easier and safer, public recognition, pay rises, promotions, bonuses, profit sharing and equity ownership programmes.
- *Participation and job improvement.* Quality management changes the nature of jobs and of the work itself, making tasks in some cases multifaceted and, therefore, more challenging. Many employees enjoy participating in quality processes that require more of their knowledge and skills to solve problems. Although they typically receive the same (material) compensation, their job may become more desirable.
- *Public recognition.* Various quality gurus view public recognition as contributing to increasing commitment to quality (see, for example, Crosby [1984] and Juran [1988]). Some organisations have campaigns such as 'employee of the month' or 'employee of the year' whereby those employees who proved their commitment to their customers are publicly recognised and given a diploma or insignia to certify their achievement.
- *Career advancement opportunities.* Under a quality management regime, career opportunities may also be enhanced, not in a traditional way (such as by progressing more quickly from one hierarchical level to the next), but in a more lateral thinking way. Thus an individual's area of responsibility and accountability may increase or an individual might be asked to take on board different sorts of projects.
- *Appraisals.* Appraisal and self-appraisal systems are redesigned to account for quality-related tasks and knowledge. However, there is a notoriously contradictory debate as to whether such quality-related issues are to be rewarded materially or not.
- *Quality-related pay.* Some organisations use pay-for-knowledge schemes to emphasise the importance of quality training and learning. Although the monetary rewards associated with such schemes are usually small, they could affect behaviour by breaking down the notion of seniority-based wages, and by emphasising the importance of learning. Gurus, such as Crosby (1984), Deming (1986) and Ishikawa (1985), are against quality-related pay, and argue that money is a poor motivator and that numerical measures of performance are flawed. Other gurus, such as Juran (1988), argue that both material and symbolic rewards are valued by employees, and should be used in combination. Providing that firms tie quality rewards to simple performance measures, such as overall firm profitability (through profit sharing) or firm value (through employee equity ownership plans), there is more visibility and fairness, which can in turn lead to less conflict among the employees.

By now readers or learners should be familiar with the approach taken in this book, namely that HRM in the new paradigm and in the context of constant change, global competition, etc. necessitates a quality assurance approach. This is emphasised and contextualised throughout this book, but finds prominence against the background of dealing with the major challenge to organisations: to renew continually, and to effectively manage change or to face decline.

## 20.14 Conclusion

This chapter sought to highlight the primacy of place of HRM in organisational renewal. If today's work environment is seldom marked by long-term careers, inflexible contracts, and unwavering loyalty, companies must necessarily frequently face ongoing change. The constants and guarantees of the past are no longer with us, and this together with the ever-changing knowledge economy, implies the necessity to embrace and carefully manage change.

The organisation of the present is a dynamic system of people, ideas and knowledge, and goods or products. Human resources expertise is vital in the quest to ease organisational change by promoting the new norms and approaches of organisational renewal, and by actively endorsing and proactively engaging with organisational development (ensuring a shift in and optimisation of organisational culture and leadership and management structures).

## Summary

- Organisational renewal is the purposeful effort to alter the structure and processes of an organisation so as to make it more effective and productive. It is the attempt to improve the company throughout. There can be no renewal by the organisation as a whole unless individuals and groups in the organisation are willing to alter patterns of behaviour, adopt new attitudes, and embrace different beliefs.
- Organisational renewal is usually stimulated by changes in the environment. The general environment for any organisation includes technological, economic, ecological, demographic, legal, political, and cultural factors. Change in these spheres seems to be occurring at an already rapid but accelerating rate. However, within this general environmental constellation are the specific, powerful forces of globalisation, technology, and information and knowledge management. Rapid and profound changes are constantly occurring in these domains. Other pressures for organisational renewal stem from rapid product obsolescence, the changing nature of the workforce, and demands for higher quality of work-life.
- Factors that spur renewal are not new, and some are as old as human history itself. Globalisation is as old as Marco Polo's adventures, Prince Henry the Navigator's exploits, or Christopher Columbus's 'discovery' of the Americas. Knowledge, said the Athenian Hellenic more than 2000 years ago, is power. Data leads to information, information to knowledge, and knowledge to action, which, in turn, leads to results. There is, thus, nothing new about information-based businesses, much of whose organisational renewal is based on information and knowledge strategies.
- Speed is directly linked to technology, which is essential for organisational renewal. An indicator of an organisation's ability to retain its competitive edge is the rate at which it renews itself. Increasingly, this rate lies not only in the skills the people in the organisation possess, but also in the innovations and technologies the organisation is willing to introduce.
- Together with these innovations and technologies, are goals and values essential for organisational renewal. Goals and values represent the primary determinant of behaviour. In human resources management, the focus on renewal, as we have seen, expresses itself in such processes as change, transformation, development, learning, and adaptiveness.
- It is clear that not only renewal, but also change is essential if organisations wish to survive, and therefore the role of managers, and particularly human resources managers, is critical to determine the need for change, identify obstacles to change, implement change, and evaluate its success or failure. Managers also must be alert to the fact that change does not occur in isolation, but involves a complex set of relationships. The decision of an organisation to buy, sell or merge with another organisation has major human resources repercussions which need to be closely observed.
- The management of quality in dealing with change cannot be overlooked. Quality assurance is a HRM constant, and it plays a vital role in keeping abreast of

the fast moving complex and changing world of today, a world in which organisations have to continually renew, but also to remain competitive.

## Case study
## The Kitty Group

The Kitty Group is a company that was founded in the early 1950s in South Africa. It specialises in the production of knowledge and the dissemination of information. For decades since its formation, it preferred to employ persons of particular racial, cultural, and gender backgrounds.

Of its 1000 plus employees, 90 per cent were from one racial group. The remaining five per cent were from another racial group. The latter occupied only menial positions and performed servile roles. The lowest ranks in the organisation were entirely staffed by women.

But with the changes that occurred in South Africa in 1994, the Kitty Group saw its chances of survival greatly reduced because a large source of its revenue was from government, either through grants or contracts.

The senior management of the Kitty company came to the conclusion that in order to survive, the organisation must renew itself, not only in order to be competitive in a suddenly open market, but also to be politically legitimate in a changed environment.

Subsequent to 1995, the Kitty Group undertook to implement renewal strategies, such as the following:

- *Recruitment.* The old recruitment policy was eliminated and in its stead a new one prescribed that, should a post become available, every possible effort was to be made to attract suitably qualified and/or experienced candidates from previously excluded groups. Advertisements for a vacancy were also to state that suitable experience should receive a higher consideration. Posts were also advertised simultaneously inside and outside the organisation.

- *Selection and appointment.* Candidates from previously excluded groups were selected, as far as possible, to meet the renewal goals. The criteria employed were as follows:
  - Firstly, preference was given to any suitable candidate from a designated group who was an employee of the Kitty organisation.
  - If no suitable candidate was available, preference was given to a candidate from outside the organisation who met the requirements.
  - If no suitable candidate was available, then all other Kitty employees who qualified for the post were to be considered.
  - If still no suitable candidate was available, then all other suitable candidates were to be considered.
- *Promotion.* This procedure followed the recruitment strategy outlined above, the essence of which was that candidates from designated groups were to be considered first for any promotion in an existing vacancy.
- *Training and career development.* Appropriate opportunities for training and career development were extended, first to the staff from designated groups, and then to the rest of the staff equally, regardless of race, colour, or gender.
- *Accountability.* The chief executive of the Kitty group bore full responsibility for the policy. But line management was responsible for its implementation. Clearly stated objectives regarding the efforts and process used to support and implement this policy, were to form part of their critical performance areas.
- *Targets and time frames.* To ensure that representation was effected throughout the organisation, the company aimed to have members of previously excluded groups forming at least 55 per cent of its staff complement by June 1999. The organisation set the following targets:

Kitty's Renewal Strategies
(All figures reflect percentages)

| Category | Current (1994) | 1996 | 1999 |
|---|---|---|---|
| Management | 7.8 | 33.3 | 50 |
| Researchers Professional | 22.6 | 36 | 50 |
| Support | 23.3 | 45 | 50 |
| Technical Support | 46.9 | 50 | 60 |
| Clerical/Secretarial General | 29.9 | 50 | 60 |
| Assistants | 100 | on merit | on merit |
| TOTALS | 26.6 | 43.8 | 54.6 |

## Questions

1  How successful was the renewal strategy as reflected in the table above?
2  Was the form of renewal strategy followed by the Kitty Group necessary?
3  Explain how HRM is part of organisational renewal.

## Chapter questions

1  What do you understand organisational renewal to be?
2  What role may affirmative action play in organisational renewal?
3  What role may employment equity plans play in organisational renewal?
4  Discuss environmental factors and their relationship to organisational renewal.
5  What do you consider as the conditions for successful renewal?
6  Explain the fears that are induced by change.
7  Discuss the key strategies for managing resistance to change.
8  What negative reactions flow from change, and what managerial interventions may be used to counter these reactions?
9  Critically discuss the principles of managing change.

## Bibliography

BURNES, B. 1992. *Managing change: A strategic approach to organisational development and renewal.* (Pitman), Pearson Education (UK).

CHANG, R.Y. 1994. *Mastering change management: A practical to turning obstacles into opportunities.* Richard Chang Associates, Irvine, California.

CHARLTON, G. 2000. *Human habits of highly effective organisations.* Van Schaik, Pretoria.

CROSBY, P. 1984. *Quality without tears: The art of hassle-free management.* McGraw-Hill Companies, New York.

DAWSON, P. 2003. *Understanding organizational change. The contemporary experience of people at work.* Sage Publications, London.

DEMING, W.E. 1986. *Out of crisis.* MIT Press, Cambridge, MA.

HARIGOPAL, K. 2001. *Management of organisational change. Leveraging transformation.* Response Books, New Delhi.

HARVEY, D.F. & BROWN, D.R. 1996. *An experiential approach to organization development.* (Prentice-Hall), Pearson Education Inc.

ISHIKAWA, K. 1985. *What is total quality control? The Japanese way.* (Prentice-Hall), Pearson Education Inc.

JURAN, J.M. 1988. *Quality control handbook.* McGraw-Hill Companies, New York.

KAST, R. & ROSENZWEIZ, JAMES E., 1985. *Organization and Management: A system and contingency approach, 4th edition.* McGraw-Hill Companies, New York.

KELEMEN, M.L. 2003. *Managing quality.* Sage Publications, London.

KOTTER, J.P. 1996. *Leading change.* Harvard Business School Press, Boston.

KOTTER, J.P. 1999. *What leaders really do.* Harvard Business School Press, Boston.

KRIEG, M. 2002. 'Fundamentals for change'. *People Dynamics,* 20(5):25–26. Reprinted with permission of Copyright Clearance Center.

LAWLER, E.E. 1996. *From the ground up. Six principles for building the new logic corporation.* Jossey-Bass, San Francisco.

LOMBARD, B.U. 1998. *Unbundling corporate management.* Lex Patria, Johannesburg.

NELSON, D. & QUICK, J. 1997. *Organizational*

behaviour: Foundations, realities and challenges. West Publishing Company, Minneapolis.

SENGE, P.M. 1990. *The fifth discipline: The art and practice of the learning organisation.* Century Press, London.

STONE, R.J. 2002. *Human resource management, 4th edition.* John Wiley & Sons, Australia.

SWANEPOEL, B.J., ERASMUS, B.J., VAN WYK, M. & SCHENK, H. 2000. *South African human resources management. Theory and practice, 2nd edition.* Juta, Cape Town.

VAN DYK, P.S., NEL, P.S., VAN Z. LOEDOLFF, P. & HAASBROEK, G.D. 2001. *Training management. A multidisciplinary approach to human resources development in southern Africa, 3rd edition.* Oxford University Press, Cape Town.

WATERMAN, R.A. 1987. *The renewal factor, 3rd edition.* Bantam Books, New York.

# part six

## Strategic and international human resources management

# 21

# Interdependency between organisational strategy and strategic human resources management

PS Nel and A Werner

## Learning outcomes

At the end of this chapter the learner should be able to:

- Explain the basic concepts that constitute strategy.
- Explain the concept of strategic human resources management.
- Define strategy and identify the strategic process elements.
- Explain the relation of decision-making to the strategy formulation process.
- Demonstrate the integration of an HRM strategy with the overall organisational strategy.
- Explain the relation between organisational strategy and human resources development.

## Key words and concepts

- functional level strategic planning
- human resources planning
- human resources management development
- levels of planning
- long-term planning
- mission
- operational planning
- organisation environment
- organisational values
- strategic business planning
- Strategic Business Unit (SBU)
- strategic human resources management
- strategic management
- strategy
- vision

## Illustrative case
### LL Bean

LL Bean is a company that sells a wide range of men's, women's and children's clothing, as well as outdoor and camping gear. Over the years the company has gained a very good reputation for its excellent customer service. However, when the company failed to win a popular award for their service, management decided to take a hard look at itself. Management realised that although the company had good customer service, it achieved it in an unproductive way. Instead of offering and honouring a no-questions-asked-money-back guarantee (customers could bring back products any time), customers were expected to be satisfied with the products and services in the first place. The management of LL Bean decided to embark on a Total Quality Management (TQM) strategy. The first part of the strategy focused on changing the knowledge, skills, and attitudes of managers and employees, and the second part on changing the processes in the company. TQM involves managing a business in such a way that customer satisfaction is achieved in the most efficient and effective way by totally involving people in improving the way work is done. The human resources department played a vital role in the planning, implementation and facilitation of the TQM process. Everyone in the organisation (including the president) became involved in discussions about what TQM meant for managers and employees, cross-functional teams were established with specific tasks, and more quality workshops were held. A survey was conducted to determine the extent to which managers reinforced a TQM culture in the company. Feedback sessions between management and employees were held and based on the results of the survey and feedback sessions, action plans were formulated. In addition, the human resources department facilitated the development of a new performance management and compensation or reward system to reinforce the desired behaviours.

In the whole process the human resources department had to redefine itself. Total quality was in the hand of employees, but the human resources department provided the support systems. The human resources department had to re-engineer itself from being functionally organised to being more customer-organised. Human resources was moved into customer areas by setting up service teams to support each area. It retained a core resource center which provided expertise to support the decentralised service teams.

In a follow-up survey almost all employees indicated that they felt strongly committed to LL Beans' goals.

SOURCE: www.workforce.com

## 21.1  Introduction

In order for an organisation to maximise its competitiveness, it is imperative that its human resources should be managed successfully. Human resources practices are only effective if they are aligned with the strategic direction of the business, make business sense, are focused on business operations, and executed professionally. HRM plays a major role in clarifying the organisation's human resources challenges and developing solutions for them. There is a strong trend towards a new, non-traditional form of human resources department, one that is no longer simply a service provider, but which has moved to become a strategic partner and contributor to corporate goals. In short, a human resources department that adds real value to the organisation.

With the recurring low productivity that characterises South African organisations and the great shortage of professional and highly skilled employees, management has finally accepted that people are the only sustainable competitive advantage of an organisation. This shift in focus is welcomed by human resources practitioners in South Africa, but the ball is now in their court to meet the expectations of top management in this regard.

This book deals with run of the mill aspects of HRM; strategic aspects are regarded as advanced subject matter. For this reason, strategy will only be briefly discussed on the basis of the principal learning components as shown in Figure 21.1.

**Figure 21.1** Principal learning components of strategic human resources management

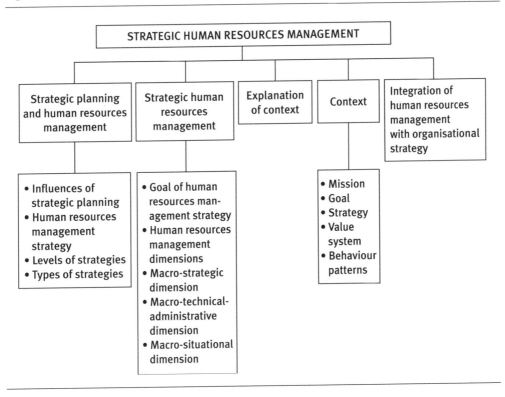

**Figure 21.2** A pyramidal framework for strategic management

## 21.2 The vocabulary of strategy

The general concepts or terms used in describing any organisational strategy are given in Figure 21.2 and are briefly discussed here.

An organisational vision, mission, values, and strategy are only meaningful if employees participate in the formulation of these concepts, and if they translate and integrate them into everyday behaviour:

- *Vision:* This represents the goal or raison d'être of the organisation. A vision describes, in an exciting and passionate way, the direction the company wants to take (Schultz et el. 2003:251). The time frame might be anywhere from six months to five years in the future.
- *Mission:* This refers to the business in which the organisation is involved and represents a general plan of how the organisation aims to achieve its objectives and is explained in more detail elsewhere in this chapter.
- *Values:* These are expressed in the manner in which the organisation and its people handle customers, suppliers and each other.
- *Objectives:* The end result that the organisation wants to achieve is derived from its mission. Objectives generally represent the task that the organisation wishes to carry out.

### Case-in-point

'PepsiCo's success is the result of superior products, high standards of performance, distinctive competitive strategies and the high integrity of our people. Our mission is to be the world's premier consumer products company focused on convenience foods and beverages. We seek to produce healthy financial rewards to investors as we provide opportunities for growth and enrichment to our employ-

ees, our business partners and the communities in which we operate. And in everything we do, we strive for honesty, fairness and integrity.'

Are you able to identify the mission, broad strategies and values of PepsiCo? How can human resources assist PepsiCo in achieving its business objectives?

SOURCE: www.pepsico.com

- *Strategy:* This refers to the long-term plans developed by top management, usually for periods of two to ten years or even longer. These plans are used to evaluate and seize opportunities, as well as to allocate resources. Strategy includes plans to create new products, to purchase other organisations, to sell unprofitable sections of the business, to make shares available, and to enter international markets. Anthony et al. (1999:10) add an additional dimension by defining it as follows: 'The formulation of organizational missions, goals, and objectives, as well as action plans for achievement, that explicitly recognize the competition and the impact of outside environmental forces.'
- *Tactical business plans:* These are short-term plans to implement the activities and objectives contained in the strategy. These plans usually cover a period of a year or less. They keep the organisation on the course determined by its strategic plan. Tactical plans enable the organisation to react to changes in the environment, while at the same time concentrating on the overall strategy. Management should review and adapt the tactical business plan from time to time.
- *People:* These are all the employees of the organisation – from top management to the lowest level. They may be regarded as the power base for all the components of the pyramid. People are an organisation's only sustainable competitive advantage. Werner (in Schultz et al. 2003:37) states

that the more human resources is utilised effectively, the more it develops. The above confirms the main theme of this book, i.e. that the basic building block of organisational success is individual performance orientation.

## 21.3 The relation between strategic planning and human resources management

Organisations recognise that there is a critical relation between an organisation's human resources and its contribution to the achievement of organisational objectives. Human resources is concerned with decisions that have a long-term impact on the employment and development of people in the organisation, and on relations which exist between its management and staff. It is important that human resources managers are involved in the planning of future business activities and expansions. Dougherty (2002:180) states that competent HR professionals should be able to demonstrate how their investments in human capital will provide a reasonable rate of return, and their prescribed changes will be compatible with other HR practices and with the technological and strategic changes that take place within and outside the organisation.

According to Ivancevich (2001:8), the strategic importance of HRM implies the following:

- Analysing and solving problems from a profit-orientated, not just a service-orientated, approach.
- Assessing and interpreting costs or benefits of such HRM issues as productivity, salaries and benefits, recruitment, training, absenteeism, overseas relocation, layoffs, meetings, and attitude surveys.
- Using planning models that include realistic, challenging, specific, and meaningful goals.
- Preparing reports on HRM solutions to

problems encountered by the organisation.
- Training the human resources staff and emphasising the strategic importance of HRM and the importance of contributing to the organisation's profits.

The need for a strategic perspective on human resources management is realised as an organisation grows larger and more complex. The new strategic accountability of HRM implies that it must show that it contributes to the mission and goals of the organisation. Systematic planning is required for the people needed to staff the organisation. A lack of adequate talent may be the single major constraint in the ability to sustain future company growth. Strategic HRM is a practical step towards more comprehensive employee planning and development.

The following are the advantages of integrating strategic planning and human resources management:
- Improved understanding of the implications of strategic organisational planning for human resources.
- Proactive recruitment of the required and experienced human resources.
- Improved human resources development activities.
- Improved analysis and control of costs related to human resources, by providing more objective criteria for payroll, labour market, training, and other expenses.

We believe that strategic management and planning should also include strategic human resources planning from the outset due to the benefits it has for an organisation. Anthony et al. (1999:16) fully support this view by stating that: 'The key idea behind overall strategic management is to coordinate all of the company's resources, including human resources, in such a way that everything a company does contributes to carrying out its strategy. If all the resources are integrated within an overall, appropriate strategy, additional value to the company is generated by the effective combination of integrated forces.'

It is therefore obvious that synergy is obtained whereby extra benefit or value is realised when resources have been combined and coordinated effectively. This is therefore the focus of this chapter, and warrants a separate chapter in the book.

## 21.4   The strategic business planning process

Authors writing about strategic business planning usually make some assumptions about it, as it is difficult to pinpoint all its detail. It is usually derived from a SWOT (Strengths, Weaknesses, Opportunities, and Threats) analysis. Although the strategic planning is usually complex, it does operate as a sequential process.

According to Rothwell and Kazanas (1994a:3) strategic business planning is a process in which decision makers have to focus their attention on the following:
- *Clarify purposes.* What is the purpose of the organisation? What should it be?
- *Select goals and objectives.* What is the organisation trying to achieve? How can achievement be measured?
- *Identify present strengths and weaknesses.* What is the organisation doing well? Not so well?
- *Analyse future threats and opportunities.* What opportunities or threats will the external environment pose to the organisation in the future?
- *Compare strengths and weaknesses to threats and opportunities.* How can the organisation take advantage of future opportunities and avert future threats posed by the environment, considering its present internal strengths and weaknesses?
- *Decide on long-term strategy.* What should be the long-term direction (strategy) pursued by an organisation so that it can take advantage of opportunities and avert threats posed by the environment?
- *Implement strategy.* What changes need to be made inside the organisation so that

its chosen strategy can be pursued with the greatest likelihood of success?
- *Evaluate strategy.* How well do decision makers think the strategy will work? How well is it working? How well has it worked?

Mondy et al. (1999:144), however, claim that strategic planning in organisations can logically be divided into four steps. These are discussed below.

### 21.4.1 Step 1: Determination of the organisational mission

It is important to determine an organisation's mission because it forms the total of its purpose. It also answers the question of what the organisation's management is trying to do, i.e. should it maximise profits or pursue stability of earnings, etc. This process, however, also includes management decision-making to determine which direction it is to take (for example, a competitive compensation strategy, improving diversity, being a market leader or innovator, etc.)

A statement of purpose can also be the economic rationale for an organisation's existence (Rothwell and Kazanas 1994a:4). To address this issue, decision makers should ask:
- In what areas of business activity should the firm operate?
- How much opportunity does a business activity offer the organisation in terms of growth? Flexibility? Stability? Return on investment?
- What does it take to succeed in the business?
- What are the organisation's capabilities?
- How well do the organisation's capabilities match up to what is needed to succeed in the business?
- What is the organisation's likelihood of success in the business activity?
- What methods of doing business can be considered?
- How do these choices compare on the basis of feasibility?

- How do these choices compare on the basis of potential profitability?
- What business activities should the organisation enter into in the future? What should be its purpose?

These aspects can only be effectively answered if various strategies and levels of business planning are analysed. In this regard, four elements can be identified, namely:

- The *goal* of an organisation is the most philosophical part of the mission. It provides an explanation of the raison d'être of the organisation; in other words, for whom or for whose benefit the effort is made. Campbell and Tawadey (1990:2–3) state that 'some chief executives dedicate their companies to the shareholders, arguing that the company exists to create wealth for the shareholders.' This is probably true for small and medium-sized organisations, but according to the authors is not necessarily applicable to very large organisations.
- *Strategy* is the second element of the definition of a mission. It is the business rationale of an organisation's mission. It relates behaviour and decisions to the goal of the organisation. In order to formulate a strategy, management has to describe and define the domain in which the organisation intends to operate and compete. A strategy serves no purpose unless it is transformed into behaviour patterns and decisions. A strategy should spell out what action and behaviour it requires if it is to have an influence on the organisation.
- *Organisational values* are beliefs that support the organisation's management style and determine its attitude towards employees and shareholders, as well as its ethics.
- *Behaviour standards* are part of the organisation's way of doing business. It refers to how managers have come to feel as to what is important to effectively run the organisation. These behaviour standards are not only defined by the organi-

sation's strategy, but also by its values. It therefore means that there are two reasons for doing something in an organisation. The first is a strategic or commercial reason, and the second a moral or value-based reason.

The mission will be healthy if all the previously mentioned components form a tightly knit whole. The question thus arises as to how important a mission is for human resources management. There are three advantages for employees who identify with the mission of the organisation. First, employees are more motivated and will work more intelligently if they believe in what they are doing and trust the organisation for which they are working. Second, staff selection and training. Organisations with strong values find it easier to recruit, select, promote, train, and develop employees of the right calibre. It is implicitly a self-selection process, since prospective employees whose values and outlook on life do not agree with those of the organisation, will prefer not to join the organisation, or will resign at a very early stage. Third, and most important, is better cooperation and mutual trust. Employees with a sense of mission find it easier to work together, to respect each other and to search for solutions that will benefit the organisation as a whole, and not just individual departments.

## 21.4.2 Step 2: Assessment of the organisation and its environment

After the mission has been determined, an organisation must assess its position in the external environment. It will also identify what the organisation must do to retain or improve its competitive position regarding its products or services. This process must also be linked up with the organisation's internal competencies to assess where it should be going. Consequently, the organisation's strengths should be maximised and weaknesses minimised.

According to Prinsloo (2000:30), the

process should involve a strategic analysis which should take the following factors into consideration:

- Internal environment:
  - people (management and employees, capacity, skill, morale, etc.)
  - capital (gearing availability, cash flow management, investment, etc.)
  - systems (reliability)
  - product (brand, price, specialisation, quality, differentiation)
  - plant/equipment (capacity, technology fit)
  - spread of infrastructure
  - service
  - market segments
  - customers (profile, perceptions, etc.)
  - suppliers (terms, reliability, bargaining power)
- Client needs or wants:
  - products (range, quality, quantity)
  - service (availability, backup, distribution)
  - price (discount, credit, cash, affordability)
  - trends
  - sensitivity (push all factors)
- Competition:
  - market share
  - growth rate
  - profitability
  - technology fit
  - product range
  - flexibility
  - customers
  - suppliers
  - infrastructure
  - tactics or weapons
- External environment:
  - social
  - economic
  - technological
  - political or legislative
  - stakeholders (shareholders, unions, suppliers, financiers)
  - global trends

Once this is undertaken, the organisation's decision makers would know where they stand vis-à-vis the environment and competitors in terms of their own position.

### 21.4.3 Step 3: Setting of specific objectives or direction

These activities are aimed at attaining a common approach regarding what the organisation aims to achieve. They therefore improve the process of management so that it is focused on what it must do to achieve objectives.

In order to determine its position, gap analysis must take place to move from the current to the desired situation. This means that various scenarios should have been compiled which would include a worst, best, and most likely scenario. The decision makers then have to take decisions to pursue the objectives they have decided upon.

### 21.4.4 Step 4: Determination of strategies to accomplish those objectives

Specific strategies which can be drawn up would include financial budgets and the communication to the relevant parties of how these are to be accomplished. The strategies decided upon would probably bring about change in one or more of the following: leadership ability, organisational structure, human resources utilisation, etc.

This entails an execution framework to achieve the decisions that have been taken, by compiling appropriate strategies at the appropriate levels in the organisation. This is outlined in more detail below.

## 21.5  Strategy and levels of planning

Strategic planning should be followed up by considering at which level what occurs. This would be dependent on what the organisation regards as its core business. For example, if a business produced a single product, then a single strategic plan would cover all aspects. However, where multiple activities are applicable, various levels exist and need to be addressed. There are consequently several levels of planning to roll out the various strategies of the organisation. Functions such as production, finance, marketing, supply chain, and human resources have their own strategies, each related to business strategy and supportive of it if multiple activities and products exist.

The various levels are discussed below.

### 21.5.1 Grand strategy

According to Swanepoel et al. (2003:169), a grand strategy can be described as a comprehensive general approach that guides an organisation's major actions. It is also called the corporate level strategic plan, and outlines the overall character and purpose of the organisation, the businesses it will enter and leave, and the way resources will be distributed amongst those businesses.

The responsibility to compile it is that of the corporate chief executive and the corporate board of directors. The grand strategy defines the overall character of the organisation, the ways it competes, and the means by which the organisation's goals and objectives are to be achieved. This grand strategy of an organisation thus ties together all other plans so that they do not work at cross-purposes (Johnson and Scholes 2002:16–17).

### 21.5.2 Business strategy

This is the plan for a single business within an organisation, which its top management adopts in order to be competitive and to manage that particular business. This is important because many organisations have interests in different businesses and top management has a difficult time organising the varied activities. A way to deal with this is to create a Strategic Business Unit (SBU) so as to emphasise its relative autonomy.

### 21.5.3 Strategic business unit

This is regarded as any part of an organisation that is treated separately for strategic planning

purposes. It can either be a single business or a collection of related businesses. At the Strategic Business Unit (SBU) level, decision makers focus on questions such as:

- What specific products or services does the SBU produce?
- Who are the SBU's clients?
- How can the SBU best compete in its particular product or service segments?

These questions are quite different from those considered at the corporate level, where grand strategy necessarily focuses on overall corporate mission and on methods of tying together distinct SBUs into a corporate portfolio of businesses.

Many organisations nowadays set up SBUs as separate profit centres, which gives them practically full autonomy. In practice, SBU operations are the responsibility of Deputy Managing Directors of organisations.

### 21.5.4 Functional strategy

This is the plan for one activity within an enterprise. It is, therefore, a narrow area of activity which is focused upon. Functions include finance, marketing, logistics, production and operations, and human resources. Any major department is also a function. Functional strategies are in a sense secondary or 'down stream' to corporate or business strategies, but nevertheless an integral part of strategic management.

Functional strategy therefore means the planned direction for key activity areas within an organisation.

The functional strategy is also part of a planning hierarchy that reflects differing concerns and time periods. There are three levels of planning in this regard, namely: strategic, coordinative, or tactical:

- *Strategic planning* is chiefly the concern of top-level managers. It is directed towards achieving long-term goals and objectives over several years. Strategic plans are uncertain and involve high degrees of risk. They help decision makers anticipate changes in a largely uncontrollable external environment, and play a high-stakes game in organisational success or failure. In practice, it entails the following:

- The concern of top management.
- Long-term time horizon.
- Encompasses the entire organisation.
- External primary focus.
- *Coordinative planning* is intermediate-term. It is primarily the concern of middle-level managers. Less risky than strategy-making, coordinative plans determine how certain areas of a business deploy resources to reach objectives by following the policies and strategies that have been established in the strategic planning process. In practice, it entails the following:
  - The concern of middle managers.
  - Intermediate-term horizon.
  - Encompasses only part of the organisation.
  - Internal primary focus.
- *Tactical or operational planning* is short-term. It is the primary concern of first-line supervisors. Annual budgets are expressions of operational plans. It is less

risky than strategic or coordinative plans because operational plans involve scheduling and moving needed resources. These plans are tied to their longer-term strategic and coordinative counterparts. In practice, it entails the following:

- The concern of supervisors.
- Short-term time horizon.
- Encompasses only a small segment of an organisation's full range of activities.
- Internal primary focus.

It must, however, be borne in mind that due to the reciprocal interdependence between the various strategies, it must be integrated, and this forms the major challenge of strategic management by an organisation's decision makers and top management.

## 21.6 Strategic management

According to Swanepoel et al. (2003: 169–170), strategic management is a process at the top level of the organisation which entails planning, organising, leading, and controlling. At this level the focus is on the success of the organisation as a whole in the long run. Strategic management is therefore regarded as the process of examining both the present and future environments, formulating the company's objectives and making, implementing, and controlling decisions focused on achieving the organisation's objectives in the present and future environments.

Strategic management, however, cannot be regarded as rational decision-making and related behaviour. Unfortunately, issues such as the socio-organisational side of management become important, and therefore the ideology of managers and their motivations, as well as their perceptions of their organisations, play a significant role in what they do. It is also clear that these issues impact on how an organisation's strategic HRM evolves. Let us now focus on strategic human resources management.

## 21.7 Strategic human resources management

In view of what has been discussed, Swanepoel et al. (2003:172–3) state that strategic human resources management is 'those long-term, top-level management decisions and actions regarding employment relationships that are made and performed in a way that is fully integrated with the overall general strategic management of organisations.' It entails synchronising and integrating the organisation's strategic business needs and plans with all those aspects stemming from and relating to the management of its employees.

Therefore by involving human resources considerations when the overall strategy is formulated, human resources contributes to the achieving of a strategic advantage for the organisation because of the synergy that is achieved throughout the organisation's activities. It is consequently obvious that strategic human resources management cannot be viewed as separate from or subordinate to the formulation as well as the implementation of business or corporate strategy. If, for example, human resources requirements are compiled for a strategy of innovation, it will be vastly different from a relocation or start-up section of the business to compete in a neighbouring country. Innovation will entail beating the competition and providing improved products or services. The strategy can only be considered and be effective if management is willing to employ and train workers who will be creative and flexible in their employment endeavours.

According to Anthony et al. (1999:14), the characteristics of a strategic approach to human resources management are that it:

- Explicitly recognises the impact of the outside environment.
- Explicitly recognises the impact of competition and the dynamics of the labour market.
- Has a long-range focus (three to five years).
- Focuses on the issue of choice and decision-making.
- Considers all personnel, not just hourly or operational employees.
- Is integrated with overall corporate strategy and functional strategies.

### 21.7.1 Formulating a human resources management strategy

This process involves top management decisions and actions regarding appropriate strategies for the management of human resources within the context of the internal and external environment. According to Swanepoel et al. (2003:173–4), strategic choices must be made within the context of environmental constraints. This is because an organisation's success is dependent upon its ability to match or fit the variety in the environment in which it operates. Anthony et al. (1999:59), however, point out that all strategies are situational, and that a proper strategy for any particular organisation will depend on the unique situation it faces. What works for one organisation may not necessarily be applicable to another. There must, however, be a fit between the organisation and its environment for any particular organisation to make it work for it. This entails a focus that includes:

- A scanning of the environment to create the necessary fit.
- Considering the organisation's mission in terms of its human resources management approach.
- Deciding on an appropriate HRM strategy.
- Establishment of a human resources management business plan.

The aforementioned is essential because the human resources management strategy and the HRM business plan must fit into a particular organisation's grand strategy. In other words, the human resources management business plan's purpose should basically be to operationalise or bring about the concept of fit between general business strategy and the human resources management strategy. Although the selection or choice of an appropriate HRM strategy must itself ensure that there is an alignment between business and human resources management, the various elements of the business plan must clarify how the necessary fit will be achieved.

These issues clearly demonstrate the link between the various strategies so as to ultimately ensure that human resources utilisation contributes to the goal achievement of the organisation, which means that key areas and strategic priorities must consistently be revisited and redesigned where necessary. It may, for example, be necessary to rewrite job descriptions, to recruit new employees with different characteristics, to update the employment equity plan for the further transformation of an organisation, etc. These aspects were discussed in preceding chapters, but in summary, involve four foci:

- *Individual level considerations*, for example, job redesign, horizontal work redesign, vertical work redesign, ergonomic work redesign, flexibility in work, etc.
- *Group level considerations* of work organisation, such as restructuring work teams, etc.
- *Organisational level considerations*, for instance, changing the organisation structure, focusing on different types of structures, etc.
- *Structural considerations* regarding human resources management functions, for example, redefining the job of the human resources specialist, changing the reporting position of the human resources department in an organisation by doing away with a corporate human resources department and relocating it to a SBU, etc.

Various other views also exist with regard to strategic human resources management, and are presented below.

## 21.7.2 The view of Cascio

A different view is that of Cascio (1995:42), who states that strategic human resources

management simply means getting everybody from the top of the company to the bottom to do things and to implement the strategy of the business as effectively as possible. As a resource, people must be used to fit the strategic needs of the company. The relationship between strategic business needs, people as a resource, and human resources management has led to the development of a framework, which Cascio termed the 5-P model.

Cascio's (1995:42) strategic business needs set the 5-P model in motion. Organisations define (or redefine) such needs during times of turbulence. These needs reflect management's overall plan for survival, growth, adaptability and profitability. The strategic human resources management activities are listed as follows:

- *Philosophy* expresses statements defining business values and culture. It will express how to treat and value people.
- *Policies* express shared values (guidelines). They will establish guidelines for action on people-related business issues and HR programmes.
- *Programmes* are articulated as human resources strategies. They will coordinate efforts to facilitate change to address major people-related business issues.
- *Practices* for leadership, managerial, and operational roles. They will motivate needed role behaviours.
- *Processes* express the formulation and implementation of other activities. They will define how these activities are carried out.

## 21.7.3 The view of Van Dyk

South African organisations cannot successfully compete in the labour market for scarce human resources in all fields of specialisation due to a general lack of availability of skilled human resources. Furthermore, certain skills will be required that will not be available on the open labour market. This is due to emigration of skilled people, poor education policy, lack of funding and the legacies of apartheid, to name but a few. This poses a great challenge to HRM and, more than ever before, there will be a need for interaction between human resources managers and other functional and line managers in organisations. Figure 21.3 shows some of these interfaces, the most important of which are briefly discussed below, as well as the types of interaction and information that human resources managers will have to obtain at a strategic level.

It is clear from Figure 21.3 that management of human resources, with a view to successful human resources development, is a comprehensive task. From a systems and quality assurance point of view, the macro-variables (mega-trends) that have an effect on organisational strategy also have a profound effect on human resources. A proactive strategic approach implies that an analysis of the strengths and weaknesses of the available human resources must be done in order to adapt the strategy agreed upon for every substrategy (such as logistics), both qualitatively and quantitatively. This must be done in the form of a human resources audit of every functional department and its sub-strategy to determine the current state of affairs and to extrapolate the figures for future requirements in the various labour categories (managers, professionals, skilled workers, semiskilled workers, and unskilled workers) for the various functional departments in order to ensure future organisational success.

Another important aspect that human resources managers of organisations must develop, particularly in our times of high technology and information, is new job profiles, since it is expected that the nature of jobs will change drastically in the future.

As a result of technological and other job-related innovations, many jobs will become obsolete and new ones will emerge. For this reason it is essential for organisations to develop new job profiles and to use them as a concept for compiling a skills inventory that can serve as a basis for the strategic human resources management of the organisation.

It is certain that the success of future human resources activities will depend on integrating human resources strategies with the overall organisational strategy, as well as on the interaction between the managements of the various business units to determine what inputs are required for sound human resources management.

Let us now focus on the critical element of skills development from a strategic human resources development point of view.

## 21.8 Strategic human resources development

According to Van Dyk et al. (2001:106–8), strategic human resources development (SHRD) means the process of changing an organisation, stakeholders outside it, groups inside it, and people employed by it through planned learning, so that they possess the knowledge and skills needed for the future. There is a critical shortage of skilled human resources in South Africa, which must be addressed if the country is to become globally competitive. Strategic human resources development helps implement strategic business plans and human resources plans by cultivating the skills of people inside the firm or changing the knowledge and skills of stakeholders outside it. In this regard the possible relationship between strategic business plans, human resources plans, and strategic human resources development can be presented as follows:

- The point of departure is the mission and grand strategy which indicates the long-term direction of an organisation.
- From this the other functional plans of the organisation flow, which would include marketing, finance, supply chain, products, etc. A simultaneous flow is the human resources plans or strategy, which directs the long-term human resources direction of the organisation and also indicates the nature of skills which ought to be required.
- From the human resources strategy, the human resources development strategy flows, which is aimed at the development

**Figure 21.3** A strategic human resources management model

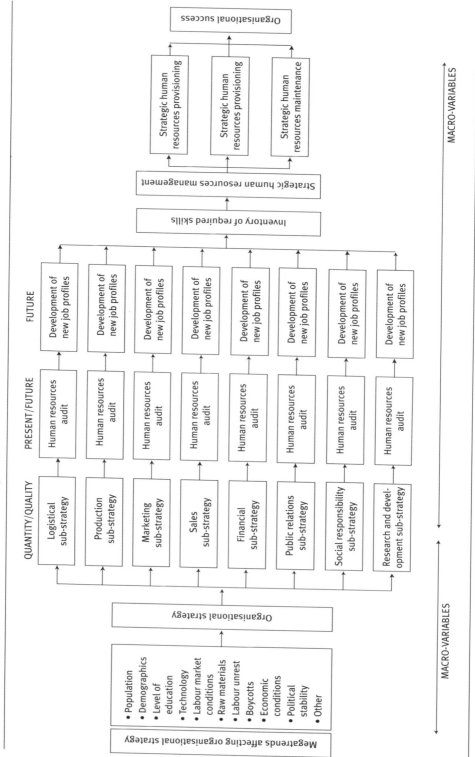

of human resources over time. On the other hand, more specific plans flow from this, such as recruitment, promotion policy, particular training and development issues, etc.

- The cycle is completed by evaluating whether human resources development departmental plans are contributing to the organisation's objective achievement by having developed human resources available as and when required.

Strategic human resources development is therefore more holistic than traditional human resources development. The growth of strategic human resources development is an organisational strategy for the human resources development effort which guides the direction of an organisation. In strategic human resources development, the focus of planning centres around the roles and responsibilities of everyone – human resources development practitioners, line managers, and participants. This focus on human resources development effort – a broad undertaking in which many people have roles to play – differs from mere human resources development department planning.

A further distinction between traditional and strategic human resources development concerns experience. Experience denotes awareness based on participation in past problem solving. It occupies a central place in most human endeavours. Everyone has heard the old saying, 'experience is the best teacher'. Many people believe that 95 per cent of all learning occurs through experience. However, the trouble is that experience is not always appropriate in preparing for the future. There are many reasons why this is so. New knowledge is created faster today than it was in the past. Computers increase the speed with which information can be processed – but not the speed at which human beings can absorb it or use it. Organisations face more competition and must anticipate competitive challenges if they are to survive. The same principle applies to individuals who are competing with others for career success.

A new approach to human resources development is therefore needed to cope with a future that is not always like the past. This approach should help individuals anticipate the knowledge and skills needed in the future rather than react after problems become apparent. Strategic human resources development does this.

This is not to say that strategic human resources development always differs from its traditional counterpart. Traditional human resources development and strategic human resources development coincide when the external environment of the organisation, individual, or job is relatively stable. If the future is likely to be like the past, then traditional and strategic human resources development intersect. But if the future is likely to be utterly unlike the past due to external environmental change, then strategic human resources development is appropriate for equipping people with new knowledge and skills.

By applying strategic HRM development effectively, organisations will certainly be better equipped to face the challenges of the future of global competition and simultaneously be more productive locally.

## 21.9   Conclusion

In this chapter, an overview was given of the essential elements of strategy. Strategy is a prerequisite for any effective human resources management in particular. It was also pointed out that organisational strategy, with all its facets (such as business strategy, and functional strategy including the various levels of planning) are all important prerequisites to embarking on any human resources management activities. It was furthermore highlighted that vision, mission, organisational values, and standards of behaviour form the nucleus of elements which impact on decision makers in their efforts to decide on the direction an organisation is to take so as to achieve a competitive edge and to remain competitive.

# Summary

- Strategic human resources management is the handling and overseeing of human capital with an eye to the future and the long-term, and in accordance with established policies and procedures. In ensuring that individual employers and employees get the maximum benefit from the work experience, over time, strategic human resources is inseparable from corporate and business objectives. It is clear that an interdependent relationship exists between an organisation's grand strategy and its approach to strategic HRM. If either are poorly formulated or executed, the chances decrease rapidly for an organisation to be successful. The synergy between human resources management and organisational effectiveness should therefore never be under-estimated.
- It is also evident that the development of human resources should be undertaken from a strategic point of view as this would be the optimal way for the organisation to have the right quality and quantity of human resources available to achieve its objectives in the most competitive and efficient way. It is a fact that human resources, particularly if managed strategically, remains the greatest asset any organisation can have, because effective knowledge management of its human resources is to be the ultimate success weapon of any organisation in the decades to come.
- Human resources management is as important as any other form of corporate management. Strong and exemplary leadership in addressing workplace inter-relationships, personal dynamics, and individual needs and wants, is no less significant, for example, than good and confident leadership in merchandising and the marketing of a physical product. It is especially true nowadays that the respect of the individual, his/her knowledge, and his/her competencies and ambitions, be merged with respect for the company, its image, its branding, and its products. The sustainability of people and the sustainability of the organisation are one and the same.

## Case study
## Paving the way to profitability

The HR team at Bayer's Corp Myerstown production facility initiated a 'Roadmap for Change' process that ultimately helped the plant became profitable.

During the seven months before the plant became the property of Bayer, it had changed ownership three times. This was a lot of change for a company that had been producing prescription pharmaceuticals for more than half a century. Employees, who experienced job insecurity because of previous lay-offs, were uncertain about what it would be like working for Bayer. Morale was low. Line-managers had their own worries, as they were required to run a 24-hour a day, seven-day-a-week production schedule with a workforce that was weary of takeovers. The plant was also operating in red for some time.

Managers realised that given competitive forces and the rate of change in their industry, they had to streamline operations to secure the future of the plant. The plant had no plant manager for the last year and a half. The functional department managers, including the HR manager, had to run the plant. It was realised that employees had to be involved if they wanted to make a turnaround.

A six-person HR team embarked on a present-state analysis. They selected 93 employees at random to participate in seven focus groups to get a clear indication of what was happening at the plant. A focus group consists of stakeholders (employees in this case) who openly share their thoughts and feelings in a relaxed a casual and informal atmosphere. The responses were carefully recorded and then analysed. In this case employees had to answer questions such as: Why do people work here? And, why do people leave here?

The HR team summarised the responses and got all other employees to comment on the findings. Employees mentioned good things (pay and benefits), but also 30 issues that required attention. This kind of interaction was new to employees – the previous management style was top-down and reactive, rather than proactive.

A new Plant Manager, John O'Neill, was appointed. He formed another cross-functional employee team consisting of 18 employees. The team was called the 'Roadmap for Change' team. This team condensed the 30 previously raised issues into five key issues:

1  Define site goals or strategies and communicate them to employees in interactive employee conferences.
2  Develop a site communication process.
3  Develop role descriptions and competency profiles for hourly employees and supervisors.
4  Identify perceived inconsistencies in practices and policies, and determine appropriate action.
5  Develop a performance measurement process.

These employees also developed a plan to implement these changes and communicate changes and results to all employees on a regular basis. Knowing employees were skeptical of new management programmes in the past (which failed every time), plant manager O'Niell and the HR team addressed workers at an all-employee meeting about the site strategy and goal: 'To be clearly recognised as Bayer Consumer Care's most efficient site in this region in terms of safety, customer service, value-added manufacturing or packing, and cost effectiveness'. The 'Myerstown Information Exchange', an electronic newsletter, was sent to members of the site management team, who in turn discussed the information with their employees. It was important to get everyone on the same page, and involve people with issues that affected them.

The company also instituted the 'Productivity Plus' programme into the compensation plan. The programme established a scorecard of key performance measures such as right-first-time quality and cost management.

The 'Roadmap for Change' had numerous positive outcomes. Schedule attainment, quality, waste-reduction, and safety all improved, while job satisfaction increased and financial goals were attained.

In the end, the Myerstown site has become the model for other Bayer facilities to emulate. Instead of following, now the group is leading. And it looks like there's a clear road ahead.

SOURCE: www.workforce.com

## Questions

1  What is the purpose or mission of Bayer Corporation?
2  Conduct a SWOT analysis of Bayer Corporation for the period before changes were instituted.
3  Identify the strategy or strategies followed at Bayer Corporation to achieve its goals.
4  What role did HRM play in the change process?

## Experiential exercise

PURPOSE: To compare various organisations in terms of relevant strategic aspects.

TASK (to be completed in advance): Step 1. Divide into groups of two. Each group should choose a specific organisation to prevent duplication and then collect information about the organisation's vision, mission, values and HRM strategies. This information can be obtained from the organisation itself, newspapers, corporate reports, and organisational websites.

Step 2. Each group presents an overview of the collected material to the class and indicates how the HRM strategy supports the organisational goals.

# Chapter questions

1  Describe the general vocabulary of strategy.
2  Discuss the importance of integrating HRM strategy into organisational strategy.
3  Use a diagram to explain the integration of human resources strategy with the overall organisational strategy.
4  Draw up a list of examples to differentiate between the following concepts in your organisation:
   - organisation strategy
   - grand strategy
   - strategic business unit strategy
   - functional strategy
5  Describe organisational level considerations of work organisation you would adjust in your organisation to achieve the organisation's objectives.
6  From a strategic management perspective, how would you go about integrating decisions concerning employment to ensure a highly competent and achievement-orientated staff complement. Use your accumulated knowledge of the employment process to answer this question.

# Bibliography

ANTHONY, W.P., PERREWÉ, P. & KACMAR, K.M. 1999. *Human resource management. A strategic approach, 3rd edition.* Dryden Press, New York.

BIRCHALL, D. & LYONS, L. 1995. *Creating tomorrow's organisation – Unlocking the benefits of Future Work.* (Pitman), Pearson Education (UK).

CAMPBELL, A. & TAWADEY, K. 1990. *Mission and business philosophy: Waning employee commitment.* Billings, London.

CASCIO, W.F. 1995. Managing human resources: Productivity, quality of work life, profits. McGraw-Hill Companies, New York.

CHARLTON, G. 2000. *Human habits of highly effective organisations.* Van Schaik, Pretoria.

DOUGHERTY, D. 2002. *Human resource strategy.*
McGraw-Hill Companies, New York.

DOWLING, P.J., WELCH, D.E. & SCHULER, R.S. 1999. *International human resource management. Managing people in a multinational context, 3rd edition.* South Western College Publishing, Melbourne.

IVANCEVICH, J.M. 2001. *Human resource management, 8th edition.* McGraw-Hill Companies, New York.

JOHNSON, G. & SCHOLES, K. 2002. *Exploring corporate Strategy: Text and cases, 6th edition.* (Prentice-Hall), Pearson Education (UK).

MONDY, R.W., NOE, R.M. & PREMEAUX, S.R. 1999. *Human resource management, 7th edition.* (Prentice-Hall), Pearson Education Inc.

OGILVIE-THOMPSON, J. 1993. 'People management critical for business'. *Human Resources Management,* 9(5).

PLEVEL, M.J., NELLIS, S., LANE, F. & SCHULER, R.S. 1994. 'Linking HR with business strategy'. *Organizational Dynamics,* 22(3).

PRINSLOO, R. 2000. 'Strategic planning model'. *People Dynamics,* 18(1):30–31. Reprinted with permission of Copyright Clearance Center.

ROTHWELL, W.J. & KAZANAS, H.C. 1994a. *Planning and managing human resources: Strategic planning for personnel management.* Massachusetts HRD Press, Amherst.

ROTHWELL, W.J. & KAZANAS, H.C. 1994b. *Human resources development: A strategic approach.* Massachusetts HRD Press, Amherst.

SCHULTZ, H., BAGRAIM, J., PORTGIETER, T., VIEDGE, C. & WERNER, A. 2003. *Organisational behaviour. A contemporary South African perspective.* Van Schaik, Pretoria.

SWANEPOEL, B.J., ERASMUS, B.J, VAN WYK, M. & SCHENK, H. 2003. *South African human resources management: Theory and practice, 3rd edition.* Juta, Cape Town.

TAYLOR, T., BEECHLER, S. & NAPIER, N. 1996. 'Toward an integrative model of strategic international human resources management'. *Academy of Management Review,* 21(4):959.

TYSON, S. 1995. *Human resource strategy. Towards a general theory of human resource management.* (Pitman), Pearson Education (UK).

VAN DYK, P.S., NEL, P.S., LOEDOLFF, P. VAN Z & HAASBROEK, G.D. 2001. *Training management: A multidisciplinary approach to human resources development in South Africa, 3rd edition.* Oxford University Press, Cape Town.

## Websites

American Department of Labour:
   www.stats.bls.gov
International Business Machine (IBM):
   www.ibm.com
American affirmative action register:
   www.aar-eeo.com
Fortune magazine: www.fortune.com

# 22

# Human Resources Information Systems

## A Werner

## Learning outcomes

At the end of this chapter the learner should be able to:

- Appreciate the role of a Human Resources Information System (HRIS).
- Discuss the myths that surround the use of HRISs.
- Recommend a systematic plan for implementing an HRIS in an organisation.
- Discuss the components of an HRIS.
- Discuss the areas in HRM where information systems are utilised.
- Explain how HRISs can be used as a diagnostic and decision-making tool with regard to selected organisational variables.
- Comment on employees' privacy and the use of HRISs.
- Discuss quality assurance in HRISs.

## Key words and concepts

- business intelligence
- Decision Support System (DSS)
- Enterprise Resource Planning (ERP)
- Human Resources Information Systems (HRISs)
- Management Information System (MIS).

## Illustrative case
## Automated recruitment at Nike

Nike has increased the efficiency (time and cost) and effectiveness of its recruitment services by adopting an applicant tracking system, called Resumix. Before the system was implemented, job applicants had to submit a separate resumé for each job for which they applied. The old system did not provide a mechanism to store information from unsolicited job applications, with the result that more than 35 000 submitted applications forms were thrown away. With the new system, information from each resumé is scanned in and stored in a database for retrieval at a later stage. Key items, such as job history, education, and experience are used to guide storing and retrieval. If a suitable job becomes available, the applicant is informed automatically. The new system also enables managers to cross-reference resumés.

The company now runs less newspaper ads, and the ads are more general in nature, generating a greater variety of candidates. The time to fill positions has also been reduced considerably.

SOURCE: Noe et al. (2000:591)

## 22.1 Introduction

There is no question about it: we are in the electronic and information age where systems, software, and databases manage vast reservoirs of data. In this environment, business intelligence is taking on a new meaning. Organisations use modern technology to find the most profitable customers, identify the best marketing techniques, identify parts and equipment that need replacement, control production, manage finances, sales, and fulfil a vast number of other functions. The Human Resources Information System (HRIS) forms part of the organisation's larger Management Information System (MIS). An HRIS is used to collect, record, store, analyse, distribute, and retrieve data concerning the organisation's human resources.

It has increasingly become important for the human resources department to fulfil a bigger role in the strategic direction of the company and to affect internal and external change. The strategic value of human resources management lies in the ability to distribute relevant and accurate information to key decision makers in the organisation and to ensure that the respondents are able to interpret and utilise the information. This function is called the Decision Support System (DSS).

Advances in computing technology always present a paradox: the promise of well-managed information, time and cost savings, and the threat of an inability to handle the technical maintenance or application of the system. However, for a company to be dominant in today's markets it must be able to react to change, successfully participating in and managing events and turning them to competitive advantage. Although Information Technology (IT) is responsible for assembling and maintaining the technology, IT specialists are hardly able to determine the information needs within a business. The driving force behind a HRIS is the human resources department, which must provide a conceptual framework of what is required. Putting all the pieces into place is not an easy task. It is by nature complex and sometimes very frustrating to ensure that the data is correct, that it flows correctly, and that people know how to use the analytical tools sitting on their desktops. But once it is working, success becomes more of a reality than a gamble.

In this chapter we will explore the myths surrounding the use of HRISs. We will investigate the areas in which HRISs are generally applied and the way they can be used as a diagnostic and decision-making tool with regard to absenteeism, labour turnover, job satisfaction, and job equity. Quality assurance in HRISs will also be considered.

## 22.2 Components of an HRIS

An HRIS consists of four distinct components. These include hardware, software, data, and the users. These components are interrelated, and defects in one can affect one or more of the other components.

- *Hardware* refers to all the physical, tangible parts of a computer, such as the central processing unit, keyboard, display screen, printer, disks and compact disks (CDs).
- *Software* refers to the instructions that are built into a computer or computer program to make it work. Software enables a computer. Software is divided into two categories. System software includes the operating system and all the utilities that enable the computer to perform. Windows is an example of system software. Applications software includes actual programs used by the user for a specific purpose. Examples of software are word

processors such as Word Perfect, MS Word or Apple Works, spreadsheets and database management systems, such as payroll and employee record systems.

- *Data* are distinct pieces of information, usually formatted in a special way. Examples of data include: employee's name, number, job title, job skills, educational level, performance rating, and attendance status.
- *User* refers to anyone who uses a computer. Users of HRISs include human resources practitioners, data-entry specialists, managers, and employees. The users have access to designated information components, and not the total HRIS.

## 22.3  The myths of HRISs

Human resources practitioners and other key decision makers within organisations often have misconceptions about the installation and use of information technology in the human resources department (Witschger 1999). These misconceptions have led to the slow introduction of HRISs into organisations. These include:

- *HRISs will solve all human resources information problems.* HRISs automate existing processes. If the manual systems used are of high quality, then software will speed up the operation, make it more vital, visible and timely. If the manual system is not well managed, the software will expose these shortcomings. For example, HRISs cannot produce a well-presented absenteeism report with missing or incorrect information. However, they can produce a bad report at a very high speed.
- *HRISs will eliminate jobs in the human resources department.* HRISs seldom result in job losses due to automation in the human resources department. Staff members who previously had the mundane task of recording or filing information, can now direct their efforts to what they are supposed to be doing: serving management as is appropriate, and contribut-

ing more effectively to the strategic goals of the organisation.

- *HRISs are complex and therefore expensive.* HRISs are much less complex than accounting systems. A key factor, however, is the amount of information that is tracked for employees, applicants, jobs, etc. The storing, reporting and calculation process is basic.
- *HRISs take a long time to implement.* A well managed, manual HR function in a small to mid-size organisation can be implemented within a week or two. Automation implies the conversion of existing programmes into computerised ones. The same historical data are used. It is possible that the current procedure has to be adjusted to the computerised system, but the basic elements of the process will stay the same.
- *HRISs require expensive and intensive training.* A well designed software program merely automates tasks that are already performed. Intensive training will only become necessary if the human resources function was not performed well before. In this case, the introduction of the programme can only benefit the organisation, and the costs and time spent on training will be justified.
- *Customising HRISs requires very expensive consultants.* The human resources department must analyse its information system needs carefully before making a decision about what system and software to acquire. It is important to choose a system that is very close to the identified needs. Most programs have customisation options that allow for flexibility.
- *HRISs require constant involvement from the IT department.* A well designed and well implemented system does not require constant IT involvement.
- *Technical support is not readily available for HRIS support.* Information about the quality of after-sales technical support from the supplier can be obtained from other customers, and from pre-sales queries and efforts. It is best to negotiate

after-sales technical support for a defined period as well as a retainer fee.

From the above discussion it is clear that a decision regarding a specific HRIS should only be made after a thorough study of the human resources information needs and the products and services of reputable suppliers. Introducing a computerised system provides an organisation with an opportunity to simultaneously upgrade their existing processes and procedures.

## 22.4 Steps in the implementation of an HRIS

Organisations need to carefully think and plan when an HRIS is to be implemented. The purpose of such a system should be made readily apparent and the users should receive special attention. Byars and Rue (1989:526) outline the following steps in the implementation of an HRIS:

- *Step 1: Inception of the idea.* The person who initiates the idea of implementing an HRIS system should clearly motivate his/her idea by illustrating how it will assist management in making decisions.
- *Step 2: Feasibility study.* The feasibility study should indicate the benefits of an HRIS in terms of less labour, less material, and increased accuracy, in comparison to the cost of such a system. The study might indicate that it is not feasible to implement an HRIS.
- *Step 3: Selecting a project team.* The project team must include a human resources representative, and representatives from both management information systems and payroll.
- *Step 4: Defining the requirements.* A statement of the requirements spells out what the HRIS will do. This will include reports to be produced, and outline how users collect and prepare data, obtain approvals, complete forms, and retrieve data.
- *Step 5: Vendor analysis.* Here the available

hardware and software are considered against the organisational needs and budget allowances. Detailed information about how a package will meet organisational needs should be elicited. Based on this analysis a decision is made whether to buy an 'off-the-shelf' package or one that is developed internally.

- *Step 6: Package contract negotiation.* A contract with the chosen vendor stipulates the vendor's responsibilities with regard to software, installation service, maintenance, training and documentation.
- *Step 7: Training.* Members of the project team are trained first in how to use the system before carefully selected members from other departments are trained.
- *Step 8: Tailoring the system.* The system can be adjusted to suit specific organisational needs, but care should be taken not to cause technical problems.
- *Step 9: Collecting the data.* Before the start-up of the system, data must be collected and entered into the system.
- *Step 10: Testing the system.* The purpose of testing is to verify the output of HRM and to ensure that the desirable results are achieved.
- *Step 11: Starting up.* Start-up commences when all data and current actions are put into the system, and reports produced. Best is to start the system during a quiet time.
- *Step 12: Running in parallel.* Running the new and old system simultaneously allows for a comparison of the two systems so as to detect any inaccuracies.
- *Step 13: Maintenance.* During the maintenance phase, people settle down and get used to the system.
- *Step 14: Evaluation.* Specific factors to consider in the evaluation phase include the value of reports, the system's response time, its update facility, integration with the payroll system, ability to answer specific functional questions on request, as well as the cost of implementing and maintaining the system.

## 22.5  HRM application areas of HRISs

HRISs are built on a modular basis to allow flexibility. These modules or components are inter-related and use the same basic database. 'Best practice' for human resources software is founded on:

- An extensive database for a wide range of employee-employer information.
- A significant 'data-sensitive' historical capacity.
- Easy-to-use reporting and analysis capability, available with a broad user community.

### 22.5.1 Employee data maintenance

Employee data collection, capturing, and maintenance form the core of the information system in HRM. These tasks address information such as the employee's name, personnel number, identity number, address, family particulars, date of employment, job information, salary comparison data, qualifications, competencies, and other basic information required by the organisation. The employee data component supports all other human resources information. Any change made in the information in this component is immediately reflected in all other components that use the same data.

### 22.5.2 Financial planning

This component allows the human resources manager to simulate the financial impact of salary and benefit changes. Based on this information, the manager can recommend an increase strategy that remains within the overall budget goal.

### 22.5.3 Payroll processing

The payroll component handles the entire payroll process, including regulations, tax considerations, and deductions. It can also be used to develop appropriate compensation and benefits, and to track individual employ-

ees as well as groups of employees so as to spot compensation trends in the organisation. In addition, it can handle stock purchase and stock option plans. Information about salary grades, job classification, and salary ranges form the basis of this component.

### 22.5.4 Equity management

This component enables employers to formulate an employment equity plan in line with the new regulations published by the Department of Labour in 1999. It provides a profile of the workforce and the skill development of employees, and handles the development of an equity plan.

### 22.5.5 Competency management

A competency system package tracks the skill levels of employees, and develops compensation and training to match employees' and organisational needs. Both the manager's as well as the employee's evaluations of training needs can be entered. This component contains information on internal and external training courses, training course evaluations, instructors, costs, and enrollment facilities. It also provides individual profiles containing information on qualifications, training received in-house and outside, results of courses, financial reimbursements, and training needs.

### 22.5.6 Recruitment and selection

This component keeps record of vacant positions and candidates for those vacancies. It tracks resumés and matches candidates with the requirements of the vacant positions. It records the length of times vacancies exist and compares the visit-to-offer and offer-to-acceptance ratios. Information kept of applicants includes personal details, educational background, work experience, etc. This component allows the organisation to locate the most successful interviewer, recruitment source, and recruitment area.

**Table 22.1** Examples of HR software available in South Africa

| Application area | Package | Description |
| --- | --- | --- |
| Roster planning | Quickshift | A system that automatically generates staff rosters for shift work. Supplied by Omega Digital. |
| Payroll | Accsys Peopleware Solutions | A fully integrated modular human resources and payroll system. Supplied by Accsys. |
| Equity management | Employment Equity Software | Makes provision for a workforce profile, skills development report, analysis of employment policies, practices, procedures and work environment, equity plan, and benchmarking. Supplied by Van Zyl Rudd and associates. |
| Competency management | Peodesy | Supports all HR tasks through a modular system. Supplied by FSA-Contact. |
| Recruitment and Selection | Assis | A fully integrated staff recruitment system. Supplied by CPS-Computerised Personnel Systems. |
| Time and attendance | Paywise | An integrated personnel or administration system that combines accounting and time recording functions. Supplied by Paywise Software. |
| Human resources planning | Third Foundation Manpower Planning | Provides a comprehensive package covering affirmative action, employee development, performance management, post profiling, and related functions. Supplied by Third Foundation Systems. |
| Self-help desk | PWA Empower | An Internet or intranet workflow enabled solution with a manager and employee self-service function. Provided by EmSoft. |

## 22.5.7 Time and attendance

This component tracks the number of hours worked by using magnetic strip cards or PC-based systems instead of time clock or hand-written timecards. This information is also used in the wage and salary administration component. It can also provide information on the amount of time lost due to absenteeism, the causes, costs involved, personal absence profiles, and group records.

## 22.5.8 Risk management

This component monitors whether people in specific positions have updated driver's licenses, safety training, and even physical examinations.

## 22.5.9 Human resources planning

This module is used to estimate future HRM needs by analysing current job occupation,

**Figure 22.1** A typical advertisement for an HRIS found in professional magazines

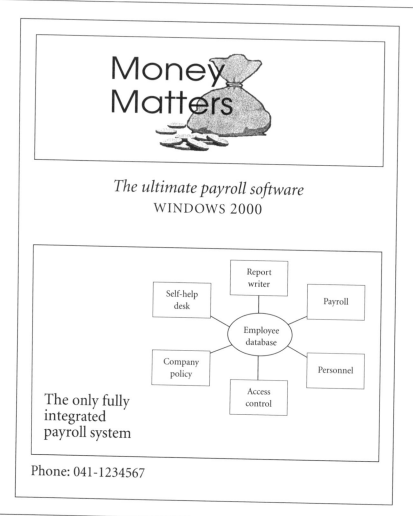

turnover, transfers, promotions (as well as the related skill levels), and retirements.

### 22.5.10 Self-help desk

This is a relatively new addition to HRISs, which provides many new opportunities for the employer-employee relationship. Traditionally, the human resources department has been viewed as a 'query office'. The self-help desk frees the human resources depart-

ment from this function, allowing it to spend more time on strategic or organisational issues. The employee self-help desk is linked to the organisation's intranet and allows employees to have instant access to information relevant to the user.

The self-help desk can be used for the following purposes:

- *Personal information:* the employee has the opportunity to review, confirm and change personal information such as marital status, dependents, emergency contacts, and beneficiaries.

- *Suggestions:* the employee self-help desk provides an outlet for their ideas and complaints.
- *Organisation bulletin:* employees access the bulletin or submit their creative contributions.
- *Company policies:* employees have instant and permanent access to all relevant policies and procedures, such as for grievances and discipline, sexual harassment, benefits, and other rules governing the workplace.
- *Financial benefits:* benefit statements, investment modelling, stock options, and other options.
- *New forms:* information can be collected quickly and efficiently for example in cases where employees have to exercise an option.
- *Socialisation:* the corporate culture is reinforced by exposing employees to the mission, goals, expectations, behavioural norms, and results of the company.

The self-help desk allows both the human resources department and the employee to spend their time more productively by reducing time spent on requesting information, filling out forms and following up on them. It reduces paperwork and provides an anonymous form and equal service to everyone.

## 22.6 The utilisation of HRISs as a diagnostic and decision-making tool with regard to selected organisational variables

A statistic often quoted by IBM Corporation in New York indicates that the average company only uses two to four per cent of the data that resides in its systems. The rest of the information never sees the light of a computer monitor (Greengard 1999:103–4).

Organisations vary with respect to what extent they utilise human resources information. The ideal is that the organisation will exhibit a high competency and capability to handle information, and make use of human resources software to support well articulated and aligned business goals across all HR disciplines. The dynamic environment in which organisations operate necessitates a learning culture. Calculated decision-making and constructive problem solving are based on accurate and timely information that generate knowledge and understanding.

### Case-in-point

At Forbes Pty (Ltd.) the human resources department illustrated how they added value to the organisation. The HRIS revealed that exceptionally high levels of labour turnover were experienced in the analytical chemistry department. Employees from this department, as well as those who left the company, were surveyed. It became evident that these employees considered themselves as knowledge workers and required more opportunities for personal achievement and independence, and that they wanted to be fairly rewarded for the value they added to the organisation. The recruitment and training costs of analytical chemists were determined, and a business case was presented for retaining these employees. This move not only saved the company money, but also increased the motivational levels of the analytical chemists.

The ability to conduct research and utilise the findings appropriately is critically important to HR practitioners and managers.

### 22.6.1 Areas of human resources-related research

In contrast to basic research, which has the aim of generating theoretical knowledge to create a better understanding about a given subject for future use, applied research is aimed at solving a particular practical problem immediately. Basic research is mostly done under the guidance of an academic or research institution, while applied research is done within organisations.

Research in organisations can be planned and conducted on human resources aspects such as:

- The equity status of the organisation in accordance with the Employment Equity Act.
- The absenteeism status within various sections or departments and the main causes of the problem if it proves to exist.
- The labour turnover rate and the nature of a labour turnover problem.
- The job satisfaction of employees.
- The current organisational culture in comparison to the desired culture.
- The reasons for the slow implementation of a mentoring programme.
- Training needs analysis.
- The alignment of individual performance management applications with the organisational goals.
- Competency assessment of employees.

The following section will focus on the application of human resources information with regard to the management of employment equity, absenteeism, labour turnover, and employee satisfaction.

## Employment equity

The Employment Equity Act requires that employers prepare and implement an employment equity plan that complies with the new regulations published by the Department of Labour in 1999. These regulations stipulate the exact manner in which designated employers must analyse their workforce and the relevant information that must appear in their equity reports. Chapter 6 covers employment equity and affirmative action.

The introduction of various software programs has made the procedural application of the Employment Equity Act easier. Some of these programs enable the employer to:

- Compile a profile of the workforce in terms of designated groups, non-designated groups, occupational categories, occupational levels, and permanent and non-permanent employees.
- Compile a report of the skills development of employees.
- Analyse the organisation's employment policies, practices, procedures, and the working environment.
- Compile the organisation's equity plan.
- Benchmark itself against similar organisations.

## Absenteeism

A search on the Internet for information on absenteeism revealed more than 10 000 absence-related websites. This is an indication of the magnitude of this problem! On the other hand, the new logical organisation is result-driven and not behaviour-orientated. In an emerging virtual environment absenteeism is becoming less and less important. Before management embarks on a programme to control and reduce absenteeism, it should first consider whether attendance is linked to performance outcomes or not.

Absenteeism is defined as the non-attendance of an employee when scheduled to work. Research on absenteeism is important due to the potentially disruptive effect it has on operations within the organisation and as well as the related costs involved. Absenteeism is regarded as withdrawal behaviour when it is used as a way to escape an undesirable working environment. Figure 22.2 illustrates the cost of absenteeism in small businesses as established by a survey done in America in 1998. It plainly shows that absenteeism can be expensive.

- *Factors contributing to absenteeism:* The human resources practitioner must be sensitive to the fact that people do get sick and that they do encounter life problems that might prevent them from attending work. However, it is also a fact that people do abuse the sick leave that they are granted by the organisation for

**Figure 22.2** Costs related to absenteeism

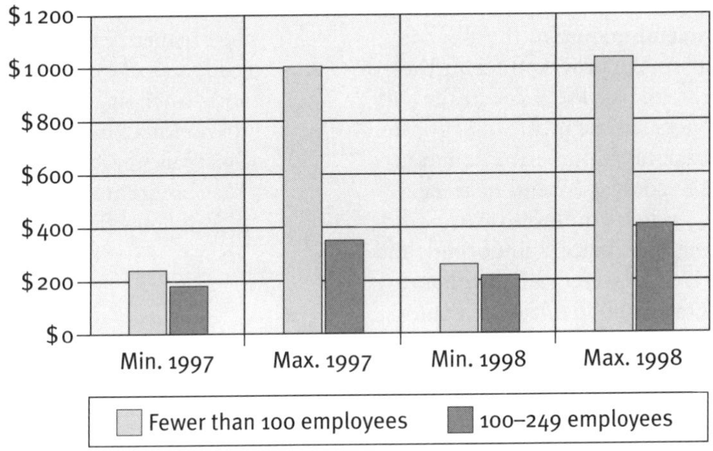

SOURCE: 'Business owner's toolkit' (www.toolkit.cch.com). ©CCH Inc.

various reasons. The same cold that won't prevent us from attending a social meeting, becomes a convenient excuse not to attend work. These reasons can be explained as follows:

- *Met expectations:* New employees enter an organisation with certain expectations relating to the opportunities to apply their skills and abilities, equal treatment, receiving respect, or enjoying satisfactory working conditions. If the employee's expectations are not met, the employee could abuse sick leave as a mechanism to withdraw temporarily from the job or the job situation.
- *Job-person match:* If an employee's personality, abilities, and skills are not congruent with the job requirements, the person becomes either bored or stressed, and withdraws from the situation by being absent. If there is a good match between the job characteristics and personal characteristics of the employee, the person will rather accept responsibility and stay committed to her/his job.

- *Organisational culture:* If a permissive absence culture exists within an organisation, employees will consider sick leave as a benefit that needs to be utilised, or it will be lost. On the other hand, if unnecessary absence is frowned upon by either management or the co-workers, the employee will think twice before abusing sick leave.
- *Absence categories:* For the sake of accurate recording and analysis, absenteeism is divided into three categories:
  - *Sick absence* occurs when a person is absent due to a reported illness, whether genuine or not. The company policy will state at what stage a medical certificate is required.
  - *Authorised absence* occurs when the employee is absent for any reason other than illness, and it is accepted by management. Employees should be encouraged to seek permission beforehand if the situation allows for it.
  - *Unexcused absence* is considered as unacceptable and should not be tolerated. Progressive discipline is used to handle this problem.

- *Recording absenteeism:* The HRIS makes it very easy to record individual absences. The most basic information required is the person's name and employee number, days absent, and reason for the absence. Some HRISs make provision for further information, such as the name of the doctor who issued the medical certificate. The contemporary approach is to counsel employees as soon as a trend in absenteeism is detected. Employees are reminded that their attendance is important, and assistance is offered in dealing with any problem. Once individual absence information is entered, group records and trends can be followed. Group records include absenteeism measurements per section, department, race, gender, skill level, etc. These distinctions allow for more effective problem detection and problem solving.
- *Measuring absenteeism.* Measuring absenteeism allows us to determine the extent and nature (reasons) of absenteeism in order to take appropriate corrective action if necessary. Two measures are generally used:
  - *Total time lost* gives the percentage of work time lost due to absenteeism. The international norm is three per cent. However, the question is raised whether organisations that compete in world markets should be content with an absenteeism norm of three per cent. The total time lost index is calculated as follows:

$$\text{Total time lost} = \frac{\text{Total number of days lost due to absence over the period}}{\text{Average number of employees} \times \text{total workdays over the period}} \times 100\%$$

  - *Absence frequency* gives an indication of the number of absence incidents per employee. An incident is one spell of absence, irrespective of duration. A high absence frequency rate suggests that absence incidents are of a shorter duration, and thus more disruptive to the organisation. It is easier and less costly to make contingency plans when it is known that an employee will be absent for a longer period than for short, unexpected absence incidents. The absence frequency rate is calculated as follows and expressed as a ratio:

$$\text{Absence frequency} = \frac{\text{Number of absence incidents over the period}}{\text{Average number of employees employed over the period}}$$

The total time lost index and frequency ratio is determined for every group of employees and every category of absence, namely sick absence, authorised absence and unexcused absence.

- *Analysis of absenteeism measurements.* The recording and measurement of absenteeism figures has absolutely no value if it is not interpreted and acted upon. The measurement of absenteeism should be used as a diagnostic tool to identify organisational problems. A comparison between different departments and worker groups can pinpoint trends. If most days are lost due to sick absence and a large number of employees are involved, it might be an indication of withdrawal behaviour. If authorised absence is a problem, the organisation's policy and involvement of supervisors should be considered. Lastly, unexcused absence is unacceptable under any circumstances. It can be reduced by properly communicated and applied disciplinary procedures. Figure 22.3 illustrates some of the options available for the analysis of absence by means of an absence software program.

**Figure 22.3** Group trends menu of an absence software program

Absenteeism programme – group trends

| | |
|---|---|
| ▶ Department/section | ▶ Education |
| ▶ Age | ▶ Length of service |
| ▶ Gender and race related | ▶ Residential area |
| ▶ Marital status | ▶ Go to Main menu |

## Labour turnover

Labour turnover is the movement of employees in and out of the boundaries of the organisation. Transfers are thus not considered as labour turnover. Labour turnover is considered as the permanent withdrawal from the work situation. Labour turnover can be disruptive and costly to an organisation. The stability of the work group is influenced by staff turnover, and new employees must be recruited, employed, and trained. A certain amount of labour turnover can be beneficial, however, if it provides the organisation with new, enthusiastic employees who bring creative ideas with them. Labour turnover is influenced by the prevailing economic climate, the nature of the organisation, and the type of employee.

- *Causes of labour turnover.* Unmet expectations and the person-work relationship will influence labour turnover (as in the case of absenteeism). Individual factors that have an effect are age, education, background, and personality. Employees sometimes remain in an organisation for a long period because they have built up a good relationship with co-workers.
- *Controllable and uncontrollable labour turnover.* Labour turnover is divided into controllable and uncontrollable turnover, depending on management's ability to prevent it or not. Voluntary resignations and dismissals are regarded as controllable. Voluntary resignations can be controlled if management provides better

leadership, wages, opportunities, working conditions, etc. Dismissals can be prevented through proper employment, training, policies, and procedures. Only controllable labour turnover is included in the measurement of labour turnover. Uncontrollable labour turnover includes death, permanent illness, pregnancy, retirement, and retrenchment. These are recorded, yet not included, in the measurement of labour turnover, as no reasonable action from management can reduce or prevent them.

- *Recording of labour turnover.* Information required for the measurement of labour turnover includes the employee's name and personnel number, date of entry and departure and reasons given.
- *Measurement and analysis of labour turnover.* Labour turnover is measured by calculating the Labour Turnover Rate (LTO), Median Length Of Service (MLOS) and percentage of Voluntary resignations (%V). The LTO indicates the percentage of people who left the organisation due to controllable reasons. The LTO is calculated as an annual figure to make comparison possible. The norm for labour turnover is dependent on the type of worker and industry, the economic conditions, and the geographical area. It is recommended that labour turnover is compared over a period of time and with similar groups or organisations.

$$LTO = \frac{V+D \text{ (voluntary resignations and dismissals)}}{\text{Average number of employees over period}} \times \frac{100}{1}$$

$$\% V = \frac{V}{V+D} \times \frac{100}{1}$$

MLOS = median length of service (middle figure)

The MLOS indicates at what stage of employment employees have left. The MLOS differs from the average length of service in the sense that a median refers to the middle figure. The MLOS is indicated in months. Should the length of service of employees who left be 1, 2, 2, 3, 4, 5 and 6 months respectively, the MLOS will be 3 months. A short MLOS indicates problems with employment, induction, training, and mentoring. A long MLOS indicates problems with advancement opportunities, or resistance to changes in the organisation.

The %V indicates the percentage of leavers who left voluntarily as opposed to being dismissed. A high %V indicates employee dissatisfaction with the organisation, whereas a low %V indicates a high rate of dismissals, thus dissatisfaction on the part of the organisation. The MLOS and %V must be interpreted together.

The above analysis is an indication of the course of action that should be taken in order to reduce labour turnover. If a high percentage of employees leave the organisation voluntarily soon after employment, the employment, induction and placement practices should be re-evaluated. If many employees are dismissed, employment practices as well as training should be reconsidered.

Employees who leave after a reasonable time period often feel that they have started to stagnate and leave for better opportunities or more challenges. If many employees leave after a long service with the company, it will be an indication that changes have taken place that they found difficult to cope with. Resistance to

change should be managed by informing and involving employees in advance of changes.

## Job satisfaction

High absenteeism and labour turnover figures might be an indication of dissatisfaction in the organisation. Greenberg and Baron (1995:169) define job satisfaction as individuals' cognitive, affective and evaluative reaction to their jobs. Although a direct relationship has not been found between job dissatisfaction and performance, it is generally agreed that job satisfaction influences absenteeism, labour turnover, commitment, and organisational citizenship. Research has found differences in the levels of satisfaction of white-collar personnel (managerial and professional people) and blue-collar workers, older people and younger people, more experienced and less experienced people, women and men, and people belonging to minority and majority groups.

- Factors contributing to job satisfaction. Two main groups of factors contribute to job satisfaction; namely personal factors and organisational factors. Personal factors refer mainly to personality, status and seniority, general life satisfaction and the extent to which the job characteristics are congruent with personal characteristics. Organisational factors refer to the following:
  - *Pay and benefits:* People perceive their remuneration as an indication of what they are worth to the organisa-

tion. The principle of equitable pay is very important. People compare what they put into the organisation to what they get out, and to what other people put in and get out. Negative inequity leads to job dissatisfaction.

■ *The work itself:* People have a preference for interesting and challenging tasks that provide opportunities for self-actualisation and recognition.

■ *The supervisor:* Job satisfaction is influenced by the amount of technical and social support extended by the supervisor.

■ *Relationship with co-workers:* Whereas the first three factors have a strong influence on job satisfaction, the relationship an employee has with co-workers only influences job satisfaction moderately. People with a strong career orientation may place less emphasis on social relations.

■ *Working conditions:* People become dissatisfied if they work in an overcrowded, dark, dirty or noisy place. Adequate working conditions are taken for granted, and not noticed.

● Measurement of job satisfaction. Various reliable and valid instruments are available to measure job satisfaction systematically. These include:

■ *Rating scales:* A rating scale is a questionnaire in which people report their reactions to their jobs. The Job Descriptive Index (JDI), for example, is a questionnaire in which employees describe whether or not each of several adjectives describes a particular aspect of their job. Questions deal with the work itself, pay, promotional opportunities, supervision, and co-workers. The advantage of a rating scale is that it is easy and quick to fill in and that norms are usually available for comparisons.

■ *Critical Incidents:* Here employees are given an opportunity to describe situations or events in their jobs that either made them very satisfied or

very dissatisfied. For example, employees might indicate situations where they received special recognition or situations where they were treated rudely. The researcher will examine the replies in order to identify underlying themes.

■ *Interviews:* Structured interviews are preferable, since they provide a basis for comparison and ensure that important aspects are covered. On the other hand, an unstructured approach allows the employee to express any thought on his/her mind that might not be covered by a structured interview.

Conducting a job satisfaction survey in an organisation tends to create expectations in employees that positive changes will be instituted. Not attending to obvious problems, may aggravate any existing dissatisfaction.

## 22.7 HRISs and employees' privacy

One of the major concerns about HRISs is that it is easier for someone in the organisation to invade the privacy of other employees. For this reason, organisations should carefully consider their policies regarding access to, and the release of, HRIS data, as well as the legal and ethical implications thereof. It poses the greatest threat to privacy when the employee does not retain the right to authorise the release of information.

Ivancevich (2001:145) recommends the following steps in minimising the risk to privacy in an HRIS:

● Determine the best method to collect data.

● Limit the information to what is necessary for a business decision.

● Let employees know what kind of information is kept on the data system and how it will be used.

● Allow employees to inspect and correct information on the system.

- Keep sensitive information separate.
- Limit the use of personal information to what it is absolutely necessary for business decisions.
- Disclose personal information about employees to outsiders only after they have given consent.

## 22.8 HRISs and quality assurance

HRISs provide the human resources department with an excellent opportunity to contribute constructively to the strategic goals of the organisation by providing timely and accurate information to support key decision-making. The ultimate purpose of human resources information systems is not to collect an intensive database of information, but to use the information to assist the organisation in adapting to internal and external environmental changes.

The distinguishing best-practice characteristics of an HRIS are highly integrated and complete databases, broad self-service access by employees and managers, harnessed intranet and Internet connectivity, and a tightly aligned link between the goals of the business and human resources activities.

## 22.9 Conclusion

It is impossible to make informed decisions in an organisation without timely and accurate information. The human resources department is responsible for maintaining a user-friendly database relating to all human issues and information. Although the advent of computers has made this function easier, it has also created more expectations. The human resources department has to prove that it does contribute directly to the strategic vision of the organisation.

## Summary

- The function of an HRIS is to collect, record, store, analyse, distribute, and retrieve data concerning the organisation's human resources.
- Various myths surround the implementation and utilisation of HRISs in organisations. These myths cause resistance to change and lead to the slow introduction of such systems into organisations. Many of the problems associated with HRISs can be avoided if the implementation thereof is carefully planned.
- HRISs consist of hardware, software, data and users. HRISs can be applied in every aspect of human resources management, such as recruitment, salary administration, skills development, equity management, and performance management. A new addition is a self-help desk that is linked to the intranet to assist employees with personal inquiries and allow them to communicate their ideas and suggestions to either the human resources department or other users in the organisation.
- The HRIS serves as a diagnostic and decision-making tool in the organisation. Specific areas where it can be utilised as a databank and research tool include absenteeism and labour turnover control, employment equity management, and the monitoring of job satisfaction.
- Employees' right to privacy should be taken into account in the implementation and use of an HRIS.
- Quality assurance in HRISs is crucial. Effective decision-making is only possible if it is based on accurate, complete, and timely information. Managers must be trained in the use of technological decision-making tools.

## Case study

Honey Distributors is an organisation that imports and distributes a wide range of delicacies to hotels and shops in South Africa. The company recently decided to introduce a HRIS to ease administration around HRM issues. A representative from management information systems was requested to buy and implement the necessary system. A date was set for discontinuing the manual system and commencing the new system. On this date, and also immediately afterwards, numerous problems were encountered. A few are listed below:

- Inaccurate data and calculations.
- Too few people trained to operate the system.
- Lack of technical support from vendor.
- Incompatibility of some of the additional models with the payroll.

After a few months and extra, unanticipated expenses to sort out problems, it was decided that the implementation of the new system was not worthwhile in terms of time and cost. But by now it was too late, and the company had to carry the burden of a new HRIS.

## Question

By considering the steps in the implementation of an HRIS, how could the above problems have been prevented in the first place?

## Experiential exercise No. 1

PURPOSE: To get an overview of the human resources-related software used in a specific organisation.

INTRODUCTION: Organisations use HRIS to gather, analyse and communicate information.

TASK: Step 1. Visit a local organisation that uses an HRIS and inquire about the type of software they use, how it is used and by whom it is used. Collect examples of how the information is used to make decisions in the organisation.

Step 2. Present an overview of the visit to the class and compare information collected.

## Experiential exercise No. 2

PURPOSE: To evaluate the job satisfaction levels of employees in an organisation.

INTRODUCTION: Information about the job satisfaction levels of employees in an organisation can be used to anticipate problems that could lead to excessive absenteeism and labour turnover.

TASK: Compile a questionnaire consisting of about 15 questions to determine the job satisfaction levels of employees. Administer the questionnaire to at least 10 employees working in the same department. Analyse and compare the responses collected.

## Chapter questions

1 How can the realisation of the myths surrounding the introduction of HRISs into organisations be prevented?
2 Discuss the implementation of an HRIS in an organisation.
3 How can information regarding absenteeism be used to pinpoint more specific problems in the organisation?
4 It has been mentioned that organisations store a vast amount of information in their data systems without using it. How can information about labour turnover be used to pinpoint problems and to take corrective action?
5 Which method will you select to collect information about the job satisfaction levels of employees?

## Bibliography

BERGH, Z.C. & THERON, A.L. 2003. *Psychology in the work context, 2nd edition.* Oxford University Press, Johannesburg.

BYARS, L.L. & RUE, L.W. 1989. *Human resources management, 5th edition.* Irwin, Chicago.

GREENBERG, J. & BARON, R.A. 1995. *Behavior in organizations. Understanding and managing the human side of work, 5th edition.* (Prentice-Hall), Pearson Education Inc.

GREENGARD, S. 1999. 'Mine your corporate data

with business intelligence'. *Workforce*, 78(1): 103–104 (www.workforceonline.com/archive/article/22/04/53.php). Reprinted with permission of Copyright Clearance Center.

IVANCEVICH, J.M. 2001. *Human resources management, 8th edition*. McGraw-Hill Companies, New York.

IVANCEVICH, J.M. & MATTESON, M.T. 1999. *Organizational behavior and mancgement, 5th edition*. Irwin, Chicago.

KREITNER, R. & KINICKI, A. 2001. *Organizational behaviour, 5th edition*. Irwin, Chicago.

LA POINTE, J.R. 1999. 'HR software products are rarely finished'. *Workforce*, 78(10):90–92 (www.workforceonline.com/archive/feature/22/22/76/223214.php). Reprinted with permission of Copyright Clearance Center.

MULLINS, L.J. 1996. *Management and organisational behaviour, 4th edition*. (Pitman), Pearson Education (UK).

NOE, R.A., HOLLENBECK, J.R., GERHART, B. & WRIGHT, P.M. 2000. *Human resources management – Gaining a competitive advantage, 3rd edition*. McGraw-Hill Companies, New York.

ROBBINS, S.P. 1998. *Organizational behavior, 8th edition*. (Prentice-Hall), Pearson Education Inc.

VAN DER MERWE, R. & MILLER, S. 1988. *Measuring absence and labour turnover*. Lexicon, Johannesburg.

WITSCHGER, J. 1999. 'Eight myths of HRMS software' (www.workforceonline.com/archive/article/22/02/41.php). Reprinted with permission of Copyright Clearance Center.

## Websites

Q Data DynamiQue: www.dynamique.co.za
Department of Labour: www.labour.gov.za
Equity employment software:
    www.equityact.co.za
    www.emsoft.co.za
    www.vanzylrudd.co.za

# 23

# International human resources management

HB Schultz and PS Nel

## Learning outcomes

At the end of this chapter the learner should be able to:

- Provide an overview of current global changes.
- Describe factors affecting HRM in global markets.
- Explain the stages of corporate international involvement.
- Compare the approaches to managing an international subsidiary.
- Discuss the problems faced by the expatriate.
- Suggest guidelines for dealing with the problems faced by repatriates.
- Describe the competencies that affect the selection of expatriates.
- Apply relevant human resources policies to expatriates.

## Key words and concepts

- ethnocentric
- expatriate
- geocentric
- global corporation
- host or local country
- parent or home company
- polycentric
- regiocentric
- repatriate

## Illustrative case

### The unhappy hiker

Judith Terry was very excited when her husband, Rodney, was transferred to the Hong Kong subsidiary of Plain Gold Investments. Both Judith and Rodney were Chartered Accountants and had met while studying at the University of Cape Town. They waited until they had completed their Articles before they got married. The arrival of their two daughters was well planned, and Judith was able to continue working and achieving her career goals while the girls were growing up. The children were now teenagers and Rodney was doing very well for himself at Plain Gold. Judith felt that the time was right for an overseas posting.

Judith was very eager to launch into this new phase of her life, and she was optimistic about the opportunities that awaited her in the Far East. She was aware that statistics showed that accompanying spouses who relocate globally with their partners rarely get jobs. But she had a strategy: she took the time to ensure that the girls were settled into their new school, she made sure that their new home was running efficiently, and she made friends in both the local and South African community in the district where they were living.

However, Judith did not foresee how difficult it would be to work overseas, even though she easily obtained a work visa. She soon found a position in an accountancy firm, but quickly discovered that the typical work schedule of 10-hour days, six days a week made it impossible for her to attend to her husband's and children's needs, without her work commitment suffering. She was amazed at the work ethic and cultural differences in Hong Kong, which were totally strange to her South African viewpoint. It seemed that dual-career families were not encouraged because corporate expectations of employees were so high that family life suffered if staff members were completely loyal to their company goals.

And so Judith found herself joining the ranks of unhappy global spouses who 'hiked' from one temporary position to the next, unable to commit herself to local managers who believed that expatriates are transient, struggling with child-care needs and language barriers, even though English was spoken throughout the city. She was still unaware that the most common reason listed for internal assignment failure is lack of partner satisfaction, and this applied directly to her situation.

Although the challenge is daunting, companies and their global HR managers are beginning to consider shorter assignments because they are less disruptive, and are ensuring that the needs of the accompanying spouse are adequately addressed before finalising arrangements for an international work relocation.

SOURCE: Solomon (2001)

## 23.1  Introduction

Throughout this book, it is emphasised that human resources management is an integral part of all business, which is at present experiencing an expansion of its environment into global markets. It is becoming more and more commonplace for companies to export their products, build plants or subsidiaries in other countries, or to enter into alliances with other companies in foreign markets. The main reason for this phenomenon is that companies attempt to gain a competitive advantage by exploiting new markets with a large number of potential new customers, or by capitalising on the lower labour costs for relatively unskilled jobs in the new country, and to find safe places in which to do business. Physically, South Africa finds itself in the middle of the map of the world, displaying how important our country's location is in relation to the world's business markets (see Figure 23.1).

We have excellent examples of current global changes to illustrate how human resources management is now forced to contribute towards gaining a competitive advantage in a global economy. The discussion in this chapter is based on these global changes, some of which are addressed below.

In this chapter, attention will be given to:

- Factors affecting HRM in global markets including culture, education or human capital, political or legal system, and the economic system.
- The stages of international involvement.
- The mix of host countries and expatriate employees.
- Problems faced by the expatriate.
- Problems faced by the repatriate.
- International human resources management policies.

**Figure 23.1** South Africa in relation to world markets

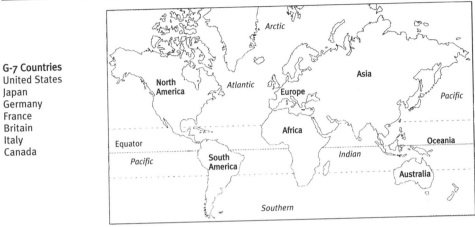

G-7 Countries
United States
Japan
Germany
France
Britain
Italy
Canada

**South Africa's ranking in the 2002 World Economic Forum's Competitive Survey:**
Growth Competitiveness: 32
Microeconomic Competitiveness Index Rank: 29

Source: www.weforum.org

## 23.2    An overview of current global changes

### 23.2.1 The European Economic Community (EEC)

The European Economic Community (EEC), which began in 1992, is a confederation of most of the European nations, that agreed to enter into free trade with one another. Because of their close proximity, these countries experienced that their economies were very much intertwined. The European Commission (EC) is the regulating body to oversee trade between these countries. Under the EC the legal regulations between these participating countries have become almost uniform. The absence of such uniformity was somewhat of a problem before. The regulations in Germany, for example, were vastly different from a country such as Italy. This has to a large extent disappeared due to the introduction of the common monetary unit (the euro), which became effective in 2002. The EEC is now the second largest free market in the world after the Asia-Pacific Economic Cooperation (APEC) agreement, which has 47 per cent of world trade and 61 per cent of the world's GDP. (See details of APEC elsewhere.)

Scullion and Brewster (2001) have identified eight important factors about Europe:

1   The dismantling of barriers to the movement of goods, capital and labour through the development of the European Union (EU).

2   Research suggests a growing emphasis on regionalisation where there is more restricted access to headquarters in places such as the US.

3   There has been a rapid growth in the numbers of small- and medium-sized enterprises.

4   Europe is more densely populated with highly industrialised countries in a smaller geographical area than anywhere else in the world.

5   Expatriation in Europe may not involve sending people 'overseas'.

6    Since the collapse of communism in Central and Eastern European (CEE) states, there was a significant growth of Foreign Direct Investment (FDI), of which a major contributor was the eastward flow of western European business activity.

7    The development of the EU and its civil service and its many agencies and higher levels of public sector employment, along with other contributing factors, means that 'not-for-profit' international organisations are more common in Europe.

8    A greater collectivism is found in Europe than in the USA, and European companies are more experienced at working with trade unions and other stakeholders.

## 23.2.2 The Unification of Germany

From 1949 (after World War II) until 1989, Germany was divided into East Germany under Soviet rule with a socialist economic system, and West Germany with a capitalist economy. In 1990, steps were taken to re-unify East and West Germany, thereby entering the two countries as a unity into the global market. The East German integration into a capitalist economy posed tremendous human resources management problems. Under the socialist government in East Germany, every citizen was guaranteed a job (causing overstaffing, low motivation, little incentive to maximise profits, and a general state of a lack of competitiveness). The fact that wages were relatively low compared to high skills, compensated to a large extent, making former East Germany a viable proposition for foreign companies seeking to invest. The unification process still remains a constant challenge to human resources management to merge two very diverse workforces.

## 23.2.3 The North American Free Trade Agreement (NAFTA)

The United States of America and Canada entered into a free trade agreement in 1989. The North American Free Trade Agreement (NAFTA), however, has more recently brought Mexico into this agreement, which will probably open a free market larger than the EEC. This will lead to an increase of US investment in Mexico resulting from the lower labour cost for low skilled employees. On a macro-level, it may result in a large portion of low-skilled jobs being moved to Mexico, thereby lowering employment opportunities for low-skilled Americans.

## 23.2.4 The Soviet Union

After the unification of Germany and the fall of the Berlin Wall, there was a move on the part of countries controlled by the Soviet Union to convert their economies to a capitalist system. This movement resulted in an opening up of markets and the privatising of government-owned enterprises. For the last few decades these countries were deprived of private or foreign investment, which has now changed completely. These major changes offer interesting challenges to human resources management, ranging from training and culture management, to the normal activities of HRM, all of which were absent in the communist past.

## 23.2.5 Asia-Pacific Economic Cooperation (APEC)

Since its birth in 1989, APEC has become a leading forum in the Asia-Pacific region for strengthening regional links and pursuing common trade and economic goals, whilst it has 41 per cent of the world's population. Economic Leaders from the APEC member economies meet annually to develop strategies for promoting growth and economic development in the Asia-Pacific region. They also hold informal discussions on current regional and international issues. Ministers, government officials and all sectors of business and industry also cooperate to reduce the barriers to trade and investment. The building of human resources has become a new focal point in establishing cooperation between governments, businesses, and the academic sector with views toward establishing a life-long education system creating a learning society (Rongxia 2001).

### 23.2.6 New alliances during times of terrorism

Wars and disasters have changed the scope of HRM over the years, but the profound effects of the September 11 and Bali bombing terrorist attacks have marked the dawn of a new era in the global economy. Because of globalisation and the ease of travel and communication worldwide, it has been increasingly popular to move employees to other countries for further experience or roles unable to be filled by locals. Following September 11, employee safety, security, and preparedness have become focal points for HRM managers, with thousands of employees in large organisations scattered all over the world.

Prior to the recent terrorist attacks, expatriates would be given a hardship premium with the expectation that they would take care of their own security. According to Krentzel (2001), in the more controversial countries, such as Russia, parts of South America, and the Middle East, high security compounds have been set up for expatriates. More attention is being paid to preparing employees before they leave their country of origin, making clear the availability of Employee Assistance Programmes (EAPs) and Emergency Response Plans (ERPs). This is highlighted by the aftermath of Afghanistan and the subsequent terrorist activities in Bali.

It may be possible that in light of the heightened Iraq conflict over the last few years and controversy over North Korea's nuclear policy, new alliances may be formed and old alliances broken as countries decide where their allegiance lies. Scullion and Brewster (2001) identify that lawful expatriates have started to be subjected to tough interviewing from the US Immigration and Naturalisation Service. There is also a 20-day waiting period on applications to the USA for men aged 16–45 from mainly Muslim countries.

## 23.3 Factors affecting human resources management in global markets

Various authors (Gomez-Mejia et al. 1998; Jackson 2002) have identified certain factors which impact upon human resources management in global markets. They include diverse cultural, educational, economic, political, and legal environments.

### 23.3.1 Culture

The ability to understand and balance cultural values and practices regarding things such as the importance of work, how status is determined, the relationship of work to the whole person and the group, the perceived value of experience versus training and development, the desire for change and how people from different cultures view what is happening in the world, form an important part of the task of the international manager.

Different cultures cultivate different beliefs. A general overview reveals the following: German managers, more than others, believe that creativity is important for career success, and focus on preparations for functional careers. British managers, on the other hand, believe that the ability to create the right image and to get noticed for what they do is essential for career success. French managers view an organisation as an authority network where the power to organise and control originates from their position in the hierarchy. Cultures such as those in Singapore and Jamaica socialise individuals to accept uncertainty and take each day as it comes. People from these cultures tend to be easier going and flexible regarding different views. Cultures in Greece and Portugal socialise their people to seek security through technology, law, and religion – in the process providing clear rules how to behave. In Japan and Germany strong roles are given to men. Japan and China have a long-term orientation with a focus on the future and values such as saving and persistence. Countries and regions with a more short-term orientation include the United States of America, Russia, and West Africa.

It is important to be prepared for the mannerisms, slang, and intercultural communication to avoid offending the local culture. For example, and according to Dadoo et al. (2001:176), something as simple as silence can be interpreted differently. Eastern societies value silence as a sign of interpersonal sensitivity, mutual respect, personal dignity, affirmation, and wisdom. The West finds silence to be more socially disagreeable, such as a sign of lacking attention or initiative.

Trompenaars and Wooliams (1999) explore seven major dimensions in which cultures differ. Five of these dimensions relate to solving problems in human relationships. They look at how different cultures balance the everyday dilemmas of dealing with rules and relationships, the individual within the group, how status is given and earned, how emotions are expressed, and what is considered private and what public.

The sixth dimension deals with how culture relates to their environment – do people seek to control it, or to accept and adapt to it? The seventh looks at how different cultures relate to time, how they perceive the relative importance and degree of integration of the past, the present and the future, and how they organise time within this.

Finally, it is important to emphasise that culture is closely intertwined and has a strong impact upon other factors, i.e. education, human capital, the political or legal system, and the economic system. If a culture values education highly, it is obvious that members of the community will strive to improve their knowledge and skills. Laws are a direct result of how the inhabitants of a country view right and wrong. Culture and the economic system are closely intertwined, as values will determine to a large extent which economic system will be adopted.

## 23.3.2 Education or human capital

It is significant that the Pacific Rim countries such as Japan, Taiwan, Singapore, and Korea, which lead the world in productivity and quality despite limited natural resources, have gained their competitive edge through their people. Their heavy investment in education and training is providing the rewards.

Human capital can be described as the productive capabilities of individuals – that is the knowledge, skills and experience that in themselves have economic value. Different countries have different levels of human capital. The shortage of human capital in the USA results from jobs being created requiring skills beyond those of most of the new entrants into the labour market. The same applies in West Germany, where a shift in types of production has taken place, requiring highly skilled workers, and resulting in a human capital shortage for the higher-skilled jobs.

Where free education is offered, as in the Netherlands and the former Soviet Bloc, a high level of human capital becomes available. In contrast, a low level of human capital is available in Third World countries as a result of a low investment in education. From a practical point of view, countries with low human capital levels manage to attract investments in facilities that require low skills and low wage levels. On the other hand, companies in developed countries like the USA locate currently unionised low-skill/high-wage manufacturing and assembling jobs in Mexico. They manage to obtain low-skilled workers in Mexico for substantially lower wages. Japan ships its low-skill work to neighbouring countries, while maintaining its high-skill work at home.

## 23.3.3 Political or legal system

The political or legal system by its nature is closely linked to the culture in which it operates. Norms and values are normally reflected in the legal regulations, which again are directly manifested in the practices of human resources management regarding training, employment, lay-offs, compensation, industrial relations, etc. Through legislation, norms and values in a specific country will indicate clearly in what direction they are moving. The United States of America was, for example, the first country to eliminate discrimination based on sex or colour in the workplace. Employees in Germany were granted the legal right to co-determination at the company plant and industrial level. The implication of this is that employees, who serve on the supervisory council, have a direct influence over important decisions that influence them directly. Another good example of the influence of the political or legal system is the European Economic Charter, of 9 December 1989, which provides for the social rights of workers, including freedom of movement, freedom of choice of own occupation, right to be fairly compensated, guarantee of social protection via social security benefits, freedom of association and collective bargaining, equal treatment for men and women, safe and healthy work environment, etc.

Finally, an important concern for multinational corporations is whether human resources policies will be created at corporate headquarters and transplanted to local companies or created by local companies in accordance with local laws and customs. According to Cherrington and Middelton (1995:130), employment policies, such as conditions of employment, retirement, termination, discrimination, and workers' rights differ greatly from country to country.

## 23.3.4 The economic system

The economic system can be broadly described as the manner in which society produces and distributes its goods and services. The world today is to a large extent divided into capitalist and socialist blocks. This demarcation, together with economic factors such as exchange rates, availability of raw material, labour cost, technology and level of innovation, all play an important role in the decision as to where a corporate head office will conduct its business.

It is obvious that the economic system operating in a country has a very definite impact upon the profitability of a company and also more specifically on the human resources management in the organisation. The tax system, as part of the economic system, for example, has a profound influence upon profitability. In capitalist countries, attempts are made to reward the individual by allowing him/her to keep as much of their earnings as possible. The higher taxes in socialist countries provide for those services which the employee receives 'free'. In capitalist countries the individual's salary is a reflection of the quality of human capital. The highly skilled worker will receive more than his/her lower-skilled counterpart. The investment in human capital will thus be a fairly accurate barometer of the level of economic development in a particular country, which will be valuable information for a corporate head office to consider when doing business in a foreign country.

## 23.3.5 Women expatriates

Women on international assignments have at least as much success as their male counterparts, but are placed overseas less often. The main contributor to the increase in women being assigned internationally is the rise in the number of women in middle to upper management.

According to Jackson (2002:95), women have not been recognised as candidates for foreign assignments because of assumptions and myths that women do not want to be international managers or that women may be discriminated against. Influential considerations are:

- *Organisational factors:* such as women being faced with the glass ceiling over and above their competencies and skills.
- *Socio-cultural factors:* host country barriers such as women being prejudiced against in certain countries, such as some Middle East countries.
- *Societal factors:* dual career issues, such as the women partner having the better paid job, but having to move together with her male partner who has accepted an expatriate position.

There are, according to Nel (1997), some advantages and disadvantages to being a female international manager. Women have the advantage that they are more visible and accessible in an international setting and are more committed and motivated to go over-seas and more committed to making the assignment work. Further advantages include their interpersonal skills, flexibility, and the fact they are not expected to act as local women and are seen as foreigners. One disadvantage experienced by women is the difficulty in getting sent abroad in the first place, and if they are sent it may only be for a short assignment. Having weighed the advantages and disadvantages, it is safe to realise that there are some misconceptions and prejudices, which are slowly dissolving and opening new doors for women expatriates.

## 23.4 The stages of international involvement

Before we examine how an organisation becomes involved in international business, it is important to understand what the term 'international company' means. Pitfield (1996: 12) categorises international companies as:

- Traditional, or 'colonial' companies, which were established as the result of international commercial activity and followed the political models of their nation-states.
- Modern, or domestic 'highfliers', which developed from a sound national base and expanded their operations into the international market in the face of local competition.
- Fast-movers resulting from mergers and acquisitions, which moved from a strong home or regional base to acquire complementary organisations in other parts of the world.

A further model has emerged in recent years: the international company resulting from alliances in order to achieve the benefits of global operation. One of the most prominent examples of alliances in this region is South African Airways, which has forged alliances with many powerful international airlines.

Gómez-Mejía et al. (1998:516–8) indicate how firms progress through five stages as they internationalise their operations and adapt their HR practices to diverse cultural, economic, political, and legal environments.

- *Stage 1.* In this stage the firm's market is exclusively domestic, and primarily local and/or national forces dictate human resources practices such as staffing, training, and compensation. Many South African companies are still operating within this stage, but to become globally competitive they will have to consider expanding their operations.
- *Stage 2.* Dessler (1997:671) states that exporting is often the first choice when a company decides to expand overseas. The company retains production facilities within domestic borders, but even though few employees expect to be posted over-seas, human resources practices should be geared towards managerial incentives, appropriate training and staffing strategies that focus on the demands of international customers. In South Africa, the elimination of trade barriers is contributing to the number of firms that fall into Stage 2. Besides exporting, companies can also enter into franchising and licensing agreements, which place them in Stage 2 of internationalisation.
- *Stage 3.* Many firms move some of their operations out of the home country, particularly for parts assembly. These facilities tend to be under close control of corporate headquarters, and most top managers are expatriates (citizens of the home country). Human resources practices must emphasise the selection, training, and compensation of expatriates, and the development of personnel policies for local employees.
- *Stage 4.* When an organisation reaches stage 4, it has a parent firm based in the home country to coordinate a fully-fledged multinational corporation, which

operates manufacturing and marketing facilities in several countries. Although many personnel decisions affecting foreign branches are made at corporate headquarters, foreign operations are still managed by expatriates, resulting in complex human resources practices dealing with diverse ethnic and cultural groups in multiple countries.

- *Stage 5.* Marketing experts believe that the multinational corporation is facing demise, as the new global transnational corporation becomes more prominent. These corporations have weak ties to any given country, operations are highly decentralised and each business unit makes personnel decisions with little or no control from corporate headquarters. They sell the same products in the same way everywhere (such as the Sony Walkman), and the organisation freely hires employees from any country.

  Human resources practices at stage 5 attempt to create a shared corporate culture rather than a national identity. Managers are usually trained in the home country and may receive some exposure at corporate headquarters before being sent on international assignments.

Pitfield (1996:6) notes that the traditional expatriate manager is rapidly declining in status as the speed of international travel and communications means that the opportunity for developing local nationals to run local operations becomes more obvious. In addition, 'third country nationals' demonstrate their ability in an overseas operational area and are then posted to other parts of the world to broaden and build their experience.

Organisations are increasingly using 'troubleshooters' to perform the interface role between headquarters and local operations. They are highly mobile, able to solve problems in a wide variety of cultural environments, and then move on to the next international assignment.

The advent of trustworthy and efficient phone, fax, video, Internet, and electronic mail links has also brought about the rise of the stay-at-home international manager, who is rarely called upon to travel abroad, but who has significant contact and responsibility for aspects of the international operation.

## 23.5 The mix of host country and expatriate employees

When a firm opens a foreign branch, thus passing into stage 3 of internationalisation, issues of control between the parent and the host subsidiary companies become important, as well as concerns about management and human resources issues (Beardwell and Holden 1997:702).

### 23.5.1 Approaches to managing an international subsidiary

There are four main approaches to managing an international subsidiary:

- *The ethnocentric approach.* In this approach parent company nationals fill all key positions. Direct control over the host country subsidiary is established and is common in the early stages of internationalisation. Direct control may also be exercised if there is lack of qualified host country nationals. According to Nel (1997), organisations use this approach when they are in the infant stages of internationalisation (multi-domestic stage).
- *The geocentric approach.* The use of the geocentric approach involves the parent company deliberately searching on a worldwide or regional basis for the best staff to fill key positions. Transnational firms in stage 5 tend to follow this approach as it enables the development of an international executive team.
- *The regiocentric approach.* The regiocentric approach allows the movement of staff within geographic operations of a multinational corporation and offers the opportunity for development of management succession programmes.

- *The polycentric approach.* Nel (1997) identifies this approach when an organisation is in a multinational stage of development and the local organisation is seen as independent. The expatriate manager is employed to assist the local organisation in developing management structures and providing support.

## 23.5.2 Using parent company and host country employees

Expatriates usually hold key positions, and it makes little financial sense to pay high salaries (usually based on the home country's pay systems) and to finance relocation costs, if foreign nationals can competently fill these positions. In addition, many countries require that a certain percentage of the workforce be local citizens. The use of expatriates generally increases when:

- Sufficient local talent is not available, as in developing countries.
- An important part of the firm's overall business strategy is the creation of a corporate-wide global vision.
- International units and domestic operations are highly interdependent, for example, in certain production processes that require all divisions of a corporation, both international and domestic, to work closely with one another.
- The political situation is unstable.
- There are significant cultural differences between the host country and the home country, demanding cross-cultural sensitivity.

---

## Encounter 23.1

'September 11' and '9–11' are phrases that have catapulted the issue of expatriate safety to the top of the list for global managers. Even though these terrorist activities were aimed at America, personal security for foreign expatriates working for American firms is a serious issue. American companies have quickly reacted by creating crisis management planning, and companies worldwide that deal with foreign assignments for their employees should take note of what the Americans are saying.

'Find out where all of your expats are right now.' This may sound simplistic but a surprising number of HR managers and security directors don't know exactly where everyone is.

'Make sure your assignees know how to conduct themselves.' Expats should not advertise that they are from an American company by wearing 'Nikes' or 'Reeboks', or lots of jewellery.

'Create a phone tree.' Construct a telephone list for expats where everyone has a few people to call in case of an emergency.

'Find out what other companies are doing.' Contact other companies in the expats' area and keep up to date with their emergency plans.

'Become familiar with places to which you are sending people.' Inform your expats about their locations, facilities, and risk areas.

'Create a crisis team and a crisis plan.' This is the team that will make decisions about expats and will know if there is trouble brewing in certain areas.

'Take advantage of security information.' Use web sites and information services to update you on activities in specific neighbourhoods, such as the anniversary of an uprising and expected demonstrations.

SOURCE: Solomon (2001:22–30)

---

## 23.6 Problems faced by the expatriate

Before discussing the problems facing expatriates, it is necessary to distinguish between the various types of international employees. 'Expatriate' is the term used for an employee sent by a company in one country to manage operations in a different country. There are, however, different types of expatriates. Parent country nationals are employees who were born and live in the parent country. Host country nationals are those employees who were born and raised in the host country. Third country nationals are employees born in a country other than the parent country or host country, but who work in the host country.

Apart from the above distinctions, companies are referred to as multinational or international companies when operating globally. International companies become multinational when they build facilities in a number of different countries in an attempt to capitalise on lower production or distribution costs in different locations. A third type of organisation, the global organisation, competes in state-of-the art, top quality products and services on the basis of the lowest cash possible. The global company will emphasise flexibility, and wants customisation of products to meet the needs of particular clients.

The global company will thus proactively consider the cultures, human capital, political or legal systems and economic systems to determine where production facilities can be located to provide a competitive advantage. This will result in less hierarchical structures emphasising decentralised decision-making.

The compensation package of an expatriate manager is obviously very high. Likewise, the cost of an unsuccessful expatriate returning early will be significant. It is therefore important not to under-estimate assignments to the contribution towards the company's profitability. The major issues that contribute towards effective management of expatriates include selection, training and development, compensation, and re-acculturation (re-entering of their home country).

Understanding the reasons why many international assignments end in failure can assist in reducing the high failure rates of expatriates. Gómez-Mejía et al. (1998:522) mention seven factors that account for most failures:

- *Career blockage.* International companies usually believe that the career planning of their expatriates is well taken care of. However, after the initial excitement of moving abroad has worn off, many employees perceive that their careers are stagnating while their counterparts at home are climbing the corporate ladder. This perception is due to the fact that the majority of firms do not identify the technical, managerial and interpersonal competencies required by expatriates, nor do they link international competencies and experiences to career planning.

- *Culture shock.* Expatriates who cannot adjust to a different cultural environment experience the phenomenon called culture shock, and try to impose the home country's values on the host country's employees, instead of learning to work within the new culture. Escalating cultural clashes and misunderstandings may then force the expatriate to return to more familiar surroundings.

- *Lack of pre-departure cross-cultural training.* Only about one-third of multinationals provide any cross-cultural training to expatriates, and this tends to be rather cursory. Many expatriates, especially women, feel that they are not accorded proper respect when having to undergo business rituals in the host country which they do not understand. Advance knowledge of what to expect could pre-empt embarrassing situations.

- *Over-emphasis on technical qualifications.* Often expatriates who have impressive credentials in the home office are regarded as natural choices for starting up a new international facility or troubleshooting when technical difficulties arise. However, these same traits may not be perceived as relevant in the host country, and the latter's workplace practices may be regarded as unacceptable to the expatriate. It appears that cultural sensitivity is more important than technical skills in an overseas assignment.

- *Getting rid of a troublesome employee.* In some cases, organisations see an international assignment as an easy way of resolving difficult interpersonal situations or political conflicts at the home office. This can have disastrous effects, especially if the expatriate is not selected according to the competencies required for carrying out the assignment.

- *Family problems.* Very often the expatriate's spouse and children are unable or unwilling to adapt to life in another country. Coupled with the stress experienced when trying to function in unfamiliar surroundings, this problem can easily result in an aborted international assignment. Surprisingly, very few companies provide any type of counselling programme for the families of expatriates, especially when one spouse in a dual-career couple is asked to make a career sacrifice in order to allow the other's development. Torrington and Hall (1995:663–4) add that economic development and geographic location, especially if the host is a third-world country, exacerbate the problem of the expatriate's family adapting to a new lifestyle.

- *Spouse or partner pressure.* According to Jackson (2002), a further important consideration is that an overseas assignment often falls on the spouse or partner of the employee, which frequently includes the coordination of the move. They also lack a local support structure at the new location and are often not included in the familiarisation programme of the host organisation where the 'contract spouse' gets all the support at work. This is an area often neglected by human resources managers.

## 23.7 Problems faced by the repatriate

Dessler (1997:687) explains that repatriation is the process of moving back to the parent company and country from the foreign assignment. Many companies do not anticipate the problems which may be faced by the repatriate and consequently do not adopt a proactive approach to making the transition as smooth as possible.

### 23.7.1 Common repatriation problems

Even if the expatriation phase has proceeded smoothly, there are five common problems that many repatriates have to deal with, namely:

- *Lack of respect for acquired skills.* In many cases the repatriate, who has gained a wealth of information and valuable skills on a foreign assignment, is not accorded the recognition and appreciation s/he deserves. If the international assignment has lasted several years, the repatriate may be regarded as being out of touch with the situation at corporate headquarters. Very few repatriates believe that overseas assignments enhance their career development, and Gómez-Mejía et al. (1998:524) report that most companies do not take advantage of what their expatriates have learnt overseas.

- *Poor planning for return position.* Often the home office repatriates an employee without giving much thought to what his/her new career assignment will be. The repatriate may suffer much anxiety regarding the uncertainty of the position s/he will hold on her/his return, especially if s/he experiences a loss of status in the position s/he is expected to assume.

- *Reverse culture shock.* Extended international assignments can result in internalisation of the host country's norms and customs. Expatriates are usually unaware of how much psychological change they have undergone until they return home and experience a culture to which they have been unaccustomed for a long time. This may result in reverse culture shock, leading to alienation, a sense of uprootedness, and even disciplinary problems. The repatriate's family may also suffer when having to re-establish old friendships and habits.

- *Loss of status.* Repatriates face the risk of losing their status in the organisation, especially on extended assignments. This can lead to repatriates coming home to a different organisation structure, with appointments to leading positions within an organisation taken by those who have maintained their grounding in the parent organisation.

- *Loss of income.* Because of the financial support provided when an employee and her/his family take on a foreign assignment, there may be a considerable drop of actual income and other support, such as schooling for children.

### 23.7.2 Guidelines for dealing with the repatriate

Although repatriation problems are common, Dessler (1997:687) offers a number of steps that progressive multinational companies can take:

- *Write repatriation agreements.* These agreements guarantee that the expatriate will not spend longer than a stipulated period abroad and that on return, a mutually acceptable job will be made available.
- *Assign a sponsor.* A senior manager at the parent company can be assigned to keep the expatriate informed of significant corporate changes, monitor the expatriate's career interests and ensure that s/he is considered for key openings on return.
- *Provide career counselling.* Formal career counselling sessions provide the opportunity to ensure that job assignments meet the expatriate's needs on return to the parent company.
- *Keep communications open.* Parent companies can keep expatriates informed of home office business affairs by holding management meetings abroad, frequent home leave, and regularly scheduled meetings at headquarters. Rapid advances in technology also allow frequent and interactive communication by means of faxes, email, and video conferencing sessions.
- *Offer financial support.* Companies who have the financial means can assist the expatriate in maintaining his/her residence in the home country, which can alleviate settling-in problems when the family returns.
- *Develop re-orientation programmes.* Adjustment back into the home culture can be facilitated through re-orientation programmes, which the repatriate and his/her family can attend.

## 23.8 Selecting expatriates and applying relevant human resources policies

If the parent company carefully plans and executes its international human resources management policies, many of the problems that face expatriates when undertaking an overseas assignment can be alleviated.

### 23.8.1 Factors that influence the choice of expatriates

Research undertaken by Henley Management College in the United Kingdom indicates that certain specific competencies are required if managers are to operate successfully in the international area (Pitfield 1996:9–12). These competencies include:

- *Familiarity with a variety of cultures.* Multicultural exposure, 'longish' periods abroad, and frequent working visits to overseas operations contribute significantly to the ability of the international manager to operate successfully.
- *Real experience of different cultures.* Genuine cultural contact, perhaps staying in the home of one of the host country's local managers, and obtaining firsthand information of the pervading culture by using local transport systems, contribute to an awareness of cultural differences.
- *Acceptance of mobility.* The Henley studies reveal that managers are much less willing to move abroad than in the past, especially when considering issues relating to property prices, children's schooling, overseas allowances, and foreign exchange controls. The extent of company support for families and personal circumstances can be a deciding factor in choosing to move, particularly if there are dual-career difficulties.
- *Cultural sensitivity and flexibility.* Successful international managers have acquired sensitivity and flexibility in different management cultures before they arrive in the host country. Some of the

issues that they may face include:

- Recognising that the purpose of meetings can differ in different countries.
- Understanding that the use of first names may not be acceptable.
- Realising that attitudes to time and punctuality may differ.
- Accepting that demonstrations of hospitality are often required before business can be conducted.
- Recognising that the balance of work and social relationships can differ markedly between different cultures.
- Cultivating an awareness that ethical issues such as 'bribery' may be viewed in a different light in the host country.

- *Knowledge of languages.* Although the international language of business is English, it is wise to have a social knowledge of other languages to express thanks, gratitude, admiration, and to demonstrate that an effort has been made to move towards the culture of the host country.
- *Information technology communication skills.* The mobile international manager requires high-level IT skills in order to be able to communicate effectively with headquarters and other subsidiaries.

Jackson (2002:88) adds that the following are essential when choosing expatriates for a foreign assignment:

- *Technical ability:* the ability to do the job is of course a prerequisite.
- *Managerial skills:* those skills that are associated with being an effective manager are important.
- *Diplomatic skills:* an ability to deal with others, negotiate, and to represent the parent company on foreign assignment; this may even involve interaction with politicians and government officials in some developing countries.
- *Personal motives:* a positive reason for wanting to take on foreign assignments.
- *Emotional stability and maturity:* this involves having the staying power and emotional maturity to maintain equilibri-

um in a foreign environment as well as being non-judgmental in relationships with others.

Based on the above required competencies, the focus of human resources management policies is directed towards the areas of recruitment and selection, training, remuneration, performance management, and labour relations.

## 23.8.2 Recruitment and selection

Although necessity may demand that an organisation, which has little experience of overseas operations, use external recruitment, people within the organisation may already possess some of the required competencies. These employees should be identified and development activity should be based on those skills that are lacking. Although recruitment for overseas assignments should include both employees identified by the company, and internal and external applications, Dessler (1997:681) recommends that adaptability screening be used in all recruitment efforts to assess the possible expatriate's potential in handling the foreign transfer. A psychologist or a psychiatrist usually conducts this process.

Realistic previews of what to expect in the new job and a different culture are essential, as is an evaluation of the extent to which the future expatriate possesses those qualities perceived to contribute to the success of the international assignee. According to Dessler (1997:681), the qualities are:

- Job knowledge and motivation.
- Relational skills.
- Flexibility and adaptability.
- Extra-cultural openness.
- Family situation.

Recruiting and selecting the wrong person for an overseas operation can cost an organisation a considerable amount. According to Dowling et al. (1999), expatriate failure will have direct and indirect costs. Direct costs include airfares, relocation expenses, salary, and training. These will vary according to the level of position the expatriate held, exchange rates, and the country of destination. Indirect costs may be loss of market share, difficulty with government host officials, poor morale, and decreased productivity.

### 23.8.3 Training

A crucial question when preparing expatriates to take up their new assignments is: What sort of special training do overseas candidates need? Dessler (1997:683) prescribes a four-level approach:

- Level 1, where training focuses on the impact of cultural differences.
- Level 2, which aims at an awareness of how attitudes influence behaviour.
- Level 3, where training provides factual knowledge about the target country.
- Level 4, which introduces skill-building in language and adjustment and adaptation skills.

Gómez-Mejía et al. (1998:529) also stress the importance of a cross-cultural approach to training that provides the skills required to deal with a wide range of people with different values. These authors identify three approaches to cross-cultural training:

- *The information-giving approach,* which lasts less than a week and provides indispensable briefings and a little language training.
- *The affective approach,* which lasts from one to four weeks and provides psychological and managerial skills needed to perform effectively during a moderate-length assignment.
- *The impression approach,* which lasts from one to two months and provides the manager with field experiences and extended language training.

This readiness training is depicted in Figure 23.2. The parent company must also give attention to the career development opportunities offered to the expatriate. Gómez-Mejía et al. (1998:528–9) state that headquarters should at least position the international assignment as a step towards advancement

Figure 23.2 Training for overseas assignment

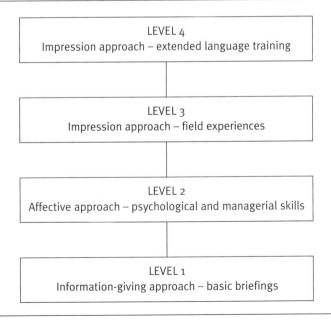

within the firm, and should provide support for expatriates by maintaining contact through a mentor at the home office, or allowing the employee to visit the home office occasionally to foster a sense of belonging and reduce re-entry shock.

### 23.8.4 Remuneration or benefit issues

Pitfield (1996:29) mentions that some of the most stressful aspects of understanding overseas assignments relate to the financial implications of spending a period abroad. Areas which must be addressed by the home office are: a removal allowance, salary structure, pension arrangements, tax issues, overseas allowance, home visits, family arrangements, and a local or home-based compensation package. Gómez-Mejía et al. (1998:529–530) believe that planning compensation for expatriates requires that management follows three important guidelines:

- Provide the expatriate with a disposable income that is equivalent to what s/he would receive at home.
- Provide an 'add-on' incentive for accepting an international assignment.
- Avoid having expatriates fill the same jobs held by locals or lower-ranking jobs.

### 23.8.5 Managing the performance of expatriates

One of the complications of managing and appraising the expatriate's performance is the question of who will undertake this responsibility. Allowing only host country management to conduct the exercise may result in distorted cultural differences. On the other hand, parent country managers may be so geographically distanced from the expatriate that their input would not be valid. Dessler (1997:685–6) provides five suggestions for improving the performance management of expatriates:

- Stipulate the assignment's difficulty level and take difficulty-level differences into account during the appraisal period.

- Weight the evaluation more toward the on-site manager's appraisal than toward the home-site manager's distant perceptions.
- Allow home-site managers to use a former expatriate from the same overseas location to provide background advice.
- Modify normal performance criteria to fit the overseas position.
- Encourage the expatriate to offer relevant insights into the functioning of the operation and the interdependencies of the domestic and foreign operations.

## Case-in-point

Companies have long accepted the high cost of expatriate assignments as the price of doing business in the global arena. But companies can minimise this cost, although they seldom do it effectively.

Mary Rowe, director of *Motorola's* global assignment centre, explains that when overseas assignments last much longer than anticipated, or when their original purpose changes, expatriates are 'localised', without compromising the assignment or hindering the assignee. The localisation process migrates employees away from their expatriate packages and into the host country economy, usually by eliminating some of the expatriate's allowances immediately, and gradually phasing out others.

Motorola has three categories of expatriate assignments, which simplifies the decision on when to localise. In the first category, international transferees understand from the start that the job is located in another country and that they will be treated as a local country hire within the host country salary structure. Secondly, they have 'wind-downs', where an employee has been on an assignment for five to six years and s/he is approached to become a local hire, this person will have become used to expatriate benefits, so these benefits are wound down over a period of time.

A third scenario occurs when an expatriate has been on assignment for a shorter period of time, but the position itself has moved to the host country and is no longer an expatriate assignment. In this case benefits are converted immediately.

The savings that come from localising expatriates outweigh the drawbacks. Driven by a desire for cost containment, companies are making the decision to localise sooner rather than later in the assignment life cycle.

SOURCE: Joinson (2002)

## 23.8.6 International labour relations

Substantial differences in labour relations practices are to be found among the world's countries and regions. Labour relations policies should focus on answering the following questions in order to prepare the international manager for his/her assignment abroad:

- Does collective bargaining take place industry-wide or regionally, or does it occur at plant level?
- What degree of autonomy and decision-making power do unions in the host country possess?
- To what extent is collective bargaining undertaken by employer organisations?
- How formal are recognition agreements in the host country?
- Does the host country practise closed-shop or open-shop agreements?
- Are labour/management contracts legally binding or 'gentlemen's agreements'?
- What are the content and scope of bargaining issues?
- How are grievances, disciplinary offences, and strikes handled in the host country?
- What is the local government's role in labour relations?
- To what extent is worker participation encouraged?

It must also be realised that there are various and often deep-seated differences in the approach to employment relations in various countries due to the historical evolution thereof or political differences. It should be accepted that when it comes to the 'current state of employment relations', South Africa is not the same as other countries. An example is that South Africa currently has a 'labour government' in power. Elsewhere, an expatriate may be posted to where a 'conservative government' is in power, with a concomitant approach to employment relations.

Furthermore, it may be that the state of the host country's economy might be vastly different from that of South Africa. The expatriate person may then, for example, be faced with a buoyant or depressed economy, all of which would have different influences on the practice of employment relations in a particular business or the country where the expatriate works.

## 23.9  Conclusion

According to Gunn (2002), the 21st century will see more women in foreign assignments. Currently there are only 10 to 20 per cent woman expatriates, with an increasing number of women moving into middle- and upper-management positions where the opportunity for women and their families to move abroad is more likely.

There has been a considerable paradigm shift since the September 11 attacks and subsequent terrorism, which has reformed the way HRM management will be handled in the 21st century. Due to the recent terrorist attacks and looming conflicts in the Middle East and Asia, security has been tightened for expatriates, with current expatriate employees and their families having their backgrounds investigated, and it is predicted that extra security precautions will become part of the HRM checklist for vetting potential international assignees. On the other hand, and according to Watt et al. (2002), Employee Assistance Programmes (EAPs) have never been as important as now with a greater requirement for counselling, the development of emergency procedures, and business recovery programmes.

## Summary

It is clear that companies embarking on international business initiatives must have a clear knowledge of global trends and the ways in which international assignments can be managed effectively. To do this, problems facing expatriates and repatriates must be obviated by means of proactive planning, implementation, and maintenance of the exercise. Distinct international human resources policies must be formulated to ensure that quality standards are upheld. Such policies should include the following:

- The impact of future global business trends must be considered when planning the management of international assignments.
- An international company can follow the traditional, modern, fast-mover, or alliance model. Companies progress through various stages of international business, expanding from a pure domestic market, through the export stage, to an extension of operations out of the home country, before a multinational corporation undertakes manufacturing and marketing in several countries. The global transnational corporation has weak ties in any given country and operations are highly decentralised.
- Parent companies must decide whether to follow an ethnocentric, polycentric, geocentric, or regiocentric approach to managing an international subsidiary. These approaches dictate the mix of host country and expatriate employees.
- Some of the problems that expatriates may experience include career blockage, culture shock, a lack of pre-departure cross-cultural training, an overemphasis on technical qualifications, being sent on an overseas assignment to resolve difficult interpersonal situations or political conflicts and family problems experienced by the expatriate's spouse and children.

- On return to their home country, repatriates often face a lack of respect for the skills they have acquired, a loss of status, poor planning for their position when they return, and reverse culture shock.
- International managers need a familiarity with a variety of cultures, real experience of different cultures, acceptance of mobility, cultural sensitivity and flexibility, knowledge of languages, and IT communication skills. International human resources policies must focus on recruitment and selection, training, remuneration and benefit issues, performance management, and international labour relations.
- Quality assurance in international HRM is a prerequisite for competitive success.

## Case study
### André's Asian experience

André Taupo had been back in Johannesburg for two months after an exciting three years working abroad in a subsidiary of Saubona Foods (Pty) Ltd. As he sat in his empty office looking out at the city skyline, André reviewed his situation. Well, he had to admit, for him it had been an exciting and challenging time since his position there as finance manager had been a promotion. More importantly, it had brought him in contact with different work approaches and procedures, and he had interacted with fellow expatriates now also working at headquarters as well as some Malaysians also working at headquarters. Even though his previous position had been in the Asia-Pacific Regional Office, it had not provided him with the same exposure as he enjoyed in the Malaysian subsidiary. André knew that he had gained valuable experience and self-confidence as a result.

It has not all been excitement, though, for the family. Jenna, his wife, did not complain, but André knew that she faced a difficult time because of his international assignment. One reason was because his two teenage children had to attend the International School located a considerable distance from the Malaysian subsidiary, which meant they only came 'home' on weekends to Kuala Lumpur. It made life particularly lonely for Jenna who was then not working in the Malaysian subsidiary. She did admit that she often missed her work as a sociologist. Jenna was having trouble back home finding employment – her previous department in a local government division had been closed down due to reduced government funding.

Both children enjoyed the international environment at the school, and had adjusted better than André had expected. Coming back to South Africa, though, was proving to be traumatic. His elder son, John, had not been accepted into his chosen university course due to non-recognition of the accreditation of the International School, or at least that was what John claimed. His younger son, Chris, wasn't adjusting easily either.

Dinner the previous night had not been a happy occasion, but tonight would be worse, André knew. How was he going to explain that the family had made such sacrifices to further his career that was going nowhere? Headquarters in Johannesburg has decided to reorganise the entire global operation and, as a result, the Regional Office was to be upgraded to a Regional Headquarters, and located in Kuala Lumpur. André knew that it made sound business sense, since most of the Asian-Pacific activity was centred around the Malaysian facility and Asia and to a lesser extent the Indian markets. To retain its regional headquarters in Manila on the grounds of sentiment was unthinkable in such a highly competitive industry. 'But where does that leave me? All the work from the regions was transferred to Kuala Lumpur. My position will now be filled by someone from either headquarters or, more probably, from Manila. My boss made it quite clear that I could move back to Malaysia if I wanted to or face a downgrading of my position. I could not have asked the family to move back anyway,' thought André. The situation was compounded by the news that several of his colleagues in the regional office had been made redundant in Manila. 'My acceptance of the international assignment has been career suicide – and not just for me,' André thought. 'I will have to see if there are positions available at headquarters, otherwise I am not going to be able to face Jenna and the boys tonight. Surely another organisation will value my international experience.'

## Questions

1. What would your answers be to Jenna if you were André and had decided to not go back to Kuala Lumpur and had to find another job, or worst of all, face downgrading of the position as reward for going on an expatriate contract?

2. What support structures do you propose the organisation's HR department should have in place to help and support André's family to overcome the difficult expatriate time they had?

3. Draw up some differences and similarities between a country of your choice and South African culture, which are of importance for a person to operate effectively as an expatriate.

## Experiential exercise

PURPOSE: To instill an awareness in learners that cultural differences within the borders of South Africa can be just as diverse as international cultural diversity.

INTRODUCTION: Because of the multitude of different language and race groups in South Africa, it is sometimes difficult for people to understand why others behave in the way in which they do.
Understanding each other makes acceptance easier and will contribute to a harmonious and united nation.

TASK (20 minutes): Divide into groups of four or five, if possible containing representatives of different South African race and/or language groups. Select two or three traditional customs, such as a wedding, a funeral, a 'coming-of-age' ritual or initiation. Learners must discuss differences and similarities in the chosen customs between the race and/or language groups.

The feedback received from the class will enable the instructor to compile a list of similar and different characteristics in our cultures. How could these differences and similarities affect the development of human resources policies within South Africa?

## Chapter questions

1  Various predictions have been made concerning the way in which global corporations will conduct their business in the future. How do you think human resources managers should react to these predicted trends?

2  Describe the stages through which firms progress as they internationalise their operations. At what stage are the majority of South African companies currently operating in the international arena?

3  What specific conditions would determine an ethnocentric, polycentric, geocentric, and regiocentric approach to international staffing?

4  What recommendations would you make to human resources managers to alleviate the problems faced by expatriates?

5  Develop a programme that your company can use to reduce repatriation problems of returning expatriates.

6  Most South Africans have had to function in another culture at some stage in their lives. Whether this culture has been marked by racial, language, or religious differences, we have had to face up to the fact that the differences of the human race outweigh the similarities. Think of a time when you have faced obstacles in another culture (perhaps in a job situation, in the classroom, or in a shop). What were the major obstacles that you faced? How did you deal with them? Was this a stressful experience? What skills would have enabled you to deal better with the situation?

## Bibliography

BEARDWELL, I. & HOLDEN, L. 1997. *Human resource management: A contemporary perspective, 2nd edition.* (Pitman), Pearson Education (UK).

BENNIS, W. & MISCHE, M. 1995. *The 21st century organization: Reinventing through re-engineering.* Pfeiffer & Co, San Diego.

CASCIO, W.F. 1995. *Managing human resources: Productivity, quality of work Life, profits, 4th edition.* McGraw-Hill Companies, New York.

CHERRINGTON, D. & MIDDLETON, L.A. 1995. 'An introduction to global business issues'. *HR Magazine*, 40(6):129–135. Reprinted with permission of Copyright Clearance Center.

CUCULLU, G. 1998. 'Living in the Lion City'. *Global Workforce*, 3(6):10–11.

DADOO, Y., GHYOOT, V., LEPHOKO, D. & LUBBE, G. 2001. *Multicultural sensitivity for managers.* Tsebanang Group, Rant en Dal.

DESSLER, G. 1997. *Human resource management, 7th edition.* (Prentice-Hall), Pearson Education Inc.

DOWLING, P.J., WELCH, D.E. & SCHULER, R.S. 1999. *International human resource management: Managing people in a multinational context, 3rd edition.* South-Western College Publishing, Mason.

GÓMEZ-MEJÍA, L.R., BALKIN, D.B. & CARDY, R.L. 1998. *Managing human resources, 2nd edition.* (Prentice-Hall), Pearson Education Inc.

GUNN, E. 2002. 'Why women abroad need coping strategies' www.expatica.com/hr.asp?pad=234,345,&item_id=27204 (accessed 12 February 2003).

JACKSON, T. 2002. *International HRM: A cross-cultural approach.* Sage Publications, London.

JOINSON, C. 2002. 'No returns'. *HR Magazine*, 47(11), www.shrm.org/hrmagazine/

articles/1102/1102joinson.asp (accessed 5 February 2003). Reprinted with permission of Copyright Clearance Center.

KEMSKE, F. 1998. 'HR 2008: A forecast based on our exclusive study'. *Workforce*, 77(1):46–60. www.workforceonline.com (accessed 29 January 2003). Reprinted with permission of Copyright Clearance Center.

KRENTZEL, E. 2001. 'Expat Safety in a Time of Terror', www.expatica.com/hr.asp?pad=234, 346,&item_id=27028 (accessed 5 December 2002).

NEL, P. 1997. *Acculturation and the adjustment of the expatriate manager and his spouse.* Unpublished dissertation, Faculty of Economic and Management Sciences, University of Pretoria, Pretoria.

PITFIELD, M. 1996. *Developing international managers.* Herts: Technical Communications.

RONGXIA, L. 2001. 'APEC Meeting on Human Resources', www.bjreview.com.cn/2001/ 200123/NationalIssues-200123(A).htm (accessed 17 February 2003).

SCULLION, H. & BREWSTER, C. 2001. 'The management of exptriates: Message from Europe'. *Journal of World Business*, 36(4):346.

SOLOMON, C.M. 1994. 'How does your global talent measure up?' *Personnel Journal*, 73(10):96–108. Reprinted with permission of Copyright Clearance Center.

SOLOMON, C.M. 1995. 'Learning to manage host-country nationals'. *Personnel Journal*,

74(1):60–67. Reprinted with permission of Copyright Clearance Center.

SOLOMON, C.M. 2001. 'Keeping expatriates safe'. *Workforce*, 80(10):22–30. Reprinted with permission of Copyright Clearance Center.

TORRINGTON, D. & HALL, L. 1995. *Personnel management: Human Resource Management in action, 3rd edition.* (Prentice-Hall), Pearson Education (UK).

TROMPENAARS, F. & WOOLIAMS. P. 1999. 'First-class accommodation'. *People Management*, 22, April.

WATT, J. et al. 2002. 'Life Goes On'. *HR Magazine*, 47(9):42. Reprinted with permission of Copyright Clearance Center.

## Websites

Thunderbird School of International Management: www.t-bird.edu/

Across Frontiers International: www.acrossfrontiers.com

Craighead Global Knowledge: www.craighead.com

Kroll Associates: www.krollassociates.com

Society for Human Resource Management Global Forum: www.shrmglobal.org

The Manager: www.themanager.org/knowledgebase/HR/ Future.htm

International Business Culture, Customs and Etiquette: www.executiveplanet.com/index2.jsp

# 24

# The future of human resources management

HB Schultz and PS Nel

## Learning outcomes

At the end of this chapter the learner should
be able to:

- Describe the employee and organisation
  of the future.
- Compile a developmental plan for a
  human resources practitioner, based on
  the evolving role of the HR professional.
- Discuss how the human resources department can add value to the organisation
  by cultivating knowledge workers.
- Explain the contribution of the human
  resources professional to achieving strategic customer orientation.
- Discuss how sound human resources
  practices can contribute to shareholder
  value.
- Briefly discuss the need for superior quality assurance in the future role of HRM.

## Key words and concepts

- continuum
- heterogeneous workforce
- intellectual capital
- knowledge workers
- mindset
- paradigm
- phoenix leader
- shareholder value
- value chain
- value proposition
- visionary

## Illustrative case

### A blueprint for human resources health

When South Auckland and Waitemata Health
merged to form Health Alliance as a shared
human resources service, the outcome was
something of a blueprint for a new-look
human resources structure. It is divided into
three. The central unit focuses on transactional functions such as recruitment, and then
there are 'embedded' human resources managers in each business unit and a separate
'centre of human resources expertise'.

The latter comprises senior human

resources specialists who function at a more strategic level and provide support and advice related to occupational health and safety, plus areas such as training, or leadership development.

At the same time, the Alliance got 'a lot smarter' about its human resources processes, says its general manager, human resources, Andre Norton. 'As a result, even though we've increased employee numbers, we're on track to save around a million dollars. So it's been quite a radical reform, but based around some smart process mapping and technology to support that.'

For instance, recruitment is web-enabled and uses a United States application, called Hire.com, to attract and filter potential recruits. Instead of running full ads, the Alliance now runs banner ads directing people to its website. Applications are done online and anyone interested in jobs with any health district can lodge their contact details and qualifications.

This particular feature resulted in one position, that of a burns surgeon at Auckland's Middlemore Hospital, basically being filled in five minutes. When the vacancy was lodged, the software matched it with a United Kingdom applicant who had the right qualifications and automatically dispatched an email. He replied straight away and was subsequently hired for the job.

Having a shared human resources function has also enabled the Alliance to look at the whole concept of knowledge sharing and collaborating in ways that benefit both organisations, says Norton. That includes looking 'outside the box' for new solutions to chronic skills shortages as well as initiating various cross-organisational human resources projects. It also includes developing a common framework for performance management, for instance 'one other thing this structure offers is a potential human resources career path. We can bring new graduates in to work in the transactional centre doing mainly recruiting work. Once they gain knowledge of the wider

organisation, they can move into human resources manager roles and do more general human resources work. Then they can move into more specialised centres of expertise work. In a tough industry like healthcare, there has traditionally been a high turnover of staff. I think we can look to attract a better quality of talent and hang onto them a bit longer,' says Norton.

SOURCE: Jayne (2002:28)

## 24.1  Introduction

This chapter is the culmination of all chapters in part 6 of the book, and should be read as a whole, since issues such as strategic and international human resources management as well as human resources information systems all impact on HR practitioners' efforts to meet future challenges in their organisations.

The issues discussed in various other chapters also impact on the future of human resources, such as organisational renewal and change management (see Chapter 20). In this context human resources management plays a key role in contributing to an organisation's bottom line via the quality assurance process, as well as by adding value via various other processes.

Unfortunately there are perceptions that human resources is behind in the behavioural change curve in organisations and should therefore speed up to rightfully earn its place as a core function in an organisation's activities in order to add value and contribute via quality assurance.

Important contributions to successful future human resources management are, firstly, an established profession worldwide. Secondly, there is a change from being a human resources manager in an organisation to being a strategic partner in an organisation's attempts to reach its goals. Thirdly, there is a need for human resources to be part of the top management team. Fourthly, human resources managers need to have competencies in both human resources work and general business management in an organisation.

According to Hamilton (2003:10), it is clear that in the first decade of the new millennium the focus of future human resources management is to be on excellence. It is also partly reliant on the fact that organisations are now operating in an increasingly competitive and complex world. Furthermore, stakeholders' demands will lead to an increase in focus on the 'soft' areas of ethics and culture management – once again areas in which HR functionaries specialise, and in which they can make a positive contribution.

With the aforementioned in mind, an envisaged picture of the employee and organisation of the future is first addressed. The role of the human resources professional must evolve in order to meet the challenges of change. This particular issue is discussed in depth. The information age has brought with it the requirements of so-called knowledge workers. The way in which the human resources department can add value to the organisation through knowledge workers, and its role to enhance shareholder value, are also debated. Finally, we turn our attention to the survival of human resources professionals through the development of strategic customer orientation.

Further aspects are, firstly, staffing and employee challenges need to be competently addressed in human resources management. Secondly, globalisation and evolving workplace relationships need to be addressed competently by human resources managers. And thirdly, demographic changes in the population and workforce of industries and countries need to be proactively addressed. In the future many tasks will be outsourced, so 'employ' also means to work for another entity or contractors. The future hours of work are likely to be chaotic, with the catch phrase being '7x24x52' service, thus ensuring that some staff are available all of the time – midnights and weekends. And, in this climate, employees resign and need to be replaced at a rate higher than ever. They require time off to study, and look after their aged parents.

## 24.2 The employee and the organisation of the future

Rapid changes and advances in technology, medicine, and new mindsets during the last three decades of the 20th century have resulted in a worldwide heterogeneous workforce that has diverse approaches to the way in which work is regarded. The employee and organisation of the future are focused on below.

### 24.2.1 Employee values

According to Allen (2003:27), the immediate future generation starting to enter the labour market is going to have a greater influence on global business than before. It is predicted to become more diverse in terms of age, ethnicity, and racial background. It is therefore unlikely that one set of values will characterise all employees. For example, 'traditionalists', born between 1927 and 1945, tend to be uncomfortable challenging the status quo and authority; 'baby boomers', born between 1946 and 1960, view work as a means to self-fulfilment, and 'baby busters', the so-called 'generation-X' (born between 1961 and 1979), value unexpected rewards for work accomplishments, opportunities to learn new things, praise, recognition, and time with the manager. Lastly, 'generation-Y', also known as 'millennials, echo boomers and nexters', born between 1980 and 1995, act as a group. This group tends to:

- Think differently, behave differently, and have different aspirations.
- Look for instant gratification, have no loyalties to employers who give nothing back, and vote with their feet.

Furthermore it must be noted that 'generation-Y' has the characteristics needed for the leaders of the future. These are:

- Ease with the requirements of technology, diversity, and uncertainty.
- Familiar with a complex mix of routine

and non-routine tasks.
- Flexible, multiskilled risk takers who can multitask.
- A job for life is not in the equation of their makeup.

The values of 'generation-Y' employees are regarded as follows:
- free agent
- highly transient
- optimistic
- highly idealistic
- entrepreneurial
- respect wisdom not authority
- confident achievers
- sociable
- life-style driven

Allen (2003:28–9) states that the talent of 'generation-Y' must be developed, as it would become critical if organisations wish to compete successfully in the future. The strategies and values are as follows:
- Developing a learning organisation requiring a highly individualised process of goal setting, development planning and organisational culture that supports this as a legitimate work activity.
- Providing challenging and meaningful work that taps into their talents and creates opportunities to enhance their skills.
- Catering to a highly transient population by providing opportunities to move between offices, locations, and projects.
- Job redesign to establish a project approach to work. Transparent boundaries to maintain positive relationships with past employees so that they might return at a later stage.
- Coaching and mentoring with the 'wise heads' to capitalise on the wisdom of a veteran they respect.
- Educating leaders. The manager's task is increasingly a matter of not telling the worker what to do, but rather to clear the obstacles from the path that they choose.

Cutting edge organisations must therefore understand what drives 'generation-Y' em-

ployees in order to track and keep the people they need for the future. It is a fact that four different generations of employees are working side by side in organisations, and this must be focused on in the management of employees in organisations. This is particularly important in view of the fact that by the year 2005, the baby boomers born in the 15 years after the World War II will start reaching retirement age.

The September 11 events have also resulted in an important change in values. Previously, values were (in order of priority): career, wealth, health, family and home. Probart (2002:32) states that these values changed after the terror attacks to family, God, health, country and home. This analysis reveals that 'softer' issues, such as religion and family, are substituting tangible values, such as money and careers.

Not only is the labour pool changing as far as current employee values are concerned, but there is also an increasing demand for:
- Work/life balance.
- Paid parental leave.
- Increasing opportunities for consultation and better communication flows.

Organisations which are unable to attract, retain, and motivate excellent staff, are going to have difficulty surviving, let alone growing in the future. Human resources managers should therefore be able to:
- Recruit the very best people who are not only capable of carrying out today's tasks, but also have the potential to grow into tomorrow's roles.
- Quickly induct and acculturate new people into the organisation.

These new people need to clearly understand 'the way we do things around here' and the strengths of the organisation's culture.

Glade (2002:15) also makes the comment that the recruitment and retention of talented staff in a tight labour market is difficult. Innovative solutions are now emerging such as boomerang bonuses, that is, enticements for those who leave an organisation and are shown an 'open door' through which they can return together with benefits and seniority that previously did not exist.

## 24.2.2 Drivers of change

According to Hughes (2002), the driver of change for organisations of the future is to obtain a best fit, which means to have a closer look at external fit between an organisation's policies and practices and its overall competitive strategy, thereby making the organisation more effective. Other aspects, which have generally been found to be important for the future, relate to technology. Information is more accessible and has joined people electronically in ways that impact on organisations and work relationships. As pointed out in the previous section a knowledge-based workforce will turn many employees into 'volunteers' in the future, because they could choose to work elsewhere for equal or more money. This means that they work in an organisation by choice, not by obligation. The challenge is to turn worker knowledge into productivity and to leverage intellectual capital.

Ison and Barton (2003:35) also highlight drivers for change and indicate that successful organisations of the future must provide the following for their employees:
- A flexible, innovative work environment.
- Clear leaderships and accountabilities.
- A customer-focused environment.
- Open communication channels.
- Effective recruitment processes.
- Retention focused on key skills.
- Effective performance management.
- Competitive guaranteed rewards.
- Flexible packages with an appropriate mix of total rewards.
- Pay linked to business performance.
- Ownership opportunities.

Watt et al. (2002:42) point out that another driver for change has been the recent financial scandals such as Enron and WorldCom. Corporations are looking closer at their book keeping and business practice, which has led to a closer watch on incentives and bonuses given to staff, including the organisations' leaders. Whenever a CEO's salary increases and benefits are made known, there are questions about their justification.

In his presentation to delegates at the Institute of Personnel and Development annual conference in 2000, Dave Ulrich expressed the view that senior managers and HR professionals can collaborate to deliver customer-focused culture, talent, speed, learning, and leadership to their organisation. This approach requires HR practitioners to be drivers of change, and not merely respondents to it.

## 24.2.3 Forces shaping the future

Organisations must be completely flexible in the 21st century because markets are chaotic and resource needs are unpredictable. Individuals must be correspondingly flexible and self-reliant as there is no one-way to think about or do anything any more (Tulgan 2000:1).

Since the September 11 attacks on the World Trade Center in New York and subsequent terrorism, there has been a considerable paradigm shift in the relationship between cultures and religions. The world has been redefined by these attacks in such a way that old alliances are being broken and new ones established. The HRM function now needs to pay closer attention to the protocols and strategies of employing and deploying people within the global business environment. Additional security has been, and will continue to be, implemented as part of the screening of potential employees.

Global demographic changes are becoming a dramatic challenge for HR practitioners. The world population is growing at 9 000 per hour, and a factor of the increasingly aging population is the large percentage of the workforce over the age of 60 (Probart 2002:32).

Lynda Gratton (2003), a leading human resources strategist at London Business School, states that traditionally, organisations have a hierarchical mindset that forms an obstacle to a democratic organisation in which employees are given choices about their employment direction. She outlines three challenges facing human resources professions in organisations today. Firstly, human resources management needs to become more vocal and influential in the boardroom alongside the financial and marketing directors. Secondly, quantitative skills, such as the measurement of human capital and the understanding of organisational structure and dynamics, need to be brought to the human resources management role. And, thirdly, HRM needs to develop a new set of skills and competencies around visioning, systems thinking, organisational development, and change management.

Gratton (2003:23) also identifies various issues to be considered for human resources management in the future:

- How can human resources management add value? What can be outsourced, taken on by line managers, or simply stopped? How can human resources management manage outsourcing?
- Who has the skills of a strategic partner? How can these skills be developed?
- From a structural perspective, how can human resources managers develop organisations capable of knowledge dissemination and innovation?
- How can human resources managers ensure that employees remain engaged and committed during times of turbulence?

Another force that will shape the future, is that the leadership of organisations in general is moving from 'power and position' leaders, to empowering leaders who give their employees autonomy while 'steering the ship'. A leader leads people and a manager manages things. Jayne (2002:29) states that there is a drive towards achieving a win-win ideal with a growth surge in coaching and mentoring, team building, leadership development, upskilling and personal development providing a 'work/life' balance. These, along with tech-nological advances and increased outsourcing, are encroaching on the traditional human resources management roles such as recruiting, administration, payroll, performance assessment, and training.

During the last few years on the world stage, there has also been an increase in labour-elected governments in major Western countries including the USA, UK, Germany, Australia, Canada, South Africa, and New Zealand. Human resources management needs to focus on the changing faces of government to maintain its ideals and policies, viewing any changes in legislation as a way to form a strategy for the organisation. For instance, more attention needs to be paid to individuals and the maintenance of their employment, rather than corporate 'slash and burn' styles, which tend to be the underlying focus of the hard right-wing governments. With the increase of labour governments there has been a re-emergence of trade unions. Human resources management needs to learn about the shifts in political and trade foci in order to gain the greater benefits of working with the current system, as well as being well prepared for any sudden shifts over election times and cooperative decisions made at summits such as APEC and NAFTA.

According to Watt et al. (2002), another new force shaping the future is Employee Assistance Programmes (EAPs), which have never been as important as now. It places a greater requirement for counselling, the development of emergency procedures, and business recovery programmes, all of which HRM will have to take responsibility for in the future.

Vinassa (2002:4) introduced the necessity that organisations must deal with AIDS as a serious force shaping the future, since it is not only a human resources-driven issue in an organisation, but also central to the organisation strategy. Therefore, human resources practitioners must ensure that organisations address this critically. 'Many large companies are already redefining the AIDS challenge. They previously saw it as primarily a human resources issue. Now they acknowledge that it is the single most important strategic issue facing South African business' (Vinassa 2002:4). Human resources departments can still make a major contribution to the value adding of an organisation by promoting organisation-wide awareness, and addressing the AIDS pandemic facing organisations in Southern Africa (which is the greatest challenge of the new millennium so far). The following statistics illustrate the gravity of the situation and ought to be taken into consideration not only by the HRM staff of organisations, but also by the entire management since HIV/AIDS has become a national pandemic (Sunter and Whiteside 2000).

The HIV/AIDS situation by the end of 1990 was as follows:

- Life expectancy in South Africa was 63 years.
- Fewer than 1 000 AIDS deaths occurred for the year.
- Less than 0.5 per cent of the population was HIV positive.

The HIV/AIDS situation at the end of 2000 was as follows:

- 12 per cent HIV positive population, which is approximately 5 million.
- Average life expectancy of the population was approximately 56.5 years.
- 250 000 persons were AIDS sick.
- 1 600 newly infected persons per day.
- 200 000 AIDS deaths for the year.

The situation is anticipated to be as follows by the end of 2010. The particular impact on business as well appears to paint the following picture:

- By 2010 the gross domestic product is to be down by approximately 17 per cent, since it is envisaged to decrease between one per cent and two per cent per year from 2000.
- Loss of approximately 10 per cent of the workforce.
- 8 million newly infected persons.
- 80 per cent of the current HIV positive population, which was approximately 5 million in 2000, will be dead or sick with

AIDS by 2010.
- Indirect costs to organisations could add another 10 per cent to the remuneration budget of organisations by 2005, and approximately 15 per cent by 2010.

All in all, this is a serious challenge facing the human resources profession, since it impacts on all facets of an organisation, and will need integrated action and top management support to combat it effectively.

Ulrich (2000) believes that the skills and assumptions of many HR professionals are outdated. These people managers can no longer assume that the challenges ahead are bureaucratic. They need to take a strategic lead in combining the capabilities and competencies of their organisations in the areas of global management, culture change, and intellectual capital.

In outlining the forces that shape the future, Hamilton (2003:10) states that organisations are now starting to understand that:

- Strategic competitive advantage is not the ability to manufacture quickly and cheaply.
- Strategic competitive advantage is being able to meet the customer's needs brilliantly.

## 24.3 An evolving role for human resources management

Gibson et al. (2000:451) believe that the future role of human resources professionals will be greatly influenced by the forces for change at work in our organisations. Comprehending the implications of these forces requires organisational learning processes which involve the capacity to absorb new information, process that information in the light of previous experience, and act on the information in new and potentially risky ways. Only through such learning experiences will organisations survive in the 21st century.

According to Bates (2002), human resources practitioners who aspire to leadership roles within the profession will have to become more strategic, more proactive, and more involved in the overall business of their organisations. The most successful HR people will be those who can think 'from the outside in', from the customer back to the organisation. HR professionals are expected to know the business well enough to align human capital with business needs, and to look for problems to solve. The human resources function must prepare itself for an outsourcing explosion that allows an outside firm to do most of the transactional HR functions more cheaply than the organisation itself. The outsourcing route frees practitioners to do more strategic work within the organisation, shifting the focus away from training and process to the outcomes; away from a people function to an organisation function.

Numerous authors (for example, Brewster et al. 2000:216; Hamilton 2003:10–11 and Noe et al. 2000:566) agree that a new model for the role of human resources management is necessary. The new model must emphasise the strategic function of human resources professionals as business partners. To become a fully-fledged partner in business, the human resources department must evaluate its role, practices, and effectiveness. In the past, human resources managers have concentrated on transactional and traditional activities. These activities are still necessary, but transformational activities now assume their rightful place.

Transactional activities are the day-to-day transactions, such as benefits administration, record keeping, and employee services, and are low in strategic value. Traditional activities can be classified as performance management,

training, recruiting, selection, compensation, and employee relations functions. These activities have moderate strategic value. Transformational activities create long-term capability and adaptability for the firm, and they include knowledge management, management development, cultural change, and strategic redirection and renewal. These activities have the greatest strategic value for the organisation. Jayne (2002:28) also outlines the following competencies for human resources professionals for the future:

- Change management. Instead of coming in after and patching up mess-ups, human resources managers must be smarter and savvier, and more actively involved in managing organisational change.
- A better understanding of what it means to be strategic in human resources.
- More knowledge about e-human resources technology, employee self-service, e-recruiting, e-learning, e-performance measures.
- Human resources professionals must keep doing the basic human resources administration as well as it was done in the past, but also improve it dramatically.

The time allocation for the various human resources activities now becomes the most important element of this model, and the rapid pace of change dictates that time allocation must be flexible, with the activities taking place on a time continuum such as depicted in Figure 24.1.

Ulrich (1998:87–91) takes the idea of continuum further, and uses the concept to describe what the future role of human

**Figure 24.1** A continuum of human resources activities

resources management might be. These continua are depicted in Figure 24.2.

- *Administrative versus strategic roles.* The human resources function has evolved from administrative to strategic, but if the administrative work is not done efficiently, accurately, and timeously, strategic roles will suffer. The ongoing challenge is to balance these roles.
- *Existing versus transformed versus disappearing human resources departments.* Some practitioners argue that the department should rediscover values and administrative processes; some believe that the department should be transformed into an elite strategic corps of

business partners; while yet others believe that human resources departments should disappear and be outsourced.

- *Human resources professional versus line manager versus staff.* Who should do human resources work? Role and accountabilities will be discussed for the next few years, but will almost certainly persist along a continuum.
- *Metaphors for human resources professionals.* Multiple roles will exist for practitioners, and behaviour will be shaped according to the descriptions of leaders, architects, stewards, partners, and players.
- *Aggressiveness of human resources professionals.* The debate will rage as to when

**Figure 24.2** The role of the human resources professional

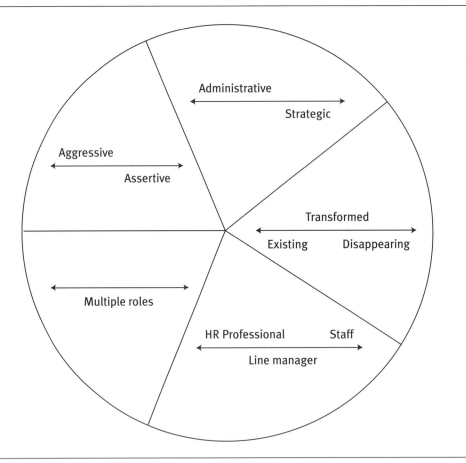

practitioners should become more assertive and take a stand. Their roles will at different times require advocacy, acquiescence, and proactive and reactive approaches.

## Encounter 24.1

HR ONLINE

An organisation wishing to make itself attractive for potential employees might use the following words in a recruitment advertisement:

'Behold our Internet-based human resources department! It is efficient, focused, and streamlined. It grants our employees more time to be team players and organisational partners! Do you want to work for us?'

These words would probably make an impact, provided they are true! Numerous companies have gone the Internet-based HR way and have not regretted it. Here is what some of them have to say.

Jeff Anthony, senior vice-president of corporate development at PSS/world Medical Inc., a medical supplies distributor, manages the HR services of the company's 5 000 employees throughout its 100 offices by means of an Internet-based service for handling employee information. Jeff says he has achieved his objective of turning the HR department into a completely paperless function. It has reduced errors and avoided lots of redundant work.

The American Family Mutual Insurance Company's (AFMIC) brand and content manager of HR, Russ Evansen, has put his HR department online and converted many administrative functions to self-service functions using the Internet, including salary planning, work-schedule changes, and promotions. Employees who dealt primarily with these functions on paper in the past were redeployed in a newly designed HR division. The division has a director and is staffed with HR business partners who work with company leaders on strategic business issues. He says, 'Online initiatives resulted in offline advances.'

The online initiative of AFMIC has been divided into three distinct groups. Non-management employees can access a section that deals with routine requests concerning policy, vacation days, and sick days. A higher level of daily requests is handled in a second division that oversees compensation, hiring and terminations. The concerns of the third group, officers, consist of their own compensation and benefit information.

The HR department is now able to focus on key issues and justify an increased return on investment.

SOURCE: Jaroneczyk (2001:18)

What are the competencies that human resources professionals themselves believe they will need in the future? The following figure (Figure 24.3) indicates, in rank order, the feelings of current practitioners in a Workforceonline (2000) survey regarding the functions of HR professionals to ensure high standards and in executing their jobs:

Glade (2002:15) states that the human resources professional must have the traditional competencies, but in future also integrate competencies which are to become important, such as being an organisational development expert, strategic thinker, etc. In order to achieve this, the following expertise needs to be pursued to be a competent HR professional in future as is shown in Figure 24.4.

**Figure 24.3** It is the function of the human resources professional to ensure the highest standards of:

1  Communication skills.
2  Problem solving.
3  Leadership.
4  Recruiting or staffing.
5  Adherence to employment law.
6  Training and development.
7  Technology.
8  Forecasting.
9  Compensation design.
10  Benefits design and administration.
11  Accounting or finance.
12  Record keeping.

**Figure 24.4** Future integrative competencies of the human resources professional:

- Relationship builder.
- Exceptional communicator.
- Conflict resolver.
- Creative HR leader.
- Assisting line managers in pursuing the business strategy.
- Increasing an organisation's capacity for rapid change.
- Address changed circumstances in business.

Hamilton (2003:10) outlines additional skills with regard to the human resources management professionals' role, namely to be able to operate in the following areas:

- The way an organisation operates.
- To demonstrate and practise a clear understanding of complex systems and cultures in organisations.
- To manage the interactions between individuals and groups to ensure the organisation is able to achieve its desired outcome with the help of the human resources department.

Ulrich (2000) points out that HR professionals must build and maintain credibility within their organisations. He maintains that this is done by being accurate, consistent, meeting commitments, developing abilities to be at ease with colleagues, behaving with integrity, relating their actions to those of the business, confronting when appropriate, and thinking laterally.

Lastly, and according to Gratton (2003:23), the future of relationships between human resources, line managers, and CEOs also needs to be revisited. This means that they need to work very closely together. The human resources team has to be a very confident 'mirror' of what is happening in the company and must be adept at understanding employee motivations and aspirations. At the same time it needs to be highly sophisticated in its understanding of key human resources practices and processes. Delivering choice is more complex than simply treating every employee in the same manner.

## 24.4 Adding value in the knowledge-based economy

Despite the rather radical changes in the environment of the human resources management function, where human resources activities have become decentralised, outsourced, in-sourced, or even absorbed by line managers, there has been a stronger recognition of the links between how people are managed and the bottom line. Human resources managers recognise that they are accountable for business results through effective management practices. The softer side of competitiveness reflects the shift towards a knowledge-based economy. In the industrial world today, roughly 15 per cent of the active population physically touch a product in the production process. The other 85 per cent add value by the creation, management and transfer of information. A modern economy, thus, depends heavily on the human factor as a key to success.

With this in mind, the human resources management function will continue to play an important role in making organisations more effective and competitive. The changing image of human resources management as a bureaucracy to a strategic partner, by integrating business issues with human resources solutions, is evident. Fitz-enz (2000) states that knowledge is not a technical issue, it is a human issue, and offers human resources managers the chance to be at the heart of the most important force in the 21st century, namely information.

According to Laabs (2000:52–56), human resources professionals of the future will add value by becoming 'phoenix' leaders. Phoenix leaders are defined by their ability to make five essential contributions:

- They allow issues that confront the organisation to emerge.

- They use the people to resolve those issues.
- They prioritise and allocate resources to address those issues.
- They set ownership free so that everyone can deal with those issues.
- They stimulate learning.

Dahmen (2002:29) came up with some answers to the question of how best human resources can add value to the business bottom line and what is best human resources practice. He identifies seven 'REs', which are presented as follows:

- *REView.* A key competence strategic human resources managers need is the ability to review the state of a business. They have to understand how people management aligns with a business' direction at all levels and how much it costs in relation to the value it generates.
- *REcruit and REtain.* Anyone who wants to add value has to understand how to attract key personnel and provide them with an environment that makes them want to stay.
- *RE-win.* Keeping track of former employees when they take parental leave or work for another organisation, and be able to win back their skill input at an appropriate time.
- *REnewal.* It is 'big picture' skills that involve understanding when an organisation needs to change its purpose or product. That means a keen grasp of market and customer behaviour, competition, client needs, etc. Human resources practices that give renewal a high priority are considered to add real value to an organisation.
- *REdesign.* Providing an organisation with a new shape, defining its blueprint, and achieving culture changes as a focus for human resources practitioners.
- *REsult.* While the first six points represent the investment in human resources, this has to do with the return on that investment. While historically, human resources was responsible for results based around

individual performance, it now has a more strategic involvement with bottom line success (or otherwise) of an organisation.

Dahmen (2002:29) also states that these winning competencies help highlight trends for human resources' future, which includes the following: firstly, human resources is moving out of the backroom and becoming a function that has a strong external rather than a mainly internal focus. Secondly, at an individual level, human resources is focusing on talent pools – identifying, attracting, retaining, developing, and choosing who gets key attention and how. The recruit, retain, and re-win strategies will all revolve around these talent pools. Thirdly, the human resources winners have an organisational or big picture focus that enables them to see how best to utilise talent within the structure and to redesign the whole if needed. Fourthly, human resources and the bottom line are not strange animals to each other – they need to be linked, and successful human resources people will be able to define what they deliver to the bottom line. This view is also supported by Parmenter (2002:36), where similar claims are made in terms of how human resources can add to a company's bottom line.

---

## Encounter 24.2

WHAT WILL THE HUMAN RESOURCES ARENA LOOK LIKE IN 2020?

Answering this question, Roger E Herman, of The Herman Group (Greensboro, North Carolina, USA), states that one area that will continue on its current path is that of outsourcing. Although several generalists will manage the corporate and strategic human resources function, recruitment, selection, record keeping, and compensation and benefits administration will be outsourced, mainly on an electronic basis.

A major portion of the workforce will be contingent labour, and human resources professionals will require a substantially different set of skills for recruiting, negotiating, managing, and servicing a very flexible workforce. Many workers will be free agents, and a large number will sell their services through an international network of brokers.

Benefits will be self-designed and self-managed, relieving employers from carrying out this administrative burden. Most employment arrangements will be established though individual negotiation, and wage and salary specialists, together with employee relations specialists, will play a much different role in the future.

SOURCE: www.workforceonline.com

The research of Lipiec (2001:144) focused on the future role of human resources management, and is presented in Table 24.1. It is based on a survey of human resources practitioners. It is indicated that a greater emphasis must be placed on the strategic role of human resources management. It is also clear that in terms of increased competition, the role of the human resources manager will rely more on intellectual capital, i.e. how to retain and manage the knowledge of the workers. Management must therefore devise ways to motivate workers in a changing reality and find ways to retain them.

### 24.4.1 Human resources contributions to shareholder value

A major development regarding future human resources management, which has come to the fore in recent times, is to determine the value of the various human resources functions as they impact on adding value to the organisation. This is not only in terms of internal efficiency, but according to Grigg (2003:30–1), should also be reflected in human resources management's contribution to shareholder value. In this regard, managers have tried for years to measure the return on people practices to allow them to only choose those which would allow an organisation the best return on their investment in human resources. The development of the Watson Wyatt Human Capital Index (HCI) has enabled organisations to identify shareholder value increases. For example, if the key human resources practices in an organisation can be improved, it could lead to a substantial increase in market value. The HCI is a single, simple set of measures that quantifies exactly which human resources practices have the most effect on increasing, or decreasing, shareholder value.

According to Grigg (2003:30), research to compile the survey detail has identified 49 specific human resources practices that play the greatest role in increasing shareholder value, which again has been summarised into the following dimensions, each of which is briefly discussed below:

- *Total rewards and accountability and value*

**Table 24.1** Skills and competencies that will be required from human resources managers

| Skills and competencies that will be required from human resources managers | Percentage of responses regarded as very important |
|---|---|
| Change management | 49.60% |
| Teamwork | 42.10% |
| Classic tools of HRM | 37.40% |
| General management | 32.40% |
| Consulting, communication | 33.80% |
| Business | 32.40% |
| International and multicultural management | 24.20% |
| Concepts and theories of HRM | 17.20% |

SOURCE: Lipiec (2001:145)

*creation.* This aspect focuses on rewarding employees for good work and refusing to accept sub-performance. In future, the human resources function should therefore focus on building the right mix of short-, medium- and long-term rewards to increase performance. It is estimated that this aspect could increase shareholder value by 16.5 per cent.

- *Collegiality and flexibility.* Great leadership and less hierarchical culture that encourage employee contribution combine to create a nine per cent increase in shareholder value. In this regard, globally, and bearing in mind the characteristics of best business practices, the human resources function should focus on the following:
  - A 'single status' culture.
  - Flexible working arrangements.
  - An environment that encourages innovation.
  - Employee input as to how their work is done.
  - Trust and integrity associated with organisation leadership.
  - Focus on the customer.
- *Recruiting and retention excellence and value creation.* In the future, human resources management ought to pay even more attention to this critical element of a business. However, it is a worldwide trend in increasing productivity to do more with fewer employees. This implies doing the following:
  - Keeping voluntary turnover low.
  - Stronger commitment to job security.
  - Stepping up efforts to use formal strategies, aligning them with business plans, bringing co-workers into the hiring process, and offering new employees extensive orientation.
  - Selecting candidates that would be able to 'hit the ground running'.
  - Attempting to establish a reputation as a great place to work, in other words to regard the employer as exceptionally good.

Should the human resources management function be able to do this well in future, it may contribute up to 7.9 per cent in shareholder value.

- *Communications integrity and value creation.* It will be the role of human resources practitioners to enhance shareholder value in future and therefore enhance the role of the human resources management function by improving the communication and integrity of an organisation.

  It would mean that employees should have access to multiple communication channels and that they should be informed about and be aligned with an organisation's goals and objectives. This aspect would also allow an organisation to improve intellectual capital, knowledge sharing, and financial performance.

  It is particularly important that the human resources management function strives to increase the opening up of communication channels and to improve the transparency in an organisation.

  In terms of predictions, these aspects could increase the shareholder value by 7.1 per cent.

- *Focused human resources service technologies and value creation.* In the future, human resources departments should focus on increasing the use of human resources technology. This would entail the following:
  - Improving accuracy, service and cost effectiveness of all employees in an organisation.
  - Less quantifiable goals are enhancing communication and promoting organisational culture.

This aspect could increase shareholder value by 6.5 per cent.

## Case-in-point
### Corporate HR can contribute to the bottom line

Exbeck, a US-based engineering contracting project management firm, has harnessed its human resources more effectively to maintain its competitive profile. This has involved centralising the corporate HR function and positioning it as a full business partner.

Over the past decade, organisations have faced international recession and developments that have reduced market opportunities. This has placed additional pressures on individual firms to maintain their competitive profile. Exbeck consists of about 100 companies worldwide that design, construct, procure and test investment projects for process producers in sectors such as oil, gas, chemical production, steel productions, and electricity generation. The company has endured many pressures, but found it was good at winning tenders, although it experienced operational difficulties in completing projects within budgets. An internal business review found that the group's HR management team was underutilised.

Previous budget overruns had often centred on employee development and resourcing problems. The HR function had become inflexible and the management and deployment of HR was completely reactive. Exbeck devised its own programme of internal restructuring and management development. This programme repositioned the corporate HR function as a full business partner in project planning, project tendering and project management. By promoting the corporate HR function, Exbeck sought to improve operating procedures and improve the operating relationship between project management and functional management.

As a result, Exbeck's corporate HR function became a central player in project management, assuming full control of management development, and with the res-

ponsibility for monitoring financial performance in a new framework for project management.

SOURCE: Clarke (2001)

The human resources management function can make a contribution to the organisation by ensuring that the right people are recruited, the right environment is created, and that human resources supports creative thinking. This will lead to increased productivity, which will greatly enhance the value of the human resources department's contribution to an organisation's success while adding shareholder market value to the organisation.

## 24.5 Strategic customer orientation

Global environments and organisational strategy will govern the future of human resources management. Organisational strategy refers to the way the organisation positions itself in its setting in relation to its stakeholders given the organisation's resources, capabilities, and mission. Strategic choice refers to the idea that an organisation interacts with its environment instead of being totally determined by external forces (McShane and Von Glinow 2000:585).

Noe et al. (2000:569) state that a customer orientation is one of the most important changes in the attempt by the human resources function to become strategic. A customer orientation entails three defining steps:

1 Human resources practitioners must identify their customers in the form of line managers, the strategic planning team, and all employees.
2 The products of the human resources department must be identified in the form of high-quality employees, information and recommendations for the planning process, and fair compensation and benefit programmes and decisions.

3   Human resources professionals must identify the technologies required to satisfy customer needs.

This customer orientation is essential in creating the organisation of the future. Human resources professionals must learn how to encourage the creativity and commitment that they wanted to express when they first joined the organisation, and they must figure out how to re-engage people in the important work of organising. This is what strategic customer orientation is all about.

Sullivan (2002) lists the following as the basic elements of excellent customer service:

- Gathering information on the customers' expectations and needs, and then exceeding these expectations.
- Providing the customer with information without them having to ask for it.
- Rapid, honest, accurate and friendly responses.
- Assessing whether the customers' needs were met, during and after the process.

What are some of the ways in which the human resources department can aim for the goal of strategic customer orientation? Laabs (2000:52–6) believes that the challenge is to discover which areas of an organisation need human resources leadership and which need HRM, and at what times. Furthermore, if an organisation is to be perceived as more strategic, more valuable, and more reliable, then the thought needs to be what customers want from the vendor, and how well the vendor will deliver it, and how it will improve the organisation's brand image. This implies that human resources practitioners must think like business partners, with a product to be developed, marketed, and reliably delivered to the customers who need their services. These ideas are summarised in Figure 24.5:

Fitz-enz (2000) maintains that human resources professionals must also begin to think in terms of human capital business management, rather than concentrating on a human resources programme. Human resources programmes are tools to assist in

**Figure 24.5** Eight steps to developing strategic customer orientation

1   Identify your customer's needs and perceptions.
2   Craft an identity based on customer needs.
3   Develop a mission statement to guide you through change.
4   Align human resources practices with the goals of customer service.
5   Improve the image of the human resources department.
6   Market the achievements of the human resources department.
7   Validate the improvements of the human resources department with customers external to the organisation.
8   Subject the human resources department to self-scrutiny.

managing expensive human capital. It is imperative to move from mechanical to electronic distribution channels, and to think in terms of the external customer. The objective of human resources departments should be to help managers cut costs, move more quickly, produce more with less, and improve quality.

Caudron (2000:30–2) declares that if human resources practitioners wish to prevent their own jobs from being outsourced, they must understand what work is required for their own organisation to be successful, and then determine the most efficient way to accomplish that work. As Roger Herman (in Caudron 2000:30–2), management consultant and president of The Herman Group, explains: 'We're moving into a much different world and we cannot survive tomorrow using the same approaches we used yesterday, let alone today.'

## 24.6  Quality assurance in the future role of human resources management

The identification and quantification of intellectual capital and its relationship to an organisation's current and future plans and goals is of utmost importance. The recognition of intellectual capital acknowledges that the future of an enterprise mainly depends on the uniqueness, abilities, and experience of the organisation's employees. Many organisations have realised the need to re-organise their human resources functions so as to obtain the quality results required in the area of intellectual capital. This re-organisation for the sake of quality assurance is intensifying the trend for organisations to have small corporate human resources functions, whose role is to provide overall strategy and policy advice, and to decentralise all other aspects of the department.

The decentralisation of the human resources function involves having some staff reporting to line managers, who draw specialist advice and consulting skills in areas such as compensation, recruitment, and organisational development. Human resources staff at the business unit level are becoming like account executives, as they identify business and human resources needs, contract for the required help, and charge for services they have provided. The business of adding value is inextricably linked to the business of providing quality service.

There must also be a move away from the approach that personnel are the greatest assets organisations have, to staff being resourceful humans. To treat personnel like assets actually misses the point, because it makes personnel think that they are an organisation's biggest cost element. Furthermore, to call personnel assets will not lead to any change in organisational structure. The approach should be to see personnel as a source of income and not a hidden cost. The difference between human resources and resourceful humans is that personnel are both an organisation's biggest cost and probably its biggest source of ideas, creativity, innovations, revenue, and income. Therefore a quality approach in terms of the role and functions of personnel should also be interwoven into the equation in managing human resources.

Furthermore, in a quality assurance context, perhaps human resources needs to be rechristened to adapt to its changing role. Describing people as a 'resource' or as 'human capital' suggests their acquisition and use is subject to the same sort of supply/demand mechanisms as other business inputs. If the supply is short, employers compete harder and pay more. In times of over-supply, they pay less. But people come equipped with a much more complex set of motivations. Discovering and catering for those is helping promote the growth of a conglomeration of new people-empowering practices – from leadership development and mentoring, to values identification and community engagement. This might be the future direction – to rather see people as investments in future productivity.

## 24.7 Conclusion

The world in which employers operate is becoming increasingly complex. The environment both inside and outside organisations is changing at a faster and faster rate. The various stakeholders are putting higher demands upon the organisation and these demands are often contradictory. All these changes and demands involve the employees and their interactions with the organisation. The people who are experts at managing this interface are the human resources professionals. Successful organisations will need to utilise their skills to ensure their progress can continue in the future.

Organisations thus need to take their competitors seriously in order to determine in what area they can obtain a competitive advantage. The three areas that stand out are an obsession with quality, the client, and technology. Within this new world-class scenario the management of human resources has also undergone a significant transformation. Like all business activities, human resources management should focus on making a significant contribution towards the bottom line.

In 1871, the noted English artist and writer John Ruskin (1819–1900) wrote:

In order that people may be happy in their work, these three things are needed: they must be fit for it, they must not do too much of it, and they must have a sense of success in it.

HRM leadership must be more vocal and influential in the boardroom so that there can be a more strategic approach to the maintenance of human capital, empowering employees, and providing a more democratic organisation overall. Burchell (2002) identifies that there will be a considerable shift towards a more strategic role versus an operational role over the next five to ten years which is more in line with hard management. It is important that human resources management identify these major shifts early in order to develop the quality systems to support a strategic role as governments and international alliances change.

## Summary

- The employee and organisation of the future will emerge from the values that employees hold, depending on whether the worker is a 'traditionalist', 'baby boomer', or 'baby buster'.
- Drivers for change, in the form of technology and a knowledge-based workforce, are shaping the future of all employees and the organisations in which they work.
- Organisations must be completely flexible and learning processes are needed to be able to contend with the forces of change.
- The new model for the role of human resources management emphasises the strategic function of human resources professionals as business partners, allowing transformational activities to dominate. The future role of the practitioner will probably be found along numerous continua.
- The image of the human resources department will change from that of a bureaucracy to a strategic partner, intent on adding value to the organisation by integrating business issues with human resources solutions.
- Human resources professionals of the future will add value by becoming 'phoenix' leaders who understand and master the challenges of delivering as opposed to doing.
- Human resources professionals must develop a strategic customer orientation by identifying their customers, their products, and the technologies required to satisfy customer needs.
- Many organisations have reorganised their human resources functions to obtain the quality results required in the area of intellectual capital.
- Organisation management focuses more on human resources values with regard to shareholder values.
- The trend has intensified for organisations to have small corporate human resources functions, whose role is to provide overall strategy and policy advice, and to decentralise all other aspects of the department.

## Case study
## How the dream became a reality

Joe W Forehand, Andersen Consulting's Managing Partner and CEO is quoted as saying, 'The issue of human performance is now a top CEO issue and it's the one that occupies most of my time. I believe that this is the one key issue that the CEO must put their stamp on in order to make progress happen.'

In 1989, Andersen Consulting broke away from Arthur Andersen, the accounting and tax business created in the 1950s. Andersen Consulting was formed as a legally separate commercial enterprise devoted to business and technology consulting. The 'business divorce' was not without pain, and the development of Andersen Consulting into a company that defined the consulting market makes interesting reading.

During the last decade of the 20th century it became apparent that Andersen Consulting was becoming top-heavy and was unable to define where exactly the core of the consultancy lay. Financial services, people-related issues and technological matters are relatively unrelated fields, and the need to diversify was clear. Andersen Consulting's involvement in the Enron scandal almost destroyed credibility in the company and the decision to split the organisation was taken. Accenture was born and started trading as a separate entity to Andersen Consulting.

Go to www.ac.com, and click through 'Message from Our CEO', 'Our History', and 'Annual Report' to obtain the background to this case. Type in the words 'Human+Resources' in the Search area and review the following hyper links:

- Careers-United Kingdom-Graduates-Human Resources.
- Personnel Attention.
- Change Management – Thought Leadership – The Changing Face of Human Resources.

## Question

Write an essay on the evolution of the human resources department of Andersen Consulting. Comment on whether you think the HR department is proactive and visionary, or whether it has brought the philosophy of Arthur Andersen with it from the 1980s.

## Experiential exercise

PURPOSE: To analyse the roles of human resources professionals in a selected organisation and to determine whether these roles conform to the anticipated roles of human resources professionals in the future.

INTRODUCTION: Many human resources departments are still engrossed in performing transactional and traditional functions, while business initiatives and strategies are calling for transformational activities. This experiential exercise will allow the learner to gain a better understanding of the nature of the human resources practitioner's job, and to gain insight into the interface between human resources and line managers.

TASK: This assignment may be undertaken individually or by groups of learners. Locate a human resources manager to interview. You may select a human resources generalist or specialist. After the manager understands the research project and agrees to cooperate, conduct the interview, which should take about 45 minutes to one hour.

Also interview a line manager in the same organisation to gain his or her views of human resources management. Your objective is to prepare a report of eight to ten pages indicating the results of the interviews. The report will culminate with recommendations regarding areas where the human resources department should be concentrating on intensifying its transformational role.

The report will use the following framework:

- A description of the overall operations and role of the human resources department.
- The type of interaction between human resources and line managers.
- The extent to which the organisation's HRM practices conform to theoretical prescriptions. If differences are found, discuss why they exist.

## Chapter questions

1   In 1996, *Fortune* columnist Thomas A Stewart suggested that the human resources function as we know it should be blown up. Do you agree with this statement? Motivate your answer. If there were certain parts of the function that you feel should be eradicated, how would you do it? Has this already started to

happen? If you feel that you do not have enough knowledge to answer this question, approach a human resources professional for an expert opinion.

2   Why have the roles and activities of the human resources department changed over the last twenty years, and how effectively do you think practitioners have responded?

3   What factors can you identify in your organisation to enhance shareholder value through better human resources management?

4   What recommendations would you make to human resources managers to develop a strategic customer orientation?

# Bibliography

ALLEN, C. 2003. 'You should care'. *Employment Review, Australia,* 1(1):27–29.

AYCAN, Z. 2001. 'Human resource management in Turkey. Current issues and future challenges'. *International Journal of Manpower,* 22(3):252–260.

BATES, S. 2002. 'Facing the future'. *HR Magazine,* 47(7):23–25. Reprinted with permission of Copyright Clearance Center.

BIRCHFIELD, D. 2002. 'Future trends for human resources'. *Management,* 49(10):20.

BREWSTER, C., DOWLING, P. GROBLER, P., HOLLAND, P. & WARNICH, S. 2000. *Contemporary issues in human resource management: Gaining a competitive advantage.* Oxford University Press, Cape Town.

BURCHELL, N. 2002. *2000–2010 future directions for HR in New Zealand,* Unpublished report. UNITEC Institute of Technology, Auckland, New Zealand.

BURTON, L. 2003. 'The next big thing'. *People Dynamics,* 21(2):22–23. Reprinted with permission of Copyright Clearance Center.

CAUDRON, S. 2000. 'Jobs disappear when work becomes more important'. *Workforceonline,* 79(1):30–32. Reprinted with permission of Copyright Clearance Center.

CLARKE, I. 2001. 'Corporate human resources and "bottom-line" financial performance'. *Personnel Review,* 28(3):33–41. ©Emerald

Group Publishing.

COLLINS, R. 2002. 'Accelerating change, ambiguity and dualisms'. *Human Resources,* 7(1):14–15.

DAHMEN, C. 2002. 'The recipe for HR success'. *New Zealand Management,* 49(10):29.

DAVIDSON, L. 1999. 'Top 12 future HR competencies'. *Workforceonline,* 78(2) (www.workforce.com). Reprinted with permission of Copyright Clearance Center.

FITZ-ENZ, J. 2000. 'Blueberries from Chile'. *Workforceonline,* www.workforceonline.com/archive/ (accessed 14 March 2003). Reprinted with permission of Copyright Clearance Center.

GIBSON, J.L., IVANCEVICH, J.M. & DONNELLY, JR. 2000. *Organizations: Behavior, structure, processes,* 10th edition. Irwin, Chicago.

GLADE, B. 2002. 'Emerging trends in HR – A view from a big place'. *Human Resources,* 7(1):14–15.

GRATTON, L. 2003. 'The next big thing'. *People Dynamics,* 21(2):22–23. Reprinted with permission of Copyright Clearance Center.

GRIGG, V. 2003. 'Linking HR to shareholder value'. *Employment Review, Australia,* 1(1):30–31.

HAMILTON, N. 2003. 'HR'$ currency'. *Employment Review, Australia,* 1(1):10–11.

HUGHES, J.M.C. 2002. 'HRM and universalism: Is there one best way?' *International Journal of Contemporary Hospitality Management,* 14(5):221–228.

ISON, J. & BARTON, P. 2003. 'Future Fillips'. *Employment Review, Australia,* 1(1):34–35.

JARONECZYK, J. 2001. 'Internet-based HR'. *Internet World,* 7(19):18–23. Reprinted with permission of Reprint Management Systems. ©2001, Penton Media Inc. All rights reserved.

JAYNE, V. 2002. 'At the crossroads. Is human resource management on the right track? And where exactly is it headed?' *New Zealand Management,* 49(10):26–30. Reprinted with permission of Profile Publishing Ltd. www.management. co.nz

LAABS, J. 2000. 'Strategic HR won't come easily'. *Workforceonline,* 79(1):52–56. Reprinted with permission of Copyright Clearance Center.

LACAYO, R. & RIPLEY, A. 2003. 'Persons of the

year 2002'. *Time Magazine,*
www.time.com/time/personoftheyear/2002/po
yintro.html (12 March 2003).

LIPIEC, J. 2001. 'Human resources management
perspective at the turn of the century'. *Public
Personnel Management,* 30(2):145.

MCSHANE, S.L. & VON GLINOW, M.A. 2000.
*Organizational behavior.* Irwin/McGraw-Hill
Companies, New York.

NOE, R.A., HOLLENBECK, J.R., GERHART, B. &
WRIGHT, P.M. 2000. *Human resources management – Gaining a competitive advantage,
3rd edition.* McGraw-Hill Companies, New
York.

OTHMAN, R.B. & POON, J.M.L. 2000. 'What
shapes HRM? A multivariate examination'.
*Employee Relations,* 22(5):467–480.

PARMENTER, D. 2002. 'How HR adds value'. *New
Zealand Management,* 49(10):36–37.

PROBART, R. 2002. ,In search of international
trends in HR management'. *Management
Today,* 18(9):32–33.

SULLIVAN, J. 2000. '10 Tenets of 21st century HR'.
*Workforceonline,* 79(1):54
(www.workforce.com).

SULLIVAN, J. 2002. 'Staffing – The worst customer service process in the world?'
www.erexchange.com (accessed 12 March
2003). Reprinted with permission of
Copyright Clearance Center.

SUNTER, C. & WHITESIDE, A. 2000. *AIDS. The
challenge for South Africa.* (Human &
Rousseau), NB Publishers, Cape Town.

TULGAN, B. 2000. 'Four key forces shaping the
future'. *Workforceonline,* www.workforceon-
line.com/archive (accessed 19 February 2003).
Reprinted with permission of Copyright
Clearance Center.

ULRICH, D. 1998. 'The future calls for change'.
*Workforceonline,* 77(1):87–91

(www.workforce.com). Reprinted with permission of Copyright Clearance Center.

ULRICH, D. 2000. 'The way ahead for HR specialists'. *Human Resource Management
International Digest,* 8(1).

VINASSA, A. 2002. 'Measure, monitor and
manage'. *People Dynamics,* 20(5):4–5.
Reprinted with permission of Copyright
Clearance Center.

WATT, J. et al. 2002. 'Life goes on'. *HR Magazine,*
47(9):42. Reprinted with permission of
Copyright Clearance Center.

WORKFORCEONLINE. 2000. 'Survey', www.work-
forceonline.com/archive/article/64 (accessed
24 February 2000). Reprinted with permission
of Copyright Clearance Center.

# Websites

The fifth discipline: www.wbur.org
Lessons in Leadership conference:
    www.lessonsinleadership.com
Thought leaders: www.gwsae.org
The leader's new work:
    www.home.nycap.rr.com/klarsen/learnorg/
    senge2
The human resources value chain:
    www.tigger.stthomas.edu/mccr
Workforceonline:
    www.workforceonline.com/archive/article/64
    www.tompeters.com
    www.themanager.org/knowledgebase/HR/
    Future.htm
    www.reportfinder.com
    www.cpavision.org/visionh/wpaper07b.cfm
    www.sfutures.com/weg-Ink1.thm
    www.workforce.com
    www.e-hresources.com/April2002.htm
    www.hr-guide.com

# Index

Page references in italics indicate tables and figures.